The American Promise

A COMPACT HISTORY

★ Unknown American artist, *The Sargent Family*, 1800.

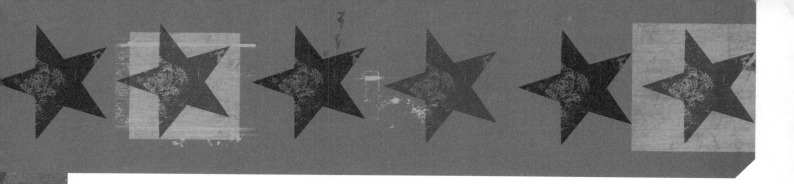

The American Promise

A COMPACT HISTORY FOURTH EDITION

Volume I: To 1877

JAMES L. ROARK *Emory University*

MICHAEL P. JOHNSON *Johns Hopkins University*

PATRICIA CLINE COHEN *University of California, Santa Barbara*

SARAH STAGE *Arizona State University*

ALAN LAWSON *Boston College*

SUSAN M. HARTMANN *The Ohio State University*

BEDFORD/ST. MARTIN'S

Boston • New York

FOR BEDFORD/ST. MARTIN'S

Publisher for History: Mary Dougherty
Director of Development for History: Jane Knetzger
Senior Developmental Editor: Laura Arcari
Senior Production Editor: Christina M. Horn
Assistant Production Manager: Joe Ford
Executive Marketing Manager: Jenna Bookin Barry
Associate Editor: Lynn Sternberger
Editorial Assistant: Robin Soule
Production Assistants: David Ayers, Alexis Biasell, and Alexandra Leach
Senior Art Director: Anna Palchik
Text Design: Brian Salisbury
Copyeditor: Sybil Sosin
Map Editor: Charlotte Miller
Indexer: Leoni Z. McVey
Photo Research: Pembroke Herbert/Sandi Rygiel, Picture Research Consultants & Archives, Inc.
Cover Design: Billy Boardman
Cover and Title Page Art: Unknown American artist, *The Sargent Family,* 1800. The Granger Collection, New York.
Cartography: Mapping Specialists, Ltd.
Composition: Macmillan Publishing Solutions
Printing and Binding: RR Donnelley and Sons

President: Joan E. Feinberg
Editorial Director: Denise B. Wydra
Director of Marketing: Karen R. Soeltz
Director of Editing, Design, and Production: Marcia Cohen
Assistant Director of Editing, Design, and Production: Elise S. Kaiser
Managing Editor: Elizabeth M. Schaaf

Library of Congress Control Number: 2009924719

Manufactured in the United States of America.
4   3   2   1   0   9
f   e   d   c   b   a

For information, write: Bedford/St. Martin's, 75 Arlington Street, Boston, MA 02116 (617-399-4000)

ISBN-10: 0-312-53406-X ISBN-13: 978-0-312-53406-6 (combined edition)
ISBN-10: 0-312-53407-8 ISBN-13: 978-0-312-53407-3 (Vol. I)
ISBN-10: 0-312-53408-6 ISBN-13: 978-0-312-53408-0 (Vol. II)

1   Ancient America: **Before 1492**   3

2   Europeans Encounter the New World, **1492–1600**   25

3   The Southern Colonies in the Seventeenth Century, **1601–1700**   49

4   The Northern Colonies in the Seventeenth Century, **1601–1700**   75

5   Colonial America in the Eighteenth Century, **1701–1770**   101

6   The British Empire and the Colonial Crisis, **1754–1775**   129

7   The War for America, **1775–1783**   155

8   Building a Republic, **1775–1789**   181

9   The New Nation Takes Form, **1789–1800**   205

10   Republicans in Power, **1800–1824**   227

11   The Expanding Republic, **1815–1840**   251

12   The New West and Free North, **1840–1860**   279

13   The Slave South, **1820–1860**   307

14   The House Divided, **1846–1861**   333

15   The Crucible of War, **1861–1865**   357

16   Reconstruction, **1863–1877**   385

Appendices   **A-1**

Glossary of Historical Terms   **G-1**

Spot Artifact Credits   **CR-1**

Index   **I-1**

★ CONTENTS

Maps, Figures, and Tables   xxi

Special Features   xxv

Preface   xxvii

About the Authors   xxxv

Ancient America
Before 1492   3

Opening Vignette: *Archaeological discovery proves that humans have inhabited America for more than 10,000 years*   3

Archaeology and History   4

The First Americans   5

    African and Asian Origins   5

    Paleo-Indian Hunters   6

HISTORICAL QUESTION: Who Were the First Americans?   8

Archaic Hunters and Gatherers   8

    Great Plains Bison Hunters   11

    Great Basin Cultures   11

    Pacific Coast Cultures   11

    Eastern Woodland Cultures   12

Agricultural Settlements and Chiefdoms   12

    Southwestern Cultures   13

    Woodland Burial Mounds and Chiefdoms   15

Native Americans in the 1490s   16

The Mexica: A Mesoamerican Culture   20

Conclusion: The World of Ancient Americans   21

Reviewing the Chapter   22

Europeans Encounter the New World

1492–1600   25

Opening Vignette: *Queen Isabella of Spain supports Christopher Columbus's risky plan to sail west across the Atlantic*   25

Europe in the Age of Exploration   27

Mediterranean Trade and European Expansion   27

A Century of Portuguese Exploration   28

A Surprising New World in the Western Atlantic   29

The Explorations of Columbus   29

The Geographic Revolution and the Columbian Exchange   32

Spanish Exploration and Conquest   33

The Conquest of Mexico   34

The Search for Other Mexicos   34

New Spain in the Sixteenth Century   36

The Toll of Spanish Conquest and Colonization   40

Spanish Outposts in Florida and New Mexico   42

DOCUMENTING THE AMERICAN PROMISE: Justifying Conquest   38

The New World and Sixteenth-Century Europe   42

The Protestant Reformation and the European Order   43

New World Treasure and Spanish Ambitions   43

Europe and the Spanish Example   43

Conclusion: The Promise of the New World for Europeans   45

Reviewing the Chapter   46

The Southern Colonies in the Seventeenth Century

1601–1700   49

Opening Vignette: *Pocahontas "rescues" John Smith*   49

An English Colony on the Chesapeake   51

The Fragile Jamestown Settlement   51

Cooperation and Conflict between Natives and Newcomers   53

From Private Company to Royal Government   54

A Tobacco Society   55

Tobacco Agriculture   56

A Servant Labor System   57

Cultivating Land and Faith   59

DOCUMENTING THE AMERICAN PROMISE: Virginia Laws Governing Servants and Slaves   60

The Evolution of Chesapeake Society   62

Social and Economic Polarization   62

Government Policies and Political Conflict   63

Bacon's Rebellion   64

Religion and Revolt in the Spanish Borderland   65

Toward a Slave Labor System   66

The West Indies: Sugar and Slavery   66

Carolina: A West Indian Frontier   67

Slave Labor Emerges in the Chesapeake   68

GLOBAL COMPARISON: Migration to the New World from Europe and Africa, 1492–1700   69

Conclusion: The Growth of English Colonies Based on Export Crops and Slave Labor   70

Reviewing the Chapter   72

The Northern Colonies in the Seventeenth Century

1601–1700   75

4

Opening Vignette: *Roger Williams is banished from Puritan Massachusetts* 75

Puritan Origins: The English Reformation 76

Puritans and the Settlement of New England 78

The Pilgrims and Plymouth Colony 78

The Founding of Massachusetts Bay Colony 79

The Evolution of New England Society 81

Church, Covenant, and Conformity 82

Government by Puritans for Puritanism 83

The Splintering of Puritanism 84

Religious Controversies and Economic Changes 85

The Founding of the Middle Colonies 88

From New Netherland to New York 88

New Jersey and Pennsylvania 90

Toleration and Diversity in Pennsylvania 90

The Colonies and the English Empire 91

Royal Regulation of Colonial Trade 91

King Philip's War and the Consolidation of Royal Authority 93

BEYOND AMERICA'S BORDERS: New France and the Indians: The English Colonies' Northern Borderlands 94

Conclusion: An English Model of Colonization in North America 97

Reviewing the Chapter 98

Colonial America in the Eighteenth Century

1701–1770   101

5

Opening Vignette: *The Robin Johns experience horrific turns of fortune in the Atlantic slave trade* 101

A Growing Population and Expanding Economy in British North America 102

New England: From Puritan Settlers to Yankee Traders 103

Natural Increase and Land Distribution 103

Farms, Fish, and Atlantic Trade 104

SEEKING THE AMERICAN PROMISE: A Sailor's Life in the Eighteenth-Century Atlantic World 106

The Middle Colonies: Immigrants, Wheat, and Work 108

German and Scots-Irish Immigrants 108

Pennsylvania: "The Best Poor [White] Man's Country" 109

The Southern Colonies: Land of Slavery 112

The Atlantic Slave Trade and the Growth of Slavery 112

Slave Labor and African American Culture 116

Tobacco, Rice, and Prosperity 117

Unifying Experiences 117

Commerce and Consumption 118

Religion, Enlightenment, and Revival 119

Borderlands and Colonial Politics in the British Empire 121

GLOBAL COMPARISON: Large Warships in European Navies, 1660–1760 122

Conclusion: The Dual Identity of British North American Colonists 124

Reviewing the Chapter 126

The British Empire and the Colonial Crisis 6
1754–1775   129

Opening Vignette: *Loyalist governor Thomas Hutchinson stands his ground in radical Massachusetts*   129

The Seven Years' War, 1754–1763   130
   French-British Rivalry in the Ohio Country   130
   The Albany Congress and Intercolonial Defense   133
   The War and Its Consequences   134
   British Leadership, Pontiac's Uprising, and the Proclamation of 1763   135

HISTORICAL QUESTION: How Long Did the Seven Years' War Last in Indian Country?   136

The Sugar and Stamp Acts, 1763–1765   138
   Grenville's Sugar Act   138
   The Stamp Act   139
   Resistance Strategies and Crowd Politics   140
   Liberty and Property   141

The Townshend Acts and Economic Retaliation, 1767–1770   142
   The Townshend Duties   142
   Nonconsumption and the Daughters of Liberty   143
   Military Occupation and "Massacre" in Boston   144

The Tea Party and the Coercive Acts, 1770–1774   145
   The Calm before the Storm   145
   Tea in Boston Harbor   146
   The Coercive Acts   146
   Beyond Boston: Rural Massachusetts   147
   The First Continental Congress   148

Domestic Insurrections, 1774–1775   149
   Lexington and Concord   149
   Rebelling against Slavery   150

Conclusion: How Far Does Liberty Go?   151

Reviewing the Chapter   152

The War for America 7
1775–1783   155

Opening Vignette: *Deborah Sampson masquerades as a man to join the Continental army*   155

The Second Continental Congress   156
   Assuming Political and Military Authority   157
   Pursuing Both War and Peace   158
   Thomas Paine, Abigail Adams, and the Case for Independence   159
   The Declaration of Independence   160

The First Year of War, 1775–1776   160
   The American Military Forces   160
   The British Strategy   161
   Quebec, New York, and New Jersey   162

GLOBAL COMPARISON: How Tall Were Eighteenth-Century Men on Average?   162

The Home Front   163
   Patriotism at the Local Level   163
   The Loyalists   165
   Who Is a Traitor?   168
   Financial Instability and Corruption   169

BEYOND AMERICA'S BORDERS: Prisoners of War in the Eighteenth Century   166

The Campaigns of 1777–1779: The North and West   169
   Burgoyne's Army and the Battle of Saratoga   169
   The War in the West: Indian Country   171
   The French Alliance   172

The Southern Strategy and the End of the War   173
   Georgia and South Carolina   173
   The Other Southern War: Guerrillas   174
   Surrender at Yorktown   174
   The Losers and the Winners   175

Conclusion: Why the British Lost   177

Reviewing the Chapter   178

Building a Republic 8
1775–1789 181

Opening Vignette: *James Madison comes of age in the midst of revolution* 181

The Articles of Confederation 183

Congress, Confederation, and the Problem of Western Lands 183

Running the New Government 184

The Sovereign States 185

The State Constitutions 185

Who Are "the People"? 185

Equality and Slavery 187

SEEKING THE AMERICAN PROMISE: A Slave Sues for Her Freedom 188

The Confederation's Problems 190

Financial Chaos and Paper Money 191

The Treaty of Fort Stanwix 192

Land Ordinances and the Northwest Territory 193

Shays's Rebellion, 1786–1787 194

The United States Constitution 195

From Annapolis to Philadelphia 196

The Virginia and New Jersey Plans 196

Democracy versus Republicanism 197

Ratification of the Constitution 197

The Federalists 198

The Antifederalists 198

The Big Holdouts: Virginia and New York 200

Conclusion: The "Republican Remedy" 201

Reviewing the Chapter 202

The New Nation Takes Form 9
1789–1800 205

Opening Vignette: *Brilliant and brash, Alexander Hamilton becomes a polarizing figure in the 1790s* 205

The Search for Stability 206

Washington Inaugurates the Government 207

The Bill of Rights 208

The Republican Wife and Mother 208

Hamilton's Economic Policies 209

Agriculture, Transportation, and Banking 209

The Public Debt and Taxes 212

The First Bank of the United States and the *Report on Manufactures* 213

The Whiskey Rebellion 214

BEYOND AMERICA'S BORDERS: France, Britain, and Woman's Rights in the 1790s 210

Conflicts West, East, and South 215

To the West: The Indians 215

Across the Atlantic: France and Britain 218

To the South: The Haitian Revolution 219

Federalists and Republicans 220

The Election of 1796 220

The XYZ Affair 221

The Alien and Sedition Acts 222

Conclusion: Parties Nonetheless 223

Reviewing the Chapter 224

Republicans in Power
1800–1824   **227**

Opening Vignette: *The Shawnee chief Tecumseh attempts to forge a pan-Indian confederacy*   **227**

Jefferson's Presidency   **228**

   Turbulent Times: Election and Rebellion   **229**

   The Jeffersonian Vision of Republican Simplicity   **229**

   The Promise of the West: The Louisiana Purchase and the Lewis and Clark Expedition   **232**

   Challenges Overseas: The Barbary Wars   **234**

   More Transatlantic Troubles: Impressment and Embargo   **234**

HISTORICAL QUESTION: How Could a Vice President Get Away with Murder?   **230**

The Madisons in the White House   **235**

   Women in Washington City   **235**

   Indian Troubles in the West   **236**

   The War of 1812   **237**

   Washington City Burns: The British Offensive   **238**

Women's Status in the Early Republic   **239**

   Women and the Law   **240**

   Women and Church Governance   **240**

   Female Education   **241**

Monroe and Adams   **242**

   From Property to Democracy   **242**

   The Missouri Compromise   **243**

   The Monroe Doctrine   **245**

   The Election of 1824   **245**

   The Adams Administration   **246**

Conclusion: Republican Simplicity Becomes Complex   **247**

Reviewing the Chapter   **248**

The Expanding Republic
1815–1840   **251**

Opening Vignette: *The rise of Andrew Jackson, symbol of a self-confident and expanding nation*   **251**

The Market Revolution   **252**

   Improvements in Transportation   **253**

   Factories, Workingwomen, and Wage Labor   **255**

   Bankers and Lawyers   **256**

   Booms and Busts   **257**

The Spread of Democracy   **258**

   Popular Politics and Partisan Identity   **258**

   The Election of 1828 and the Character Issue   **258**

   Jackson's Democratic Agenda   **259**

Jackson Defines the Democratic Party   **260**

   Indian Policy and the Trail of Tears   **260**

   The Tariff of Abominations and Nullification   **262**

   The Bank War and Economic Boom   **263**

Cultural Shifts, Religion, and Reform   **264**

   The Family and Separate Spheres   **264**

   The Education and Training of Youths   **265**

   The Second Great Awakening   **267**

   The Temperance Movement and the Campaign for Moral Reform   **268**

   Organizing against Slavery   **268**

GLOBAL COMPARISON: Changing Trends in Age at First Marriage for Women   **265**

BEYOND AMERICA'S BORDERS: Transatlantic Abolition   **270**

Van Buren's One-Term Presidency   **272**

   The Politics of Slavery   **272**

   Elections and Panics   **272**

Conclusion: The Age of Jackson or the Era of Reform?   **274**

Reviewing the Chapter   **276**

The New West and Free North
1840–1860   279

Opening Vignette: *With the support of his wife, Abraham Lincoln struggles to survive in antebellum America*   279

Economic and Industrial Evolution   280
   Agriculture and Land Policy   281
   Manufacturing and Mechanization   281
   Railroads: Breaking the Bonds of Nature   282

Free Labor: Promise and Reality   284
   The Free-Labor Ideal: Freedom plus Labor   284
   Economic Inequality   285
   Immigrants and the Free-Labor Ladder   287

GLOBAL COMPARISON: Nineteenth-Century School Enrollment and Literacy Rates   286

The Westward Movement   287
   Manifest Destiny   288
   Oregon and the Overland Trail   288
   The Mormon Exodus   290
   The Mexican Borderlands   291

Expansion and the Mexican-American War   293
   The Politics of Expansion   293
   The Mexican-American War, 1846–1848   294
   Victory in Mexico   296
   Golden California   297

HISTORICAL QUESTION: Who Rushed for California Gold?   298

Reforming Self and Society   300
   The Pursuit of Perfection: Transcendentalists and Utopians   300
   Woman's Rights Activists   301
   Abolitionists and the American Ideal   302

Conclusion: Free Labor, Free Men   303

Reviewing the Chapter   304

The Slave South
1820–1860   307

Opening Vignette: *Slave Nat Turner leads a revolt to end slavery*   307

The Growing Distinctiveness of the South   308
   Cotton Kingdom, Slave Empire   309
   The South in Black and White   310
   The Plantation Economy   311

DOCUMENTING THE AMERICAN PROMISE: Defending Slavery   312

Masters, Mistresses, and the Big House   316
   Plantation Masters   316
   Plantation Mistresses   317

Slaves and the Quarter   319
   Work   319
   Family, Religion, and Community   320
   Resistance and Rebellion   322

Black and Free: On the Middle Ground   323
   Precarious Freedom   323
   Achievement despite Restrictions   323

The Plain Folk   324
   Plantation Belt Yeomen   324
   Upcountry Yeomen   325
   Poor Whites   325
   The Culture of the Plain Folk   327

The Politics of Slavery   327
   The Democratization of the Political Arena   327
   Planter Power   328

Conclusion: A Slave Society   328

Reviewing the Chapter   330

The House Divided

1846–1861   333

The Crucible of War

1861–1865   357

Opening Vignette: *Abolitionist John Brown takes his war against slavery to Harpers Ferry, Virginia*   333

The Bitter Fruits of War   334

The Wilmot Proviso and the Expansion of Slavery   334

The Election of 1848   336

Debate and Compromise   336

The Sectional Balance Undone   338

The Fugitive Slave Act   338

Uncle Tom's Cabin   339

The Kansas-Nebraska Act   339

Realignment of the Party System   341

The Old Parties: Whigs and Democrats   341

The New Parties: Know-Nothings and Republicans   341

The Election of 1856   343

SEEKING THE AMERICAN PROMISE: "A Purse of Her Own": Petitioning for the Right to Own Property   344

Freedom under Siege   345

"Bleeding Kansas"   346

The *Dred Scott* Decision   347

Prairie Republican: Abraham Lincoln   348

The Lincoln-Douglas Debates   348

The Union Collapses   349

The Aftermath of John Brown's Raid   349

Republican Victory in 1860   351

Secession Winter   352

Conclusion: Slavery, Free Labor, and the Failure of Political Compromise   353

Reviewing the Chapter   354

Opening Vignette: *Runaway slave William Gould enlists in the U.S. navy*   357

"And the War Came"   358

Attack on Fort Sumter   359

The Upper South Chooses Sides   359

The Combatants   360

How They Expected to Win   360

Lincoln and Davis Mobilize   362

Battling It Out, 1861–1862   363

Stalemate in the Eastern Theater   363

Union Victories in the Western Theater   365

The Atlantic Theater   366

International Diplomacy   366

GLOBAL COMPARISON: European Cotton Imports, 1860–1870   368

Union *and* Freedom   368

From Slaves to Contraband   368

From Contraband to Free People   369

War of Black Liberation   370

The South at War   371

Revolution from Above   371

Hardship Below   371

The Disintegration of Slavery   374

SEEKING THE AMERICAN PROMISE: The Right to Fight: Black Soldiers in the Civil War   372

The North at War   374

The Government and the Economy   374

Women and Work on the Home Front   375

Politics and Dissent   376

Grinding Out Victory, 1863–1865   377

Vicksburg and Gettysburg   377

Grant Takes Command   378

The Election of 1864   379

The Confederacy Collapses   379

Conclusion: The Second American Revolution   381

Reviewing the Chapter   382

Reconstruction
1863–1877

16

385

Opening Vignette: *James T. Rapier emerges in the early 1870s as Alabama's most prominent black leader* 385

Wartime Reconstruction 386

"To Bind Up the Nation's Wounds" 387

Land and Labor 387

The African American Quest for Autonomy 388

DOCUMENTING THE AMERICAN PROMISE: The Meaning of Freedom 390

Presidential Reconstruction 392

Johnson's Program of Reconciliation 392

White Southern Resistance and Black Codes 392

Expansion of Federal Authority and Black Rights 394

Congressional Reconstruction 395

The Fourteenth Amendment and Escalating Violence 395

Radical Reconstruction and Military Rule 396

Impeaching a President 397

The Fifteenth Amendment and Women's Demands 398

The Struggle in the South 398

Freedmen, Yankees, and Yeomen 399

Republican Rule 399

White Landlords, Black Sharecroppers 401

Reconstruction Collapses 402

Grant's Troubled Presidency 403

Northern Resolve Withers 404

White Supremacy Triumphs 405

An Election and a Compromise 406

Conclusion: "A Revolution But Half Accomplished" 407

Reviewing the Chapter 408

I. Documents A-1

The Declaration of Independence A-1

The Constitution of the United States A-3

Amendments to the Constitution (including the six unratified amendments) A-7

II. Facts and Figures: Government, Economy, and Demographics A-13

Presidential Elections A-13

Presidents, Vice Presidents, and Secretaries of State A-16

Supreme Court Justices A-19

Federal Spending and the Economy, 1790–2007 A-20

Population Growth, 1630–2000 A-21

Birthrate, 1820–2000 A-22

Life Expectancy, 1900–2000 A-22

Major Trends in Immigration, 1820–2000 A-22

III. Research Resources in U.S. History A-23

Bibliographies and Indexes A-23

Primary Resources A-23

Internet Resources A-24

Glossary of Historical Terms G-1

Spot Artifact Credits CR-1

Index I-1

CHAPTER 1

Map 1.1   Continental Drift   6

Spot Map   Beringia   6

Map 1.2   Native North American Cultures   10

Spot Map   Ancient California Peoples   11

Spot Map   Southwestern Cultures   13

Spot Map   Major Mississippian Mounds, AD 800–1500   15

Figure 1.1   Native American Population in North America, about 1492 (Estimated)   17

Map 1.3   Native North Americans about 1500   18

CHAPTER 2

Map 2.1   European Trade Routes and Portuguese Exploration in the Fifteenth Century   28

Spot Map   Columbus's First Voyage to the New World, 1492–1493   30

Map 2.2   European Exploration in Sixteenth-Century America   31

Spot Map   Cortés's Invasion of Tenochtitlán, 1519–1521   34

Map 2.3   Sixteenth-Century European Colonies in the New World   37

Spot Map   Roanoke Settlement, 1585–1590   44

CHAPTER 3

Map 3.1   Chesapeake Colonies in the Seventeenth Century   56

Spot Map   Settlement Patterns along the James River   59

Map 3.2   The West Indies and Carolina in the Seventeenth Century   68

CHAPTER 4

Map 4.1   New England Colonies in the Seventeenth Century   80

Figure 4.1   Population of the English North American Colonies in the Seventeenth Century   86

Map 4.2   Middle Colonies in the Seventeenth Century   88

Map 4.3   American Colonies at the End of the Seventeenth Century   92

Spot Map   King Philip's War, 1675   93

CHAPTER 5

Map 5.1   Europeans and Africans in the Eighteenth Century **104**

Map 5.2   North American Atlantic Trade in the Eighteenth Century **105**

Spot Map   Patterns of Settlement, 1700–1770 **111**

Map 5.3   The Atlantic Slave Trade **113**

Table 5.1 Slave Imports, 1451–1870 **113**

Map 5.4   Zones of Empire in Eastern North America **121**

Spot Map   Spanish Missions in California **124**

CHAPTER 6

Map 6.1   European Areas of Influence and the Seven Years' War, 1754–1763 **131**

Spot Map   Ohio River Valley, 1753 **132**

Map 6.2   Europe Redraws the Map of North America, 1763 **135**

Spot Map   Pontiac's Uprising, 1763 **135**

Map 6.3   Lexington and Concord, April 1775 **149**

CHAPTER 7

Spot Map   Battle of Bunker Hill, 1775 **158**

Map 7.1   The War in the North, 1775–1778 **164**

Map 7.2   Loyalist Strength and Rebel Support **168**

Spot Map   Battle of Saratoga, 1777 **170**

Map 7.3   The Indian War in the West, 1777–1782 **172**

Map 7.4   The War in the South, 1780–1781 **173**

Spot Map   Siege of Yorktown, 1781 **175**

CHAPTER 8

Map 8.1   Cession of Western Lands, 1782–1802 **184**

Spot Map   Legal Changes to Slavery, 1777–1804 **187**

Spot Map   Treaty of Fort Stanwix **192**

Spot Map   Shays's Rebellion, 1786–1787 **194**

Map 8.2   Ratification of the Constitution, 1788–1790 **199**

CHAPTER 9

Spot Map	Major Roads in the 1790s	212
Map 9.1	Travel Times from New York City in 1800	213
Map 9.2	Western Expansion and Indian Land Cessions to 1810	216
Spot Map	Haitian Revolution, 1791–1804	219

CHAPTER 10

Map 10.1	The Louisiana Purchase and the Lewis and Clark Expedition	233
Spot Map	The *Chesapeake* Incident, June 22, 1807	235
Spot Map	Battle of Tippecanoe, 1811	237
Map 10.2	The War of 1812	238
Map 10.3	The Missouri Compromise, 1820	244
Map 10.4	The Election of 1824	246

CHAPTER 11

Map 11.1	Routes of Transportation in 1840	253
Spot Map	Cotton Textile Industry, ca. 1840	255
Table 11.1	Growth of Newspapers, 1820–1840	258
Map 11.2	The Election of 1828	259
Map 11.3	Indian Removal and the Trail of Tears	261

CHAPTER 12

Map 12.1	Railroads in 1860	283
Spot Map	Plains Indians and Trails West in the 1840s and 1850s	288
Map 12.2	Major Trails West	289
Map 12.3	Texas and Mexico in the 1830s	292
Spot Map	Texas War for Independence, 1836	292
Map 12.4	The Mexican-American War, 1846–1848	295
Map 12.5	Territorial Expansion by 1860	297

CHAPTER 13

Map 13.1	Cotton Kingdom, Slave Empire: 1820 and 1860	309
Spot Map	The Upper and Lower South	309
Figure 13.1	Black and White Populations in the South, 1860	310
Map 13.2	The Agricultural Economy of the South, 1860	314

Spot Map   Immigrants as a Percentage of State Populations, 1860   **315**

Spot Map   The Cotton Belt   **324**

Spot Map   Upcountry of the South   **325**

CHAPTER 14

Spot Map   Mexican Cession, 1848   **335**

Map 14.1   The Election of 1848   **336**

Map 14.2   The Compromise of 1850   **338**

Spot Map   Gadsden Purchase, 1853   **340**

Map 14.3   The Kansas-Nebraska Act, 1854   **340**

Map 14.4   Political Realignment, 1848–1860   **342**

Spot Map   "Bleeding Kansas," 1850s   **346**

Map 14.5   The Election of 1860   **352**

Spot Map   Secession of the Lower South, December 1860–
                February 1861   **352**

CHAPTER 15

Map 15.1   Secession, 1860–1861   **360**

Figure 15.1   Resources of the Union and Confederacy   **361**

Map 15.2   The Civil War, 1861–1862   **364**

Spot Map   Peninsula Campaign, 1862   **365**

Spot Map   Battle of Glorieta Pass, 1862   **366**

Spot Map   Vicksburg Campaign, 1863   **377**

Spot Map   Battle of Gettysburg, July 1–3, 1863   **377**

Map 15.3   The Civil War, 1863–1865   **378**

CHAPTER 16

Spot Map   Reconstruction Military Districts, 1867   **396**

Figure 16.1   Southern Congressional Delegations, 1865–1877   **400**

Map 16.1   A Southern Plantation in 1860 and 1881   **402**

Map 16.2   The Election of 1868   **403**

Spot Map   Grant's Proposed Annexation of the Dominican Republic   **404**

Map 16.3   The Reconstruction of the South   **406**

Map 16.4   The Election of 1876   **407**

Beyond America's Borders

New France and the Indians: The English Colonies' Northern Borderlands 94

Prisoners of War in the Eighteenth Century 166

France, Britain, and Woman's Rights in the 1790s 210

Transatlantic Abolition 270

Documenting the American Promise

Justifying Conquest 38

Virginia Laws Governing Servants and Slaves 60

Defending Slavery 312

The Meaning of Freedom 390

Global Comparison

Migration to the New World from Europe and Africa, 1492–1700 69

Large Warships in European Navies, 1660–1760 122

How Tall Were Eighteenth-Century Men on Average? 162

Changing Trends in Age at First Marriage for Women 265

Nineteenth-Century School Enrollment and Literacy Rates 286

European Cotton Imports, 1860–1870 368

Historical Question

Who Were the First Americans? 8

How Long Did the Seven Years' War Last in Indian Country? 136

How Could a Vice President Get Away with Murder? 230

Who Rushed for California Gold? 298

Seeking the American Promise

A Sailor's Life in the Eighteenth-Century Atlantic World 106

A Slave Sues for Her Freedom 188

"A Purse of Her Own": Petitioning for the Right to Own Property 344

The Right to Fight: Black Soldiers in the Civil War 372

GETTING STUDENTS TO OPEN THE BOOK IS ONE of the biggest hurdles instructors face. *The American Promise: A Compact History* grew from the concerns most frequently voiced by instructors: that students often find history boring, unfocused, and difficult and their textbooks lifeless and overwhelming. We asked ourselves how our text could address these concerns and engage students in ways that would help them understand and remember the main developments in American history. To make the political, social, economic, and cultural changes vivid and memorable and to portray fully the diversity of the American experience, we stitched into our narrative the voices of hundreds of contemporaries — from presidents to pipe fitters and sharecroppers to suffragists — whose ideas and actions shaped their times and whose efforts still affect our lives. More maps and illustrations than in any other brief book — including hundreds of artifacts that highlight material culture — engage, inform, and make the past tangible to students. By incorporating a rich selection of authentic American voices and contemporaneous illustrations, we seek to capture history as it happened and to create a compelling narrative that captures students' interests and sparks their historical imagination.

From the beginning, *The American Promise* has been shaped by our firsthand knowledge that the survey course is the most difficult to teach and the most difficult to take. Collectively, we have logged considerably more than a century in introductory American history classrooms in institutions that range from small community colleges to large research universities. Our experience as teachers informs every aspect of our text, beginning with its framework. In our classrooms, we have found that students need **both** the structure a political narrative provides and the insights gained from examining social and cultural experience. To write a comprehensive, balanced account of American history, we focused on the public arena — the place where politics intersects social and cultural developments — to show how Americans confronted the major issues of their day and created far-reaching historical change.

Our title, *The American Promise*, reflects our emphasis on human agency and our conviction that American history is an unfinished story. For millions, the nation has held out the promise of a better life, unfettered worship, representative government, democratic politics, and other freedoms seldom found elsewhere. But none of these promises has come with guarantees. As we see it, much of American history is a continuing struggle over the definition and realization of the nation's promise. Abraham Lincoln, in the midst of what he termed the "fiery trial" of the Civil War, pronounced the nation "the last best hope of Earth." That hope has been marred by compromises, disappointments, and denials, but it lives still. Barack Obama declared that it is the "promise that has always set this country apart," adding that "when that promise was in jeopardy, ordinary men and women — students and soldiers, farmers and teachers, nurses and janitors — found the courage to keep it alive."

In developing the fourth edition, we sought to provide an alternative for colleagues searching for an affordable text with all the features of a full-length text. Many of our competitors continue to chase after the goals we achieved with this book: to offer a readable, accessible, briefer text that really works for students and teachers. With so many choices, we've been deeply gratified by the continued success of the compact edition. The fourth edition rests solidly on our original goals and premises. We continue to pair all the color, pedagogy, and features of a full-length text with a briefer narrative at a lower price. As authors, we continue to do our own abridgment to make a narrative that is both brief and rich with memorable details. To engage students more fully in the American story, we've given the book a new look, redesigned all of the book's maps, added a new biographical feature, and found new ways to position American history in the global world in which students live. Finally, in our quest to make this book even easier to study from, we've strengthened the pedagogical aids to provide students with greater guidance in reading, understanding, and remembering American history. Like America itself over the centuries, the fourth edition of *The American Promise: A Compact History* is both recognizable and new.

Features

From the beginning, readers have proclaimed this textbook a visual feast, richly illustrated in ways that extend and reinforce the narrative. The fourth edition offers almost **500** contemporaneous **illustrations**. In our effort to make history tangible, we include over **200 artifacts**—from boots and political buttons to guns and sewing machines—that emphasize the importance of material culture in the study of the past and enrich the historical account. **Comprehensive captions** for the illustrations in the book entice students to delve deeper into the text itself.

Our highly regarded **map program**, with **170** maps in all, rests on the old truth that "History is not intelligible without geography." Each chapter offers, on average, three **full-size maps** showing major developments in the narrative and two or three **spot maps** embedded in the narrative that emphasize detail from the discussion. To help students think critically about the role of geography in American history, we include **one critical-thinking map exercise** per chapter. New maps in the fourth edition highlight such topics as the Treaty of Fort Stanwix, Zululand and Cape Colony in 1878, major sources of oil in 1980, the recent conflict in Iraq, and the election of 2008.

To draw students in, each chapter begins with a colorful **opening vignette** featuring lively accounts of individuals or groups who embody the central themes of the chapter. New vignettes in this edition include, among others, Queen Isabella supporting Columbus's expedition to the New World, the Robin Johns's experiences in the Atlantic slave trade, Deborah Sampson masquerading as a man to join the Continental army, Alexander Hamilton as a polarizing figure, James T. Rapier emerging in the early 1870s as Alabama's most prominent black leader, Frances Willard participating in the creation of the Populist Party in 1892, and congresswoman Helen Gahagan Douglas during the Cold War.

As part of our ongoing efforts to make this the most teachable and readable survey text available, we paid renewed attention to the fourth edition's pedagogy. Chapters are constructed to preview, reinforce, and review the narrative in the most memorable and engaging ways possible. Designed to help students get the most out of their reading, each chapter includes **chapter outlines**, **review questions** that check the comprehension of main ideas, and boldfaced **key terms**. **Reviewing the Chapter** sections at the end of each chapter help students prepare for exams, with key terms, review questions repeated from within the narrative, **Making Connections** questions that ask students to think about broad developments, and **Suggested Readings**. These comprehensive reading and study tools offer students all the support of a full-sized text.

An enriched array of special features reinforces the narrative and offers teachers more points of departure for assignments and discussion. We've developed two new special features for this edition. To increase the book's emphasis on human agency, we've added **new Seeking the American Promise essays**. Biographical in nature, each essay explores a different promise of America—from the promise of freedom to the promise of home ownership, for example—while recognizing that the promises fulfilled for some have meant promises denied to others. Students connect to the broader themes through the stories of Americans such as Elizabeth Freeman, a slave who sued for her freedom in 1781, and paraplegic Beverly Jones, who sued for access under the Americans with Disabilities Act in her home state of Tennessee.

To support our increased emphasis on the global context of U.S. history, this edition also debuts fourteen **new Global Comparison figures** that showcase data visually with an emphasis on global connections. Features are focused on a wide range of topics, from comparing "Nineteenth-Century School Enrollment and Literacy Rates" worldwide to "Energy Consumption per Capita" in 1980.

Fresh topics in our three enduring special features further enrich this edition. Each **Documenting the American Promise** feature juxtaposes three or four primary documents to dramatize the human dimension of major events and show varying perspectives on a topic or issue. Feature introductions and document headnotes contextualize the sources, and Questions for Analysis and Debate promote critical thinking about primary sources. New topics in this edition include "Virginia Laws Governing Servants and Slaves," "Defending Slavery," and "The Final Push for Woman Suffrage." **Historical Question** essays pose and interpret specific questions of continuing interest so as to demonstrate the depth and variety of possible answers, thereby countering the belief of many beginning students that historians simply gather facts and string them together in a chronological narrative. Students recognize that history is an interpretive enterprise by joining in the questioning of, arguing about, and wrestling with the past. New questions in this edition include "Who Were the

First Americans?"; "Progressives and Conservation: Should Hetch Hetchy Be Dammed or Saved?"; and "Why Did the Allies Win World War II?" In addition, 50 percent of the **Beyond America's Borders** features are new. These essays seek to widen students' perspectives and help students see that this country did not develop in isolation. New essays as varied as "Prisoners of War in the Eighteenth Century" and "Imperialism, Colonialism, and the Treatment of the Sioux and the Zulu" consider the reciprocal connections between the United States and the wider world and challenge students to think about the effects of transnational connections over time.

Textual Changes

Because students live in an increasingly global world and benefit from making connections with the world outside the United States, we have substantially increased our attention to the global context of American history in the fourth edition. In addition to the two global features—Beyond America's Borders and the Global Comparison figures—the transnational context of American history has been integrated throughout the narrative as appropriate, including a new section on international diplomacy during the Civil War and a comparison of the welfare state in the United States and Europe during the Cold War. By contributing to a broader notion of American history, these additions help students understand more fully the complex development of their nation's history and help prepare them to live in the twenty-first century.

In our ongoing effort to offer a comprehensive text that braids all Americans into the national narrative, we have increased our attention to women's history. In addition to enhancing our coverage of women in the narrative—including a new section on women's education in the early Republic and more on woman suffrage—we've added eleven new vignettes and features focused around women. These additions continue to position women firmly in the national narrative while introducing students in more depth to women such as Queen Liliuokalani, Frances Willard, and Helen Gahagan Douglas, among others who have contributed to this nation's story.

To strengthen coverage and increase clarity and accessibility, we reorganized certain chapters. In particular, reorganization in Chapter 11, "The Expanding Republic, 1815–1840," and Chapter 12, "The New West and Free North, 1840–1860,"

provides clearer themes with smoother transitions. Chapter 17—newly titled "The Contested West"—has also been reorganized to incorporate the latest scholarship on the colonization of the West and to accommodate an expanded treatment of the struggles of Native Americans.

Staying abreast of current scholarship is a primary concern of ours, and this edition reflects that keen interest. We incorporated a wealth of new scholarship in myriad ways to benefit students. Readers will note that we made good use of the latest works on a number of topics, such as the French and Indian borderlands, the education of women in the early Republic, the Barbary wars, Denmark Vesey, black soldiers in the Civil War, the colonization of the West and the struggles of Native Americans in response to it, and American imperialism in Hawaii, as well as providing up-to-date coverage of the George W. Bush administration, the Middle East, Hurricane Katrina, the Iraq War, the 2008 election of Barack Obama, and the recent economic downturn.

Flexible Format

To accommodate the different ways that the American history survey is taught, *The American Promise: A Compact History*, Fourth Edition, is published in several versions:

- Combined edition (Chapters 1–31): paperback or e-Book
- Volume I, To 1877 (Chapters 1–16): paperback or e-Book
- Volume II, From 1865 (Chapters 16–31): paperback or e-book

For more information on the e-Book, see below.

Supplements

Developed with our guidance and thoroughly revised to reflect the changes in the fourth edition, the comprehensive collection of free and premium resources accompanying the textbook provide a host of practical learning and teaching aids. We learned much from the book's community of adopters, and we broadened the scope of the supplements to create a learning package that responds to the real needs of instructors and students. Many of the new media options not only will save you and your students time and money but also will add sound to the voices, movement to the images, and interactivity to the documents that help bring history to life. Cross-references in the textbook to the Online Study Guide and to the primary source reader signal the tight integration of the core text with the supplements.

For Students

Print Resources

Reading the American Past: Selected Historical Documents, **Fourth Edition.** Edited by Michael P. Johnson (Johns Hopkins University), one of the authors of *The American Promise,* and designed to complement the textbook, *Reading the American Past* provides a broad selection of more than 150 primary source documents, as well as editorial apparatus to help students understand the sources. Emphasizing the important social, political, and economic themes of U.S. history courses, 32 new documents (at least one per chapter) were added to provide a multiplicity of perspectives on environmental, western, ethnic, and gender history and to bring a global dimension to the anthology. Available free when packaged with the text and now available as an e-book (see below).

NEW *Rand McNally Atlas of American History.* This collection of more than 80 full-color maps illustrates key events and eras from early exploration, settlement, expansion, and immigration to U.S. involvement in wars abroad and on U.S. soil. Introductory pages for each section include brief overviews, timelines, graphs, and photos to quickly establish a historical context. Available for $3 when packaged with the text.

Maps in Context: A Workbook for American History. Written by historical cartography expert Gerald A. Danzer (University of Illinois at Chicago), this skill-building workbook helps students comprehend essential connections between geographic literacy and historical understanding. Organized to correspond to the typical U.S. history survey course, *Maps in Context* presents a wealth of map-centered projects and convenient pop quizzes that give students hands-on experience working with maps. Available free when packaged with the text.

The Bedford Glossary for U.S. History. This handy supplement for the survey course gives students clear, concise definitions of the political, economic, social, and cultural terms used by historians and contemporary media alike. The terms are historically contextualized to aid comprehension. Available free when packaged with the text.

U.S. History Matters: A Student Guide to U.S. History Online, **Second Edition.** This resource, written by Alan Gevinson, Kelly Schrum, and Roy Rosenzweig (all of George Mason University), provides an illustrated and annotated guide to 250 of the most useful Web sites for student research in U.S. history as well as advice on evaluating and using Internet sources. This essential guide is based on the acclaimed "History Matters" Web site developed by the American History Social Project and the Center for History and New Media. Available free when packaged with the text.

Bedford Series in History and Culture. More than 100 titles in this highly praised series combine first-rate scholarship, historical narrative, and important primary documents for undergraduate courses. Each book is brief, inexpensive, and focused on a specific topic or period. Package discounts are available.

Historians at Work Series. Brief enough for a single assignment yet meaty enough to provoke thoughtful discussion, each volume in this series examines a single historical question by combining unabridged selections by distinguished historians, each with a different perspective on the issue, with helpful learning aids. Package discounts are available.

Trade Books. Titles published by sister companies Farrar, Straus and Giroux; Henry Holt and Company; Hill and Wang; Picador; St. Martin's Press; and Palgrave Macmillan are available at a 50 percent discount when packaged with Bedford/St. Martin's textbooks. For more information, visit **bedfordstmartins .com/tradeup**.

Student Course Guides for *Shaping America: U.S. History to 1877* **and** *Transforming America: U.S. History since 1877.* These guides by Kenneth G. Alfers (Dallas County Community College District) are designed for students using *The American Promise* in conjunction with the Dallas TeleLearning telecourses *Shaping America* and *Transforming America.* Lesson overviews, assignments, objectives, and focus points provide structure for distance learners, while enrichment ideas, suggested readings, and brief primary sources extend the unit lessons. Practice tests help students evaluate their mastery of the material.

New Media Resources

NEW *The American Promise: A Compact History e-Book.* This electronic version of the fourth edition offers students unmatched value—the complete text of the print book with easy-to-use highlighting, searching, and note-taking tools, at a significantly reduced price.

NEW *Reading the American Past e-Book.* An online version of the fourth edition of *Reading the American Past* offers more than 150 primary source documents and editorial apparatus to aid students' understanding of the sources. This e-Book allows you to add an electronic dimension to your class or to integrate sources with your existing online course.

FREE Online Study Guide at bedfordstmartins .com/roarkcompact. The popular Online Study Guide for *The American Promise: A Compact History* is a free learning tool to help students master themes and information presented in the textbook and improve their historical skills. Assessment quizzes let students evaluate their comprehension, and a wide range of quizzing, map, and primary document analysis activities provides them with the opportunity for further study. Instructors can monitor students' progress through the online Quiz Gradebook or receive e-mail updates.

Audio Reviews. These 25- to 30-minute chapter summaries of each chapter in *The American Promise: A Compact History*, Fourth Edition, highlight the major themes of the text and help reinforce student learning. They fit easily into students' lifestyles and provide a practical way for them to study.

Online Bibliography at bedfordstmartins.com/ roark compact. Organized by book chapter and topic, the online bibliography provides an authoritative and comprehensive list of references to jump-start student research.

Jules R. Benjamin's *A Student's Online Guide to History Reference Sources* at bedfordstmartins .com/roarkcompact. This Web site provides links to history-related databases, indexes, and journals, plus contact information for state, provincial, local, and professional history organizations.

Bedford Bibliographer at bedfordstmartins .com/roarkcompact. This simple but powerful Web-based tool assists students with the process of collecting sources and generates bibliographies in four commonly used documentation styles.

Diana Hacker's *Research and Documentation Online* at bedfordstmartins.com/roarkcompact. This Web site provides clear advice on how to integrate primary and secondary sources into research papers, how to cite sources correctly, and how to format in MLA, APA, *Chicago*, or CBE style.

The St. Martin's Tutorial on Avoiding Plagiarism at bedfordstmartins.com/roark compact. This online tutorial reviews the consequences of plagiarism and explains what sources to acknowledge, how to keep good notes, how to organize research, and how to integrate sources appropriately. The tutorial includes exercises to help students practice integrating sources and recognize acceptable summaries.

Critical Thinking Modules at bedfordstmartins .com/roarkcompact. This Web site offers more than two dozen online modules for interpreting maps and audio, visual, and textual sources centered on events covered in the U.S. history survey.

For Instructors

Print Resources

Transparencies. This set of full-color acetate transparencies includes all full-size maps and many other images from *The American Promise* to help instructors present lectures and teach students important map-reading skills. A correlation guide showing how the transparencies align with the compact edition appears in the Instructor's Resource Manual and at bedfordstmartins.com/roarkcompact.

New Media Resources

Instructor's Resource Manual at bedfordstmartins .com/roarkcompact/catalog. This popular manual by Sarah E. Gardner (Mercer University) and Catherine A. Jones (Johns Hopkins University) offers both experienced and first-time instructors tools for presenting textbook material in exciting and engaging ways—learning objectives, annotated chapter outlines, lecture strategies, tips for helping students with common misconceptions and difficult topics, and suggestions for in-class activities, including using film and video, ways to start discussions, topics for debate, and analyzing primary sources. The new edition includes model answers for the questions in the book as well as a chapter-by-chapter guide to all of the supplements available with *The American Promise: A Compact History*. An extensive guide for first-time teaching assistants and sample syllabi are also included.

Instructor's Resource CD-ROM. This disc provides instructors with ready-made and customizable PowerPoint multimedia presentations built around chapter outlines, maps, figures, and selected images from the textbook plus jpeg versions of all maps and figures and of selected images. Also included are chapter questions formatted in PowerPoint and MS Word for use with i<clicker, a classroom response system, and blank outline maps in PDF format.

Computerized Test Bank. The test bank offers over 80 exercises per chapter, including multiple-choice, matching, map, and short and long essay questions. The answer key includes textbook page numbers, correct answers, and model essay responses. Instructors can customize quizzes, add or edit both questions and answers, and export questions to a variety of formats, including WebCT and Blackboard. The disc includes separate test banks for the associated telecourses *Shaping America* and *Transforming America*.

Book Companion Site at bedfordstmartins .com/roark compact. This companion Web site gathers all the electronic resources for the text, including the Online Study Guide and related Quiz Gradebook, at a single Web address providing convenient links to lecture, assignment, and research materials such as PowerPoint chapter outlines and the digital libraries at Make History.

Make History at bedfordstmartins.com/ roarkcompact. Comprising the content of our five acclaimed online libraries—Map Central, the Bedford History Image Library, DocLinks, HistoryLinks, and PlaceLinks, Make History provides one-stop access to relevant digital content including maps, images, documents, and Web links. Students and instructors alike can browse this free, easy-to-use database by course, topic, date, or resource type and can download the content they find. Instructors can also create entire collections of content and store them online for later use or post their collections to the Web to share with students.

Content for Course Management Systems. A variety of student and instructor resources developed for this textbook are ready for use in course management systems such as WebCT, Blackboard, and other platforms. This e-content includes nearly all of the offerings from the book's Online Study Guide as well as the book's test bank and the test banks from the associated telecourses *Shaping America* and *Transforming America*.

Reel Teaching. A valuable tool for enhancing media-rich lectures, short segments in VHS and DVD format are available to qualified adopters from the award-winning telecourses *Shaping America* and *Transforming America* by Dallas Tele-Learning at the LeCroy Center for Educational Telecommunications.

***The American Promise* via Telecourse.** *The American Promise* has been selected as the textbook for the award-winning U.S. history telecourses *Shaping America: U.S. History to 1877* and *Transforming America: U.S. History since 1877* by Dallas TeleLearning at the LeCroy Center for Educational Telecommunications, Dallas County Community College District. Guides for students and instructors fully integrate the narrative of *The American Promise* into each telecourse. For more information on these distance-learning opportunities, visit the Dallas Tele-Learning Web site at **http://telelearning.dcccd.edu,** e-mail **tlearn@dcccd.edu,** or call 972-669-6650.

Videos and Multimedia. A wide assortment of videos and multimedia CD-ROMs on various topics in American history is available to qualified adopters.

Acknowledgments

We gratefully acknowledge all of the helpful suggestions from those who have read and taught from the previous editions of *The American Promise: A Compact History*, and we hope that our many classroom collaborators will be pleased to see their influence in the fourth edition. In particular, we wish to thank the talented scholars and teachers who gave generously of their time and knowledge to review this book; their critiques and suggestions contributed greatly to the published work: Virginia Bellows, *Tulsa Community College;* Deborah Blackwell, *Texas A&M;* Harry Carpenter, *Western Piedmont Community College;* John Duke, *Alvin Community College;* Ronald B. Frankum, *Millersville University;* Barry Gidcomb, *Columbia State Community College;* Cecilia Gowdy-Wygant, *Front Range Community College–Westminster;* Eric

Hall, *Purdue University;* Arnette Hawkins, *University of Toledo;* Laurie Hochstetler, *Western Washington University;* David Howard-Pitney, *De Anza College;* Patricia Kaiser, *Erie Community College;* Carol Keller, *San Antonio College;* Ross Kennedy, *Illinois State University;* Peggy Lambert, *Kingwood College (a North Harris Montgomery Community College District school);* John Leiby, *Paradise Valley Community College;* Susan Oliver, *Cerritos College;* Anne Paulet, *Humboldt State University;* Dr. Patrick Reagan, *Tennessee Technological University;* Dan Rezny, *St. Charles County Community College;* Walter Sargent, *University of Maine–Farmington;* Jeff Smith, *Lindenwood University;* Norton Wheeler, *Washburn University;* and James Whitt, *Ozarks Technical Community College.*

A project as complex as this requires the talents of many individuals. First, we would like to acknowledge our families for their support, forbearance, and toleration of our textbook responsibilities. Pembroke Herbert and Sandi Rygiel of Picture Research Consultants, Inc., contributed their unparalleled knowledge, soaring imagination, and diligent research to make possible the extraordinary illustration program.

We would also like to thank the many people at Bedford/St. Martin's who have been crucial to this project. No one contributed more than developmental editor Laura Arcari, who managed the entire revision and oversaw the development of each chapter. The results of her dedication to excellence and commitment to creating the best textbook imaginable are evident on every page. We greatly appreciate the acute intelligence and indomitable good humor that Laura brought to this revision. Thanks also go to associate editor Lynn Sternberger, for her assistance managing

the reviews, and editorial assistant Robin Soule, who provided unflagging assistance and who coordinated the turnover of manuscript. We are also grateful to Jane Knetzger, director of development for history; William Lombardo, executive editor; and Mary Dougherty, publisher, for their support and guidance. For their imaginative and tireless efforts to promote the book, we want to thank Jenna Bookin Barry, executive marketing manager; John Hunger, senior history specialist; and Amanda Byrnes, senior marketing associate. With great skill and professionalism, Christina Horn, senior production editor, pulled together the many pieces related to copyediting, design, and typesetting, with the able assistance of David Ayers and the guidance of managing editor Elizabeth Schaaf and assistant managing editor John Amburg. Senior production supervisor Joe Ford oversaw the manufacturing of the book. Designer Brian Salisbury, copyeditor Sybil Sosin, and proofreaders Andrea Martin and Angela Hoover Morrison attended to the myriad details that help make the book shine. Leoni McVey provided an outstanding index. The book's gorgeous covers were designed by Billy Boardman. New media associate editor Marissa Zanetti, associate editor Jack Cashman, and new media production associate Rebecca Merrill made sure that *The American Promise: A Compact History* remains at the forefront of technological support for students and instructors. Editorial director Denise Wydra provided helpful advice throughout the course of the project. Finally, Charles H. Christensen, former president, took a personal interest in *The American Promise* from the start, and Joan E. Feinberg, president, guided all editions through every stage of development.

James L. Roark

Born in Eunice, Louisiana, and raised in the West, James L. Roark received his B.A. from the University of California, Davis, and his Ph.D. from Stanford University. His dissertation won the Allan Nevins Prize. He has taught at the University of Nigeria, Nsukka; the University of Nairobi, Kenya; the University of Missouri, St. Louis; and, since 1983, Emory University, where he is Samuel Candler Dobbs Professor of American History. In 1993, he received the Emory Williams Distinguished Teaching Award, and in 2001–2002 he was Pitt Professor of American Institutions at Cambridge University. He has written *Masters without Slaves: Southern Planters in the Civil War and Reconstruction* (1977). With Michael P. Johnson, he is author of *Black Masters: A Free Family of Color in the Old South* (1984) and editor of *No Chariot Let Down: Charleston's Free People of Color on the Eve of the Civil War* (1984). He has received research assistance from the American Philosophical Society, the National Endowment for the Humanities, and the Gilder Lehrman Institute of American History. Active in the Organization of American Historians and the Southern Historical Association, he is also a fellow of the Society of American Historians.

Michael P. Johnson

Born and raised in Ponca City, Oklahoma, Michael P. Johnson studied at Knox College in Galesburg, Illinois, where he received a B.A., and at Stanford University in Palo Alto, California, where he earned his Ph.D. He is currently professor of history at Johns Hopkins University in Baltimore, having previously taught at the University of California, Irvine; San Jose State University; and LeMoyne (now LeMoyne-Owen) College in Memphis. His publications include *Toward a Patriarchal Republic: The Secession of Georgia* (1977); with James L. Roark, *Black Masters: A Free Family of Color in the Old South* (1984) and *No Chariot Let Down: Charleston's Free People of Color on the Eve of the Civil War* (1984); *Abraham Lincoln, Slavery, and the Civil War: Selected Speeches and Writings* (2001); *Reading the American Past: Selected Historical Documents*, the documents reader for *The American Promise*; and articles that have appeared in the *William and Mary Quarterly*, the *Journal of Southern History, Labor History,* the *New York Review of Books,* the *New Republic,* the *Nation,* and other journals. Johnson has been awarded research fellowships by the American Council of Learned Societies, the National Endowment for the Humanities, and the Center for Advanced Study in the Behavioral Sciences and Stanford University, and the Times Mirror Foundation Distinguished Research Fellowship at the Huntington Library. He has directed a National Endowment for the Humanities Summer Seminar for College Teachers and has been honored with the University of California, Irvine, Academic Senate Distinguished Teaching Award and the University of California, Irvine, Alumni Association Outstanding Teaching Award. He won the *William and Mary Quarterly* award for best article and the Organization of American Historians ABC-CLIO *America: History and Life* Award for best American history article. He is an active member of the Society of American Historians, the American Historical Association, the Organization of American Historians, and the Southern Historical Association.

Patricia Cline Cohen

Born in Ann Arbor, Michigan, and raised in Palo Alto, California, Patricia Cline Cohen earned a B.A. at the University of Chicago and a Ph.D. at the University of California, Berkeley. In 1976, she joined the history faculty at the University of California, Santa Barbara. In 2005–2006 she received the university's Distinguished Teaching Award. Cohen has written *A Calculating People: The Spread of Numeracy in Early America* (1982; reissued 1999) and *The Murder of Helen Jewett: The Life and Death of a Prostitute in Nineteenth-Century New York* (1998). She has also published articles on quantitative literacy, mathematics education, prostitution, and murder in journals including the *Journal of Women's History, Radical History Review,* the *William and Mary Quarterly,* and the *NWSA Journal.* Her scholarly work has received support from the National Endowment for the Humanities, the National Humanities Center, the University of California President's Fellowship in the Humanities, the Mellon Foundation, the American Antiquarian Society, the Schlesinger Library, and the Newberry Library. She is an active associate of the Omohundro Institute of Early American History and Culture, sits on the advisory council of the Society for the History of the Early American Republic, and is past president of the Western Association of Women Historians. She has served as chair of the history department, as chair of the Women's Studies Program, and as acting dean of the humanities and fine arts at the University of California at Santa Barbara. In 2001–2002 she was the Distinguished Senior Mellon Fellow at the American Antiquarian Society. Currently she is working on a book about women's health advocate Mary Gove Nichols.

Sarah Stage

Sarah Stage was born in Davenport, Iowa, and received a B.A. from the University of Iowa and a Ph.D. in American studies from Yale University. She has taught U.S. history for more than twenty-five years at Williams College and the University of California, Riverside. Currently she is professor of Women's Studies at Arizona State University at the West campus in Phoenix. Her books include *Female Complaints: Lydia Pinkham and the Business of Women's Medicine* (1979) and *Rethinking Home Economics: Women and the History of a Profession* (1997), which has been translated for a Japanese edition. Among the fellowships she has received are the Rockefeller Foundation Humanities Fellowship, the American Association of University Women dissertation fellowship, a fellowship from the Charles Warren Center for the Study of History at Harvard University, and the University of California President's Fellowship in the Humanities. She recently returned from China where she was a visiting scholar at Beijing University and Sichuan University.

Alan Lawson

Born in Providence, Rhode Island, Alan Lawson received his B.A. from Brown University and his M.A. from the University of Wisconsin. After army service and experience as a high school teacher, he earned his Ph.D. from the University of Michigan. Since winning the Allan Nevins Prize for his dissertation, Lawson has served on the faculties of the University of California, Irvine; Smith College; and, currently, Boston College. He has written *The Failure of Independent Liberalism* (1971) and coedited *From Revolution to Republic* (1976). While completing the forthcoming *Ideas in Crisis: The New Deal and the Mobilization of Progressive Experience,* he has published book chapters and essays on political economy, the cultural legacy of the New Deal, multiculturalism, and the arts in public life. He has served as editor of the *Review of Education* and the *Intellectual History Newsletter* and contributed articles to those journals as well as to the *History of Education Quarterly.* He has been active in the field of American studies as director of the Boston College American studies program and as a contributor to the *American Quarterly.* Under the auspices of the United States Information Agency, Lawson has been coordinator and lecturer for programs to instruct faculty from foreign nations in the state of American historical scholarship and teaching.

Susan M. Hartmann

Professor of history at Ohio State University, Susan M. Hartmann received her B.A. from Washington University and her Ph.D. from the University of Missouri. After specializing in the political economy of the post–World War II period and publishing *Truman and the 80th Congress* (1971), she expanded her interests to the field of women's history, publishing many articles and three books: *The Home Front and Beyond: American Women in the 1940s* (1982); *From Margin to Mainstream: American Women and Politics since 1960* (1989); and *The Other Feminists: Activists in the Liberal Establishment* (1998). Her work has been supported by the Truman Library Institute, the Rockefeller Foundation, the National Endowment for the Humanities, the American Council of Learned Societies, and the Woodrow Wilson International Center for Scholars. At Ohio State she has served as director of women's studies, and in 1995 she won the Exemplary Faculty Award in the College of Humanities. Hartmann has taught at the University of Missouri, St. Louis, and Boston University, and she has lectured on American history in Australia, Austria, France, Germany, Greece, Japan, Nepal, and New Zealand. She is a fellow of the Society of American Historians and has served on award committees of the American Historical Association, the Organization of American Historians, the American Studies Association, and the National Women's Studies Association. She has also served on the Board of Directors at the Truman Library Institute. Her current research is on gender and the transformation of politics since 1945.

The American Promise

A COMPACT HISTORY

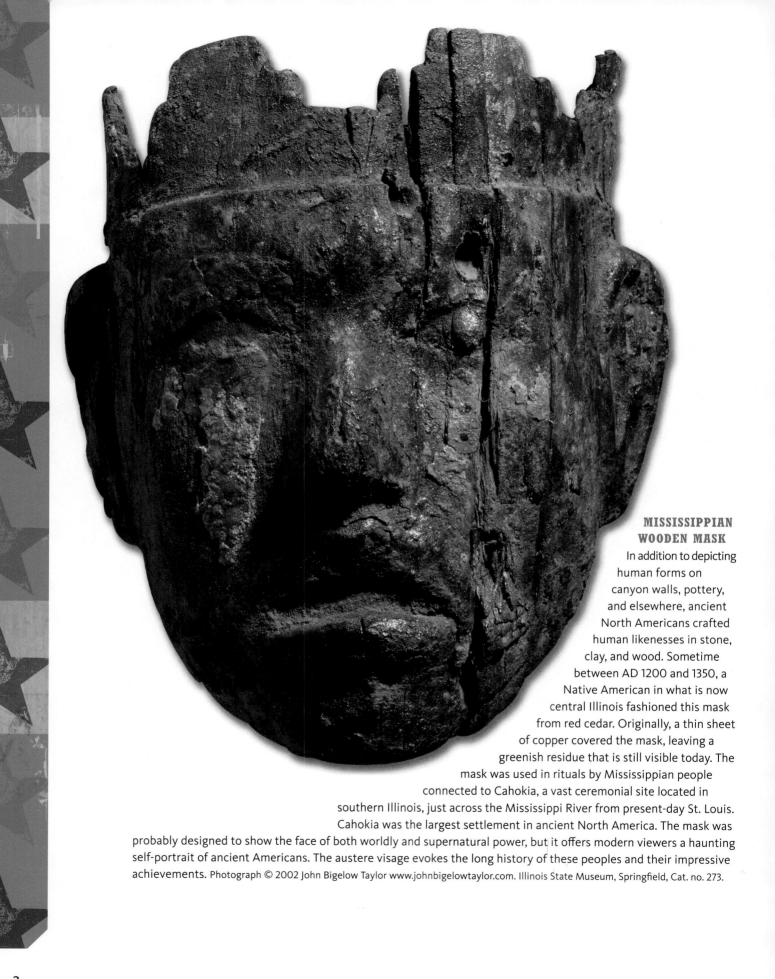

MISSISSIPPIAN WOODEN MASK

In addition to depicting human forms on canyon walls, pottery, and elsewhere, ancient North Americans crafted human likenesses in stone, clay, and wood. Sometime between AD 1200 and 1350, a Native American in what is now central Illinois fashioned this mask from red cedar. Originally, a thin sheet of copper covered the mask, leaving a greenish residue that is still visible today. The mask was used in rituals by Mississippian people connected to Cahokia, a vast ceremonial site located in southern Illinois, just across the Mississippi River from present-day St. Louis. Cahokia was the largest settlement in ancient North America. The mask was probably designed to show the face of both worldly and supernatural power, but it offers modern viewers a haunting self-portrait of ancient Americans. The austere visage evokes the long history of these peoples and their impressive achievements. Photograph © 2002 John Bigelow Taylor www.johnbigelowtaylor.com. Illinois State Museum, Springfield, Cat. no. 273.

Ancient America

BEFORE 1492

GEORGE McJUNKIN, THE MANAGER OF THE CROWFOOT RANCH near Folsom, New Mexico, rode out to mend fences and to look for missing cattle after a violent rainstorm in August 1908. An American of African descent, McJunkin had been born a slave in Texas and had been riding horses since he was a boy. After he became free at the end of the Civil War in 1865, McJunkin worked as a cowboy in Colorado and New Mexico before becoming the Crowfoot manager in 1891. Now, as he rode across the ranch, McJunkin noticed that floodwater had washed away the bank of a gulch called Wild Horse Arroyo and exposed a deposit of stark white bones. Curious, he dismounted and chipped away at the deposit until he uncovered an entire fossilized bone. The bone was much larger than the parched skeletons of range cattle and buffalo that McJunkin often saw, so he saved it, hoping someday to identify it.

Four years later, in 1912, McJunkin met Carl Schwachheim, a white man in Raton, New Mexico, and the two men became friends. McJunkin told Schwachheim about the fossil deposit he had discovered. Ten years later, after McJunkin's death, Schwachheim finally drove out to Wild Horse Arroyo and dug out several bones. But, like McJunkin, he could not identify any animal that had such big bones.

In 1926, Schwachheim delivered cattle to the stockyards in Denver, and he took some of the fossilized bones to the Denver Museum of Natural History and showed them to J. D. Figgins, a paleontologist who was an expert on fossils of ancient animals. Figgins immediately recognized the significance of the bones and a few months later began an excavation of the Folsom site that revolutionized knowledge about the first Americans.

When Figgins began his dig at Folsom, archaeologists — individuals who examine **artifacts**, or material remains, left by long-vanished peoples as part of the study of **archaeology** — believed that Native Americans had arrived relatively recently in the Western Hemisphere, probably no more than three or four thousand years earlier, when, experts assumed, they had paddled small boats across the icy waters of the Bering Strait from what is now Siberia. At Folsom, Figgins learned that the bones McJunkin had first spotted belonged to twenty-three giant bison, a species known to have been extinct for at least 10,000 years.

Previewing the Chapter

Archaeology and History 4
Q: Why do historians rely on the work of archaeologists to write the history of ancient America?

The First Americans 5
Q: Why were humans able to migrate into North America after 15,000 BP?

Archaic Hunters and Gatherers 8
Q: Why did Archaic Native Americans shift from big-game hunting to foraging and smaller-game hunting?

Agricultural Settlements and Chiefdoms 12
Q: How did the availability of food influence the distribution of the Native American population across the continent?

Native Americans in the 1490s 16
Q: Why did some Native Americans set fire to the land?

The Mexica: A Mesoamerican Culture 20
Q: How did the payment of tribute influence the Mexican empire?

Conclusion: The World of Ancient Americans 21

George McJunkin This photo shows McJunkin a few years after he discovered the Folsom site but about fifteen years before anyone understood the significance of his find. He appears here in his work clothes on horseback, as he probably was when he made the discovery. The fossilized bones he discovered belonged to an extinct bison species that was much larger than modern bison; the horns of the ancient animal often spanned six feet, wide enough for McJunkin's horse to have stood sideways between them. Eastern New Mexico University, Blackwater Draw Site, Portales, New Mexico 88130.

More startling, Figgins found nineteen flint spear points among the bones (**Folsom points**, they have since been called). Since no random natural process could have produced the finely crafted Folsom points, they seemed to prove that human beings had been alive at the same time as the giant bison. One spear point proved conclusively that the giant bison, the spear points, and the human beings who made them were contemporaries. One Folsom point remained stuck between two ribs of a giant bison, where a Stone Age hunter had plunged it more than 10,000 years earlier. No longer could anyone doubt that human beings had inhabited North America for at least ten millennia.

The Folsom discovery sparked other major finds of ancient artifacts that continue to this day. Since the 1930s, archaeologists have revolutionized our knowledge about ancient Americans. They have learned a great deal about the Folsom-era hunters who killed giant bison with flint-tipped spears, as well as about their ancestors who first arrived in North America and their descendants who built southwestern pueblos, eastern burial mounds, and much else. Most of the artifacts made by ancient Americans have been lost, have been destroyed by animals or natural deterioration, or still lie buried under geological deposits that accumulated for millennia. But archaeologists' careful study of the rare ancient artifacts that have been discovered has revealed much about the long, complex history of ancient Americans.

The story is necessarily incomplete and controversial because evidence that would resolve uncertainties and settle disputes no longer exists or awaits discovery. But archaeologists have learned enough in the last eighty years to understand where ancient Americans came from and many basic features of the complex cultures they created and passed along to their descendants, some of whom stood on the beach of a small island in the Caribbean in 1492 and watched Christopher Columbus and his men row ashore.   ★

Archaeology and History

Archaeologists and historians share the desire to learn about people who lived in the past, but they usually employ different methods to obtain information. Both archaeologists and historians study artifacts as clues to the activities and ideas of the humans who created them. They concentrate, however, on different kinds of artifacts. Archaeologists tend to focus on physical objects such as bones, spear points, pots, baskets, jewelry, clothing, and buildings. Historians direct their attention mostly to writings, including personal and private jottings such as letters and diary entries, and an enormous variety of public documents, such as laws, speeches, newspapers, and court cases. Although historians are interested in other artifacts and archaeologists do not neglect written sources if they exist, the characteristic concentration of historians on writings and of archaeologists on other physical objects denotes a rough cultural and chronological boundary between the human beings studied by the two groups of scholars, a boundary marked by the use of writing.

Writing is defined as a system of symbols that record spoken language. Writing originated among ancient peoples in China, Egypt, and Central America about eight thousand years ago, within the most recent 2 percent of the four hundred millennia that modern human beings (*Homo sapiens*) have existed. Writing came into use even later in most other places in the world. The ancient

Americans who inhabited North America in 1492, for example, possessed many forms of symbolic representation, but not writing.

The people who lived during the millennia before writing were biologically nearly identical to us. Their DNA was the template for ours. But unlike us, they did not use writing to communicate across space and time. They invented hundreds of spoken languages; they moved across the face of the globe, learning to survive in almost every natural environment; they chose and honored leaders; they traded, warred, and worshipped; and, above all, they learned from and taught each other. Much of what we would like to know about their experiences remains unknown because it took place before writing existed.

Archaeologists specialize in learning about people who did not document their history in writing. They study the millions of artifacts these people created. They also scrutinize soil, geological strata, pollen, climate, and other environmental features to reconstruct as much as possible about the world ancient peoples inhabited. Although no documents chronicle ancient Americans' births and deaths, pleasures and pains, archaeologists have learned to make artifacts, along with their natural and human environment, tell a great deal about the people who used them.

This chapter relies on studies by archaeologists to sketch a brief overview of ancient America, the long first phase of the history of the United States. Ancient Americans and their descendants resided in North America for thousands of years before Europeans arrived. For their own reasons and in their own ways, they created societies and cultures of remarkable diversity and complexity. Because they did not use written records, their history cannot be reconstructed with the detail and certainty made possible by writing. But it is better to abbreviate and oversimplify ancient Americans' history than to ignore it.

Q: Why do historians rely on the work of archaeologists to write the history of ancient America?

The First Americans

The first human beings to arrive in the Western Hemisphere emigrated from Asia. They brought with them hunting skills, weapon- and tool-making techniques, and a full range of other forms of human knowledge developed millennia earlier in Africa, Europe, and Asia. These first Americans hunted large mammals, such as the mammoths they had learned in Europe and Asia to kill, butcher, and process for food, clothing, building materials, and many other purposes. Most likely, these first Americans wandered into the Western Hemisphere more or less accidentally, hungry and in pursuit of their prey.

African and Asian Origins Human beings lived elsewhere in the world for hundreds of thousands of years before they reached the Western Hemisphere. They lacked a way to travel to the Western Hemisphere because millions of years before humans existed anywhere on the globe, North and South America became detached from the gigantic common landmass scientists now call Pangaea. About 240 million years ago, powerful forces deep within the earth fractured Pangaea and slowly pushed the continents apart to approximately their present positions (Map 1.1). This process of **continental drift** encircled the land of the Western Hemisphere with large oceans that isolated it from the other continents long before early human beings (*Homo erectus*) first appeared in Africa about two million years ago. (Hereafter in this chapter, the abbreviation *BP*—archaeologists' notation for "years before the present"—is used to indicate dates earlier than two thousand years ago. Dates more recent than two thousand years ago are indicated with the common and familiar notation *AD*—for example, AD 1492.)

More than a million and a half years after *Homo erectus* appeared, or about 400,000 BP, modern humans (*Homo sapiens*) evolved in Africa. All human beings throughout the world today are descendants of these ancient Africans. Slowly, over many millennia, *Homo sapiens* migrated out of Africa and into Europe and Asia. Unlike North and South America, Europe and Asia retained land connections to Africa, making this migration possible. The enormous oceans isolating North and South America from the Eurasian landmass kept human beings away for roughly 97 percent of the time *Homo sapiens* have been on earth.

Two major developments made it possible for human beings to migrate to the Western Hemisphere. First, humans successfully adapted to the frigid environment near the Arctic Circle. Second, changes in the earth's climate reconnected North America to Asia.

By about 25,000 BP, *Homo sapiens* had spread from Africa throughout Europe and Asia. People, probably women, had learned to use bone needles to sew animal skins into warm clothing that permitted them to become permanent residents of extremely cold regions such as northeastern Siberia.

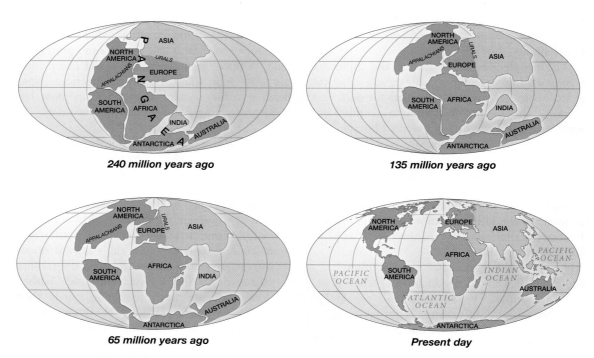

240 million years ago

135 million years ago

65 million years ago

Present day

MAP 1.1 Continental Drift
Massive geological forces separated North and South America from other continents eons before human beings evolved in Africa in the past 1.5 million years.

A few of these ancient Siberians clothed in animal hides walked to North America on land that now lies submerged beneath the sixty miles of water that currently separates easternmost Siberia from westernmost Alaska. During the last global cold spell—the Wisconsin glaciation, which endured from about 25,000 BP to 14,000 BP—snow piled up in glaciers, causing the sea level to drop as much as 350 feet below its current level. The falling sea level exposed what experts refer to as a land bridge between Asian Siberia and American Alaska. This land bridge, which scientists call **Beringia**, opened a pathway hundreds of miles wide between the Eastern and Western Hemispheres.

Siberian hunters presumably roamed Beringia for centuries in search of game animals. Grasses and small shrubs that covered Beringia supported herds of mammoths, bison, and numerous smaller animals. As the hunters ventured farther and farther east, they eventually became pioneers of human life in the Western Hemisphere. Their migrations probably had very little influence on their own lives, which

continued more or less in the age-old ways they had learned from their Siberian ancestors. Although they did not know it, their migrations revolutionized the history of the world.

Archaeologists refer to these first migrants and their descendants for the next few millennia as **Paleo-Indians**. They speculate that these Siberian hunters traveled in small bands of no more than twenty-five people. How many such bands arrived in North America before Beringia disappeared beneath the sea will never be known.

When they came is hotly debated by experts. The first migrants probably arrived sometime after 15,000 BP. Scattered and inconclusive evidence suggests that they may have arrived several thousand years earlier. (See "Historical Question," page 8.) Certainly, humans who originated in Asia inhabited the Western Hemisphere by 13,500 BP.

Paleo-Indian Hunters When humans first arrived in the Western Hemisphere, massive glaciers covered most of present-day Canada. A narrow corridor not entirely obstructed by ice ran along the eastern side of Canada's Rocky Mountains, and most archaeologists believe that Paleo-Indians probably migrated through the ice-free passageway

Beringia

in pursuit of game. They may also have traveled along the Pacific coast in small boats, hunting marine life and hopscotching from one desirable landing spot to another. At the southern edge of the glaciers, Paleo-Indians entered a hunters' paradise. North, Central, and South America teemed with wildlife that had never before confronted wily two-legged predators armed with razor-sharp spears. The abundance of game presumably made hunting relatively easy. Ample food permitted the Paleo-Indian population to grow. Within a thousand years or so, Paleo-Indians had migrated to the tip of South America and virtually everywhere else in the Western Hemisphere, as proved by discoveries of their spear points in numerous excavations that followed George McJunkin's Folsom find.

Early Paleo-Indians used a distinctively shaped spearhead known as a **Clovis point**, named for the place in New Mexico where it was first excavated. Archaeologists' discovery of Clovis points throughout North and Central America in sites occupied between 13,500 BP and 13,000 BP provides evidence that these nomadic hunters shared a common ancestry and way of life. Paleo-Indians hunted mammoths and bison—judging from the artifacts and bones that have survived from this era—but they probably also hunted smaller animals. Concentration on large animals, when possible, made sense because just one mammoth kill supplied hunters with meat for weeks or, if dried, for months. In addition to food, mammoth kills provided hides and bones for clothing, shelter, tools, and much more.

Clovis Spear Straightener Clovis hunters used this bone spear straightener about 11,000 BP at a campsite in Arizona, where archaeologists discovered it lying among the butchered remains of two mammoth carcasses and thirteen ancient bison. Similar objects often appear in ancient sites in Eurasia, but this is the only bone artifact yet discovered in a Clovis-era site in North America. Presumably Clovis hunters stuck their spear shafts through the opening and then grasped the handle of the straightener and moved it back and forth along the length of the shaft to remove imperfections and make the spear a more effective weapon. Arizona State Museum, University of Arizona.

About 11,000 BP, Paleo-Indians confronted a major crisis. The mammoths and other large mammals they hunted became extinct. The extinction was gradual, stretching over several hundred years. Scientists are not completely certain why it occurred, although environmental change probably contributed to it. About this time, the earth's climate warmed, glaciers melted, and sea levels rose. Mammoths and other large mammals probably had difficulty adapting to the warmer climate. Many archaeologists also believe, however, that Paleo-Indians probably contributed to the extinctions in the Western Hemisphere by killing large animals more rapidly than they could reproduce. Although this overkill hypothesis is disputed by some experts, similar environmental changes had occurred for millions of years without triggering the large mammal extinctions that followed the arrival of Paleo-Indian hunters. Whatever the causes, Paleo-Indian hunters faced a radical change in the natural environment within just a few thousand years of their arrival in the Western Hemisphere—namely, the extinction of large mammals. After the extinction, Paleo-Indians literally inhabited a new world.

Paleo-Indians adapted to the drastic environmental change of the big-game extinction by making at least two important changes in their way of life. First, hunters began to prey more intensively on smaller animals. Second, Paleo-Indians devoted more energy to foraging—that is, to collecting wild plant foods such as roots, seeds, nuts, berries, and fruits. When Paleo-Indians made these changes, they replaced the apparent uniformity of the big-game-oriented Clovis culture with great cultural diversity adapted to the many natural environments throughout the hemisphere, ranging from icy tundra to steamy jungles.

These post-Clovis adaptations to local environments resulted in the astounding variety of Native American cultures that existed when Europeans arrived in AD 1492. By then, more than three hundred major tribes and hundreds of lesser groups inhabited North America alone. Hundreds more lived in Central and South America. Hundreds of other ancient American cultures had disappeared or transformed themselves as their people constantly adapted to environmental change and other challenges.

> North, Central, and South America teemed with wildlife that had never before confronted wily two-legged predators armed with razor-sharp spears.

Q: Why were humans able to migrate into North America after 15,000 BP?

Who Were the First Americans?

To learn where the first humans who migrated to the Western Hemisphere came from and when they arrived requires following a trail that has grown very cold during the past 15,000 or more years. After millennia of erosion and environmental change, much of the land they walked, hunted, and camped on is now submerged and inaccessible, not only beneath the Bering Sea but also along the Atlantic and Pacific coasts of North America, where rising sea levels have flooded previously exposed coastal plains. Archaeologists have located numerous Paleo-Indian sites, but many of them (such as the Folsom site) date to hundreds of centuries after the first migrants arrived. Kill sites often yield spear points and large animal bones, but Paleo-Indian human skeletal remains are very rare. Yet evidence that Paleo-Indians inhabited the Western Hemisphere is overwhelming and indisputable. Human craftsmanship is the only plausible explanation for Clovis points, and carbon dating establishes that the oldest Clovis sites are about 13,500 years old.

Scattered and controversial evidence suggests, however, that Clovis peoples were not the first arrivals. Human coprolites (fossilized feces) recently discovered in the Paisley Caves in Oregon appear to date from about a thousand years before the Clovis culture. Along with the Meadowcroft site in Pennsylvania and the Monte Verde excavation in Chile, the Oregon evidence suggests that these ancient Americans arrived earlier than and differed from the later Clovis peoples. But if the first Americans already lived in Oregon, Pennsylvania, and Chile 14,000 or more years ago, when did they first arrive and from where?

Some experts hypothesize that pre-Clovis peoples sailed or floated across the Pacific from Australia, which had human inhabitants by at least 35,000 BP. Another speculation posits ancient Australians sailing first to Antarctica and then up the west coast of South America. These proposals of ancient Australians or Southeast Asians as the first Americans strike most scholars as far-fetched. The Pacific is too wide and tempestuous for these ancient peoples and their small boats to have survived a long transoceanic trip. The Polynesian islands lie much closer to Australia than does the Western Hemisphere, and human beings did not make that shorter journey until about 3,500 years ago.

Ancient Siberians had the means (hunting skills and adaptation to the frigid climate), motive (pursuit of game animals), and opportunity (the Beringian land bridge) to become the first humans to arrive in America, and most archaeologists believe they did just that. But when they came is difficult to determine, since the Beringian land bridge existed for thousands of years. The extreme rarity of the earliest archaeological sites in North America also makes it difficult to estimate with confidence when pre-Clovis hunters arrived. A rough guess is 15,000 BP, although it might have been considerably earlier. The scarcity of pre-Clovis sites discovered so far strongly suggests that these ancient Americans were few in number (compared to the much more numerous Clovis-era Paleo-Indians), very widely scattered, and ultimately unsuccessful in establishing permanent residence in the hemisphere. Although they and their descendants may have survived in America for a millennium or more, pre-Clovis peoples appear to have died out. The sparse archaeological evidence discovered to date does not suggest that they evolved into Clovis peoples.

Exactly how Clovis culture emerged remains a mystery. Close counterparts of Clovis points—the signature artifacts of North American Clovis sites—have not been found in Siberia or elsewhere outside America. Clovis culture, according to the archaeological evidence, appears to have arisen, flourished, and spread rapidly, as if it were an improvisation by newly arrived immigrants—an improvisation that perhaps never occurred among the people the immigrants left behind. Although Clovis peoples evidently were not the first humans to arrive in the Western Hemisphere, they may well represent the first Paleo-Indians to establish a permanent American presence.

To investigate where the mysterious first Americans came from, experts have supplemented archaeological evidence with careful study of modern-day Native Americans. Although many millennia separate today's Native Americans from those ancient hunters, most scholars agree that telltale

Archaic Hunters and Gatherers

Archaeologists use the term *Archaic* to describe both the many different hunting and gathering cultures that descended from Paleo-Indians and the long period of time when those cultures dominated the history of ancient America, roughly from 10,000 BP

to somewhere between 4000 BP and 3000 BP. The term usefully describes the era in the history of ancient America that followed the Paleo-Indian big-game hunters and preceded the development of agriculture. It denotes a **hunter-gatherer** way of life that persisted in North America long after European colonization.

Like their Paleo-Indian ancestors, **Archaic Indians** hunted with spears, but they also took clues to the identity of the first Americans can be gleaned from dental, linguistic, and genetic evidence collected from their descendants who still live throughout the hemisphere.

Detailed scientific analyses of the teeth of thousands of ancient and modern Native Americans have identified distinctive dental shapes—such as incisors with a scooped-out inner surface—commonly found among ancient Siberians, ancient Americans, and modern Native Americans, but rare elsewhere. This dental evidence strongly supports the Asian origins and Beringian migration route of the first Americans with descendants among contemporary Native Americans.

Linguistic analysis of more than a thousand modern Native American languages suggests that they cluster into three principal groups that appear to result from three separate ancient migrations. Aleut, spoken from Alaska across northern Canada to Greenland, seems to have been brought by the most recent migrants, who arrived about 4000 BP. Na-Dené, restricted to western Canada, appears to have arrived with migrants who came about 5,000 years earlier. Amerind is by far the most common group of Native American languages. Some form of Amerind is spoken by Native Americans throughout the hemisphere, the consequence (presumably) of its arrival with the earliest wave of ancient migrants around 13,000 BP. This migration chronology and linguistic analysis remains controversial among experts, but it is consistent with geological evidence of the Beringian land bridge and archaeological evidence of Clovis peoples. Taken together, the evidence suggests that Clovis peoples spoke some ancient form of Amerind.

Genetic research into the mutation rate of DNA inside mitochondria (tiny intracellular structures that carry out metabolic functions and are believed to mutate at a predictable rate) demonstrates that many modern Native Americans share genetic characteristics commonly found in Asians. Calculating the evolutionary time estimated to account for the subtle differences between Asian and Native American strains of mitochondrial DNA suggests a much earlier migration from Asia, possibly around 25,000 BP or before. But like the other high-tech evidence, this genetic evidence is sharply disputed by experts.

Fascinating as the genetic, linguistic, and dental studies are, they are unlikely to win widespread support among experts until they can be firmly corroborated by archaeological

★ **Clovis Artifacts** These Clovis-era artifacts were excavated from five mammoth kill sites in the United States. All the stone points show the signature Clovis shape with the distinctive flaking along the edges. The smaller points display a notched indentation at the bottom for tying the points to spear shafts. The largest stone implements in the photograph probably served as knives for butchering game or scrapers for cleaning hides. The bone object with a hole in one end was used to straighten spear shafts by scraping away imperfections. The slender bone rod is precisely inscribed with orderly serrations; its purpose is unknown. Experts speculate that it may have been used to flake chips to make spear points or attached to the end of a spear shaft to strengthen the connection between the shaft and the point. These artifacts illustrate the variety of Clovis objects found throughout the Western Hemisphere and their underlying similarity. Archaeologists believe that the commonalities in Clovis artifacts document a widely shared Clovis culture brought into being by ancient Americans who spread it across thousands of miles and many human generations. © Peter A. Bostrom.

evidence that, so far, has not been found. As a recent U.S. government study of the earliest Americans concluded, "How far back in time initial colonization [of America] occurred, how many separate migrations took place, whether all these migrations were successful, and the geographical and biological affinities of these founding populations remain ambiguous, and are subjects currently under intensive investigation by archaeologists."

Who were the first Americans? Thus far, no conclusive answer to this historical question has been found.

---

smaller game with traps, nets, and hooks. Unlike their Paleo-Indian predecessors, most Archaic peoples used a variety of stone tools to prepare food from wild plants. A characteristic Archaic artifact is a grinding stone used to pulverize seeds into edible form. Most Archaic Indians migrated from place to place to harvest plants and hunt animals. They usually did not establish permanent villages, although

they often returned to the same river valley or fertile meadow from year to year. In certain regions with especially rich resources—such as present-day California and the Pacific Northwest—the developed permanent settlements. Archaic peop followed these practices in distinctive ways i different environmental regions of North A (Map 1.2).

Bering
Strait

180°

160°W

140°W

120°W

100°W

80°W

60°W

40°W

20°W

60°N

40°N

20°N

Thule

ARCTIC

NORTHWEST COAST

ROCKY MTS.

Columbia R.

Snake R.

Missouri R.

L. Superior

L. Huron

L. Michigan

L. Ontario

L. Erie

GREAT PLAINS

SIERRA NEVADA

CALIFORNIA

GREAT
BASIN

Chumash

Colorado R.

Pueblo
Bonito

Folsom

Gila R.

Anasazi

Hohokam

Mogollon

SOUTH-
WESTERN

Pecos R.

Rio Grande

Hopewell

Adena

Cahokia

Ohio R.

Cumberland R.

Arkansas R.

Tennessee R.

Mississippi R.

Poverty
Point

APPALACHIAN MTS.

EASTERN WOODLANDS

ATLANTIC
OCEAN

PACIFIC
OCEAN

Gulf of
Mexico

MESO-AMERICAN

Caribbean Sea

Ancient North American site

N
W   E
S

| 0 | 500 | 1,000 miles |
| 0 | 500 | 1,000 kilometers |

MAP 1.2 Native North American Cultures

Environmental conditions defined the boundaries of the broad zones of cultural similarity among ancient North Americans.

READING THE MAP: What crucial environmental features set the boundaries of each cultural region? (The topography indicated on Map 1.3, "Native North Americans about 1500," may be helpful.)

CONNECTIONS: How did environmental factors and variations affect the development of different groups of Native American cultures? Why do you think historians and archaeologists group cultures together by their regional positions?

FOR MORE HELP ANALYZING THIS MAP, see the map activity for this chapter in the Online Study Guide at bedfordstmartins.com/roarkcompact.

Great Plains Bison Hunters After the extinction of large game animals, some hunters began to concentrate on bison in the huge herds that grazed the grassy, arid plains stretching for hundreds of miles east of the Rocky Mountains. For almost a thousand years after the big-game extinctions, Archaic Indians hunted bison with Folsom points like those found at the site discovered by George McJunkin.

Like their nomadic predecessors, Folsom hunters moved constantly to maintain contact with their prey. Great Plains hunters developed trapping techniques that made it easy to kill large numbers of animals. At the original Folsom site, careful study of the bones McJunkin found suggests that early one winter hunters drove bison into the narrow gulch and speared twenty-three of them. At other sites, Great Plains hunters stampeded bison herds over cliffs, then slaughtered the animals that plunged to their deaths.

Bows and arrows reached Great Plains hunters from the north about AD 500. They largely replaced spears, which had been the hunters' weapons of choice for millennia. Bows permitted hunters to wound animals from farther away, arrows made it possible to shoot repeatedly, and arrowheads were easier to make and therefore less costly to lose than the larger, heavier spear points. But these new weapons did not otherwise alter age-old techniques of bison hunting on the Great Plains. Although we tend to imagine ancient Great Plains bison hunters on horseback, in fact they hunted on foot, like their Paleo-Indian ancestors. Horses that had existed in North America millions of years earlier had long since become extinct. Horses did not return to the Great Plains until Europeans imported them in the decades after 1492, when Native American bison hunters acquired them and soon became expert riders.

Great Basin Cultures Archaic peoples in the Great Basin between the Rocky Mountains and the Sierra Nevada inhabited a region of great environmental diversity. Some Great Basin Indians lived along the shores of large marshes and lakes that formed during rainy periods. They ate fish of every available size and type, catching them with bone hooks and nets. Other cultures survived in the foothills of mountains between the blistering heat on the desert floor and the cold, treeless mountain heights. Hunters killed deer, antelope, and sometimes bison, as well as smaller game such as rabbits, rodents, and snakes. These broadly defined zones of habitation changed constantly, depending largely on the amount of rain.

Despite the variety and occasional abundance of animals, Great Basin peoples relied on plants as their most important food source. Unlike meat and fish, plant food could be collected and stored for long periods to protect against shortages caused by the fickle rainfall. Many Great Basin peoples gathered ample supplies of piñon nuts as a dietary staple. By diversifying their food sources and migrating to favorable locations to collect and store them, Great Basin peoples adapted to the severe environmental challenges of the region and maintained their Archaic hunter-gatherer way of life for centuries after Europeans arrived in AD 1492.

Pacific Coast Cultures The richness of the natural environment made present-day California the most densely settled area in all of ancient North America. The land and ocean offered such ample food that **California peoples** remained hunters and gatherers for hundreds of years after AD 1492. The diversity of California's environment also encouraged corresponding diversity among native peoples. The mosaic of Archaic settlements in California included about five hundred separate tribes speaking some ninety languages, each with local dialects. No other region of comparable size in North America exhibited such cultural variety.

The Chumash, one of the many California cultures, emerged in the region surrounding what is now Santa Barbara about 5000 BP. Comparatively plentiful food resources—especially acorns—permitted Chumash people to establish relatively permanent villages. Conflict, evidently caused by competition for valuable acorn-gathering territory, frequently broke out among the villages, as documented by Chumash skeletons that display signs of violent deaths. Although few other California cultures achieved the population density and village settlements of the Chumash, all shared the hunter-gatherer way of life and reliance on acorns as a major food source.

Another rich natural environment lay along the Pacific Northwest coast. Like the Chumash, **Northwest peoples** built more or less permanent villages. After about 5500 BP, they concentrated on catching whales and large quantities of salmon, halibut, and other fish, which they dried to last throughout the year. They also traded with

Ancient California Peoples

people who lived hundreds of miles from the coast. Fishing freed Northwest peoples to develop sophisticated woodworking skills. They fashioned elaborate wood carvings that denoted wealth and status, as well as huge canoes for fishing, hunting, and conducting warfare against neighboring tribes. Much of the warfare among Archaic northwesterners grew out of attempts to defend or gain access to prime fishing sites.

Eastern Woodland Cultures East of the Mississippi River, Archaic peoples adapted to a forest environment that included many local variants, such as the major river valleys of the Mississippi, Ohio, Tennessee, and Cumberland; the Great Lakes region; and the Atlantic coast (see Map 1.2). Throughout these diverse locales, Archaic peoples followed similar survival strategies.

Woodland hunters stalked deer as their most important prey. Deer supplied **Woodland peoples** with food as well as hides and bones that they crafted into clothing, weapons, needles, and many other tools. Like Archaic peoples elsewhere, Woodland Indians gathered edible plants, seeds, and nuts, especially hickory nuts, pecans, walnuts, and acorns. About 6000 BP, some Woodland groups established more or less permanent settlements of 25 to 150 people, usually near a river or lake that offered a wide variety of plant and animal resources. The existence of such settlements has permitted archaeologists to locate numerous Archaic burial sites that suggest Woodland people had a life expectancy of about eighteen years, a relatively short time to learn all the skills necessary to survive, reproduce, and adapt to change.

Ceramic Jar This handsome jar, crafted about 2000 BP by a Woodland potter (probably a woman), illustrates the usefulness of ceramic pots for storage and cooking and exhibits the human delight in decorative artistry. Gilcrease Museum, Tulsa, Oklahoma.

Around 4000 BP, Woodland cultures added two important features to their basic hunter-gatherer lifestyles: agriculture and pottery. Gourds and pumpkins that were first cultivated thousands of years earlier in Mexico spread north to Woodland peoples through trade and migration. Woodland peoples also began to cultivate local species such as sunflowers, as well as small quantities of tobacco, another import from South America. Corn was the most important plant food carried to North America by traders and migrants from Mexico, and it became a significant Woodland food crop around 2500 BP. Most likely, women learned how to plant, grow, and harvest these crops as an outgrowth of their work gathering edible wild plants. Cultivated crops added to the quantity, variety, and predictability of Woodland food sources, but they did not alter Woodland peoples' dependence on gathering wild plants, seeds, and nuts.

Like agriculture, pottery also probably originated in Mexico. Traders and migrants probably brought pots into North America along with Central and South American seeds. Pots were more durable than baskets for cooking and storage of food and water, but they were also much heavier and therefore were shunned by nomadic peoples. The permanent settlements of Woodland peoples made the heavy weight of pots much less important than their advantages compared to leaky and fragile baskets. While pottery and agriculture introduced changes in Woodland cultures, ancient Woodland Americans retained the other basic features of their Archaic hunter-gatherer lifestyle, which persisted in most areas to 1492 and beyond.

Q: **Why did Archaic Native Americans shift from big-game hunting to foraging and smaller-game hunting?**

Agricultural Settlements and Chiefdoms

Among Eastern Woodland peoples and most other Archaic cultures, agriculture supplemented, but did not replace, hunter-gatherer subsistence strategies. Reliance on wild animals and plants required most Archaic groups to remain small and mobile. But beginning about 4000 BP, distinctive southwestern cultures slowly began to depend on agriculture and to build permanent settlements. Later, around 2500 BP, Woodland peoples in the vast Mississippi valley began to construct **burial mounds** and other earthworks that suggest the existence of social and political hierarchies that archaeologists term **chiefdoms**.

Ancient Agriculture Dropping seeds into holes punched in cleared ground by a pointed stick, known as a "dibble," this ancient American farmer sows a new crop while previously planted seeds — including the corn and beans immediately opposite him — bear fruit for harvest. Created by a sixteenth-century European artist, the drawing misrepresents who did the agricultural work in many ancient American cultures — namely, women rather than men. However, the three-foot dibble would have been used as shown here. The Pierpont Morgan Library/Art Resource, NY; Jerry Jacka Photography.

FOR MORE HELP ANALYZING THIS IMAGE, see the visual activity for this chapter in the Online Study Guide at **bedfordstmartins.com/ roarkcompact**.

Although the hunter-gatherer lifestyle never entirely disappeared, the development of agricultural settlements and chiefdoms represented important innovations to the Archaic way of life.

Southwestern Cultures Ancient Americans in present-day Arizona, New Mexico, and southern portions of Utah and Colorado developed cultures characterized by agriculture and multiunit dwellings called **pueblos**. All **southwestern peoples** confronted the challenge of a dry climate and unpredictable fluctuations in rainfall that made the supply of wild plant food very unreliable. These ancient Americans probably adopted agriculture in response to this basic environmental condition.

About 3500 BP, southwestern hunters and gatherers began to cultivate corn, their signature food crop. Corn had been grown in Central and South America since about 7000 BP, and it slowly traveled up to North America with migrants and traders. In the centuries after

Southwestern Cultures

3500 BP, corn eventually became the most important cultivated crop for ancient Americans throughout North America. In the Southwest, the demands of corn cultivation encouraged hunter-gatherers to restrict their migratory habits in order to tend the crop. A vital consideration was access to water. Southwestern Indians became irrigation experts, conserving water from streams, springs, and rainfall and distributing it to thirsty crops.

About AD 200, small farming settlements began to appear throughout southern New Mexico, marking the emergence of the Mogollon culture. Typically, a Mogollon settlement included a dozen pit houses, each made by digging out a rounded pit about fifteen feet in diameter and a foot or two deep and then erecting poles to support a roof of branches or dirt. Larger villages usually had one or two bigger pit houses that may have been the predecessors

Hohokam "Cigarettes"
Ancient Hohokam smokers in present-day Arizona stuffed these reeds (which probably grew near their irrigation canals) with shredded tobacco. They wrapped cotton thread around each reed to protect their fingers from heat while they inhaled the smoke of the burning tobacco. When hunting or tending their crops, Hohokam smokers probably found these "cigarettes" more convenient than their heavier and more cumbersome stone or ceramic pipes, which were better suited for sedentary occasions. Jerry Jacka Photography.

they traveled north. Hohokam people built sizable platform mounds and ball courts characteristic of many Mexican cultures. About AD 1400, Hohokam culture declined for reasons that remain a mystery, although the rising salinity of the soil caused by centuries of irrigation probably caused declining crop yields and growing food shortages.

North of the Hohokam and Mogollon cultures, in a region that encompassed southern Utah and Colorado and northern Arizona and New Mexico, the **Anasazi** culture began to flourish about AD 100. The early Anasazi built pit houses on mesa tops and used irrigation much like their neighbors to the south. Beginning around AD 1000 (again, it is not known why), some Anasazi began to move to large, multistory cliff dwellings whose spectacular ruins still exist at Mesa Verde, Colorado, and elsewhere. Other Anasazi communities—like the one whose impressive ruins can be visited at Chaco Canyon, New Mexico—erected huge stone-walled pueblos with enough rooms to house everyone in the settlement. Pueblo Bonito at Chaco Canyon, for example, contained more than eight hundred rooms. Anasazi pueblos and cliff dwellings typically included one or more kivas used for secret ceremonies, restricted to men, that sought to communicate with the supernatural world.

Drought began to plague the region about AD 1130, and it lasted for more than half a century, triggering the disappearance of Anasazi culture. By AD 1200, the large Anasazi pueblos had been abandoned. The prolonged drought probably intensified conflict among pueblos and made it impossible to depend on the techniques of irrigated agriculture that had worked for centuries. Some Anasazi migrated toward regions with more reliable rainfall and settled in Hopi, Zuñi, and Acoma pueblos that their descendants in Arizona and New Mexico have occupied ever since.

of the circular **kivas**, the ceremonial rooms that became a characteristic of nearly all southwestern settlements. About AD 900, Mogollon culture began to decline, for reasons that remain obscure. Its descendants included the Mimbres people in southwestern New Mexico, who crafted spectacular pottery adorned with human and animal designs. By about AD 1250, the Mimbres culture disappeared, for reasons unknown.

Around AD 500, while the Mogollon culture prevailed in New Mexico, other ancient people migrated from Mexico to southern Arizona and established the distinctive Hohokam culture. Hohokam settlements used sophisticated grids of irrigation canals to plant and harvest crops twice a year. Hohokam settlements reflected the continuing influence of Mexican cultural practices that migrants brought with them as

Mexican Ball Court Model The Mexica and other ancient Central American peoples commonly built special courts (or playing fields) for their intensely competitive ball games. This rare model of a ball court, made in Mexico sometime between 2200 BP and AD 250, shows a game in progress, complete with players and spectators. Players wore padded belts and used their hips to hit the hard rubber ball through the goal. Spectators watched intently, not only to admire the skills of the players but also because a lot was at stake. Spectators bet on the games, and losing players were often killed. A few ball courts have been excavated in North America, providing compelling evidence of one of the many connections between ancient Mexicans and North Americans. Yale University Art Gallery. Stephen Carlton Clark, B.A. 1903, Fund.

Pueblo Bonito, Chaco Canyon, New Mexico About AD 1000, Pueblo Bonito stood at the center of Chacoan culture, which extended over more than 20,000 square miles in the region at the intersection of present-day Utah, Colorado, Arizona, and New Mexico. The numerous circular kivas show the significance of ceremonies and rituals to the people of Chaco Canyon. Major buildings appear to have been aligned to mark the spring and winter solstices and the phases of the lunar cycle, suggesting that the ceremonies at Chaco Canyon may have symbolized the potent connections between earth and sky, between humans and the omnipotent celestial ruler. Richard Alexander Cooke III.

FOR MORE HELP ANALYZING THIS IMAGE, see the visual activity for this chapter in the Online Study Guide at bedfordstmartins.com/roarkcompact.

Woodland Burial Mounds and Chiefdoms No other ancient Americans created dwellings similar to pueblos, but around 2500 BP, Woodland cultures throughout the vast area drained by the Mississippi River began to build burial mounds. The size of the mounds, the labor and organization required to erect them, and differences in the artifacts buried with certain individuals suggest the existence of a social and political hierarchy that archaeologists term a *chiefdom*. Experts do not know the name of a single chief, nor do they know the organizational structure a chief headed. But the only way archaeologists can account for the complex and labor-intensive burial mounds and artifacts found in them is to assume that one person—whom scholars term a *chief*—commanded the labor and obedience of very large numbers of other people, who made up the chief's chiefdom.

Between 2500 BP and 2100 BP, Adena people built hundreds of burial mounds radiating from central Ohio. In the mounds, the Adena usually accompanied burials with grave goods that included

Major Mississippian Mounds, AD 800–1500

spear points and stone pipes as well as thin sheets of mica (a glasslike mineral) crafted into shapes of birds, beasts, and human hands. Over the body and grave goods Adena people piled dirt into a mound. Sometimes burial mounds were constructed all at once, but often they were built up slowly over many years. About 2100 BP, Adena culture evolved into the more elaborate **Hopewell culture**, which lasted about 500 years. Centered in Ohio, Hopewell culture extended throughout the enormous drainage of the Ohio and Mississippi rivers. Hopewell people built larger mounds than their Adena predecessors and filled them with more magnificent grave goods.

Burial was probably reserved for the most important members of Hopewell groups. Most people were cremated. Burial rituals appear to have brought many people together to honor the dead person and to help build the mound. Hopewell mounds were often one hundred feet in diameter and thirty feet high. Grave goods at Hopewell sites testify to the high quality of Hopewell crafts and to a thriving trade network that ranged from Wyoming to Florida. Archaeologists believe that Hopewell chiefs probably played an important role in this sprawling interregional trade.

Hopewell culture declined about AD 400 for reasons that are obscure. Archaeologists speculate that bows and arrows, along with increasing reliance on agriculture, made small settlements more self-sufficient and, therefore, less dependent on the central authority of the Hopewell chiefs who were responsible for the burial mounds.

Four hundred years later, another mound-building culture flourished. The **Mississippian culture** emerged in the floodplains of the major southeastern river systems about AD 800 and lasted until about AD 1500. Major Mississippian sites included huge mounds with platforms on top for ceremonies and for the residences of great chiefs. Most likely, the ceremonial mounds and ritual practices derived from Mexican cultural expressions that were carried north by traders and migrants. The largest Mississippian site was **Cahokia**, whose remnants can be seen in Illinois near the confluence of the Mississippi and Missouri rivers.

At Cahokia, more than one hundred mounds were grouped around large open plazas. Monk's Mound, the largest, covered sixteen acres at its base and was one hundred feet tall. Dwellings may have housed as many as thirty thousand inhabitants, easily qualifying Cahokia as the largest settlement in ancient North America. At Cahokia and other Mississippian sites, people evidently worshipped a sun god; the mounds probably elevated elites nearer to the sun's supernatural power. One Cahokia burial mound suggests the authority a great chief exercised. One man—presumably the chief—was buried with the bodies of more than sixty people who had been killed at the time of burial, including fifty young women who had been strangled. Such a mass sacrifice illustrates the coercive power of a Cahokia chief.

Cahokia and other Mississippian cultures dwindled by AD 1500. When Europeans arrived, most of the descendants of Mississippian cultures, like those of the Hopewell culture, lived in small dispersed villages supported by hunting and gathering supplemented by agriculture. Clearly, the conditions that caused large chiefdoms to emerge—whatever they were—had changed, and chiefs no longer commanded the sweeping powers they had once enjoyed.

Q: **How did the availability of food influence the distribution of the Native American population across the continent?**

Native Americans in the 1490s

About thirteen millennia after Paleo-Indians first migrated to the Western Hemisphere, a new migration—this time from Europe—began in 1492 with the journey of Christopher Columbus. In the decades before 1492, Native Americans continued to employ their ancestors' time-tested survival strategies of hunting, gathering, and agriculture. Those strategies succeeded in both populating and shaping the new world Europeans encountered.

By the 1490s, Native Americans lived throughout North America, but their total population is a subject of spirited debate among scholars. Some experts claim Native Americans numbered 18 million to 20 million, while others place the population at no more than a million. A prudent estimate is about 4 million. On the eve of European colonization, the small island nation of England had about the same number of people as all of North America. The vastness of North America meant the population density was low, just 60 people per hundred square miles, compared to more than 8,000 in England. Compared to England and elsewhere in Europe, Native Americans were spread thin across the land because of their survival strategies of hunting, gathering, and agriculture.

Regions in North America with abundant resources had relatively high populations. About one-fifth of Native Americans lived along the West Coast in food-rich California and the Pacific Northwest, where the population density was, respectively, six times greater and four times greater than the average for the whole continent (Figure 1.1). The food-scarce vastness of the Great Plains, Great Basin, and Arctic regions held about one-quarter of Native Americans, but the population density was extremely low, roughly one-tenth the continental average. About a quarter of Native Americans resided in the arid Southwest, where irrigation and intensive agriculture permitted a population density about twice the continental average. But even in California, the most densely inhabited region of North America, population density was just one-twentieth of England's.

The enormous Woodland region east of the Mississippi River was home to about one-third of Native Americans, whose population density approximated the continental average. Eastern Woodland peoples clustered into three broad linguistic and cultural groups: Algonquian, Iroquoian, and Muskogean. **Algonquian tribes** inhabited the Atlantic seaboard, the Great Lakes region, and much of the upper Midwest (Map 1.3). The relatively mild climate along the Atlantic permitted the coastal Algonquians to grow corn and other crops as well as to hunt and fish. Around the Great Lakes and in northern New England, however, cool summers and severe winters made agriculture impractical. Instead, the Abenaki, Penobscot, Chippewa, and other tribes concentrated

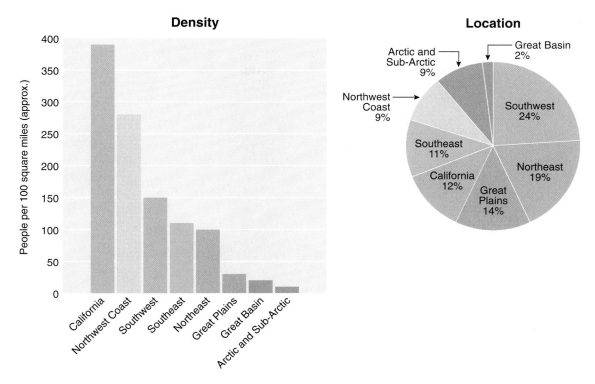

Density

People per 100 square miles (approx.)

Location

Arctic and Sub-Arctic 9%
Great Basin 2%
Northwest Coast 9%
Southwest 24%
Southeast 11%
California 12%
Great Plains 14%
Northeast 19%

FIGURE 1.1 Native American Population in North America, about 1492 (Estimated)
The population density on the enormous expanses of the Great Plains, Great Basin, and Arctic regions was very low, although in total about a quarter of all native North Americans resided in these areas. Overall, the population density in North America was less than 1 percent of the population density of England, which helps explain why European colonists tended to view North America as a comparatively empty wilderness.

on hunting and fishing, using canoes both for transportation and for gathering wild rice.

Inland from the Algonquian region, **Iroquoian tribes** occupied territories centered in Pennsylvania and upstate New York, as well as the hilly upland regions of the Carolinas and Georgia. Three features distinguished Iroquoian tribes from their neighbors. First, their success in cultivating corn and other crops allowed them to build permanent settlements, usually consisting of several bark-covered longhouses up to one hundred feet long and housing five to ten families. Second, Iroquoian societies adhered to matrilineal rules of descent. Property of all sorts belonged to women. Women headed family clans and even selected the chiefs (normally men) who governed the tribes. Third, for purposes of war and diplomacy, an Iroquoian confederation—including the Seneca, Onondaga, Mohawk, Oneida, and Cayuga tribes—formed the League of Five Nations, which remained powerful well into the eighteenth century.

Muskogean peoples spread throughout the woodlands of the Southeast, south of the Ohio River and east of the Mississippi. Including the Creek, Choctaw, Chickasaw, and Natchez tribes, Muskogeans inhabited a bountiful natural environment that provided abundant food from hunting,

gathering, and agriculture. Remnants of the earlier Mississippian culture still existed in Muskogean religion. The Natchez, for example, worshipped the sun and built temple mounds modeled after those of their Mississippian ancestors.

Great Plains peoples accounted for about one out of seven Native Americans. Inhabiting the huge region west of the Eastern Woodland people and east of the Rocky Mountains, many tribes had migrated to the Great Plains within the past century or two, forced westward by Iroquoian and Algonquian tribes. Some Great Plains tribes—especially the Mandan and Pawnee—farmed successfully, growing both corn and sunflowers. But the Teton Sioux, Blackfeet, Comanche, Cheyenne, and Crow on the northern plains and the Apache and other nomadic tribes on the southern plains depended on buffalo (American bison) for their subsistence.

Southwestern cultures included about a quarter of all native North Americans. These descendants of the Mogollon, Hohokam, and Anasazi cultures lived in settled agricultural communities, many of them pueblos. They continued to grow corn, beans, and squash using methods they had refined for centuries. However, their communities came under attack by a large number of warlike Athapascan tribes

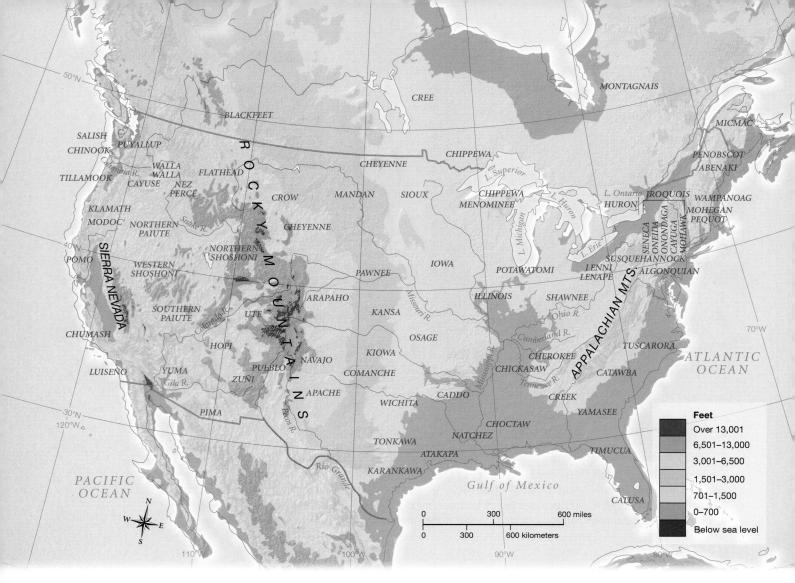

MAP 1.3 Native North Americans about 1500
Distinctive Native American peoples resided throughout the area that, centuries later, would become the United States. This map indicates the approximate location of some of the larger tribes about 1500. In the interest of legibility, many other peoples who inhabited North America at the time are omitted from the map.

who invaded the Southwest beginning around AD 1300. The Athapascans—principally Apache and Navajo—were skillful warriors who preyed on the sedentary pueblo Indians, reaping the fruits of agriculture without the work of farming.

About a fifth of all native North Americans resided along the Pacific coast. In California, abundant acorns and nutritious marine life continued to support high population densities, but they retarded the development of agriculture. Similar dependence on hunting and gathering persisted along the Northwest coast, where fishing reigned supreme. Salmon was so abundant that at The Dalles, a prime fishing site on the Columbia River on the border of present-day Oregon and

Washington, Northwest peoples caught millions of pounds of salmon every summer and traded it as far away as California and the Great Plains. Although important trading centers existed throughout North America, particularly in the Southwest, it is likely that The Dalles was the largest Native American trading center in North America.

While trading was common, all native North Americans in the 1490s still depended on hunting and gathering for a major portion of their food. Most of them also practiced agriculture. Some used agriculture to supplement hunting and gathering; for others, the balance was reversed. People throughout North America used bows, arrows, and other weapons for hunting and warfare. None

THE PROMISE OF TECHNOLOGY

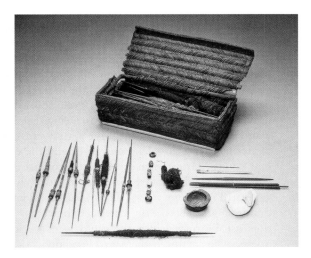

Ancient American Weaving The workbasket of a master weaver shown here illustrates the technology of ancient American textile production. Found in the Andes in a woman's grave dating from one thousand years ago, the workbasket contains tools for every stage of textile production. Weaving — like other activities such as cooking, hunting, and worship — depended above all on human knowledge passed from one person to another in cycle after cycle of teaching and learning. But the cycle of teaching and learning was fragile. A weaver's knowledge could die with her if she had not taught it to somebody else. Wars, famines, droughts, epidemics, and other disasters could extinguish technological knowledge along with its possessors. The technology of weaving practiced by the owner of this workbasket was developed by the women she learned from and passed on to the women she taught. Museum of Fine Arts, Boston. Gift of Charles H. White, 02.680.

of them employed writing, expressing themselves instead in many other ways: drawings sketched on stones, wood, and animal skins; patterns woven in baskets and textiles; designs painted on pottery, crafted into beadwork, or carved into effigies; and songs, dances, religious ceremonies, and burial rites.

These rich and varied cultural resources of Native Americans did not include features of life common in Europe during the 1490s. Native Americans did not use wheels; sailing ships were unknown to them; they had no large domesticated animals such as horses, cows, or oxen; their use of metals was restricted to copper. However, the absence of these European conveniences mattered less to native North Americans than their own cultural adaptations to the natural environment local to each tribe and to the social environment among neighboring peoples. That great similarity — adaptation to natural and social environments — underlay all the cultural diversity among native North Americans.

It would be a mistake, however, to conclude that native North Americans lived in blissful harmony with nature and each other. Archaeological sites provide ample evidence of violent conflict among Native Americans. Skeletons bear the marks of wounds as well as of ritualistic human sacrifice and even cannibalism. Religious, ethnic, economic, and familial conflicts must have occurred, but they remain in obscurity because they left few archaeo-

logical traces. In general, fear and anxiety must have been at least as common among Native Americans as feelings of peace and security.

Native Americans not only adapted to the natural environment; they also changed it in many ways. They built thousands of structures, from small dwellings to massive pueblos and enormous mounds, permanently altering the landscape. Their gathering techniques selected productive and nutritious varieties of plants, thereby shifting the balance of local plants toward useful varieties. The first stages of North American agriculture, for example, probably resulted from Native Americans gathering wild seeds and then sowing them in a meadow for later harvest. It is almost certain that fertile and hardy varieties of corn were developed this way, first in Mexico and later in North America. To clear land for planting corn, Native Americans set fires that burned off thousands of acres of forest.

Native Americans also used fires for hunting. Great Plains hunters often started fires to force buffalo together and make them easy to slaughter. Eastern Woodland, Southwest, and Pacific coast Indians also set fires to hunt deer and other valuable prey. Hunters crouched downwind from a brushy area while their companions set a fire upwind;

> *The absence of European conveniences mattered less to native North Americans than their own cultural adaptations to the natural environment.*

as animals raced out of the burning underbrush, hunters killed them.

Throughout North America, Indians started fires along the edges of woods to burn off shrubby undergrowth and encroaching tree seedlings. These burns encouraged the growth of tender young plants that attracted deer and other game animals, bringing them within convenient range of hunters' weapons. The burns also encouraged the growth of sun-loving food plants that Indians relished, such as blackberries, strawberries, and raspberries.

Because fires set by Native Americans usually burned until they ran out of fuel or were extinguished by rain or wind, enormous regions of North America were burned over. In the long run, fires created and maintained light-dappled meadows for hunting and agriculture, cleared entangling underbrush from forests, and promoted a diverse and productive natural environment. Fires, like other activities of Native Americans, shaped the landscape of North America long before Europeans arrived in 1492.

Q: **Why did some Native Americans set fire to the land?**

The Mexica: A Mesoamerican Culture

The indigenous population of the New World (the Western Hemisphere) numbered roughly 80 million in the 1490s, about the same as the population of Europe. Almost all these people lived in Mexico and Central and South America. Like their much less numerous North American counterparts, they too lived in a natural environment of tremendous diversity. They too developed hundreds of cultures, far too numerous to catalog here. But among all these cultures, the **Mexica** stood out. (Europeans often called these people Aztecs, a name the Mexica did not use.) Their empire stretched from coast to coast across central Mexico, encompassing between 8 million and 25 million people (experts disagree about the total population). We know more about the Mexica than about any other Native American society of the time, principally because of their massive monuments and their Spanish conquerors' well-documented interest in subduing them. Their significance in the history of the New World after 1492 dictates a brief discussion of their culture and society.

The Mexica began their rise to prominence about 1325, when small bands settled on a marshy island in Lake Texcoco, the site of the future city of Tenochtitlán, the capital of the Mexican empire.

Resourceful, courageous, and cold-blooded warriors, the Mexica often hired out as mercenaries for richer, more settled tribes.

By 1430, the Mexica succeeded in asserting their dominance over their former allies and leading their own military campaigns in an ever-widening arc of empire building. Despite pockets of resistance, by the 1490s the Mexica ruled an empire that covered more land than Spain and Portugal combined and contained almost three times as many people.

The empire exemplified the central values of Mexican society. The Mexica worshipped the war god Huitzilopochtli. Warriors held the most exalted positions in the social hierarchy, even above the priests who performed the sacred ceremonies that won Huitzilopochtli's favor. In the almost constant battles necessary to defend and to extend the empire, young Mexican men exhibited the courage and daring that would allow them to rise in the carefully graduated ranks of warriors. The Mexica considered capturing prisoners the ultimate act of bravery. Warriors usually turned over the captives to Mexican priests, who sacrificed them to Huitzilopochtli by cutting out their hearts. The Mexica believed that human sacrifice fed the sun's craving for blood, which kept the sun aflame and prevented the fatal descent of everlasting darkness and chaos.

The empire contributed far more to Mexican society than victims for sacrifice. At the most basic level, the empire functioned as a military and political system that collected **tribute** from subject peoples. The Mexica forced conquered tribes to pay tribute in goods, not money. Tribute redistributed to the Mexica as much as one-third of the goods produced by conquered tribes. It included everything from candidates for human sacrifice to textiles and basic food products such as corn and beans, as well as exotic luxury items such as gold, turquoise, and rare bird feathers.

Tribute reflected the fundamental relations of power and wealth that pervaded the Mexican empire. The relatively small nobility of Mexican warriors, supported by a still smaller priesthood, possessed the military and religious power to command the obedience of thousands of non-noble Mexicans and of millions of other non-Mexicans in subjugated colonies. The Mexican elite exercised their power to obtain tribute and thereby to redistribute wealth from the conquered to the conquerors, from the commoners to the nobility, from the poor to the rich. This redistribution of wealth made possible the achievements of Mexican society that eventually amazed the Spaniards: the huge cities, fabulous temples, teeming markets, and luxuriant gardens, not to mention the storehouses stuffed with gold and other treasures.

On the whole, the Mexica did not interfere much with the internal government of conquered regions.

Mexican Human Sacrifice This graphic portrait of human sacrifice was drawn by a Mexican artist in the sixteenth century, after the Spanish conquest. It shows the typical routine of human sacrifice practiced by the Mexica for centuries before Europeans arrived. The victim climbed the temple steps, then was stretched over a stone pillar (notice the priest's helper holding the victim's legs) to make it easier for the priest to plunge a stone knife into the victim's chest, cut out the still-beating heart, and offer it to the bloodthirsty gods. The body of the previous victim has already been pushed down from the temple heights and is about to be dragged away. The Mexica's blood-caked priests and temples repulsed the Spanish conquerors, who considered human sacrifice barbaric. The intent watchfulness among the people portrayed at the base of the temple suggests their keen interest in the gory spectacle was a way of obtaining favors from supernatural powers. Scala/Art Resource, NY; Biblioteca Nazionale, Florence, Italy.

Instead, they usually permitted the traditional ruling elite to stay in power—so long as they paid tribute. The conquered provinces received very little in return from the Mexica, except immunity from punitive raids. Subjugated communities felt exploited by the constant payment of tribute to the Mexica. By depending on military conquest and constant collection of tribute, the Mexica failed to create among their subjects a belief that Mexican domination was, at some level, legitimate and equitable. The high level of discontent among subject peoples constituted the soft, vulnerable underbelly of the Mexican empire, a fact Spanish intruders exploited after AD 1492 to conquer the Mexica.

Q: **How did the payment of tribute influence the Mexican empire?**

Conclusion: The World of Ancient Americans

Ancient Americans shaped the history of human beings in the New World for more than twelve thousand years. They established continuous human habitation in the Western Hemisphere from the time the first big-game hunters crossed Beringia until 1492 and beyond. Much of their history remains irretrievably lost because they relied on oral rather than written communication. But much can be pieced together from artifacts they left behind, like the Folsom points among the bones discovered by George McJunkin. Ancient Americans achieved their success through resourceful adaptation to the hemisphere's many and ever-changing natural environments. They also adapted to social and cultural changes caused by human beings—such as marriages, deaths, political struggles, and warfare—but the sparse evidence that has survived renders those adaptations almost entirely unknowable. Their creativity and artistry are unmistakably documented in the artifacts they left at kill sites, camps, and burial mounds. Those artifacts sketch the only likenesses of ancient Americans we will ever have—blurred, shadowy images that are indisputably human but forever silent.

In the five centuries after 1492—just 4 percent of the time human beings have inhabited the Western Hemisphere—Europeans and their descendants began to shape and eventually to dominate American history. Native American peoples continued to influence major developments of American history for centuries after 1492. But the new wave of strangers that at first trickled and then flooded into the New World from Europe and Africa forever transformed the peoples and places of ancient America.

Reviewing the Chapter

★ KEY TERMS

Explain each term's significance

WHO

Paleo-Indians (p. 6)

Archaic Indians (p. 8)

California peoples (p. 11)

Northwest peoples (p. 11)

Woodland peoples (p. 12)

southwestern peoples (p. 13)

Anasazi (p. 14)

Hopewell culture (p. 15)

Mississippian culture (p. 16)

Algonquian tribes (p. 16)

Iroquoian tribes (p. 17)

Mexica (p. 20)

WHAT

artifacts (p. 3)

archaeology (p. 3)

Folsom points (p. 4)

continental drift (p. 5)

Beringia (p. 6)

Clovis point (p. 7)

hunter-gatherer (p. 8)

burial mounds (p. 12)

chiefdoms (p. 12)

pueblos (p. 13)

kivas (p. 14)

Cahokia (p. 16)

tribute (p. 20)

FOR PRACTICE QUIZZES AND OTHER STUDY TOOLS, see the Online Study Guide at **bedfordstmartins.com/roarkcompact**.

★ REVIEW QUESTIONS

Use key terms and dates to support your answer

1. Why do historians rely on the work of archaeologists to write the history of ancient America? (pp. 4–5)

2. Why were humans able to migrate into North America after 15,000 BP? (pp. 5–7)

3. Why did Archaic Native Americans shift from big-game hunting to foraging and smaller-game hunting? (pp. 8–12)

4. How did the availability of food influence the distribution of the Native American population across the continent? (pp. 12–16)

5. Why did some Native Americans set fire to the land? (pp. 16–20)

6. How did the payment of tribute influence the Mexican empire? (pp. 20–21)

★ MAKING CONNECTIONS

Draw on key terms, timeline, and review questions

1. Explain the different approaches historians and archaeologists bring to studying people in the past. How do the different sources they draw on shape their accounts of the human past? In your answer, cite specific examples from the history of ancient America.

2. Discuss Native Americans' strategies for surviving in the varied climates of North America. How did their different approaches to survival contribute to the diversity of Native American cultures?

3. For more than twelve thousand years, Native Americans both adapted to environmental change in North America and produced significant changes in the environments around them. Discuss specific examples of Native Americans' adaptation to environmental change and the changes they caused in the North American landscape.

4. Rich archaeological and manuscript sources have enabled historians to develop a detailed portrait of the Mexica on the eve of European contact. How did the Mexica establish and maintain their expansive empire?

★ SUGGESTED READINGS

Karen Olsen Bruhns and Karen R. Stothert, *Women in Ancient America* (1999). An informative account of ancient American women, who are often overlooked in other books.

Colin G. Calloway, *One Vast Winter Count: The Native American West before Lewis and Clark* (2003). A fascinating overview of Native Americans in the West.

Michael D. Coe and Rex Koontz, *Mexico: From the Olmecs to the Aztecs* (5th ed., 2002). An authoritative survey of ancient Mexico.

Tim Flannery, *The Eternal Frontier: An Ecological History of North America and Its Peoples* (2001). A sweeping ecological history of North American plants and animals covering millions of years.

Charles C. Mann, *1491: New Revelations of the Americas before Columbus* (2006). An accessible account of recent archaeological evidence about ancient Americans.

FOR MORE BOOKS ABOUT TOPICS IN THIS CHAPTER, see the Online Bibliography at **bedfordstmartins.com/roarkcompact**.

FOR ADDITIONAL FIRSTHAND ACCOUNTS OF THIS PERIOD, see Chapter 1 in Michael Johnson, ed., *Reading the American Past*, Fourth Edition.

FOR WEB SITES, IMAGES, AND DOCUMENTS RELATED TO TOPICS AND PLACES IN THIS CHAPTER, visit Make History at **bedfordstmartins.com/roarkcompact**.

★ TIMELINE

ca. 400,000 BP	• Modern humans (*Homo sapiens*) evolve in Africa.
ca. 75,000–45,000 BP and ca. 25,000–14,000 BP	• Wisconsin glaciation exposes Beringia land bridge between Siberia and Alaska.
ca. 15,000 BP	• First humans arrive in North America.
ca. 13,500–13,000 BP	• Paleo-Indians in North and Central America use Clovis points to hunt big game.
ca. 11,000 BP	• Mammoths and many other big-game prey of Paleo-Indians become extinct.
ca. 10,000–3000 BP	• Archaic hunter-gatherer cultures dominate ancient America.
ca. 7000 BP	• Corn cultivation begins in Central and South America.
ca. 4000 BP	• Some Eastern Woodland peoples grow gourds and pumpkins and begin making pottery.
ca. 3500 BP	• Southwestern cultures begin corn cultivation.
ca. 2500 BP	• Eastern Woodland cultures start to build burial mounds. • Some Eastern Woodland peoples begin to cultivate corn.
ca. 2500–2100 BP	• Adena culture develops in Ohio.
ca. 2100 BP–AD 400	• Hopewell culture emerges in Ohio and Mississippi valleys.
ca. AD 200–900	• Mogollon culture develops in New Mexico.
ca. AD 500	• Bows and arrows appear in North America south of Arctic.
ca. AD 500–1400	• Hohokam culture develops in Arizona.
ca. AD 800–1500	• Mississippian culture flourishes in Southeast.
ca. AD 1000–1200	• Anasazi peoples build cliff dwellings at Mesa Verde and pueblos at Chaco Canyon.
ca. AD 1325–1500	• Mexica conquer neighboring peoples and establish Mexican empire.
AD 1492	• Christopher Columbus arrives in New World, beginning European colonization.

BP is an abbreviation used by archaeologists for "years before the present."

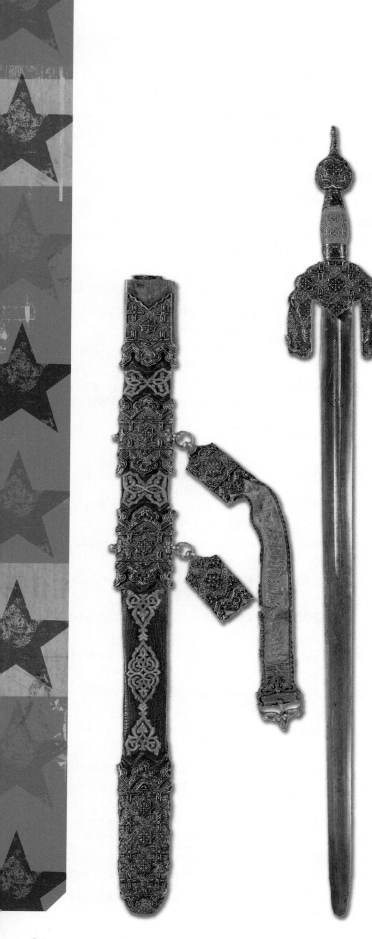

SPANISH SWORD In the hands of a strong Spaniard mounted on horseback, this sixteenth-century sword was a fearsome weapon that could slice through cloth, leather, flesh, bone, and even some metals with deadly effect. Ancient Americans did not possess the Spaniards' highly developed technology of metallurgy, which created a strong, relatively lightweight sword honed to a razor-sharp edge. When Christopher Columbus showed swords to the Native Americans he initially encountered, "they took them by the edge and through ignorance cut themselves," he noted in his journal. Swords proved to be indispensable weapons in the Spaniards' military and political conquest of Native Americans during the sixteenth century. Few battle swords and scabbards displayed the elaborate decoration seen here. The decorative motif derives from the artistic traditions of the centuries-long Muslim presence on the Iberian Peninsula, which Spanish warriors and monarchs such as Queen Isabella finally ended in 1492. Such magnificent decoration communicated the ironfisted power of important government officials who might never have wielded a sword in combat. Both ceremonial swords and battle swords were crucial instruments in the Spaniards' creation of the first European empire in the New World.
Museo del Ejercito — Colección/Archivo Oronoz.

CHAPTER 2

Europeans Encounter the New World

1492–1600

TWO BABIES WERE BORN in southern Europe in 1451, separated by about seven hundred miles and a chasm of social, economic, and political power. The baby girl, Isabella, was born in a king's castle in what is now Spain. The baby boy, Christopher, was born in the humble dwelling of a weaver near Genoa in what is now Italy. Forty-one years later, the lives and aspirations of these two people intersected in southern Spain and permanently changed the history of the world.

Isabella was named for her mother, the Portuguese second wife of King John II of Castile, whose monarchy encompassed the large central region of present-day Spain. Isabella grew up amid the swirling countercurrents of dynastic rivalries and political conflict. Her father died when she was three, and her half-brother, Henry, assumed the throne. Henry proved an ineffective ruler who made many enemies among the nobility and the clergy. When Isabella was fourteen, Henry's rivals launched a campaign to overthrow him and replace him with her brother, Alfonso.

By then, Isabella had received an excellent education from private tutors who were bishops in the Catholic Church. Her learning helped her become a strong, resolute woman. Henry tried to control her by bringing her to his court, where he could watch her. When Alfonso died in 1468, Henry plotted to undermine her independence by arranging her marriage to one of several eligible sons of European monarchs. Isabella refused to accept Henry's choices for her husband and likewise refused to cooperate with Henry's enemies by rebelling and seeking to overthrow him. Instead, she maneuvered to obtain Henry's consent that she would succeed him as monarch, and then she selected Ferdinand, a man she had never met, to be her husband. A year younger than Isabella, Ferdinand was the king of Aragon, a region encompassing a triangular slice of northeastern Spain bordering France and the Mediterranean Sea. The couple married in 1469, and Isabella became queen when Henry died in 1474.

Queen Isabella and King Ferdinand fought to defeat other claimants to Isabella's throne, to unite the monarchies of Spain under their rule, to complete the long campaign known as the **Reconquest** to eliminate Muslim strongholds on the Iberian Peninsula, and to purify Christianity. A pious

Previewing the Chapter

Europe in the Age of Exploration 27

Q: *Why did European exploration expand dramatically in the fifteenth century?*

A Surprising New World in the Western Atlantic 29

Q: *How did Columbus's landfall in the Caribbean help revolutionize Europeans' understanding of world geography?*

Spanish Exploration and Conquest 33

Q: *Why did New Spain develop a society highly stratified by race and national origin?*

The New World and Sixteenth-Century Europe 42

Q: *How did Spain's conquests in the New World shape Spanish influence in Europe?*

Conclusion: The Promise of the New World for Europeans 45

woman, Isabella supported the Inquisition in 1478 to identify and punish heretics, especially Jewish converts. Catholic Church officials believed that many of these converts were "false Christians" who openly embraced Christianity but secretly remained faithful to Judaism.

In their intense decades-long campaign to defend Christianity, persecute Jews, and defeat Muslims, Isabella and Ferdinand traveled throughout their realm, staying a month or two in one place after another, meeting local notables, hearing appeals and complaints, and impressing all with their regal splendor. Although Isabella understood the importance of displaying the magnificence of her royal court, she was a serious, sober ruler who read Latin and had a personal library of some four hundred books, a rarity among fifteenth-century monarchs.

Tagging along in the royal cavalcade of advisers, servants, and assorted hangers-on that moved around Spain in 1485 was Christopher Columbus, a deeply religious man obsessed with obtaining support for his scheme to sail west across the Atlantic Ocean to reach China and Japan. An experienced sailor, Columbus had become convinced that it was possible to reach the riches of the East by sailing west. Columbus pitched his idea to the king of Portugal in 1484. The king's geography experts declared Columbus's proposal impossible: The globe was too big, the ocean between Europe and China was too wide, and no sailors or ships could possibly withstand such a long voyage.

Rejected in Portugal, Columbus made his way to the court of Isabella and Ferdinand in 1485 and joined their entourage until he finally won an audience with the monarchs in January 1486. They too rejected his plan. Columbus tried again to interest the Portuguese king, without success. Doggedly, he went back to Spain in 1489 and managed to meet privately with Isabella, whose army was attacking the last major Muslim stronghold at Granada. When Granada surrendered early in 1492, Isabella and Ferdinand once again asked their experts to consider Columbus's plan, and again they rejected it. But Isabella soon changed her mind. In hopes of expanding the wealth and influence of the monarchy, she summoned Columbus and in mid-April 1492 agreed to support his risky scheme.

Columbus hurriedly organized his expedition, and just before sunrise on August 3, 1492, three ships under his command caught the tide out of a harbor in southern Spain and sailed west. Barely two months later, in the predawn moonlight of October 12, 1492, Columbus glimpsed an island on the western horizon. At daybreak, he rowed ashore, and as the curious islanders crowded around, he claimed possession of the land for Isabella and Ferdinand of Spain.

Columbus's encounters with Isabella and those islanders in 1492 transformed the history of the world and unexpectedly made Spain the most important European power in the Western Hemisphere for more than a century. Long before 1492, other Europeans had restlessly expanded the limits of the world known to them, and their efforts helped make possible Columbus's voyage. But without Isabella's sponsorship, it is doubtful that Columbus could have made his voyage. With her support and his own unflagging determination, Columbus blazed a watery trail to a world that neither he nor anyone else in Europe knew existed. As

Spanish Tapestry This detail from a lavish sixteenth-century tapestry depicts Columbus (kneeling) receiving a box of jewels from Queen Isabella (whose husband, King Ferdinand, stands slightly behind her) in appreciation for his voyages to the New World. These gifts and others signified the monarchs' elation about the immense promise of the lands and peoples that Columbus encountered. The exact nature of that promise did not become clear until after the deaths of both Columbus and Isabella, when Cortés invaded and eventually conquered Mexico between 1519 and 1521. © Julio Conoso/Corbis Sygma.

Isabella, Ferdinand, and subsequent Spanish monarchs sought to reap the rewards of what they considered their emerging empire in the West, they created a distinctively Spanish colonial society that conquered and killed Native Americans, built new institutions, and extracted great wealth that enriched the Spanish monarchy and made Spain the envy of other Europeans. ★

Europe in the Age of Exploration

Historically, the East—not the West—attracted Europeans. Around the year 1000, Norsemen ventured west across the North Atlantic and founded a small fishing village at L'Anse aux Meadows on the tip of Newfoundland that lasted only a decade or so. After the world's climate cooled, choking the North Atlantic with ice, the Norse left. Viking sagas memorialized the Norse "discovery," but it had virtually no other impact in the New World or in Europe. Instead, wealthy Europeans developed a taste for luxury goods from Asia and Africa, and merchants competed to satisfy that taste. As Europeans traded with the East and with one another, they acquired new information about the world they inhabited. A few people—sailors, merchants, and aristocrats—took the risks of exploring beyond the limits of the world known to Europeans. Those risks were genuine and could be deadly. But sometimes they paid off in new information, new opportunities, and eventually the discovery of a world entirely new to Europeans.

Mediterranean Trade and European Expansion
From the twelfth through the fifteenth centuries, spices, silk, carpets, ivory, gold, and other exotic goods traveled overland from Persia, Asia Minor, India, and Africa and then were funneled into continental Europe through Mediterranean trade routes (Map 2.1). Dominated primarily by the Italian cities of Venice, Genoa, and Pisa, this lucrative trade enriched Italian merchants and bankers, who fiercely defended their near monopoly of access to Eastern goods. The vitality of the Mediterranean trade offered few incentives to look for alternatives. New routes to the East and the discovery of new lands were the stuff of fantasy.

Preconditions for turning fantasy into reality developed in fifteenth-century Europe. In the mid-fourteenth century, Europeans suffered a catastrophic epidemic of bubonic plague. The Black Death, as it was called, killed about a third of the European population. This devastating pestilence had major long-term consequences. By drastically reducing the population, it made Europe's limited supply of food more plentiful for survivors. Many survivors inherited property from plague victims, giving them new chances for advancement.

Understandably, most Europeans perceived the world as a place of alarming risks where the delicate balance of health, harvests, and peace could quickly be tipped toward disaster by epidemics, famine, and violence. Most people protected themselves from the constant threat of calamity by worshipping the supernatural, by living amid kinfolk and friends, and by maintaining good relations with the rich and powerful. But the insecurity and uncertainty of fifteenth-century European life also encouraged a few people to take greater risks, such as embarking on dangerous sea voyages through uncharted waters to points unknown.

Exploration promised fame and fortune in European societies to those who succeeded, whether they were kings or commoners. Monarchs such as Isabella who hoped to enlarge their realms and enrich their dynasties also had reasons to sponsor journeys of exploration. More territory meant more subjects who could pay more taxes, provide more soldiers, and participate in more commerce, magnifying the monarch's power and prestige. Voyages of exploration also could stabilize the monarch's regime by diverting unruly noblemen toward distant lands. Some explorers, such as Columbus, were commoners who hoped to be elevated to the aristocracy as a reward for their daring achievements.

Scientific and technological advances also helped set the stage for exploration. The invention of movable type by Johannes Gutenberg around 1450 in Germany made printing easier and cheaper, stimulating the diffusion of information, including news of discoveries, among literate Europeans. By 1400, crucial navigational aids employed by maritime explorers such as Columbus were already available: compasses; hourglasses, which allowed for the calculation of elapsed time, useful in estimating speed; and the astrolabe and quadrant, which were devices for determining latitude. Many people throughout fifteenth-century Europe knew about these and other technological advances. The Portuguese were the first to use them in a campaign to sail beyond the limits of the world known to Europeans.

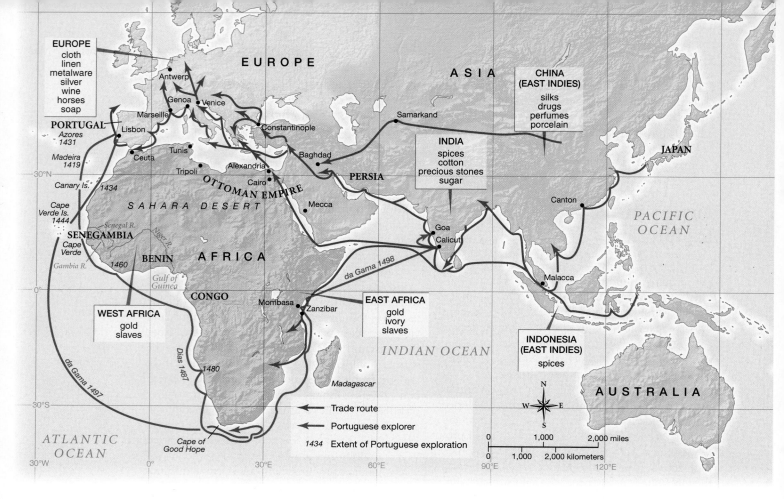

MAP 2.1 **European Trade Routes and Portuguese Exploration in the Fifteenth Century**
The strategic geographic position of Italian cities as a conduit for overland trade from
Asia was slowly undermined during the fifteenth century by Portuguese explorers who
hopscotched along the coast of Africa and eventually found a sea route that opened the
rich trade of the East to Portuguese merchants.

A Century of Portuguese Exploration Portugal
devoted far more energy and wealth to the geographical exploration of the world between 1415
and 1460 than all the other countries of Europe
combined. Facing the Atlantic on the Iberian
Peninsula, the Portuguese lived on the fringes of the
thriving Mediterranean trade. As a Christian kingdom, Portugal cooperated with Spain in the Reconquest, the centuries-long drive to expel the Muslims
from the Iberian Peninsula. The religious zeal that
propelled the Reconquest also justified expansion
into what the Portuguese considered heathen lands.
A key victory came in 1415 when Portuguese forces
conquered Ceuta, the Muslim bastion at the mouth
of the Strait of Gibraltar that had blocked Portugal's
access to the Atlantic coast of Africa.

The most influential advocate of Portuguese exploration was **Prince Henry the Navigator**, son of the
Portuguese king (and great-uncle of Queen Isabella
of Spain). From 1415 until his death in 1460,
Henry collected the latest information about sailing

techniques and geography, supported new crusades
against the Muslims, sought fresh sources of trade to
fatten Portuguese pocketbooks, and pushed explorers
to go farther still. African expeditions also promised
to wrest wheat fields from their Moroccan owners
and to obtain gold, the currency of European trade.

Neither the Portuguese nor anybody else in
Europe knew the immensity of Africa or the length
or shape of its coastline, which, in reality, fronted the
Atlantic for more than seven thousand miles—about
five times the considerable distance from Genoa,
Columbus's hometown, to Lisbon, the Portuguese
capital. At first, Portuguese mariners cautiously
hugged the west coast of Africa, seldom venturing
beyond sight of land. By 1434, they had reached the
northern edge of the Sahara Desert, where strong
westerly currents swept them out to sea. They soon
learned to ride those currents far away from the
coast before catching favorable winds that turned
them back toward land, a technique that allowed
them to reach Cape Verde by 1444 (see Map 2.1).

To stow the supplies necessary for long periods at sea and to withstand the battering of waves in the open ocean, the Portuguese developed the caravel, a sturdy ship that became explorers' vessel of choice. In caravels, Portuguese mariners sailed into and around the Gulf of Guinea and as far south as the Congo by 1480.

Fierce African resistance confined Portuguese expeditions to coastal trading posts, where they bartered successfully for gold, slaves, and ivory. Powerful African kingdoms welcomed Portuguese trading ships loaded with iron goods, weapons, textiles, and ornamental shells. Portuguese merchants learned that establishing relatively peaceful trading posts on the coast was far more profitable than attempting the violent conquest and **colonization** of inland regions. In the 1460s, the Portuguese used African slaves to develop sugar plantations on the Cape Verde Islands, inaugurating an association between enslaved Africans and plantation labor that would be transplanted to the New World in the centuries to come.

About 1480, Portuguese explorers began a conscious search for a sea route to Asia. In 1488, Bartolomeu Dias sailed around the Cape of Good Hope at the southern tip of Africa and hurried back to Lisbon with the exciting news that it appeared to be possible to sail on to India and China. In 1498, after ten years of careful preparation, Vasco da Gama commanded the first Portuguese fleet to sail to India. Portugal quickly capitalized on the commercial potential of da Gama's new sea route. By the early sixteenth century, the Portuguese controlled a far-flung commercial empire in India, Indonesia, and China (collectively referred to as the East Indies). Their new sea route to the East eliminated overland travel and allowed Portuguese merchants to charge much lower prices for the Eastern goods they imported and still make handsome profits.

Portugal's African explorations during the fifteenth century broke the monopoly of the old Mediterranean trade with the East, dramatically expanded the world known to Europeans, established a network of Portuguese outposts in Africa and Asia, and developed methods of sailing the high seas that Columbus employed on his revolutionary voyage west.

Q: **Why did European exploration expand dramatically in the fifteenth century?**

A Surprising New World in the Western Atlantic

In retrospect, the Portuguese seemed ideally qualified to venture across the Atlantic. They had pioneered the frontiers of seafaring, exploration, and geography for almost a century. However, Portuguese and most other experts believed that sailing west across the Atlantic to Asia was literally impossible. The European discovery of America required someone bold enough to believe that the experts were wrong and the risks were surmountable. That person was **Christopher Columbus**. His explorations inaugurated a geographical revolution that forever altered Europeans' understanding of the world and its peoples, including themselves. Columbus's landfall in the Caribbean originated a thriving exchange between the people, ideas, cultures, and institutions of the Old and New Worlds that continues to this day.

The Explorations of Columbus Columbus went to sea when he was about fourteen, and he eventually made his way to Lisbon, where he married Felipa Moniz, whose father had been raised in the household of Prince Henry the Navigator. Through Felipa, Columbus gained access to explorers' maps and information about the tricky currents and winds encountered in sailing the Atlantic. Columbus himself ventured into the Atlantic frequently and at least twice sailed to the central coast of Africa.

Like other educated Europeans, Columbus believed that the earth was a sphere and that theoretically it was possible to reach the East Indies by sailing west. With flawed calculations, he estimated that Asia was only about 2,500 miles away, a shorter distance than Portuguese ships routinely sailed between Lisbon and the Congo. In fact, the shortest distance to Japan from Europe's jumping-off point was nearly 11,000 miles. Convinced by his erroneous calculations, Columbus became obsessed with a scheme to prove he was right.

In 1492, after years of unsuccessful lobbying in Portugal and Spain, plus overtures to England and France, Columbus finally won financing for his journey from the Spanish monarchs, Isabella and Ferdinand. They saw Columbus's venture as an inexpensive gamble: The potential loss was small, but the potential gain was huge.

After scarcely three months of frantic preparation, Columbus and his small fleet—the *Niña* and *Pinta*, both caravels, and the *Santa María*, a larger merchant vessel—headed west. Six weeks after leaving the Canary Islands, where he stopped for

Columbus's First Voyage to the New World, 1492–1493

supplies, Columbus landed on a tiny Caribbean island about three hundred miles north of the eastern tip of Cuba.

Columbus claimed possession of the island for Isabella and Ferdinand and named it San Salvador, in honor of the Savior, Jesus Christ. He called the islanders "Indians," assuming that they inhabited the East Indies somewhere near Japan or China. The islanders called themselves **Tainos**, which in their language meant "good" or "noble." The Tainos inhabited most of the Caribbean islands Columbus visited on his first voyage, as had their ancestors for more than two centuries. An agricultural people, the Tainos grew cassava, corn, cotton, tobacco, and other crops. Instead of dressing in the finery Columbus had expected to find in the East Indies, the Tainos "all . . . go around as naked as their mothers bore them," Columbus wrote. Although Columbus concluded that the Tainos "had no religion," in reality they worshipped gods they called *zemis*, ancestral spirits who inhabited natural objects such as trees and stones. The Tainos mined a little gold, but they had no riches. "It seemed to me that they were a people very poor in everything," Columbus wrote.

What the Tainos thought about Columbus and his sailors we can only surmise, since they left no written documents. At first, Columbus got the impression that the Tainos believed the Spaniards came from heaven. But

after six weeks of encounters, Columbus decided that "the people of these lands do not understand me nor do I, nor anyone else that I have with me, [understand] them. And many times I understand one thing said by these Indians . . . for another, its contrary." The confused communication between the Spaniards and the Tainos suggests how strange each group seemed to the other. Columbus's perceptions of the Tainos were shaped by European attitudes, ideas, and expectations, just as the Tainos' perceptions of the Europeans were no doubt colored by their own culture.

Columbus and his men understood that they had made a momentous discovery, but they found it frustrating. Although the Tainos proved friendly, they did not have the riches Columbus expected to find in the East. In mid-January 1493, he started back to Spain, where Queen Isabella and King Ferdinand were overjoyed by his news. With a voyage that had lasted barely eight months, Columbus appeared to have catapulted Spain from the position of an also-ran in the race for a sea route to Asia into that of a serious challenger to Portugal, whose explorers had not yet sailed to India or China. The Spanish monarchs elevated Columbus to the nobility and awarded him the title "Admiral of the Ocean Sea."

Soon after Columbus returned to Spain, the Spanish monarchs rushed to obtain the pope's support for their claim to the new lands in the West. When the pope, a Spaniard, complied, the Portuguese feared their own claims to recently discovered territories were in jeopardy. To protect their claims, the Portuguese and Spanish monarchs negotiated the **Treaty of Tordesillas** in 1494. The treaty drew an imaginary line eleven hundred miles west of the Canary Islands (Map 2.2). Land discovered west of the line (namely, the islands that Columbus discovered and any additional land that might be located) belonged to Spain; Portugal claimed land to the east (namely, its African and East Indian trading empire).

Isabella and Ferdinand moved quickly to realize the promise of their new claims. In the fall of 1493, they dispatched Columbus once again, this time with a fleet of seventeen ships and more than a thousand men who planned to locate the Asian mainland, find gold, and get rich. Before Columbus died in 1506, he returned to the New World two more times (in 1498 and 1502) without relinquishing his belief that the East Indies were there, someplace. Other explorers continued to search for a passage to

Taino Zemi Basket

This basket is an example of the effigies Tainos made to represent zemis, or deities. The effigy illustrates the artistry of the basket maker, almost certainly a Taino woman. Crafted sometime between 1492 and about 1520, the effigy demonstrates that the Tainos readily incorporated goods obtained through contacts with Europeans into their own traditional beliefs and practices. The basket maker used African ivory and European mirrors as well as Native American fibers, dyes, and designs. © The Trustees of the British Museum.

MAP 2.2 European Exploration in Sixteenth-Century America

This map illustrates the approximate routes of early European explorations of the New World.

READING THE MAP: Which countries were most actively exploring the New World? Which countries were exploring later than others?

CONNECTIONS: What were the motivations behind the explorations? What were the motivations for colonization?

FOR MORE HELP ANALYZING THIS MAP, see the map activity for this chapter in the Online Study Guide at bedfordstmartins.com/roarkcompact.

the East or some other source of profit. Before long, however, prospects of beating the Portuguese to Asia began to dim along with the hope of finding vast hoards of gold. Nonetheless, Columbus's discoveries forced sixteenth-century Europeans to think about the world in new ways: It was possible to sail from Europe to the western rim of the Atlantic and return to Europe, and, most important, across the Atlantic lay lands and peoples entirely unknown to Europeans.

The Geographic Revolution and the Columbian Exchange Within thirty years of Columbus's initial discovery, Europeans' understanding of world geography underwent a revolution. An elite of perhaps twenty thousand people with access to Europe's royal courts and trading centers learned the exciting news about global geography. But it took a generation of additional exploration before they could comprehend the larger contours of Columbus's discoveries.

European monarchs hurried to stake their claims to the newly discovered lands. In 1497, King Henry VII of England, who had spurned Columbus a decade earlier, sent John Cabot to look for a **Northwest Passage** to the Indies across the North Atlantic (see Map 2.2). Cabot reached the tip of Newfoundland, which he believed was part of Asia, and hurried back to England, where he assembled a small fleet and sailed west in 1498. But he was never heard from again.

Three thousand miles to the south, a Spanish expedition landed on the northern coast of South America in 1499 accompanied by Amerigo Vespucci, an Italian businessman. In 1500, Pedro Álvars Cabral commanded a Portuguese fleet bound for the Indian Ocean that accidentally made landfall on the coast of Brazil as it looped westward into the Atlantic.

By 1500, European experts knew that several large chunks of land cluttered the western Atlantic. A few cartographers speculated that these chunks were connected to one another in a landmass that was not Asia. In 1507, Martin Waldseemüller, a German cartographer, published the first map that showed the New World separate from Asia; he named the land America, in honor of Amerigo Vespucci.

Two additional discoveries confirmed Waldseemüller's speculation. In 1513, Vasco Núñez de Balboa crossed the Isthmus of Panama and reached the Pacific Ocean. Clearly, more water lay between the New World and Asia. How much water **Ferdinand Magellan** discovered when he led an expedition to circumnavigate the globe in 1519. Sponsored by King Charles I of Spain, Magellan's voyage took him first to the New World, around the southern tip of South America, and into the Pacific late in November 1520. Crossing the Pacific took almost four months, decimating his crew with hunger and thirst. Magellan himself was killed by Philippine tribesmen. A remnant of his expedition continued on to the Indian Ocean and managed to transport a cargo of spices back to Spain in 1522.

In most ways, Magellan's voyage was a disaster. One ship and 18 men crawled back from an expedition that had begun with five ships and more than 250 men. But the geographic information it provided left no doubt that America was a continent separated from Asia by the enormous Pacific Ocean. Magellan's voyage made clear that it was possible to sail west to reach the East Indies, but that was a terrible way to go. After Magellan, most Europeans who sailed west set their sights on the New World, not on Asia.

Columbus's arrival in the Caribbean anchored the western end of what might be imagined as a sea bridge that spanned the Atlantic, connecting the Western Hemisphere to Europe. Somewhat like the Beringian land bridge traversed by the first Americans millennia earlier (see chapter 1), the new sea bridge reestablished a connection between the Eastern and Western Hemispheres. The Atlantic Ocean, which had previously isolated America from Europe, became an aquatic highway, thanks to sailing technology, intrepid seamen, and their European sponsors. This new sea bridge launched the **Columbian exchange**, a transatlantic trade of goods, people, and ideas that has continued ever since.

Spaniards brought novelties to the New World that were commonplace in Europe, including Christianity, iron technology, sailing ships, firearms, wheeled vehicles, horses and other domesticated animals, and much else. Unknowingly, they also smuggled along many Old World microorganisms that caused devastating epidemics of smallpox, measles, and other diseases that would kill the vast majority of Indians during the sixteenth century and continue to decimate survivors in later centuries. European diseases made the Columbian exchange catastrophic for Native Americans. In the long term, these diseases were decisive in transforming the dominant peoples of the New World from descendants of Asians, who had inhabited the hemisphere for millennia, to descendants of Europeans and Africans, the recent arrivals from the Old World by way of the newly formed sea bridge.

Ancient American goods, people, and ideas made the return trip across the Atlantic. Europeans were introduced to New World foods such as corn and potatoes that became important staples in European diets, especially for poor people. Columbus's sailors became infected with syphilis in sexual encounters with New World women and unwittingly carried the deadly parasite back to Europe. New World tobacco created a European fashion for smoking that ignited quickly and has yet to be extinguished. But for almost a generation after 1492, this Columbian exchange did not reward the Spaniards with the riches they yearned to find.

Q: How did Columbus's landfall in the Caribbean help revolutionize Europeans' understanding of world geography?

Columbian Exchange The arrival of Columbus in the New World started an ongoing transatlantic exchange of goods, people, and ideas. The Spaniards brought domesticated animals from the Old World, including horses, cattle, goats, chickens, cats, and sheep. The novelty of such animals is demonstrated by the Nahuatl words the Mexican people initially used to refer to these strange new beasts. For a horse, they used the Nahuatl word for deer; a cat was a "little cougar"; a sheep was referred to with the word for cotton, linking the animal with its fibrous woolen coat. The Spaniards brought many other alien items, such as cannons, which the Mexica at first termed "fat fire trumpets," and guitars, which the Mexica called "rope drums." The Spaniards also carried Old World microorganisms that caused devastating epidemics of smallpox, measles, and other diseases (center). Ancient American people, goods, and ideas made the return trip across the Atlantic. In 1493, Columbus told Isabella and Ferdinand about an amazingly productive New World plant he called maize, his version of the Taino word *mahiz*, which means "life-giver." This maize, or corn, goddess (left) crafted in Peru about a thousand years before Columbus arrived in the New World suggests ancient Americans' worship of corn. Within a generation after 1493, corn had been carried across the Atlantic and was growing in Europe, the Middle East, Africa, India, and China. Smoking tobacco, like the cigar puffed by an ancient Mayan lord (right), became such a fashion in Europe that some came to believe, as a print of two men relaxing with their pipes was captioned, "Life Is Smoke." The strangeness of New World peoples and cultures also reinforced Europeans' notions of their own superiority. Although the Columbian exchange went in both directions, it was not a relationship of equality. Europeans seized and retained the upper hand. Bildarchiv Preussischer Kulturbesitz/Art Resource, NY; Arxiu Mas; Collection of Dr. Francis Robicsek.

Spanish Exploration and Conquest

During the sixteenth century, the New World helped Spain become the most powerful monarchy in both Europe and the Americas. Initially, Spanish expeditions reconnoitered the Caribbean, scouted stretches of the Atlantic coast, and established settlements on the large islands of Hispaniola, Puerto Rico, Jamaica, and Cuba. Spaniards enslaved Caribbean tribes and put them to work growing crops and mining gold. But the profits from these early ventures barely covered the costs of maintaining the settlers. After almost thirty years of exploration, the promise of Columbus's discovery seemed illusory.

In 1519, however, that promise was fulfilled, spectacularly, by Hernán Cortés's march into Mexico. By about 1545, Spanish conquests extended from northern Mexico to southern Chile, and New World riches filled Spanish treasure chests. Cortés's expedition served as the model for Spaniards' and other Europeans' expectations that the New World could yield bonanza profits for its conquerors.

The Conquest of Mexico

Hernán Cortés, an obscure nineteen-year-old Spaniard seeking adventure and the chance to make a name for himself, arrived in the New World in 1504. He fought in the conquest of Cuba and elsewhere in the Caribbean. In 1519, the governor of Cuba authorized Cortés to organize an expedition of about six hundred men and eleven ships to investigate rumors of a fabulously wealthy kingdom somewhere in the interior of the mainland.

A charismatic and confident man, Cortés could not speak any Native American language. Landing first on the Yucatán peninsula, he had the good fortune to receive from a local chief the gift of a fourteen-year-old girl named **Malinali** who spoke several native languages, including Mayan and Nahuatl, the language of the Mexica, the most powerful people in what is now Mexico and Central America (see chapter 1). Malinali, whom the Spaniards called Marina, soon learned Spanish and became Cortés's interpreter. She was the Spaniards' essential conduit of communication with the Indians. "Without her help," wrote one of the Spaniards who accompanied Cortés, "we would not have understood the language of New Spain and Mexico." With her help, Cortés talked and fought with Indians along the Gulf coast of Mexico, trying to discover the location of the fabled kingdom.

In the capital of the Mexican empire Tenochtitlán, the emperor **Montezuma** heard about some strange creatures sighted along the coast. (Montezuma and his people are often called Aztecs, but they called themselves Mexica.) Montezuma sent representatives to bring the strangers large quantities of food and perhaps postpone their dreaded arrival in the capital. Before the Mexican messengers served food to the Spaniards, they sacrificed several hostages and soaked the food in their blood. This fare disgusted the Spaniards and might have been enough to turn them back to Cuba. But along with the food, the Mexica also brought the

> The great capital of the Mexican empire "looked as if it had been ploughed up," one of Cortés's soldiers remembered.

Cortés's Invasion of Tenochtitlán, 1519–1521

→ Cortés's original route, 1519
→ Cortés's retreat, 1520
→ Cortés's return route, 1520–1521

Gulf of Mexico

Texcoco · Otumba · Zautla · Jalapa
Tlaxcala · Veracruz
Tenochtitlán · Cholula

0 25 50 mi.
0 25 50 km.

Spaniards another gift, a "disk in the shape of a sun, as big as a cartwheel and made of very fine gold," as one of the Mexica recalled. Here was conclusive evidence that the rumors of fabulous riches heard by Cortés had some basis in fact.

In August 1519, Cortés marched inland to find Montezuma. Leading about 350 men armed with swords, lances, and muskets and supported by ten cannons, four smaller guns, and sixteen horses, Cortés had to live off the land, establishing peaceful relations with indigenous tribes when he could and killing them when he thought necessary. On November 8, 1519, Cortés reached Tenochtitlán. Montezuma came out to welcome the Spaniards. After presenting Cortés with gifts, Montezuma ushered the Spaniards to the royal palace and showered them with lavish hospitality. Quickly, Cortés took Montezuma hostage and held him under house arrest, hoping to make him a puppet through which the Spaniards could rule the Mexican empire. This uneasy peace existed for several months until one of Cortés's men led a brutal massacre of many Mexican nobles, causing the people of Tenochtitlán to revolt. They murdered Montezuma, who seemed to them a Spanish puppet, and they mounted a ferocious assault on the Spaniards. On June 30, 1520, Cortés and about a hundred other Spaniards fought their way out of Tenochtitlán and retreated about one hundred miles to Tlaxcala, a stronghold of bitter enemies of the Mexica. The friendly Tlaxcalans—who had long resented Mexican power—allowed Cortés to regroup, obtain reinforcements, and plan a strategy to conquer Tenochtitlán.

In the spring of 1521, Cortés and tens of thousands of Indian allies laid siege to the Mexican capital. With a relentless, scorched-earth strategy, Cortés finally defeated the last Mexican defenders on August 13, 1521. The great capital of the Mexican empire "looked as if it had been ploughed up," one of Cortés's soldiers remembered.

The Search for Other Mexicos

Lured by their insatiable appetite for gold, **conquistadors** quickly fanned out from Tenochtitlán in search of other sources of treasure. The most spectacular prize fell to **Francisco Pizarro**, who conquered

Cortés Arrives in Tenochtitlán This portrayal of the arrival of Cortés and his army in the Mexican capital illustrates the importance of Malinali, who stands at the front of the Spaniards' procession, serving as their translator and intermediary with Montezuma (not pictured), who has come out to greet the invaders. Painted by a Mexican artist after the conquest, the work contrasts Cortés — dressed as a Spanish gentleman, respectfully doffing his hat to Montezuma, and accompanied by his horse and African groom — with his soldiers, who are armed and ready for battle. The painting displays the choices confronted by the Mexica: Accept the pacific overtures of Cortés or face the lances, swords, and battle-axes of the Spanish soldiers. Also notable is the importance of the Indian porters who carried the Spaniards' food and other supplies. What do you think was the significance of the winged image on the flag? Bibliothèque Nationale de France.

the **Incan empire** in Peru. The Incas controlled a vast, complex region that contained more than nine million people and stretched along the western coast of South America for more than two thousand miles. In 1532, Pizarro and his army of fewer than two hundred men captured the Incan emperor Atahualpa and held him hostage. As ransom, the Incas gave Pizarro the largest treasure yet produced by the conquests: gold and silver equivalent to half a century's worth of precious-metal production in Europe. With the ransom safely in their hands, the Spaniards executed Atahualpa. The Incan treasure proved that at least one other Mexico did indeed exist, and it spurred the search for others.

Juan Ponce de León had sailed along the Florida coast in 1513. Encouraged by Cortés's success, he went back to Florida in 1521 to find riches, only to be killed in battle with Calusa Indians. A few years later, Lucas Vázquez de Ayllón explored the Atlantic coast north of Florida to present-day South Carolina. In 1526, he established a small settlement on the Georgia coast that he named **San Miguel de Gualdape**, the first Spanish attempt to establish a foothold in what is now the United States. This settlement was soon swept away by sickness and hostile Indians. Pánfilo de Narváez surveyed the Gulf coast from Florida to Texas in 1528. The Narváez expedition ended disastrously with a shipwreck on the Texas coast near present-day Galveston.

In 1539, **Hernando de Soto**, a seasoned conquistador who had taken part in the conquest of Peru, set out with nine ships and more than six hundred men to find another Peru in North America. Landing in Florida, de Soto literally slashed his way through much of southeastern North America for three years, searching for the rich, majestic civilizations he believed were there. After the brutal slaughter of many Native Americans and much hardship, de Soto died in 1542 and his men turned back to Mexico, disappointed.

Tales of the fabulous wealth of the mythical Seven Cities of Cíbola also lured **Francisco Vásquez de Coronado** to search the Southwest and Great Plains of North America. In 1540, Coronado left northern Mexico with more than three hundred Spaniards, a thousand Indians, and a priest who claimed to know the way to what he called "the greatest and best of the discoveries." Cíbola turned out to be a small Zuñi pueblo of about a hundred families. When the Zuñi shot arrows at the Spaniards, Coronado attacked the pueblo and routed the defenders after a hard battle. Convinced that the rich cities must lie somewhere over the horizon, Coronado kept moving all the way to central Kansas before deciding in 1542 that the rumors he had pursued were just that.

Juan Rodríguez Cabrillo led a maritime expedition in 1542 that sailed along the coast of California. Cabrillo died on Santa Catalina

Artifacts of Spanish Conquest

The Spaniards reveled in their victories over the Mexica and other native peoples in the New World. About 1522, Cortés sent this Mexican shield as a trophy of conquest to a bishop in Spain. Made by a Mexican featherworker and probably looted from its Mexican owner by Cortés's soldiers, the shield was constructed of reeds, reinforced by sticks and rawhide, and decorated with feathers of exotic Central American birds. The animal outlined in strips of gold on the shield probably depicts the coyote effigy of Mexican warriors. The shield displayed the artistry of the Mexica as well as their weakness: Feathers, reeds, and coyotes were no match for the Spaniards' steel, gunpowder, and Christianity. Contrast the vulnerability of the featherwork shield to the Spaniards' razor-sharp swords, and the comparative invulnerability of the Spanish war helmet to the Mexica's wooden spears and stone points. Like the shield, the helmet was a sign of the Spaniards' technological superiority, which both made conquest possible and justified it: People of feathers and reeds should be conquered by people of steel. The gold ingot was another trophy of conquest. Shortly after Cortés and his army entered Tenochtitlán, they found the treasure-house of Montezuma filled with golden artifacts. The Spaniards confiscated the treasure and melted the golden artworks into ingots slightly bent to allow them to be strapped in belts around the soldiers' waists. In 1521, when the Mexica revolted against the Spaniards and temporarily drove them out of Tenochtitlán, many of Cortés's soldiers were forced to drop their heavy waistbands of gold in order to escape. This gold ingot, excavated in Mexico City in 1982, is probably one dropped by the retreating Spaniards. The ingot hints of the looting and destruction that accompanied conquest. Museum of Volkerkunde, Vienna; Wallace Collection, London, UK/Bridgeman Art Library; Museo Nacional de Antropologia, conaculta-inah, 10-220012.

Island, offshore from present-day Los Angeles, but his men sailed on to Oregon, where a ferocious storm forced them to turn back toward Mexico.

These probes into North America by de Soto, Coronado, and Cabrillo persuaded other Spaniards that although enormous territories stretched northward, their inhabitants had little to loot or exploit. After a generation of vigorous exploration, the Spaniards concluded that there was only one Mexico and one Peru.

New Spain in the Sixteenth Century For all practical purposes, Spain was the dominant European power in the Western Hemisphere during the sixteenth century (Map 2.3). Portugal claimed the giant territory of Brazil under the Tordesillas treaty but was far more concerned with exploiting its hard-won trade with the East Indies than in colonizing the New World. England and France were absorbed by domestic and diplomatic concerns in Europe and largely lost interest in America until late in the century. In the decades after 1519, the Spaniards created the distinctive colonial society of **New Spain** that showed other Europeans how the New World could be made to serve the purposes of the Old.

The Spanish monarchy claimed ownership of most of the land in the Western Hemisphere and gave the conquistadors permission to explore and plunder. (See "Documenting the American Promise," page 38.) The crown took one-fifth, called the "royal fifth," of any loot confiscated and allowed the conquerors to divide the rest. In the end, most conquistadors received very little after the plunder was divided among leaders such as Cortés and his favorite officers. To compensate his disappointed battle-hardened soldiers, Cortés gave them towns the Spaniards had subdued.

The distribution of conquered towns institutionalized the system of ***encomienda***, which empowered the conquistadors to rule the Indians and the lands in and around their towns. Encomienda transferred to the Spanish *encomendero* (the man who "owned" the town) the tribute that the town had previously paid to the Mexican empire. In theory, encomienda involved a reciprocal relationship between the encomendero and "his" Indians. In return for the tribute and labor of the Indians, the encomendero was supposed to be responsible for their material well-being, to guarantee order and justice in the town, and to encourage the Indians to convert to Christianity.

Catholic missionaries labored earnestly to convert the Indians to Christianity. Missionaries fervently believed that God expected them to save the Indians' souls by convincing them to abandon their old sinful beliefs and to embrace the one true Christian faith. But after baptizing tens of thousands of Indians, the missionaries learned that many Indians continued to worship their own gods. Most priests came to believe that the Indians were lesser beings inherently incapable of fully understanding Christianity.

In practice, encomenderos were far more interested in what the Indians could do for them than in what they or the missionaries could do for the Indians. Encomenderos subjected the Indians to chronic overwork, mistreatment, and abuse. Economically, however, encomienda recognized a fundamental reality of New Spain: The most important treasure the Spaniards could plunder from the New World was not gold but uncompensated Indian labor. To exploit that labor, New Spain's richest natural resource, encomenderos

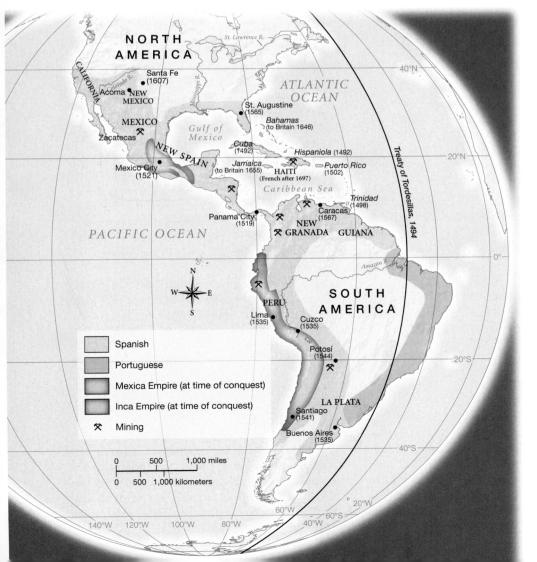

MAP 2.3 Sixteenth-Century European Colonies in the New World
Spanish control spread throughout Central and South America during the sixteenth century, with the important exception of Portuguese Brazil. North America, though claimed by Spain under the Treaty of Tordesillas, remained peripheral to Spain's New World empire.

Justifying Conquest

The immense riches Spain reaped from its New World empire came largely at the expense of the Indians. A few individual Spaniards raised their voices against the brutal exploitation of the Indians. Their criticisms prompted the Spanish monarchy to formulate an official justification of conquest that, in effect, blamed the Indians for resisting Spanish dominion.

DOCUMENT 1
Montecino's 1511 Sermon

In 1511, a Dominican friar named Antón Montecino delivered a blistering sermon that astonished the Spaniards gathered in the church in Santo Domingo, headquarters of the Spanish Caribbean.

Your greed for gold is blind. Your pride, your lust, your anger, your envy, your sloth, all blind. . . . You are in mortal sin. And you are heading for damnation. . . . For you are destroying an innocent people. For they are God's people, these innocents, whom you destroyed. By what right do you make them die? Mining gold for you in your mines or working for you in your fields, by what right do you unleash enslaving wars upon them? They have lived in peace in this land before you came, in peace in their own homes. They did nothing to harm you to cause you to slaughter them wholesale. . . . Are you not under God's command to love them as you love yourselves? Are you out of your souls, out of your minds? Yes. And that will bring you to damnation.

SOURCE: Zvi Dor-Ner, *Columbus and the Age of Discovery* (New York: William Morrow, 1991), 220–21.

DOCUMENT 2
The Requerimiento

Montecino returned to Spain to bring the Indians' plight to the king's attention. In 1512 and 1513, King Ferdinand met with philosophers, theologians, and other advisers and concluded that the holy duty to spread the Christian faith justified conquest. To buttress this claim, the king had his advisers prepare the Requerimiento. According to the Requerimiento, Indians who failed to welcome Spanish conquest and all its blessings deserved to die. Conquistadors were commanded to read the Requerimiento to the Indians before any act of conquest. Beginning in 1514, they routinely did so, speaking in Spanish while other Spaniards brandishing unsheathed swords stood nearby.*

On the part of the King . . . [and] queen of [Spain], subduers of the barbarous nations, we their servants notify and make known to you, as best we can, that the Lord our God, living and eternal, created the heaven and the earth, and one man and one woman, of whom you and we, and all the men of the world, were and are descendants. . . .

God our lord gave charge to one man called St. Peter, that he should be lord and superior to all the men in the world, that all should obey him, and that he should be the head of the whole human race, wherever men should live . . . and he gave him the world for his kingdom and jurisdiction.

And he commanded him to place his seat in Rome, as the spot most fitting to rule the world from. . . . This man was called Pope, as if to say, Admirable Great Father and Governor of men. The men who lived in that time obeyed that St. Peter and took him for lord, king, and superior of the universe. So also they have regarded the others who after him have been elected to the pontificate, and so has it been continued even till now, and will continue till the end of the world.

One of these pontiffs, who succeeded that St. Peter as lord of the world . . . made donation of these islands and mainland to the aforesaid king and queen [of Spain] and to their successors. . . .

forced Indians to work when, where, and how Spaniards pleased.

Encomienda engendered two groups of influential critics. A few of the missionaries were horrified at the brutal mistreatment of the Indians. The cruelty of the encomenderos made it difficult for priests to persuade the Indians of the tender mercies of the Spaniards' God. "What will [the Indians] think about the God of the Christians," Friar Bartolomé de Las Casas asked, when

So their highnesses are kings and lords of these islands and mainland by virtue of this donation; and . . . almost all those to whom this has been notified, have received and served their highnesses, as lords and kings, in the way that subjects ought to do, with good will, without any resistance, immediately, without delay, when they were informed of the aforesaid facts. And also they received and obeyed the priests whom their highnesses sent to preach to them and to teach them our holy faith; and all these, of their own free will, without any reward or condition have become Christians, and are so, and the highnesses have joyfully and graciously received them, and they have also commanded them to be treated as their subjects and vassals; and you too are held and obliged to do the same. Wherefore, as best we can, we ask and require that you consider what we have said to you, and that you take the time that shall be necessary to understand and deliberate upon it, and that you acknowledge the Church as the ruler and superior of the whole world, and the high priest called Pope, and in his name the king and queen [of Spain] our lords, in his place, as superiors and lords and kings of these islands and this mainland by virtue of the said donation, and that you consent and permit that these religious fathers declare and preach to you. . . .

If you do so . . . we . . . shall receive you in all love and charity, and shall leave you your wives and your children and your lands free without servitude, that you may do with them and with yourselves freely what you like and think best, and they shall not compel you to turn to Christians unless you yourselves, when informed of the truth, should wish to be converted to our holy Catholic faith. . . . And besides this, their highnesses award you many privileges and exemptions and will grant you many benefits.

But if you do not do this or if you maliciously delay in doing it, I certify to you that with the help of God we shall forcefully enter into your country and shall make war against you in all ways and manners that we can, and shall subject you to the yoke and obedience of the Church and of their highnesses; we shall take you and your wives and your children and shall make slaves of them, and as such shall sell and dispose of them as their highnesses may command; and we shall take

away your goods and shall do to you all the harm and damage that we can, as to vassals who do not obey and refuse to receive their lord and resist and contradict him; and we protest that the deaths and losses which shall accrue from this are your fault, and not that of their highnesses, or ours, or of these soldiers who come with us.

The Indians who heard the Requerimiento could not understand Spanish, of course. No native documents survive to record the Indians' thoughts upon hearing the Spaniards' official justification for conquest, even when it was translated into a language they recognized. But one conquistador reported that when the Requerimiento was translated for two chiefs in Colombia, they responded that if the pope gave the king so much territory that belonged to other people, "the Pope must have been drunk."

SOURCE: Adapted from A. Helps and M. Oppenheim, eds., *The Spanish Conquest in America and Its Relation to the History of Slavery and to the Government of the Colonies*, 4 vols. (London and New York, 1900–1904), 1:264–67.

Questions for Analysis and Debate

1. How did the Requerimiento answer the criticisms of Montecino? According to the Requerimiento, why was conquest justified? What was the source of the Indians' resistance to conquest?

2. What arguments might a critic like Montecino have used to respond to the Requerimiento's justification of conquest? What arguments might the Mexican leader Montezuma have made against those of the Requerimiento?

3. Was the Requerimiento a faithful expression or a cynical violation of the Spaniards' Christian faith?

they see their friends "with their heads split, their hands amputated, their intestines torn open? . . . Would they want to come to Christ's sheepfold after their homes had been destroyed, their children imprisoned, their wives raped, their cities devastated, their maidens deflowered, and their provinces laid waste?" Las Casas and other outspoken missionaries softened few hearts among the encomenderos, but they did win some sympathy for the Indians from the Spanish monarchy and royal bureaucracy. The Spanish monarchy moved to abolish encomienda in an effort to replace swashbuckling old conquistadors with royal bureaucrats as the rulers of New Spain.

In 1549, a reform called the *repartimiento* limited the labor an encomendero could command from his Indians to forty-five days per year from each adult male. The repartimiento, however, did not challenge the principle of forced labor, nor did it prevent encomenderos from continuing to cheat, mistreat, and overwork their Indians. Slowly, repartimiento replaced encomienda as the basic system of exploiting Indian labor.

The practice of coerced labor in New Spain grew directly out of the Spaniards' assumption that they were superior to the Indians. As one missionary put it, the Indians "are incapable of learning. . . . [They] are more stupid than asses and refuse to improve in anything." Therefore, most Spaniards assumed, Indians' labor should be organized by and for their conquerors. Spaniards seldom hesitated to use violence to punish and intimidate recalcitrant Indians.

From the viewpoint of Spain, the single most important economic activity in New Spain after 1540 was silver mining. Spain imported more New World gold than silver in the early decades of the century, but that changed with the discovery of major silver deposits at Potosí, Bolivia, in 1545 and Zacatecas, Mexico, in 1546. The mines required large capital investments and many miners. Typically, a few Spaniards supervised large groups of Indian miners, who were supplemented by African slaves later in the sixteenth century.

> One colonist wrote to his brother in Spain, "Don't hesitate [to come]. . . . This land [New Spain] is as good as ours [in Spain], for God has given us more here than there, and we shall be better off."

For the Spaniards, life in New Spain after the conquests was relatively easy. Although the riches they won fell far short of their expectations, encomienda gave them a comfortable, leisurely life that was the envy of many Spaniards back in Europe. As one colonist wrote to his brother in Spain, "Don't hesitate [to come]. . . . This land [New Spain] is as good as ours [in Spain], for God has given us more here than there, and we shall be better off."

During the century after 1492, about 225,000 Spaniards settled in the colonies. Virtually all of them were poor young men of common (non-

noble) lineage who came directly from Spain. Laborers and artisans made up the largest proportion, but soldiers and sailors were also numerous. Throughout the sixteenth century, men vastly outnumbered women, although the proportion of women grew from about one in twenty before 1519 to nearly one in three by the 1580s.

The gender and number of Spanish settlers shaped two fundamental features of the society of New Spain. First, Europeans never made up more than 1 or 2 percent of the total population. Although the Spaniards ruled New Spain, the population was almost wholly Indian. Second, the shortage of Spanish women meant that Spanish men frequently married Indian women or used them as concubines. For the most part, the relatively few women from Spain married Spanish men, contributing to a tiny elite defined by European origins.

The small number of Spaniards, the masses of Indians, and the frequency of intermarriage created a steep social hierarchy defined by perceptions of national origin and race. Natives of Spain — *peninsulares* (people born on the Iberian Peninsula) — enjoyed the highest social status in New Spain. Below them but still within the white elite were **creoles**, the children born in the New World to Spanish men and women. Together, peninsulares and creoles made up barely 1 or 2 percent of the population. Below them on the social pyramid was a larger group of **mestizos**, the offspring of Spanish men and Indian women, who accounted for 4 or 5 percent of the population. Some mestizos worked as artisans and labor overseers and lived well, and a few rose into the ranks of the elite, especially if their Indian ancestry was not obvious from their skin color. Most mestizos, however, were lumped with the Indians, the enormous bottom slab of the social pyramid.

The society of New Spain established the precedent for what would become a pronounced pattern in the European colonies of the New World: a society stratified sharply by social origin and race. All Europeans of whatever social origin considered themselves superior to Native Americans; in New Spain, they were a dominant minority in both power and status.

The Toll of Spanish Conquest and Colonization
By 1560, the major centers of Indian civilization had been conquered, their leaders overthrown, their religion held in contempt, and their people forced to work for the Spaniards. Profound demor-

alization pervaded Indian society. As a Mexican poet wrote:

> Nothing but flowers and songs of sorrow are left
>   in Mexico . . .
> where once we saw warriors and wise men. . . .
> We are crushed to the ground; we lie in ruins.
> There is nothing but grief and suffering in
>   Mexico.

Adding to the culture shock of conquest and colonization was the deadly toll of European diseases. As conquest spread, the Indians succumbed to virulent epidemics of measles, smallpox, and respiratory illnesses. They had no immunity to these diseases because they had not been exposed to them before the arrival of Europeans. The isolation of the Western Hemisphere before 1492 had protected ancient Americans from the contagious diseases that had raged throughout Eurasia for millennia. The new post-1492 sea bridge eliminated that isolation, and by 1570, the Indian population of New Spain had fallen about 90 percent from what it was when Columbus arrived. The destruction of the Indians was a catastrophe unequaled in human history. A Mayan Indian recalled that when sickness struck his village, "great was the stench of the dead. . . . The dogs and vultures devoured the bodies. The mortality was terrible." For most Indians, New Spain was a graveyard.

Mixed Races The residents of New Spain maintained a lively interest in each person's racial lineage. These eighteenth-century paintings illustrate forms of racial mixture common in the sixteenth century. In the first painting, a Spanish man and an Indian woman have a mestizo son; in the fourth, a Spanish man and a woman of African descent have a mulatto son; in the fifth, a Spanish woman and a mulatto man have a *morisco* daughter. The many racial permutations led the residents of New Spain to develop an elaborate vocabulary of ancestry. The child of a morisco and a Spaniard was a *chino*; the child of a chino and an Indian was a *salta abas*; the child of a salta abas and a mulatto was a *lobo*; and so on. Can you detect hints of some of the meanings of racial categories in the clothing depicted in these paintings? Bob Schalkwijk/INAH.

FOR MORE HELP ANALYZING THIS IMAGE, see the visual activity for this chapter in the Online Study Guide at bedfordstmartins.com/roarkcompact.

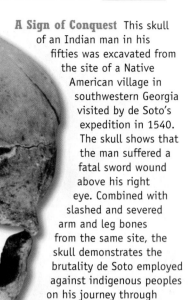

A Sign of Conquest This skull of an Indian man in his fifties was excavated from the site of a Native American village in southwestern Georgia visited by de Soto's expedition in 1540. The skull shows that the man suffered a fatal sword wound above his right eye. Combined with slashed and severed arm and leg bones from the same site, the skull demonstrates the brutality de Soto employed against indigenous peoples on his journey through the Southeast. No native weapons could have inflicted the wounds left on this skull and the other bones. Robert L. Blakely.

For the Spaniards, Indian deaths meant that the most valuable resource of New Spain—Indian labor—dwindled rapidly. By the last quarter of the sixteenth century, Spanish colonists felt the pinch of a labor shortage. To help supply laborers, the colonists began to import African slaves. In the years before 1550, while Indian labor was still adequate, only 15,000 slaves were imported from Africa. Even after Indian labor began to decline, the relatively high cost of African slaves kept imports low, totaling approximately 36,000 from 1550 to the end of the century. During the sixteenth century, New Spain continued to rely primarily on a shrinking number of Indians.

Spanish Outposts in Florida and New Mexico After the explorations of de Soto, Coronado, and Cabrillo, officials in New Spain lost interest in North America. The monarchy claimed that Spain owned North America and insisted that a few North American settlements be established to give some tangible reality to its claims. Settlements in Florida would have the additional benefit of protecting Spanish ships from pirates and privateers who lurked along the southeastern coast, waiting for the Spanish treasure fleet sailing toward Spain.

In 1565, the Spanish king sent Pedro Menéndez de Avilés to create settlements along the Atlantic coast of North America. In early September, Menéndez founded St. Augustine in Florida, the first permanent European settlement within what became the United States. By 1600, St. Augustine had a population of about five hundred, the only remaining Spanish beachhead on the vast Atlantic shoreline of North America.

More than sixteen hundred miles west of St. Augustine, the Spaniards founded another outpost in 1598. Juan de Oñate led an expedition of about five hundred people to settle northern Mexico, now called New Mexico, and claim the booty rumored to exist there. After a two-month journey from Mexico, Oñate and his companions reached pueblos near present-day Albuquerque and Santa Fe. He solemnly convened the pueblos' leaders and received their oath of loyalty to the Spanish king and the Christian God. Oñate sent out scouting parties to find the legendary treasures of the region and to locate the ocean, which he believed must be nearby. Meanwhile, many of his soldiers planned to mutiny, and relations with the Indians deteriorated. When Indians in the Acoma pueblo revolted against the Spaniards, Oñate ruthlessly suppressed the uprising, killing eight hundred men, women, and children. Although Oñate's response to the **Acoma pueblo revolt** reconfirmed the Spaniards' military superiority, he did not bring peace or stability to the region. After another pueblo revolt occurred in 1599, many of Oñate's settlers returned to Mexico, leaving New Mexico as a small, dusty assertion of Spanish claims to the North American Southwest.

Q: **Why did New Spain develop a society highly stratified by race and national origin?**

The New World and Sixteenth-Century Europe

The riches of New Spain helped make the sixteenth century the Golden Age of Spain. After the deaths of Queen Isabella and King Ferdinand, their sixteen-year-old grandson became King Charles I of Spain in 1516. Three years later, just as Cortés ventured into Mexico, Charles I used judicious bribes to secure his selection as Holy Roman Emperor Charles V. His empire encompassed more territory than that of any other European monarch. He used the wealth of New Spain to protect the sprawling empire and promote his interests in the fierce dynastic battles of sixteenth-century Europe. He also sought to defend orthodox Christianity from the insurgent heresy of the Protestant Reformation. The power of the Spanish monarchy spread the clear message throughout sixteenth-century Europe that a New World empire could bankroll Old World ambitions.

The Protestant Reformation and the European Order

In 1517, **Martin Luther**, an obscure Catholic priest in central Germany, initiated the **Protestant Reformation** by publicizing his criticisms of the Catholic Church. Luther's ideas won the sympathy of many Catholics, but they were considered extremely dangerous by church officials and monarchs such as Charles V who believed that just as the church spoke for God, they ruled for God.

Luther preached a doctrine known as "justification by faith": Individual Christians could obtain salvation and life everlasting only by having faith that God would save them. Giving offerings to the church, following the orders of priests, or participating in church rituals would not put believers one step closer to heaven. Also, the only true source of information about God's will was the Bible, not the church. By reading the Bible, any Christian could learn as much about God's commandments as any priest. Indeed, Luther called for a "priesthood of all believers."

In effect, Luther charged that the Catholic Church was in many respects fraudulent. He insisted that priests were unnecessary for salvation and that they encouraged Christians to violate God's will by promoting religious practices not specifically commanded by the Bible. The church, Luther declared, had neglected its true purpose of helping individual Christians understand the spiritual realm revealed in the Bible and had wasted its resources in worldly conflicts of politics and wars. Luther hoped his ideas would reform the Catholic Church, but instead they ruptured forever the unity of Christianity in western Europe.

Charles V pledged to exterminate Luther's Protestant heresies. The wealth pouring into Spain from the New World fueled his efforts to defend orthodox Catholic faith against Protestants, as well as against Muslims in eastern Europe and against any nation bold or foolhardy enough to contest Spain's supremacy. As the wealthiest and most powerful monarch in Europe, Charles V, followed by his son and successor Philip II, assumed responsibility for upholding the existing order of sixteenth-century Europe.

New World Treasure and Spanish Ambitions

Both Charles V and Philip II fought wars throughout the world during the sixteenth century. Mexican silver funneled through the royal treasury and was dissipated in military adventures that served the goals of the monarchy but did little to benefit most Spaniards.

American wealth fueled Spanish ambitions, making the Spanish monarchy rich and powerful among the states of Europe. But Charles V's and Philip II's expenses for constant warfare far outstripped the revenues arriving from New Spain. To help meet military expenditures, both kings raised taxes in Spain more than fivefold during the sixteenth century. When taxes failed to produce enough revenue to fight its wars, the monarchy borrowed heavily from European bankers. By the end of the sixteenth century, interest payments on royal debts swallowed two-thirds of the crown's annual revenues. In retrospect, the riches from New Spain proved a short-term blessing but a long-term curse.

Sixteenth-century Spaniards did not see it that way. As they looked at their accomplishments in the New World, they saw unmistakable signs of progress. They had added enormously to their knowledge and wealth. They had built mines, cities, Catholic churches, and even universities on the other side of the Atlantic. Their military, religious, and economic achievements gave them great pride and confidence.

Europe and the Spanish Example

The lessons of sixteenth-century Spain were not lost on Spain's European rivals. Spain proudly displayed the fruits of its New World conquests. In 1520, for example, the German artist Albrecht Dürer wrote in his diary that he "marveled over the subtle ingenuity of the men in these distant lands" who created such "things . . . [as] a sun entirely of gold, a whole fathom [six feet] broad." But the most exciting news about "the men in these distant lands" was that they could serve the interests of Europeans, as Spain had shown. With a few notable exceptions, Europeans saw the New World as a place for the expansion of European influence, a place where, as one Spaniard wrote, Europeans could "give to those strange lands the form of our own."

France and England tried to follow Spain's example. Both nations warred with Spain in Europe, preyed on Spanish treasure fleets, and ventured to the New World, where they too hoped to find an undiscovered passageway to the East Indies or another Mexico or Peru.

In 1524, France sent Giovanni da Verrazano to scout the Atlantic coast of North America from North Carolina to Canada, looking for a Northwest Passage (see Map 2.2). Eleven years later, France probed farther north with Jacques Cartier's voyage up the St. Lawrence River. Encouraged, Cartier returned to the region with

Algonquian Ceremonial Dance When the English artist John White visited the coast of present-day North Carolina in 1585 as part of Raleigh's expedition, he painted this watercolor portrait of an Algonquian ceremonial dance. This and White's other portraits are the only surviving likenesses of sixteenth-century North American Indians that were drawn from direct observation in the New World. White's portrait captures the individuality of these Indians' appearances and gestures while depicting a ceremony that must have appeared bizarre and alien to a sixteenth-century Englishman. The significance of this ceremonial dance is still a mystery, although the portrait's obvious signs of order, organization, and collective understanding show that the dancing Indians knew what it meant. Copyright © The British Museum.

FOR MORE HELP ANALYZING THIS IMAGE, see the visual activity for this chapter in the Online Study Guide at bedfordstmartins.com/roarkcompact.

a group of settlers in 1541, but the colony they established—like the search for a Northwest Passage—came to nothing.

English attempts to follow Spain's lead were slower but equally ill-fated. Not until 1576, almost eighty years after John Cabot's voyages, did the English try again to find a Northwest Passage. This time Martin Frobisher sailed into the frigid waters of northern Canada (see Map 2.2). His sponsor was the Cathay Company, which hoped to open trade with China. Like many other explorers, Frobisher was mesmerized by the Spanish

Roanoke Settlement, 1585–1590

example and was sure he had found gold. But the tons of "ore" he hauled back to England proved worthless, the Cathay Company collapsed, and English interests shifted southward to the giant region on the northern margins of New Spain.

English explorers' attempts to establish North American settlements were no more fruitful than their search for a northern route to China. Sir Humphrey Gilbert led expeditions in 1578 and 1583 that made feeble efforts to found colonies in Newfoundland until Gilbert vanished at sea. Sir Walter Raleigh organized an expedition in 1585 to settle **Roanoke** Island off the coast of present-day North Carolina. The first group of explorers left no colonists on the island, but two years later, Raleigh sent a contingent of more than one hundred settlers to Roanoke under John White's leadership. White went back to England for supplies, and when he returned to Roanoke in 1590, the colonists had disappeared, leaving only the word *Croatoan* (whose meaning is unknown) carved in a tree. The Roanoke colonists most likely died from a combination of natural causes and unfriendly Indians. By the end of the century, England had failed to secure a New World beachhead.

Q: How did Spain's conquests in the New World shape Spanish influence in Europe?

Conclusion: The Promise of the New World for Europeans

The sixteenth century in the New World belonged to the Spaniards who employed Columbus and to the Indians who greeted him as he stepped ashore. Isabella of Spain helped initiate the Columbian exchange between the New World and the Old that massively benefited first Spain and later other Europeans and that continues to this day. The exchange also subjected Native Americans to the ravages of European diseases and Spanish conquest. Spanish explorers, conquistadors, and colonists forced the Indians to serve the interests of Spanish settlers and the Spanish monarchy. The exchange illustrated one of the most important lessons of the sixteenth century: After millions of years, the Atlantic no longer was an impermeable barrier separating the Eastern and Western Hemispheres. After the voyages of Columbus, European sailing ships regularly bridged the Atlantic and carried people, products, diseases, and ideas from one shore to the other.

No European monarch could forget the seductive lesson taught by Spain's example: The New World could vastly enrich the Old. Spain remained a New World power for almost four centuries, and its language, religion, culture, and institutions left a permanent imprint. By the end of the sixteenth century, however, other European monarchies had begun to contest Spain's dominion in Europe and to make forays into the northern fringes of Spain's New World preserve. To reap the benefits the Spaniards enjoyed from their New World domain, the others had to learn a difficult lesson: how to deviate from Spain's example. That discovery lay ahead.

Reviewing the Chapter

★ KEY TERMS

Explain each term's significance

WHO

Queen Isabella (p. 25)

Prince Henry the Navigator (p. 28)

Christopher Columbus (p. 29)

Tainos (p. 30)

Ferdinand Magellan (p. 32)

Hernán Cortés (p. 34)

Malinali (p. 34)

Montezuma (p. 34)

Francisco Pizarro (p. 34)

Hernando de Soto (p. 35)

Francisco Vásquez de Coronado (p. 35)

Juan Rodríguez Cabrillo (p. 35)

Martin Luther (p. 43)

WHAT

Reconquest (p. 25)

colonization (p. 29)

Treaty of Tordesillas (p. 30)

Northwest Passage (p. 32)

Columbian exchange (p. 32)

conquistadors (p. 34)

Incan empire (p. 35)

San Miguel de Gualdape (p. 35)

New Spain (p. 36)

encomienda (p. 37)

repartimiento (p. 40)

peninsulares (p. 40)

creoles (p. 40)

mestizos (p. 40)

Acoma pueblo revolt (p. 42)

Protestant Reformation (p. 43)

Roanoke (p. 45)

FOR PRACTICE QUIZZES AND OTHER STUDY TOOLS, see the Online Study Guide at **bedfordstmartins.com/roarkcompact.**

★ REVIEW QUESTIONS Q:

Use key terms and dates to support your answers

1. Why did European exploration expand dramatically in the fifteenth century? (pp. 27–29)

2. How did Columbus's landfall in the Caribbean help revolutionize Europeans' understanding of world geography? (pp. 29–32)

3. Why did New Spain develop a society highly stratified by race and national origin? (pp. 33–42)

4. How did Spain's conquests in the New World shape Spanish influence in Europe? (pp. 42–45)

★ MAKING CONNECTIONS

Draw on key terms, timeline, and review questions

1. The Columbian exchange exposed people on both sides of the Atlantic to surprising new people and goods. It also produced dramatic demographic and political transformations in the Old World and the New. How did the Columbian exchange lead to redistributions of power and population? Discuss these changes, being sure to cite examples from both contexts.

2. Despite inferior numbers, the Spaniards were able to conquer the Mexica and maintain control of the colonial hierarchy that followed. Why did the Spanish conquest of the Mexica succeed, and how did the Spaniards govern the conquered territory to maintain their dominance?

3. Spanish conquest in North America brought new peoples into constant contact. How did the Spaniards' and Indians' perceptions of each other shape their interactions? In your answer, cite specific examples and consider how perceptions changed over time.

4. How did the astonishing wealth generated for the Spanish crown by its conquest of the New World influence European colonial exploration throughout the sixteenth century? In your answer, discuss the ways in which it both encouraged and limited interest in exploration.

★ SUGGESTED READINGS

J. H. Elliott, *Empires of the Atlantic World: Britain and Spain in America, 1491–1830* (2006). A masterful comparison of British and Spanish empires in the New World.

John L. Kessell, *Spain in the Southwest: A Narrative History of Colonial New Mexico, Arizona, Texas, and California* (2002). The story of the long legacy of New Spain in what is now the U.S. Southwest.

Kenneth F. Kiple and Stephen V. Beck, eds., *Biological Consequences of European Expansion, 1450–1800* (1997). A careful analysis of the major biological consequences of the Columbian exchange.

Diarmaid MacCulloch, *The Reformation: A History* (2004). A sweeping, authoritative overview of the historic rupture of Christianity.

Hugh Thomas, *Conquest: Montezuma, Cortés, and the Fall of Old Mexico* (2002). The amazing history of the conquest of Mexico.

FOR MORE BOOKS ABOUT TOPICS IN THIS CHAPTER, see the Online Bibliography at **bedfordstmartins.com/roarkcompact**.

FOR ADDITIONAL FIRSTHAND ACCOUNTS OF THIS PERIOD, see Chapter 2 in Michael Johnson, ed., *Reading the American Past*, Fourth Edition.

FOR WEB SITES, IMAGES, AND DOCUMENTS RELATED TO TOPICS AND PLACES IN THIS CHAPTER, visit Make History at **bedfordstmartins.com/roarkcompact**.

★ TIMELINE

1480	• Portuguese ships reach Congo.
1488	• Bartolomeu Dias rounds Cape of Good Hope.
1492	• Christopher Columbus lands on Caribbean island that he names San Salvador.
1493	• Columbus makes second voyage to New World.
1494	• Portugal and Spain negotiate Treaty of Tordesillas.
1497	• John Cabot searches for Northwest Passage.
1498	• Vasco da Gama sails to India.
1513	• Vasco Núñez de Balboa crosses Isthmus of Panama.
1517	• Protestant Reformation begins in Germany.
1519	• Hernán Cortés leads expedition to find wealth in Mexico. • Ferdinand Magellan sets out to sail around the world.
1520	• Mexica in Tenochtitlán revolt against Spaniards.
1521	• Cortés conquers Mexica at Tenochtitlán.
1532	• Francisco Pizarro begins conquest of Peru.
1535	• Jacques Cartier explores St. Lawrence River.
1539	• Hernando de Soto explores southeastern North America.
1540	• Francisco Vásquez de Coronado starts to explore Southwest and Great Plains.
1542	• Juan Rodríguez Cabrillo explores California coast.
1549	• Repartimiento reforms begin to replace encomienda.
1565	• St. Augustine, Florida, settled.
1576	• Martin Frobisher explores northern Canadian waters.
1587	• English settle Roanoke Island.
1598	• Juan de Oñate explores New Mexico.
1599	• Pueblos revolt against Oñate.

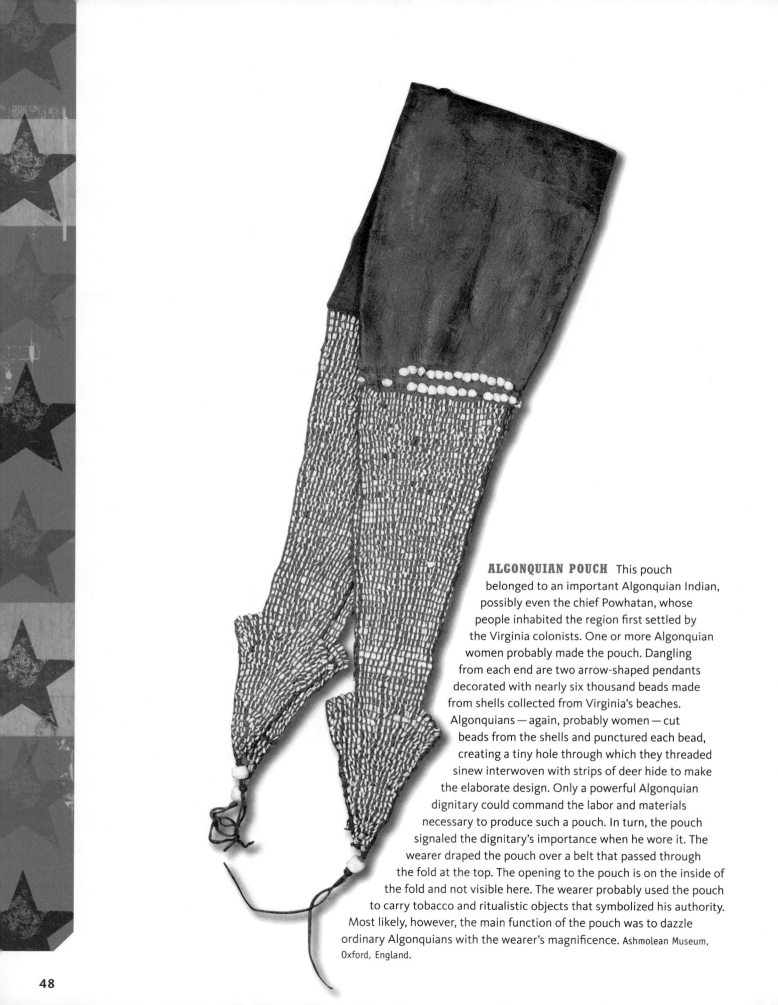

ALGONQUIAN POUCH This pouch belonged to an important Algonquian Indian, possibly even the chief Powhatan, whose people inhabited the region first settled by the Virginia colonists. One or more Algonquian women probably made the pouch. Dangling from each end are two arrow-shaped pendants decorated with nearly six thousand beads made from shells collected from Virginia's beaches. Algonquians — again, probably women — cut beads from the shells and punctured each bead, creating a tiny hole through which they threaded sinew interwoven with strips of deer hide to make the elaborate design. Only a powerful Algonquian dignitary could command the labor and materials necessary to produce such a pouch. In turn, the pouch signaled the dignitary's importance when he wore it. The wearer draped the pouch over a belt that passed through the fold at the top. The opening to the pouch is on the inside of the fold and not visible here. The wearer probably used the pouch to carry tobacco and ritualistic objects that symbolized his authority. Most likely, however, the main function of the pouch was to dazzle ordinary Algonquians with the wearer's magnificence. Ashmolean Museum, Oxford, England.

The Southern Colonies in the Seventeenth Century

1601–1700

IN DECEMBER 1607, barely six months after arriving at Jamestown with the first English colonists, **Captain John Smith** was captured by warriors of **Powhatan**, the supreme chief of about fourteen thousand **Algonquian Indians** who inhabited the coastal plain of present-day Virginia, near the Chesapeake Bay. According to Smith, Powhatan "feasted him after their best barbarous manner." Then, Smith recalled, "two great stones were brought before Powhatan: then as many [Indians] as could layd hands on [Smith], dragged him to [the stones], and thereon laid his head, and being ready with their clubs, to beate out his braines." At that moment, **Pocahontas**, Powhatan's eleven-year-old daughter, rushed forward and "got [Smith's] head in her armes, and laid her owne upon his to save him from death." Pocahontas, Smith wrote, "hazarded the beating out of her owne braines to save mine, and . . . so prevailed with her father, that I was safely conducted [back] to James towne." This romantic story of an Indian maiden rescuing a white soldier and saving Jamestown — and ultimately English colonization (gaining control of land primarily through settlement) of North America — has been enshrined in the writing of American history since 1624, when Smith published his *Generall Historie of Virginia*. Historians believe that this episode happened more or less as Smith described it. But Smith did not understand why Pocahontas acted as she did. Many commentators have claimed that her love for Smith caused her to rebel against her father's authority. Pocahontas herself left no document that explains her motives; most likely, she could not write. Everything known about her comes from the pen of Smith or other Englishmen. When their writings are considered in the context of what is known about the Algonquian society Pocahontas was born into, her actions appear in an entirely different light.

Most likely, when Pocahontas intervened to save Smith, she was a knowing participant in an Algonquian ceremony that expressed Powhatan's supremacy and his ritualistic adoption of Smith as a subordinate chief, or *werowance*. What Smith interpreted as Pocahontas's saving him from certain death was instead a ceremonial enactment of Powhatan's willingness to incorporate Smith and the white strangers at Jamestown into Powhatan's

Previewing the Chapter

An English Colony on the Chesapeake 51

Q: *Why did Powhatan pursue largely peaceful relations with the Jamestown settlement?*

A Tobacco Society 55

Q: *Why did the vast majority of European immigrants to the Chesapeake come as indentured servants?*

The Evolution of Chesapeake Society 62

Q: *Why did Chesapeake colonial society become increasingly polarized between 1650 and 1670?*

Religion and Revolt in the Spanish Borderland 65

Q: *Why did the Pueblo Indians revolt against Spanish missionaries in 1680?*

Toward a Slave Labor System 66

Q: *Why had slave labor largely displaced indentured servant labor by 1700 in Chesapeake tobacco production?*

Conclusion: The Growth of English Colonies Based on Export Crops and Slave Labor 70

Matoaks als Rebecka daughter to the mighty Prince Powhatan Emperour of Attanoughkomouck als Virginia converted and baptized in the Christian faith, and Wife to the worll Mr Tho: Rolff.

Ætatis suæ 21 A 1616.

Pocahontas in England Shortly after Pocahontas and her husband, John Rolfe, arrived in England in 1616, she posed for this portrait dressed in English clothing suitable for a princess. The portrait captures the dual novelty of England for Pocahontas and of Pocahontas for the English. Ornate, courtly clothing probably signified to English observers that Pocahontas was royalty and to Pocahontas that the English were accepting her as befitted the "Emperour" Powhatan's daughter. The mutability of Pocahontas's identity is displayed in the identification of her as "Matoaks" or "Rebecka." National Portrait Gallery, Smithsonian Institution/Art Resource, NY.

empire. The ceremony displayed Powhatan's power of life or death and his willingness to give protection to those who acknowledged his supremacy—in this case, the interlopers at Jamestown. By appearing to save Smith, Pocahontas was probably acting out Smith's new status as an adopted member of Powhatan's extended family. Rather than a rebellious, love-struck girl, Pocahontas was almost certainly a dutiful daughter playing the part prescribed for her by her father and her culture.

Smith went back to England about two years after the adoption ritual. In the meantime, Pocahontas frequently visited the English settlement and often brought gifts of food from her father. Powhatan routinely attached his sons and daughters to subordinate tribes as an expression of his protection and his dominance. It appears that Pocahontas's attachment to the English colonists grew out of Powhatan's attempt to treat the tribe of white strangers at Jamestown as he did other tribes in his empire — an attempt that failed.

In 1613, after relations between Powhatan and the English colonists had deteriorated into bloody raids by both parties, the colonists captured Pocahontas and held her hostage at Jamestown. Within a year, she converted to Christianity and married one of the colonists, a widower named **John Rolfe**. After giving birth to a son named Thomas, Pocahontas, her husband, and the new baby sailed for England in the spring of 1616. There, promoters of the Virginia colony dressed her as a proper Englishwoman and even arranged for her to go to a ball attended by the king and queen.

When John Smith heard that Pocahontas was in London, he went to see her. According to Smith, Pocahontas said, "You did promise Powhatan what was yours should bee his, and he the like to you; you called him father, being in his land a stranger, and by the same reason so must I doe you." It seems likely that Pocahontas believed her incorporation into English society was a counterpart of the adoption ritual Powhatan had staged for John Smith in Virginia back in 1607.

Pocahontas died in England in 1617. Her son, Thomas, ultimately returned to Virginia, and by the time of the American Revolution, his descendants numbered in the hundreds. But the world Thomas Rolfe and his descendants inhabited was shaped by a reversal of the power ritualized when his mother "saved" John Smith. By the end of the seventeenth century, Native Americans no longer dominated the newcomers who had arrived in the Chesapeake with John Smith.

During the seventeenth century, English colonists learned how to deviate from the example of New Spain (see chapter 2) by growing tobacco, a crop Native Americans had cultivated in small quantities for centuries. The new settlers, however, grew enormous quantities of tobacco, far more than they could chew, smoke, or sniff themselves, and they exported most of it to England. Instead of incorporating Powhatan's people into their new society, the settlers encroached on Indian land and built new societies on the foundation of tobacco agriculture and transatlantic trade.

Producing large crop surpluses for export required hard labor and people who were willing — or could be forced — to do it. For the most part, the Native Americans refused to be conscripted into the colonists' fields. Instead, the settlers depended on the labor of family members, indentured servants, and, by the last third of the seventeenth century, African slaves.

By the end of the century, the southern colonies had become sharply different both from the world dominated by Powhatan when the Jamestown settlers first arrived and from contemporary English society. In ways unimaginable to Powhatan, Pocahontas, and John Smith, the colonists paid homage to the international market and the English monarch by working mightily to make a good living growing crops for sale to the Old World. ★

An English Colony on the Chesapeake

When James I became king of England in 1603, he eyed North America as a possible location for English colonies that could be as profitable as the Spanish colonies. Although Spain claimed all of North America under the 1494 Treaty of Tordesillas (see chapter 2), King James believed that England could encroach on the outskirts of Spain's New World empire.

In 1606, London investors organized the **Virginia Company**, a joint-stock company. English merchants had pooled their capital and shared risks for many years by using joint-stock companies for trading voyages to Europe, Asia, and Africa. The Virginia Company, however, had larger ambitions: to establish a colony in North America that might somehow benefit England as Spain's New World empire had rewarded Spain. King James granted the company more than six million acres in North America. In effect, the king's land grant was a royal license to poach on both Spanish claims and Powhatan's chiefdom.

The Virginia Company investors hoped to found an empire that would strengthen England both overseas and at home. Richard Hakluyt, a strong proponent of colonization, claimed that a colony would provide work for swarms of poor "valiant youths rusting and hurtfull by lack of employment" in England. Colonists could buy English goods and supply products that England now had to import from other nations. More trade and more jobs would benefit many people in England, but the Virginia Company investors risked their capital because they fervently hoped to reap quick profits from the new colony.

Enthusiastic reports from the Roanoke voyages twenty years earlier (see chapter 2) claimed that in Virginia, "the earth bringeth foorth all things in aboundance . . . without toile or labour." Even if these reports were exaggerated, investors reasoned, maybe some valuable exotic crop could be grown profitably. Maybe rich lodes of gold and silver awaited discovery, as they had in New Spain. Or maybe quick and easy profits could be grabbed in an occasional raid on the gold and silver stashed in the holds of Spanish ships that cruised up the Atlantic coast on their way to Spain. Such hopes failed to address the difficulties of adapting European desires and expectations to the New World already inhabited by Native Americans. The Jamestown settlement struggled to survive for nearly two decades, until the royal government replaced the private Virginia Company, which never earned a penny for its investors.

Secotan Village This engraving, published in 1612, was copied from an original drawing John White made in 1585 when he visited the village of Secotan on the coast of North Carolina. The drawing provides a schematic view of daily life in the village, which may have resembled one of Powhatan's settlements. White noted on the original that the fire burning behind the line of crouching men was "the place of solemne prayer." The large building in the lower left was a tomb where the bodies of important leaders were kept. Dwellings similar to those illustrated on John Smith's map of Virginia (see page 52) lined a central space where men and women ate. Corn is growing in the fields along the right side of the village. The engraver included hunters shooting deer at the upper left. Hunting was probably never so convenient — no such hunters or deer appear in White's original drawing. This drawing conveys the message that Secotan was orderly, settled, religious, harmonious, and peaceful (notice the absence of fortifications), and very different from English villages. Princeton University Libraries, Department of Rare Books and Special Collections.

FOR MORE HELP ANALYZING THIS IMAGE, see the visual activity for this chapter in the Online Study Guide at bedfordstmartins.com/roarkcompact.

The Fragile Jamestown Settlement In December 1606, the ships *Susan Constant, Discovery,* and *Godspeed* carried 144 Englishmen toward Virginia. They arrived at the mouth of the

Chesapeake Bay on April 26, 1607. That night while the colonists rested on shore, one of them later recalled, a band of Indians "creeping upon all foure, from the Hills like Beares, with their Bowes in their mouthes," attacked and dangerously wounded two men. The attack gave the colonists an early warning that the North American wilderness was not quite the paradise described by the Virginia Company's publications in England. A few weeks later, they went ashore on a small peninsula in the midst of Powhatan's chiefdom. With the memory of their first night in America fresh in their minds, they quickly built a fort, the first building in the settlement they named **Jamestown**.

The Jamestown fort showed the colonists' awareness that they needed to protect themselves from Indians and Spaniards. Spain planned to wipe out Jamestown when the time was ripe, but that time never came. Powhatan's people defended Virginia as their own. For weeks, the settlers and Powhatan's warriors skirmished repeatedly. English muskets and cannons repelled Indian attacks on Jamestown, but the Indians' superior numbers and knowledge of the Virginia wilderness made it risky for the settlers to venture far beyond the peninsula. Late in June 1607, Powhatan sensed a stalemate and made peace overtures.

The settlers soon confronted dangerous, invisible threats: disease and starvation. During the summer, many of the Englishmen lay "night and day groaning in every corner of the Fort most pittiful to heare," wrote George Percy, one of the settlers. By September, fifty colonists had died. The colonists increased their misery by bickering among themselves, leaving crops unplanted and food supplies shrinking. "For the most part [the settlers] died of meere famine," Percy wrote; "there were never Englishmen left in a forreigne Countrey in such miserie as wee were in this new discovered Virginia."

Powhatan's people came to the rescue of the weakened and demoralized Englishmen. Early in September 1607, they began to bring corn to the colony for barter. Accustomed to eating food

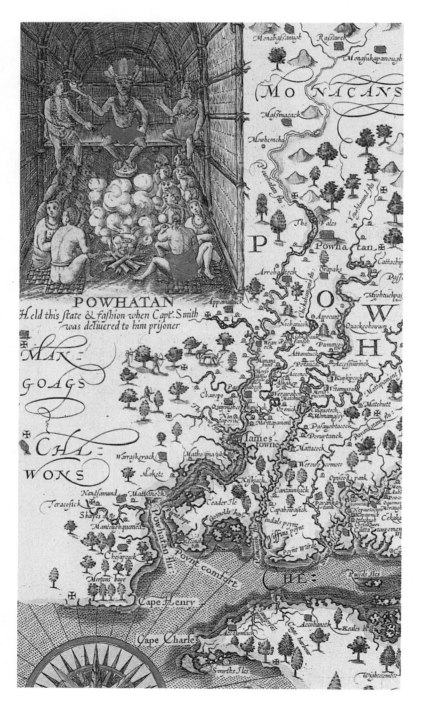

John Smith's Map of Virginia In 1612, John Smith published a detailed map that showed not only geographic features of early Virginia but also the limits of exploration (indicated by small crosses), the locations of the houses of the Indian "kings" (indicated by red boxes), and "ordinary houses" of indigenous people (indicated by dots). The map shows the early settlers' intense interest in knowing where the Indians were — and were not. Notice the location of Jamestown (upriver from Point Comfort) and of Powhatan's residence at the falls (just to the right of the large P outside the hut on the upper left side). The drawing of Powhatan surrounded by some of his many wives was almost certainly made by an English artist who had never been to Virginia or seen Powhatan but tried to imagine the scene as described by John Smith. Princeton University Libraries, Department of Rare Books and Special Collections.

derived from wheat, English people considered corn the food "of the barbarous Indians which know no better . . . a more convenient food for swine than for man." The famished Jamestown colonists soon overcame their prejudice against corn. Captain John Smith recalled that the settlers were so hungry "they would have sould their soules" for half a basket of Powhatan's corn. Indians' corn acquired by both trade and plunder managed to keep 38 of the original settlers alive until a fresh supply of food and 120 more colonists arrived from England in January 1608.

It is difficult to exaggerate the fragility of the early Jamestown settlement. Although the Virginia Company sent hundreds of new settlers to Jamestown each year, each of them eager to find the paradise promised by the company, few survived. When a new group of colonists arrived in 1610, they found only 60 of the 500 previous settlers still alive. The Virginia Company continued to pour people into the colony, promising in a 1609 pamphlet that "the place will make them rich." But most settlers went instead to early graves.

Cooperation and Conflict between Natives and Newcomers Powhatan's people stayed in contact with the English settlers but maintained their distance. The Virginia Company boasted that the settlers bought from the Indians "the pearles of earth [corn] and [sold] to them the pearles of heaven [Christianity]." In fact, few Indians converted to Christianity, and the English devoted scant effort to proselytizing. Marriage between Indian women and English men also was rare, despite the acute shortage of English women in Virginia in the early years. Few settlers other than John Smith troubled to learn the Indians' language.

Powhatan's people regarded the English with suspicion, for good reason. Although the settlers often made friendly overtures to the Indians, they did not hesitate to use their guns and swords to enforce English notions of proper Indian behavior. More than once, the Indians refused to trade their corn to the settlers, evidently hoping to starve them out. Each time, the English broke the boycott by attacking the uncooperative Indians, pillaging their villages, and confiscating their corn.

The Indians retaliated against English violence, but for fifteen years they did not organize an all-out assault on the European intruders, probably for several reasons. Although Christianity held few attractions for the Indians, the power of the settlers' God impressed them. One chief told John Smith that "he did believe that our [English] God as much exceeded theirs as our guns did their bows and arrows." Powhatan probably concluded that

these powerful strangers would make better allies than enemies. As allies, the English strengthened Powhatan's dominance over the tribes in the region. They also traded with his people, usually exchanging European goods for corn. Native Virginians had some copper weapons and tools before the English arrived, but they quickly recognized the superiority of the intruders' iron and steel knives, axes, and pots, and they traded eagerly to obtain them. The trade that supplied the Indians with European conveniences provided the English settlers with a necessity: food.

But why were the settlers unable to feed themselves for more than a decade? First, as the staggering death rate suggests, many settlers were too sick to be productive members of the colony. Second, very few farmers came to Virginia in the early years. Instead, most of the newcomers were gentlemen and their servants. In John Smith's words, these men "never did know what a day's work was." The proportion of gentlemen in Virginia in the early years was six times greater than in England, a reflection of the Virginia Company's urgent need for investors and settlers. John Smith declared repeatedly that in Virginia "there is no country to pillage [as in New Spain]. . . . All you can expect from [Virginia] must be by labor." For years, however, colonists clung to English notions that gentlemen should not work with their hands and tradesmen should work only in trades for which they had been trained. These ideas made more sense in labor-rich England than in labor-poor Virginia. In the meantime, the colonists depended on the Indians' corn for food.

The persistence of the Virginia colony created difficulties for Powhatan's chiefdom. Steady contact between natives and newcomers spread European diseases among the Indians, who suffered deadly epidemics in 1608 and between 1617 and 1619. The settlers' insatiable appetite for corn introduced other tensions within Powhatan's villages. To produce enough corn for their own survival and for trade with the English required the Indians to spend more time and effort growing crops. Since Native American women did most of the agricultural work, their burden increased along with the cultural significance of their chief crop. The corn surplus grown by Indian women was bartered for desirable English goods such as iron pots, which replaced the baskets and ceramic jugs Native Americans had used for millennia. Growing enough corn to feed the English boosted the workload of Indian women and altered age-old patterns of village life. But from the Indians'

Becaufe many doe defire to know the manner
of their Language, I haue inferted thefe few words.

KA katorawincs yowo. What call you this.

Nemarough, a man.

Crenepo, a woman.

Marowancheffo, a boy.

Yehawkans, Houfes.

Matchcores, Skins, or garments.

Mockafins, Shooes.

Tuffan, Beds. *Pokatawer,* Fire.

Attawp, A bow. *Attonce,* Arrowes.

Monacookes, Swords.

Aumoubhowgh, A Target.

Pawcuffacks, Gunnes.

Tomahacks, Axes.

Tockahacks, Pickaxes.

Pamefacks, Kniues.

Accowprets, Sheares.

Pawpecones, Pipes. *Mattaffin,* Copper *Vffawaffin,* Iron, Braffe, Silver, or any white mettall. *Muffes,* Woods.

Attaffkuff, Leaues, weeds, or graffe.

Chepfin, Land. *Shacquohocan.* A ftone.

Wepenter, A cookold.

Suckahanna, Water. *Noughmaff,* Fifh.

Copotone, Sturgeon.

Weghfhaughes, Flefh.

Sawwehone, Bloud.

Netoppew, Friends.

Marrapough, Enemies.

Maskapow, the worft of the enemies.

Mawchick chammay, The beft of friends

Cafacunnakack, peya quagh acquintan vttafantafough, In how many daies will there come hither any more Englifh Ships.

Their Numbers.

Necut, 1. *Ningh,* 2. *Nuff,* 3. *Yowgh,* 4. *Paranske,* 5. *Comotinch,* 6. *Toppawoff,* 7 *Nuffwafh,* 8. *Kekatawgh,* 9. *Kaskeke* 10 **They count no more but by tennes as followeth.**

Cafe, how many.

Ninghfapooeksku, 20.

Nuffapooeksku, 30.

Yowghapooeksku, 40.

Parankeftafsapoockfku, 50.

Comatinchtafsapoockfku, 60.

Nuffwafhtafsapoockfku, 70.

Kekatanghtafsapoockfku, 90.

Necuttoughtyfinough, 100.

Necuttwevnquaough, 1000.

Rawcofowghs, Dayes.

Kefkowghes, Sunnes:

Toppquough. Nights.

Nepawwefhowghs, Moones.

Pawpaxfoughes, Yeares.

Pummahumps, Starres.

Ofies, Heavens.

Okees, Gods.

Quiyoughcofoughs, Pettie **Gods**, **and** their affinities.

Righcomoughes, Deaths.

Kekughes, Liues.

Mowchick woyawgh tawgh noeragh kaquere mecher, I am very hungry? what fhall I eate?

Tawnor nehiegh Powhatan, Where dwels Powhatan.

Mache, nehiegh yourowgh, Orapaks. Now he dwels a great way hence at Orapaks.

Vittapitchewayne anpechitchs nehawper Werowacomoco, You lie, he ftaid ever at Werowacomoco.

Kator nehiegh mattagh neer vttapitchewayne, Truely he is there I doe not lie.

Spaughtynere keragh werowance mawmarinough kekatē wawgh peyaquaugh. Run you then to the King Mawmarynough and bid him come hither.

Vtteke, e peya weyack wighwhip, Get you gone, & come againe quickly.

Kekaten Pokahontas patiaquagh niugh tanks manotyens neer mowchick rawrenock audowgh, Bid Pokahontas bring hither two little Baskets, and I will giue her white Beads to make her a Chaine.   *FINIS.*

massacre arrived [March 22], a number of savages visited many of our people in their dwellings, and while partaking with them of their meal[,] the savages, at a given signal, drew their weapons and fell upon us murdering and killing everybody they could reach[,] sparing neither women nor children, as well inside as outside the dwellings." In all, the Indians killed 347 colonists, nearly a third of the English population. But the attack failed to dislodge the colonists. In the aftermath, the settlers unleashed a murderous campaign of Indian extermination that in a few years pushed the Indians beyond the small circumference of white settlement. Before 1622, the settlers knew that the Indians, though dangerous, were necessary to keep the colony alive. After 1622, most colonists considered the Indians their perpetual enemies.

From Private Company to Royal Government

The 1622 uprising came close to achieving Opechancanough's goal of pushing the colonists back into the Atlantic — so close that it prompted a royal investigation of affairs in Virginia. The investigators discovered that the appalling mortality among the colonists was caused more by disease and mismanagement than by Indian raids. In 1624, King James revoked the charter of the Virginia Company and made Virginia a **royal colony**, subject to the direction of the royal government rather than to the company's private investors, an arrangement that lasted until 1776.

The king now appointed the governor of Virginia and his council, but most other features of local government established under the Virginia Company remained intact. In 1619, for example, the company had inaugurated the **House of Burgesses**, an assembly of representatives (called burgesses) elected by the colony's inhabitants. (Historians do not know exactly which settlers were considered inhabitants and were thus qualified to vote.) Under the new royal government, laws passed by the burgesses had to be approved by the

viewpoint, the most important fact about the always-hungry English colonists was that they were not going away.

Powhatan died in 1618, and his brother **Opechancanough** replaced him as supreme chief. In 1622, Opechancanough organized an all-out assault on the English settlers. As an English colonist observed, "When the day appointed for the

Advertisement for Jamestown Settlers Virginia imported thousands of indentured servants to labor in the tobacco fields, but the colony also advertised in 1631 for settlers like those pictured here. The notice features men and women equally, although men heavily outnumbered women in the Chesapeake region. How would the English experiences of the individuals portrayed in the advertisement have been useful in Virginia? Why would such individuals have wanted to leave England and go to Virginia? If indentured servants had been pictured, how might they have differed in appearance from these people? Harvard Map Collection, Pusey Library, Harvard University.

king's bureaucrats in England rather than by the company. Otherwise, the House of Burgesses continued as before, acquiring distinction as the oldest representative legislative assembly in the English colonies. Under the new royal government, all free adult men in Virginia could vote for the House of Burgesses, giving it a far broader and more representative constituency than the English House of Commons.

The demise of the Virginia Company marked the end of the first phase of colonization of the Chesapeake region. From the first 105 adventurers in 1607, the population had grown to about 1,200 by 1624. Despite mortality rates higher than during the worst epidemics in London, new settlers still came. Their arrival and King James's willingness to take over the struggling colony reflected a fundamental change in Virginia. After years of fruitless experimentation, it was becoming clear that English settlers could make a fortune in Virginia by growing tobacco.

Q: **Why did Powhatan pursue largely peaceful relations with the Jamestown settlement?**

A Tobacco Society

Tobacco grew wild in the New World, and Native Americans used it for thousands of years before Europeans arrived. Columbus observed Indians smoking tobacco on his first voyage to the New World. Many other sixteenth-century European explorers noticed the Indians' habit of "drinking smoke." During the sixteenth century, Spanish colonists in the New World sent tobacco to Europe, where it was an expensive luxury used sparingly by a few. During the next century, English colonists in North America sent so much tobacco to European markets that it became an affordable indulgence used often by many people.

Initially, the Virginia Company had no plans to grow and sell tobacco. "As for tobacco," John Smith wrote, "we never then dreamt of it." John Rolfe—Pocahontas's husband-to-be—planted West Indian tobacco seeds in 1612 and learned that they flourished in Virginia. By 1617, the colonists had grown enough tobacco to send the first commercial shipment to England, where it sold for a high price. After that, Virginia pivoted from a colony of rather aimless adventurers who had difficulty growing enough corn to feed themselves into a society of dedicated planters who grew as much tobacco as possible.

Dedicated they were. By 1700, nearly 100,000 colonists lived in the Chesapeake region, encompassing Virginia, Maryland, and northern North Carolina (Map 3.1). They exported more than 35 million pounds of tobacco, a fivefold increase in per capita production since 1620. Clearly, Chesapeake colonists mastered the demands of tobacco agriculture, and the "Stinkinge Weede" (a seventeenth-century Marylander's term for tobacco) also mastered the colonists. Settlers lived by the rhythms of tobacco agriculture, and their endless need for labor attracted droves of English indentured servants to work in the tobacco fields.

Tobacco Agriculture A demanding crop, tobacco required close attention and a great deal of hand labor year-round. Primitive tools and methods made this intensive cycle of labor taxing. Like the Indians, the colonists "cleared" fields by cutting a ring of bark from each tree (a procedure known as "girdling"), thereby killing the tree. Girdling brought sunlight to clearings but left fields studded with tree stumps, making the use of plows impractical. Instead, colonists used heavy hoes to till their tobacco fields. To plant, a visitor observed, they "just make holes [with a stick] into which they drop the seeds," much as the Indians did. Growing tobacco with such methods left little time for idleness, but the colonists enjoyed the fruits of their labor. "Everyone smokes while working or idling," one traveler reported, including "men, women, girls, and boys, from the age of seven years."

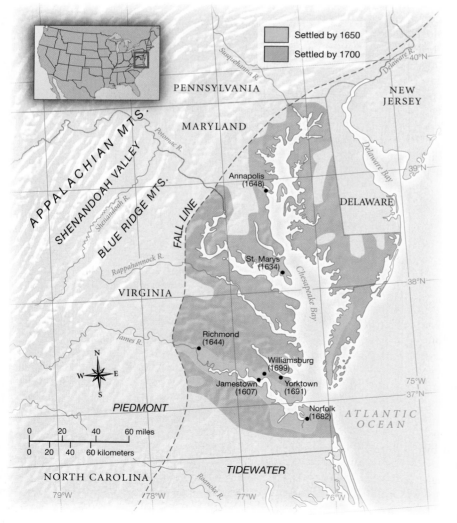

MAP 3.1 Chesapeake Colonies in the Seventeenth Century

The intimate association between land and water in the settlement of the Chesapeake in the seventeenth century is illustrated by this map. The fall line indicates the limit of navigable water, where rapids and falls prevented farther upstream travel. Although Delaware had excellent access to navigable water, it was claimed and defended by the Dutch colony at New Amsterdam (discussed in chapter 4) rather than by the English settlements in Virginia and Maryland shown on this map.

READING THE MAP: Using the notations on the map, create a chronology of the establishment of towns and settlements. What physical features correspond to the earliest habitation by English settlers?

CONNECTIONS: Why was access to navigable water so important? Given the settlers' need for defense against native tribes, what explains the distance between settlements?

FOR MORE HELP ANALYZING THIS MAP, see the map activity for this chapter in the Online Study Guide at bedfordstmartins.com/roarkcompact.

Tobacco Plantation This print illustrates the processing of tobacco on a seventeenth-century plantation. Workers cut the mature plants and put the leaves in piles to wilt (left foreground and center background). After the leaves dried somewhat, they were suspended from poles in a drying barn (right foreground), where they were seasoned before being packed in casks for shipping. Sometimes, tobacco leaves were left to dry in the fields (center background). The print suggests the labor demands of tobacco by showing twenty-two individuals, all but two of them actively at work with the crop. The one woman, hand in hand with a man in the left foreground, may be on her way to work on the harvested leaves, but it is more likely that she and the man are overseeing the labor of their servants or employees. From "About Tobacco," Lehman Brothers.

The English settlers worked hard because their labor promised greater rewards in the Chesapeake region than in England. One colonist proclaimed that "the dirt of this Province affords as great a profit to the general Inhabitant, as the Gold of Peru doth to . . . the Spaniard." Although he exaggerated, it was true that a hired man could expect to earn two or three times more in Virginia's tobacco fields than in England. Better still, in Virginia land was so abundant that it was extremely cheap compared to land in England.

By the mid-seventeenth century, common laborers could buy a hundred acres for less than their annual wages—an impossibility in England. New settlers who paid their own transportation to the Chesapeake received a grant of fifty acres of free land (termed a **headright**). The Virginia Company initiated headrights to encourage settlement, and the royal government continued them for the same reason.

A Servant Labor System Headrights, cheap land, and high wages gave poor English folk powerful incentives to immigrate to the New World. Yet many potential immigrants could not scrape together the money to pay for a trip across the Atlantic. Their poverty and the colonists' crying need for labor formed the basic context for the creation of a servant labor system.

About 80 percent of the immigrants to the Chesapeake during the seventeenth century were **indentured servants**. Twenty Africans arrived in Virginia in 1619, and they probably were enslaved, although scanty records make it uncertain. Until the 1670s, however, only a small number of slaves labored in Chesapeake tobacco fields. (Large numbers of slaves came in the eighteenth century, as chapter 5 explains.) A few indentured servants of African descent served out their terms of servitude and became free. A few slaves purchased their way out of bondage and lived as free people, even owning land and using the local courts to resolve disputes, much as freed white servants did. A small number of Native Americans also became servants. But the overwhelming majority of indentured servants were white immigrants from England. Instead of a slave society, the seventeenth-century Chesapeake region was fundamentally a society of white servants and ex-servants.

To buy passage aboard a ship bound for the Chesapeake, an English immigrant had to come up with about £5, roughly a year's wages for an English servant or laborer. Earning wages at all was difficult in England since job opportunities were shrinking. Many country landowners needed fewer farmhands because they shifted from growing crops to raising sheep in newly enclosed fields.

Unemployed people drifted into seaports such as Bristol, Liverpool, and London, where they learned about the plentiful jobs in North America. Unable to pay for their trip across the Atlantic, poor immigrants agreed to a contract called an indenture, which functioned as a form of credit. By signing an indenture, an immigrant borrowed the cost of transportation to the Chesapeake from a merchant or ship captain in England. To repay this loan, the indentured person agreed to work as a servant for four to seven years in North America.

Once the indentured person arrived in the colonies, the merchant or ship captain sold his right to the immigrant's labor to a local tobacco planter. To obtain the servant's labor, the planter paid about twice the cost of transportation and agreed to provide the servant with food and shelter during the term of the indenture. When the indenture expired, the planter owed the former servant "freedom dues," usually a few barrels of corn and a suit of clothes.

Ideally, indentures allowed poor immigrants to trade their most valuable assets—their freedom and their ability to work—for a trip to the New World and a period of servitude followed by freedom in a land of opportunity. Planters reaped more immediate benefits. Servants meant more hands to grow more tobacco. A planter expected a servant to grow enough tobacco in one year to cover the price the planter paid for the indenture. Servants' labor during the remaining three to six

years of the indenture promised a handsome profit for the planter. No wonder one Virginian declared, "Our principall wealth . . . consisteth in servants." But roughly half of all servants became sick and died before serving out their indentures, reducing planters' gains and destroying the servants' hopes. Planters still profited, however, since they received a headright of fifty acres of land from the colonial government for every newly purchased servant.

About three out of four servants were men between the ages of fifteen and twenty-five when they arrived in the Chesapeake. Typically, they shared the desperation of sixteen-year-old Francis Haires, who indentured himself for seven years because, according to his contract, "his father and mother and All friends [are] dead and he [is] a miserable wandering boy." Like Francis, most servants had no special training or skills, although the majority had some experience with agricultural work. "Hunger and fear of prisons bring to us onely such servants as have been brought up to no Art or Trade," one Virginia planter complained. A skilled craftsman could obtain a shorter indenture, but few risked coming to the colonies since their prospects were better in England.

Women were almost as rare as skilled craftsmen in the Chesapeake and more ardently desired. In the early days of the tobacco boom, the Virginia Company shipped young single women servants to the colony as prospective wives for male settlers willing to pay "120 weight [pounds] of the best leaf tobacco for each of them," in effect getting both a wife and a servant. The company reasoned that, as one official wrote in 1622, "the plantation can never flourish till families be planted, and the respect of wives and children fix the people on the soil." The company's efforts as a marriage broker proved no more successful than its other ventures. Women remained a small minority of the Chesapeake population until late in the seventeenth century.

The servant labor system perpetuated the gender imbalance. Although female servants cost about the same as males and generally served for the same length of time, only about one servant in four was a woman. Planters preferred male servants for field work, although many servant women hoed and harvested tobacco fields. Most women servants also did household chores such as cooking, washing, cleaning, gardening, and milking.

Servants—whether men or women, whites or blacks, English or African—tended to work together and socialize together. During the first half century of settlement, racial intermingling occurred, although the small number of blacks made it infrequent. Courts punished sexual relations between blacks and whites, but the number of court cases shows that sexual desire readily crossed the color line. In general, the commonalities of servitude caused servants—regardless of their race and gender—to consider themselves apart from free people, whose ranks they longed to join eventually.

Servant life was harsh by the standards of seventeenth-century England and even by the frontier standards of the Chesapeake. Unlike servants in England, Chesapeake servants had no control over who purchased their labor—and thus them—for the period of their indenture. Many servants were bought and sold several times before their indenture expired. A Virginia servant protested in 1623 that his master "hath sold me for £150 sterling like a damnd slave." But tobacco planters' need for labor muffled complaints about treating servants as property.

For servants, the promise of indentured servitude that loomed large in their decision to leave England and immigrate to the Chesapeake often withered when they confronted the rigors of labor in the tobacco fields. James Revel, an eighteen-year-old thief punished by being indentured to a Virginia tobacco planter, declared he was a "slave" sent to hoe "tobacco plants all day" from dawn to dark. Severe laws aimed to keep servants in their place. (See "Documenting the American Promise," page 60.) Punishments for petty crimes stretched servitude far beyond the original terms of indenture. Richard Higby, for example, received six extra years of servitude for killing three hogs. After midcentury, the Virginia legislature added three or more years to the indentures of most servants by requiring them to serve until they were twenty-four years old.

Women servants were subject to special restrictions and risks. They were prohibited from marrying until their servitude had expired. A servant woman, the law assumed, could not serve two masters at the same time: one who owned her indentured labor and another who was her husband. However, the predominance of men in the Chesapeake population inevitably pressured women to engage in sexual relations. About a third of immigrant women were pregnant when they married. Pregnancy and childbirth sapped a woman's strength, and a new child diverted her attention,

reducing her usefulness as a servant. As a rule, if a woman servant gave birth to a child, she had to serve two extra years and pay a fine. However, for some servant women, premarital pregnancy was a path out of servitude: The father of an unborn child sometimes purchased the indenture of the servant mother-to-be, then freed and married her.

> **A Virginia servant protested in 1623 that his master "hath sold me for £150 sterling like a damnd slave."**

Harsh punishments reflected four fundamental realities of the servant labor system. First, planters' hunger for labor caused them to demand as much labor as they could get from their servants, including devising legal ways to extend the period of servitude. Second, servants hoped to survive their servitude and use their freedom to obtain land and start a family. Third, servants' hopes frequently conflicted with planters' demands. Since servants saw themselves as free people in a temporary status of servitude, they often made grudging, halfhearted workers. Finally, planters put up with this contentious arrangement because the alternatives were less desirable.

Planters could not easily hire free men and women because land was readily available and free people preferred to work for themselves on their own land. Nor could planters depend on much labor from family members. The preponderance of men in the population meant that families were few, were started late, and thus had few children. And, until the 1680s and 1690s, slaves were expensive and hard to come by. Before then, masters who wanted to expand their labor force and grow more tobacco had few alternatives to buying indentured servants.

Cultivating Land and Faith Villages and small towns dotted the rural landscape of seventeenth-century England, but in the Chesapeake, acres of wilderness were interrupted here and there by tobacco farms. Tobacco was such a labor-intensive crop that one field worker could tend only about two acres of the plants in a year (an acre is slightly smaller than a football field), plus a few more acres for food crops. A successful farmer needed a great deal more land, however, because tobacco quickly exhausted the fertility of the soil. Since each farmer cultivated only 5 or 10 percent of his land at any one time, a "settled"

Settlement Patterns along the James River

Virginia Laws Governing Servants and Slaves

Servants and slaves often chafed at the terms of their servitude. Masters usually punished unruly servants and slaves privately. But the Virginia legislature also enacted numerous laws to reinforce masters' rule over servants and slaves. The following selections from seventeenth-century Virginia laws illustrate the emerging legal distinctions between servants, slaves, and free people, as well as between English settlers, Africans, and Native Americans.

DOCUMENT 1
Law Punishing Runaway Servants, 1661

Runaway servants—both white and black—plagued masters. The enactment of this law suggests that by the 1660s, masters sought government help to punish runaways.

Whereas there are diverse loitering runaways in this country who very often absent themselves from their masters service and sometimes in a long time cannot be found, that losse of the time and the charge in the seeking them often exceeding the value of their labor: Bee it therefore enacted that all runaways that shall absent themselves from their said masters service shalbe lyable to make satisfaction by service after the times by custome or indenture is expired (vizt.) double their times of service soe neglected, and if the time of their running away was in the crop or the charge of recovering them extraordinary[,] the court shall lymitt a longer time of service proportionable to the damage the master shall make appear he hath susteyned. . . . And in case any English servant shall run away in the company of any negroes who are incapable of making satisfaction by addition of a time, it is enacted that the English soe running away in the company with them shall[,] at the time of service to their owne masters [is] expired, serve the masters of the said negroes for their absence soe long as they should have done by this act if that had not beene slaves, every christian in company serving his proportion; and if the negroes be lost or dye in such time of their being run away, the christian servants in company with them shall by proportion among them, either pay fower thousand five hundred pounds of tobacco . . . or fower years service for every negroe soe lost or dead.

SOURCE: William Waller Hening, ed., *The Statutes at Large; Being a Collection of All the Laws of Virginia*, 18 vols. (1809–1823), 2:116–17.

DOCUMENT 2
Law Making Slave Status Inherited from Mother, 1662

In 1662, Virginia lawmakers specified that the children of slave mothers inherited their mothers' slave status. This law overturned the precedent of English law, which provided that children inherited their fathers' status. In practice, the Virginia law meant that if a white man had a child with a female slave, the child was a slave. However, if a male slave had a child with a white woman, the child was free. The law also punished all sexual relations across the color line.

Whereas some doubts have arisen whether children got by any Englishman upon a negro woman should be slave or ffree, Be it therefore enacted and declared . . . that all children borne in this country shalbe held bond or free only according to the condition of the mother. And that if any christian shall commit fornication with a negro man or woman, hee or shee soe offending shall pay double the ffines imposed by the former act.

SOURCE: William Waller Hening, ed., *The Statutes at Large; Being a Collection of All the Laws of Virginia*, 18 vols. (1809–1823), 2:170.

DOCUMENT 3
Law Specifies That Baptism Does Not Free Slaves, 1667

Virginia legislators declared in 1667 that slaves who converted to Christianity did not thereby become free. Lawmakers officially assured masters that slavery and Christianity were legally compatible, permitting Christianity to be taught to slaves without jeopardizing their slave status.

Whereas some doubts have arisen whether children that are slaves by birth, and by the charity and piety of their

owners made pertakers of the blessed sacrament of baptisms, should by vertue of their baptisme be made ffree; It is enacted and declared . . . that the conferring of baptisme doth not alter the condition of the person as to his bondage or ffreedome; that diverse masters, ffreed from this doubt, may more carefully endeavour the propagation of christianity by permitting children, though slaves, or those of greater growth if capable to be admitted to that sacrament.

SOURCE: William Waller Hening, ed., *The Statutes at Large; Being a Collection of All the Laws of Virginia*, 18 vols. (1809–1823), 2:170.

DOCUMENT 4
Law Makes Killing a Slave Legal, 1669

If a servant assaulted a master, the master could legally extend the servants' period of servitude as punishment. A master had no similar legal remedy to inflict on an obstreperous slave, since a slave was already enslaved for life. In 1669, the Virginia legislature gave masters a green light to use any force they deemed necessary, including death, to control unruly slaves. Lawmakers declared that killing a slave was not murder, but instead was justifiable and legal.

Whereas the only law in force for the punishment of refractory servants resisting their master, mistris or overseer cannot be inflicted upon negroes, nor the obstinacy of many of them by other then violent meanes supprest, Be it enacted and declared . . . [that] if any slave resist his master (or other by his masters order correcting him) and by the extremity of the correction should chance to die, that his death shall not be accompted a ffelony, but the master (or that other person appointed by the master to punish him) be acquit from molestation, since it cannot be presumed that prepensed malice (which alone makes murther ffelony) should induce any man to destroy his owne estate.

SOURCE: William Waller Hening, ed., *The Statutes at Large; Being a Collection of All the Laws of Virginia*, 18 vols. (1809–1823), 2:270.

DOCUMENT 5
Law Authorizes Force to Suppress Rebellious Slaves, Indians, and Servants, 1672

In 1672, the Virginia legislature authorized all white colonists to use any necessary force to suppress rebellious slaves, Indians, and servants. In effect, the law deputized white colonists to use deadly force against runaways. Lawmakers also encouraged Indians to help apprehend runaways, providing a reward for any fugitives turned over to white authorities.

Forasmuch as it hath beene manifested to this grand assembly that many negroes have lately beene, and now are out in rebellion in sundry parts of this country, and that noe meanes have yet beene found for the apprehension and suppression of them from whome many mischiefs of a very dangerous consequence may arise to the country if either other negroes, Indians or servants should happen to fly forth and joyne with them; for the prevention of which, be it enacted . . . that if any negroe, molatto, Indian slave, or servant for life, runaway and shalbe persued . . . , it shall and may be lawful for any person who shall endeavour to take them, upon the resistance of such negroe, molatto, Indian slave, or servant for life, to kill or wound him or them soe resisting. . . . And if it happen that such negroe, molatto, Indian slave, or servant for life doe dye of any wound in such their resistance . . . the master or owner of such shall receive satisfaction from the publique for [value of the slave]. . . . And it is further enacted that the neighbouring Indians doe and hereby are required and enjoyned to seize and apprehend all runaways whatsoever that shall happen to come amongst them, and to bring them before some justice of the peace who . . . shall pay unto the said Indians . . . a recompence.

SOURCE: William Waller Hening, ed., *The Statutes at Large; Being a Collection of All the Laws of Virginia*, 18 vols. (1809–1823), 2:299–300.

Questions for Analysis and Debate

1. According to these laws, how did slaves differ from servants? What boundaries did these laws draw among the various peoples in servitude?

2. According to these laws, what characterized colonists from England? What terms did the laws use to refer to English colonists? How did those terms differ from the words used to describe slaves?

3. In what ways did these laws reflect important developments that occurred in the southern colonies in the 1660s and 1670s? In what ways do the laws document an emerging hierarchy of race and class?

area comprised swatches of cultivated land surrounded by forest. Arrangements for marketing tobacco also contributed to the dispersion of settlements. Tobacco planters sought land that fronted a navigable river in order to minimize the work of transporting the heavy barrels of tobacco onto ships. A settled region thus resembled a lacework of farms stitched around waterways.

Most Chesapeake colonists were nominally Protestants. Attendance at Sunday services and conformity to the doctrines of the Church of England were required of all English men and women. Few clergymen migrated to the Chesapeake, however, and too few of those who did were models of righteousness and piety. Certainly, some colonists took their religion seriously. Church courts punished fornicators, censured blasphemers, and served notice on parishioners who spent Sundays "goeing a fishing." But on the whole, religion did not awaken the zeal of Chesapeake settlers, certainly not as it did the zeal of New England settlers in these same years (see chapter 4). What quickened the pulse of most Chesapeake folk was a close horse race, a bloody cockfight, or—most of all—an exceptionally fine tobacco crop. The religion of the Chesapeake colonists was Anglican, but their faith lay in the turbulent, competitive, high-stakes gamble of survival as tobacco planters.

The situation was similar in the Catholic colony of Maryland. In 1632, England's King Charles I granted his Catholic friend **Lord Baltimore** about six and a half million acres in the northern Chesapeake region. In return, the king specified that Lord Baltimore pay him the token rent of "two Indian arrowheads" a year. Lord Baltimore intended to create a refuge for Catholics, who suffered severe discrimination in England. He fitted out two ships, the *Ark* and the *Dove*; gathered about 150 settlers; and sent them to the new colony, where they arrived on March 25, 1634. However, Maryland failed to live up to Baltimore's hopes. The colony's population grew very slowly for twenty years, and most settlers were Protestants rather than Catholics. The religious turmoil of the Puritan Revolution in England (discussed in chapter 4) spilled across the Atlantic, creating conflict between Maryland's few Catholics—most of them wealthy and prominent—and the Protestant majority, most of them neither wealthy nor prominent. During the 1660s, Maryland began to attract settlers, mostly Protestants, as readily as Virginia. Although Catholics and the Catholic faith continued to exert influence in Maryland, the colony's society, economy, politics, and culture became nearly indistinguishable from Virginia's. Both colonies shared a devotion to tobacco, the true faith of the Chesapeake.

> **Q:** Why did the vast majority of European immigrants to the Chesapeake come as indentured servants?

The Evolution of Chesapeake Society

The system of indentured servitude sharpened inequality in Chesapeake society by the midseventeenth century, propelling social and political polarization that culminated in 1676 with Bacon's Rebellion. The rebellion prompted reforms that stabilized relations between elite planters and their lesser neighbors and paved the way for a social hierarchy that muted differences of landholding and wealth and amplified racial differences. Amid this social and political evolution, one thing did not change: Chesapeake colonists' dedication to growing tobacco.

Social and Economic Polarization
The first half of the seventeenth century in the Chesapeake was the era of the **yeoman**—a farmer who owned a small plot of land sufficient to support a family and tilled largely by servants and a few family members. A small number of elite planters had larger estates and commanded ten or more servants. But for the first several decades, few men lived long enough to accumulate fortunes sufficient to set them much apart from their neighbors. On the whole, a rough frontier equality characterized free families in the Chesapeake until about 1650.

Until midcentury, the principal division in Chesapeake society was less between rich and poor planters than between free farmers and unfree servants. Although these two groups contrasted sharply in their legal and economic status, their daily lives had many similarities. Servants looked forward to the time when their indentures would expire and they would become free and eventually own land.

Three major developments splintered the equality during the third quarter of the century. First, as planters grew more and more tobacco, the ample supply depressed tobacco prices in European markets. Cheap tobacco reduced planters' profits and made saving enough to become landowners more difficult for freed servants. Second, because the mortality rate in the Chesapeake colonies declined, more and more servants survived their indentures, and landless freemen became more numerous and grew more discontented. Third, declining mortality also encouraged the formation of a planter elite. By living longer, the most successful planters compounded their success. The wealthiest planters also began to serve as merchants, marketing crops for their less successful neighbors, importing English goods for sale, and extending credit to hard-pressed customers.

By the 1670s, the society of the Chesapeake had become polarized. Landowners—the planter elite and the more numerous yeoman planters—clustered around one pole. Landless colonists, mainly freed servants, gathered at the other. Each group eyed the other with suspicion and mistrust. For the most part, planters saw landless freemen as a dangerous rabble rather than as fellow colonists with legitimate grievances. Governor William Berkeley feared the political threat to the governing elite posed by "six parts in seven [of Virginia colonists who] . . . are poor, indebted, discontented, and armed."

Government Policies and Political Conflict In general, government and politics strengthened the distinctions in Chesapeake society. The most vital distinction separated servants and masters, and the colonial government enforced it with an iron fist. Poor men such as William Tyler complained that "nether the Governor nor Counsell could or would doe any poore men right, but that they would shew favor to great men and wronge the poore." Most Chesapeake colonists, like most Europeans, assumed that "great men" should bear the responsibilities of government. Until 1670, all freemen could vote, and they routinely elected prosperous planters to the legislature. No former servant served in either the governor's council or the House of Burgesses after 1640. Yet Tyler and other poor Virginians believed that the "great men" used their government offices to promote their selfish personal interests rather than governing impartially.

As discontent mounted among the poor during the 1660s and 1670s, colonial officials tried to keep political power in safe hands. Beginning in 1661, for example, **Governor William Berkeley** did not call an election for the House of Burgesses for fifteen years. In 1670, the House of Burgesses outlawed voting by poor men, permitting only men who headed households and were landowners to vote.

The king also began to tighten the royal government's control of trade and to collect substantial revenue from the Chesapeake. A series of navigation acts funneled the colonial trade exclusively

Inside a Poor Planter's House The houses of seventeenth-century Chesapeake settlers were typically "earth-fast": The structural timbers that framed the house were simply placed in holes in the ground, and the floor was packed dirt. No seventeenth-century house was substantial enough to survive until today. This photo shows a carefully documented reconstruction of the interior of a poor planter's house at Historic St. Mary's City, Maryland. The wall of this one-room dwelling with a loft features a window with a shutter but no glass. When the shutter was closed, the only source of light was a candle or a fire. Notice the rustic, unfinished bench, table, and walls. These meager furnishings were usually accompanied by a storage chest and some bedding, but not a bed. If and when a planter became more prosperous, a bed was likely to be the first acquisition, suggesting that the lack of a good night's sleep was one of the planter's major discomforts. Image courtesy of Historic St. Mary's City.

into the hands of English merchants and shippers. The **Navigation Acts** of 1650 and 1651 specified that colonial goods had to be transported in English ships with predominantly English crews. A 1660 act required colonial products to be sent only to English ports, and a 1663 law stipulated further that all goods sent to the colonies must pass through English ports and be carried in English ships manned by English sailors. Taken together, these navigation acts reflected the English government's mercantilist assumptions about the colonies: What was good for England should determine colonial policy.

Assumptions about **mercantilism** also underlay the import duty on tobacco inaugurated by the Navigation Act of 1660. The law assessed an import tax of two pence on every pound of colonial tobacco brought into England, about the price a Chesapeake tobacco farmer received. The tax gave the king a major financial interest in the size of the tobacco crop. During the 1660s, these tobacco import taxes yielded about a quarter of all English customs revenues, an impressive sign of the growing importance of the Chesapeake colonies in England's Atlantic empire.

Bacon's Rebellion Colonists, like residents of European monarchies, accepted social hierarchy and inequality as long as they believed that government officials ruled for the general good. When rulers violated that precept, ordinary people felt justified in rebelling. In 1676, **Bacon's Rebellion** erupted as a dispute over Virginia's Indian policy. Before it was over, the rebellion convulsed Chesapeake politics and society, leaving in its wake death, destruction, and a legacy of hostility between the great planters and their poorer neighbors.

Opechancanough, the Algonquian chief who had led the Indian uprising of 1622 in Virginia, mounted another surprise attack in 1644 and killed about five hundred Virginia colonists in two days. During the next two years of bitter fighting, the colonists eventually gained the upper hand, capturing and murdering the old chief. The treaty that concluded the war established policies toward the Indians that the government tried to maintain for the next thirty years. The Indians relinquished all claims to land already settled by the English. Wilderness land beyond the fringe of English settlement was supposed to be reserved exclusively for Indian use. The colonial government hoped to minimize contact between settlers and Indians and thereby maintain the peace.

If the Chesapeake population had not grown, the policy might have worked. But the number of land-hungry colonists, especially poor, recently freed servants, continued to multiply. In their quest for land, they pushed beyond the treaty limits of English settlement and encroached steadily on Indian land. During the 1660s and 1670s, violence between colonists and Indians repeatedly flared along the advancing frontier. The government, headquartered in the tidewater region near the coast, far from the danger of Indian raids, took steps to calm the disputes and reestablish the peace. Frontier settlers thirsted for revenge against what their leader, **Nathaniel Bacon**, termed "the protected and Darling Indians." Bacon proclaimed his "Design not only to ruine and extirpate all Indians in Generall but all Manner of Trade and Commerce with them." Indians were not the only enemies Bacon and his men singled out. Bacon also urged the colonists to "see what spounges have suckt up the Publique Treasure." He charged that **grandees**, or elite planters, operated the government for their private gain, a charge that made sense to many colonists. Bacon crystallized the grievances of the small planters and poor farmers against both the Indians and the colonial rulers in Jamestown.

Hoping to maintain the fragile peace on the frontier in 1676, Governor Berkeley pronounced Bacon a rebel, threatened to punish him for treason, and called for new elections of burgesses who, Berkeley believed, would endorse his get-tough policy. To Berkeley's surprise, the elections backfired. Almost all the old burgesses were voted out of office, and they were replaced by local leaders, including Bacon. The legislature was now in the hands of minor grandees who, like Bacon, chafed at the rule of the elite planters.

In June 1676, the new legislature passed a series of reform measures known as Bacon's Laws. Among other changes, the laws gave local settlers a voice in setting tax levies, forbade officeholders from demanding bribes or other extra fees for carrying out their duties, placed limits on holding multiple offices, and restored the vote to all freemen. Under pressure, Berkeley pardoned Bacon and authorized his campaign of Indian warfare. But elite planters soon convinced Berkeley that Bacon and his men were a greater threat than Indians.

When Bacon learned that Berkeley had once again branded him a traitor, he declared war against Berkeley and the other grandees. For three months, Bacon's forces fought the Indians, sacked the grandees' plantations, and attacked Jamestown. Berkeley's loyalists retaliated by plundering the homes of Bacon's supporters. The fighting continued until late October, when Bacon unexpectedly died, most likely from dysentery, and several English ships arrived to bolster Berkeley's strength. With the rebellion crushed, Berkeley hanged several of Bacon's allies and destroyed farms that belonged to Bacon's supporters.

The rebellion did nothing to dislodge the grandees from their positions of power. If anything, it strengthened them. When the king learned of the turmoil in the Chesapeake and its devastating effect on tobacco exports and customs duties, he ordered an investigation. Royal officials replaced Berkeley with a governor more attentive to the king's interests, nullified Bacon's Laws, and instituted an export tax on every hogshead of tobacco as a way of paying the expenses of government without having to obtain the consent of the tight-fisted House of Burgesses.

In the aftermath of Bacon's Rebellion, tensions between great planters and small farmers gradually lessened. Bacon's Rebellion showed, a governor of Virginia said, that it was necessary "to steer between . . . either an Indian or a civil war." The ruling elite concluded that it was safer for the colonists to fight the Indians than to fight each other, and the government made little effort to restrict settlers' encroachment on Indian land. Tax cuts also were welcomed by all freemen. The export duty on tobacco imposed by the king allowed the colonial government to reduce taxes by 75 percent between 1660 and 1700. In the long run, however, the most important contribution to political stability was the declining importance of the servant labor system. During the 1680s and 1690s, fewer servants arrived in the Chesapeake, partly because of improving economic conditions in England. Accordingly, the number of poor, newly freed servants also declined, reducing the size of the lowest stratum of free society. In 1700, as many as one-third of the free colonists still worked as tenants on land owned by others, but the social and political distance between them and the great planters did not seem as important as it had been in 1660. The main reason was that by 1700, the Chesapeake was in the midst of transition to a slave labor system that minimized the differences between poor farmers and rich planters and magnified the differences between whites and blacks.

Q: **Why did Chesapeake colonial society become increasingly polarized between 1650 and 1670?**

Religion and Revolt in the Spanish Borderland

While English colonies in the Chesapeake grew and prospered with the tobacco trade, the northern outposts of the Spanish empire in New Mexico and Florida stagnated. Instead of attracting settlers and growing crops for export, New Mexico and Florida appealed to Spanish missionaries seeking to harvest Indian souls. The missionaries baptized thousands of Indians in Spanish North America during the seventeenth century, but they also planted the seeds of Indian uprisings against Spanish rule.

Few Spaniards came to New Spain's northern borderland during the seventeenth century. Only about fifteen hundred Spaniards lived in Florida, and roughly twice as many inhabited New Mexico. One royal governor complained that "no [Spaniard] comes . . . to plow and sow [crops], but only to eat and loaf." In both colonies, Indians outnumbered Spaniards ten or twenty to one.

Royal officials seriously considered eliminating both colonies because their costs greatly exceeded their benefits. Every three years, a caravan from Mexico brought wagons full of goods to outposts in New Mexico. Florida required even larger subsidies because it housed a garrison of soldiers as well as missionaries who persuaded the Spanish government that instead of being losing propositions, the colonies represented golden opportunities to convert heathen Indians to Christianity. Stirrups

Spanish Stirrup This seventeenth-century stirrup used by Spaniards on the northern frontier of New Spain illustrates the use of elaborate ornamentation and display to convey a sense of Spanish power. It is no accident that the stirrup is in the shape of a Christian cross, a vivid symbol of the Spaniards' belief in the divine source of their authority.
© George H. H. Huey.

adorned with Christian crosses on soldiers' saddles proclaimed the faith behind the Spaniards' swords, and vice versa. Royal officials hoped that the missionaries' efforts would pacify the Indians and be a relatively cheap way to preserve Spanish footholds in North America.

Dozens of missionaries came to Florida and New Mexico, as one announced, to free the Indians "from the miserable slavery of the demon and from the obscure darkness of their idolatry." The missionaries believed that the Indians' religious beliefs and rituals were idolatrous devil worship and that their way of life was barbaric. The missionaries followed royal instructions that Indians should be taught "to live in a civilized manner, clothed and wearing shoes . . . [and] given the use of . . . bread, linen, horses, cattle, tools, and weapons, and all the rest that Spain has had." In effect, the missionaries sought to convert the Indians not just into Christians but also into surrogate Spaniards.

The missionaries supervised the building of scores of Catholic churches across Florida and New Mexico. Typically, they conscripted Indian women and men to do the construction. Adopting practices common elsewhere in New Spain, they forced the Indians both to work and to pay tribute in the form of food, blankets, and other goods. Although the missionaries congratulated themselves on the many Indians they converted, their coercive methods subverted their goals. A missionary reported that an Indian in New Mexico asked him, "If we [missionaries] who are Christians caused so much harm and violence [to Indians], why should they become Christians?"

The Indians retaliated repeatedly against Spanish exploitation, but the Spaniards suppressed the violent uprisings by taking advantage of the disunity among the Indians, much as Cortés did in the conquest of Mexico (see chapter 2). In 1680, however, **Pueblo Indians** organized a unified revolt under the leadership of **Popé**, who ordered his followers, as one recounted, to "break up and burn the images of the holy Christ, the Virgin Mary, and the other saints, the crosses, and everything pertaining to Christianity." During the Pueblo Revolt, the Indians desecrated churches, killed two-thirds of the Spanish missionaries, and drove the Spaniards out of New Mexico to present-day El Paso, Texas. The Spaniards managed to return to New Mexico by the end of the seventeenth century, but only by curtailing the missionaries and reducing labor exploitation. Florida Indians never mounted a unified attack on Spanish rule, but they too organized sporadic uprisings and resisted conversion, causing a Spanish official

to report by the end of the seventeenth century that "the law of God and the preaching of the Holy Gospel have now ceased."

Q: Why did the Pueblo Indians revolt against Spanish missionaries in 1680?

Toward a Slave Labor System

During the sixteenth century, Spaniards and Portuguese in the New World supplemented Indian laborers with enslaved Africans. On this foundation, European colonizers built African **slavery** into the most important form of coerced labor in the New World. During the seventeenth century, English colonies in the West Indies followed the Spanish and Portuguese examples and developed sugar plantations with slave labor. In the English North American colonies, however, a slave labor system did not emerge until the last quarter of the seventeenth century. During the 1670s, settlers from **Barbados** brought slavery to the new English mainland colony of Carolina, where the imprint of the West Indies remained strong for decades. In Chesapeake tobacco fields at about the same time, slave labor began to replace servant labor, marking the transition toward a society of freedom for whites and slavery for Africans.

The West Indies: Sugar and Slavery The most profitable part of the English New World empire in the seventeenth century lay in the Caribbean (Map 3.2). The tiny island of Barbados, colonized in the 1630s, was the jewel of the English West Indies. During the 1640s, Barbadian planters began to grow sugarcane with such success that a colonial official proclaimed Barbados "the most flourishing Island in all those American parts, and I verily believe in all the world for the production of sugar." Sugar commanded high prices in England, and planters rushed to grow as much as they could. By midcentury, annual sugar exports from the English Caribbean totaled about 150,000 pounds; by 1700, exports reached nearly 50 million pounds.

Sugar transformed Barbados and other West Indian islands. Poor farmers could not afford the expensive machinery that extracted and refined sugarcane juice. Planters with the necessary capital to grow sugar got rich. By 1680, the wealthiest Barbadian sugar planters were, on average, four times richer than tobacco grandees in the Chesapeake. The sugar grandees differed from their

Sugar Plantation This portrait of a Brazilian sugar plantation shows the house of the Brazilian owners, attended by numerous slaves. Cartloads of sugarcane are being hauled to the mill, which is powered by a waterwheel (far right), where the cane will be squeezed between rollers to extract the sugary juice. The juice will then be distilled over a fire tended by the slaves (at the left end of the mill) until it has the desired consistency and purity. Notice that all of the working people are of African descent, and probably all of them are slaves. How did the artist differentiate slaves from their owners? Courtesy of the John Carter Brown Library at Brown University.

Chesapeake counterparts in another crucial way: The average sugar baron in Barbados owned 115 slaves in 1680.

African slaves planted, cultivated, and harvested the sugarcane that made West Indian planters wealthy. (See "Global Comparison.") Beginning in the 1640s, Barbadian planters purchased thousands of slaves to work their plantations, and the African population on the island mushroomed. During the 1650s, when blacks made up only 3 percent of the Chesapeake population, they had already become the majority on Barbados. By 1700, slaves constituted more than three-fourths of the island's population.

For slaves, work on a sugar plantation was a life sentence to brutal, unremitting labor. Slaves suffered high death rates. Since slave men outnumbered slave women two to one, few slaves could form families and have children. These grim realities meant that in Barbados and elsewhere in the West Indies, the slave population did not grow by natural reproduction. Instead, planters continually purchased enslaved Africans. Although sugar plantations did not gain a foothold in North America in the seventeenth century, the West Indies nonetheless exerted a powerful influence on the development of slavery in the mainland colonies.

Carolina: A West Indian Frontier The early settlers of what became South Carolina were immigrants from Barbados. In 1663, a Barbadian planter named John Colleton and a group of seven other men obtained a charter from England's King Charles II to establish a colony south of the Chesapeake and north of the Spanish territories in Florida. The men, known as "proprietors," hoped to siphon settlers from Barbados and other colonies and encourage them to develop a profitable export crop comparable to West Indian sugar and Chesapeake tobacco. Following the Chesapeake example, the proprietors offered headrights of up to 150 acres of land for each settler. In 1670, they established the colony's first permanent English settlement, Charles Towne (later spelled Charleston) (see Map 3.2).

As the proprietors had planned, most of the early settlers were from Barbados. In fact, Carolina was the only seventeenth-century English colony to be settled principally by colonists from other colonies rather than from England. The Barbadian immigrants brought their slaves with them. More than a fourth of the early settlers were slaves, and as the colony continued to attract settlers from Barbados, the black population multiplied. By 1700, slaves made up about half the population of Carolina. The new colony's close association with Barbados caused

MAP 3.2 The West Indies and Carolina in the Seventeenth Century

Although Carolina was geographically close to the Chesapeake colonies, it was culturally closer to the West Indies in the seventeenth century because its early settlers — both blacks and whites — came from Barbados. South Carolina maintained strong ties to the West Indies for more than a century, long after the arrival of many later settlers from England, Ireland, France, and elsewhere.

> The new colony's close association with Barbados caused English officials to refer routinely to "Carolina in ye West Indies."

English officials to refer routinely to "Carolina in ye West Indies."

The Carolinians experimented unsuccessfully to match their semitropical climate with profitable export crops of tobacco, cotton, indigo, and olives. In the mid-1690s, colonists identified a hardy strain of rice and took advantage of the knowledge of rice cultivation among their many African slaves to build rice plantations. Settlers also sold livestock and timber to the West Indies, as well as another "natural resource": They captured and enslaved several thousand local Indians and sold them to Caribbean planters. Both economically and socially, seventeenth-century Carolina was a frontier outpost of the West Indian sugar economy.

Slave Labor Emerges in the Chesapeake By 1700, more than eight out of ten people in the southern colonies of English North America lived

in the Chesapeake. Until the 1670s, almost all Chesapeake colonists were white people from England. By 1700, however, one out of eight people in the region was a black person from Africa. A few black people had lived in the Chesapeake since the 1620s, but the black population grew fivefold between 1670 and 1700 as hundreds of tobacco planters made the transition from servant to slave labor.

For planters, slaves had several obvious advantages over servants. Although slaves cost three to five times more than servants, slaves never became free. Since the mortality rate had declined by the 1680s, planters could reasonably expect a slave to live longer than a servant's period of indenture. Slaves also promised to be a perpetual labor force, since children of slave mothers inherited the status of slavery.

Slaves had another important advantage over servants: They could be controlled politically. Bacon's Rebellion had demonstrated how disruptive former servants could be when their expectations were not met. A slave labor system promised

Migration to the New World from Europe and Africa, 1492–1700

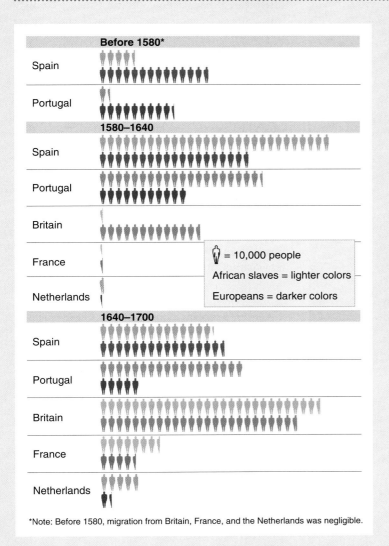

Before 1580*

Spain

Portugal

1580–1640

Spain

Portugal

Britain

France

Netherlands

 = 10,000 people

African slaves = lighter colors

Europeans = darker colors

1640–1700

Spain

Portugal

Britain

France

Netherlands

*Note: Before 1580, migration from Britain, France, and the Netherlands was negligible.

Before 1640, Spain and Portugal reaped the rewards of their sixteenth-century voyages of discovery by sending four out of five European migrants to the New World, virtually all of them bound for New Spain or Brazil. But from 1640 to 1700, more migrants came from England than from any other European nation and nearly as many as from all other European nations combined, a measure of the growing significance of England's colonies in both the Caribbean and North America during the seventeenth century.

While few enslaved Africans were carried across the Atlantic before 1580, after 1580 more enslaved Africans than Europeans arrived in New World colonies, an outgrowth of the enormous expansion of slave labor in the European colonies. Between 1580 and 1640, Spanish and Portuguese colonies pioneered in the use of large numbers of slaves, especially in sugarcane fields, and other nations quickly followed suit. Only a comparatively few enslaved Africans were carried to English North American tobacco and rice fields before 1700 (not shown separately in this figure). Overall, from the voyages of Columbus to 1700, more Africans than Europeans crossed the Atlantic to the New World, and virtually all of them were slaves. Of the total number of Africans, roughly what fraction were taken to the colonies of each nation during each of the three periods? What might explain the shifts in the destinations of enslaved Africans? Were those shifts comparable to shifts among European immigrants?

to avoid the political problems caused by the servant labor system. Slavery kept discontented laborers in permanent servitude, and their color was a badge of their bondage.

The slave labor system polarized Chesapeake society along lines of race and status: All slaves were black, and nearly all blacks were slaves; almost all free people were white, and all whites were free or only temporarily bound in indentured servi-

tude. Unlike Barbados, however, the Chesapeake retained a vast white majority. Among whites, huge differences of wealth and status still existed. By 1700, more than three-quarters of white families had neither servants nor slaves. Nonetheless, poor white farmers enjoyed the privileges of free status. They could own property, get married, have families, and bequeath their property and their freedom to their descendants; they could

Suonatori

African Musicians An Italian missionary in seventeenth-century Angola drew this portrait of three African musicians playing local wind, percussion, and stringed instruments. The textiles worn around their waists probably came from Europe and were traded for African goods that most likely included slaves. The small white cross on the chest of the man in the middle may be a symbol of conversion to Christianity, a mark of the missionary artist's efforts. Private Collection.

In contrast to slaves in Barbados, most slaves in the seventeenth-century Chesapeake colonies had frequent and close contact with white people. Slaves and white servants performed the same tasks on tobacco plantations, often working side by side in the fields. Slaves took advantage of every opportunity to slip away from white supervision and seek out the company of other slaves. Planters often feared that slaves would turn such seemingly innocent social pleasures to political ends, either to run away or to conspire to strike against their masters. Slaves often did run away, but they were usually captured or returned after a brief absence. Despite planters' nightmares, slave insurrections did not occur.

Although slavery resolved the political unrest caused by the servant labor system, it created new political problems. By 1700, the bedrock political issue in the southern colonies was keeping slaves in their place, at the end of a hoe. The slave labor system in the southern colonies stood roughly midway between the sugar plantations and black majority of Barbados to the south and the small farms and homogeneous villages that developed in seventeenth-century New England to the north (see chapter 4).

Q: Why had slave labor largely displaced indentured servant labor by 1700 in Chesapeake tobacco production?

move when and where they wanted; they could associate freely with other people; they could serve on juries, vote, and hold political office; and they could work, loaf, and sleep as they chose. These privileges of freedom—none of them possessed by slaves—made lesser white folk feel they had a genuine stake in the existence of slavery, even if they did not own a single slave. By emphasizing the privileges of freedom shared by all white people, the slave labor system reduced the tensions between poor folk and grandees that had plagued the Chesapeake region in the 1670s.

Conclusion: The Growth of English Colonies Based on Export Crops and Slave Labor

By 1700, the colonies of Virginia, Maryland, and Carolina were firmly established. The staple crops they grew for export provided a livelihood for many, a fortune for a few, and valuable revenues for shippers, merchants, and the English monarchy. Their societies differed markedly from English society in most respects, yet the colonists considered themselves English people who happened to live in North America. They claimed the same rights and privileges as English men and women, while they denied those rights and privileges to Native Americans and African slaves.

The English colonies also differed from the example of New Spain. Settlers and servants flocked to English colonies, in contrast to Spaniards who trickled into New Spain. Few English missionaries sought to convert Indians to Protestant Christianity, unlike the numerous Catholic missionaries in the Spanish settlements in New Mexico and Florida. Large quantities of gold and silver never materialized in English North America. English colonists never adopted the system of encomienda (see chapter 2) because the Indians in these areas were too few and too hostile and their communities too small and decentralized compared with those of the Mexica. Yet some forms of coerced labor and racial distinction that developed in New Spain had North American counterparts,

as English colonists employed servants and slaves and defined themselves as superior to Indians and Africans.

By 1700, the remnants of Powhatan's people still survived. As English settlement pushed north, west, and south of the Chesapeake Bay, the Indians faced the new colonial world that Powhatan and Pocahontas had encountered when John Smith and the first colonists had arrived at Jamestown. By 1700, the many descendants of Pocahontas's son, Thomas, as well as other colonists and Native Americans, understood that the English had come to stay.

Reviewing the Chapter

★ KEY TERMS

Explain each term's significance

WHO
Captain John Smith (p. 49)
Powhatan (p. 49)
Algonquian Indians (p. 49)
Pocahontas (p. 49)
John Rolfe (p. 50)
Opechancanough (p. 54)
Lord Baltimore (p. 62)
Governor William Berkeley (p. 63)
Nathaniel Bacon (p. 64)
Pueblo Indians (p. 66)
Popé (p. 66)

WHAT
Virginia Company (p. 51)
Jamestown (p. 52)
royal colony (p. 54)
House of Burgesses (p. 54)
tobacco (p. 55)
headright (p. 57)
indentured servants (p. 57)
yeoman (p. 62)
Navigation Acts (p. 63)
mercantilism (p. 64)
Bacon's Rebellion (p. 64)
grandees (p. 64)
slavery (p. 66)
Barbados (p. 66)

FOR PRACTICE QUIZZES AND OTHER STUDY TOOLS, see the Online Study Guide at **bedfordstmartins.com/roarkcompact**.

★ REVIEW QUESTIONS Q:

Use key terms and dates to support your answers

1. Why did Powhatan pursue largely peaceful relations with the Jamestown settlement? (pp. 51–55)

2. Why did the vast majority of European immigrants to the Chesapeake come as indentured servants? (pp. 55–62)

3. Why did Chesapeake colonial society become increasingly polarized between 1650 and 1670? (pp. 62–65)

4. Why did the Pueblo Indians revolt against Spanish missionaries in 1680? (pp. 65–66)

5. Why had slave labor largely displaced indentured servant labor by 1700 in Chesapeake tobacco production? (pp. 66–70)

★ MAKING CONNECTIONS

Draw on key terms, timeline, and review questions

1. Given the extraordinary vulnerability of the Jamestown settlement in its first two decades, why did its sponsors and settlers not abandon it? In your answer, discuss the challenges the settlement faced and the benefits different participants in England and the New World hoped to derive from their efforts.

2. Tobacco dominated European settlement in the seventeenth-century Chesapeake. How did tobacco agriculture shape the region's development? In your answer, be sure to address the demographic and geographic features of the colony.

3. Bacon's Rebellion highlighted significant tensions within Chesapeake society. What provoked the rebellion, and what did it accomplish? In your answer, be sure to consider causes and results in the colonies and in England.

4. In addition to making crucial contributions to the economic success of seventeenth-century English colonies, Native Americans and enslaved Africans influenced colonial politics. Describe how European colonists' relations with these populations contributed to political friction and harmony within the colony.

★ SUGGESTED READINGS

S. Max Edelson, *Plantation Enterprise in Colonial South Carolina* (2006). A compelling environmental and economic history of the creation of South Carolina plantations.

April Hatfield, *Atlantic Virginia: Intercolonial Relations in the Seventeenth Century* (2003). A fascinating analysis of relations among colonies in the Atlantic world.

Edmund S. Morgan, *American Slavery, American Freedom: The Ordeal of Colonial Virginia* (1975). A classic account of seventeenth-century Virginia by an eminent historian.

John Ruston Pagan, *Anne Orthwood's Bastard: Sex and Law in Early Virginia* (2003). A revealing case study of sex and the law in the early Chesapeake.

Helen C. Rountree, *Pocahontas, Powhatan, Opechancanough: Three Indian Lives Changed by Jamestown* (2005). The story of how English settlement changed the lives of three notable Native Americans.

FOR MORE BOOKS ABOUT TOPICS IN THIS CHAPTER, see the Online Bibliography at **bedfordstmartins.com/roarkcompact**.

FOR ADDITIONAL FIRSTHAND ACCOUNTS OF THIS PERIOD, see Chapter 3 in Michael Johnson, ed., *Reading the American Past*, Fourth Edition.

FOR WEB SITES, IMAGES, AND DOCUMENTS RELATED TO TOPICS AND PLACES IN THIS CHAPTER, visit Make History at **bedfordstmartins.com/roarkcompact**.

★ TIMELINE

1606	• Virginia Company receives royal charter.
1607	• English colonists found Jamestown settlement; Pocahontas "rescues" John Smith.
1607–10	• Starvation plagues Jamestown.
1612	• John Rolfe begins to plant tobacco in Virginia.
1617	• First commercial tobacco shipment leaves Virginia for England. • Pocahontas dies in England.
1618	• Powhatan dies; Opechancanough becomes chief of the Algonquians.
1619	• First Africans arrive in Virginia. • House of Burgesses begins to meet in Virginia.
1622	• Opechancanough leads first Indian uprising against Virginia colonists.
1624	• Virginia becomes royal colony.
1632	• King Charles I grants Lord Baltimore land for colony of Maryland.
1634	• Colonists begin to arrive in Maryland.
1640s	• Barbados colonists begin to grow sugarcane with labor of African slaves.
1644	• Opechancanough leads second Indian uprising against Virginia colonists.
1660	• Navigation Act requires colonial tobacco to be shipped to English ports.
1663	• Royal charter is granted for Carolina colony.
1670	• Charles Towne, South Carolina, founded.
1670–1700	• Slave labor system emerges in Carolina and Chesapeake colonies.
1676	• Bacon's Rebellion.
1680	• Pueblo Revolt.

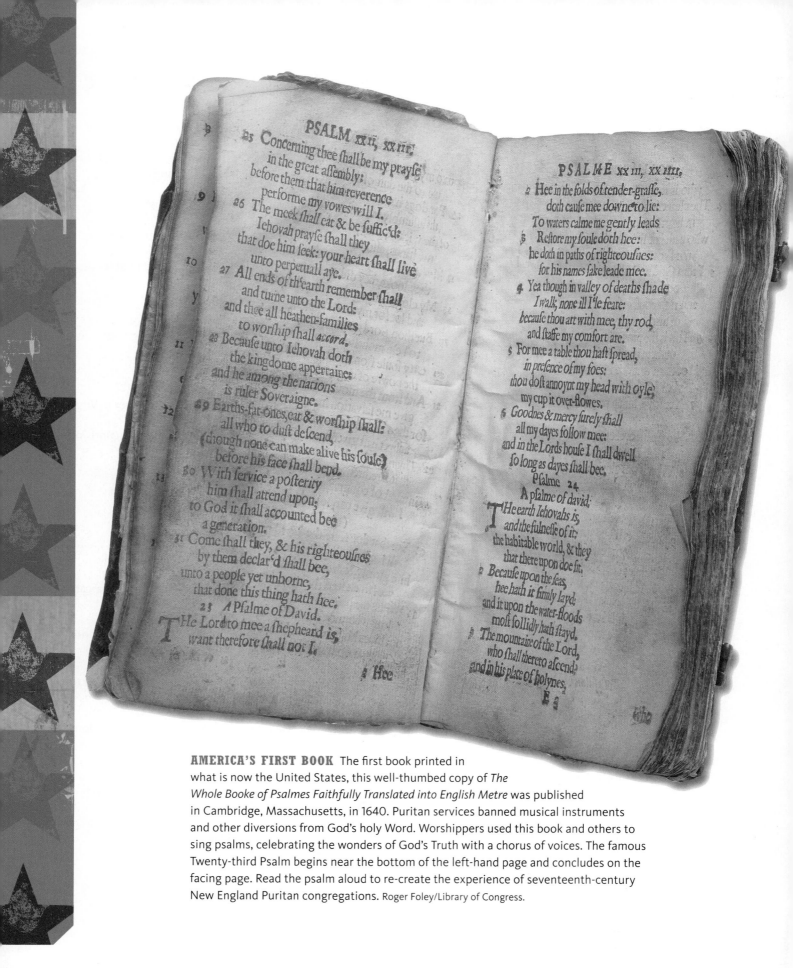

AMERICA'S FIRST BOOK The first book printed in what is now the United States, this well-thumbed copy of *The Whole Booke of Psalmes Faithfully Translated into English Metre* was published in Cambridge, Massachusetts, in 1640. Puritan services banned musical instruments and other diversions from God's holy Word. Worshippers used this book and others to sing psalms, celebrating the wonders of God's Truth with a chorus of voices. The famous Twenty-third Psalm begins near the bottom of the left-hand page and concludes on the facing page. Read the psalm aloud to re-create the experience of seventeenth-century New England Puritan congregations. Roger Foley/Library of Congress.

The Northern Colonies in the Seventeenth Century

1601–1700

ROGER WILLIAMS AND HIS WIFE, MARY, arrived in Massachusetts in February 1631. Fresh from a superb education at Cambridge University, the twenty-eight-year-old Williams was "a godly [Puritan] minister," noted Governor John Winthrop. Winthrop's Boston church asked Williams to become its minister, but he refused because the church had not openly rejected the corrupt Church of England. New England's premier Puritan church was not pure enough for **Roger Williams**.

Williams and his wife moved to Plymouth colony for two years. While there, he spent a great deal of time among the Narragansett Indians. "My soul's desire was to do the natives good," he said. Williams believed that "Nature knows no difference between Europeans and [Native] Americans in blood, birth, [or] bodies . . . God having made of one blood all mankind." He sought to learn about the Indians' language, religion, and culture, without trying to convert them to Christianity. Williams insisted that the colonists respect the Indians' religion and culture since all human beings — Christians and non-Christians alike — should live according to their consciences as revealed to them by God.

Williams condemned English colonists for their "sin of unjust usurpation" of Indian land. He believed that English claims were legally, morally, and spiritually invalid. In contrast, Massachusetts officials defended colonists' settlement on Indian land. If land "lies common, and hath never been replenished or subdued, [it] is free to any that possess or improve it," Governor Winthrop explained. Besides, he said, "if we leave [the Indians] sufficient [land] for their use, we may lawfully take the rest, there being more than enough for them and us." Winthrop's arguments prevailed, but Williams refused to knuckle under. "God Land," he said, "[is] as great a God with us English as God Gold was with the Spaniards."

In 1633, Williams became the minister of the church in Salem, Massachusetts. Like other New England Puritans, the members of the Salem church had solemnly agreed to "Covenant with the Lord and one with another; and doe bynd our selves in the presence of God, to walke together in all his waies, according as he is pleased to reveale himself unto us in his Blessed word of truth [the Bible]." Most New England Puritans believed that churches and

Previewing the Chapter

**Puritan Origins:
The English Reformation 76**

Q: *Why did Henry VIII initiate the English Reformation?*

Puritans and the Settlement of New England 78

Q: *Why did the Puritans immigrate to North America?*

The Evolution of New England Society 81

Q: *Why did Massachusetts Puritans adopt the Halfway Covenant?*

The Founding of the Middle Colonies 88

Q: *How did Quaker ideals shape the colony of Pennsylvania?*

The Colonies and the English Empire 91

Q: *Why did the Glorious Revolution in England lead to uprisings in the American colonies?*

Conclusion: An English Model of Colonization in North America 97

governments should enforce both godly belief and behavior according to biblical rules. They claimed that "the Word of God is . . . clear." In contrast, Williams believed that the Bible shrouded the Word of God in "mist and fog." Williams pointed out that devout and pious Christians could and did differ about what the Bible said and what God expected. That observation led him to denounce the emerging New England order as impure, ungodly, and tyrannical.

Williams also disagreed with the New England government's requirement that everyone attend church services. He argued that forcing people who were not Christians to attend church was wrong in four major ways. First, Williams preached, it was akin to requiring "a dead child to suck the breast, or a dead man [to] feast." The only way for any person to become a true Christian was by God's gift of faith revealed to the person's conscience. Second, churches should be reserved exclusively for those already converted, separating "holy from unholy . . . [and] godly from ungodly." He said requiring everybody to attend church was "False Worshipping" that promoted "spiritual drunkenness and whoredom, a soul sleep and a soul sickness." Third, the government had no business ruling on spiritual matters. Williams termed New England's regulation of religious behavior "spiritual rape" that inevitably would lead governments to use coercion and violence to enforce their misguided ways. Finally, Williams believed that governments should tolerate all religious beliefs because only God knows the Truth; no person and no religion can understand God with absolute certainty. "I commend that man," Williams wrote, "whether Jew, or Turk, or Papist, or whoever, that steers no otherwise than his conscience dares." In Williams's view, toleration of religious belief and liberty of conscience were the only paths to religious purity and political harmony.

New England's leaders denounced Williams's arguments. One minister wrote that Williams sought "liberty to enfranchise all false Religions," which was "the greatest impiety in the World." Genuine liberty, he said, was "to contend earnestly for the Truth; to preserve unity of Spirit, Faith, ordinances, to be all like minded, of one accord." Like-minded New Englanders banished Williams for his "extreme and dangerous" opinions. He escaped from an attempt to ship him back to England and in the winter of 1636 spent fourteen weeks walking south to Narragansett Bay, "exposed to the mercy of an howling Wilderness in Frost and Snow." There he founded the colony of Rhode Island, which enshrined "Liberty of Conscience" as a fundamental ideal and became a refuge for other dissenters.

Although New England's leaders expelled Williams from their holy commonwealth, his dissenting ideas arose from orthodox Puritan doctrines. By urging believers to search for evidence of God's grace, Puritanism encouraged the faithful to listen for God's whisper of Truth and faith. Puritanism combined rigid insistence on conformity to God's law and aching uncertainty about how to identify and act upon it. Despite the best efforts of New England's leaders to define their way as God's Way, Puritanism inspired believers such as Roger Williams to draw their own conclusions and stick to them.

During the seventeenth century, New England's Puritan zeal — exemplified by Roger Williams and his persecutors — cooled. The goal of founding a holy New England faded. Late in the century, the new "middle" colonies of New York, New Jersey, and Pennsylvania, featuring greater religious and ethnic diversity than New England, were founded. Religion remained important throughout all the colonies, but it competed with the growing faith that the promise of a better life required less focus on salvation and more attention to worldly concerns of family, work, and trade.

As settler populations increased throughout the English mainland colonies, settlements encroached on Indian land, causing violent conflict to flare up repeatedly. Political conflict also arose among colonists, particularly in response to major political upheavals in England. By the end of the seventeenth century, the English monarchy exerted greater control over North America and the rest of its Atlantic empire. The lifeblood of the empire, however, remained the continual flow of products, people, and ideas that pulsed between England and the colonies, energizing both.   ★

Puritan Origins: The English Reformation

The religious roots of the **Puritans** who founded New England reached back to the Protestant Reformation, which arose in Germany in 1517 (see chapter 2). The Reformation spread quickly to other countries, but the English church initially remained within the Catholic fold and continued its allegiance to the pope in Rome. King Henry VIII, who reigned from 1509 to 1547, understood that the Reformation offered him an opportunity to break with Rome and take control of the church in England. In 1534, Henry formally initiated the **English Reformation**. At his insistence, Parliament passed the Act of Supremacy, which outlawed the Catholic Church and proclaimed the king "the only supreme head on earth of the Church of England." Henry seized the vast properties of the Catholic Church in England as well as the privilege of appointing bishops and others in the church hierarchy.

In the short run, the English Reformation allowed Henry VIII to achieve his political goal of controlling the church. In the long run, however, the Reformation brought to England the political and religious turmoil that Henry had hoped to avoid. Henry himself sought no more than a halfway Reformation. Protestant doctrines held no attraction for Henry; in almost all matters of religious belief and practice, he remained an orthodox Catholic. Many English Catholics wanted to revoke the English Reformation; they hoped to return the Church of England to the pope and to restore Catholic doctrines and ceremonies. But many other English people insisted on a genuine, thoroughgoing Reformation; these people came to be called Puritans.

During the sixteenth century, Puritanism was less an organized movement than a set of ideas and religious principles that appealed strongly to many dissenting members of the Church of England. They sought to purify the Church of England by eliminating what they considered the offensive features of Catholicism. For example, they demanded that the church hierarchy be abolished and that ordinary Christians be given greater control over religious life. They wanted to do away with the rituals of Catholic worship and instead emphasize an individual's relationship with God developed through Bible study, prayer, and introspection.

Although there were many varieties and degrees of Puritanism, all Puritans shared a desire to make the English church thoroughly Protestant.

The fate of Protestantism waxed and waned under the monarchs who succeeded Henry VIII. When he died in 1547, the advisers of the new king, Edward VI — the nine-year-old son of Henry and his third wife, Jane Seymour — initiated religious reforms that moved in a Protestant direction. The tide of reform reversed in 1553 when Edward died and was succeeded by Mary I, the daughter of Henry and Catherine of Aragon, his first wife. Mary was a steadfast Catholic, and shortly after becoming queen, she married Philip II of Spain, Europe's most powerful guardian of Catholicism. Mary attempted to restore the pre-Reformation Catholic Church. She outlawed Protestantism in England and persecuted those who refused to conform, sentencing almost three hundred to burn at the stake.

The tide turned again in 1558 when Mary died and was succeeded by Elizabeth I, the daughter of Henry and his second wife, Anne Boleyn. During her long reign, Elizabeth reaffirmed the English Reformation and tried to position the English church between the extremes of Catholicism and Puritanism. Like her father, she was less concerned with theology than with politics. Above all, she desired a church that would strengthen the monarchy and the nation. By the time Elizabeth died in 1603, many people in England looked on Protestantism as a defining feature of national identity.

Queen Elizabeth's Funeral Procession The death of Elizabeth I in 1603 created uncertainty about the balance of Protestantism and Catholicism in England. Since Elizabeth had no children, James, the son of the staunch Catholic queen Mary II, assumed the throne and soon cracked down on Protestants, especially Puritans. This contemporary painting shows Elizabeth's casket, with a gilded effigy of her on the lid, pulled by four steeds and shaded by a black canopy held aloft by knights. The knights are surrounded by courtiers carrying flags emblazoned with royal insignia. The funeral procession combined mourning with an opulent display of royal magnificence, reminding viewers that the splendor of the monarchy would survive the death of the queen. Courtesy of the Trustees of the British Library.

When Elizabeth's successor, James I, became king, English Puritans petitioned for further reform of the Church of England. James authorized a new translation of the Bible, known ever since as the King James version. However, neither James I nor his son Charles I, who became king in 1625, was receptive to the ideas of Puritan reformers. James and Charles moved the Church of England away from Puritanism. They enforced conformity to the Church of England and punished dissenters, both ordinary Christians and ministers. In 1629, Charles I dissolved Parliament—where Puritans were well represented—and initiated aggressive anti-Puritan policies. Many Puritans despaired about continuing to defend their faith in England and began to make plans to emigrate. Some left for Europe, others for the West Indies. The largest number set out for America.

Q: Why did Henry VIII initiate the English Reformation?

Puritans and the Settlement of New England

Puritans who emigrated aspired to escape the turmoil and persecution of England and to build a new, orderly, Puritan version of England. Puritans established the first small settlement in New England in 1620, followed a few years later by additional settlements by the Massachusetts Bay Company. Allowed self-government through royal charter, these Puritans were in a unique position to direct the new colonies according to their faith. Their faith shaped the colonies they established in almost every way. Although many New England colonists were not Puritans, Puritanism remained a paramount influence in New England's religion, politics, and community life during the seventeenth century.

The Pilgrims and Plymouth Colony One of the first Protestant groups to emigrate, later known as **Pilgrims**, espoused an unorthodox view known as separatism. These **Separatists** sought to withdraw—or separate—from the Church of England, which they considered hopelessly corrupt. In 1608, they moved to Holland; by 1620, they realized that they could not live and worship there as they had hoped. **William Bradford**, a leader of the Separatists, believed that

> That first winter "was most sad and lamentable," Bradford wrote later. "In two or three months' time half of [our] company died . . . being the depth of winter, and wanting houses and other comforts [and] being infected with scurvy and other diseases."

America promised to better protect their children's piety and preserve their community. Separatists obtained permission to settle in the extensive territory granted to the Virginia Company (see chapter 3). To finance their journey, they formed a joint-stock company with English investors. The investors provided the capital; the Separatists provided their labor and lives and received a share of the profits for seven years. In August 1620, the Pilgrim families boarded the *Mayflower*, and after eleven weeks at sea, all but one of the 102 immigrants arrived at the outermost tip of Cape Cod, in present-day Massachusetts.

The Pilgrims realized immediately that they had landed far north of the Virginia grants and had no legal authority to settle in the area. To provide order and security as well as a claim to legitimacy, they drew up the **Mayflower Compact** on the day they arrived. They pledged to "covenant and combine ourselves together into a civil Body Politick, for our better Ordering and Preservation." The signers (all men) agreed to enact and obey necessary and just laws.

The Pilgrims settled at Plymouth in 1620 and elected William Bradford their governor. That first winter "was most sad and lamentable," Bradford wrote later. "In two or three months' time half of [our] company died . . . being the depth of winter, and wanting houses and other comforts [and] being infected with scurvy and other diseases." In the spring, **Wampanoag Indians** rescued the floundering Plymouth settlement. First Samoset, then Squanto befriended the settlers. Both had learned English from previous contacts with sailors and fishermen who had visited the coast to dry fish and make repairs years before the Plymouth settlers arrived. Samoset arranged for the Pilgrims to meet and establish good relations with Massasoit, the Wampanoag chief whose territory included Plymouth. Squanto, Bradford recalled, "was a special instrument sent of God for their [the Pilgrims'] good. . . . He directed them how to set their corn, where to take fish, and to procure other commodities, and was also their pilot to bring them to unknown places." With the Indians' guidance, the Pilgrims managed to harvest enough food to guarantee their survival through the coming winter, an occasion they celebrated in the fall of 1621 with a feast of thanksgiving attended by Massasoit and other Wampanoags.

Still, the Plymouth colony remained precarious. Only seven dwellings were erected that first year; half the original colonists died; and a new group of threadbare, sickly settlers arrived in November 1621, requiring the colony to adopt stringent food rationing. The colonists quarreled with their London investors, who became frustrated when

Plymouth failed to produce the expected profits. These struggles to survive constantly frustrated the London investors, but the Pilgrims persisted, living simply and coexisting in relative peace with the Indians. They paid the Wampanoags when settlers gradually encroached on Indian land. By 1630, Plymouth had become a small permanent settlement, but it failed to attract many other English Puritans.

The Founding of Massachusetts Bay Colony

In 1629, shortly before Charles I dissolved Parliament, a group of Puritan merchants and country gentlemen obtained a royal charter for the **Massachusetts Bay Company**. The charter provided the usual privileges granted to joint-stock companies, including land for colonization that spanned present-day Massachusetts, New Hampshire, Vermont, Maine, and upstate New York. In addition, a unique provision of the charter permitted the government of the Massachusetts Bay Company to be located in the colony rather than in England. This provision allowed Puritans to exchange their status as a harassed minority in England for self-government in Massachusetts.

To lead the emigrants, the stockholders of the Massachusetts Bay Company elected **John Winthrop**, a prosperous lawyer and landowner, to serve as governor. In March 1630, eleven ships crammed with seven hundred passengers sailed for Massachusetts; six more ships and another five hundred emigrants followed a few months later. Winthrop's fleet arrived in Massachusetts Bay in

early June. Unlike the Separatists, Winthrop's Puritans aspired to reform the corrupt Church of England (rather than separate from it) by setting an example of godliness in the New World. Winthrop and a small group chose to settle on the peninsula that became Boston, and other settlers clustered at promising locations nearby (Map 4.1).

In a sermon to his companions aboard the *Arbella* while they were still at sea—probably the most famous sermon in American history—Winthrop proclaimed the cosmic significance of their journey. The Puritans had "entered into a covenant" with God to "work out our salvation under the power and purity of his holy ordinances," Winthrop declared. This sanctified agreement with God meant that the Puritans had to make "extraordinary" efforts to "bring into familiar and constant practice" religious principles that most people in England merely preached. To achieve their pious goals, the Puritans had to subordinate their individual interests to the common good. "We must be knit together in this work as one man," Winthrop preached. "We must delight in each other, make others' conditions our own, rejoice together, mourn together, labor and suffer together." The stakes could not be higher, Winthrop told his listeners: "We must consider that we shall be as a city upon a hill. The eyes of all people are upon us."

That belief shaped seventeenth-century New England as profoundly as tobacco shaped the Chesapeake.

Seal of Massachusetts Bay Colony In 1629, the Massachusetts Bay Company designed this seal depicting an Indian man inviting English settlers to "come over and help us." Of course, such an invitation was never issued. The seal was an attempt to lend an aura of altruism to the Massachusetts Bay Company's colonization efforts. In English eyes, the Indian man obviously needed help. The only signs that he was more civilized than the pine trees flanking him are his girdle of leaves, his bow and arrow, and his miraculous use of English. In reality, colonists in Massachusetts and elsewhere were far less interested in helping Indians than in helping themselves. For the most part, that suited the Indians, who wanted no "help" from the colonists. Courtesy of Massachusetts Archives.

FOR MORE HELP ANALYZING THIS IMAGE, see the visual activity for this chapter in the Online Study Guide at bedfordstmartins.com/roarkcompact.

MAP 4.1 New England Colonies in the Seventeenth Century

New Englanders spread across the landscape town by town during the seventeenth century. (For the sake of legibility, only a few of the more important towns are shown on the map.)

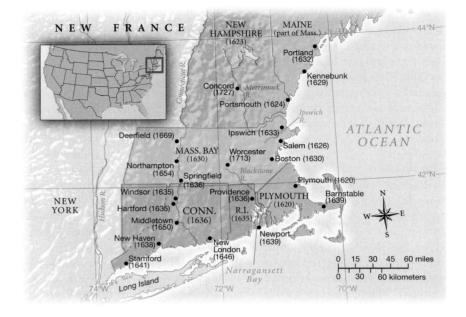

Winthrop's vision of a city on a hill fired the Puritans' fierce determination to keep their covenant and live according to God's laws, unlike the backsliders and compromisers who accommodated to the Church of England. Their determination to adhere strictly to God's plan charged nearly every feature of life in seventeenth-century New England with a distinctive, high-voltage piety.

The new colonists, as Winthrop's son John wrote later, had "all things to do, as in the beginning of the world." Unlike the early Chesapeake settlers, the first Massachusetts Bay colonists encountered few Indians because the local population had been almost entirely exterminated by an epidemic probably caused by contact with Europeans more than a decade earlier. Still, as in the Chesapeake, the colonists fell victim to deadly ailments. But Winthrop maintained a confidence that proved infectious. He wrote to his wife, "I like so well to be heer as I do not repent my comminge. . . . I would not have altered my course, though I had forseene all these Afflictions." And each year from 1630 to 1640, ship after ship followed in the wake of Winthrop's fleet. In all, more than twenty thousand new settlers came, their eyes focused on the Puritans' city on a hill.

Often, when the Church of England cracked down on a Puritan minister in England, he and many of his followers moved together to New England. Smaller groups of English Puritans moved to the Chesapeake, Barbados, and elsewhere in the New World, including New Amsterdam (present-day New York). By 1640, New England had one of the highest ratios of preachers to population in all of Christendom. A few ministers sought to carry the message of Christianity to the Indians, accompanied by instructions replacing what missionary John Eliot termed the Indians' "unfixed, confused, and ungoverned . . . life, uncivilized and unsubdued to labor and order." For the most part, however, the colonists focused less on saving Indians' souls than on saving their own.

The occupations of New England immigrants reflected the social origins of English Puritans. On the whole, the immigrants came from the middle ranks of English society. The vast majority were either farmers or tradesmen, including carpenters, tailors, and textile workers. Indentured servants, whose numbers dominated the Chesapeake settlers, accounted for only about a fifth of those headed for New England. Most New England immigrants paid their way to Massachusetts, even though the journey often took their life savings. They were encouraged by the promise of bounty in New England reported in Winthrop's letter to his son: "Here is as good land as I have seen there [in England]. . . . Here can be no want of anything to those who bring means to raise [it] out of the earth and sea."

In contrast to Chesapeake newcomers, New England immigrants usually arrived as families. In fact, more Puritans came with family members than did any other group of immigrants in all of American history. Unlike immigrants to the Chesapeake, women and children made up a solid majority in New England.

As Winthrop reminded the first settlers in his *Arbella* sermon, each family was a "little commonwealth" that mirrored the hierarchy among all God's creatures. Just as humankind was subordinate to God, so young people were subordinate to their elders, children to their parents, and wives to their husbands. The immigrants' family ties reinforced their religious beliefs with universally understood notions of hierarchy and mutual dependence. Whereas immigrants to the Chesapeake were disciplined mostly by the coercions of servitude and the caprices of the tobacco market, immigrants to New England entered a social order defined by the interlocking institutions of family, church, and community.

Q: Why did the Puritans immigrate to North America?

The Evolution of New England Society

The New England colonists, unlike their counterparts in the Chesapeake, settled in small towns, usually located on the coast or by a river (see Map 4.1). Massachusetts Bay colonists founded 133 towns during the seventeenth century, each with one or more churches. Church members' fervent piety, buttressed by the institutions of local government, enforced remarkable religious and social conformity in the small New England settlements. During the century, tensions within the Puritan faith and changes in New England communities splintered religious orthodoxy and weakened Puritan zeal. By 1700, however, Puritanism still maintained a distinctive influence in New England.

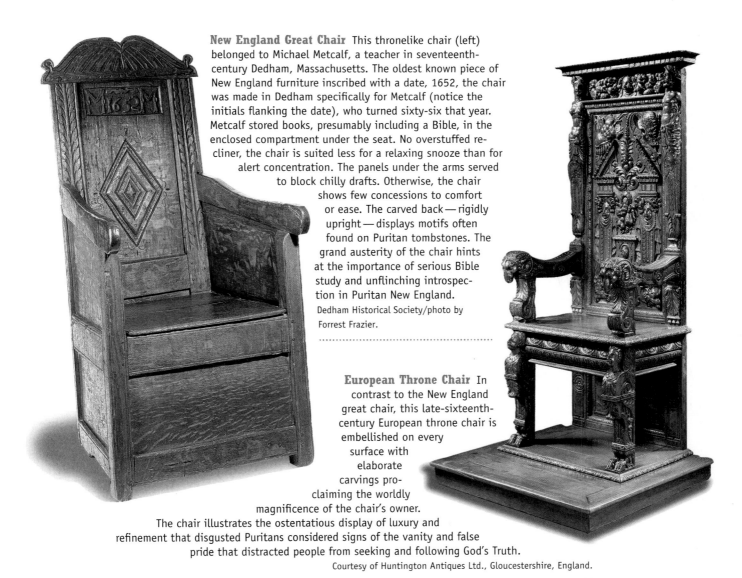

New England Great Chair This thronelike chair (left) belonged to Michael Metcalf, a teacher in seventeenth-century Dedham, Massachusetts. The oldest known piece of New England furniture inscribed with a date, 1652, the chair was made in Dedham specifically for Metcalf (notice the initials flanking the date), who turned sixty-six that year. Metcalf stored books, presumably including a Bible, in the enclosed compartment under the seat. No overstuffed recliner, the chair is suited less for a relaxing snooze than for alert concentration. The panels under the arms served to block chilly drafts. Otherwise, the chair shows few concessions to comfort or ease. The carved back — rigidly upright — displays motifs often found on Puritan tombstones. The grand austerity of the chair hints at the importance of serious Bible study and unflinching introspection in Puritan New England. Dedham Historical Society/photo by Forrest Frazier.

European Throne Chair In contrast to the New England great chair, this late-sixteenth-century European throne chair is embellished on every surface with elaborate carvings proclaiming the worldly magnificence of the chair's owner. The chair illustrates the ostentatious display of luxury and refinement that disgusted Puritans considered signs of the vanity and false pride that distracted people from seeking and following God's Truth. Courtesy of Huntington Antiques Ltd., Gloucestershire, England.

Church, Covenant, and Conformity Puritans believed that the church consisted of men and women who had entered a solemn covenant with one another and with God. Each new member of the covenant had to persuade existing members that she or he had fully experienced conversion. By 1635, the Boston church had added more than 250 names to the four original subscribers to the covenant.

Puritans embraced a distinctive version of Protestantism derived from **Calvinism**, the doctrines of John Calvin, a sixteenth-century Swiss Protestant theologian. Calvin insisted that Christians strictly discipline their behavior to conform to God's commandments announced in the Bible. Like Calvin, Puritans believed in **predestination**—the idea that the all-powerful God, before the creation of the world, decided which few human souls would receive eternal life. Only God knows the identity of these fortunate predestined individuals—the "elect" or "saints."

THE

VVorld turn'd upfide down:

OR,

A briefe defcription of the ridiculous Fafhions of thefe diftracted Times.

By T. J. a well-willer to King, Parliament and Kingdom.

London : Printed for John Smith. 1647.

The Puritan Challenge to the Status Quo *The World Turn'd Upside Down*, a pamphlet printed in London in 1647, satirizes the Puritan notion that the contemporary world was deeply flawed. The pamphlet refers to the "distracted Times" of the Puritan Revolution in England. The drawing on the title page ridicules criticisms of English society that also were common among New England Puritans. Courtesy of the Trustees of The British Library.

FOR MORE HELP ANALYZING THIS IMAGE, see the visual activity for this chapter in the Online Study Guide at bedfordstmartins.com/roarkcompact.

Nothing a person did in his or her lifetime could alter God's inscrutable choice or provide assurance that the person was predestined for salvation with the elect or damned to hell with the doomed multitude. The gloomy inevitability and exclusivity of predestination contrasted sharply with Catholic doctrines that all human beings could potentially be granted eternal life by God, acting through the Catholic Church.

Despite the looming uncertainty about God's choice of the elect, Puritans believed that if a person lived a rigorously godly life—constantly winning the daily battle against sinful temptations—his or her behavior was likely to be a hint, a visible sign, that he or she was one of God's chosen few. Puritans thought that "sainthood" would become visible in individuals' behavior, especially if they were privileged to know God's Word as revealed in the Bible.

The connection between sainthood and saintly behavior, however, was far from certain. Some members of the elect, Puritans believed, had not heard God's Word as revealed in the Bible, and therefore their behavior did not necessarily signal their sainthood. One reason Puritans required all town residents to attend church services was to enlighten anyone who was ignorant of God's Truth. The slippery relationship between saintly behavior—observable by anybody—and God's predestined election—invisible and unknowable to anyone—caused Puritans to worry constantly that individuals who acted like saints were fooling themselves and others. Nevertheless, Puritans thought that **visible saints**—persons who passed their demanding tests of conversion and church membership—probably, though not certainly, were among God's elect.

Members of Puritan churches ardently hoped that God had chosen them to receive eternal life and tried to demonstrate saintly behavior. Their covenant bound them to help each other attain salvation and to discipline the entire community by saintly standards. Church members kept an eye on the behavior of everybody in town. Infractions of morality, order, or propriety were reported to Puritan elders, who summoned the wayward to a church inquiry. By overseeing every aspect of life, the visible saints enforced a remarkable degree of righteous conformity in Puritan communities. Total conformity, however, was never achieved. Ardent Puritans differed among themselves; non-Puritans shirked orthodox rules.

Despite the central importance of religion, churches played no direct role in the civil government of New England communities. Puritans did not want to mimic the Church of England, which they considered a puppet of the king rather than an independent body that served the Lord. They were determined to insulate New England churches from the contaminating influence of the civil state and its merely human laws. Although ministers were the most highly respected figures in New England towns, they were prohibited from holding government office.

Puritans had no qualms, however, about their religious beliefs influencing New England governments. As much as possible, the Puritans tried to bring public life into conformity with their view of God's law. For example, fines were issued for Sabbath-breaking activities such as working, traveling, playing a flute, smoking a pipe, and visiting neighbors. Puritans mandated other purifications of what they considered corrupt English practices. They refused to celebrate Christmas or Easter because the Bible did not mention either one. They outlawed religious wedding ceremonies; couples were married by a magistrate in a civil ceremony (the first wedding in Massachusetts performed by a minister occurred in 1686). They prohibited elaborate clothing and finery such as lace trim and short sleeves — "whereby the nakedness of the arm may be discovered." They banned cards, dice, shuffleboard, and other games of chance, as well as music and dancing. The distinguished minister Increase Mather insisted that "Mixt or Promiscuous Dancing . . . of Men and Women"

could not be tolerated since "the unchaste Touches and Gesticulations used by Dancers have a palpable tendency to that which is evil." On special occasions, Puritans proclaimed days of fasting and humiliation, which, as one preacher boasted, amounted to "so many Sabbaths more."

Government by Puritans for Puritanism

It is only a slight exaggeration to say that seventeenth-century New England was governed by Puritans for Puritanism. The charter of the Massachusetts Bay Company empowered the company's stockholders, known as freemen, to meet as a body known as the General Court and make the laws needed to govern the company's affairs. The colonists transformed this arrangement for running a joint-stock company into a structure for governing the colony. Hoping to ensure that godly men would decide government policies, the General Court expanded the number of freemen in 1631 to include all male church members. Only freemen had the right to vote for governor, deputy governor, and other colonial officials. As new settlers were recognized as freemen, the size of the General Court grew too large to meet conveniently. So in 1634, the freemen in each town agreed to send two deputies to the General Court to act as the colony's legislative assembly. All other men were classified as "inhabitants," and they had the right to vote, hold office, and participate fully in town government. A "town meeting," composed of a town's inhabitants and freemen, chose the selectmen and

Old Ship Meeting House Built in Hingham, Massachusetts, in 1681, this meetinghouse is one of the oldest surviving buildings used for church services in English North America. The unadorned walls and windows reflect the austere religious aesthetic of New England Puritanism. The family pews mark boundaries of kinship and piety visible to all. The elevated pulpit bathed in light signals the illumination of God's Word as preached by the minister. Old Ship Church, Hingham, Mass., photo by Bruce Benedict.

other officials who administered local affairs. New England town meetings routinely practiced a level of popular participation in political life that was unprecedented elsewhere in the world during the seventeenth century. Almost every adult man could speak out in town meetings and fortify his voice with a vote. However, all women—even church members—were prohibited from voting, and towns did not permit "contrary-minded" men to become or remain inhabitants. Although town meeting participants wrangled from time to time, widespread political participation tended to reinforce conformity to Puritan ideals.

One of the most important functions of New England government was land distribution. Settlers who desired to establish a new town entered a covenant and petitioned the General Court for a grant of land. The court granted town sites to suitably pious petitioners but did not allow settlement until the Indians who inhabited a grant agreed to relinquish their claim to the land, usually in exchange for manufactured goods. For instance, William Pynchon purchased the site of Springfield, Massachusetts, from the Agawam Indians for "eighteen fathams [arm's lengths] of Wampum, eighteen coates, 18 hatchets, 18 hoes, [and] 18 knives."

Having obtained their grant, town founders apportioned land among themselves and any newcomers they permitted to join them. Normally, each family received a house lot large enough for an adjacent garden as well as one or more strips of agricultural land on the perimeter of the town. Although there was a considerable difference between the largest and smallest family plots, most clustered in the middle range—roughly fifty to one hundred acres—resulting in a more nearly equal distribution of land in New England than in the Chesapeake.

The physical layout of New England towns encouraged settlers to look inward toward their neighbors, multiplying the opportunities for godly vigilance. Most people considered the forest that lay just beyond every settler's house an alien environment that was interrupted here and there by those oases of civilization, the towns. Footpaths connecting one town to another were so rudimentary that even John Winthrop once got lost within half a mile of his house and spent a sleepless night in the forest, circling the light of his small campfire and singing psalms.

The Splintering of Puritanism Almost from the beginning, John Winthrop and other leaders had difficulty enforcing their views of Puritan orthodoxy. In England, persecution as a dissenting minority had unified Puritan voices in opposition to the Church of England. In New England, the promise of a godly society and the Puritans' emphasis on individual Bible study led New Englanders toward different visions of godliness. Puritan leaders, however, interpreted dissent as an error caused either by a misguided believer or by the malevolent power of Satan. Whatever the cause, errors could not be tolerated.

Shortly after banishing Roger Williams, Winthrop confronted another dissenter, this time a devout Puritan woman steeped in Scripture and absorbed by religious questions: **Anne Hutchinson**. The mother of fourteen children, Hutchinson settled into her new home in Boston in 1634, and women gathered there to hear her weekly lectures on recent sermons. As one listener observed, she was a "Woman that Preaches better Gospell then any of your blackcoates . . . [from] the Ninneversity."

Hutchinson expounded on the sermons of John Cotton, her favorite minister. Cotton stressed what he termed the **covenant of grace**—the idea that individuals could be saved only by God's grace in choosing them to be members of the elect. Cotton contrasted this familiar Puritan doctrine with the **covenant of works**, the erroneous belief that a person's behavior—one's works—could win God's favor and ultimately earn a person salvation. Belief in the covenant of works and in the possibility of salvation for all was known as **Arminianism**. Cotton's sermons strongly hinted that many Puritans, including ministers, embraced Arminianism, which claimed—falsely, Cotton declared—that human beings could influence God's will. Anne Hutchinson agreed with Cotton. Her lectures emphasized her opinion that many of the colony's leaders affirmed the Arminian covenant of works. Like Cotton, she preached that only God's covenant of grace led to salvation.

The meetings at Hutchinson's house alarmed her nearest neighbor, John Winthrop, who believed that she was subverting the good order of the colony. In 1637, Winthrop had formal charges brought against Hutchinson and denounced her lectures as "not tolerable nor comely in the sight of God nor fitting for your sex." He told her, "You have stept out of your place, you have rather bine a Husband than a Wife and a preacher than a Hearer; and a Magistrate than a Subject."

In court, Winthrop interrogated Hutchinson, fishing for a heresy he could pin on her. Winthrop and other Puritan elders referred to Hutchinson and her followers as **antinomians**, people who believed that Christians could be saved by faith alone and did not need to act in accordance with God's law as set forth in the Bible and as interpreted by the colony's leaders. Hutchinson nimbly defended herself against the accusation of antinomianism. Yes, she acknowledged, she believed that men and women were saved by faith alone; but no, she did not deny the need to obey God's law. "The Lord hath let me see which was the clear ministry and which the wrong," she said. Finally, Winthrop had cornered her. How could she tell which ministry was which? "By an immediate revelation," she replied, "by the voice of [God's] own spirit to my soul." Winthrop spotted in this statement the heresy of prophecy, the view that God revealed his will directly to a believer instead of exclusively through the Bible, as every right-minded Puritan knew.

In 1638, the Boston church formally excommunicated Hutchinson. The minister decreed, "I doe cast you out and . . . deliver you up to Satan that you may learne no more to blaspheme[,] to seduce and to lye. . . . I command you . . . as a Leper to withdraw your selfe out of the Congregation." Banished, Hutchinson and her family moved first to Roger Williams's Rhode Island and then to present-day New York, where she and most of her family were killed by Indians.

The strains within Puritanism exemplified by Anne Hutchinson and Roger Williams caused communities to splinter repeatedly during the seventeenth century. **Thomas Hooker**, a prominent minister, clashed with Winthrop and other leaders over the composition of the church. Hooker argued that men and women who lived godly lives should be admitted to church membership even if they had not experienced conversion. This issue, like most others in New England, had both religious and political dimensions, for only church members could vote in Massachusetts. In 1636, Hooker led an exodus of more than eight hundred colonists from Massachusetts to the Connecticut River valley, where they founded Hartford and neighboring towns. In 1639, the towns adopted the Fundamental Orders of Connecticut, a quasi-constitution that could be altered by the vote of freemen, who did not have to be church members, though nearly all of them were.

Other Puritan churches divided and subdivided throughout the seventeenth century as acrimony developed over doctrine and church government. Sometimes churches split over the appointment of a controversial minister. Sometimes families who had a long walk to the meetinghouse simply decided to form their own church nearer their houses. These schisms arose from ambiguities and tensions within Puritan belief. As the colonies matured, other tensions developed as well.

Religious Controversies and Economic Changes

A revolutionary transformation in the fortunes of Puritans in England had profound consequences in New England. Disputes between King Charles I and Parliament, dominated by Puritans, escalated in 1642 to civil war in England, a conflict known as the **Puritan Revolution**. Parliamentary forces led by the staunch Puritan Oliver Cromwell were victorious, executing Charles I in 1649 and proclaiming England a Puritan republic. From 1649 to 1660, England's rulers were not monarchs who suppressed Puritanism but believers who championed it. In a half century, English Puritans had risen from a harassed group of religious dissenters to a dominant power in English government.

When the Puritan Revolution began, the stream of immigrants to New England dwindled to a trickle, creating hard times for the colonists. They could no longer consider themselves a city on a hill setting a godly example for humankind. Puritans in England, not New England, were reforming English society. Furthermore, when immigrant ships became rare, the colonists faced sky-high prices for scarce English goods and few customers for their own colonial products. As they searched to find new products and markets, they established the enduring patterns of New England's economy.

New England's rocky soil and short growing season ruled out cultivating the southern colonies' crops of tobacco and rice that found ready markets in Atlantic ports. Exports that New Englanders could not get from the soil they took instead from the forest and the sea. During the first decade of settlement, colonists traded with the Indians for animal pelts, which were in demand in Europe. By the 1640s, furbearing animals had become scarce unless traders ventured far beyond the frontiers of English settlement. Trees from the seemingly limitless forests of New England proved a longer-lasting resource. Masts for ships and staves for barrels of Spanish wine and West Indian sugar were crafted from New England timber.

The most important New England export was fish. During the turmoil of the Puritan Revolution, English ships withdrew from the rich North Atlantic fishing grounds, and New England fishermen quickly took their place. Dried, salted codfish found markets in southern Europe and the West Indies. The fish trade also stimulated colonial shipbuilding and trained generations of fishermen, sailors, and merchants, creating a commercial network that endured for more than a century. But this export economy remained peripheral to most New England colonists. Their lives revolved around their farms, their churches, and their families.

Although immigration came to a standstill in the 1640s, the population continued to boom, doubling every twenty years. In New England, almost everyone married, and women often had eight or nine children. Long, cold winters minimized the warm-weather ailments of the southern colonies and reduced New England mortality.

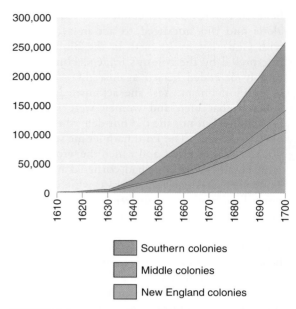

FIGURE 4.1 **Population of the English North American Colonies in the Seventeenth Century** The colonial population grew at a steadily accelerating rate during the seventeenth century. New England and the southern colonies each accounted for about half the total colonial population until after 1680, when growth in Pennsylvania and New York contributed to a surge in the population of the middle colonies.

David, Joanna, and Abigail Mason This 1670 painting depicts the children of Joanna and Anthony Mason, a wealthy Boston baker. The artist lavished attention on the children's elaborate clothing. Fashionable slashed sleeves, fancy lace, silver-studded shoes, six-year-old Joanna's and four-year-old Abigail's necklaces, and nine-year-old David's silver-headed cane suggest not only the Masons' wealth but also their desire to display and memorialize their possessions and adornments. The painting hints that the children themselves were adornments—young sprouts of the Mason lineage, which could afford such finery. The portrait is unified not by signs of warm affection, innocent smiles, or familial solidarity, but by trappings of wealth and sober self-importance. The painting expresses the growing respect for wealth and its worldly rewards in seventeenth-century New England. Fine Arts Museums of San Francisco. Gift of Mr. and Mrs. John D. Rockefeller III.

The descendants of the immigrants of the 1630s multiplied, boosting the New England population to roughly equal that of the southern colonies (Figure 4.1).

During the second half of the seventeenth century, under the pressures of steady population growth and integration into the Atlantic economy, the red-hot piety of the founders cooled. After 1640, the population grew faster than church membership. All residents attended sermons on pain of fines and punishment, but many could not find seats in the meetinghouses. Boston's churches in 1650 could house only about a third of the city's residents. By the 1680s, women were the majority of church members throughout New England. In some towns, only 15 percent of the adult men were members. A growing fraction of New Englanders, especially men, embraced what one historian has termed "horse-shed Christianity": They attended sermons but loitered outside near the horse shed, gossiping about the weather, fishing, their crops, or the scandalous behavior of neighbors. This slackening of piety led the

Puritan minister Michael Wigglesworth to ask, in verse:

> How is it that I find
>   In stead of holiness Carnality;
> In stead of heavenly frames an Earthly mind,
>   For burning zeal luke-warm Indifferency,
> For flaming love, key-cold Dead-heartedness.

Most alarming to Puritan leaders, many of the children of the visible saints of Winthrop's generation failed to experience conversion and attain full church membership. Puritans tended to assume that sainthood was inherited—that the children of visible saints were probably also among the elect. Acting on this premise, churches permitted saints to baptize their infant sons and daughters, symbolically cleansing them of their contamination with original sin. As these children grew up during the 1640s and 1650s, however, they seldom experienced the inward transformation that signaled conversion and qualification for church membership. The problem of declining church membership and the watering-down of Puritan orthodoxy became urgent during the 1650s when the children of saints, who had grown to adulthood in New England but had not experienced conversion, began to have children themselves. Their sons and daughters—the grandchildren of the founders of the colony—could not receive the protection that baptism afforded against the terrors of death because their parents had not experienced conversion.

Puritan churches debated what to do. To allow anyone, even the child of a saint, to become a church member without conversion was an unthinkable retreat from fundamental Puritan doctrine. In 1662, a synod of Massachusetts ministers reached a compromise known as the **Halfway Covenant**. Unconverted children of saints would be permitted to become "halfway" church members. Like regular church members, they could baptize their infants. But unlike full church members, they could not participate in communion or have the voting privileges of church membership. The Halfway Covenant generated a controversy that sputtered through Puritan churches for the remainder of the century. With the Halfway Covenant, Puritan churches came to terms with the lukewarm piety that had replaced the founders' burning zeal.

Nonetheless, New England communities continued to enforce piety with holy rigor. Beginning in 1656, small bands of

Quakers—members of the Society of Friends, as they called themselves—began to arrive in Massachusetts. Many of their beliefs were at odds with orthodox Puritanism. Quakers believed that God spoke directly to each individual through an "inner light," and that individuals needed neither a preacher nor the Bible to discover God's Word. Maintaining that all human beings were equal in God's eyes, Quakers refused to conform to mere temporal powers such as laws and governments unless God requested otherwise. For example, Quakers refused to observe the Sabbath because, they insisted, God had not set aside any special day for worship, expecting believers to worship faithfully every day. Women often took a leading role in Quaker meetings, in contrast to Puritan congregations, where women usually outnumbered men but remained subordinate.

New England communities treated Quakers with ruthless severity. Some Quakers were branded on the face "with a red-hot iron with [an] H. for heresie." When Quakers refused to leave Massachusetts, Boston officials hanged four of them between 1659 and 1661.

Witches Show Their Love for Satan Mocking pious Christians' humble obeisance to God, witches willingly debased themselves by standing in line to kneel and kiss Satan's buttocks—or so it was popularly believed. This seventeenth-century print portrays Satan with clawlike hands and feet, the tail of a rodent, the wings of a bat, and the head of a lustful ram attached to the torso of a man. Notice that women predominate among the witches eager to express their devotion to Satan and to do his bidding. UCSF Library/Center for Knowledge Management.

New Englanders' partial success in realizing the promise of a godly society ultimately undermined the intense appeal of Puritanism. In the pious Puritan communities of New England, leaders tried to eliminate sin. In the process, they diminished the sense of utter human depravity that was the wellspring of Puritanism. By 1700, New Englanders did not doubt that human beings sinned, but they were more concerned with the sins of others than with their own.

Witch trials held in Salem, Massachusetts, signaled the erosion of religious confidence and assurance. In 1692, the frenzied Salem proceedings accused more than one hundred people of witchcraft, a capital crime. The Salem court executed nineteen accused witches, signaling enduring belief in the supernatural origins of evil and gnawing doubt about the strength of Puritan New Englanders' faith.

Q: Why did Massachusetts Puritans adopt the Halfway Covenant?

The Founding of the Middle Colonies

South of New England and north of the Chesapeake, a group of middle colonies were founded in the last third of the seventeenth century. Before the 1670s, few Europeans settled in the region. For the first two-thirds of the seventeenth century, the most important European outpost in the area was the relatively small Dutch colony of New Netherland. By 1700, however, the English monarchy had seized New Netherland, renamed it New York, and encouraged the creation of a Quaker colony in Pennsylvania led by **William Penn**. Unlike the New England colonies, the middle colonies of New York, New Jersey, and Pennsylvania originated as land grants by the English monarch to one or more proprietors, who then possessed both the land and the extensive, almost monarchical, powers of government (Map 4.2). These middle colonies attracted settlers of more diverse European origins and religious faiths than were found in New England.

From New Netherland to New York In 1609, the Dutch East India Company dispatched Henry Hudson to search for a Northwest Passage to the Orient. Hudson sailed along the Atlantic coast and ventured up the large river that now bears his name until it dwindled to a stream that obviously did not lead to China. A decade later, the Dutch government granted the West India Company—a group

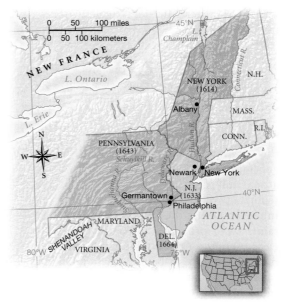

MAP 4.2 Middle Colonies in the Seventeenth Century
For the most part, the middle colonies in the seventeenth century were inhabited by settlers who clustered along the Hudson and Delaware rivers. The vast geographic extent of the colonies shown in this map reflects land grants authorized in England. Most of this area was inhabited by Native Americans rather than settled by colonists.

of Dutch merchants and shippers—exclusive rights to trade with the Western Hemisphere. In 1626, Peter Minuit, the resident director of the company, purchased Manhattan Island from the Manhate Indians for trade goods worth the equivalent of a dozen beaver pelts. New Amsterdam, the small settlement established at the southern tip of Manhattan Island, became the principal trading center in New Netherland and the colony's headquarters.

Unlike the English colonies, New Netherland did not attract many European immigrants. Like New England and the Chesapeake colonies, New Netherland never realized its sponsors' dreams of great profits. The company tried to stimulate immigration by granting patroonships—allotments of eighteen miles of land along the Hudson River—to wealthy stockholders who would bring fifty families to the colony and settle them as serflike tenants on their huge domains. Only one patroonship succeeded; the others failed to attract settlers, and the company eventually recovered much of the land.

Though few in number, New Netherlanders were remarkably diverse, especially compared

New Amsterdam The settlement on Manhattan Island — complete with a windmill — appears in the background of this 1673 Dutch portrait of New Amsterdam. Wharves connect Manhattan residents to the seaborne commerce of the Atlantic world. In the foreground, the Dutch artist placed native inhabitants of the mainland, drawing them in such a way that they resemble Africans rather than Lenni Lenape (Delaware) Indians. Dutch merchants carried tens of thousands of African slaves to New World ports, including New Amsterdam. The artist probably had never seen Indians, had never been to New Amsterdam, and depended on well-known artistic conventions about the appearance of Africans to create his Native Americans. The portrait contrasts orderly, efficient, businesslike New Amsterdam with the exotic natural environment of America, to which the native woman clings as if she is refusing to succumb to the culture represented by those neat rows of rectangular houses across the river. © Collection of the New-York Historical Society.

with the homogeneous English settlers to the north and south. Religious dissenters and immigrants from Holland, Sweden, France, Germany, and elsewhere made their way to the colony. A minister of the Dutch Reformed Church complained to his superiors in Holland that several groups of Jews had recently arrived, adding to the religious mixture of "Papists, Mennonites and Lutherans among the Dutch [and] many Puritans . . . and many other atheists . . . who conceal themselves under the name of Christians." The West India Company struggled to govern the motley colonists. Peter Stuyvesant, governor from 1647 to 1664, tried to enforce conformity to the Dutch Reformed Church, but the company declared that "the consciences of men should be free and unshackled," making a virtue of New Netherland necessity. The company never permitted the colony's settlers to form a representative government. Instead, the company appointed government officials who established policies, including taxes, that many colonists deeply resented.

In 1664, New Netherland became New York. Charles II, who became king of England in 1660 when Parliament restored the monarchy, gave his brother James, the Duke of York, an enormous grant of land that included New Netherland. Of course, the Dutch colony did not belong to the king of England, but that legal technicality did not deter the king or his brother. The duke quickly organized a small fleet of warships, which

William Penn This portrait was drawn about a decade after the founding of Pennsylvania. At a time when extravagant clothing and a fancy wig proclaimed that the wearer was an important person, Penn is portrayed informally, lacking even a coat, his natural hair neat but undressed—all a reflection of his Quaker faith. Penn's full face and double chin show that his faith did not make him a stranger to the pleasures of the table. No hollow-cheeked ascetic or wild-eyed enthusiast, Penn appears sober and observant, as if sizing up the viewer and reserving judgment. The portrait captures the calm determination—anchored in faith—that inspired Penn's hopes for his new colony. Historical Society of Pennsylvania.

appeared off Manhattan Island in late summer 1664, and demanded that Stuyvesant surrender. With little choice, he did.

As the new proprietor of the colony, the Duke of York exercised almost the same unlimited authority over the colony as had the West India Company. The duke never set foot in New York, but his governors struggled to impose order on the unruly colonists. Like the Dutch, the duke permitted "all persons of what Religion soever, quietly to inhabit . . . provided they give no disturbance to the publique peace, nor doe molest or disquiet others in the free exercise of their religion." This policy of religious toleration was less an affirmation of liberty of

> **Quakers allowed women to assume positions of religious leadership. "In souls there is no sex," they said.**

conscience than a recognition of the reality of the most heterogeneous colony in seventeenth-century North America.

New Jersey and Pennsylvania The creation of New York led indirectly to the founding of two other middle colonies, New Jersey and Pennsylvania (see Map 4.2). In 1664, the Duke of York subdivided his grant and gave the portion between the Hudson and Delaware rivers to two of his friends. The proprietors of this new colony, New Jersey, quarreled and called in a prominent English Quaker, William Penn, to arbitrate their dispute. Penn eventually worked out a settlement that continued New Jersey's proprietary government. In the process, Penn became intensely interested in what he termed a "holy experiment" of establishing a genuinely Quaker colony in America.

Unlike most Quakers, William Penn came from an eminent family. His father had served both Cromwell and Charles II and had been knighted. Born in 1644, the younger Penn trained for a military career, but the ideas of dissenters from the reestablished Church of England appealed to him, and he became a devout Quaker. By 1680, he had published fifty books and pamphlets and spoken at countless public meetings, although he had not won official toleration for Quakers in England.

The Quakers' concept of an open, generous God who made his love equally available to all people manifested itself in behavior that continually brought them into conflict with the English government. Quaker leaders were ordinary men and women, not specially trained preachers. Quakers allowed women to assume positions of religious leadership. "In souls there is no sex," they said. Since all people were equal in the spiritual realm, Quakers considered social hierarchy false and evil. They called everyone "friend" and shook hands instead of curtsying or removing their hats—even when meeting the king. These customs enraged many non-Quakers and provoked innumerable beatings and worse. Penn was jailed four times for such offenses, once for nine months.

Despite his many run-ins with the government, Penn remained on good terms with Charles II. Partly to rid England of the troublesome Quakers, in 1681 Charles made Penn the proprietor of a new colony of some 45,000 square miles called Pennsylvania.

Toleration and Diversity in Pennsylvania
Quakers flocked to Pennsylvania in numbers exceeded only by the great Puritan migration to

New England fifty years earlier. Between 1682 and 1685, nearly eight thousand immigrants arrived, most of them from England, Ireland, and Wales. They represented a cross section of the artisans, farmers, and laborers who predominated among English Quakers. Quaker missionaries also encouraged immigrants from the European continent, and many came, giving Pennsylvania greater ethnic diversity than any other English colony except New York. The Quaker colony prospered, and the capital city, Philadelphia, soon rivaled New York as a center of commerce. By 1700, the city's five thousand inhabitants participated in a thriving trade exporting flour and other food products to the West Indies and importing English textiles and manufactured goods.

Penn was determined to live in peace with the Indians who inhabited the region. His Indian policy expressed his Quaker ideals and contrasted sharply with the hostile policies of the other English colonies. As he explained to the chief of the Lenni Lenape (Delaware) Indians, "God has written his law in our hearts, by which we are taught and commanded to love and help and do good to one another . . . [and] I desire to enjoy [Pennsylvania lands] with your love and consent." Penn instructed his agents to obtain the Indians' consent by purchasing their land, respecting their claims, and dealing with them fairly.

Penn declared that the first principle of government was that every settler would "enjoy the free possession of his or her faith and exercise of worship towards God." Accordingly, Pennsylvania tolerated Protestant sects of all kinds as well as Roman Catholicism. All voters and officeholders had to be Christians, but the government did not compel settlers to attend religious services, as in Massachusetts, or to pay taxes to maintain a state-supported church, as in Virginia.

Despite its toleration and diversity, Pennsylvania was as much a Quaker colony as New England was a stronghold of Puritanism. Penn had no hesitation about using civil government to enforce religious morality. One of the colony's first laws provided severe punishment for "all such offenses against God, as swearing, cursing, lying, profane talking, drunkenness, drinking of healths, [and] obscene words . . . which excite the people to rudeness, cruelty, looseness, and irreligion."

As proprietor, Penn had extensive powers subject only to review by the king. He appointed a governor, who maintained the proprietor's power to veto any laws passed by the colonial council, which was elected by property owners

who possessed at least one hundred acres of land or who paid taxes. The council had the power to originate laws and administer all the affairs of government. A popularly elected assembly served as a check on the council; its members had the authority to reject or approve laws framed by the council.

Penn stressed that the exact form of government mattered less than the men who served in it. In Penn's eyes, "good men" staffed Pennsylvania's government because Quakers dominated elective and appointive offices. Quakers, of course, differed among themselves. Members of the assembly struggled to win the right to debate and amend laws, especially tax laws. They finally won the battle in 1701 when a new Charter of Privileges gave the proprietor the power to appoint the council and in turn stripped the council of all its former powers and gave them to the assembly, which became the only single-house legislature in all the English colonies.

Q: How did Quaker ideals shape the colony of Pennsylvania?

The Colonies and the English Empire

Proprietary grants to faraway lands were a cheap way for the king to reward friends. As the colonies grew, however, the grants became more valuable. After 1660, the king took initiatives to channel colonial trade through English hands and to consolidate royal authority over colonial governments. Occasioned by such economic and political considerations and triggered by King Philip's War between colonists and Native Americans, these initiatives defined the basic relationship between the colonies and England that endured until the American Revolution (Map 4.3).

Royal Regulation of Colonial Trade English economic policies toward the colonies were designed to yield customs revenues for the monarchy and profitable business for English merchants and shippers. Also, the policies were intended to divert the colonies' trade from England's enemies, especially the Dutch and the French.

The Navigation Acts of 1650, 1651, 1660, and 1663 (see chapter 3) set forth two fundamental rules governing colonial trade. First, goods shipped to and from the colonies had to be transported in English ships using primarily

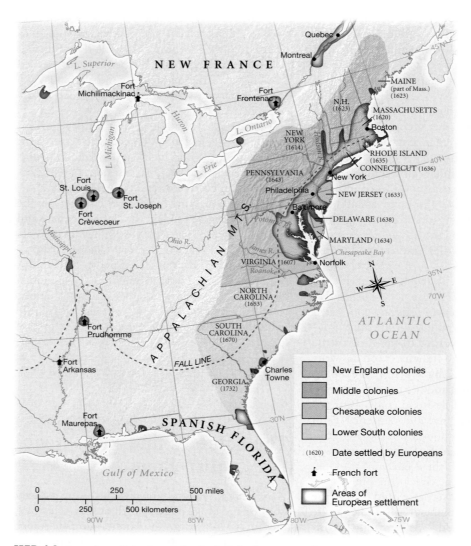

MAP 4.3 American Colonies at the End of the Seventeenth Century

By the end of the seventeenth century, settlers inhabited a narrow band of land that stretched more or less continuously from Boston to Norfolk, with pockets of settlement farther south. The colonies' claims to enormous tracts of land to the west were contested by Native Americans as well as by France and Spain.

READING THE MAP: What geographic feature acted as the western boundary for colonial territorial claims? Which colonies were the most settled and which the least?

CONNECTIONS: The map divides the colonies into four regions. Can you think of an alternative organization? On what criteria would it be based?

FOR MORE HELP ANALYZING THIS MAP, see the map activity for this chapter in the Online Study Guide at **bedfordstmartins.com/roarkcompact**.

English crews. Second, the Navigation Acts listed ("enumerated," in the language of the time) colonial products that could be shipped only to England or to other English colonies. While these regulations prevented Chesapeake planters from shipping their tobacco directly to the European continent, they interfered less with the commerce of New England and the middle colonies, whose principal exports — fish, lumber, and flour — were not enumerated and could legally be sent directly to their most important markets in the West Indies.

Pine Tree Shilling Currency was in short supply in the colonies. Since England prohibited the export of its coins, the precious currency circulating in the North American colonies tended to be Spanish, Dutch, French, or Portuguese. In violation of English rules that forbade colonies from issuing their own currency, John Hull, a wealthy Boston merchant and shipowner, began to mint coins in 1652. Shown here is one of his pine tree shillings, both sides boldly announcing its Massachusetts/New England origins. A shilling was worth twelve pennies; twenty shillings equaled one pound sterling. Despite Hull's attempt to ease the currency shortage, the legal tender most colonists used consisted of such commonly available items as bushels of corn or wheat, skins of beavers or deer, and, following Native American practice, wampum. Courtesy of the Museum of the American Numismatic Association.

By the end of the seventeenth century, colonial commerce was defined by regulations that subjected merchants and shippers to royal supervision and gave them access to markets throughout the English empire. In addition, colonial commerce received protection from the English navy. By 1700, colonial goods (including those from the West Indies) accounted for one-fifth of all English imports and for two-thirds of all goods reexported from England to the European continent. In turn, the colonies absorbed more than one-tenth of English exports. The commercial regulations gave economic value to England's proprietorship of the American colonies.

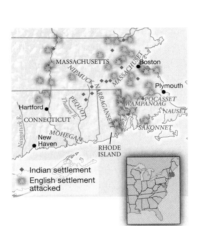

King Philip's War, 1675

Indian settlement
English settlement attacked

King Philip's War and the Consolidation of Royal Authority The monarchy also took steps to exercise greater control over colonial governments. Virginia had been a royal colony since 1624; Maryland, South Carolina, and the middle colonies were proprietary colonies with close ties to the crown. The New England colonies possessed royal charters, but they had developed their own distinctively Puritan governments. Charles II, whose father, Charles I, had been executed by Puritans in England, took a particular interest in harnessing the New England colonies more firmly to the English empire. The occasion was a royal investigation following **King Philip's War**.

In 1675, warfare between Indians and colonists erupted in the Chesapeake and New England. Massachusetts settlers had massacred hundreds of Pequot Indians in 1637, but they had established relatively peaceful relations with the more potent Wampanoags. In the decades that followed, New Englanders steadily encroached on Indian land, and in 1675 the Wampanoags struck back with attacks on settlements in western Massachusetts. **Metacomet**—the chief of the Wampanoags (and son of Massasoit), whom the colonists called King Philip—probably neither planned the attacks nor masterminded a conspiracy with the Nipmucks and the Narragansetts, as the colonists feared. But when militias from Massachusetts and other New England colonies counterattacked all three tribes, a deadly sequence of battles killed more than a thousand colonists and thousands more Indians. The Indians destroyed thirteen English settlements and partially burned another half dozen. By the spring of 1676, Indian warriors ranged freely within seventeen miles of Boston. The colonists finally defeated the Indians, principally with a scorched-earth policy of burning their food supplies. King Philip's War left the New England colonists with an enduring hatred of Indians, a large war debt, and a devastated frontier. And in 1676, an agent of the king arrived to investigate whether New England was abiding by English laws.

New France and the Indians: The English Colonies' Northern Borderlands

North of New England, French explorers, traders, and missionaries carved out a distinctive North American colony that contrasted, competed, and periodically fought with the English colonies to the south.

King Louis XIV officially made New France a royal colony in 1663, but by then representatives of France had been active for more than a century in the region that stretched along the St. Lawrence River to the Great Lakes and beyond. The explorer Jacques Cartier sailed into the St. Lawrence in 1535 and claimed the region for France. Cartier's attempts to found a permanent colony failed, but French ships followed in his wake and began to trade with Native Americans for wild animal pelts. By the seventeenth century, the fur trade had become the economic foundation of New France.

Wealthy consumers in France and elsewhere in Europe coveted the thick, lustrous furs grown by beavers, bears, wolves, and other mammals during the frigid winters of what is now eastern Canada. Skilled French furriers cut and sewed the animal skins into fashionable hats, coats, and other garments prized by consumers to stay warm and to display their wealth and good taste. Aware of the strong demand for North American furs, the French monarchy granted monopoly rights to a succession of fur-trading companies. The crown hoped to channel the fur trade through French hands into the broader European market and to compete against rival Dutch traders, whose headquarters at Albany (in what is now New York) funneled North American furs down the Hudson River to markets in the Netherlands. The French monarchy also hoped the fur trade would allow the creation of a North American colony on the cheap.

The fur trade required little investment other than the construction and staffing of trading outposts at Quebec, Montreal, and elsewhere. In exchange for textiles and various metal trade goods, the Iroquois, Huron, Ottawa, Ojibwa, and other Native Americans did the arduous, time-consuming, and labor-intensive work of tracking, trapping, and skinning the animals and transporting the pelts—usually by canoe—to French traders waiting for business in their fortifications on the St. Lawrence. The fur trade harnessed the knowledge and skills learned by Native Americans over many millennia to drain the northern wilderness of animal pelts. Unlike the English colonies, which attracted numerous settlers to engage in agriculture and produce food as well as valuable export crops of tobacco, rice, and wheat, New France needed only a few colonists to keep the trading posts open and to maintain friendly relations with their Indian suppliers. By 1660, English colonists in North America outnumbered their French counterparts by more than 20 to 1.

After England seized control of New York in 1664, English fur traders replaced the Dutch at Albany and eagerly competed to divert the northern fur trade away from New France. By then, the Iroquois—strategically located between the supply of furs to the north and west, New France to the east, and New York to the south—had become middlemen, collecting pelts from Huron, Ottawa, and other Indians and swapping them with French or English traders, depending on which offered the better deal. Able to mobilize scores of fierce warriors to threaten European traders (as well as their Indian suppliers) with traditional Native American weapons and firearms obtained mostly from the English, the Iroquois managed to play the French and English off against each other and to maintain a near choke hold on the supply of furs.

Native Americans preferred English trade goods, which tended to be of higher quality and less expensive than those available at French outposts, but New France cultivated better relationships with the Indians. When English colonists had the required military strength, they seldom hesitated to kill Indians, especially those who occupied land the colonists craved. The small number of colonists in New France never had as much military power as the English colonists to mobilize against the Indians. Instead of separating themselves from the Native Americans, as the English colonists usually did, the French colonists sought to stay on relatively peaceful and friendly terms with them. French men commonly married or cohabited with Indian women, an outgrowth of both the shortage of French women among the colonists and the relative acceptance of such couplings, compared to the strong taboo prevalent in the English colonies.

Jesuit missionaries led the spiritual colonization of New France. Zealous enemies of what they considered Protestant heresies and stout defenders of Catholicism,

★ **The Fur Trade in New France** A seventeenth-century drawing (left) illustrates the importance of canoes in the fur trade to both Native Americans and Europeans, who used them to traverse the waterways of New France. Strong, lightweight, and easy to repair with bark, wood, and pitch, all readily available in the wilderness, canoes carried not just furs, but also people, ideas, and diseases along the watery arteries of trade in New France. This drawing shrinks the size of the canoes in comparison to the people. In reality, most canoes could carry three or four people, and sometimes many more. A portrait (right) of a prosperous seventeenth-century Frenchman wearing a heavy fur coat illustrates the European demand for North American pelts. What does this portrait suggest about the living conditions inside affluent French households? Drawing: Bibliothèque Nationale de France; Portrait: Bridgeman Art Library.

the Jesuits fanned out to Indian villages throughout New France, determined to convert the Native Americans and to preserve the colony as a Catholic stronghold. The missionaries focused on Huron villages, posing a challenge to Iroquois control of the fur supply and increasing Iroquois hostility toward New France. Unwittingly, the missionaries also spread European diseases among the Native Americans, repeatedly causing deadly epidemics. Above all, the missionaries worked hand in hand with the fur traders and royal officials to make New France a low-cost Catholic colony on the thinly defended borders of the predominantly Protestant English colonies.

To extend the boundaries of New France far to the west and south, almost encircling the English colonies along the Atlantic coast, royal officials in 1673 sponsored a voyage by the explorer Louis Jolliet and the priest Jacques Marquette to explore the vast interior of the North American continent by canoeing down the Mississippi River to what is now Arkansas. There they learned

from local Indians that the river did not drain into the Pacific Ocean, opening the pathway to Asia they had hoped to find, but rather into the Gulf of Mexico. Jolliet and Marquette made grandiose claims to the Mississippi valley, but these claims amounted to little more than a colored patch on European maps since these assertions were not defended on the ground.

England and France clashed repeatedly in North America over the fur trade and in a colonial extension of their rivalry at home. English forces captured Quebec in 1629 but returned it to French control three years later. European conflict between France and England spread to North America during King William's War (1689–1697), during which the colonists and their Indian allies carried out numerous deadly raids. These raids had no permanent consequences in the seventeenth century except to mark the boundary between New France and the English colonies as a bloody, contested zone controlled by none of its claimants or inhabitants.

Wampanoag War Club This seventeenth-century war club was used to kill King Philip, according to the Anglican missionary who obtained it from Indians early in the eighteenth century. Although the missionary's tale is probably a legend, the club is certainly a seventeenth-century Wampanoag weapon that might well have been used in King Philip's War. The heavy ball carved into the head of the club could deliver a disabling, even fatal, blow. Unlike a bow and arrow, the club needed to be wielded at very close range. For this reason, it was most useful against a wounded or utterly unaware enemy. Courtesy of the Fruitlands Museums, Harvard, Massachusetts.

Not surprisingly, the king's agent found all sorts of deviations from English rules, and the monarchy decided to govern New England more directly. In 1684, an English court revoked the Massachusetts charter, the foundation of the distinctive Puritan government. Two years later, royal officials incorporated Massachusetts and the other colonies north of Maryland into the **Dominion of New England**. To govern the dominion, the English sent Sir **Edmund Andros** to Boston. Some New England merchants cooperated with Andros, but most colonists were offended by his flagrant disregard of such Puritan traditions as keeping the Sabbath. Worst of all, the Dominion of New England invalidated all land titles, confronting every landowner in New England with the horrifying prospect of losing his or her land.

Events in England, however, permitted Massachusetts colonists to overthrow Andros and retain title to their property. When Charles II died in 1685, he was succeeded by his brother James II, a zealous Catholic. James's aggressive campaign to appoint Catholics to government posts engendered such unrest that in 1688, a group of Protestant noblemen in Parliament invited the Dutch ruler William III of Orange, James's son-in-law, to claim the English throne.

When William III landed in England at the head of a large army, James fled to France, and William III and his wife, Mary II (James's daughter), became corulers in the relatively bloodless "Glorious Revolution," reasserting Protestant influence in England and its empire. Rumors of the revolution raced across the Atlantic and emboldened colonial uprisings against royal authority in Massachusetts, New York, and Maryland.

In Boston in 1689, rebels tossed Andros and other English officials in jail, destroyed the Dominion of New England, and reestablished the former charter government. New Yorkers followed the Massachusetts example. Under the leadership of Jacob Leisler, rebels seized the royal governor in 1689 and ruled the colony for more than a year. That same year in Maryland, the Protestant Association, led by John Coode, overthrew the colony's pro-Catholic government, fearing it would not recognize the new Protestant king.

But these rebel governments did not last. When King William III's governor of New York arrived in 1691, he executed Leisler for treason. Coode's men ruled Maryland until the new royal governor arrived in 1692 and ended both Coode's rebellion and Lord Baltimore's proprietary government. In Massachusetts, John Winthrop's city on a hill became another royal colony in 1691. The new charter said that the governor of the colony would be appointed by the king rather than elected by the colonists' representatives. But perhaps the most unsettling change was the new qualification for voting. Possession of property replaced church membership as a prerequisite for voting in colony-wide elections. Wealth replaced God's grace as the defining characteristic of Massachusetts citizenship.

Much as colonists chafed under increasing royal control, they still valued English protection from hostile neighbors. While the northern colonies were distracted by the Glorious Revolution, French forces from the fur-trading regions along the Great Lakes and in Canada attacked villages in New England and New York. (See "Beyond America's Borders," page 94.) Known as King William's War, the conflict with the French was a colonial outgrowth of William's war against France in Europe. The war dragged on until 1697 and ended inconclusively in both Europe and the colonies. But it made clear to many colonists that along with English royal government came a welcome measure of military security.

Q: **Why did the Glorious Revolution in England lead to uprisings in the American colonies?**

Conclusion: An English Model of Colonization in North America

By 1700, the diverse English colonies in North America had developed along lines quite different from the example New Spain had set in 1600. In the North American colonies, English immigrants and their descendants created societies of settlers unlike the largely Indian societies in New Spain ruled by a tiny group of Spaniards. Although many settlers came to North America from other parts of Europe and a growing number of Africans arrived in bondage, English laws, habits, ideas, and language dominated all the colonies.

Economically, the English colonies thrived on agriculture and trade instead of mining silver and exploiting Indian labor as in New Spain. Southern colonies grew huge crops of tobacco and rice with the labor of indentured servants and slaves, while farmers in the middle colonies planted wheat and New England fishermen harvested the sea. Although servants and slaves could be found throughout the North American colonies, many settlers depended principally on the labor of family members. Relations between settlers and Native Americans often exploded in bloody warfare, but Indians seldom served as an important source of labor for settlers, as they did in New Spain.

Protestantism prevailed in the North American settlements, relaxed in some colonies and strait-laced in others. The convictions of Puritanism that motivated John Winthrop and others to build a new England in the colonies became muted as the New England colonies matured and dissenters such as Roger Williams multiplied. Catholics, Quakers, Anglicans (members of the Church of England), Jews, and others settled in the middle and southern colonies, creating considerable religious toleration, especially in Pennsylvania and New York.

Politics and government differed from colony to colony, although the imprint of English institutions and practices existed everywhere. And everywhere, local settlers who were free adult white men had an extraordinary degree of political influence, far beyond that of colonists in New Spain or ordinary citizens in England. A new world of settlers that Columbus could not have imagined, that Powhatan only glimpsed, had been firmly established in English North America by 1700. During the next half century, that English colonial world would undergo surprising new developments built on the achievements of the seventeenth century.

Reviewing the Chapter

★ KEY TERMS

Explain each term's significance

WHO

Roger Williams (p. 75)

Puritans (p. 76)

Pilgrims (p. 78)

Separatists (p. 78)

William Bradford (p. 78)

Wampanoag Indians (p. 78)

John Winthrop (p. 79)

visible saints (p. 82)

Anne Hutchinson (p. 84)

antinomians (p. 84)

Thomas Hooker (p. 85)

Quakers (p. 87)

William Penn (p. 88)

Metacomet (p. 93)

Edmund Andros (p. 96)

WHAT

English Reformation (p. 76)

Mayflower Compact (p. 78)

Massachusetts Bay Company (p. 79)

Calvinism (p. 82)

predestination (p. 82)

covenant of grace (p. 84)

covenant of works (p. 84)

Arminianism (p. 84)

Puritan Revolution (p. 85)

Halfway Covenant (p. 87)

King Philip's War (p. 93)

Dominion of New England (p. 96)

FOR PRACTICE QUIZZES AND OTHER STUDY TOOLS, see the Online Study Guide at **bedfordstmartins.com/roarkcompact**.

★ REVIEW QUESTIONS Q:

Use key terms and dates to support your answers

1. Why did Henry VIII initiate the English Reformation? (pp. 76–78)

2. Why did the Puritans immigrate to North America? (pp. 78–81)

3. Why did Massachusetts Puritans adopt the Halfway Covenant? (pp. 81–88)

4. How did Quaker ideals shape the colony of Pennsylvania? (pp. 88–91)

5. Why did the Glorious Revolution in England lead to uprisings in the American colonies? (pp. 91–96)

★ MAKING CONNECTIONS

Draw on key terms, timeline, and review questions

1. How did the religious dissenters who flooded into the northern colonies address the question of religious dissent in their new homes? Comparing two colonies, discuss their different approaches and the implications of those approaches for colonial development.

2. In his sermon aboard the *Arbella*, John Winthrop spoke of the Massachusetts Bay Colony as "a city upon a hill." What did he mean? How did this expectation influence life in New England during the seventeenth century? In your answer, be sure to consider the relationship between religious and political life in the colony.

3. Religious conflict and political turmoil battered England in the seventeenth century. How did political developments in England affect life in the colonies? In your answer, consider the establishment of the colonies and the crown's attempts to exercise authority over them.

4. Although both were settled by the English, colonial New England was dramatically different from the colonial Chesapeake. How did they differ and why? In your answer, consider the economies, systems of governance, and patterns of settlement in each colony.

★ SUGGESTED READINGS

Virginia DeJohn Anderson, *Creatures of Empire: How Domestic Animals Transformed Early America* (2004). An innovative study of the influence of domestic animals on humans and the natural environment in early America.

David D. Hall, *Worlds of Wonder, Days of Judgment: Popular Religious Belief in Early New England* (1989). A fascinating survey of popular religious belief in the context of Puritan New England.

Donna Merwick, *The Shame and the Sorrow: Dutch-Amerindian Encounters in New Netherland* (2006). A revealing analysis of often-overlooked Native Americans in New Netherlands.

Mary Beth Norton, *In the Devil's Snare: The Salem Witchcraft Crisis of 1692* (2002). An authoritative analysis of the cultural crosscurrents that influenced the Salem witchcraft crisis.

Nathaniel Philbrick, *Mayflower: A Story of Courage, Community, and War* (2006). A lively narrative of the Plymouth settlement.

Russell Shorto, *The Island at the Center of the World: The Epic Story of Dutch Manhattan and the Forgotten Colony That Shaped America* (2004). A vivid account of the Dutch colony that became New York.

FOR MORE BOOKS ABOUT TOPICS IN THIS CHAPTER, see the Online Bibliography at **bedfordstmartins.com/roarkcompact**.

FOR ADDITIONAL FIRSTHAND ACCOUNTS OF THIS PERIOD, see Chapter 4 in Michael Johnson, ed., *Reading the American Past,* Fourth Edition.

FOR WEB SITES, IMAGES, AND DOCUMENTS RELATED TO TOPICS AND PLACES IN THIS CHAPTER, visit Make History at **bedfordstmartins.com/roarkcompact**.

★ TIMELINE

1534	• King Henry VIII breaks with Roman Catholic Church; English Reformation begins.
1609	• Henry Hudson searches for Northwest Passage.
1620	• Plymouth colony founded.
1626	• Manhattan Island purchased; New Amsterdam founded.
1629	• Massachusetts Bay Company receives royal charter.
1630	• John Winthrop leads Puritan settlers to Massachusetts Bay.
1636	• Rhode Island colony established. • Connecticut colony founded.
1638	• Anne Hutchinson excommunicated.
1642	• Puritan Revolution inflames England.
1649	• English Puritans win civil war and execute Charles I.
1656	• Quakers arrive in Massachusetts and are persecuted there.
1660	• Monarchy restored in England; Charles II becomes king.
1662	• Many Puritan congregations adopt Halfway Covenant.
1664	• English seize Dutch colony, rename it New York. • Colony of New Jersey created.
1675	• King Philip's War.
1681	• William Penn receives charter for colony of Pennsylvania.
1686	• Dominion of New England created.
1688	• England's Glorious Revolution; William III and Mary II become new rulers.
1692	• Salem witch trials.

PRINTED HANDKERCHIEF This eighteenth-century handkerchief instructs servants about the life-changing virtue of industry and the vice of idleness. The story of the good servant, William Goodchild, and the bad servant, Jack Idle, starts in the upper left corner and proceeds clockwise around the handkerchief. While William stays busy at his loom, "Sluggard" Jack loafs and will be "cloathed in Rags." While William kneels and prays on Sunday, Jack fights, then foolishly goes to sea. "Faithful Servant" William is rewarded by his master with greater responsibilities, then with marriage to the boss's daughter. Soon enough, William rises to sheriff of London, a step on his path to the "Riches and Honour" of the city's highest office, mayor. Jack, in contrast, commits robbery, is turned in by his coworkers, and is finally carted off to execution because of his "own Iniquities." William's "Frugality & Industry" lead to the colonial "Trade & Commerce" (lower left) that were the lifeblood of the eighteenth-century British empire, while idle servants who avoided the gallows, unlike Jack, ended up in the colonies hoeing tobacco alongside slaves (lower right). The handkerchief displays a parable of eighteenth-century values from the perspective of masters who sought frugal, industrious, and obedient servants rather than those who were profligate, lazy, and disorderly. Ideally, the parable suggests, servants' obedience to their masters would displace their subordination to God. What does the parable suggest about the values of freedom and individualism? How might the parable be different if it adopted the viewpoint of servants rather than masters or of female servants rather than males? How might a seventeenth-century version of this parable differ, if at all? Colonial Williamsburg Foundation.

CHAPTER 5

Colonial America in the Eighteenth Century

1701–1770

THE BROTHERS AMBOE ROBIN JOHN and Little Ephraim Robin John and their cousin Ancona Robin John lived during the 1750s and 1760s in Old Calabar on the Bight of Biafra in West Africa. The Robin Johns were part of a slave-trading dynasty headed by their kinsman Grandy King George, one of the most powerful leaders of the Efik people. Grandy King George owned hundreds of slaves whom he employed to capture and trade for still more slaves in the African interior. He sold these captives to captains of European slave ships seeking to fill their holds with human cargo for the transatlantic voyage to the sugar, tobacco, and rice fields in the New World. During the half century after 1725, Old Calabar exported about 80,000 slaves, almost all of them aboard British ships. It was a major contributor to the massive flow of more than 1.2 million slaves from the Bight of Biafra to the New World during the eighteenth century.

Grandy King George nearly monopolized the Old Calabar slave trade during the 1760s, allowing him to live in luxury, surrounded by fine British trade goods. British slave ship captains and Grandy King George's African rivals resented his choke hold on the supply of slaves and in 1767 conspired to trap the king and the Robin Johns, seize hundreds of their slaves, and destroy the king's monopoly. In the bloody melee, Grandy King George managed to escape, but other members of his family were less fortunate. Amboe Robin John was beheaded by the leader of the African attackers. Little Ephraim and Ancona Robin John were enslaved, packed aboard the ship *Duke of York* with more than 330 other slaves, and transported across the Atlantic to the West Indian island of Dominica, which the British had recently acquired from the French.

Unlike most slaves, the Robin Johns understood, spoke, and even wrote English, an essential skill they had learned as slave traders in Old Calabar. A French physician bought the Robin Johns and, according to Ancona, "treated [them] . . . upon ye whole not badly." After seven months, the Robin Johns escaped from their owner and boarded a ship "determined to get home," Little Ephraim wrote. But the ship captain took them to Virginia instead and sold them as slaves to a merchant who traded between the Chesapeake and Bristol, England. Their new master "would tie me up & whip me many times for nothing at all," Ancona testified, adding that he "was exceedingly badly

Previewing the Chapter

A Growing Population and Expanding Economy in British North America 102

Q: *How did the North American colonies achieve the remarkable population growth of the eighteenth century?*

New England: From Puritan Settlers to Yankee Traders 103

Q: *Why did settlement patterns in New England change from the seventeenth to the eighteenth century?*

The Middle Colonies: Immigrants, Wheat, and Work 108

Q: *Why did immigrants flood into Pennsylvania during the eighteenth century?*

The Southern Colonies: Land of Slavery 112

Q: *How did slavery influence the society and economy of the southern colonies?*

Unifying Experiences 117

Q: *What experiences tended to unify the colonists in British North America during the eighteenth century?*

Conclusion: The Dual Identity of British North American Colonists 124

Colonial Slave Drum An African in Virginia made this drum sometime around the beginning of the eighteenth century. He probably was enslaved in Africa, transported across the Atlantic in the hold of a slave ship, and sold to a tobacco planter in the Chesapeake. The drum combines deerskin and cedarwood from North America with African workmanship and designs. During rare moments of respite from their work, slaves played drums to accompany dances learned in Africa. They also drummed out messages from plantation to plantation. Whites knew that slaves used drums for communication, but they could not decipher the meanings of the rhythms and sounds. Fearful that drums signaled rebellious uprisings, whites outlawed drumming but could not eliminate it. Most likely, the messages sent included lamentations about the drummers' lives of bondage.
© The Trustees of the British Museum.

man ever I saw." After their master died in 1772, the Robin Johns heard that a slave ship from Old Calabar had recently arrived in Virginia, and the captain promised to take them back to Africa if they would run away and come aboard his ship. Instead, he took the Robin Johns to Bristol and sought to sell them as slaves yet again.

While imprisoned "in this Deplorable condition" on a ship in Bristol harbor, the Robin Johns managed to smuggle letters to a Bristol slave trader they had known and dealt with in Old Calabar. With help from him and other English sympathizers, the Robin Johns appeared before Lord Mansfield, the chief justice of England, and appealed for their freedom on the grounds that they "were free people . . . [who] had not done anything to forfeit our liberty" and were thus unjustly enslaved. After complex negotiations, they won legal recognition of their freedom.

As free Africans in Bristol, the Robin Johns converted to Christianity under the ministry of the famous Methodists John and Charles Wesley. Although the Robin Johns had many friends and admirers among English Methodists, they longed to return to Africa. In 1774, they sailed from Bristol as free men on another slave ship bound for Old Calabar, where they resumed their careers as slave traders.

The Robin Johns' unrelenting quest to escape enslavement and redeem their freedom was shared but not realized by millions of Africans who were victims of slave traders such as Grandy King George and numberless merchants, ship captains, and colonists. They came involuntarily to the New World. In contrast, tens of thousands of Europeans voluntarily crossed the Atlantic to seek opportunities in North America — opportunities many purchased by agreeing to several years of contractual servitude. Both groups illustrate the undertow of violence and deceit just beneath the surface of the eighteenth-century Atlantic commerce linking Britain, Africa, the West Indies, and British North America. In the flux and uncertainty of the eighteenth-century world, many, like the Robin Johns, turned to the consolations of religious faith as a source of meaning and hope in an often cruel and unforgiving society.

The flood of free and unfree migrants crossing the Atlantic contributed to unprecedented population growth in eighteenth-century British North America. In contrast, Spanish and French colonies in North America remained thinly populated outposts of European empires interested principally in maintaining a toehold in the vast continent. While adaptations to varied natural, economic, and social environments reinforced regional differences among New England, the middle colonies, and the southern colonies, other commercial, cultural, and political trends built common experiences, aspirations, and assumptions among the British colonists. These unifying trends would lay the groundwork for what became the United States of America in 1776.   ★

A Growing Population and Expanding Economy in British North America

The most important fact about eighteenth-century British America is its phenomenal population growth: In 1700, colonists numbered about 250,000; by 1770, they tallied well over 2 million. An index of the emerging significance of colonial North America is that in 1700, there were nineteen

people in England for every American colonist; by 1770, there were only three. The eightfold growth of the colonial population signaled the maturation of a distinctive colonial society. That society was by no means homogeneous. Colonists of different ethnic groups, races, and religions lived in varied environments under thirteen different colonial governments, all of them part of the British empire.

In general, the growth and diversity of the eighteenth-century colonial population derived from two sources: immigration and **natural increase** (growth through reproduction). Natural increase contributed about three-fourths of the population growth, immigration about one-fourth. Immigration shifted the ethnic and racial balance among the colonists, making them by 1770 less English and less white than ever before. Fewer than 10 percent of eighteenth-century immigrants came from England; about 36 percent were Scots-Irish, mostly from northern Ireland; 33 percent arrived from Africa, almost all of them slaves; nearly 15 percent had left the many German-language principalities (the nation of Germany did not exist until 1871); and almost 10 percent came from Scotland. In 1670, more than 9 out of 10 colonists were of English ancestry, and only 1 out of 25 was of African ancestry. By 1770, only about half of the colonists were of English descent, while more than 20 percent descended from Africans. Thus, by 1770, the people of the colonies had a distinctive colonial—rather than English—profile (Map 5.1).

The booming population of the colonies hints at a second major feature of eighteenth-century colonial society: an expanding economy. In 1700, after almost a century of settlement, nearly all the colonists lived within fifty miles of the Atlantic coast. The almost limitless wilderness stretching westward made land relatively cheap. Land in the colonies commonly sold for a fraction of its price in the Old World. The abundance of land in the colonies made labor precious, and the colonists always needed more. The insatiable demand for labor was the fundamental economic environment that sustained the mushrooming population. Economic historians estimate that free colonists (those who were not indentured servants or slaves) had a higher standard of living than the majority of people elsewhere in the Atlantic world. The unique achievement of the eighteenth-century colonial economy was this modest economic welfare of the vast bulk of the free population.

Q: How did the North American colonies achieve the remarkable population growth of the eighteenth century?

New England: From Puritan Settlers to Yankee Traders

The New England population grew sixfold during the eighteenth century but lagged behind the growth in the other colonies. Most immigrants chose other destinations because of New England's relatively densely settled land and because Puritan orthodoxy made these colonies comparatively inhospitable to religious dissenters and those indifferent to religion. As the population grew, many settlers in search of farmland dispersed from towns, and Puritan communities lost much of their cohesion. Nonetheless, networks of economic exchange laced New Englanders to their neighbors, to Boston merchants, and to the broad currents of Atlantic commerce. In many ways, trade became a faith that competed strongly with the traditions of Puritanism.

Natural Increase and Land Distribution The New England population grew mostly by natural increase, much as it had during the seventeenth century. Nearly every adult woman married. Most married women had children—often many children, thanks to the relatively low mortality rate in New England. The perils of childbirth gave wives a shorter life expectancy than husbands, but wives often lived to have six, seven, or eight babies.

"Dummy Board" of Phyllis, a New England Slave This life-size portrait of a slave woman named Phyllis, a mulatto who worked as a domestic servant for her owner, Elizabeth Hunt Wendell, was painted sometime before 1753. Known as a "dummy board," it was propped against a wall or placed in a doorway or window to suggest that the residence was occupied and to discourage thieves. Phyllis's dress and demeanor suggest that she was capable, orderly, and efficient. She illustrates the integration of the mundane tasks of housekeeping with the shifting currents of transatlantic commerce. Although tens of thousands of slaves were brought from Africa to British North America during the eighteenth century, Phyllis was probably not one of them. Instead, she was most likely born in the colonies of mixed black and white parentage. Courtesy of Historic New England.

FOR MORE HELP ANALYZING THIS IMAGE, see the visual activity for this chapter in the Online Study Guide at bedfordstmartins.com/roarkcompact.

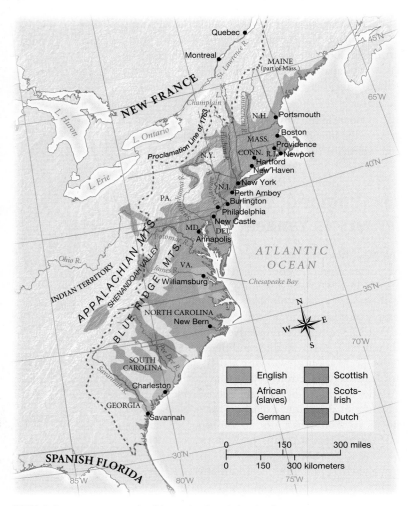

MAP 5.1 Europeans and Africans in the Eighteenth Century
This map illustrates regions where Africans and certain immigrant groups clustered. It is important to avoid misreading the map. Predominantly English and German regions, for example, also contained colonists from other places. Likewise, regions where African slaves resided in large numbers also included many whites, slave masters among them. The map suggests the diversity of eighteenth-century colonial society.

During the seventeenth century, New England towns parceled out land to individual families. In most cases, the original settlers practiced **partible inheritance**—that is, they subdivided land more or less equally among sons. By the eighteenth century, the original land allotments had to be further subdivided to accommodate grandsons and great-grandsons, and many plots of land became too small to support a family. Sons who could not hope to inherit sufficient land to farm had to move away from the town where they were born.

During the eighteenth century, colonial governments in New England abandoned the seventeenth-century policy of granting land to towns. Needing revenue, the governments of both Connecticut and Massachusetts sold land directly to individuals, including speculators. Now money, rather than membership in a community bound by a church covenant, determined whether a person could obtain land. The new land policy eroded the seventeenth-century pattern of settlement. As colonists moved, they tended to settle on individual farms rather than in the towns and villages that characterized the seventeenth century. New Englanders still depended on their relatives and neighbors, but far more than in the seventeenth century, they regulated their behavior in newly settled areas by their own individual choices.

Farms, Fish, and Atlantic Trade A New England farm was a place to get by, not to get rich. New England farmers grew food for their families, but their fields did not produce huge marketable surpluses. Instead of one big crop, a farmer grew many small ones. If farmers had extra, they sold to or traded with neighbors. Poor roads made travel difficult, time-consuming, and expensive, especially with bulky and heavy agricultural goods. The one major agricultural product the New England colonies exported—livestock—walked to market on its own legs. By 1770, New Englanders had only one-fourth as much wealth per capita as free colonists in the southern colonies.

As consumers, New England farmers participated in a diversified commercial economy that linked remote farms to markets throughout the Atlantic world. Merchants large and small stocked imported goods—British textiles, ceramics, and metal goods; Chinese tea; West Indian sugar; and Chesapeake tobacco. Farmers' needs supported local shoemakers, tailors, wheelwrights, and carpenters. Larger towns, especially Boston,

The growing New England population pressed against a limited amount of land. Compared to colonies farther south, New England had less land for the expansion of settlement (see Map 5.1). Moreover, as the northernmost group of British colonies, New England had contested northern and western frontiers. Powerful Native Americans, especially the Iroquois and Mahican tribes, jealously guarded their territory. The French (and Catholic) colony of New France also menaced the British (and mostly Protestant) New England colonies when provoked by colonial or European disputes. (See chapter 4, "Beyond America's Borders," page 94.)

MAP 5.2 North American Atlantic Trade in the Eighteenth Century
This map illustrates the economic outlook of the colonies in the eighteenth century—east toward the Atlantic world rather than west toward the interior of North America. The long distances involved in the Atlantic trade and the uncertainties of ocean travel suggest the difficulties Britain experienced governing the colonies and regulating colonial commerce.

housed skilled tradesmen such as cabinetmakers, silversmiths, and printers. Shipbuilders tended to do better than other artisans because they served the most dynamic sector of the New England economy.

Many New Englanders made their fortunes at sea, as they had since the seventeenth century. Fish accounted for more than a third of New England's eighteenth-century exports; livestock and timber made up another third. The West Indies absorbed two-thirds of all New England's exports. Slaves on Caribbean sugar plantations ate dried, salted codfish caught by New England fishermen, filled barrels crafted from New England timber with molasses and refined

sugar, and loaded those barrels aboard ships bound ultimately for Europeans with a sweet tooth. Almost all of the rest of New England's exports went to Britain and continental Europe (Map 5.2). This Atlantic commerce benefited the entire New England economy, providing jobs for laborers and tradesmen as well as for ship captains, clerks, merchants, and sailors. (See "Seeking the American Promise," page 106.)

Merchants dominated Atlantic commerce. The largest and most successful New England merchants lived in Boston at the hub of trade between local folk and the international market. Merchants not only bought and sold goods, but they also owned and insured the ships that carried

A Sailor's Life in the Eighteenth-Century Atlantic World

Although most eighteenth-century North American colonists made their livings on farms, tens of thousands manned the vessels that ferried people, animals, commodities, consumer goods, ideas, microorganisms, and much more from port to port throughout the Atlantic world. Built almost entirely from wood crafted into hulls, masts, and fittings and from fiber twisted into ropes or woven into sails, ships were the most complex machines in the eighteenth century. Sailing them required learning a specialized vocabulary that was indecipherable to landlubbers. When the mate shouted "The Helm's A-Lee, Fore-Sheet, Fore Top-Bowline, Jib and Stay-Sail Sheets Let Go!" the seamen had no time to ask questions and fumble around. They needed to know how to handle the intricacies of a vessel's working parts quickly, smoothly, and reliably. The ship, the cargo, and their own lives depended on such knowledge and dexterity. They also had to endure hard physical labor for weeks or months on end in a cramped space packed with cargo and crew. Sailors followed "one of the hardest and dangerousest callings," one old salt declared.

Despite the certainty of strenuous work and spartan accommodations, young men like Ashley Bowen made their way to wharves in small ports such as Marblehead, Massachusetts—Bowen's hometown—or large commercial centers such as Boston, Philadelphia, New York, and Charleston. There they boarded vessels and launched lives of seafaring, seeking the promise of a future wafted on the surface of the deep rather than rooted below the surface of the soil.

Born in 1728, Bowen grew up in Marblehead, one of the most important fishing ports in North America. Like other boys who lived in or near ports, Bowen probably watched ships come and go; heard tales of adventure, disaster, and intrigue; and learned from neighbors and pals how to maneuver small, shallow-draft boats within sight of land. Young girls sometimes learned to handle small boats, but they almost never worked as sailors aboard Atlantic vessels. When Bowen was only eleven years old, he sailed as a ship's boy aboard a vessel captained by the father of a friend who traveled down the coast to North Carolina to pick up a load of tar bound for Bristol, England. Upon arrival in Bristol, the crew—except underage Bowen and his friend—were pressed (that is, forced, involuntarily) into the British navy. The vessel picked up a new crew and a cargo of coal in Wales and carried it to Boston, where Bowen, now twelve, arrived with a yearlong seafaring education under his belt.

Most commonly, young men first went to sea when they were fifteen to eighteen years old. Like Bowen, they were single, living with their parents, and casting about for work. They usually sailed with friends, neighbors, or kinfolk, and they sought an education in the ways of the sea. Also like Bowen, they aspired to earn wages, to rise in the ranks eventually from seaman to mate and possibly to master (the common term for captain), to save enough to marry and support a family, and after twenty years or so to retire from the rigors of the seafaring life with a "competency"—that is, enough money to live modestly.

It typically took about four years at sea to become a fully competent seaman. Shortly after Bowen returned from his first voyage, his father apprenticed him to a sea captain for seven years. In return for a hefty payment, the captain agreed to tutor young Bowen in the art of seafaring, which ideally promised to ease his path to become a captain himself. In reality, the captain employed him as a cabin boy, taught him little except to obey, and beat him for trivial mistakes, causing Bowen to run away after four years of servitude.

Now seventeen years old, Bowen had already sailed to dozens of ports in North America, the West Indies, the British Isles, and Europe. For the next eighteen years, he shipped out as a common seaman on scores of vessels carrying nearly every kind of cargo afloat on the

the merchandise throughout the Atlantic world. Shrewd, diligent, and lucky merchants could make fortunes. The magnificence of a wealthy Boston merchant's home stunned John Adams, a thrifty Massachusetts lawyer who became a leader during the American Revolution and ultimately the second president of the United States. To Adams, the merchant's house seemed fit "for a noble Man, a Prince." Such luxurious Boston homes contrasted with the modest dwellings of

Atlantic. He sailed mostly aboard merchant freighters, but he also worked on whalers, fishing boats, privateers, and warships. He survived sickness, imprisonment, foul weather, accidents, and innumerable close calls. But when he retired from seafaring at age thirty-five, he still had not managed to attain command. In twenty-four years at sea, he had worked as either a common seaman or a mate, with the exception of two or three voyages that he commanded. He tried again and again to be hired as a shipmaster, but shipowners refused to employ him despite his experience. For whatever reason, when shipowners eyed Bowen, they did not see a man they would trust to command their vessels.

Careful study of other eighteenth-century colonial seamen discloses that Bowen did better than some, about as well as many, and less well than the most successful. Unlike Bowen, about three out of ten seamen died at sea. Many drowned or died as a result of injuries, but most succumbed to tropical diseases usually picked up in the West Indies. Bowen had a hardy constitution and lived to the age of eighty-five. After his retirement, he worked in Marblehead as a rigger, crafting nautical fittings for sailing vessels. Like Bowen, about three out of ten seamen spent their entire seafaring careers as seamen or mates, earning five dollars a month or so in wages. This was roughly comparable to wages for farm laborers, who often received payment in kind rather than in currency. About one in four seamen attained the status and improved earnings of shipmasters. Masters earned two to five times as much as common seamen and could profit handsomely from the privilege of carrying and selling their own private cargoes in available space aboard the vessels they commanded.

Although Ashley Bowen failed to attain the ultimate goal of his seafaring career, he maintained his connection to seafaring with his trade as a rigger, and he lived out his life in Marblehead within sight, sound, and smell of the sea. When Bowen was about sixty, he wrote the only autobiography ever written by an eighteenth-century common seaman, chronicling the promise, achievements, adventures, and problems of a seafaring life. When Bowen, like thousands of other seafarers in the colonies, looked at the world, his gaze did not turn west toward the farms and forests of the interior, but east toward the promise of the masts and sails in the harbor and the Atlantic deep beyond.

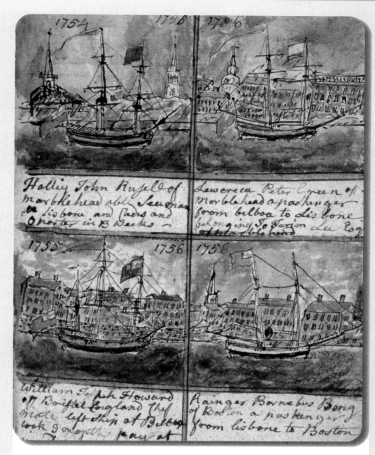

★ **Ashley Bowen's Journal** Ashley Bowen painted these watercolors of ships he sailed aboard in 1754, 1755, and 1756. Befitting an experienced seaman, he paid attention to the distinctive rigging and flags of each vessel, and he kept notes about the vessels' owners, masters, mates, passengers, and destinations. As the focus of Bowen's fascination, the vessels dwarf the buildings of Marblehead, Massachusetts, in the background. To Bowen, each ship had distinctive features. Can you spot the differences that caught his eye? Why might such differences be important to Bowen? Photo courtesy of The Marblehead Historical Society, Marblehead, MA.

Adams and other New Englanders, an indication of the polarization of wealth that developed in Boston and other seaports during the eighteenth century. By 1770, the richest 5 percent of Bostonians owned about half the city's wealth; the poorest two-thirds of the population owned less than one-tenth.

While the rich got richer and everybody else had a smaller share of the total wealth, the incidence of genuine poverty did not change much. About

5 percent of New Englanders qualified for poor relief throughout the eighteenth century. Overall, colonists were better off than most people in England. A Connecticut traveler wrote from England in 1764, "We in New England know nothing of poverty and want, we have no idea of the thing, how much better do our poor people live than 7/8 of the people on this much famed island."

The contrast with English poverty had meaning because the overwhelming majority of New Englanders traced their ancestry to England. New England was more homogeneously English than any other colonial region. People of African ancestry (almost all of them slaves) numbered more than fifteen thousand by 1770, but they barely diversified the region's 97 percent white majority. In the Narragansett region of Rhode Island, large landowners imported numerous slaves to raise livestock. But most New Englanders had little use for slaves on their family farms. Instead, slaves were concentrated in towns, especially Boston, where most of them worked as domestic servants and laborers.

By 1770, the population, wealth, and commercial activity of New England differed from what they had been in 1700. Ministers still enjoyed high status, but Yankee traders had replaced Puritan saints as the symbolic New Englanders. Atlantic commerce competed with religious convictions in ordering New Englanders' daily lives.

Q: **Why did settlement patterns in New England change from the seventeenth to the eighteenth century?**

The Middle Colonies: Immigrants, Wheat, and Work

In 1700, almost twice as many people lived in New England as in the middle colonies of Pennsylvania, New York, New Jersey, and Delaware. But by 1770, the population of the middle colonies had multiplied tenfold—mainly from an influx of German, Irish, Scottish, and other immigrants—and nearly equaled the population of New England. Immigrants made the middle colonies a uniquely diverse society. By 1800, barely one-third of Pennsylvanians and less than half the total population of the middle colonies traced their ancestry to England.

German and Scots-Irish Immigrants Germans made up the largest contingent of migrants from the European continent to the middle colonies. By 1770, about 85,000 Germans had arrived in the colonies. Their fellow colonists often referred to them as **Pennsylvania Dutch**, an English corruption of *Deutsch*, the word the immigrants used to describe themselves.

Most German immigrants came from what is now southwestern Germany, where, one observer noted, peasants were "not as well off as cattle elsewhere." German immigrants included numerous artisans and a few merchants, but the great majority were farmers and laborers. Economically, they represented "middling folk," neither the poorest (who could not afford the trip) nor the better-off (who did not want to leave).

Weathercock To twenty-first-century eyes, this mid-eighteenth-century rooster seems an appropriate weather vane for a farmhouse or barn. In fact, it crowned the first Lutheran church in Schoharie, New York, where it reminded believers of Christ's prediction at the Last Supper that his devoted disciple Peter would betray him three times before the cock crowed. Lutheran and German Reform churches often displayed such weathercocks to warn that even the most devout and faithful Christians frequently succumbed to the weaknesses of the flesh and the temptations of sin. Schoharie County Historical Society, Old Stone Fort Museum.

By the 1720s, Germans who had established themselves in the colonies wrote back to their friends and relatives, as one reported, "of the civil and religious liberties [and] privileges, and of all the goodness I have heard and seen." Such letters prompted still more Germans to pull up stakes and embark for America, to exchange the miserable certainties of their lives in Europe for the uncertain attractions of life in the middle colonies.

Similar motives propelled the **Scots-Irish**, who considerably outnumbered German immigrants. The "Scots-Irish" actually hailed from northern Ireland, Scotland, and northern England. Like the Germans, the Scots-Irish were Protestants, but with a difference. Most German immigrants worshiped in Lutheran or German Reformed churches; many others belonged to dissenting sects such as the Mennonites, Moravians, and Amish, whose adherents sought relief from persecution they had suffered in Europe for their refusal to bear arms and to swear oaths, practices they shared with the Quakers. In contrast, the Scots-Irish tended to be militant Presbyterians who seldom hesitated to bear arms or swear oaths. Like German settlers, however, Scots-Irish immigrants were clannish, residing when they could among relatives or neighbors from the old country.

In the eighteenth century, wave after wave of Scots-Irish immigrants arrived, culminating in a flood of immigration in the years just before the American Revolution. Deteriorating economic conditions in northern Ireland, Scotland, and England pushed many toward America. Most of the immigrants were farm laborers or tenant farmers fleeing droughts, crop failures, high food prices, or rising rents. They came, they told inquisitive British officials, because of "poverty," "tyranny of landlords," and their desire to "do better in America."

Both Scots-Irish and Germans probably heard the common saying "Pennsylvania is heaven for farmers [and] paradise for artisans," but they almost certainly did not fully understand the risks of their decision to leave their native lands. Ship captains, aware of the hunger for labor in the colonies, eagerly signed up the penniless emigrants as **redemptioners**, a variant of indentured servants. A captain would agree to provide transportation to Philadelphia, where redemptioners would obtain the money to pay for their passage by borrowing it from a friend or relative who was already in the colonies or, as most did, by selling themselves as servants. Many redemptioners traveled in family groups, unlike impoverished Scots-Irish emigrants, who usually traveled alone and paid for their passage by contracting as indentured servants before they sailed to the colonies.

Redemptioners and indentured servants were packed aboard ships "as closely as herring," one migrant observed. Seasickness compounded by exhaustion, poverty, poor food, bad water, inadequate sanitation, and tight quarters encouraged the spread of disease. When one ship finally approached land, a traveler wrote, "everyone crawls from below to the deck . . . and people cry for joy, pray, and sing praises and thanks to God." Unfortunately, their troubles were far from over. Redemptioners and indentured servants had to stay on board until somebody came to purchase their labor. Unlike indentured servants, redemptioners negotiated independently with their purchasers about their period of servitude. Typically, a healthy adult redemptioner agreed to four years of labor. Indentured servants commonly served five, six, or seven years.

Pennsylvania: "The Best Poor [White] Man's Country"

New settlers, whether free or in servitude, poured into the middle colonies because they perceived unparalleled opportunities, particularly in Pennsylvania, "the best poor Man's Country in the World," as an indentured servant wrote in 1743. Although the servant reported that "the Condition of bought Servants is very hard" and masters often failed to live up to their promise to provide decent food and clothing, opportunity abounded because there was more work to be done than workers to do it.

Most servants toiled in Philadelphia, New York City, or one of the smaller towns or villages. Artisans, small manufacturers, and shopkeepers prized the labor of male servants. Female servants made valuable additions to households, where nearly all of them cleaned, washed, cooked, or minded children. From the masters' viewpoint, servants were a bargain. A master could purchase five or six years of a servant's labor for approximately the wages a common laborer would earn in four months. Wageworkers could walk away from their jobs when they pleased, and they did so often enough to be troublesome for employers. Servants, however, could not walk away; they were legally bound to work for their masters until their terms expired.

Since a slave cost at least three times as much as a servant, only affluent colonists could afford the long-term investment in slave labor. Like many other prosperous urban residents, Benjamin Franklin purchased a few slaves after he became wealthy. But most farmers in the middle colonies used family labor, not slaves. Wheat, the most widely grown crop, did not require more labor than farmers could typically muster from relatives, neighbors, and a hired hand or two. Consequently, although people of African ancestry (almost all slaves) increased to more than thirty thousand in the middle colonies by 1770, they accounted for only about 7 percent of the total population and much less outside the cities.

Most slaves came to the middle colonies and New England after a stopover in the West Indies, as the Robin Johns did. Very few came directly from Africa. Enough slaves arrived to prompt colonial assemblies to pass laws that punished slaves much more severely than servants for the same transgressions. But in cases of abuse, servants—unlike slaves—could charge masters with violating the terms of their indenture contracts. Small numbers of slaves managed to obtain their freedom, though few of them as dramatically as the Robin Johns. But free African Americans did not escape whites' firm convictions about black inferiority and white supremacy.

Whites' racism and blacks' lowly social status made African Americans scapegoats for European Americans' suspicions and anxieties. In 1741, when arson and several unexplained thefts plagued New York City, officials suspected a murderous slave

Bethlehem, Pennsylvania This view of the small community of Bethlehem, Pennsylvania, in 1757 dramatizes the profound transformation of the natural landscape wrought in the eighteenth century by highly motivated human labor. Founded by Moravian immigrants in 1740, Bethlehem must have appeared at first like the dense woods on the upper left horizon. In less than twenty years, precisely laid-out orchards and fields replaced forests and glades. By carefully penning their livestock (lower center right) and fencing their fields (lower left), farmers safeguarded their livelihoods from the risks and disorders of untamed nature. Individual farmsteads (lower center) and impressive multistory brick town buildings (upper center) integrated the bounty of the land with the delights of community life. Few eighteenth-century communities were as orderly as Bethlehem, but many effected a comparable transformation of the environment. Print Collection, Miriam and Ira D. Wallack Division of Art, Prints and Photographs, The New York Public Library. Astor, Lenox, and Tilden Foundations.

FOR MORE HELP ANALYZING THIS IMAGE, see the visual activity for this chapter in the Online Study Guide at bedfordstmartins.com/roarkcompact.

conspiracy and executed thirty-one slaves. Although slaves were certifiably impoverished, they were not among the poor for whom the middle colonies were reputed to be the best country in the world.

Immigrants swarmed to the middle colonies because of the availability of land. The Penn family encouraged immigration to bring in potential buyers for their enormous tracts of land in Pennsylvania. From the beginning, Pennsylvania followed a policy of negotiating with Indian tribes to purchase additional land. This policy reduced the violent frontier clashes more common elsewhere in the colonies.

Few colonists drifted beyond the northern boundaries of Pennsylvania. Owners of the huge estates in New York's Hudson valley preferred to rent rather than sell their land, and therefore they attracted fewer immigrants. The **Iroquois Indians** dominated the lucrative fur trade of the St. Lawrence valley and eastern Great Lakes, and they vigorously defended their territory from colonial encroachment. Few settlers chose to risk having their scalps lifted by Iroquois warriors in northern New York when they could settle instead in the comparatively safe environs of Pennsylvania.

The price of farmland depended on soil quality, access to water, distance from a market town, and extent of improvements. One hundred acres of improved land that had been cleared, plowed, fenced, and ditched, and perhaps had a house and barn built on it, cost three or four times more than the same acreage of uncleared, unimproved land. Since the cheapest land always lay at the margin of settlement, would-be farmers tended to migrate to promising areas just beyond already improved farms. By midcentury, settlement had reached the eastern slopes of the Appalachian Mountains, and newcomers spilled south down the fertile valley of the Shenandoah River into western Virginia and the Carolinas. Thousands of settlers migrated from the middle colonies through this back door to the South.

Farmers made the middle colonies the breadbasket of North America. They planted a wide variety of crops to feed their families, but they grew wheat in abundance. Flour milling was the number one industry and flour the number one export, constituting nearly three-fourths of all exports from the middle colonies. For farmers, the grain market in the Atlantic world proved risky but profitable. Grain prices rose steadily after 1720. By 1770, a bushel of wheat was worth twice as much (adjusted for inflation) as it had been fifty years earlier.

The standard of living in rural Pennsylvania was probably higher than in any other agricultural region of the eighteenth-century world. The comparatively widespread prosperity of all the middle colonies permitted residents

Patterns of Settlement, 1700–1770

Mrs. Charles Willing This portrait of Mrs. Charles Willing of Philadelphia illustrates the prosperity achieved by numerous women and men in the eighteenth-century colonies. Painted by the Philadelphia artist Robert Feke in 1746, the portrait depicts the close connections between Europe and the North American colonies made possible by the thriving transatlantic commerce. Scholars have discovered that Anna Maria Garthwaite, an established textile designer in Spitalfields — a silk-weaving center near London — designed the material used to make Mrs. Willing's dress. A Spitalfields weaver, Simeon Julins, then wove the fabric and sold it to a merchant, who exported it to Philadelphia in 1744.

Mrs. Willing must have spotted the silk in a shop and purchased enough to have this fashionable gown made for her portrait. The portrait demonstrates that, like other prosperous colonists, Mrs. Willing kept abreast of the latest London fashions available in the shops of colonial merchants. Courtesy, Winterthur Museum, gift of Mrs. George P. Bissell Jr.

to indulge in a half-century shopping spree for British imports. The middle colonies' per capita consumption of imported goods from Britain more than doubled between 1720 and 1770, far outstripping the per capita consumption of British goods in New England and the southern colonies.

At the crossroads of trade in wheat exports and British imports stood Philadelphia. By 1776, Philadelphia had a larger population than any other city in the entire British empire except London. Merchants occupied the top stratum of Philadelphia society. In a city where only 2 percent of the residents owned enough property to qualify to vote, merchants built grand homes and dominated local government. Many of Philadelphia's wealthiest merchants were Quakers. Quaker traits of industry, thrift, honesty, and sobriety encouraged the accumulation of wealth.

In 1733, Benjamin Franklin began to publish *Poor Richard's Almanack*, which preached the likelihood of long-term rewards for tireless labor. The popularity of *Poor Richard's Almanack* suggests that many Pennsylvanians thought less  about the pearly gates than about their pocketbooks. Poor Richard's advice that "God gives all Things to Industry" might be considered the motto for the middle colonies. The promise of a worldly payoff made work a secular faith. Poor Richard advised, "Work as if you were to live 100 years, Pray as if you were to die Tomorrow." William Penn's Quaker utopia became a center of worldly affluence whose most famous citizen, Franklin, was neither a Quaker nor a utopian. Quakers remained influential, but Franklin spoke for most colonists with his aphorisms of work, discipline, and thrift that echoed Quaker rules for outward behavior.

Q: **Why did immigrants flood into Pennsylvania during the eighteenth century?**

The Southern Colonies: Land of Slavery

Between 1700 and 1770, the population of the southern colonies of Virginia, Maryland, North Carolina, South Carolina, and Georgia grew almost ninefold. By 1770, about twice as many people lived in the South as in either the middle colonies or New England. As elsewhere, natural increase and immigration accounted for the rapid population growth. Many Scots-Irish and German immigrants funneled from the middle colonies into the southern backcountry. Other immigrants were indentured servants (mostly English and Scots-Irish) who followed their seventeenth-century predecessors. But slaves made the most striking contribution to the booming southern colonies, transforming the racial composition of the population. Slavery became the defining characteristic of the southern colonies during the eighteenth century, shaping the region's economy, society, and politics.

The Atlantic Slave Trade and the Growth of Slavery The number of southerners of African ancestry (nearly all of them slaves) rocketed from just over 20,000 in 1700 to well over 400,000 in 1770. The black population increased nearly three times faster than the South's briskly growing white population. Consequently, the proportion of southerners of African ancestry grew from 20 percent in 1700 to 40 percent in 1770.

Southern colonists clustered into two distinct geographic and agricultural zones. The colonies in the upper South, surrounding the Chesapeake Bay, specialized in growing tobacco, as they had since the early seventeenth century. Throughout the eighteenth century, nine out of ten southern whites and eight out of ten southern blacks lived in the Chesapeake region. The upper South retained a white majority during the eighteenth century.

In the lower South, a much smaller cluster of colonists inhabited the coastal region and specialized in the production of rice and indigo (a plant used to make blue dye). Lower South colonists made up only 5 percent of the total population of the southern colonies in 1700 but inched upward to 15 percent by 1770. South Carolina was the sole British colony along the southern Atlantic coast until 1732, when Georgia was founded. (North Carolina, founded in 1711, was largely an extension of the Chesapeake region.) Blacks in South Carolina, in contrast to every other British mainland colony, outnumbered whites almost two to one; in some low-country districts, the ratio of blacks to whites exceeded ten to one.

The enormous growth in the South's slave population occurred through natural increase and the flourishing Atlantic slave trade (Table 5.1 and Map 5.3). Slave ships brought almost 300,000 Africans to British North America between 1619 and 1780. Of these Africans, 95 percent arrived in the South and 96 percent arrived during the

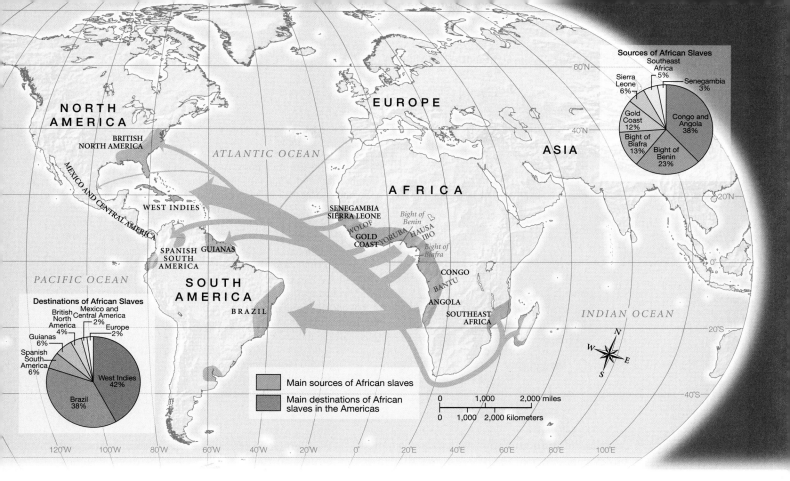

Sources of African Slaves
- Southeast Africa 5%
- Senegambia 3%
- Congo and Angola 38%
- Bight of Benin 23%
- Bight of Biafra 13%
- Gold Coast 12%
- Sierra Leone 6%

Destinations of African Slaves
- Mexico and Central America 2%
- Europe 2%
- British North America 4%
- Guianas 6%
- Spanish South America 6%
- West Indies 42%
- Brazil 38%

- Main sources of African slaves
- Main destinations of African slaves in the Americas

MAP 5.3 The Atlantic Slave Trade

Although the Atlantic slave trade lasted from about 1450 to 1870, it peaked during the eighteenth century, when more than six million African slaves were imported to the New World. Only a small fraction of these slaves were taken to British North America. Most went to sugar plantations in Brazil and the Caribbean.

READING THE MAP: Where in Africa did most slaves originate? Approximately how far was the trip from the busiest ports of origin to the two most common New World destinations?

CONNECTIONS: Why were so many more African slaves sent to the West Indies and Brazil than to British North America?

FOR MORE HELP ANALYZING THIS MAP, see the map activity for this chapter in the Online Study Guide at bedfordstmartins.com/roarkcompact.

eighteenth century. Unlike indentured servants and redemptioners, these Africans did not choose to come to the colonies. Like the Robin Johns, most of them had been born into free families in villages located within a few hundred miles of the West African coast.

Although they shared African origins, they came from many different African cultures, including Akan, Angolan, Asante, Bambara, Gambian, Igbo, and Mandinga, among others. They spoke different languages, worshipped different deities, observed different rules of kinship, grew different crops, and recognized different rulers. The most important experience they had in common was enslavement. Captured in war, kidnapped, or sold into slavery by other Africans, they were brought to the coast, sold to African traders like the Robin Johns who assembled

★ **TABLE 5.1 Slave Imports, 1451–1870**

Estimated Slave Imports to the Western Hemisphere

1451–1600	275,000
1601–1700	1,341,000
1701–1810	6,100,000
1811–1870	1,900,000

slaves for resale, and sold again to European or colonial slave traders or ship captains, who packed two hundred to three hundred or more aboard ships that carried them on the **Middle Passage** across the Atlantic and then sold them yet again to colonial slave merchants or southern planters.

Olaudah Equiano This portrait shows Equiano more than a decade after he had bought his freedom. The portrait evokes Equiano's successful acculturation to the customs of eighteenth-century England. His clothing and hairstyle reflect the fashions of a respectable young Englishman. In his *Interesting Narrative*, Equiano explained that he had learned to speak and understand English while he was a slave. He wrote that he "looked upon [the English] . . . as men superior to us [Africans], and therefore I had the stronger desire to resemble them, to imbibe their spirit and imitate their manners; I therefore embraced every occasion of improvement, and every new thing that I observed I treasured up in my memory." Equiano's embrace of English culture did not cause him to forsake his African roots. He honored his dual identity by campaigning against slavery. His *Narrative* was one of the most important and powerful antislavery documents of the time. Library of Congress.

Olaudah Equiano published an account of his enslavement that hints at the stories that might have been told by the millions of other Africans swept up in the slave trade. Equiano wrote that he was born in 1745 in the interior of what is now Nigeria. "I had never heard of white men or Europeans, nor of the sea," he recalled. One day when he was eleven years old, he was kidnapped by Africans, who sold him to other Africans, who in turn eventually sold him to a slave ship on the coast. Equiano feared that he was "going to be killed" and "eaten by those white men with horrible looks, red faces, and loose hair." Once the ship set sail, many of the slaves, crowded together in suffocating heat fouled by filth of all descriptions, died from sickness. "The shrieks of the women and the groans of the dying rendered the whole a scene of horror almost inconceivable," Equiano recalled. Most of the slaves on the ship were sold in Barbados, but Equiano and other leftovers were shipped off to Virginia, where he "saw few or none of our native Africans and not one soul who could talk to me." Equiano felt isolated and "exceedingly miserable" because he "had no person to speak to that I could understand." Finally, the captain of a tobacco ship bound for England purchased Equiano, and he traveled as a slave between North America, England, and the West Indies for ten years until he succeeded in buying his freedom in 1766.

Only about 15 percent of the slaves brought into the southern colonies came aboard ships from the West Indies, as Equiano and the Robin Johns did. All the other slaves brought into the southern colonies came directly from Africa, and almost all the ships that brought them (roughly 90 percent) belonged to British merchants. Most of the slaves on board were young adults, with men usually outnumbering women two to one. Children under the age of fourteen, like Equiano, typically accounted for no more than 10 to 15 percent of a cargo.

Mortality during the Middle Passage varied considerably from ship to ship. On average, about 15 percent of the slaves died, but sometimes half or more perished. The average mortality among the white crew of slave ships was often nearly as bad. In general, the longer the voyage lasted, the more people died. Recent studies suggest that many slaves succumbed not only to virulent epidemic diseases such as smallpox and dysentery, but also to acute dehydration caused by fluid loss from perspiration, vomiting, and diarrhea combined with a severe shortage of drinking water.

Normally, an individual planter purchased at any one time a relatively small number of newly arrived Africans, or **new Negroes**, as they were called. New Negroes were often profoundly depressed, demoralized, and disoriented. Planters expected their other slaves—either those born into slavery in the colonies (often called **country-born** or **creole slaves**) or Africans who had arrived earlier—to help new Negroes become accustomed to their strange new surroundings. Planters' preferences for slaves from specific regions of Africa aided slaves' acculturation (or **seasoning**, as it was called) to the routines of bondage in the southern colonies.

The African Slave Trade The African slave trade existed to satisfy the New World's demand for labor and Europe's voracious appetite for such New World products as sugar, tobacco, and rice. African men, women, and children were kidnapped or captured in wars — typically by other Africans — and enslaved. Uprooted from their homes and kin, they were usually taken to coastal enclaves where African traders and European ship captains negotiated prices, made deals, and often branded the newly enslaved people.

The collaboration between Europeans and their African trading partners is evident in the seventeenth-century Benin bronze box (top) in the shape of a royal palace in Nigeria. The palace is guarded by two massive predatory birds and two Portuguese soldiers.

Jammed into the holds of slave ships, enslaved Africans made the dreaded Middle Passage to the New World. The model of a slave ship shown here (right) was used in parliamentary debates by antislavery leaders in Britain to demonstrate the inhumanity of shipping people as if they were cargo. The model does not show another typical feature of slave ships: weapons. Slaves vastly outnumbered the crews aboard the ships, and crew members justifiably feared slave uprisings. Benin bronze box: Staatliche Museen Zu Berlin, Preussischer Kulturbesitz; Slave ship model: Wilberforce House, Hull City Museums and Art Galleries, UK/Bridgeman Art Library.

Chesapeake planters preferred slaves from Senegambia, the Gold Coast, or — like Equiano and the Robin Johns — the Bight of Biafra, which combined accounted for 40 percent of all Africans imported to the Chesapeake. South Carolina planters favored slaves from the central African Congo and Angola regions, the origin of about 40 percent of the African slaves they imported (see Map 5.3). Although slaves within each of these regions spoke many different languages, enough linguistic and cultural similarities existed that they could usually communicate with other Africans from the same region.

Seasoning acclimated new Africans to the physical as well as the cultural environment of the southern colonies. Slaves who had just endured the Middle Passage were poorly nourished, weak, and sick. In this vulnerable state, they encountered the alien diseases of North America without having developed a biological arsenal of acquired immunities. As many as 10 to 15 percent of newly arrived Africans, sometimes more, died during their first year in the southern colonies. Nonetheless, the large number of newly enslaved Africans made the influence of African culture in the South stronger in the eighteenth century than ever before — or since.

While newly enslaved Africans poured into the southern colonies, slave mothers bore children, which caused the slave population in the South to grow rapidly. Slave owners encouraged these births. Thomas Jefferson explained, "I consider the labor of a breeding [slave] woman as no object, that a [slave] child raised every 2 years is of more profit than the crop of the best laboring [slave] man." Although slave mothers loved and nurtured their children, the mortality rate among slave children was high, and the ever-present risk of being separated by sale brought grief to many slave families. Nonetheless, the growing number of slave babies set the southern colonies apart from other New World slave societies, where mortality rates were so high that deaths exceeded births. The high rate of natural increase in the southern colonies meant that by the 1740s, the majority of southern slaves were country-born.

Slave Labor and African American Culture

Southern planters expected slaves to work from sunup to sundown and beyond. George Washington wrote that his slaves should "be at their work as soon as it is light, work til it is dark, and be diligent while they are at it." The conflict between the masters' desire for maximum labor and the slaves' reluctance to do more than necessary made the threat of physical punishment a constant for eighteenth-century slaves. Masters preferred black slaves to white indentured servants, not just because slaves served for life but also because colonial laws did not limit the force masters could use against slaves. As a traveler observed in 1740, slaves resisted their masters' demands because of their "greatness of soul"—their stubborn unwillingness to conform to their masters' definition of them as merely slaves.

Some slaves escalated their acts of resistance to direct physical confrontation with the master, the mistress, or an overseer. But a hoe raised in anger, a punch in the face, or a desperate swipe with a knife led to swift and predictable retaliation by whites. Throughout the southern colonies, the balance of physical power rested securely in the hands of whites.

Rebellion occurred, however, at Stono, South Carolina, in 1739. Before dawn on a September Sunday, a group of about twenty slaves attacked a country store, killed the two storekeepers, and confiscated the store's guns, ammunition, and powder. Enticing other slaves to join, the group plundered and burned more than half a dozen plantations and killed more than twenty white men, women, and children. A mounted force of whites quickly suppressed the rebellion. They placed the rebels' heads atop mileposts along the road, grim reminders of the consequences of rebellion. The **Stono rebellion** illustrated that eighteenth-century

> George Washington wrote that his slaves should "be at their work as soon as it is light, work til it is dark, and be diligent while they are at it."

slaves had no chance of overturning slavery and very little chance of defending themselves in any bold strike for freedom. After the rebellion, South Carolina legislators enacted repressive laws designed to guarantee that whites would always have the upper hand. No other similar uprisings occurred during the colonial period.

Slaves maneuvered constantly to protect themselves and to gain a measure of autonomy within the boundaries of slavery. In Chesapeake tobacco fields, most slaves were subject to close supervision by whites. In the lower South, the **task system** gave slaves some control over the pace of their work and some discretion in the use of the rest of their time. A "task" was typically defined as a certain area of ground to be cultivated or a specific job to be completed. A slave who completed the assigned task might use the remainder of the day, if any, to work in a garden, fish, hunt, spin, weave, sew, or cook. When masters sought to boost productivity by increasing tasks, slaves did what they could to defend their customary work assignments.

Eighteenth-century slaves also planted the roots of African American lineages that branch out to the present. Slaves valued family ties, and, as in West African societies, kinship structured slaves' relations with one another. Slave parents often gave a child the name of a grandparent, aunt, or uncle. In West Africa, kinship identified a person's place among living relatives and linked the person to ancestors in the past and to descendants in the future. Newly imported African slaves usually arrived alone, like Equiano, without kin. Often slaves who had traversed the Middle Passage on the same ship adopted one another as "brothers" and "sisters." Likewise, as new Negroes were seasoned and incorporated into existing slave communities, established families often adopted them as fictive kin.

When possible, slaves expressed many other features of their West African origins in their lives on New World plantations. They gave their children traditional dolls and African names such as Cudjo or Quash, Minda or Fuladi. They grew food crops they had known in Africa, such as yams and okra. They constructed huts with mud walls and thatched roofs similar to African residences. They fashioned banjos, drums, and other musical instruments, held dances, and observed funeral rites that echoed African practices. In these and many other ways, slaves drew upon their African heritages as much as the oppressive circumstances of slavery permitted.

Tobacco, Rice, and Prosperity Slaves' labor bestowed prosperity on their masters, British merchants, and the monarchy. The southern colonies supplied 90 percent of all North American exports to Britain. Rice exports from the lower South exploded from less than half a million pounds in 1700 to eighty million pounds in 1770, nearly all of it grown by slaves. Exports of indigo also boomed. Together, rice and indigo made up three-fourths of lower South exports, nearly two-thirds of them going to Britain and most of the rest to the West Indies, where sugar-growing slaves ate slave-grown rice. Tobacco was by far the most important export from British North America; by 1770, it represented almost one-third of all colonial exports and three-fourths of all Chesapeake exports. Under the provisions of the Navigation Acts (see chapter 4), nearly all of it went to Britain, where the monarchy collected a lucrative tax on each pound. British merchants then reexported more than 80 percent of the tobacco to the European continent, pocketing a nice markup for their troubles.

These products of slave labor made the southern colonies by far the richest in North America. The per capita wealth of free whites in the South was four times greater than that in New England and three times that in the middle colonies. At the top of the wealth pyramid stood the rice grandees of the lower South and the tobacco **gentry** of the Chesapeake. These elite families commonly resided on large estates in handsome mansions adorned by luxurious gardens, all maintained and supported by slaves.

The vast differences in wealth among white southerners engendered envy and occasional tension between rich and poor, but remarkably little open hostility. In private, the planter elite spoke disparagingly of humble whites, but in public the planters acknowledged their lesser neighbors as equals, at least in belonging to the superior — in their minds — white race. Looking upward, white yeomen and tenants (who owned neither land nor slaves) sensed the gentry's condescension and veiled contempt. But they also appreciated the gentry for granting favors, upholding white supremacy, and keeping slaves in their place. Although racial slavery made a few whites much richer than others, it also gave those who did not get rich a powerful reason to feel similar (in race) to those who were so different (in wealth).

The slaveholding gentry dominated the politics and economy of the southern colonies. In Virginia, only adult white men who owned at least one hundred acres of unimproved land or twenty-five acres of land with a house could vote. This property-holding requirement prevented about 40 percent of white men in Virginia from voting for representatives to the House of Burgesses. In South Carolina, the property requirement was only fifty acres of land, and therefore most adult white men qualified to vote. In both colonies, voters elected members of the gentry to serve in the colonial legislature. The gentry passed elected political offices from generation to generation, almost as if they were hereditary. Politically, the gentry built a self-perpetuating oligarchy — rule by the elite few — with the votes of their many humble neighbors.

The gentry also set the cultural standard in the southern colonies. They entertained lavishly, gambled regularly, and attended Anglican (Church of England) services more for social than for religious reasons. Above all, they cultivated the leisurely pursuit of happiness. They did not condone idleness, however. Their many pleasures and responsibilities as plantation owners kept them busy. Thomas Jefferson, a phenomenally productive member of the gentry, recalled that his earliest childhood memory was of being carried on a pillow by a family slave — a powerful image of the slave hands supporting the gentry's leisure and achievement.

Q: **How did slavery influence the society and economy of the southern colonies?**

Unifying Experiences

The societies of New England, the middle colonies, and the southern colonies became more sharply differentiated during the eighteenth century, but colonists throughout British North America also shared unifying experiences that eluded settlers in the Spanish and French colonies. The first was economic. All three British colonial regions had their economic roots in agriculture. Colonists sold their distinctive products in markets that, in turn, offered a more or less uniform array of goods to consumers throughout British North America. A second unifying experience was a decline in the importance of religion. Some settlers called for a revival of religious intensity, but most people focused less on religion and more on the affairs of the world than they had in the seventeenth century. Third, white inhabitants throughout British North America became aware that they shared a distinctive identity as *British* colonists. Thirteen different governments presided over these North American colonies, but all of them answered to the British monarchy. British policies governed not only trade but also military and diplomatic relations with the Indians, French, and Spanish arrayed along colonial borderlands. Royal officials who expected loyalty from the colonists often had difficulty obtaining obedience. The British colonists asserted their prerogatives as British subjects to defend their special colonial interests.

Commerce and Consumption Eighteenth-century commerce whetted colonists' appetites to consume. Colonial products spurred the development of mass markets throughout the Atlantic world. Huge increases in the supply of colonial tobacco and sugar brought the price of these small luxuries within the reach of most free whites. Colonial goods brought into focus an important lesson of eighteenth-century commerce: Ordinary people, not just the wealthy elite, would buy the things that they desired in addition to what they absolutely needed. Even news, formerly restricted mostly to a few people through face-to-face conversations or private letters, became an object of public consumption through the innovation of newspapers. With the appropriate stimulus, market demand seemed unlimited.

THE PROMISE OF TECHNOLOGY

James Franklin's Printing Press In the eighteenth century, colonial printers began to publish newspapers. In 1721, James Franklin began the *New England Courant,* a newspaper that set out to thumb its nose at officialdom of both government and religious institutions. The *Courant* pledged "to entertain the Town with the most comical and diverting Incidents of Humane Life" and to "expose the Vice and Follies of Persons of all Ranks and Degrees." Franklin's press (shown here) broadcast to the reading public dissenting opinions previously confined to private conversations. Relatively high rates of literacy gave newspapers a large audience. Newspapers were also read aloud, allowing nonreaders access to the controversial ideas, partisan accusations, and salacious rumors that printers relished. When newspapers employed the technology of printing to publish everything from political news to advertisements for a spouse, information and ideas began to spread beyond official channels to help form public opinion. Combining the old technology of printing with the new currents of commerce, dissent, and enlightenment, eighteenth-century newspapers created a novel awareness of the problems and possibilities of public life. Newport Historical Society.

The Atlantic commerce that took colonial goods to markets in Britain brought objects of consumer desire back to the colonies. British merchants and manufacturers recognized that colonists made excellent customers, and the Navigation Acts gave British exporters privileged access to the colonial market. By midcentury, export-oriented industries in Britain were growing ten times faster than firms attuned to the home market. Most British exports went to the vast European market, where potential customers outnumbered those in the colonies by more than one hundred to one. But as European competition stiffened, colonial markets became increasingly important. British exports to North America multiplied eightfold between 1700 and 1770, outpacing the rate of population growth after midcentury. When the colonists' eagerness to consume exceeded their ability to pay, British exporters willingly extended credit, and colonial debts soared.

Imported mirrors, silver plate, spices, bed and table linens, clocks, tea services, wigs, books, and more infiltrated parlors, kitchens, and bedrooms throughout the colonies. Despite the many differences among the colonists, the consumption of British exports built a certain material uniformity across region, religion, class, and status. Consumption of British exports made the colonists look and feel more British even though they lived at the edge of a wilderness an ocean away from Britain.

The rising tide of colonial consumption had other less visible but no less important consequences. Consumption presented women and men with a novel array of choices. In many respects, the choices might appear trivial: whether to buy knives and forks, teacups, or a clock. But such small choices confronted eighteenth-century consumers with a big question: What do you want? As colonial consumers defined and expressed their desires with greater frequency during the eighteenth century, they became accustomed to thinking of themselves as individuals who had the power to make decisions that influenced the quality of their lives—attitudes of significance in the hierarchical world of eighteenth-century British North America.

Religion, Enlightenment, and Revival

Eighteenth-century colonists could choose from almost as many religions as consumer goods. Virtually all of the bewildering variety of religious denominations represented some form of Christianity, almost all of them Protestant. Slaves made up the largest group of non-Christians. A few slaves converted to Christianity in Africa or after they arrived in North America, but most continued to embrace elements of indigenous African religions. Roman Catholics concentrated in Maryland as they had since the seventeenth century, but even there they were outnumbered by Protestants.

The varieties of Protestant faith and practice ranged across a broad spectrum. The middle colonies and the southern backcountry included militant Baptists and Presbyterians. Huguenots who had fled persecution in Catholic France peopled congregations in several cities. In New England, old-style Puritanism splintered into strands of Congregationalism that differed over fine points of theological doctrine. The **Congregational Church** was the official established church in New England, and all residents paid taxes for its support. Throughout the plantation South and in urban centers such as Charleston, New York, and Philadelphia, prominent colonists belonged to the Anglican Church, which received tax support in the South. But dissenting faiths grew everywhere, and in most colonies their adherents won the right to worship publicly, although the established churches retained official support.

Many educated colonists became deists, looking for God's plan in nature more than in the Bible. **Deism** shared the ideas of eighteenth-century European Enlightenment thinkers, who tended to agree that science and reason could disclose God's laws in the natural order. In the colonies as well as in Europe, **Enlightenment** ideas encouraged people to study the world around them, to think for themselves, and to ask whether the disorderly appearance of things masked the principles of a deeper, more profound natural order. From New England towns to southern drawing rooms, individuals met to discuss such matters. Philadelphia was the center of these conversations, especially after the formation of the American Philosophical Society in 1769, an outgrowth of an earlier group organized by **Benjamin Franklin**, who was a deist. Leading colonial thinkers such as Franklin and Thomas Jefferson, among many other members, communicated with each other seeking both to understand nature and to find ways to improve society. Franklin's interest in electricity, stoves, and eyeglasses exemplified the shift of focus among many eighteenth-century colonists from heaven to the here and now.

Most eighteenth-century colonists went to church seldom or not at all, although they probably considered themselves Christians. A minister in Charleston observed that on the Sabbath, "the Taverns have more Visitants than the Churches." In the leading colonial cities, church members were a small minority of eligible adults, no more than 10 to 15 percent. Anglican parishes in the South rarely claimed more than one-fifth of eligible adults as members. In some regions of rural New England and the middle colonies, church membership embraced two-thirds of eligible adults, while in other areas, only one-quarter of the residents belonged to a church. The dominant faith overall was religious indifference. As a late-eighteenth-century traveler observed, "Religious indifference is imperceptibly disseminated from one end of the continent to the other." The spread of religious indifference, of deism, of denominational

> A minister in Charleston observed that on the Sabbath, "the Taverns have more Visitants than the Churches."

George Whitefield An anonymous artist portrayed George Whitefield preaching, emphasizing the power of his sermons to transport his audience to a revived awareness of divine spirituality. Light from above gleams off his forehead. His crossed eyes and far-away gaze suggest that he spoke in a semihypnotic trance. Notice the absence of a Bible on the pulpit. Rather than elaborating on God's Word as revealed in Scripture, Whitefield speaks from his own inner awareness. The young woman bathed in light below his hands appears transfixed, her focus on some inner realm illuminated by his words. Her eyes and Whitefield's do not meet, yet the artist's use of light suggests that she and Whitefield see the same core of holy Truth. The other people in Whitefield's audience appear not to have achieved this state, failing so far to be ignited by the divine spark. National Portrait Gallery, London.

wave of revivals the **Great Awakening**. In Massachusetts during the mid-1730s, the fiery Puritan minister **Jonathan Edwards** reaped a harvest of souls by reemphasizing traditional Puritan doctrines of humanity's utter depravity and God's vengeful omnipotence. The title of Edwards's most famous sermon, "Sinners in the Hands of an Angry God," conveys the flavor of his message. In Pennsylvania and New Jersey, William Tennent led revivals that dramatized spiritual rebirth with accounts of God's miraculous powers, such as raising Tennent's son from the dead.

The most famous revivalist in the eighteenth-century Atlantic world was **George Whitefield**. An Anglican, Whitefield preached well-worn messages of sin and salvation to large audiences in England using his spellbinding, unforgettable voice. Whitefield visited the North American colonies seven times, staying for more than three years during the mid-1740s and attracting tens of thousands to his sermons, including Benjamin Franklin and Olaudah Equiano. Whitefield's preaching transported many in his audience to emotion-choked states of religious ecstasy. About one revival he wrote, "The bitter cries and groans were enough to pierce the hardest heart. Some of the people were as pale as death; others were wringing their hands; others lying on the ground; others sinking into the arms of their friends; and most lifting their eyes to heaven, and crying to God for mercy."

Whitefield's successful revivals spawned many lesser imitations. Itinerant preachers, many of them poorly educated, toured the colonial backcountry after midcentury, echoing Whitefield's medium and message as best they could. Bathsheba Kingsley, a member of Jonathan Edwards's flock, preached the revival message informally—as did an unprecedented number of other women throughout the colonies—causing her congregation to brand her a "brawling woman" who had "gone quite out of her place."

The revivals awakened and refreshed the spiritual energies of thousands of colonists struggling with the uncertainties and anxieties of eighteenth-century America. The conversions at revivals did not substantially boost the total number of church members, however. After the revivalists moved on, the routines and pressures of everyday existence reasserted their primacy in the lives of many converts. But the revivals

rivalry, and of comfortable backsliding profoundly concerned many Christians.

To combat what one preacher called the "dead formality" of church services, some ministers set out to convert nonbelievers and to revive the piety of the faithful with a new style of preaching that appealed more to the heart than to the head. Historians have termed this communicated the important message that every soul mattered, that men and women could choose to be saved, that individuals had the power to make a decision for everlasting life or death. Colonial revivals expressed in religious terms many of the same democratic and egalitarian values expressed in economic terms by colonists' patterns of consumption. One colonist noted the analogy by referring to itinerant revivalists as "Pedlars in divinity." Like consumption, revivals contributed to a set of common experiences that bridged colonial divides of faith, region, class, and status.

Borderlands and Colonial Politics in the British Empire

The plurality of peoples, faiths, and communities that characterized the North American colonies arose from the somewhat haphazard policies of the eighteenth-century British empire. Since the Puritan Revolution of the mid-seventeenth century, British monarchs had valued the colonies' contributions to trade and encouraged their growth and development. Unlike Spain and France—whose policies of excluding Protestants and foreigners kept the population of their North American colonial territories tiny—Britain kept the door to its colonies open to anyone, and tens of thousands of non-British immigrants settled in the North American colonies and raised families. The open door did not extend to trade, however, as the seventeenth-century Navigation Acts restricted colonial trade to British ships and traders. These policies evolved because they served the interests of the monarchy and of influential groups in Britain and the colonies. The policies also gave the colonists a common framework of political expectations and experiences.

At a minimum, British power defended the colonists from Indian, French, and Spanish enemies on their borders—as well as from foreign powers abroad. Each colony organized a militia, and privateers sailed from every port to prey on foreign ships. But the British navy and army bore ultimate responsibility for colonial defense. (See "Global Comparison.")

Royal officials warily eyed the small North American settlements of New France and New Spain for signs of threats to the colonies. Alone, neither New France nor New Spain jeopardized British North America, but with Indian allies, they could become a potent force that kept colonists on their guard (Map 5.4). Native Americans' impulse to defend their territory from colonial incursions warred with their desire for trade, which tugged them toward the settlers. As a colonial official observed in 1761, "A modern Indian cannot subsist

without Europeans. . . . [The European goods that were] only conveniency at first [have] now become necessity." To obtain such necessities as guns, ammunition, clothing, sewing utensils, and much

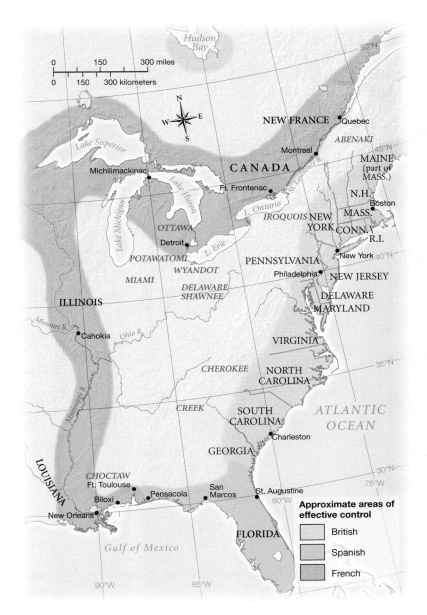

MAP 5.4 Zones of Empire in Eastern North America

The British zone, extending west from the Atlantic coast, was much more densely settled than the zones under French, Spanish, and Indian control. The comparatively large number of British colonists made them more secure than the relatively few colonists in the vast regions claimed by France and Spain or the settlers living among the many Indian peoples in the huge area between the Mississippi River and the Appalachian Mountains. Yet the British colonists were not powerful enough to dominate the French, Spanish, or Indians. Instead, they had to guard against attacks by powerful Indian groups allied with the French or Spanish.

Large Warships in European Navies, 1660–1760

1660   **1710**   **1760**

= 10 warships

England   France   England   France   England   France

Netherlands   Denmark   Netherlands   Denmark   Netherlands   Denmark

Note: Comparable data does not exist for Spain.

The large warships in England's navy usually outnumbered those of rival nations from 1660 to 1760. During the eighteenth century, the British fleet grew dramatically, while the fleets of rival nations declined. The British monarchy paid the enormous cost of building, manning, and maintaining the largest European navy because defending commerce and communication with its far-flung colonies was fundamental to the integrity of its empire. Britain's North American colonies benefited from defense by the most powerful navy in the Atlantic. However, since supremacy in the number of warships never translated automatically into supremacy in a particular naval battle, Britain's colonists constantly worried about surprise attacks by other nations, whose warships might sail into a harbor or capture a merchant vessel while British warships were someplace else. Why do you think British warships outnumbered those of their competitors? What might account for the changing numbers of warships between 1660 and 1760?

more that was manufactured largely by the British, Indians trapped beavers, deer, and other furbearing animals throughout the interior.

Colonial traders and their respective empires competed to control the fur trade. British, French, Spanish, and Dutch officials monitored the trade to prevent their competitors from deflecting the flow of furs toward their own markets. Indians took advantage of this competition to improve their own prospects, playing one trader and empire off against another. The Iroquois, for example, promised the French exclusive access to the furs and territory of the Great Lakes region and at the same time made the same pledge of exclusive rights to the British. Indian tribes and confederacies also competed among themselves for favored trading rights with one colony or another, a competition colonists encouraged.

The shifting alliances and complex dynamics of the fur trade struck a fragile balance along the frontier. The threat of violence from all sides was ever present, and the threat became reality often enough for all parties to be prepared for the worst. In the **Yamasee War of 1715**, Yamasee and Creek Indians—with French encouragement—mounted

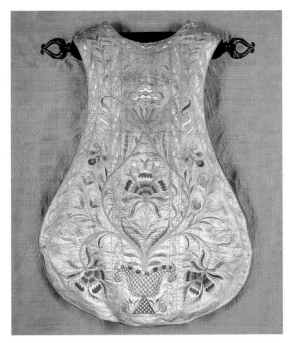

Mission Carmel This eighteenth-century drawing portrays a reception for a Spanish visitor at Mission Carmel in what is now Carmel, California. Lines of mission Indians dressed in robes flank the entrance to the chapel where a priest and his assistants await the visitor. During worship, priests wore lavishly decorated chasubles, like the one shown here from Mission Santa Clara. The intricate and colorful embroidery signified the magnificence of divine authority, embodied in the priests — God's representatives on earth — and their Spanish sponsors. The reception ritual dramatized the strict hierarchy that governed relations between Spanish missionaries, ruling officials, and the subordinate Indians. Reception: University of California at Berkeley, Bancroft Library; Chasuble: de Saisset Museum, Santa Clara University.

a coordinated attack against colonial settlements in South Carolina and inflicted heavy casualties. The Cherokee Indians, traditional enemies of the Creeks, refused to join the attack. Instead, they protected their access to British trade goods by allying with the colonists and turning the tide of battle, thus triggering a murderous rampage of revenge by the colonists against the Creek and Yamasee tribes.

Relations between Indians and colonists differed from colony to colony and from year to year. But the British colonists' nagging perceptions of menace on the frontier kept them continually hoping for help from the British to keep the Indians at bay and to maintain the essential flow of trade. In 1754, the British colonists' endemic competition with the French flared into the Seven Years' War (also known as the French and Indian War), which would inflame the frontier for years (see chapter 6). Before the 1760s, neither the British colonists nor the British themselves developed a coherent policy toward the Indians. But both agreed that Indians made deadly enemies, profitable trading partners, and powerful allies.

As a result, the British and their colonists kept an eye on the Spanish empire to the west and relations with the Indians there.

Russian hunters in search of seals and sea otters ventured along the Pacific coast from Alaska to California and threatened to become a permanent presence on New Spain's northern frontier. To block Russian access to present-day California, officials in New Spain mounted a campaign to build forts (called **presidios**) and missions there.

In 1769, an expedition headed by a military man, **Gaspar de Portolá**, and a Catholic priest, **Junípero Serra**, traveled north from Mexico to present-day San Diego, where they founded the first California mission, San Diego de Alcalá. They soon journeyed all the way to Monterey, which became the capital of Spanish California. There Portolá established a presidio in 1770 "to defend us from attacks by the Russians," he wrote. By 1772, Serra had founded other missions along the path from San Diego to Monterey.

One Spanish soldier praised the work of the missionaries, writing that "with flattery and presents [the missionaries] attract the savage Indians

Spanish Missions in California

and persuade them to adhere to life in society and to receive instruction for a knowledge of the Catholic faith, the cultivation of the land, and the arts necessary for making the instruments most needed for farming." Yet for the Indians, the Spaniards' California missions had horrendous consequences, as they had elsewhere in the Spanish borderlands. European diseases decimated Indian populations, Spanish soldiers raped Indian women, and missionaries beat Indians and subjected them to near slavery. Indian uprisings against the Spaniards occurred repeatedly, but the presidios and missions endured as feeble projections of the Spanish empire along the Pacific coast.

British attempts to exercise political power in their colonial governments met with success so long as British officials were on or very near the sea. Colonists acknowledged—although they did not always readily comply with—British authority to collect customs duties, inspect cargoes, and enforce trade regulations. But when royal officials tried to wield their authority in the internal affairs of the colonies on land, they invariably encountered colonial resistance. A governor appointed by the king in each of the nine royal colonies (Rhode Island and Connecticut selected their own governors) or by the proprietors in Maryland and Pennsylvania headed the government of each colony. The British envisioned colonial governors as mini-monarchs able to exert influence in the colonies much as the king did in Britain. But colonial governors were not kings, and the colonies were not Britain.

Eighty percent of colonial governors had been born in England, not in the colonies. Some governors stayed in England, close to the source of royal patronage, and delegated the grubby details of colonial affairs to subordinates. Even the best-intentioned colonial governors had difficulty developing relations of trust and respect with influential colonists because their terms of office averaged just five years and could be terminated at any time. Colonial governors controlled few patronage positions to secure political friendships in the colonies. Officials who administered the colonial customs service, for example, received their appointments through patronage networks centered in England rather than from colonial governors. In obedience to Britain, colonial governors fought incessantly with the colonists' assemblies. They battled over governors' vetoes of colonial legislation, removal of colonial judges, creation of new courts, dismissal of the representative assemblies, and other local issues. Some governors developed a working relationship with the colonists' assemblies. But during the eighteenth century, the assemblies gained the upper hand.

Since British policies did not clearly define the colonists' legal powers, colonial assemblies seized the opportunity to make their own rules. Gradually, the assemblies established a strong tradition of representative government analogous, in their eyes, to the British Parliament. Voters often returned the same representatives to the assemblies year after year, building continuity in power and leadership that far exceeded that of the governor.

By 1720, colonial assemblies had won the power to initiate legislation, including tax laws and authorizations to spend public funds. Although all laws passed by the assemblies (except in Maryland, Rhode Island, and Connecticut) had to be approved by the governor and then by the Board of Trade in Britain, the difficulties in communication about complex subjects over long distances effectively ratified the assemblies' decisions. Years often passed before colonial laws were repealed by British authorities, and in the meantime, the assemblies' laws prevailed.

The heated political struggles between royal governors and colonial assemblies that occurred throughout the eighteenth century taught colonists a common set of political lessons. They learned to employ traditionally British ideas of representative government to defend their own colonial interests. They learned that power in the British colonies rarely belonged to the British government.

Q: **What experiences tended to unify the colonists in British North America during the eighteenth century?**

Conclusion: The Dual Identity of British North American Colonists

During the eighteenth century, a society that was both distinctively colonial and distinctively British emerged in British North America. Tens of thousands of immigrants and slaves like the Robin Johns gave the colonies an unmistakably colonial complexion and contributed to the colonies' growing population and expanding economy. People of different ethnicities and faiths sought their fortunes in the colonies, where land was cheap, labor was dear, and — as Benjamin Franklin preached — work promised to be rewarding. Indentured servants and redemptioners risked temporary periods of bondage for the potential reward of better opportunities in the colonies than on the Atlantic's eastern shore. Slaves endured lifetime servitude, which they neither chose nor desired but from which their masters greatly benefited.

Identifiably colonial products from New England, the middle colonies, and the southern colonies flowed to the West Indies and across the Atlantic. Back came unquestionably British consumer goods along with fashions in ideas, faith, and politics. The bonds of the British empire required colonists to think of themselves as British subjects and, at the same time, encouraged them to consider their status as colonists.

People of European origin in the North American colonies of Spain and France did not share in the emerging political identity of the British colonists. They also did not participate in the cultural, economic, social, and religious changes experienced by their counterparts in British North America. Unlike the much more numerous colonists in British North America, North American Spanish and French colonists did not develop societies that began to rival the European empires that sponsored and supported them.

By 1750, British colonists in North America could not imagine that their distinctively dual identity — as British and as colonists — would soon become a source of intense conflict. But by 1776, colonists in British North America had to choose whether they were British or American.

Reviewing the Chapter

★ KEY TERMS

Explain each term's significance

WHO

Pennsylvania Dutch (p. 108)

Scots-Irish (p. 109)

redemptioners (p. 109)

Iroquois Indians (p. 111)

Olaudah Equiano (p. 114)

new Negroes (p. 114)

country-born or creole slaves (p. 114)

Benjamin Franklin (p. 119)

Jonathan Edwards (p. 120)

George Whitefield (p. 120)

Gaspar de Portolá (p. 123)

Junípero Serra (p. 123)

WHAT

natural increase (p. 102)

partible inheritance (p. 104)

Middle Passage (p. 113)

seasoning (p. 114)

Stono rebellion (p. 116)

task system (p. 116)

gentry (p. 117)

Congregational Church (p. 119)

deism (p. 119)

Enlightenment (p. 119)

Great Awakening (p. 120)

Yamasee War of 1715 (p. 122)

presidios (p. 123)

FOR PRACTICE QUIZZES AND OTHER STUDY TOOLS, see the Online Study Guide at **bedfordstmartins.com/roarkcompact**.

★ REVIEW QUESTIONS Q:

Use key terms and dates to support your answer

1. How did the North American colonies achieve the remarkable population growth of the eighteenth century? (pp. 102–03)

2. Why did settlement patterns in New England change from the seventeenth to the eighteenth century? (pp. 103–08)

3. Why did immigrants flood into Pennsylvania during the eighteenth century? (pp. 108–12)

4. How did slavery influence the society and economy of the southern colonies? (pp. 112–17)

5. What experiences tended to unify the colonists in British North America during the eighteenth century? (pp. 117–24)

★ MAKING CONNECTIONS

Draw on key terms, timeline, and review questions

1. Colonial products such as tobacco and sugar transformed consumption patterns on both sides of the Atlantic in the eighteenth century. How did consumption influence the relationship between the American colonies and Britain? In your answer, consider how it might have strengthened and weakened connections.

2. Why did the importance of religion decline throughout the colonies from the seventeenth to the eighteenth century? How did American colonists respond to these changes?

3. How did different colonies attempt to manage relations with the Indians? How did the Indians attempt to manage relationships with the Europeans? In your answer, consider disputes over territory and trade.

4. Varied immigration patterns contributed to important differences between the British colonies. Compare and contrast patterns of immigration to the middle and southern colonies. Who came, and how did they get there? How did they shape the economic, cultural, and political character of each colony?

★ SUGGESTED READINGS

Ira Berlin, *Generations of Captivity: A History of African-American Slaves* (2003). An expert overview of the rise of slavery in British North America.

George M. Marsden, *Jonathan Edwards: A Life* (2003). A thoughtful biography of the leading minister of the Great Awakening.

Simon P. Newman, *Embodied History: The Lives of the Poor in Early Philadelphia* (2003). A revealing look at the poor in the "best poor man's country."

Peter Silver, *Our Savage Neighbors: How Indian War Transformed Early America* (2008). A prize-winning study of war with Native Americans in the eighteenth century.

Randy J. Sparks, *Two Princes of Calabar: An Eighteenth-Century Odyssey* (2004). The amazing saga of two African brothers, themselves slave traders, who were enslaved and eventually managed to regain their freedom.

David Waldstreicher, *Runaway America: Benjamin Franklin, Slavery, and the American Revolution* (2004). A fascinating study of Benjamin Franklin and slavery.

FOR MORE BOOKS ABOUT TOPICS IN THIS CHAPTER, see the Online Bibliography at **bedfordstmartins.com/roarkcompact**.

FOR ADDITIONAL FIRSTHAND ACCOUNTS OF THIS PERIOD, see Chapter 5 in Michael Johnson, ed., *Reading the American Past*, Fourth Edition.

FOR WEB SITES, IMAGES, AND DOCUMENTS RELATED TO TOPICS AND PLACES IN THIS CHAPTER, visit Make History at **bedfordstmartins.com/roarkcompact**.

★ TIMELINE

1711	• North Carolina founded.
1715	• Yamasee War.
1730s	• Jonathan Edwards promotes Great Awakening.
1732	• Georgia founded.
1733	• Benjamin Franklin begins to publish *Poor Richard's Almanack*.
1739	• Stono rebellion.
1740s	• George Whitefield preaches religious revival in North America. • Majority of southern slaves are country-born.
1745	• Olaudah Equiano born.
1754	• Seven Years' War begins.
1769	• American Philosophical Society founded. • First California mission, San Diego de Alcalá, established.
1770	• Mission and presidio established at Monterey, California. • British North American colonists number more than two million.

PATRICK HENRY'S MAP DESK Like many of the leading gentry of 1760s Virginia, Patrick Henry pursued land speculation as a way to gain wealth. From 1767 to 1773, he engaged in a half dozen land ventures, buying up thousands of acres of frontier land in regions that are now part of Kentucky — purchases that would soon figure in the emerging crisis of empire. This odd little table was Henry's map desk. Its foldout extensions provided support for the large maps required to represent Virginia's vast western land claims, and its light weight allowed Henry to position it near the best light source in his law office. As is often the case with speculative purchases, Henry's land deals entailed risk: Many of his properties were occupied by the Cherokees, who did not recognize his claim of ownership. The British government, fearing war between the Indians and settlers, tried to choke off risky land speculation in 1763 by establishing an imaginary line along the crest of the Appalachian Mountains beyond which settlement was prohibited. But men like Henry continued to buy land cheap in the hope of selling dear at a later time. As a leading planter and powerful orator, Henry quickly became a spokesman in the growing imperial struggle with Britain. When he gained election to the Virginia House of Burgesses in 1765, he skillfully maneuvered that assembly into the startling repudiation of British power known as the Virginia Resolves. By 1775, he favored independence from Britain, a position that eventually would unleash settlers looking to buy land in the west. In 1776, he was elected the first governor of the Commonwealth of Virginia. Patrick Henry ultimately had seventeen children, fourteen of whom survived to adulthood. Through astute land purchases, he managed to establish each with a landed estate. Courtesy of Scotchtown, photo by Katherine Wetzel.

CHAPTER 6

The British Empire and the Colonial Crisis

1754–1775

IN 1771, THOMAS HUTCHINSON became the royal governor of the colony of Massachusetts. Unlike most royal governors, who were British aristocrats sent over by the king for short tours of duty, Hutchinson was a fifth-generation American. A Harvard-educated member of the Massachusetts elite, from a family of successful merchants, he had served two decades in the Massachusetts general assembly. In 1758, **Thomas Hutchinson** was appointed lieutenant governor, and in 1760 he also became chief justice of the colony's highest court. He lived in the finest mansion in Boston. Wealth, power, and influence were his in abundance. He was proud of his connection to the British empire and loyal to his king.

Hutchinson had the misfortune to be a loyal colonial leader during the two very tumultuous decades leading up to the American Revolution. He worked hard to keep the British and colonists aligned in interests, even promoting a plan to unify the colonies into a single defensive unit (the **Albany Plan of Union**) to ward off Indian wars. The plan of union failed, and a major war ensued — the Seven Years' War, pitting the British and colonists against the French and their Indian allies in the backcountry of the American colonies. When the war ended and the British government began to think about taxing colonists to pay for it, Hutchinson had no doubt that the new British policies were legitimate. Unwise, perhaps, in their specific formulation, but certainly legitimate.

Not everyone in Boston shared his opinion. Fervent, enthusiastic crowds protested against a succession of British taxation policies enacted after 1763 — the Sugar Act, the Stamp Act, the Townshend duties, the Tea Act, all landmark events on the road to the American Revolution. But Hutchinson maintained his steadfast loyalty to Britain. His love of order and tradition inclined him to unconditional support of the British empire, and he was, by nature, a measured and cautious man. "My temper does not incline to enthusiasm," he once wrote.

Privately, he lamented the stupidity of the British acts that provoked trouble, but his sense of duty required him to defend the king's policies, however misguided. Quickly, he became an inspiring villain to the emerging revolutionary movement. Governor Hutchinson came to personify all that

Previewing the Chapter

The Seven Years' War, 1754–1763 130
Q: How did the Seven Years' War erode relations between colonists and British authorities?

The Sugar and Stamp Acts, 1763–1765 138
Q: Why did the Sugar Act and the Stamp Act draw fierce opposition from colonists?

The Townshend Acts and Economic Retaliation, 1767–1770 142
Q: Why did British authorities send troops to occupy Boston in the fall of 1768?

The Tea Party and the Coercive Acts, 1770–1774 145
Q: Why did Parliament pass the Coercive Acts in 1774?

Domestic Insurrections, 1774–1775 149
Q: How did enslaved people in the colonies react to the stirrings of revolution?

Conclusion: How Far Does Liberty Go? 151

Thomas Hutchinson The only formal portrait of Thomas Hutchinson still in existence shows an assured young man in ruffles and hair ribbons. Decades of turmoil in Boston failed to puncture his self-confidence. Doubtless he sat for other portraits, as did all the Boston leaders in the 1760s to 1780s, but no other likeness has survived. One portrait of him hung in his summer house outside Boston; a revolutionary crowd mutilated it and stabbed out the eyes. In 1775, Hutchinson fled to Britain, the country he regarded as his cultural home, only to realize how very American he was. Courtesy of the Massachusetts Historical Society.

was wrong with British and colonial relations. The man not inclined to enthusiasm unleashed popular enthusiasm all around him. He never appreciated that irony.

In another irony, Thomas Hutchinson was actually one of the first Americans to recognize the difficulties of maintaining full rights and privileges for colonists so far from their supreme government, the king and Parliament in Britain. In 1769, when British troops occupied Boston in an effort to provide civil order, he wrote privately to a friend in England, "There must be an abridgement of what are called English liberties. . . . I doubt whether it is possible to project a system of government in which a colony three thousand miles distant from the parent state shall enjoy all the liberty of the parent state." What he could not imagine was the possibility of giving up the parent state and creating an independent government closer to home.

Thomas Hutchinson was a loyalist; in the 1750s, most English-speaking colonists were affectionately loyal to Britain. But the Seven Years' War, which Britain and its colonies fought together as allies, shook that affection, and imperial policies in the decade following the war shattered it completely. Over the course of 1763 to 1773, colonists insistently raised serious questions about American liberties and rights, especially the issues of taxation and representation. Many came to believe what Thomas Hutchinson could never credit — that a tyrannical Britain had embarked on a course to enslave the colonists by depriving them of their traditional English liberties.

The opposite of liberty was slavery, a condition of nonfreedom and coercion. Political rhetoric about liberty, tyranny, and slavery heated up emotions of white colonists during the many crises of the 1760s and 1770s. But this rhetoric turned out to be a two-edged sword. The call for an end to tyrannical slavery meant one thing when sounded by Boston merchants whose commercial shipping rights had been revoked; the same call meant something quite different in 1775 when sounded by black Americans locked in the bondage of slavery.

All of this was set in motion by the Seven Years' War. The British victory at first fortified loyalty to the mother country, but its aftermath, taxation, stirred up discussions of rights, fueled white colonists' fear of enslavement by king and Parliament, and produced a potent political vocabulary with unexpected consequences. ★

The Seven Years' War, 1754–1763

For the first half of the eighteenth century, Britain was at war intermittently with France or Spain. Often the colonists in America experienced reverberations from these conflicts, most acutely along the frontier of New France in northern New England. In the 1750s, international tensions returned, this time over events originating in America. The conflict began in 1754 over contested land in the Ohio Valley variously claimed by Virginians, Pennsylvanians, the French, and the Indians already living there. The result was the costly **Seven Years' War** (its British name), which spread in 1756 to encompass much of Europe, the Caribbean, and even

India. The American colonists experienced nearly ten years of warfare, not seven, in what they called the French and Indian War. British and American soldiers shared the hardships of battle and the glory of victory over the French and Indians. But the immense costs of the war — in money, death, and desire for revenge by losers and even winners — laid the groundwork for the imperial crisis of the 1760s between the British and Americans.

French-British Rivalry in the Ohio Country

For several decades, French traders had cultivated alliances with the Indian tribes in the Ohio Country, a frontier region they regarded as part of New France (Map 6.1). Cementing their relationships with gifts, the French established a profitable trade

Hudson Bay

GRANT TO HUDSON'S BAY COMPANY

NEWFOUNDLAND

Wolfe to Quebec

Fort Louisbourg
besieged June 8–July 26, 1758

Wolfe from Great Britain

Fort Beausejour

Amherst

NOVA SCOTIA

Port Royal

Quebec

ALGONQUIAN

NEW FRANCE

MAINE (part of MASS.)

Montreal

Amherst

St. Lawrence

L. Champlain

Fort Ticonderoga
July 8, 1758

Fort William Henry
Aug. 9, 1757

Fort Frontenac
Aug. 27, 1758

Fort Stanwix

N.H.

L. Ontario

L. Superior

L. Huron

L. Michigan

Fort Niagara
July 25, 1759

Fort Oswego

Albany

MASS.

Boston

N.Y.

CONN.

R.I.

IROQUOIS

L. Erie

Mississippi R.

Detroit

PA.

New York

N.J.

Fort Duquesne
(became Fort Pitt, 1758)

Philadelphia

Braddock's defeat
July 9, 1755

Fort Cumberland

MD.

DEL.

Fort Necessity
July 3, 1754

Ohio Company of Virginia

Ohio R.

APPALACHIAN MOUNTAINS

BRITISH COLONIES

VA.

Williamsburg

ATLANTIC OCEAN

St. Louis

LOUISIANA

NORTH CAROLINA

SOUTH CAROLINA

GEORGIA

Charleston

Savannah

Natchez

SPANISH FLORIDA

St. Augustine

New Orleans

Gulf of Mexico

Legend:

French claims

British claims

Spanish claims

Disputed British-French claims

Disputed British-Spanish claims

British forces

British victory

French victory

Fort

MAP 6.1 European Areas of Influence and the Seven Years' War, 1754–1763

In the mid-eighteenth century, France, Britain, and Spain claimed vast areas of North America, many of them already inhabited by various Indian peoples. The early flash points of the Seven Years' War were in regions of disputed claims where the French had allied with powerful native groups — the Iroquois and the Algonquian tribes — to put pressure on the westward-moving British and Americans.

of manufactured goods for beaver furs. But in the 1740s, aggressive Pennsylvania traders began to infringe on their territory, threatening to reorient Indian loyalties. Adding to the tensions, a group of enterprising Virginians, including the brothers Lawrence and Augustine Washington, formed the Ohio Company in 1747 and advanced on the same land. Their hope for profit lay not in the fur trade but in land speculation, fueled by an exploding Anglo-American population seeking fresh land.

In response to these incursions, the French sent soldiers to build a series of military forts to secure their trade routes and to create a western barrier to American population expansion. In 1753, the royal governor of Virginia, Robert Dinwiddie, himself a shareholder in the Ohio Company, sent a messenger to warn the French that they were trespassing on Virginia land.

The messenger on this dangerous mission was George Washington, younger half-brother of the Ohio Company leaders. Though only twenty-one, Washington was an ambitious youth whose

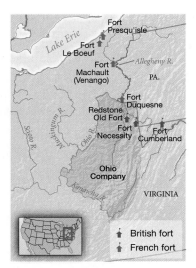

Ohio River Valley, 1753

British fort
French fort

imposing height (six feet two) and air of silent competence convinced the governor he could do the job. The middle child in a family of eight, Washington did not stand to inherit great wealth, so he sought to gain public reputation and impress the Virginia elite by volunteering for this perilous duty.

Washington returned from his mission with crucial intelligence about French military plans. Impressed, Dinwiddie appointed the youth to lead a small military expedition west to assert and, if need be, defend Virginia's claim. Imperial officials in London, concerned about the French fortifications, had authorized the governor "to repell force by force," only if the French attacked first. By early 1754, the French had built Fort Duquesne at the forks of the Ohio River; Washington's assignment was to chase the French away without actually being the aggressor.

In the spring of 1754, Washington set out with 160 Virginians and a small contingent of Mingo Indians, who were also concerned about the French military presence in the Ohio Country. The first battle of what would become known as the French and Indian War occurred early one May morning when the Mingo chief Tanaghrisson led a detachment of Washington's soldiers to a small French encampment in the woods. A brief skirmish left fourteen Frenchmen wounded. While Washington struggled to communicate with the injured French commander, Tanaghrisson and his men intervened to kill and then scalp the wounded soldiers, including the commander, probably with the aim of inflaming hostilities between the French and the colonists.

This sudden massacre violated Washington's instructions to avoid being the aggressor and raised the stakes considerably. Fearing retaliation, Washington ordered his men to fortify their position; the flimsy "Fort Necessity" was the result. Reinforcements amounting to several hundred more Virginians arrived; but the Mingos, sensing disaster and displeased by Washington's style of command, fled. (Tanaghrisson later said, "The Colonel was a good-natured man, but had no experience; he took upon him

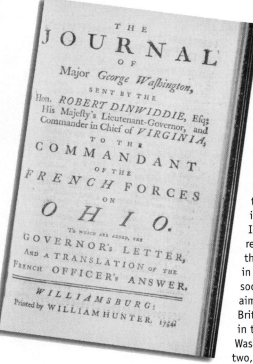

Washington's Journal, 1754
When George Washington returned from his first mission to the French, Governor Dinwiddie asked him to write a full report of what he had seen of the countryside, the Indians, and French troop strength. Washington obliged, writing about seven thousand words in less than two days (roughly equivalent to a twenty-five-page double-spaced paper). He coolly narrated scenes of personal danger: traveling in deep snow and freezing temperatures, falling off a raft into an icy river, and being shot at by a lone Indian. Dinwiddie printed Washington's report, along with his own letter and the French commander's defiant answer, in a thirty-two-page pamphlet that was soon reprinted in London. The governor's aim was to inform Virginians and British leaders about the French threat in the West. But the pamphlet suited Washington's aims as well. At age twenty-two, he became known on both sides of the Atlantic for resolute and rugged courage. Huntington Library.

Chief Hendrick and John Caldwell Dress is a symbol system that conveys status and self-presentation to others. Might it also change the way the dresser thinks about himself or herself? Chief Hendrick (top) worked closely with the British in New York to maintain the trade alliance known as the Covenant Chain. In 1740, when he was sixty, he traveled to England, was presented at the royal court, and sat for this portrait. His red coat, ruffled shirt, three-cornered hat, and cravat are all signs of a well-dressed English gentleman. But Hendrick holds a tomahawk in one hand and wampum in the other, and his long white hair is conspicuously uncurled, unlike an eighteenth-century gent's wig. John Caldwell (bottom) also holds a tomahawk, which goes with his Indian garb: feather headdress, blankets, leggings, and moccasins. During the Revolutionary War, Caldwell was stationed at Fort Detroit, a British garrison that provided aid to tribes in the Ohio Valley battling Americans. Caldwell acquired this outfit for a formal diplomatic mission to the Shawnee Indians in 1780. He took the clothes back to England and wore them for this portrait. Hendrick: Courtesy of the John Carter Brown Library at Brown University; Caldwell: The Board of Trustees of the National Museums & Galleries on Merseyside (King's Regiment Collection).

FOR MORE HELP ANALYZING THIS IMAGE, see the visual activity for this chapter in the Online Study Guide at **bedfordstmartins.com/roarkcompact**.

to command the Indians as his slaves, [and] would by no means take advice from the Indians.") In early July, over six hundred French soldiers aided by one hundred Shawnee and Delaware warriors attacked Fort Necessity, killing or wounding a third of Washington's men. The message was clear: The French would not depart from the disputed territory.

The Albany Congress and Intercolonial Defense Even as Virginians, Frenchmen, and Indians fought and died in the Ohio Country, British imperial leaders hoped to prevent a larger war. One obvious strategy was to strengthen British alliances with seemingly neutral Indian tribes. To this end, British authorities directed the governor of New York to convene a colonial conference.

In June and July 1754, twenty-four delegates from seven colonies met in Albany, New York. Also attending were Indians of the Iroquois Confederacy, an alliance of tribes inhabiting the central and western parts of present-day New York. Albany was the traditional meeting place of the Covenant Chain, first created in 1692 as a trade alliance of New York leaders and Mohawk Indians, the most easterly of the Iroquois Confederacy. In 1753, the aged Mohawk leader Hendrick accused the colonists of breaking the Covenant Chain. A prime goal of the Albany Congress was to repair trade relations with the Mohawk Indians and secure their help—or at least their neutrality—against the French threat.

Two delegates at the congress had more ambitious plans. Benjamin Franklin of Pennsylvania and Thomas Hutchinson of Massachusetts, both rising political stars, coauthored the Albany Plan of Union, a proposal for a unified colonial government limited to war and defense policies. In the course of the meeting, the Albany delegates learned of Washington's defeat at Fort Necessity and understood instantly the escalating risk of war with France; they approved the plan. Key features included a president general appointed by the crown and a

grand council meeting annually to consider questions of war, peace, and trade with the Indians. The writers of the Albany Plan humbly reaffirmed Parliament's authority; this was no bid for enlarged autonomy of the colonies.

To Franklin's surprise, not a single colony approved the Albany Plan. The Massachusetts assembly feared it was "a Design of gaining power over the Colonies," especially the power of taxation. Others objected that it would be impossible to agree on unified policies toward scores of quite different Indian tribes. The British government never backed the Albany Plan either, and soon after it appointed two superintendents of Indian affairs, one for the northern and another for the southern colonies, each with exclusive powers to negotiate treaties, trade, and land sales with all tribes.

The Indians at the Albany Congress were not impressed with the Albany Plan either. The Covenant Chain alliance with the Mohawk tribe was reaffirmed, but the other nations left without pledging to help the British battle the French. At this very early point in the Seven Years' War, the Iroquois figured that the French military presence around the Great Lakes would discourage the westward push of American colonists and therefore better serve their interests.

The War and Its Consequences By 1755, Washington's frontier skirmish had turned into a major mobilization of British and American troops against the French. The British expected a quick victory on three fronts. General Edward Braddock, recently arrived from England, marched his army toward Fort Duquesne in western Pennsylvania. Farther north, British troops moved toward Fort Niagara, critically located between Lakes Erie and Ontario. And William Johnson, a New Yorker recently appointed superintendent of Indian affairs, led forces north toward Lake Champlain, intending to defend the border against the French in Canada (see Map 6.1).

Unfortunately for the British, the French were prepared to fight and had cemented respectful alliances with many Indian tribes throughout the region. In July 1755, Braddock's army of 2,000 British soldiers rode west with Washington and Virginia militiamen (joined by just eight Oneida Indian allies) and were ambushed one day short of Fort Duquesne by 250 French soldiers and 640 Indian warriors. Nearly 1,000 on the British side were killed or wounded, including General Braddock. Washington, who was unhurt, was commended for his bravery and, at the age of twenty-two, was promoted to commander of the Virginia army.

Braddock's defeat stunned British leaders. For the next two years, they stumbled badly, deploying inadequate numbers of troops undersupplied by reluctant colonial assemblies. What finally turned the war around was the rise to power in 1757 of **William Pitt**, Britain's prime minister, a man willing to commit massive resources to fight France and its ally Spain worldwide. In America, British troops aided by American soldiers captured Forts Duquesne, Niagara, and Ticonderoga and then the French cities of Quebec and finally Montreal, all from 1758 to 1760.

The American colonists rejoiced, but the war expanded globally, with battles in the Caribbean, Austria, Prussia, and India. The British captured the French sugar islands Martinique and Guadeloupe and then invaded Spanish Cuba with an army of some four thousand provincial soldiers from New York and New England. By the end of 1762, France and Spain capitulated, and the Treaty of Paris was signed in 1763.

The triumph was sweet but short-lived. The complex peace negotiations stopped short of providing Britain with the full spoils of victory. Britain gained control of Canada, eliminating the French threat from the north. British and American title to the eastern half of North America, precisely what Britain had claimed before the war, was confirmed. But all French territory west of the Mississippi River, including New Orleans, was transferred to Spain as compensation for Spain's assistance to France during the war. Stranger still, Cuba was returned to Spain, and Martinique and Guadeloupe were returned to France (Map 6.2).

In truth, the French islands in the Caribbean were hardly a threat to Americans, for they provided a profitable trade in smuggled molasses. The main threat to the colonists came from the Indians, ignored by the Treaty of Paris. With the French gone, the Indians lost the advantage of having two opponents to play off against each other, and they now had to cope with the westward-moving Americans. Indian policy would soon become a serious point of contention between the British government and the colonists.

The British credited the mighty British army for their victory, while criticizing the inadequate and ungrateful support of the colonists. Fueling resentment, colonial smugglers kept up a lively trade in beaver pelts with French fur traders and an illegal molasses trade in the Caribbean. American traders, grumbled the British leaders, were really traitors. William Pitt was convinced that the illegal trade "principally, if not alone, enabled France to sustain and protract this long and expensive war."

Colonists read the lessons of the war differently. American soldiers had turned out in force, they claimed, but had been relegated to grunt work by arrogant British leaders and subjected to unexpectedly harsh military discipline, ranging from floggings to executions. General Braddock bragged to Benjamin Franklin that "these savages may, indeed, be a formidable enemy to your raw American militia, but upon the king's regular and disciplined troops, sir, it is impossible they should make any impression." Braddock's defeat "gave us Americans," Franklin wrote, "the first suspicion that our exalted ideas of the prowess of British regulars had not been well founded."

The human costs of the war were etched especially sharply in the minds of New England colonists. About one-third of all Massachusetts men between fifteen and thirty had seen service. Many families lost loved ones; the Cuban invasion alone cost the lives of some two thousand Americans.

The enormous expense of the war caused by Pitt's no-holds-barred military strategy cast another huge shadow over the victory. By 1763, Britain's national debt, double what it had been when Pitt took office, posed a formidable challenge to the next decade of leadership in Britain.

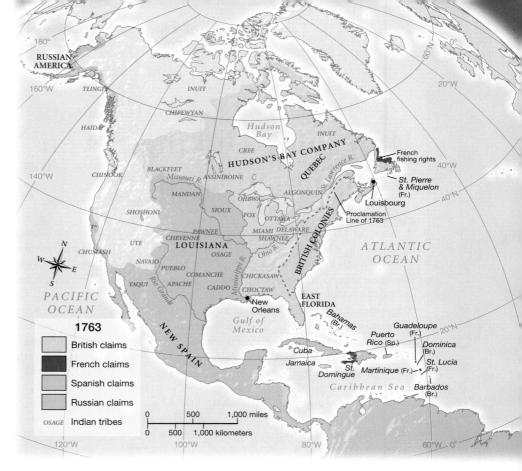

1763

- British claims
- French claims
- Spanish claims
- Russian claims
- *OSAGE* Indian tribes

MAP 6.2 Europe Redraws the Map of North America, 1763

In the peace treaty of 1763, France ceded to Britain its interior territory from Quebec to New Orleans, retaining fishing rights in the far north and several sugar islands in the Caribbean. France transferred to Spain its claim to extensive territory west of the Mississippi River.

READING THE MAP: Who actually lived on and controlled the lands ceded by France? In what sense, if any, did Britain or Spain own these large territories?

CONNECTIONS: What was the goal of the Proclamation of 1763? Could it ever have worked?

FOR MORE HELP ANALYZING THIS MAP, see the map activity for this chapter in the Online Study Guide at bedfordstmartins.com/roarkcompact.

British Leadership, Pontiac's Uprising, and the Proclamation of 1763

In 1760, in the middle of the Seven Years' War, twenty-two-year-old **George III** came to the British throne. Timid and insecure, the new king made his tutor, the Earl of Bute, an outsider to power circles in London, the head of his cabinet of ministers. Bute committed blunders and did not last long, but he made one significant decision—to keep a standing army in the colonies after the war. In both financial and political terms, this was a costly move.

The ostensible reason for stationing British troops in America was to maintain the peace between the colonists and the Indians. This was not a misplaced concern. The withdrawal of the French from North America had left their Indian allies—who did not accept defeat—in a state of alarm. Just three months after the Treaty of Paris was signed in 1763, **Pontiac**, chief of the Ottawa tribe in the northern Ohio region, attacked the British garrison near Detroit. Six more attacks on

forts quickly followed, and frontier settlements were also raided by nearly a dozen tribes from western New York, the Ohio Valley, and the Great Lakes region. By the fall, every fort west of Detroit had been captured; more than four hundred British soldiers were dead and another two thousand colonists killed or taken captive. Pontiac's uprising was quelled in December 1763 by the combined efforts of British and colonial soldiers, but tensions remained high. (See "Historical Question," page 136.)

To minimize the violence, the British government issued the **Proclamation of 1763**, forbidding colonists to settle west of the Appalachian Mountains. The Proclamation chiefly aimed to separate Indians and settlers,

Pontiac's Uprising, 1763

How Long Did the Seven Years' War Last in Indian Country?

France had been defeated on the North American continent in 1761, and the Peace of Paris officially ended the global war between France and Britain in 1763. But there was no lasting peace for the Indian nations of the Ohio Valley and Great Lakes region. In 1761, a Chippewa chief named Minavavana clearly explained the reasons in an ominous speech delivered to a British trader at Fort Michilimackinac, a British outpost that guarded the Straits of Mackinac where Lakes Huron and Michigan meet. "Englishman," he said, "although you have conquered the French, you have not yet conquered us! We are not your slaves. These lakes, these woods and mountains were left to us by our ancestors. They are our inheritance; and we will part with them to none." Furthermore, Minavavana pointedly noted, "your king has never sent us any presents, nor entered into any treaty with us, wherefore he and we are still at war; and until he does these things we must consider that we have no other father, nor friend, among the white men than the King of France."

Minavavana and other Indians of the region had cause to be alarmed. With the exit of the French, British regiments took over the French-built forts all over the old Northwest. Fort Duquesne, renamed Fort Pitt in honor of the British leader who had authorized the war-winning strategy, underwent two years of fortification. No one could mistake the new walls—sixty feet thick at their base, ten at the top—for the external facade of a friendly fur trading post. Nonmilitary Americans were moving into Fort Pitt's neighborhood, too, complicating matters.

Minavavana's complaint about the lack of British presents was a far more serious problem than the British military leaders thought. Gifts exchanged in Indian culture cemented social relationships; they symbolized honor and established obligation. Over many decades, the French had mastered the subtleties of gift exchange, distributing clothing, textiles, and hats and receiving in return calumets (ornamented ceremonial pipe stems) as symbols of friendship. The British military leaders, new to the practice, often discarded the calumets as trivial trinkets, thereby insulting the givers. Major General Jeffery Amherst was sometimes willing to offer gifts to particular Indian leaders, positioning the "gift" as a bribe in the British frame of reference. But Amherst saw extensive gift exchange as demeaning to the British, forcing them to pay tribute to people whom he considered inferior. "It is

not my intention ever to attempt to gain the friendship of Indians by presents," Amherst declared. The Indian view was the opposite: Generous givers expressed dominance and protection, not subordination, in the act of giving. Sir William Johnson, superintendent of Indian affairs, warned Amherst that he was insulting the Indians, but the imperious Amherst would not listen.

A religious revival in 1760–1761, fueled by prophetic visions, greatly enhanced the prospects of frontier war in the old Northwest. The new spiritual message was delivered by a Delaware leader named Neolin in the upper Ohio Valley. Neolin predicted a swift decline for all the tribes unless they altered their ways; gave up quarreling with each other; shunned trade in guns, alcohol, and other trade goods; and curbed their overkilling of animals for the pelt trade. Neolin's preachings spread quickly, gaining credence as the British bungled diplomacy and American settlers continued to penetrate western lands.

A renewal of commitment to Indian ways and the formation of tribal alliances led to open warfare in 1763, called (by the British) Pontiac's Rebellion. (The Indians would not have credited Pontiac with sole leadership. In its impressive and coordinated extent, the war was the work of many men.) Amherst, never a shrewd observer of Indian relations, flatly declared in April 1763 that reports of impending attack were "Meer Bugbears." By mid-May, the British commander at Detroit knew the threat was real. Pontiac, chief of the Ottawas, along with Potawatomi and Huron warriors, attacked Fort Detroit and laid siege for two months. In late May, within two weeks of Pontiac's first move, Forts Sandusky, St. Joseph, Miami, and Ouiatenon were captured by Indians, all through ruses in which Indians pretending to have peaceful business gained entry to the garrisons. Far north at Fort Michilimackinac, Ojibwas engaged in their regular sporting event, a form of lacrosse, outside the fort. After several hours of strenuous play, the ball landed near the fort's open gate, and the enthralled British spectators realized too late that the convergence of players on the ball was really a rush of warriors into the fort. The players seized tomahawks that had been hidden under blankets worn by Indian women on the sidelines. Michilimackinac fell to Ojibwa control.

By the end of June, thirteen British garrisons had either fallen or been evacuated under threat of attack. Yet the three most important forts besieged by Indians—Detroit, Niagara, and Pitt—were kept by the British. At Fort Pitt, two ostensibly friendly Delaware Indians showed up at the end of May to suggest that the British should leave to avoid attack. Fort Pitt's commander thanked them but declined their suggestion, then sent them on their way with his idea of a gift: two blankets and a handkerchief, lately used by British smallpox patients in the fort. "We hope it will have the desired effect," wrote a militiaman whose diary is the source for this story. Two months later, in July, Amherst suggested to a subordinate that spreading smallpox should be considered as a method of war: "We must use Every Stratagem in our Power to Reduce them." Annihilating the Indians was his ultimate goal; he did not flinch from what a later age would call germ or poison warfare. There is no evidence that the infected blankets actually propagated smallpox or that Amherst's suggestion was put into effect.

From late summer through the early months of 1764, Indian country was the scene of bloodshed. Indians targeted British supply routes and civilian settlements, resulting in several thousand deaths. Not all of the attacks came from Indians. In one unique event in December 1763, some fifty Pennsylvania vigilantes known as the Paxton Boys descended on a peaceful village of Conestoga Indians—friendly Indians, not very far west into Pennsylvania—and murdered and scalped twenty of them. The vigilantes, now numbering five hundred and out to make war on all Indians, marched on Philadelphia to try to capture and murder some Christian Indians held in protective custody there. British troops prevented that, but the Paxton Boys escaped punishment for their murderous attack on the Conestoga village.

In 1764, the rebellion faded. The Indians were short on ammunition; the British were tired and broke. Amherst's superiors in Britain blamed him for mishandling the conflict, and when he was recalled home, his own soldiers toasted his departure. A new military leader, Thomas Gage, took command and made good on the advice of William Johnson by distributing gifts profusely among the Indians.

Was the Seven Years' War finally over for the Indians ten years after it started? If 1764 represents an end, it was only a brief one. Periodic raids and killings punctuated the rest of the 1760s and early 1770s, climaxing in the late 1770s as Indians joined the British to fight the Americans in the Revolutionary War. Warfare and massacres extended from New England and New York down to South Carolina and Georgia, especially in the Ohio Country. The American Revolution eventually ended, at least the war between the British and the Americans, but the frontier war continued on and off until 1815, when the War of 1812 ended. Perhaps from the Indians' point of view, the Seven Years' War could be called the Sixty-One Years' War.

★ **Subduing Pontiac's Uprising** As the Indian revolt of 1763–1764 weakened, British colonel Henry Bouquet took his 1,500-man army deep into the Ohio Country to threaten and subdue the Shawnee, Delaware, and Mingo tribes. Among his soldiers was one Thomas Hutchins, a cartographer from New Jersey, who produced a detailed topographical map of the region, with this illustration in one corner. The British flag waves over Bouquet's encampment, and one tent is opened for the treaty negotiation. Bouquet and his aides command the table and chairs in the tent, while the Indians sit on a log or on the ground. Note the soldier in a kilt with a gun and sword; five hundred Scottish Highlanders were part of Bouquet's force. Attention is focused on the man standing by the fire, whose hand gestures suggest that he is speaking. Another Indian smokes a calumet pipe, a symbol of peacemaking. A third, on the log, appears to weep. Bouquet demanded the return of all captives taken by these tribes since the start of the Seven Years' War in exchange for his promise to spare Indian villages from further attack. He took two hostages from each tribe, to be held at Fort Pitt until all the captives were returned. In all, close to three hundred white captives were released. William L. Clements Library.

Silver Medal to Present to Indians After Pontiac's uprising ended, the British attempted to mend relations with the insurgent Indians by honoring them with gifts. This silver medal, minted in 1766, displays a profile of King George III on the front and a cozy depiction of an Indian and a Briton smoking a peace pipe on the back. The Latin words on the front announce George's name, title, and kingly dominions. Both this inscription and the English words on the back would have been equally unintelligible to the recipients of the gift. Imagine a conversation between an Indian chief and an English translator who tried to explain what the slogan HAPPY WHILE UNITED might mean. The scene depicted — two men with relaxed, friendly body language — illustrates HAPPY and UNITED. The WHILE, conveying a sense of temporariness and contingency, might have been trickier to explain. Why? The American Numismatic Society.

but it also limited trade with Indians to traders licensed by colonial governors, and it forbade private sales of Indian land. The Proclamation's language took care not to identify western lands as belonging to the Indians. Instead, it spoke of Indians "who live under our protection" on lands that "are reserved to them, as their Hunting Grounds." Other parts of the Proclamation of 1763 referred to American and even French colonists in Canada as "our loving subjects," entitled to English rights and privileges. The Indians were not described as British subjects.

The 1763 boundary proved impossible to enforce. Surging population growth had already sent many hundreds of settlers west of the Appalachians, and land speculators, such as those of Virginia's Ohio Company, had no desire to lose opportunities for profitable resale of their land grants. Bute's decision to post a standing army in the colonies was thus a cause for concern among western settlers, eastern speculators, and Indian tribes alike.

Q: How did the Seven Years' War erode relations between colonists and British authorities?

The Sugar and Stamp Acts, 1763–1765

Lord Bute lost power in 1763, and the young King George turned to a succession of leaders throughout the 1760s, searching for a prime minister he could trust. A half dozen ministers in seven years took turns dealing with one basic,

underlying British reality: A huge war debt needed to be serviced, and the colonists, as British subjects, should help pay it off. To many Americans, however, that proposition seemed in deep violation of what they perceived to be their rights and liberties as British subjects, and it created resentment that eventually erupted in large-scale street protests. The first provocative revenue acts were the work of Sir George Grenville, prime minister from 1763 to 1765.

Grenville's Sugar Act To find revenue, George Grenville scrutinized the customs service, which monitored the shipping trade and collected all import and export duties. Grenville found that the salaries of customs officers cost the government four times what was collected in revenue. The shortfall was due in part to bribery and smuggling, so Grenville began to insist on rigorous attention to paperwork and a strict accounting of collected duties.

The hardest duty to enforce was the one imposed by the Molasses Act of 1733 — a stiff tax of six pence per gallon on any molasses purchased from non-British sources. The purpose of the tax was to discourage trade with French Caribbean islands and redirect the molasses trade to British sugar islands, but it did not work. French molasses remained cheap and abundant because French planters on Martinique and Guadeloupe had no use for it. A by-product of sugar production, molasses was a key ingredient in rum, a drink the French scorned. Rum-loving Americans were eager to buy French molasses, and they had ignored the tax law for decades.

George Grenville, Prime Minister 1763–1765 George Grenville was a thrifty man. He worked for years in the British treasury and navy departments, banking his salary and living off the interest. His argumentative style often annoyed other politicians. He gained the prime minister's job in 1763 at a point when King George was short of competent alternatives, but the king found him irksome: "When he has wearied me for two hours, he looks at his watch, to see if he may not tire me for an hour more," King George said. The king sacked him in July 1765 for being insolent, not for his controversial colonial policies. The Earl of Halifax, Garrowby, Yorkshire.

Grenville's ingenious solution was the **Revenue Act** of 1764, popularly dubbed the **Sugar Act**. It lowered the duty on French molasses to three pence, making it more attractive for shippers to obey the law, and at the same time raised penalties for smuggling. The act appeared to be in the tradition of navigation acts meant to regulate trade, but Grenville's actual intent was to raise revenue. He was using an established form of law for new ends and accomplishing his goal by the novel means of lowering a duty.

The Sugar Act toughened enforcement policies. From now on, all British naval crews could act as impromptu customs officers, boarding suspicious ships and seizing cargoes found to be in violation. Smugglers caught without proper paperwork would be prosecuted, not in a local court with a friendly jury but in a vice admiralty court located in Nova Scotia, where a single judge presided. The implication was that justice would be sure and severe.

Grenville's hopes for the Sugar Act did not materialize. The small decrease in duty did not offset the attractions of smuggling, while the increased vigilance in enforcement led to several ugly confrontations in port cities. Reaction to the Sugar Act foreshadowed questions about Britain's right to tax Americans, but in 1764 objections to the act came principally from Americans in the shipping trades.

From the British point of view, the Proclamation of 1763 and the Sugar Act seemed to be reasonable efforts to administer the colonies. To the Americans, however, the British supervision appeared to be a disturbing intrusion into colonial practices.

The Stamp Act By his second year in office, Grenville had made almost no dent in the national debt. So in February 1765, he escalated his revenue program with the **Stamp Act**, precipitating a major conflict between Britain and the colonies over Parliament's right to tax. The Stamp Act imposed a tax on all paper used for official documents—newspapers, pamphlets, court documents, licenses, wills, ships' cargo lists—and required an affixed stamp as proof that the tax had been paid. Unlike the Sugar Act, which regulated trade, the Stamp Act was designed plainly and simply to raise money. It affected nearly everyone who used any taxed paper but, most of all, users of official documents in the business and legal communities.

Grenville was no fool. Anticipating that the stamp tax would be unpopular—Thomas Hutchinson had forewarned him—he delegated the administration of the act to Americans to avoid taxpayer hostility toward British enforcers. In each colony, local stamp distributors would be hired at a handsome salary of 8 percent of the revenue collected.

English tradition held that taxes were a gift of the people to their monarch, granted by the people's representatives. This view of taxes as a freely given gift preserved an essential concept of English political theory: the idea that citizens have the liberty to enjoy and use their property without fear of confiscation. The king could not demand money; only the House of Commons could grant it. Grenville agreed with the notion of taxation by consent, but he argued that the colonists were already "virtually" represented in Parliament. The House of Commons, he insisted, represented all British subjects, wherever they were.

Colonial leaders emphatically rejected this view, arguing that **virtual representation** could not withstand the stretch across the Atlantic. The stamp tax itself, levied by a distant Parliament on unwilling colonies, illustrated the problem. In the words of a Maryland lawyer, virtual representation was "a mere cob-web, spread to catch the unwary, and entangle the weak."

Resistance Strategies and Crowd Politics

News of the Stamp Act arrived in the colonies in April 1765, seven months before it was to take effect. There was time, therefore, to object. Governors were unlikely to challenge the law, for most of them owed their office to the king. Instead, the colonial assemblies took the lead; eight of them held discussions on the Stamp Act.

Virginia's assembly, the House of Burgesses, was the first. At the end of its May session, after two-thirds of the members had left, **Patrick Henry**, a young political newcomer, presented a series of resolutions on the Stamp Act that were debated and passed, one by one. They became known as the **Virginia Resolves**. Henry's resolutions inched the assembly toward radical opposition to the Stamp Act. The first three stated the obvious: that Virginians were British citizens, that they enjoyed the same rights and privileges as Britons, and that

self-taxation was one of those rights. The fourth resolution noted that Virginians had always taxed themselves, through their representatives in the House of Burgesses. The fifth took a radical leap by pushing the other four unexceptional statements to one logical conclusion—that the Virginia assembly alone had the right to tax Virginians.

Two more fiery resolutions were debated as Henry pressed the logic of his case to the extreme. The sixth resolution denied legitimacy to any tax law originating outside Virginia, and a seventh boldly called anyone who disagreed with these propositions an enemy of Virginia. This was too much for the other representatives. They voted down resolutions six and seven and later rescinded their vote on number five as well.

Their caution hardly mattered, however, because newspapers in other colonies printed all seven Virginia Resolves, creating the impression that a daring first challenge to the Stamp Act had occurred. Consequently, other assemblies were willing to consider even more radical questions, such as this: By what authority could Parliament legislate for the colonies without also taxing them? No one disagreed, in 1765, that Parliament had legislative power over the colonists, who were, after all, British subjects. Several assemblies advanced the argument that there was a distinction between *external* taxes, imposed to regulate trade, and *internal* taxes, such as a stamp tax or a property tax, which could only be self-imposed.

Reaction to the Stamp Act ran far deeper than political debate in assemblies. Every person whose livelihood required official paper had to decide whether to comply with the act. There were only three options: boycotting, which was within the law but impractical because of the reliance on paper; defying the law and using unstamped paper; or preventing distribution of the stamps at the source before the law took effect, thus ensuring universal noncompliance.

The first organized resistance to the Stamp Act began in Boston in August 1765 under the direction of town leaders, chief among them **Samuel Adams**, John Hancock, and Ebenezer Mackintosh. The first two, both Harvard graduates, were town officers. Adams, in his forties, had shrewd political instincts and a gift for organizing. Hancock, though not yet thirty, had recently inherited his uncle's shipping business and was one of the wealthiest men in Massachusetts. Mackintosh, the same age as Hancock, was a shoemaker and highly experienced street activist. Many other artisans, tradesmen, printers, tavern keepers, dockworkers, and sailors—the middling and lower orders—mobilized in resistance to the Stamp Act, taking the name "Sons of Liberty."

Newspapers Protest the Stamp Act The Stamp Act affected newspaper publishers more than any other businessmen. From New Hampshire to South Carolina, papers issued on October 31, 1765, used dark black mourning lines and funereal language to herald the date the Stamp Act went into effect. The editor of the *Pennsylvania Journal*, a Son of Liberty in Philadelphia, designed his paper to look like a tombstone, with coffins and skulls throughout its four pages. A New Hampshire editor dramatically declared, "I must Die, or Submit to that which is worse than Death, Be Stamped, and lose my Freedom." All colonial newspapers resumed publication within a week or two, defiantly operating without stamps. One stampless New Haven, Connecticut, editor wrote, "The press is the test of truth, the bulwark of public safety, the guardian of freedom." Library of Congress.

The plan hatched in Boston called for a large street demonstration highlighting a mock execution designed to convince Andrew Oliver, the designated stamp distributor, to resign. On August 14, 1765, a crowd of two to three thousand demonstrators, led by Mackintosh, hung an effigy of Oliver in a tree and then paraded it around town before finally beheading and burning it. In hopes of calming tensions, the royal governor Francis Bernard took no action. The flesh-and-blood Oliver stayed in hiding; the next day he resigned his office in a well-publicized announcement. The Sons of Liberty were elated.

The demonstration provided lessons for everyone. Oliver learned that stamp distributors would be very unpopular people. Francis Bernard, the royal governor, learned the limitations of his power to govern, with no police force to call on. The demonstration's leaders learned that street action was effective. And hundreds of ordinary men not only learned what the Stamp Act was all about but also gained pride in their ability to have a decisive impact on politics.

Twelve days later, a second crowd action showed how well these lessons had been learned. On August 26, a crowd visited the houses of three detested customs and court officials, breaking windows and raiding wine cellars. A fourth target was the finest dwelling in Massachusetts, owned by the stiff-necked Thomas Hutchinson. Rumors abounded that Hutchinson had urged Grenville to adopt the Stamp Act. Although he had actually done the opposite, Hutchinson refused to set the record straight, saying curtly, "I am not obliged to give an answer to all the questions that may be put me by every lawless person." The crowd attacked his house, and by daybreak only the exterior walls were standing. Governor Bernard gave orders to call out the militia, but he was told that many militiamen were among the crowd.

The destruction of Hutchinson's house brought a temporary halt to protest activities in Boston. The town meeting issued a statement of sympathy for Hutchinson, but a large reward for the arrest and conviction of rioters failed to produce a single lead. Essentially, the opponents of the Stamp Act in Boston had triumphed; no one replaced Oliver as distributor. When the act took effect on November 1, ships without stamped permits continued to clear the harbor. Since he could not bring the lawbreakers to court, Hutchinson, ever principled, felt obliged to resign his office as chief justice. He remained lieutenant governor, however, and within five years he became the royal governor.

Liberty and Property Boston's crowd actions of August sparked similar eruptions by groups calling themselves Sons of Liberty in nearly fifty towns throughout the colonies, and stamp distributors everywhere hastened to resign. One Connecticut distributor was forced by a crowd to throw his hat and powdered wig in the air while shouting a cheer for "Liberty and property!" This man fared better than another Connecticut stamp agent who was nearly buried alive by Sons of Liberty. Only when the thuds of dirt sounded on his coffin did he have a sudden change of heart, shouting out his resignation to the crowd above. Luckily, he was heard. In Charleston, South Carolina, the stamp distributor resigned after crowds burned effigies and chanted "Liberty! Liberty!"

Some colonial leaders, disturbed by the riots, sought a more moderate challenge to parliamentary authority. Twenty-seven delegates representing nine colonial assemblies met in New York City in October 1765 as the **Stamp Act Congress**. For two weeks, the men hammered out a petition about taxation addressed to the king and Parliament. Their statement closely resembled the first five Virginia Resolves, claiming that taxes were "free gifts of the people," which only the people's representatives could give. They dismissed virtual representation: "The people of these colonies are not, and from their local circumstances, cannot be represented in the House of Commons." At the same time, the delegates carefully affirmed their subordination to

Teapots for Patriots Colonists could purchase commemorative teapots to celebrate the repeal of the Stamp Act. The one heralding AMERICA: LIBERTY RESTORED proclaims NO STAMP ACT on the back. Both of these pots were British imports. Can you think of any reason why a British pottery manufacturer might also have celebrated the repeal of the Stamp Act? Do you think one or both of these teapots might have found a market in Britain, too? Remember that in 1765, teapots were just teapots; the symbolic significance of tea lay several years in the future. During the political struggles over tea in 1770–1774, no British manufacturer is known to have made a souvenir teapot for the American market. Stamp Act Repeal'd: Peabody Essex Museum, Salem, Massachusetts; Liberty Restored: Northeast Auctions, Portsmouth, New Hampshire.

Parliament and monarch in deferential language. Nevertheless, the Stamp Act Congress, by the mere fact of its meeting, advanced a radical potential—the notion of intercolonial political action.

The rallying cry of "Liberty and property" made perfect sense to many white Americans of all social ranks, who feared that the Stamp Act threatened their traditional right to liberty as British subjects. The liberty in question was the right to be taxed only by representative government. "Liberty and property" came from a trinity of concepts—"life, liberty, property"—that had come to be regarded as the birthright of freeborn British subjects since at least the seventeenth century. A powerful tradition of British political thought invested representative government with the duty to protect individual lives, liberties, and property against potential abuse by royal authority. Up to 1765, Americans had consented to accept Parliament as a body that represented them. But now, in this matter of taxation via stamps, Parliament seemed a distant body that had failed to protect Americans' liberty and property against royal authority.

Alarmed, some Americans began to speak and write about a plot by British leaders to enslave them. A Maryland writer warned that if the colonies lost "the right of exemption from all taxes without their consent," that loss would "deprive them of every privilege distinguishing freemen from slaves." The opposite meanings of *liberty* and *slavery* were utterly clear to white Americans, but they stopped short of applying similar logic to the half million black Americans they held in bondage. Many blacks, however, could see the contradiction. When a crowd of Charleston blacks paraded with shouts of "Liberty!" just a few months after white Sons of Liberty had done the same, the town militia turned out to break up the demonstration.

Politicians and merchants in Britain reacted with distress to the American demonstrations and petitions. Merchants particularly feared trade disruptions and pressured Parliament to repeal the Stamp Act. By late 1765, yet another new minister, the Marquess of Rockingham, headed the king's cabinet and sought a way to repeal the act without losing face. The solution came in March 1766: The Stamp Act was repealed, but with the repeal came the **Declaratory Act**, which asserted Parliament's right to legislate for the colonies "in all cases whatsoever." Perhaps the stamp tax had been inexpedient, but the power to tax—one prime case of a legislative power—was stoutly upheld.

Q: **Why did the Sugar Act and the Stamp Act draw fierce opposition from colonists?**

The Townshend Acts and Economic Retaliation, 1767–1770

Rockingham did not last long as prime minister. By the summer of 1766, George III had persuaded William Pitt to resume that position. Pitt appointed Charles Townshend to be chancellor of the exchequer, the chief financial minister. Facing both the old war debt and the continuing cost of stationing British troops in America, Townshend turned again to taxation. But his knowledge of the changing political climate in the colonies was limited, and his plan to raise revenue touched off coordinated boycotts of British goods in 1768 and 1769. Even women were politicized as self-styled "Daughters of Liberty." Boston led the uproar, causing the British to send peacekeeping soldiers to assist the royal governor. The stage was thus set for the first fatalities in the brewing revolution.

The Townshend Duties Townshend proposed new taxes in the old form of a navigation act. Officially called the Revenue Act of 1767, it established new duties on tea, glass, lead, paper, and painters' colors imported into the colonies, to be paid by the importer but passed on to consumers in the retail price. A year before, the duty on French molasses had been reduced from three pence to one pence per gallon, and finally the Sugar Act was pulling in a tidy revenue of about £45,000 annually. Townshend naively assumed that external taxes on transatlantic trade would be acceptable to Americans.

The **Townshend duties** were not especially burdensome, but the principle they embodied—taxation through trade duties—looked different to the colonists in the wake of the Stamp Act crisis. Although Americans once distinguished between external and internal taxes, accepting external duties as a means to direct the flow of trade, that distinction was wiped out by an external tax meant only to raise money. John Dickinson, a Philadelphia lawyer, articulated this view in a series of articles titled *Letters from a Farmer in Pennsylvania*, widely circulated in late 1767. "We are taxed without our consent. . . . We are therefore—SLAVES," Dickinson wrote, calling for "a total denial of the power of Parliament to lay upon these colonies any 'tax' whatever."

A controversial provision of the Townshend duties directed that some of the revenue generated would pay the salaries of royal governors. Before 1767, local assemblies set the salaries of their own officials, giving them significant influence over crown-appointed officeholders. Townshend wanted to strengthen the governors' position as well as to curb the growing independence of the assemblies.

Massachusetts again took the lead in protesting the Townshend duties. Samuel Adams, now an elected member of the provincial assembly, argued that any form of parliamentary taxation was unjust because Americans were not represented in Parliament. Further, he argued that the new way to pay governors' salaries subverted the proper relationship between the people and their rulers. The assembly circulated a letter with Adams's arguments to other colonial assemblies for their endorsement. As with the Stamp Act Congress of 1765, colonial assemblies were starting to coordinate their protests.

In response to Adams's letter, the new man in charge of colonial affairs in Britain, Lord Hillsborough, instructed Massachusetts governor Bernard to dissolve the assembly if it refused to repudiate the letter. The assembly refused, by a vote of 92 to 17, and Bernard carried out his instruction. In the summer of 1768, Boston was in an uproar.

Nonconsumption and the Daughters of Liberty The Boston town meeting led the way with **nonconsumption agreements** calling for a boycott of all British-made goods. Dozens of other towns passed similar resolutions in 1767 and 1768. For example, prohibited purchases in the town of New Haven, Connecticut, included carriages, furniture, hats, clothing, lace, clocks, and textiles. The idea was to encourage home manufacture and to hurt trade, causing London merchants to pressure Parliament for repeal of the duties.

Nonconsumption agreements were very hard to enforce. With the Stamp Act, there was one hated item, a stamp, and a limited number of official distributors. In contrast, an agreement to boycott all British goods required serious personal sacrifice. Some merchants were wary because it hurt their pocketbooks, and a few continued to import in readiness for the end of nonconsumption (or to sell on the side to people choosing to ignore boycotts). In Boston, such merchants found themselves blacklisted in newspapers and broadsides. A more direct blow to trade came from nonimportation agreements, but getting merchants to agree to these proved more difficult, due to fears that merchants in other colonies might continue to import goods and make handsome profits. Not until late 1768 could Boston merchants agree to suspend trade through a nonimportation agreement lasting one year starting January 1, 1769. Sixty signed the agreement. New York merchants soon followed suit, as did Philadelphia and Charleston merchants in 1769.

Edenton Tea Ladies American women in many communities renounced British apparel and tea during the early 1770s. Women in Edenton, North Carolina, publicized their pledge and drew hostile fire in the form of a British cartoon. The cartoon's message is that brazen women who meddled in politics would undermine their femininity. Neglected babies, urinating dogs, wanton sexuality, and mean-looking women would be some of the dire consequences, according to the artist. The cartoon works as humor for the British because of the gender reversals it predicts and because of the insult it directs at American men. Library of Congress.

Doing without British products, whether luxury goods, tea, or textiles, no doubt was a hardship. But it also presented an opportunity, for many of the British products specified in nonconsumption agreements were household goods traditionally under the control of the "ladies." By 1769, male leaders in the patriot cause clearly understood that women's cooperation in nonconsumption and home manufacture was beneficial to their cause. The Townshend duties thus provided an unparalleled opportunity for encouraging female patriotism. During the Stamp Act crisis, Sons of Liberty took to the streets in protest. During the difficulties of 1768 and 1769, the concept of

Daughters of Liberty emerged to give shape to a new idea—that women might play a role in public affairs. Any woman could express affiliation with the colonial protest through conspicuous boycotts of British-made goods. In Boston, more than three hundred women signed a petition to abstain from tea, "sickness excepted," in order to "save this abused Country from Ruin and Slavery." A nine-year-old girl visiting the royal governor's house in New Jersey took the tea she was offered, curtsied, and tossed the beverage out a nearby window.

Homespun cloth became a prominent symbol of patriotism. A young Boston girl learning to spin called herself "a daughter of liberty," noting that "I chuse to wear as much of our own manufactory as pocible." In the boycott period of 1768 to 1770, newspapers reported on spinning matches, or bees, in some sixty New England towns, in which women came together in public to make yarn. Nearly always, the bee was held at the local minister's house, and the yarn produced was charitably handed over to him for distribution to the poor. Newspaper accounts variously called the spinners "Daughters of Liberty" or "Daughters of Industry."

> Homespun cloth became a prominent symbol of patriotism. A young Boston girl learning to spin called herself "a daughter of liberty," noting that "I chuse to wear as much of our own manufactory as pocible."

This surge of public spinning was related to the politics of the boycott, which infused traditional women's work with new political purpose. But the women spinners were not equivalents of the Sons of Liberty. The Sons marched in streets, burned effigies, threatened hated officials, and celebrated anniversaries of their successes with raucous drinking in taverns. The Daughters manifested their patriotism quietly, in ways marked by piety, industry, and charity. The difference was due in part to cultural ideals of gender, which prized masculine self-assertion and feminine selflessness. It also was due to class. The Sons were a cross-class alliance, with leaders from the middling orders reliant on men and boys of the lower ranks to fuel their crowds. The Daughters dusting off spinning wheels and shelving their teapots were genteel ladies used to buying British goods. The difference between the Sons and Daughters also speaks to two views of how best to challenge authority: violent threats and street actions, or the self-disciplined, self-sacrificing boycott of goods?

On the whole, the anti-British boycotts were a success. Imports fell by more than 40 percent; British merchants felt the pinch and let Parliament

know it. In Boston, the Hutchinson family also endured losses, but even more alarming to the lieutenant governor, Boston seemed overrun with anti-British sentiment. The Sons of Liberty staged annual rollicking celebrations of the Stamp Act riot, and both Hutchinson and Governor Bernard concluded that British troops were necessary to restore order.

Military Occupation and "Massacre" in Boston In the fall of 1768, three thousand uniformed troops arrived to occupy Boston. The soldiers drilled conspicuously on the Common, played loud music on the Sabbath, and in general grated on the nerves of Bostonians. Although the situation was frequently tense, no major troubles occurred that winter and through most of 1769. But as January 1, 1770, approached, marking the end of the nonimportation agreement, it was clear that some merchants—such as Thomas Hutchinson's two sons, both importers—were ready to break the boycott.

Trouble began in January, when a crowd defaced the door of the Hutchinson brothers' shop with "Hillsborough paint," a potent mixture of human excrement and urine. In February, a crowd surrounded the house of customs official Ebenezer Richardson, who panicked and fired a musket, accidentally killing a young boy passing on the street. The Sons of Liberty mounted a massive funeral procession to mark this first instance of violent death in the struggle with Britain.

For the next week, tension gripped Boston. The climax came on Monday evening, March 5, 1770, when a crowd taunted eight British soldiers guarding the customs house. Onlookers threw snowballs and rocks and dared the soldiers to fire; finally one did. After a short pause, someone yelled "Fire!" and the other soldiers shot into the crowd, hitting eleven men, killing five of them.

The **Boston Massacre**, as the event quickly became called, was over in minutes. In the immediate aftermath, Hutchinson (now acting governor after Bernard's recall to Britain) showed courage in addressing the crowd from the balcony of the statehouse. He quickly removed the regiments to an island in the harbor to prevent further bloodshed, and he jailed Captain Thomas Preston and his eight soldiers for their own protection, promising they would be held for trial.

The Sons of Liberty staged elaborate martyrs' funerals for the five victims. Significantly, the one nonwhite victim shared equally in the public's veneration. Crispus Attucks, a sailor and rope maker in his forties, was the son of an African man and a Natick Indian woman. A slave in his youth, he was at the time of his death a free laborer at the Boston

The Bloody Massacre Perpetrated in King Street, Boston, on March 5, 1770 This mass-produced engraving by Paul Revere sold for sixpence per copy. In this patriot version of events, the soldiers fire on an unarmed crowd under orders of their captain. The tranquil dog is an artistic device used to signal the crowd's peaceful intent; not even a deaf dog could have held that pose during the melee. Among the five killed was Crispus Attucks, a black sailor, but Revere shows only whites among the casualties. Anne S. K. Brown Military Collection, Providence, R.I.

FOR MORE HELP ANALYZING THIS IMAGE, see the visual activity for this chapter in the Online Study Guide at **bedfordstmartins.com/ roarkcompact.**

docks. Attucks was one of the first American partisans to die in the American Revolution, and certainly the first African American.

The trial of the eight soldiers came in the fall of 1770. They were defended by two young Boston attorneys, Samuel Adams's cousin John Adams and Josiah Quincy. Because Adams and Quincy had direct ties to the leadership of the Sons of Liberty, their decision to defend the British soldiers at first seems odd. But Adams was deeply committed to the idea that even unpopular defendants deserved a fair trial. Samuel Adams respected his cousin's decision to take the case, for there was a tactical benefit as well. It showed that the Boston leadership was not lawless but could be seen as defenders of British liberty and law.

The five-day trial resulted in acquittal for Preston and for all but two of the soldiers, who were convicted of manslaughter, branded on the thumbs, and released. Nothing materialized in the trial to indicate a conspiracy or concerted plan to provoke trouble by either the British or the Sons of Liberty. To this day, the question of responsibility for the Boston Massacre remains obscure.

Q: Why did British authorities send troops to occupy Boston in the fall of 1768?

The Tea Party and the Coercive Acts, 1770–1774

In the same week as the Boston Massacre, yet another new British prime minister, Frederick North, acknowledged the harmful impact of the boycott on trade and recommended repeal of the Townshend duties. A skillful politician, Lord North took office in 1770 and kept it for twelve years; at last King George had stability at the helm. Seeking peace with the colonies and prosperity for British merchants, North persuaded Parliament to remove all the duties except the tax on tea, kept as a symbol of Parliament's power.

The renewal of trade and the return of cooperation between Britain and the colonies gave men like Thomas Hutchinson hope that the worst of the crisis was behind them. For nearly two years, peace seemed possible, but tense incidents in 1772, followed by a renewed struggle over the tea tax in 1773, precipitated a full-scale crisis that by 1775 resulted in war.

The Calm before the Storm Repeal of the Townshend duties brought an end to nonimportation. Trade boomed in 1770 and 1771, driven by pent-up demand. Moreover, the leaders of the popular movement seemed to be losing their power. Samuel Adams, for example, ran for a minor local office and lost to a conservative merchant. Then in 1772, several incidents again brought the conflict with Britain into sharp focus. One was the burning of the *Gaspée*, a Royal Navy ship pursuing suspected smugglers near Rhode Island. A British investigating commission failed to arrest anyone but announced that it would send suspects, if any were found, to Britain for trial on charges of high treason. This ruling seemed to fly in the face of the traditional English right to trial by a jury of one's peers.

When news of the *Gaspée* investigation spread, it was greeted with disbelief in other colonies. Patrick Henry, Thomas Jefferson, and Richard Henry Lee in the Virginia House of Burgesses proposed that a network of standing committees be established to link the colonies and pass along alarming news. By mid-1773, every colonial assembly except Pennsylvania's had a "committee of correspondence."

Another British action in 1772 further spread the communications network. Lord North proposed to pay the salaries of superior court justices out of the tea revenue, similar to Townshend's plan for paying royal governors. The Boston town meeting, fearful that judges would now be improperly influenced by their new paymasters, established a committee of correspondence and urged all Massachusetts towns to do likewise. The first message, circulated in December 1772, attacked the judges' salary policy as the latest proof of a British plot to undermine traditional liberties: unjust taxation, military occupation, massacre, now capped by the subversion of justice. By spring 1773, more than half the towns in Massachusetts had set up **committees of correspondence**, providing local forums for debate. These committees politicized ordinary townspeople, sparking a revolutionary language of rights and constitutional duties. They also bypassed the official flow of power and information through the colony's royal government.

The final incident shattering the relative calm of the early 1770s was the **Tea Act of 1773**. Americans had resumed buying the taxed British tea, but they were also smuggling large quantities of Dutch tea, cutting into the sales of Britain's East India Company. So Lord North proposed legislation giving favored status to the East India Company, allowing it to sell tea directly to government agents rather than through public auction to independent merchants. The hope was to lower the price of the East India tea, including the duty, below that of smuggled Dutch tea, motivating Americans to obey the law.

Tea in Boston Harbor   In the fall of 1773, news of the Tea Act reached the colonies. Parliamentary legislation to make tea inexpensive struck many colonists as an insidious plot to trick Americans into buying the dutied tea. The real goal, some argued, was the increased revenue, which would be used to pay the royal governors and judges. The Tea Act was thus a painful reminder of Parliament's claim to the power to tax and legislate for the colonies.

But how to resist the Tea Act? Nonimportation was not viable, because the tea trade was too lucrative to expect merchants to give it up willingly. Consumer boycotts seemed ineffective, because it was impossible to distinguish between dutied tea (the object of the boycott) and smuggled tea (illegal but politically clean) once it was in the teapot. The appointment of tea agents, parallel to the Stamp Act distributors, suggested one solution. In every port city, revived Sons of Liberty pressured tea agents to resign; without agents, governors yielded, and tea cargoes either landed without paperwork or were sent home.

Governor Hutchinson, however, would not bend any rules. Three ships bearing tea arrived in Boston in November 1773. They cleared customs and unloaded their other cargoes, but not the tea. Sensing the town's extreme tension, the captains wished to return to England, but Hutchinson would not grant them clearance to leave without paying the tea duty. Also, there was a time limit on the stay allowed in the harbor. After twenty days, the duty had to be paid, or local authorities would confiscate the tea.

For the full twenty days, pressure built in Boston. Daily mass meetings energized citizens from Boston and surrounding towns, alerted by the committees of correspondence. On the final day, December 16, when for a final time Hutchinson refused clearance for the ships, a large crowd gathered at Old South Church to debate a course of action. No solution emerged at that meeting, but immediately following it, 100 to 150 men, disguised as Indians, boarded the ships and dumped thousands of pounds of tea into the harbor while a crowd of two thousand watched. In admiration, John Adams wrote: "This Destruction of the Tea is so bold, so daring, so firm, intrepid and inflexible, and it must have so important Consequences."

The Coercive Acts   Lord North's response was swift and stern: He persuaded Parliament to issue the **Coercive Acts**, four laws meant to punish Massachusetts for destroying the tea. In America, those laws, along with a fifth one, the Quebec Act, were soon known as the **Intolerable Acts**.

The first act, the Boston Port Act, closed Boston harbor to all shipping as of June 1, 1774, until the destroyed tea was paid for. Britain's objective was to halt the commercial life of the city.

The second act, the Massachusetts Government Act, greatly altered the colony's charter, underscoring Parliament's claim to supremacy over Massachusetts. The royal governor's powers were augmented, and the council became an appointive, rather than elective, body. Further, the governor could now appoint all judges, sheriffs, and officers of the court. No town meeting beyond the annual spring election of town selectmen could be held without the governor's approval, and every agenda item required prior approval. Every Massachusetts town was affected.

The third Coercive Act, the Impartial Administration of Justice Act, stipulated that any royal official accused of a capital crime—for example, Captain Preston and his soldiers at the Boston Massacre—would be tried in a court in Britain. It did not matter that Preston had received a fair trial in Boston. What this act ominously suggested was that down the road, more Captain Prestons and soldiers might be firing into unruly crowds.

The fourth act, called the Quartering Act, permitted military commanders to lodge soldiers wherever necessary, even in private households. In a related move, Lord North appointed General **Thomas Gage**, commander of the Royal Army in New York, governor of Massachusetts. Thomas Hutchinson was out, relieved at long last of his duties. Military rule, including soldiers, returned once more to Boston.

The fifth act—the Quebec Act—had nothing to do with the four Coercive Acts, but it fed American fears. It confirmed the continuation of French civil law and government form, as well as Catholicism, for Quebec—all an affront to Protestant New Englanders recently denied their own representative government. The act also gave Quebec control of disputed land (and the lucrative fur trade) throughout the Ohio Valley, land also claimed by Virginia, Pennsylvania, and a number of Indian tribes.

The five Intolerable Acts spread alarm in all the colonies. If Britain could squelch Massachusetts—change its charter, suspend local government, inaugurate military rule, and on top of that give Ohio to Catholic Quebec—what liberties were secure? Fearful royal governors in a half dozen colonies dismissed the sitting assemblies, adding to the sense of urgency. A few of the assemblies defiantly continued to meet in new locations. Through the committees of correspondence, colonial leaders arranged to convene in Philadelphia in September 1774 to respond to the crisis.

Beyond Boston: Rural Massachusetts By the time delegates assembled in Philadelphia, all of Massachusetts had arrived at the brink of open insurrection. With a British general occupying the governorship and some three thousand troops controlling Boston, the revolutionary momentum shifted from urban radicals to rural farmers who protested the Massachusetts Government Act in dozens of spontaneous, dramatic showdowns. To get around the prohibition on new meetings, some towns refused to adjourn their last authorized town meeting. More defiant towns just ignored the law. Gage's call for elections for a new provincial assembly under his control sparked elections for a competing unauthorized assembly.

In all counties except one, crowds of many hundreds of armed men converged to prevent the opening of county courts run by crown-appointed jurists. No judges were physically harmed, but they were forced to resign and made to doff their judicial wigs or run a humiliating gantlet. In Suffolk County, the courts met in troop-filled Boston, making mass intimidation of judges impossible. One by one, however, the citizen jurors called to serve in court refused. By late August 1774, farmers and artisans all over Massachusetts had effectively taken local control away from the crown.

At this point in the struggle, confrontations did not lead to bloodshed. But one incident, the Powder Alarm, nearly provoked violence and showed how close New England farmers were to armed insurrection. Gage sent troops to capture a supply of gunpowder just outside Boston on September 1, and in the surprise and scramble of the attack, false news spread that the troops had fired on men defending the powder, killing six. Within twenty-four hours, several thousand armed men from Massachusetts and Connecticut streamed on foot to Boston to avenge the first blood spilled. Once the error was corrected and the crisis defused, the men returned home peaceably. But Gage could no longer doubt the speed, number, and determination of the rebellious subjects.

All this had occurred without orchestration by Boston radicals, Gage reported. But British leaders found it hard to believe, as one put it, that "a tumultuous Rabble, without any Appearance of general Concert, or without any Head to advise, or Leader to conduct" could pull off such effective resistance. Repeatedly in the years to come, the British would seriously underestimate their opponents.

Ordinary Massachusetts citizens, unfettered by the crown, began serious planning for the crisis everyone assumed would come. Town militias stockpiled gunpowder "in case of invasion." Judges who had been willing crown appointees recanted and confessed their errors—or started packing to leave. The new provincial assembly convinced towns to withhold tax money from the royal governor and divert it to military supplies. Gage beefed up fortifications around Boston, sent armed soldiers to stop meetings that quickly dispersed, and in general rattled his sword loudly. Any bolder action would have to wait until he could acquire a larger army.

The First Continental Congress Every colony except Georgia sent delegates to Philadelphia in September 1774 to discuss the looming crisis in what was later called the **First Continental Congress**. The gathering included notables such as Samuel Adams and John Adams from Massachusetts and George Washington and Patrick Henry from Virginia. A few colonies purposely sent men who opposed provoking Britain, such as Pennsylvania's Joseph Galloway, to keep the congress from becoming too radical.

Delegates sought to articulate their liberties as British subjects and the powers Parliament held over them, and they debated possible responses to the Coercive Acts. Some wanted a total ban on trade with Britain to force repeal, while others, especially southerners dependent on tobacco and rice exports, opposed halting trade. Samuel Adams and Patrick Henry were eager for a ringing denunciation of all parliamentary control. The conservative Joseph Galloway proposed a plan (quickly defeated) to create a secondary parliament in America to assist the British Parliament in ruling the colonies.

The congress met for seven weeks and produced a declaration of rights couched in traditional language: "We ask only for peace, liberty and security. We wish no diminution of royal prerogatives, we demand no new rights." But from Britain's point of view, the rights assumed already to exist were radical. Chief among them was the claim that Americans were not represented in Parliament and so each colonial government had the sole right to govern and tax its own people. The one slight concession to Britain was a carefully worded agreement that the colonists would "cheerfully consent" to trade regulations for the larger good of the empire, so long as trade regulation was not a covert means of raising revenue.

To put pressure on Britain, the delegates agreed to a staggered and limited boycott of trade: imports prohibited this year, exports the following, and rice totally exempted (to keep South Carolinians happy). To enforce the boycott, they called for a Continental Association, with chapters in each town variously called committees of public safety or of inspection, to monitor all commerce and punish suspected violators of the boycott (sometimes with a bucket of tar and a bag of feathers). Its work done in a month, the congress disbanded in October, with agreement to convene the following May.

The committees of public safety, the committees of correspondence, the regrouped colonial assemblies, and the Continental Congress were all political bodies functioning defiantly without any constitutional authority. British officials did not recognize them as legitimate, but many Americans who supported the

Tarring and Feathering Cartoon In 1774, a Boston customs collector named John Malcolm felt the sting of a Boston crowd that tarred and feathered him as punishment for extorting money from shippers. This ritualized humiliation involved stripping a man, painting him with tar, and dipping him in chicken feathers. Local committees of public safety often used threats of this treatment as a weapon to enforce boycotts. In actuality, however, it happened far less often than it was threatened. This cartoon, of English origin, is hostile to Americans, who are shown with cruelly gleeful faces, forcing tea down Malcolm's throat. The Liberty Tree has become a gallows; posted to it is the Stamp Act, upside down. The dumping of tea in the harbor is depicted in the background. Library of Congress.

patriot cause instantly accepted them. A key reason for the stability of such unauthorized governing bodies was that they were composed of many of the same men who had held elective office before.

Britain's severe reaction to Boston's destruction of the tea finally succeeded in making many colonists from New Hampshire to Georgia realize that the problems of British rule went far beyond questions of taxation. The Coercive Acts infringed on liberty and denied self-government; they could not be ignored. With one colony already subordinated to military rule and a British army at the ready in Boston, the threat of a general war was on the doorstep.

Q: Why did Parliament pass the Coercive Acts in 1774?

Domestic Insurrections, 1774–1775

Before the Second Continental Congress could meet, violence and bloodshed came to Massachusetts. Fearing the threat of domestic insurrection, General Thomas Gage requested more troops from Britain and prepared to subdue rebellion. On the other side, New England farmers prepared to defend their homes against an intrusive power they feared was bent on enslaving them. To the south, a different and inverted version of the same story began to unfold, as thousands of enslaved black men and women seized an unprecedented opportunity to

mount a different kind of insurrection — against planter-patriots who looked over their shoulders uneasily whenever they called out for liberty from the British.

Lexington and Concord During the winter of 1774–75, Americans pressed on with boycotts. Optimists hoped to effect a repeal of the Coercive Acts; pessimists stockpiled arms and ammunition. In Massachusetts, militia units known as minutemen prepared to respond at a minute's notice to any threat from the British troops in Boston.

Thomas Gage soon realized how desperate the British position was. The people, Gage wrote Lord North, were "numerous, worked up to a fury, and not a Boston rabble but the freeholders and farmers of the country." Gage requested twenty thousand reinforcements. He also strongly advised repeal of the Coercive Acts, but leaders in Britain could not admit failure. Instead, in mid-April 1775, they ordered Gage to arrest the troublemakers immediately, before the Americans got better organized.

Gage quickly planned a surprise attack on a suspected ammunition storage site at Concord, a village eighteen miles west of Boston (Map 6.3). Near midnight on April 18, 1775, British soldiers moved west across the Charles River. Boston silversmith Paul Revere and William Dawes, a tanner, raced ahead to alert the minutemen. When

> The people, Gage wrote Lord North, were "numerous, worked up to a fury, and not a Boston rabble but the freeholders and farmers of the country."

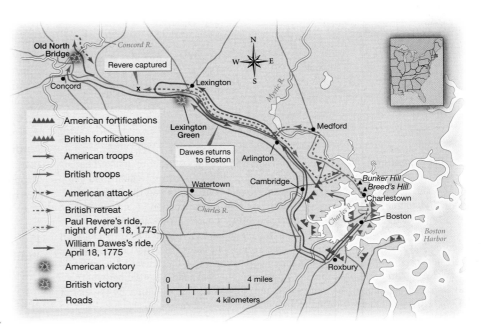

MAP 6.3 Lexington and Concord, April 1775 Under pressure from Britain, some nine hundred British forces at Boston staged a raid on a suspected patriot arms supply in Concord, Massachusetts, starting the first battle of the Revolutionary War. The routes of the two men sent to warn the patriots are marked. Paul Revere went by boat from Boston to Charlestown and then continued by horse through Medford to Lexington. William Dawes casually passed British sentries guarding the only land route out of Boston, a land bridge called the Neck, then rode his horse at full speed to Lexington. Revere and Dawes reached Samuel Adams and John Hancock, guests in a Lexington home, and urged them to flee to avoid capture. The two couriers then went on to Concord to warn residents of the impending attack.

the soldiers got to Lexington, a village five miles east of Concord, they were met by some seventy armed men assembled on the village green. The British commander barked out, "Lay down your arms, you damned rebels, and disperse." The militiamen hesitated and began to comply, turning to leave the green, but then someone—nobody knows who—fired. In the next two minutes, more firing left eight Americans dead and ten wounded.

The British units continued their march to Concord, any pretense of surprise gone. Three companies of minutemen nervously occupied the town center but offered no challenge to the British as they searched in vain for the ammunition. Finally, at Old North Bridge in Concord, troops and minutemen exchanged shots, killing two Americans and three British soldiers.

By now, both sides were very apprehensive. The British failed to find the expected arms, and the Americans failed to stop their raid. As the British returned to Boston, militia units ambushed them, bringing the bloodiest fighting of the day. In the end, 273 British soldiers were wounded or dead;

the toll for the Americans stood at about 95. It was April 19, 1775, and the war had begun.

Rebelling against Slavery News of the battles of Lexington and Concord spread rapidly. Within eight days, Virginians had heard of the fighting, and, as Thomas Jefferson reflected, "a phrenzy of revenge seems to have seized all ranks of people." The royal governor of Virginia, **Lord Dunmore**, removed a large quantity of gunpowder from the Williamsburg powder house and put it on a ship in the dead of night, out of reach of any frenzied Virginians. Next, he threatened to arm slaves, if necessary, to ward off attacks by colonists.

This was an effective threat; Dunmore understood full well how to produce panic among planters. In November 1775, he issued an official proclamation promising freedom to defecting able-bodied slaves who would fight for the British. Although Dunmore wanted to scare the planters, he had no intention of liberating all the slaves or starting a real slave rebellion. Female, young, and elderly slaves were not welcome to flee, and many were sent back to face irate masters. Astute blacks noticed that Dunmore neglected to free his own slaves. A Virginia barber named Caesar declared that "he did not know any one foolish enough to believe him [Dunmore], for if he intended to do so, he ought first to set his own free."

By December 1775, around fifteen hundred slaves in Virginia had fled to Lord Dunmore, who armed them and called them his "Ethiopian Regiment." Camp diseases quickly set in: dysentery, typhoid fever, and smallpox. When Dunmore sailed for England in mid-1776, he took just three hundred black survivors with him. But the association of freedom with the British authorities had been established, and throughout the war, thousands more southern slaves made bold to run away as soon as they heard the British army was approaching.

In the northern colonies as well, slaves clearly recognized the evolving political struggle with Britain as an ideal moment to bid for freedom. A twenty-one-year-old Boston domestic slave employed biting sarcasm in a 1774 newspaper essay to call attention to the hypocrisy of local slave owners: "How well the Cry for Liberty, and the reverse Disposition for exercise of oppressive Power over others agree,—I humbly think it does not require the Penetration of a Philosopher to Determine." This extraordinary young woman, **Phillis Wheatley**, had already gained international recognition through a book of poems endorsed by Governor Thomas Hutchinson and Boston merchant John Hancock and published in London in 1773. Possibly neither

Phillis Wheatley's Title Page Phillis, born in Africa, was sold to John Wheatley of Boston at age seven. Remarkably gifted in learning English, she published her first poem at age twelve, in 1766. By age sixteen, she could read the Bible with ease and composed many poems. Her master took her to London in 1773, where this book was published, gaining her great literary notice. Wheatley's eloquent achievement captured the attention of American leaders, and in 1776 she met with George Washington. The Wheatleys freed Phillis, but John Wheatley's early death left her without resources. An unhappy marriage to a free black man followed. Two of their three children died in infancy, and her husband deserted her. Poetry alone could not support her, and she found work in a boardinghouse. By the end of 1784, Phillis and her remaining child had died. Library of Congress.

man fully appreciated the irony of his endorsement, however, for Wheatley's poems spoke of "Fair Freedom" as the "Goddess long desir'd" by Africans enslaved in America. At the urging of his wife, Wheatley's master freed the young poet in 1775.

Wheatley's poetic ideas about freedom found concrete expression among other discontented groups. Some slaves in Boston petitioned Thomas Gage, promising to fight for the British if he would liberate them. Gage turned them down. In Ulster County, New York, along the Hudson River, two blacks were overheard discussing gunpowder, and thus a plot unraveled that involved at least twenty slaves in four villages discovered to have ammunition stashed away.

In Maryland, soon after the news of the Lexington battle arrived, blacks exhibited impatience with their status as slaves, causing one Maryland planter to report that "the insolence of the Negroes in this county is come to such a height, that we are under a necessity of disarming them. . . . We took about eighty guns, some bayonets, swords, etc." In North Carolina, a planned uprising was uncovered, and scores of slaves were arrested. Ironically, it was the revolutionary committee of public safety that ordered the whippings to punish this quest for liberty.

By 1783, when the Revolutionary War ended, as many as twenty thousand blacks had voted against slavery with their feet by seeking refuge with the British army. Most failed to achieve the liberation they were seeking. The British generally used them for menial labor, and disease, especially smallpox, devastated encampments of runaways. But some eight thousand to ten thousand persisted through the war and later, under the protection of the British army, left America to start new lives of freedom in Canada's Nova Scotia or Africa's Sierra Leone.

Q: **How did enslaved people in the colonies react to the stirrings of revolution?**

Conclusion: How Far Does Liberty Go?

The Seven Years' War set the stage for the imperial crisis of the 1760s and 1770s by creating distrust between Britain and its colonies and by running up a huge deficit in the British treasury. The years 1763 to 1775 brought repeated attempts by the British government to subordinate the colonies into taxpaying partners in the larger scheme of empire.

American resistance grew slowly but steadily over those years. In 1765, loyalist Thomas Hutchinson shared with patriot Samuel Adams the belief that it was exceedingly unwise for Britain to assert a right to taxation because Parliament did not adequately represent Americans. By temperament and office, Hutchinson had to uphold British policy. Adams, in contrast, protested the policy and made political activists out of thousands in the process.

By 1775, events propelled many Americans to the conclusion that a concerted effort was afoot to deprive them of all their liberties, the most important of which were the right to self-taxation, the right to live free of an occupying army, and the right to self-rule. Hundreds of minutemen converged on Concord, prepared to die for those liberties. April 19 marked the start of their rebellion.

Another rebellion under way in 1775 was doomed to be short-circuited. Black Americans who had experienced actual slavery listened to shouts of "Liberty!" from white crowds and appropriated the language of revolution swirling around them that spoke to their deepest needs and hopes. Defiance of authority was indeed contagious.

The emerging leaders of the patriot cause were mindful of a delicate balance they felt they had to strike. To energize the American public about the crisis with Britain, they had to politicize masses of men—and eventually women, too—and infuse them with a keen sense of their rights and liberties. But in so doing, they became fearful of the unintended consequences of teaching a vocabulary of rights and liberties. They worried that the rhetoric of enslavement might go too far.

The question of how far the crisis could be stretched before something snapped was largely unexamined in 1765. Patriot leaders in that year wanted a correction, a restoration of an ancient liberty of self-taxation that Parliament seemed to be ignoring. But events from 1765 to 1775 convinced many that a return to the old ways was impossible. Challenging Parliament's right to tax had led, step by step, to challenging Parliament's right to legislate over the colonies in any matter. If Parliament's sovereignty was set aside, who actually had authority over the American colonies? By 1775, with the outbreak of fighting and the specter of slave rebellions, American leaders turned to the king for the answer to that question.

Reviewing the Chapter

★ **KEY TERMS**

Explain each term's significance

WHO

Thomas Hutchinson (p. 129)

William Pitt (p. 134)

George III (p. 135)

Pontiac (p. 135)

Patrick Henry (p. 140)

Samuel Adams (p. 140)

Thomas Gage (p. 147)

Lord Dunmore (p. 150)

Phillis Wheatley (p. 150)

WHAT

Albany Plan of Union (p. 129)

Seven Years' War (p. 130)

Proclamation of 1763 (p. 135)

Sugar (Revenue) Act (p. 139)

Stamp Act (p. 139)

virtual representation (p. 139)

Virginia Resolves (p. 140)

Stamp Act Congress (p. 141)

Declaratory Act (p. 142)

Townshend duties (p. 142)

nonconsumption agreements (p. 143)

Boston Massacre (p. 144)

committees of correspondence (p. 146)

Tea Act of 1773 (p. 146)

Coercive (Intolerable) Acts (p. 146)

First Continental Congress (p. 148)

★ **REVIEW QUESTIONS** **Q:**

Use key terms and dates to support your answer

1. How did the Seven Years' War erode relations between colonists and British authorities? (pp. 130–38)

2. Why did the Sugar Act and the Stamp Act draw fierce opposition from colonists? (pp. 138–42)

3. Why did British authorities send troops to occupy Boston in the fall of 1768? (pp. 142–45)

4. Why did Parliament pass the Coercive Acts in 1774? (pp. 145–49)

5. How did enslaved people in the colonies react to the stirrings of revolution? (pp. 149–51)

★ **MAKING CONNECTIONS**

Draw on key terms, timeline, and review questions

1. In the mid-eighteenth century, how did Native Americans influence relations between European nations? Between Britain and the colonies?

2. Why did disputes over taxation figure so prominently in the deteriorating relations between Britain and the colonies? What else, besides taxation, aggravated colonial grievances by 1775 to cause a start to the war?

3. How did the colonists organize to oppose British power so effectively? In your answer, discuss the role of communication in facilitating the colonial resistance, being sure to cite specific examples.

FOR PRACTICE QUIZZES AND OTHER STUDY TOOLS, see the Online Study Guide at **bedfordstmartins.com/roarkcompact**.

★ SUGGESTED READINGS

Fred Anderson, *Crucible of War: The Seven Years' War and the Fate of Empire in British North America, 1754–1766* (2000). A gripping and richly detailed account of the world war that precipitated the American Revolution.

Bernard Bailyn, *The Ordeal of Thomas Hutchinson* (1974). A sympathetic portrait of an unyielding man caught in a revolution he could not countenance.

Woody Holton, *Forced Founders: Indians, Debtors, Slaves, and the Making of the American Revolution in Virginia* (1999). An account of how debt crisis, land speculation, and fears of Indian raids and slave rebellions shaped the political actions of the Virginia gentry on the eve of the Revolution.

Robert Middlekauff, *The Glorious Cause: The American Revolution, 1763–1789* (2005). A classic panoramic history of the American Revolution.

Ray Raphael, *The First American Revolution: Before Lexington and Concord* (2002). History from the bottom up: how ordinary people all over Massachusetts became insurgents in 1774 in response to a military occupation by a detested enemy.

Alfred F. Young, *The Shoemaker and the Tea Party: Memory and the American Revolution* (1999). An exploration of the life of the last surviving participant in the Boston Tea Party.

FOR MORE BOOKS ABOUT TOPICS IN THIS CHAPTER, see the Online Bibliography at **bedfordstmartins.com/roarkcompact**.

FOR ADDITIONAL FIRSTHAND ACCOUNTS OF THIS PERIOD, see Chapter 6 in Michael Johnson, ed., *Reading the American Past,* Fourth Edition.

FOR WEB SITES, IMAGES, AND DOCUMENTS RELATED TO TOPICS AND PLACES IN THIS CHAPTER, visit Make History at **bedfordstmartins.com/roarkcompact**.

★ TIMELINE

1747	• Ohio Company of Virginia formed.
1754	• Seven Years' War begins in North America. • Albany Congress proposes Plan of Union (never implemented).
1755	• Braddock defeated in western Pennsylvania.
1757	• William Pitt fully commits Britain to war effort.
1760	• Montreal falls to British. • George III becomes British king.
1763	• Treaty of Paris ends Seven Years' War. • Pontiac's uprising. • Proclamation of 1763. • Paxton Boys massacre friendly Indians in Pennsylvania.
1764	• Parliament enacts Sugar (Revenue) Act.
1765	• Parliament enacts Stamp Act. • Virginia Resolves challenge Stamp Act. • Dozens of crowd actions by Sons of Liberty. • Stamp Act Congress meets.
1766	• Parliament repeals Stamp Act and passes Declaratory Act.
1767	• Parliament enacts Townshend duties.
1768	• British station troops in Boston.
1769	• Merchants sign nonimportation agreements.
1770	• Boston Massacre. • Parliament repeals Townshend duties.
1772	• British navy ship *Gaspée* burned. • Committees of correspondence begin forming.
1773	• Parliament passes Tea Act. • Dumping of tea in Boston harbor.
1774	• Parliament passes Coercive (Intolerable) Acts. • Powder Alarm shows colonists' readiness to bear arms. • First Continental Congress meets; Continental Association formed.
1775	• Battles of Lexington and Concord. • Lord Dunmore promises freedom to defecting slaves.

CONTINENTAL ARMY UNIFORM WORN AT THE SIEGE OF FORT STANWIX, 1777 In 1775, the Continental Congress faced the daunting prospect of fielding an army to fight the largest military force in the world. Money was scarce, soldiers were hastily trained and short of equipment, and uniforms were hard to come by. (Many were purchased from France.) At the start of the war, ordinary enlisted men often wore brown work clothes, and although this outfit gave them a unified look, it did not allow for easy categorization of soldiers by their units. When General Washington finally issued dress specifications, he chose the color already preferred by many officers — dark blue — and then specified the variety of colors to be used for the facings and linings of the coat to establish the rank and the unit of each soldier. Officers especially needed distinctive clothing to distinguish them from ordinary soldiers and from other officers, so that the military hierarchy could be maintained at all times. The coat pictured here belonged to a brigadier general, Peter Gansevoort, who was twenty-eight in 1777 and in command of Fort Stanwix in the Mohawk Valley of New York. The coat has a buff-colored lining (seen inside the coattails) and bright red facings on the collar, lapels, and cuffs, marking him as a New York soldier. The color of the shoulder ribbons (red) reveals Gansevoort's rank. The ribbons could be easily replaced with a new color, enabling a man to ascend in rank without having to get a new coat. Young Gansevoort became a celebrated hero when he successfully defended Fort Stanwix against an attack by British and Indians. His grandson, the author Herman Melville, named his second son Stanwix in honor of the event.
National Museum of American History, Smithsonian Institution, Washington, D.C.

The War for America

1775–1783

LIKE MANY OF THE MEN who fought in the Revolutionary War on the American side, Robert Shurtliff of Massachusetts had multiple reasons for enlisting. Early in the war, men joined the Continental army to fight what they saw as British oppression. As the fighting dragged on, extra incentive pay and promises of future frontier acreage additionally motivated new recruits. By the war's eighth year, a severe manpower shortage caused towns to offer cash bounties of $50 in silver. Young, single, poor, and unsettled in life, Robert Shurtliff stepped up. Thanks to a tall, muscular physique and decent skill with a musket, the adventurous soldier readily won assignment in the army's elite light infantry unit.

Shurtliff's reported age was eighteen, not unusual for the new recruits of 1782. Beardless boys who had been children when the British marched on Lexington signed up for service in an army still needed after the decisive battle at Yorktown. The British refused to end their occupation of New York City until a peace treaty was signed, so for nearly two years, Washington's force of 10,000 men camped along the Hudson River north of the city, skirmishing with the enemy.

That is, 10,000 men and 1 woman. "Robert Shurtliff" was actually Deborah Sampson, age twenty-three, from Middleborough, Massachusetts. For seventeen months, Sampson masqueraded as a man, marching through woods, firing a musket, and enduring the boredom of camp. Misrepresenting her age enabled her to blend in with the beardless boys, as did her competence as a soldier. With privacy at a minimum, she faced constant risks of discovery. Soldiers slept six to a tent, "spooning" their bodies together for warmth. Somehow, Sampson managed to escape detection. Although many thousands of women served the army as cooks, laundresses, and caregivers, they were never placed in combat. Not only was Sampson defrauding the military, but she was also violating a legal prohibition on cross-dressing. Why did she run this risk?

A hard-luck childhood had left Sampson both impoverished and unusually plucky. Her father deserted the family, causing her mother to place the children in foster care. From age five forward, Deborah lived with a succession of families, learning household skills appropriate to a servant's life.

Previewing the Chapter

The Second Continental Congress 156
Q: Why were many Americans reluctant to pursue independence from Britain?

The First Year of War, 1775–1776 160
Q: Why did the British exercise restraint in their efforts to defeat the rebellious colonies?

The Home Front 163
Q: How did the patriots promote support for their cause in the colonies?

The Campaigns of 1777–1779: The North and West 169
Q: Why did the Americans need assistance from the French to ensure victory?

The Southern Strategy and the End of the War 173
Q: Why did the British southern strategy ultimately fail?

Conclusion: Why the British Lost 177

Deborah Sampson In the mid-1790s, Deborah Sampson sat for this small portrait painted by Massachusetts folk artist Joseph Stone. An engraved copy of it illustrated *The Female Review,* a short book about Sampson's unusual military career and life published in 1797. Sampson, by then a wife and mother, displays femininity in this picture. Note her long curly hair, the necklace, and the stylish gown with a low, lace-trimmed neckline filled in (for modesty's sake) with a white neckerchief. Sampson the soldier had used a cloth band to compress her breasts; Sampson the matron wore a satin band to define her bustline. Rhode Island Historical Society.

More unusually, she also learned to plow a field and to read and write. Freed from servitude at age eighteen, she earned a living as a weaver and then as a teacher, low-wage jobs but also ones without supervising bosses. Marriage would have been her normal next step, but either lack of inclination or a wartime shortage of men kept her single and "masterless," rare for an eighteenth-century woman. But like most single females, she was also poor; the $50 bounty enticed her to enlist.

Sampson was unmasked after seventeen months of service when she suffered a battle-related injury and the treatment revealed her sex. She was discharged immediately, but her fine service record kept her superiors from prosecuting her for cross-dressing. Sampson spent many years seeking a pension from the government to compensate her for her war injury, to no avail.

What eventually made Sampson famous was not her war service alone, but her effort to capitalize on it by selling her story to the public. In 1797, now a middle-aged mother of three, she told her life story (a blend of fact and fiction) in a short book. During 1802–1803, she reenacted her wartime masquerade on a speaking tour of New England and New York. Once again, she was crossing gender boundaries, since women who were not actresses normally did not speak from public stages.

Except for her disguised sex, Sampson's Revolutionary War experience was similar to that of most Americans. Disruptions affected everyone's life, whether in military service or on the home front. Wartime shortages caused women and children to take up male labor. Soldiers fought for ideas, but they also fought to earn money. Hardship was widely endured. And Sampson's quest for personal independence—a freedom from the constraints of being female—was echoed in the general quest for political independence that many Americans identified as a major goal of the war.

Political independence was not everyone's primary goal at first. For more than a year after fighting began, the Continental Congress in Philadelphia resisted declaring America's independence. Some delegates cautiously hoped for reconciliation with Britain. The congress raised an army, financed it, and sought alliances with foreign countries—all while exploring diplomatic channels for peace.

Once King George III rejected all peace overtures, Americans loudly declared their independence, and the war moved into high gear. In part a classic war with professional armies and textbook battles, the Revolutionary War was also a civil war and at times a brutal guerrilla war between committed rebels and loyalists. It also had complex ethnic dimensions, pitting Indian tribes allied with the British against others allied with the Americans. And it provided an unprecedented opportunity for enslaved African Americans to win their freedom, either by joining the British, who openly encouraged slaves to desert their masters, or by joining the Continental army and state militias, fighting alongside white Americans. ★

The Second Continental Congress

On May 10, 1775, nearly one month after the fighting at Lexington and Concord, the **Second Continental Congress** assembled in Philadelphia. The congress immediately set to work on two crucial but contradictory tasks: to raise and supply an army and to explore reconciliation with Britain.

To do the former, they needed soldiers and a commander, they needed money, and they needed to work out a declaration of war. To do the latter, however, they needed diplomacy to approach the king. But the king was not receptive, and by 1776, as the war progressed and hopes of reconciliation faded, delegates at the congress began to ponder the treasonous act of declaring independence—said by some to be plain common sense.

Assuming Political and Military Authority Like members of the First Continental Congress (see chapter 6), the delegates to the second were well-established figures in their home colonies, but they still had to learn to know and trust one another. They did not always agree. The Adams cousins John and Samuel defined the radical end of the spectrum, favoring independence. **John Dickinson** of Pennsylvania, no longer the eager revolutionary who had dashed off *Letters from a Farmer* in 1767, was now a moderate, seeking reconciliation with Britain. Benjamin Franklin, fresh off a ship from an eleven-year residence in London, was feared by some to be a British spy. Mutual suspicions flourished easily when the undertaking was so dangerous, opinions were so varied, and a misstep could spell disaster.

Most of the delegates were not yet prepared to break with Britain. Several legislatures instructed their delegates to oppose independence. Some felt that government without a king was unworkable, while others feared it might be suicidal to lose Britain's protection against its traditional enemies, France and Spain. Colonies that traded actively with Britain feared undermining their economies. Probably the vast majority of ordinary Americans were unable to envision independence. From the Stamp Act of 1765 to the Coercive Acts of 1774 (see chapter 6), the constitutional struggle with Britain had turned on the issue of parliamentary power. During that decade, almost no one had questioned the legitimacy of the monarchy.

The few men at the Continental Congress who did think that independence was desirable were, not surprisingly, from Massachusetts. Their colony had been stripped of civil government under the Coercive Acts, and their capital was occupied by the British army. Even so, those men knew that it was premature to push for a break with Britain. John Adams wrote his wife Abigail in June 1775: "America is a great, unwieldy body. Its progress must be slow. It is like a large fleet sailing under convoy. The fleetest sailors must wait for the dullest and slowest."

Yet swift action was needed, for the Massachusetts countryside was under threat of further attack. Even the hesitant moderates in the congress agreed that a military buildup was necessary. Around the country, militia units from New York to Georgia collected arms and drilled on village greens in anticipation. On June 14, the congress voted to create the **Continental army**. Choosing the commander in chief offered an opportunity to demonstrate that this was no local war of a single rebellious colony. The congress bypassed the Massachusetts general already commanding the soldiers around Boston and instead chose a Virginian, **George Washington**. Washington's appointment sent the clear message that there was widespread commitment to war beyond New England.

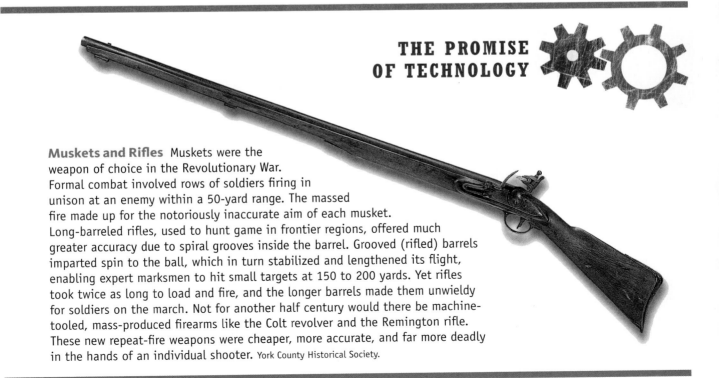

THE PROMISE OF TECHNOLOGY

Muskets and Rifles Muskets were the weapon of choice in the Revolutionary War. Formal combat involved rows of soldiers firing in unison at an enemy within a 50-yard range. The massed fire made up for the notoriously inaccurate aim of each musket. Long-barreled rifles, used to hunt game in frontier regions, offered much greater accuracy due to spiral grooves inside the barrel. Grooved (rifled) barrels imparted spin to the ball, which in turn stabilized and lengthened its flight, enabling expert marksmen to hit small targets at 150 to 200 yards. Yet rifles took twice as long to load and fire, and the longer barrels made them unwieldy for soldiers on the march. Not for another half century would there be machine-tooled, mass-produced firearms like the Colt revolver and the Remington rifle. These new repeat-fire weapons were cheaper, more accurate, and far more deadly in the hands of an individual shooter. York County Historical Society.

Next the congress drew up a document titled "A Declaration on the Causes and Necessity of Taking Up Arms," which rehearsed familiar arguments about the tyranny of Parliament and the need to defend English liberties. This declaration was first drafted by a young Virginia planter, Thomas Jefferson, a radical on the question of independence. The moderate John Dickinson, fearing that the declaration would offend Britain, was allowed to rewrite it. However, he left intact much of Jefferson's highly charged language about choosing "to die freemen rather than to live slaves." Even a man as reluctant about independence as Dickinson acknowledged the necessity of military defense against an invading army.

To pay for the military buildup, the congress authorized a currency issue of $2 million. The Continental dollars were merely paper; they were not backed by gold or silver. The delegates somewhat naively expected that the currency would be accepted as valuable on trust as it spread in the population through the hands of soldiers, farmers, munitions suppliers, and beyond.

In just two months, the Second Continental Congress had created an army, declared war, and issued its own currency. It had taken on the major functions of a legitimate government, both military and financial, without any legal basis for its authority, for it had not—and would not for a full year—declare independence from the authority of the king.

Pursuing Both War and Peace Three days after the congress established the army, one of the bloodiest battles of the Revolution occurred. The British commander in Boston, Thomas Gage, had recently received troop reinforcements, three talented generals (William Howe, John Burgoyne, and Henry Clinton), and new instructions to attack the Massachusetts rebels. But before Gage could take the offensive, the Americans fortified the hilly terrain of Charlestown, a peninsula just north of Boston, on the night of June 16, 1775.

The British generals could have closed off the peninsula to box in the Americans. But General Howe insisted on a bold frontal assault, sending 2,500 soldiers across the water and up the hill in an intimidating but potentially costly attack. The American troops, 1,400 strong, listened to the British drummers pacing the uphill march and held their fire

Battle of Bunker Hill, 1775

until the soldiers were about twenty yards away. At that distance, the musket volley was sure and deadly, and the British turned back. Twice more, General Howe sent his men up the hill and faced the same blast of firepower; each time they had to step around the bodies of men felled in the previous attempts.

On the third assault, the British took the hill, mainly because the American ammunition supply gave out, and the defenders quickly retreated. The **battle of Bunker Hill** was thus a British victory, but an expensive one. The dead numbered 226 on the British side, with more than 800 wounded; the Americans suffered 140 dead, 271 wounded, and 30 captured. As General Clinton later remarked, "It was a dear bought victory; another such would have ruined us."

Instead of pursuing the fleeing Americans, Howe retreated to Boston, unwilling to risk more raids into the countryside. If the British had had any grasp of the basic instability of the American units around Boston, they might have decisively defeated the Continental army in its infancy. Instead, they lingered in Boston, abandoning it without a fight nine months later. Howe used the time in Boston to inoculate his army against smallpox because a new epidemic of the deadly disease was spreading in port cities along the Atlantic. Inoculation worked by producing a light but real (and therefore risky) case of smallpox, followed by lifelong immunity. Howe's instinct was right: During the American Revolution, some 130,000 people on the American continent, most of them Indians, died of smallpox.

A week after Bunker Hill, when General Washington arrived to take charge of the new Continental army, he found enthusiastic but undisciplined troops. Sanitation was an unknown concept, with inadequate latrines fouling the campground. The amazed general attributed the disarray to the New England custom of letting militia units elect their own officers, which he felt undermined deference. Washington quickly imposed more hierarchy and authority. "Discipline is the soul of the army," he stated.

While military plans moved forward, the Second Continental Congress pursued its contradictory objective: reconciliation with Britain. Delegates from the middle colonies (Pennsylvania, Delaware, and New York), whose merchants depended on trade with Britain, urged that channels for negotiation remain open. In July 1775, congressional moderates led by John Dickinson engineered an appeal to the king called the Olive Branch Petition. The petition affirmed loyalty to the monarchy and blamed all the troubles on the king's ministers and on Parliament. It proposed that the American colonial assemblies be recognized as individual parliaments under the umbrella of the monarchy. By late fall 1775, however, reconciliation was out of the question. King George III rejected the Olive Branch Petition and heatedly condemned the Americans as traitors. Thereafter, it was hard to blame only ministers and not the king himself for the conflict.

Thomas Paine, Abigail Adams, and the Case for Independence Pressure for independence started to mount in January 1776, when a pamphlet titled ***Common Sense*** appeared in Philadelphia. **Thomas Paine**, its author, was an English artisan and coffeehouse intellectual who had come to America in the fall of 1774. He landed a job on a Philadelphia newspaper and soon met delegates from the Second Continental Congress. With their encouragement, he wrote *Common Sense* to lay out a lively and compelling case for complete independence.

In simple yet forceful language, Paine elaborated on the absurdities of the British monarchy. Why should one man, by accident of birth, claim extensive power over others? he asked. A king might be foolish or wicked. "One of the strongest natural proofs of the folly of hereditary right in kings," Paine wrote, "is that nature disapproves it; otherwise she would not so frequently turn it into ridicule by giving mankind *an ass for a lion.*" Calling the British king an ass broke through the automatic deference most Americans still had for the monarchy. To replace monarchy, Paine advocated republican government based on the consent of the people. Rulers, according to Paine, were only representatives of the people, and the best form of government relied on frequent elections to achieve the most direct democracy possible.

Paine's pamphlet sold more than 150,000 copies in a matter of weeks. Newspapers reprinted it; men read it aloud in taverns and coffeehouses; John Adams sent a copy to his wife, Abigail, who passed it around to neighbors in Braintree, Massachusetts. New Englanders desired independence, but other colonies, under no immediate threat of violence, remained cautious.

Abigail Adams was impatient not only for independence but also for other legal changes that would revolutionize the new country. In a series of astute letters to her husband, she outlined obstacles and gave advice. She worried that southern slave owners might shrink from a war in the name of liberty: "I have sometimes been ready to think that the passion for Liberty cannot be Equally strong in the Breasts of those who have been accustomed to deprive their fellow Creatures of theirs." And in March 1776, she expressed her hope that women's legal status would improve under the new government: "In the new Code of Laws which I suppose it will be necessary for you to make I desire you would Remember the Ladies, and be more generous and favourable to them than your ancestors." Her chief concern was husbands' legal dominion over wives: "Do not put such unlimited power into the hands of the Husbands," she advised. "Remember all Men would be tyrants if they could." Abigail Adams anticipated a more radical end to tyranny than did Thomas Paine.

> "Do not put such unlimited power into the hands of the Husbands," Abigail Adams advised. "Remember all Men would be tyrants if they could."

Abigail Adams Abigail Smith Adams was twenty-two when she sat for this pastel portrait in 1766. A wife for two years and a mother for one, Adams exhibits a steady, intelligent gaze. Pearls and a lace collar anchor her femininity, while her facial expression projects a confidence and maturity not often credited to young women of the 1760s. A decade later, she was running the family's Massachusetts farm while her husband, John, attended the Continental Congress in Philadelphia. Her frequent letters gave him the benefit of her sage advice on politics and the war. Courtesy of the Massachusetts Historical Society.

The Continental Congress was, in fact, not rewriting family law; that task was left to individual states in the 1780s. John Adams dismissed his wife's concerns. But to a male politician, Adams privately rehearsed the reasons why women (and men who were free blacks, or young, or propertyless) should remain excluded from political participation. Even though he concluded that nothing should change, at least Abigail's letter had forced him to ponder the exclusion, something few men — or women — did in 1776. Urgent talk of political independence was as radical as most could imagine.

The Declaration of Independence In addition to Paine's *Common Sense*, another factor hastening independence was the prospect of an alliance with France, Britain's archrival. France was willing to provide military supplies and naval power only if assured that the Americans would separate from Britain. By May, all but four colonies were agitating for a declaration. The holdouts were Pennsylvania, Maryland, New York, and South Carolina, the latter two containing large loyalist populations. An exasperated Virginian wrote to his friend in the congress, "For God's sake, why do you dawdle in the Congress so strangely? Why do you not at once declare yourself a separate independent state?"

In early June, the Virginia delegation introduced a resolution calling for independence. The moderates still commanded enough support to postpone a vote on the measure until July. In the meantime, the congress appointed a committee, with Thomas Jefferson and others, to draft a longer document setting out the case for independence.

On July 2, after intense politicking, all but one state voted for independence; New York abstained. The congress then turned to the document drafted by Jefferson and his committee. Jefferson began with a preamble that articulated philosophical principles about natural rights, equality, the right of revolution, and the consent of the governed as the only true basis for government. He then listed more than two dozen specific grievances against King George. The congress merely glanced at the philosophical principles, as though ideas about natural rights and the consent of the governed were accepted as "self-evident truths," just as the document claimed. The truly radical phrase declaring the natural equality of "all men" was likewise passed over without comment.

For two days, the congress wrangled over the list of grievances, especially the issue of slavery. Jefferson had included an impassioned statement blaming the king for slavery, which delegates from Georgia and South Carolina struck out. They had no intention of denouncing their labor system as an evil practice. But the congress let stand another of Jefferson's fervent grievances, blaming the king for mobilizing "the merciless Indian Savages" into bloody frontier warfare, a reference to Pontiac's uprising (see chapter 6).

On July 4, the amendments to Jefferson's text were complete, and the congress formally adopted the **Declaration of Independence**. (See appendix I, page A-1.) A month later, the delegates gathered to sign the official parchment copy, handwritten by an exacting scribe. Four men, including John Dickinson, declined to sign; several others "signed with regret . . . and with many doubts," according to John Adams. The document was then printed, widely distributed, and read aloud in celebrations everywhere. (Printed copies did not include the signers' names, for they had committed treason, a crime punishable by death.) On July 15, the New York delegation switched from abstention to endorsement, making the vote on independence unanimous.

> **Q:** **Why were many Americans reluctant to pursue independence from Britain?**

The First Year of War, 1775–1776

Both sides approached the war for America with uneasiness. The Americans, with inexperienced militias, were opposing the mightiest military power in the world. Also, their country was not unified; many people remained loyal to Britain. The British faced serious obstacles as well. Their disdain for the fighting abilities of the Americans required reassessment in light of the Bunker Hill battle. The logistics of supplying an army with food across three thousand miles of water were daunting. And since the British goal was to regain allegiance, not to destroy and conquer, the army was often constrained in its actions. These patterns — undertrained American troops and British troops strangely unwilling to press their advantage — played out repeatedly in the first year of war.

The American Military Forces Americans claimed that the initial months of war were purely defensive, triggered by the British invasion. But the war also quickly became a rebellion, an overthrowing of long-established authority. As both defenders and rebels, many Americans were highly motivated to fight, and the potential manpower that could be mobilized was, in theory, very great.

Local defense in the colonies had long rested with a militia composed of all able-bodied men over age sixteen. When the main threat to public safety was the occasional Indian attack, a local militia made sense. But such attacks were now mostly limited to the frontier. Southern militias trained with potential slave rebellions in mind, but these, too, were rare. The annual muster day in most communities had evolved into a holiday of drinking, marching, and shooting practice.

Militias were best suited for limited engagements, not for extended wars. In forming the Continental army, the congress set enlistment at one year, but army leaders soon learned that was inadequate to train soldiers and carry out campaigns. A three-year enlistment earned a new soldier a $20 bonus, while men who committed for the duration of the war were promised a postwar land grant of one hundred acres. For this inducement to be effective, of course, recruits had to believe that the Americans would win. Over the course of the war, some 230,000 men enlisted, about one-quarter of the white male adult population. (See "Global Comparison.")

Women also served in the Continental army, cooking, washing, and nursing the wounded. The British army established a ratio of one woman to every ten men; in the Continental army, the ratio was set at one woman to fifteen men. Close to 20,000 "camp followers," as they were called, served during the war, probably most of them wives of men in service. Children also tagged along, and babies were born in the camps.

Black Americans were at first excluded from the Continental army by slave owner George Washington's orders. But as manpower needs increased, northern states welcomed free blacks into service; slaves in some states could serve with their masters' permission. About 5,000 black men served in the Revolutionary War on the rebel side, nearly all from the northern states. Black Continental soldiers sometimes were segregated into separate units, as with two battalions from Rhode Island. While some of these men were draftees, others were clearly inspired by ideals of freedom in a war against tyranny. For example, twenty-three blacks gave "Liberty," "Freedom," and "Freeman" as their surnames at the time of enlistment.

Military service helped politicize Americans during the early stages of the war. In early 1776, independence was a risky, potentially treasonous idea. But as the war heated up and recruiters demanded commitment, some Americans discovered that apathy had its dangers as well. Anyone who refused to serve ran the risk of being called a traitor to the cause. Military service became a prime way of demonstrating political allegiance.

The American army was at times raw and inexperienced, and often woefully undermanned. It never had the precision and discipline of European professional armies. But it was never as bad as the British continually assumed. The British would learn that it was a serious mistake to underrate the enemy.

The British Strategy The American strategy was straightforward; to repulse and defeat an invading army. The British strategy was not nearly so clear. Britain wanted to put down a rebellion and restore monarchical power in the colonies, but the question was how to accomplish this. A decisive defeat of the Continental army was essential but not sufficient to end the rebellion, for the British would still have to contend with an armed and motivated insurgent population. Furthermore, there was no single political nerve center whose capture would spell certain victory. The Continental Congress moved from place to place, staying just out of reach of the British. During the course of the war, the British captured and occupied every major port city, but that brought no serious loss to the Americans, 95 percent of whom lived in the countryside.

Britain's delicate task was to restore the old governments, not to destroy an enemy country. Hence, the British generals were reluctant to ravage the countryside, confiscate food, or burn villages. There were thirteen distinct political entities to capture, pacify, and then restore to the crown, and they stretched in a long line from New Hampshire to Georgia. Clearly, a large land army was required for the job. Without the willingness to seize food from the locals, the British needed hundreds of supply ships bringing food for storage—hence their desire to capture the ports. The British strategy also assumed that many Americans remained loyal to the king and would come to their aid. Without a lot of loyal subjects, the plan to restore royal government made no sense.

The overall British plan was a divide-and-conquer approach, focusing first on New York, the state judged to have the greatest number of loyal subjects. New York offered a geographic advantage as well: Control of the Hudson River would allow the British to isolate the troublesome New Englanders. British armies could descend from Canada and move up from New York City along the Hudson River into western Massachusetts. Squeezed between a naval blockade on the eastern coast and army raids in the west, Massachusetts could be driven to surrender. New Jersey and Pennsylvania would fall in line, the British thought, due to loyalist strength. Virginia was a problem, like Massachusetts, but the British were confident that the Carolinas would help them isolate and subdue Virginia.

How Tall Were Eighteenth-Century Men on Average?

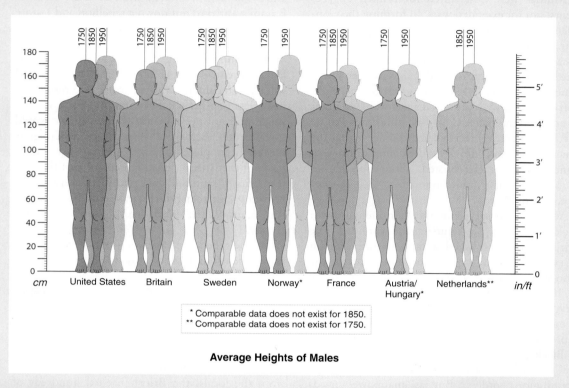

Average Heights of Males

* Comparable data does not exist for 1850.
** Comparable data does not exist for 1750.

Although individuals within a population vary in height for genetic reasons, variations between populations are generally due to differences in the basic standard of living. A key factor is inadequate nutrition, which typically stunts childhood growth and leads to shorter adults. Military enlistment records provide large data sets on height (but for males only), allowing historians to gain insight into comparative standards of living. This figure shows that American men during the Revolution were on average 8 centimeters (cm) or about 3 inches taller than British and European men, indicating an abundance of food and fewer endemic diseases than in Europe. Continental army soldiers exhibited modest but distinct regional differences, with southern soldiers an average of 1.3 cm taller than New England soldiers, while mid-Atlantic soldiers were in between. A much wider spread occurred in Britain, where officers from the gentry were a full 15 cm taller on average than soldiers recruited from the working class. What might account for these differences?

Studies of stature show that average height generally declined in the mid-nineteenth century in Europe and the United States as urbanization, industrialization, and the disease environment changed. Major gains were posted in the twentieth century, but in recent decades, average height in the United States has stagnated, while European males have continued to grow.

Quebec, New York, and New Jersey In late 1775, an American expedition was launched to capture the cities of Montreal and Quebec before British reinforcements could arrive (Map 7.1). This offensive was a clear sign that the war was not purely a reaction to the invasion of Massachusetts.

A force of New York Continentals commanded by General Richard Montgomery took Montreal easily in September 1775 and then advanced on Quebec. Meanwhile, a second contingent of Continentals led by Colonel Benedict Arnold moved north through Maine to Quebec, a punishing trek through freezing rain with woefully inadequate supplies; many men died. Arnold's determination was heroic, but in human costs, the campaign was a tragedy. Arnold and Montgomery jointly attacked Quebec in December but failed to take the city. Worse yet, they encountered smallpox, which killed more men than had battles.

The main action of the first year of the war came not in Canada, however, but in New York, so crucial to Britain. In August 1776, some 45,000 British troops (including 8,000 German mercenaries, called Hessians) under the command of General Howe landed south of New York City. General Washington had anticipated this move and had relocated his army of 20,000 south from Massachusetts. The **battle of Long Island**, in late August 1776, pitted the well-trained British "redcoats" (slang referring to their red uniforms) against a very green Continental army. Howe attacked, inflicting many casualties. A British general crowed, "If a good bleeding can bring those Bible-faced Yankees to their senses, the fever of independency should soon abate." Howe failed to press forward, however, perhaps remembering the costly victory of Bunker Hill, and Washington evacuated his troops to Manhattan Island in the dead of a foggy night.

Washington knew it would be hard to hold Manhattan, so he withdrew farther north to two forts on either side of the Hudson River. For two months, the armies engaged in limited skirmishing, but in November, Howe finally captured Fort Washington and Fort Lee, taking nearly 3,000 prisoners. (See "Beyond America's Borders," page 166.) Washington retreated quickly across New Jersey into Pennsylvania. Yet again Howe unaccountably failed to press his advantage. Had he attacked Washington's army at Philadelphia, he could have taken the city. Instead, he parked his German troops in winter quarters along the Delaware River. Perhaps he knew that many of the Continental soldiers' enlistment periods ended on December 31, making him confident the Americans would not attack him. He was wrong.

On December 25, in an icy rain, Washington stealthily moved his army across the Delaware River and at dawn made a quick capture of the unsuspecting German soldiers. This impressive victory lifted the sagging morale of the patriot side. For the next two weeks, Washington remained on the offensive, capturing supplies in a clever attack on British units at Princeton. Soon he was safe in Morristown, in northern New Jersey, where he settled his army for the winter. Washington finally had time to administer mass smallpox inoculations and see his men through the abbreviated course of the disease.

All in all, in the first year of declared war, the rebellious Americans had a few proud moments but also many worries. The inexperienced Continental army had barely hung on in the New York campaign. Washington had shown exceptional daring and admirable restraint, but what really saved the Americans was the repeated reluctance of the British to follow through militarily when they had the advantage.

Q: Why did the British exercise restraint in their efforts to defeat the rebellious colonies?

The Home Front

Battlefields alone did not determine the outcome of the war. Struggles on the home front were equally important. In 1776, each community contained small numbers of highly committed people on both sides and far larger numbers who were uncertain about whether independence was worth a war. Both persuasion and force were used to gain the allegiance of the many neutrals. Revolutionaries who took control of local government often used it to punish loyalists and intimidate neutrals, while loyalists worked to reestablish British authority. The struggle to secure political allegiance was complicated greatly by a shaky wartime economy. The creative financing of the fledgling government brought hardships as well as opportunities, forcing Americans to confront new manifestations of virtue and corruption.

Patriotism at the Local Level Committees of correspondence, of public safety, and of inspection dominated the political landscape in patriot communities. These committees took on more than customary local governance; they enforced boycotts, picked army draftees, and policed suspected traitors. They sometimes invaded homes to search for contraband goods such as British tea or textiles.

Loyalists were dismayed by the increasing show of power by patriots. A man in Westchester, New York, described his response to intrusions by committees: "Choose your committee or suffer it to be chosen by a half dozen fools in your neighborhood—open your doors to them—let them examine your tea-cannisters and molasses-jugs, and your wives' and daughters' petty coats—bow and cringe and tremble and quake—fall down and worship our sovereign lord the mob. . . . Should any pragmatical committee-gentleman come to my house and give himself airs, I shall show him the door." Oppressive or not, the local committees

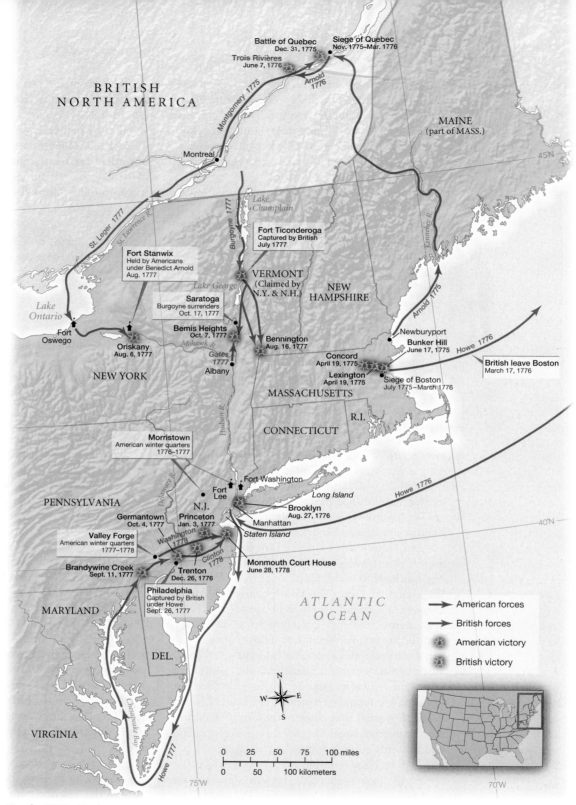

MAP 7.1 The War in the North, 1775–1778

After the early battles in Massachusetts in 1775, rebel forces invaded Canada but failed to capture Quebec. A large British army landed in New York in August 1776, turning New Jersey into a continual battle site in 1777 and 1778. Burgoyne arrived from England to secure Canada and attempted to pinch off New England along the Hudson River, but he was stopped at Saratoga in 1777 in the key battle of the early war.

READING THE MAP: Which general's troops traveled the farthest in each of these years: 1775, 1776, and 1777? How did the availability of water routes affect British and American strategy?

CONNECTIONS: Why did the French wait until early 1778 to join American forces against the British? What did France hope to gain from participating in the war?

FOR MORE HELP ANALYZING THIS MAP, see the map activity for this chapter in the Online Study Guide at bedfordstmartins.com/roarkcompact.

were rarely challenged. Their persuasive powers convinced many middle-of-the-road citizens that neutrality was not a comfortable option.

Another group new to political life—white women—increasingly demonstrated a capacity for patriotism as wartime hardships dramatically altered their work routines. Many wives whose husbands were away on military or political service took on masculine duties. Their competence to tend farms and make business decisions encouraged some to assert competence in politics as well. Abigail Adams managed the family farm in Massachusetts while John Adams was away for several years doing politics, in which Abigail took a keen interest. Eliza Wilkinson managed a South Carolina plantation and talked revolutionary politics with women friends. "None were greater politicians than the several knots of ladies who met together," she remarked, alert to the unusual turn female conversations had taken. "We commenced perfect statesmen." Women from prominent Philadelphia families took more direct action, forming the **Ladies Association** in 1780 to collect money for Continental soldiers. A published broadside, "The Sentiments of an American Woman," defended their female patriotism: "The time is arrived to display the same sentiments which animated us at the beginning of the Revolution, when we renounced the use of teas [and] when our republican and laborious hands spun the flax."

The Loyalists Around one-fifth of the American population remained loyal to the crown in 1776, and another two-fifths tried to stay neutral. With proper cultivation, this large base might have sustained the British empire in America. In general, **loyalists** had strong cultural and economic ties to England; they thought that social stability depended on a government anchored by monarchy and aristocracy. Perhaps most of all, they feared democratic tyranny. They understood that dissolving the automatic respect that subjects had for their king could lead to a society where deference to one's social betters might come under challenge. Patriots seemed to them to be unscrupulous, violent, self-interested men who simply wanted power for themselves.

The most visible loyalists (called **Tories** by their enemies) were royal officials, not only governors such as Thomas Hutchinson of Massachusetts but also local judges and customs officers. Wealthy merchants gravitated toward loyalism to maintain the trade protections of navigation acts and the British navy. Conservative urban lawyers admired the stability of British law and order. Some colonists chose loyalism simply to oppose traditional adversaries. Backcountry Carolina farmers leaned

loyalist out of resentment of the power of the lowlands gentry, generally of patriot persuasion. And, of course, southern slaves had their own resentments against the white slave-owning class and looked to Britain in hope of freedom.

Many Indian tribes hoped to remain neutral at the war's start, seeing the conflict as a civil war between English and Americans. Eventually, however, most were drawn in, many taking the British side. The powerful Iroquois Confederacy divided: The Mohawk, Cayuga, Seneca, and Onondaga peoples lined up with the British; the Oneida and Tuscarora tribes aided Americans. One young Mohawk leader, **Thayendanegea** (known also by his English name, **Joseph Brant**), traveled to England in 1775 to complain to King George about cheating American settlers. "It is very hard when we have let the King's subjects have so much of our lands for so little value," he wrote,

Joseph Brant The Mohawk leader Thayendanegea, called Joseph Brant by the Americans, had been educated in English ways at Eleazar Wheelock's New England school (which became Dartmouth College in 1769). In 1775, the thirty-four-year-old Brant traveled to England with another Mohawk to negotiate the tribe's support for the British. During his extended stay in London, he had his portrait painted by the English artist George Romney. Notice that Brant wears a metal gorget around his neck over his English shirt, along with an Indian sash, headdress, and armbands. A gorget was a piece of armor worn by feudal knights to protect the throat. Many military men, both white and Indian, wore smaller versions when they dressed formally for portraits—or for war. National Gallery of Canada.

Prisoners of War in the Eighteenth Century

The taking of captives was essential to eighteenth-century warfare, both to reduce an adversary's troop strength and to create opportunities for prisoner exchange. Although no formal international law governed the status of prisoners of war, many European nation-states had developed shared expectations of decent treatment, recognizing that captured soldiers were not common criminals subject to punishing incarceration. Among the expectations were provision of rations and such comforts as clean bedding straw. Customarily, prisoners' expenses (for food, clothes, blankets, and laundry) were paid by their own government to guarantee adequate supplies. All captives could hope for release through prisoner exchange of men of parallel rank. Officers could be ransomed or released on "parole," giving their solemn word of honor not to resume active military duty once freed.

George Washington fully expected the British to honor these customary civilities. But British leaders refused to recognize the colonies as a sovereign nation; the war was precisely about denying their independence. According to King George III, captured Americans were traitorous rebels—worse than common criminals and certainly not entitled to honorable and humane treatment.

The consequences of this point of view became apparent when the British invaded Long Island in August 1776 and captured more than a thousand Continental soldiers. Prisoners were crammed into New York City's one jail and stashed in several sugar refineries, the only large buildings in the city. In November, when another three thousand Americans surrendered at nearby Fort Washington, the British imprisoned the overflow captives on ships moored in the East River. Treatment was far from humane, and almost no means of release was honored, at least not at first. For the war's duration, some two dozen vessels anchored in Wallabout Bay, off Brooklyn, became death ships for thousands of prisoners captured from New England to Georgia.

The most infamous of these vessels was the very large HMS *Jersey*, built in the 1720s but now just a hulk stripped of its masts and guns. Built to house a crew of four hundred, the *Jersey* was packed with nearly three times that number of captives. Surviving prisoners described the dark, crowded, stinking space below-decks where men died daily, wasted and parched from extreme thirst. Prisoners were allowed on deck once a day, in shifts. Food, water, and sanitation facilities were inadequate. A twenty-year-old captive seaman described his first view of the hold: "Here was a motley crew, covered with rags and filth; visages pallid with disease, emaciated with hunger and anxiety, and retaining hardly a trace of their original appearance. Here were men . . . now shriveled by a scanty and unwholesome diet, ghastly with inhaling an impure atmosphere, exposed to contagion and disease, and surrounded with the horrors of sickness and death."

Following the European model, the prisoners were supposed to receive two-thirds the rations of regular soldiers and sailors, and the Continental Congress supplied some funds and food toward that end. But only a fraction of the provisions reached the prisons. Throughout the war, the British had trouble supplying their own soldiers, and corrupt commissaries diverted food for British use. Washington fumed at General Howe and threatened severe treatment of British prisoners; Howe remained uncooperative.

Treating the captives as common criminals instead of prisoners of war potentially triggered the Anglo-American right of habeas corpus, a central feature of English law since the thirteenth century, which guaranteed every prisoner the right to challenge his detention before a judge and learn the charges against him. To remove that possibility, Parliament voted in early 1777 to suspend habeas corpus specifically for "persons taken in the act of high treason" in any of the colonies. That suspension grievously troubled a group of Britons. The horrors of the Brooklyn prison ships were not close at hand, but there were two well-known prisons in Britain where several thousand captured American sailors languished, inadequately fed and housed. Denied prisoner-of-war privileges and denied the right to challenge their detention, these men were in legal limbo. Their British sympathizers raised funds to buy them food.

★ **The British Prisoner Ship HMS *Jersey*** American Robert Sheffield escaped from a prison ship (most likely the HMS *Jersey*) in 1778 after just six days and told a Connecticut newspaper of the torturous treatment of prisoners. "Their sickly Countenances and ghastly Looks were truly horrible," he reported. "Some [were] swearing and blaspheming; some crying, praying, and wringing their Hands, and stalking about like Ghosts and Apparitions; others delirious, void of Reason, raving, and storming; some groaning and dying—all panting for Breath; some dead and corrupting. The air so foul at Times, that a Lamp could not be kept burning, by Reason of which three Boys were not missed till they had been dead ten Days." Granger Collection.

As the war dragged on, some prisoner exchanges were negotiated when the British were desperate to regain valued officers. But for ordinary soldiers and seamen, death—or the rare escape—was their fate. Six to ten corpses left the prison ships daily and were buried along the shore by prisoner work crews. For decades after, skeletons washed out of the bay's embankments. Historians estimate that more than 15,000 men endured captivity in the New York jails and prison ships during the war. More than two-thirds of them died, a larger number than died in battle.

Nevertheless, General Washington insisted that captured British soldiers be properly treated. More than 3,000 British and Germans taken at Saratoga in 1778 spent the next five years in various locations from Massachusetts to Virginia, moving each time the theater of war drew near. Quartered in self-built barracks and guarded by local townsmen, the captives typically could cultivate small gardens, move about freely during the day, and even hire themselves out to farmers suffering wartime labor shortages. Officers with money purchased lodging with private families and mixed socially with Americans. Officers on parole enjoyed freedom to travel locally; many were allowed to keep their guns.

At the end of the war, prisoners on both sides were released and allowed to return home. But the war's end came too late for the many thousands of Americans who died in captivity.

In 1785, shortly after the Revolution, three American diplomats in Europe—Thomas Jefferson, Benjamin Franklin, and John Adams—negotiated a friendly treaty of commerce with Prussia that included a groundbreaking paragraph requiring humane treatment of prisoners of war: Prisoners "shall not be confined in dungeons, prison ships, nor prisons" and shall have "air & exercise," roomy barracks, and full rations—all concerns directly arising out of the American experience in the Revolution. It was the historic first in a series of steps leading to the twentieth-century Geneva conventions designed to protect prisoners of war.

"they should want to cheat us in this manner of the small spots we have left for our women and children to live on." Brant pledged Indian support for the king in exchange for protection from encroaching settlers. In the Ohio Country, parts of the Shawnee and Delaware tribes started out pro-American but shifted to the British side by 1779 in the face of repeated betrayals by American settlers and soldiers.

Pockets of loyalism thus existed everywhere — in the middle colonies, in the backcountry of the southern colonies, and out beyond the Appalachian Mountains in Indian country (Map 7.2). Even

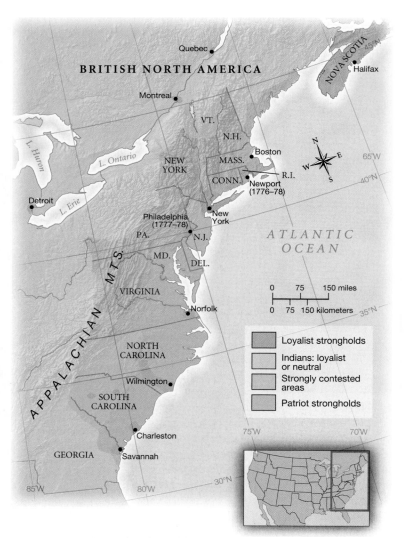

MAP 7.2 Loyalist Strength and Rebel Support
The exact number of loyalists can never be known. No one could have made an accurate count at the time, and political allegiance often shifted with the wind. This map shows the regions of loyalist strength on which the British relied — most significantly, the lower Hudson valley and the Carolina Piedmont.

New England towns at the heart of the turmoil, such as Concord, Massachusetts, had a small and increasingly silenced core of loyalists who refused to countenance armed revolution.

Loyalists were most vocal between 1774 and 1776, when the possibility of a full-scale rebellion against Britain was still uncertain. They challenged the emerging patriot side in pamphlets and newspapers. In New York City, 547 loyalists signed and circulated a broadside titled "A Declaration of Dependence" in rebuttal to the congress's July 4, 1776, declaration, denouncing the "most unnatural, unprovoked Rebellion that ever disgraced the annals of Time."

Who Is a Traitor? In June 1775, the First Continental Congress declared all loyalists to be traitors. Over the next year, state laws defined as treason acts such as provisioning the British army, saying anything that undermined patriot morale, and discouraging men from enlisting in the Continental army. Punishments ranged from house arrest and suspension of voting privileges to confiscation of property and deportation. Sometimes self-appointed committees of Tory-hunters bypassed the judicial niceties and terrorized loyalists, raiding their houses or tarring and feathering them.

Were wives of loyalists also traitors? When loyalist families fled the country, their property was typically confiscated. But if the wife stayed, courts usually allowed her to keep one-third of the property, the amount due her if widowed, and confiscated the rest. A wife who fled with her husband might have little choice in the matter. After the Revolution, descendants of refugee loyalists filed several lawsuits to regain property that had entered the family through the mother's inheritance. In one well-publicized Massachusetts case in 1805, the outcome confirmed the traditional view of women as political blank slates. The American son of loyalist refugee Anna Martin recovered her dowry property on the grounds that she had no independent will to be a loyalist.

Tarring and feathering, property confiscation, deportation, terrorism — to the loyalists, such denials of liberty of conscience and of freedom to own private property proved that democratic tyranny was more to be feared than the monarchical variety. A Boston loyalist named Mather Byles aptly expressed this point: "They call me a brainless Tory, but tell me . . . which is better — to be ruled by one tyrant three thousand miles away, or by three thousand tyrants not a mile away?" Byles was soon sentenced to deportation.

Throughout the war, probably 7,000 to 8,000 loyalists fled to England, and 28,000 found haven in Canada. But many chose to remain in the new

United States and swing with the changing political winds. In some instances, that proved difficult. In New Jersey, for example, 3,000 Jerseyites felt protected (or scared) enough by the occupying British army in 1776 to swear an oath of allegiance to the king. But then General Howe drew back to New York City, leaving them to the mercy of local patriot committees. British strategy depended on using loyalists to hold occupied territory, but the New Jersey experience showed how poorly that strategy was carried out.

Financial Instability and Corruption Wars cost money—for arms and ammunition, for food and uniforms, for soldiers' pay. The Continental Congress printed money, but its value quickly deteriorated because the congress held no reserves of gold or silver to back the currency. In practice, it was worth only what buyers and sellers agreed it was worth; the dollar eventually bottomed out at one-fortieth of its face value. States began printing paper money to pay for wartime expenses, further complicating the economy.

As the currency depreciated, the congress turned to other means to procure supplies and labor. One method was to borrow hard money (gold or silver coins) from wealthy men in exchange for certificates of debt (public securities) promising repayment with interest. The certificates of debt were similar to present-day government bonds. To pay soldiers, the congress issued land grant certificates, written promises of acreage usually located in frontier areas such as central Maine or eastern Ohio. Both the public securities and the land grant certificates quickly became forms of negotiable currency. A soldier with no cash, for example, could sell his land grant certificate to get food for his family. These certificates soon depreciated, too.

Depreciating currency inevitably led to rising prices, as sellers compensated for the falling value of the money. The wartime economy of the late 1770s, with its unreliable currency and price inflation, was extremely demoralizing to Americans everywhere. In 1778, in an effort to impose stability, local committees of public safety began to fix prices on essential goods such as flour. Inevitably, some turned this unstable situation to their advantage. Money that fell fast in value needed to be spent quickly; being in debt was suddenly advantageous because the debt could be repaid in devalued currency. A brisk black market sprang up in prohibited luxury imports, such as tea, sugar, textiles, and wines, even though these items came from Britain. A New Hampshire delegate to the congress denounced the violation of the homespun association agreements of just a few years before: "We are a crooked and perverse generation, longing for the fineries and follies of those Egyptian task masters from whom we have so lately freed ourselves."

Q: How did the patriots promote support for their cause in the colonies?

The Campaigns of 1777–1779: The North and West

In early 1777, the Continental army faced bleak choices. General Washington had skillfully avoided defeat, but the minor victories in New Jersey lent only faint optimism to the American side. Meanwhile, British troops moved south from Quebec, aiming to isolate New England from the rest of the colonies by taking control of the Hudson River. Their presence drew the Continental army up into central New York, polarizing Indian tribes of the Iroquois nation and turning the Mohawk Valley into a bloody war zone. By 1779, tribes in western New York and in Indian country in the Ohio Valley were fully involved in the Revolutionary War. Most sided with the British and against the Americans. The Americans had some success in this period, such as the victory at Saratoga, but the involvement of Indians and the continuing strength of the British forced the American government to look to France for help.

Burgoyne's Army and the Battle of Saratoga In 1777, British general John Burgoyne assumed command of an army of 7,800 soldiers in Canada and began the northern squeeze on the Hudson River valley. His goal was to capture Albany, near the intersection of the Hudson and Mohawk rivers (see Map 7.1). Accompanied by 1,000 "camp followers" (cooks, laundresses, and musicians) and some 400 Indian

A Soldier's Canteen This wooden canteen belonged to Noah Allen, whose name and regiment number are carved into the side. Allen was from the Sixth Continental Regiment from Massachusetts. Almost no piece of equipment surpassed the soldier's canteen in importance. Fort Ticonderoga Museum.

Death of Jane McCrea This 1804 painting by John Vanderlyn memorializes the martyr legend of Jane McCrea. Daughter of an American patriot family in northern New York, McCrea was in love with a young American loyalist who joined Burgoyne's army. In July 1777, she eloped to join her fiancé, guided by Indians sent by the British to escort her. But she was killed on the short journey — either shot in the crossfire of battle, as the British claimed, or murdered by savage Indians allied with the British, in the patriots' version. The American general Horatio Gates sent Burgoyne an accusatory letter. "The miserable fate of Miss McCrea was particularly aggravated by her being dressed to meet her promised husband," Gates wrote, "but she met her murderers employed by you." Gates skillfully used the story of the vulnerable, innocent maiden dressed in alluring clothes as propaganda to inspire his soldiers' drive for victory at Saratoga. Wadsworth Atheneum, Hartford.

FOR MORE HELP ANALYZING THIS IMAGE, see the visual activity for this chapter in the Online Study Guide at bedfordstmartins.com/roarkcompact.

But Howe surprised everyone by sailing south to attack Philadelphia.

To reinforce Burgoyne, British troops from Montreal came from the east along the Mohawk River, aided by Mohawks and Senecas of the Iroquois Confederacy. The British counted on loyalism among the numerous Palatine Germans living in the Mohawk Valley. But a hundred miles west of Albany, they encountered American Continental soldiers at Fort Stanwix, supported by Palatine German militiamen and Oneida Indians. Mohawk chief Joseph Brant led the Senecas and Mohawks in an ambush on the Germans and the Oneidas in a narrow ravine called **Oriskany**, killing nearly 500 out of 840 of them. On Brant's side, some 90 warriors were killed. But Fort Stanwix repelled the British and Indians and forced them to retreat (see Map 7.1). The Oriskany and Fort Stanwix battles were very deadly; they were also complexly multiethnic, pitting Indians against Indians, German Americans (the Palatines) against German mercenaries, New York patriots against New York loyalists, and English Americans against British soldiers.

The British retreat at Fort Stanwix deprived General Burgoyne of the additional troops he expected. Camped at a small village called Saratoga, he was isolated, with

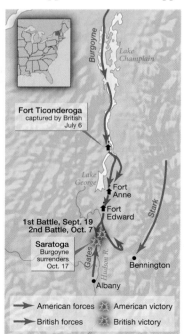

Battle of Saratoga, 1777

warriors, Burgoyne's army did not travel light. In addition to food and supplies for 9,200 people, the army carried food for the 400 horses hauling heavy artillery. Burgoyne also carted thirty trunks of personal belongings and fine wines.

In July, Burgoyne captured Fort Ticonderoga with ease. American troops stationed there spotted the approaching British and abandoned the fort without a fight. The British continued to move south, but the large army moved slowly on primitive roads through dense forests. The logical second step in isolating New England should have been to advance troops up the Hudson from New York City to meet Burgoyne. American surveillance indicated that General Howe in Manhattan was readying his men for a major move in August 1777.

food supplies dwindling and men deserting. His adversary at Albany, General Horatio Gates, began moving his army toward him. Burgoyne decided to attack first because every day his soldiers weakened. The British prevailed, but at the great cost of 600 dead or wounded redcoats. Three weeks later, an American attack on Burgoyne's forces at **Saratoga** cost the British another 600 men and most of their cannons. General Burgoyne finally surrendered to the American forces on October 17, 1777.

General Howe, meanwhile, had succeeded in occupying Philadelphia in September 1777. Figuring that the Saratoga loss was balanced by the capture of Philadelphia, the British government proposed a negotiated settlement—not including independence—to end the war. The American side refused.

Patriot optimism was not well founded. Spirits ran high, but supplies of arms and food ran precariously low. Washington moved his troops into winter quarters at Valley Forge, just west of Philadelphia. Quartered in drafty huts, the men lacked blankets, boots, stockings, and food. Some 2,000 men at Valley Forge died of disease; another 2,000 deserted over the bitter six-month encampment.

Washington blamed the citizenry for lack of support; indeed, evidence of corruption and profiteering was abundant. Army suppliers too often provided defective food, clothing, and gunpowder. One shipment of bedding arrived with blankets one-quarter their customary size. Food supplies arrived rotten. As one Continental officer said, "The people at home are destroying the Army by their conduct much faster than Howe and all his army can possibly do by fighting us."

The War in the West: Indian Country   Burgoyne's defeat in the fall of 1777 and Washington's long stay at Valley Forge up to June 1778 might suggest that the war paused for a time, and it did on the Atlantic coast. But in the interior western areas—the Mohawk Valley, the Ohio Valley, and Kentucky—the war of Indians against the American pro-independence side heated up. For native tribes, the struggle was not about taxation, representation, or monarchical rule; it was about independence, freedom, and land.

The ambush and slaughter at Oriskany in August 1777 marked the beginning of three years of terror for the inhabitants of the Mohawk Valley. Loyalists and Indians engaged in many raids on farms throughout 1778, capturing or killing the residents. In retaliation, American militiamen destroyed Joseph Brant's village but failed to capture any warriors. A month later, Brant's warriors attacked the town of Cherry Valley, killing 16 soldiers and 32 civilians.

The following summer, General Washington authorized a campaign to wreak "total destruction and devastation" on all the Iroquoian villages of central New York. Some 4,500 troops commanded by General John Sullivan implemented a campaign of terror in the fall of 1779. Forty Indian towns met with total obliteration; the soldiers looted and torched the dwellings, then burned cornfields and orchards. In a few towns, women and children were slaughtered, but in most, the inhabitants managed to escape, fleeing to the British at Fort Niagara. Thousands of Indian refugees, sick and starving, camped around the fort in one of the most miserable winters on record.

Much farther to the west, beyond Fort Pitt, another complex story of alliances and betrayals between American militiamen and Indians unfolded. Some 150,000 native people lived between the Appalachian Mountains and the Mississippi River, and by 1779, neutrality was no longer an option. Most sided with the British, but a portion of the Shawnee and Delaware tribes at first sought peace with the Americans. In mid-1778, the Delaware chief White Eyes negotiated a treaty at Fort Pitt, pledging Indian support for the Americans in exchange for supplies and trade goods. But escalating violence undermined the agreement. That fall, when American soldiers killed two friendly Shawnee chiefs, Cornstalk and Red Hawk, the Continental Congress hastened to apologize, as did the governors of Pennsylvania and Virginia, but the soldiers who stood trial for the murders were acquitted. Two months later, White Eyes, nominally an ally of and an informant for the Americans, died under mysterious circumstances, almost certainly murdered by militiamen, who repeatedly had trouble honoring distinctions between allied and enemy Indians.

West of North Carolina (today's Tennessee), the frontier war zone of the South, militias attacked Cherokee settlements in 1779, destroying thirty-six villages and burning fields and livestock. Indian raiders from north of the Ohio River, in alliance with the British, repeatedly attacked white settlements such as Boonesborough (in present-day Kentucky) (Map 7.3). In retaliation, a young Virginian, George Rogers Clark, led Kentucky militiamen into what is now Illinois, attacking and taking the British fort at Kaskaskia. Clark's men wore native clothing—hunting shirts and breech cloths—but their dress was not a sign of solidarity with the Indians. When they attacked British-held Fort Vincennes in 1779, Clark's troops tomahawked Indian captives and threw their still-live bodies into the river in a gory spectacle witnessed by the redcoats. "To excel them in barbarity is the only

> "To excel them in barbarity is the only way to make war upon Indians," George Rogers Clark announced.

way to make war upon Indians," Clark announced. And, he might have added, it was an effective way to terrorize British soldiers as well.

By 1780, very few Indians remained neutral. Violent raids by Americans drove Indians into the arms of the British at Detroit and Niagara, or into the arms of the Spanish, who still held much of the land west of the Mississippi River. Said one officer on the Sullivan campaign, "Their nests are destroyed but the birds are still on the wing." For those who stayed near their native lands, chaos and confusion prevailed. Rare as it was, Indian support for the American side occasionally emerged out of a strategic sense that the Americans were unstoppable in their westward pressure and that it was better to work out an alliance than to lose in a war. But American treatment of even friendly Indians showed that there was no winning strategy for them.

The French Alliance On their own, the Americans could not have defeated Britain, especially as pressure from hostile Indians increased. Essential help arrived as a result of the victory at Saratoga, which convinced the French to enter the war; a formal alliance was signed in February 1778. France recognized the United States as an independent nation and promised full military and commercial support. Most crucial was the French navy, which could challenge British supplies and troops at sea and aid the Americans in taking and holding prisoners of war.

Well before 1778, however, the French had been covertly providing cannons, muskets, gunpowder, and highly trained military advisers to the Americans. Monarchical France was understandably cautious about endorsing a democratic revolution attacking kingship. Instead, the main attraction of an alliance was the opportunity it provided to defeat archrival

MAP 7.3 The Indian War in the West, 1777–1782

The American Revolution involved many Indian tribes, most of them supporting the British. Iroquois Indians, with British aid, attacked American towns in New York's Mohawk Valley throughout 1778. In 1779, the Continental army marched on forty Iroquois villages in central New York and destroyed them. Shawnee and Delaware Indians to the west of Fort Pitt tangled with American militia units in 1779, while tribes supported by the British at Fort Detroit conducted raids on Kentucky settlers, who hit back with raids of their own. George Rogers Clark led Kentucky militiamen against Indians in the Illinois region. Sporadic fighting continued in the West through 1782, ending with Indian attacks on Hannastown, Pennsylvania, and Fort Henry on the Ohio River. By the late 1780s, occasional fighting resumed, sparked by American settlers pressing west onto Indian land.

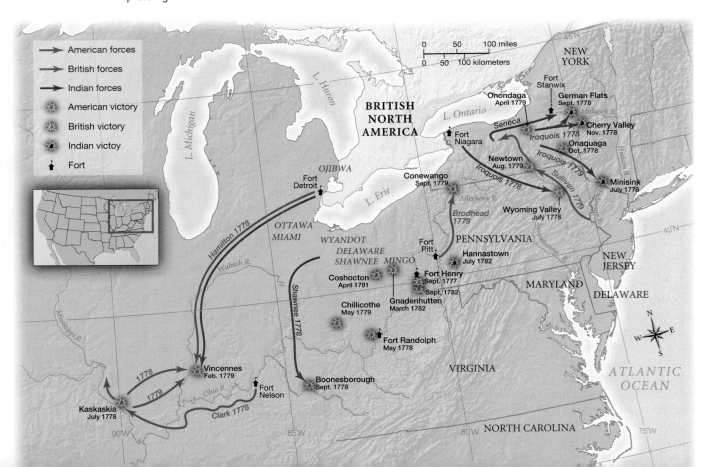

Britain. A victory would also open pathways to trade and perhaps result in France's acquiring the coveted British West Indies. Even American defeat would not be a disaster for France if the war lasted many years and drained Britain of men and money.

French support materialized slowly. The navy arrived off the Virginia coast in July 1778 but then sailed south to the West Indies to defend the French sugar-producing islands. French help would prove indispensable to the American victory, but the alliance's first months brought no dramatic victories, and some Americans grumbled that the partnership would prove worthless.

Q: Why did the Americans need assistance from the French to ensure victory?

The Southern Strategy and the End of the War

When France joined the war, some British officials wondered whether the fight was worth continuing. A troop commander, arguing for an immediate negotiated settlement, shrewdly observed that "we are far from an anticipated peace, because the bitterness of the rebels is too widespread, and in regions where we are masters the rebellious spirit is still in them. The land is too large, and there are too many people. The more land we win, the weaker our army gets in the field." The commander of the British navy argued for abandoning the war, and even Lord North, the prime minister, agreed. But the king was determined to crush the rebellion, and he encouraged a new strategy for victory focusing on the southern colonies, thought to be more persuadably loyalist. It was a brilliant but desperate plan, and ultimately unsuccessful. Southern colonists were not all that loyal and in fact were willing to engage in guerrilla warfare against the British. The southern strategy thus led to a British defeat at Yorktown and the end of the war.

Georgia and South Carolina The new strategy called for British forces to abandon New England and focus on the South, with its valuable crops—tobacco, rice, and indigo—and its large slave population, a destabilizing factor that might keep rebellious white southerners in line. Georgia and the Carolinas appeared to hold

large numbers of loyalists, providing a base for the British to recapture the southern colonies one by one, moving north to the more problematic middle colonies and saving prickly New England for last.

Georgia, the first target, fell at the end of December 1778 (Map 7.4). A small army of British soldiers occupied Savannah and Augusta, and a new royal governor and loyalist assembly were quickly installed. Taking Georgia was easy because the bulk of the Continental army was in New York and New Jersey, keeping an eye on General Henry Clinton, Howe's replacement as commander in chief, and the French were in the West Indies. The British in Georgia quickly organized twenty loyal militia units, and 1,400 Georgians swore an oath

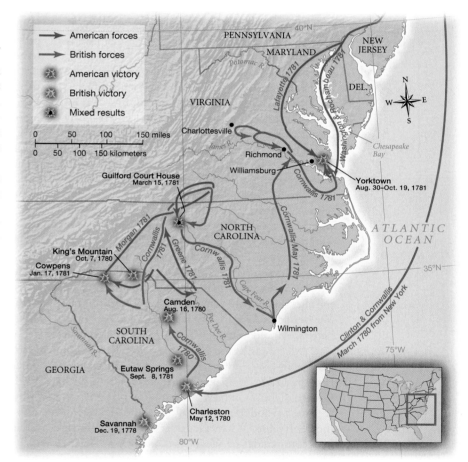

MAP 7.4 The War in the South, 1780–1781

After taking Charleston in May 1780, the British advanced into South Carolina and the foothills of North Carolina, leaving a bloody civil war in their wake. When the American general Horatio Gates and his men fled from the humiliating battle of Camden, Gates was replaced by General Nathanael Greene and General Daniel Morgan, who pulled off major victories at King's Mountain and Cowpens. The British general Cornwallis then moved north and invaded Virginia, but was bottled up and finally overpowered at Yorktown in the fall of 1781.

of allegiance to the king. So far, the southern strategy looked as if it might work.

Next came South Carolina. The Continental army put ten regiments into the port city of Charleston to defend it from attack by British troops shipped south from New York under the command of General Clinton. For five weeks in early 1780, the British laid siege to the city and took it in May 1780, sending 3,300 American soldiers, a tremendous loss, into British captivity. Again, the king's new strategy seemed to be on target.

Clinton returned to New York, leaving the task of pacifying the rest of South Carolina to General **Charles Cornwallis** and 4,000 troops. A bold commander, Lord Cornwallis quickly chased out the remaining Continentals and established military rule of South Carolina by midsummer. He purged rebels from government office and disarmed rebel militias. The export of South Carolina's main crop, rice, resumed, and as in Georgia, pardons were offered to Carolinians willing to prove their loyalty by taking up arms for the British.

By August, American troops arrived from the North to strike back at Cornwallis. General Gates, the hero of Saratoga, led 3,000 troops, half of them experienced Continental soldiers and others newly recruited militiamen, into battle against Cornwallis at **Camden**, South Carolina, on August 16 (see Map 7.4). The militiamen panicked at the sight of the approaching British cavalry and fled. When regiment leaders tried to regroup the next day, only 700 soldiers showed up; the rest were dead, wounded, captured, or still in flight. The battle of Camden was a devastating defeat and prospects seemed very grim for the Americans.

Britain's southern strategy succeeded in 1780 in part because of information about American troop movements secretly conveyed by an American traitor: **Benedict Arnold**. The hero of several American battles, Arnold was a brilliant military talent but also a deeply insecure man who never felt he got his due in either honor or financial reward. Sometime in 1779, he opened secret negotiations with General Clinton in New York, trading information for money and hinting that he could deliver far more of value. When General Washington made him commander of West Point, a new fort on the Hudson River sixty miles north of New York City, Arnold's plan crystallized. West Point controlled the Hudson; its easy capture by the British might well have meant victory in the war.

Arnold's plot to sell a West Point victory to the British was foiled in the fall of 1780 when Americans captured the man carrying plans of the fort's defense from Arnold to Clinton. News of Arnold's treason created shock waves. Arnold represented all of the patriots' worst fears about themselves: greedy self-interest, like that of the war profiteers; the unprincipled abandonment of war aims, like that of turncoat southern Tories; panic, like that of the terrified soldiers at Camden. But instead of symbolizing all that was troubling about the American side of the war, the treachery of Arnold was publicly denounced in a kind of displacement of the anxieties of the moment. Vilifying Arnold allowed Americans to stake out a wide distance between themselves and dastardly conduct. It inspired a renewal of patriotism at a particularly low moment.

The Other Southern War: Guerrillas

Shock over Gates's defeat at Camden and Arnold's treason revitalized rebel support in western South Carolina, an area that Cornwallis believed to be pacified and loyal. The backcountry of the South soon became the site of guerrilla warfare. In hit-and-run attacks, both sides burned and ravaged not only opponents' property but also the property of anyone claiming to be neutral. Loyalist militia units organized by the British were met by fierce rebel militia units whose members figured they had little to lose. In South Carolina, some 6,000 rebels met loyalist units in bloody engagements. Guerrilla warfare soon spread to Georgia and North Carolina. Both sides committed atrocities and plundered property, clear deviations from standard military practice.

The British southern strategy depended on sufficient loyalist strength to hold reconquered territory as Cornwallis's army moved north. The backcountry civil war proved this assumption false. The Americans won few major battles in the South, but they ultimately succeeded by harassing the British forces and preventing them from foraging for food. Cornwallis moved the war into North Carolina in the fall of 1780 not because he thought South Carolina was secure—it was not—but because the North Carolinians were supplying the South Carolina rebels with arms and men (see Map 7.4). Then news of a brutal massacre of loyalist units by 1,400 frontier riflemen at the battle of King's Mountain, in western South Carolina, sent him hurrying back. The British were stretched too thin to hold even two of their onetime colonies.

Surrender at Yorktown

By early 1781, the war was going very badly for the British. Their defeat at King's Mountain was quickly followed by a second major defeat at the battle of Cowpens in South Carolina in January 1781. Cornwallis retreated to North Carolina and thence to Virginia, where he captured Williamsburg in June. A raiding party proceeded to Charlottesville, the seat of government, capturing members of the Virginia assembly but not Governor Thomas Jefferson, who escaped the soldiers by a mere ten minutes. (More than a dozen of Jefferson's slaves chose this moment to seek refuge with the British.) These minor victories allowed Cornwallis to imagine he was succeeding in Virginia. He next marched to Yorktown, near the Chesapeake Bay, expecting backup troops by ship from British headquarters in New York City.

At this juncture, the French-American alliance came into play. Already, French regiments commanded by the Comte de Rochambeau had joined General Washington in Newport, Rhode Island, in mid-1780, and now in 1781 warships under the Comte de Grasse sailed from France. Washington, Rochambeau, and de Grasse fixed

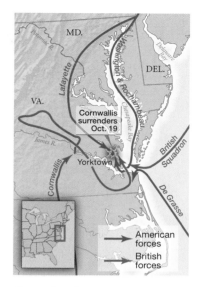

Siege of Yorktown, 1781

their attention on the Chesapeake Bay. The French fleet got there ahead of the British troop ships from New York; a five-day naval battle left the French navy in control of the Virginia coast. This proved to be the decisive factor in ending the war, because the French ships prevented any rescue of Cornwallis's army.

On land, General Cornwallis and his 7,500 troops faced a combined French and American army of 16,000. For twelve days, the Americans and French bombarded the British fortifications at

Yorktown; Cornwallis ran low on food and ammunition. An American observer noted that "the enemy, from want of forage, are killing off their horses in great numbers. Six or seven hundred of these valuable animals have been killed, and their carcasses are almost continually floating down the river." Realizing that escape was impossible, Cornwallis surrendered on October 19, 1781.

What began as a promising southern strategy in 1778 turned into a discouraging defeat. British attacks in the South had energized American resistance, as did the timely exposure of Benedict Arnold's treason. The arrival of the French fleet sealed the fate of Cornwallis at the battle of Yorktown, and major military operations came to a halt.

The Losers and the Winners The surrender at Yorktown spelled the end for the British, but two more years of skirmishes ensued. Frontier areas in Kentucky, Ohio, and Illinois blazed with battles pitting Americans against various Indian tribes. The British army still occupied three coastal cities, including New York City, and in response,

Lafayette at Yorktown An enthusiast for American liberty, the young French nobleman Lafayette came to the United States in 1777 at age twenty to volunteer his services to General Washington. After proving his leadership in several northern campaigns, he went to Virginia in 1781 to fight Cornwallis. Near Richmond, he met James, a slave belonging to William Armistead, who loaned him to Lafayette. At the siege of Yorktown, James, pretending to be an escaped slave, infiltrated the British command, giving them misinformation and bringing crucial intelligence back to Lafayette. At the surrender, Cornwallis saw James at Lafayette's headquarters and realized he'd been had. The French artist Jean Baptiste Le Paon painted the two men in 1783 without ever having laid eyes on James. His heroic portrait focuses on Lafayette; James, with plumed hat, fancy improbable costume, and generic face, is a mere ornament to his white general. James obtained his freedom in 1786 after Lafayette wrote a letter on his behalf to the Virginia assembly. In honor of his friend, he took the name James Armistead Lafayette. Art Gallery, Williams Center, Lafayette College.

"The Ballance of Power," 1780 This cartoon was published in England soon after Spain and the Netherlands declared an alliance with France to support the war in America. On the left, Britannia, a female figure representing Great Britain, cannot be moved by all the lightweights on the right side of the scale. France wears a ruffled shirt, Spain has a feather in his hat, and a Dutch boy has just hopped on, saying, "I'll do anything for Money." The forlorn Indian maiden, the standard icon representing America in the eighteenth century, sits on the scale, head in hand, wailing, "My Ingratitude is Justly punished." The poem printed below the cartoon predicts, "The Americans too will with Britons Unite." This fanciful prediction was punctured nine months after it appeared when the British surrendered to the Americans and the French at Yorktown in 1781. Print Collection, Miriam and Ira D. Wallach Division of Art, Prints, and Photographs, The New York Public Library. Astor, Lenox, and Tilden Foundations.

FOR MORE HELP ANALYZING THIS IMAGE, see the visual activity for this chapter in the Online Study Guide at bedfordstmartins.com/roarkcompact.

an augmented Continental army stayed at the ready, north of the city. Occasional clashes occurred, like the one in which light infantryman Deborah Sampson saw action and sustained a wound, thereby revealing her cross-gender masquerade.

The peace treaty took six months to negotiate. Commissioners from America, Britain, and France met in Paris and worked out eighty-two articles of peace. The first article went to the heart of the matter: "His Britannic Majesty acknowledges the said United States to be free Sovereign and independent States." Other articles set the western boundary of the new country at the Mississippi River and guaranteed that creditors on both sides could collect debts owed them in sterling money, a provision especially important to British merchants. Britain

agreed to withdraw its troops quickly; more than a decade later, this promise still had not been fully kept. The **Treaty of Paris** was signed on September 2, 1783.

Like the treaty ending the Seven Years' War, this treaty failed to recognize the Indians as players in the conflict. As one American told the Shawnee people, "Your Fathers the English have made Peace with us for themselves, but forgot you their Children, who Fought with them, and neglected you like Bastards." Indian lands were assigned to the victors as though they were uninhabited. Some Indian refugees fled west into present-day Missouri and Arkansas, and others, such as Joseph Brant's Mohawks, relocated to Canada. But significant numbers remained within the new United States, occupying their traditional homelands in areas west and north of the Ohio River. For them, the Treaty of Paris brought no peace at all; their longer war against the Americans would extend at least until 1795 and for some until 1813. Their ally, Britain, conceded defeat, but the Indians did not.

With the treaty finally signed, the British began their evacuation of New York, Charleston, and Savannah, a process complicated by the sheer numbers involved—soldiers, fearful loyalists, and runaway slaves by the thousands. In New York City, more than 27,000 soldiers and 30,000 loyalists sailed on hundreds of ships for England in the late fall of 1783. In a final act of mischief, on the November day when the last ships left, the losing side raised the British flag at the southern tip of Manhattan, cut away the ropes used to hoist it, and greased the flagpole.

Q: **Why did the British southern strategy ultimately fail?**

Conclusion: Why the British Lost

The British began the war for America convinced that they could not lose. They had the best-trained army and navy in the world; they were familiar with the landscape from the Seven Years' War; they had the willing warrior-power of most of the native tribes of the backcountry; and they easily captured every port city of consequence in America. Probably one-fifth of the population was loyalist, and another two-fifths were undecided. Why, then, did the British lose?

One continuing problem the British faced was the uncertainty of supplies. Unwilling to ravage the countryside, the army depended on a steady stream of supply ships from home. Insecurity about food helps explain their reluctance to pursue the Continental army aggressively. A further obstacle was their continual misuse of loyalist energies. Any

plan to repacify the colonies required the cooperation of the loyalists, but the British repeatedly left them to the mercy of vengeful rebels. French aid looms large in any explanation of the British defeat. Even before the formal alliance, French artillery and ammunition proved vital to the Continental army. After 1780, the French army brought a new infusion of troops to a war-weary America, and the French navy made the Yorktown victory possible. Finally, the British abdicated civil power in the colonies in 1775 and 1776, when royal officials fled to safety, and they never really regained it. For seven years, the Americans created their own government structures, from the Continental Congress to local committees and militias. Staffed by many who before 1775 had been the political elites, these new government agencies had remarkably little trouble establishing their authority to rule. The basic British goal—to turn back the clock to imperial rule—receded into impossibility as the war dragged on.

The war for America had lasted just over six years, from Lexington to Yorktown; negotiations and the evacuation took two more. It profoundly disrupted the lives of Americans everywhere. It was a war for independence from Britain, but it was more. It was a war that required men and women to think about politics and the legitimacy of authority. The precise disagreement with Britain about representation and political participation had profound implications for the kinds of governance the Americans would adopt, both in the moment of emergency and in the longer run of the late 1770s and early 1780s when states began to write their constitutions. The rhetoric employed to justify the revolution against Britain put words such as *liberty, tyranny, slavery, independence,* and *equality* into common usage. These words carried far deeper meanings than a mere complaint over taxation without representation. The Revolution unleashed a dynamic of equality and liberty that was largely unintended and unwanted by many of the American leaders of 1776. But that dynamic emerged as a potent force in American life in the decades to come.

Reviewing the Chapter

★ KEY TERMS

Explain each term's significance

WHO

John Dickinson (p. 157)

George Washington (p. 157)

Thomas Paine (p. 159)

Abigail Adams (p. 159)

loyalists (Tories) (p. 165)

Joseph Brant (Thayendanegea) (p. 165)

Charles Cornwallis (p. 174)

Benedict Arnold (p. 174)

WHAT

Second Continental Congress (p. 156)

Continental army (p. 157)

battle of Bunker Hill (p. 158)

Common Sense (p. 159)

Declaration of Independence (p. 160)

battle of Long Island (p. 163)

Ladies Association (p. 165)

battle of Oriskany (p. 170)

battle of Saratoga (p. 171)

battle of Camden (p. 174)

battle of Yorktown (p. 175)

Treaty of Paris (p. 176)

★ REVIEW QUESTIONS Q:

Use key terms and dates to support your answer

1. Why were many Americans reluctant to pursue independence from Britain? (pp. 156–60)

2. Why did the British exercise restraint in their efforts to defeat the rebellious colonies? (pp. 160–64)

3. How did the patriots promote support for their cause in the colonies? (pp. 164–69)

4. Why did the Americans need assistance from the French to ensure victory? (pp. 169–73)

5. Why did the British southern strategy ultimately fail? (pp. 173–77)

★ MAKING CONNECTIONS

Draw on key terms, timeline, and review questions

1. Even before the colonies had committed to independence, they faced the likelihood of serious military conflict. How did they mobilize for war? In your answer, discuss specific challenges they faced, noting unintended consequences of their solutions.

2. Congress's adoption of the Declaration of Independence confirmed a decisive shift in the conflict between the colonies and Britain. Why did the colonies make this decisive break in 1776? In your answer, discuss some of the arguments for and against independence.

3. The question of whether the colonists would be loyal to the new government or to the old king was pivotal during the Revolutionary War. Discuss the importance of loyalty in the outcome of the conflict. In your answer, consider both military and political strategy.

4. American colonists and British soldiers were not the only participants in the Revolutionary War. Discuss the role of Native Americans in the war. How did they shape the conflict? What benefits did they hope to gain? Did they succeed?

★ SUGGESTED READINGS

Carol Berkin, *Revolutionary Mothers: Women in the Struggle for America's Independence* (2005). A lively account of the many ways women participated in the war, including as camp followers, generals' wives, loyalists, slaves, and Indians.

Piers Mackesy, *The War for America, 1775–1783* (1964). A classic that presents the Revolution from the point of view of the British.

Pauline Maier, *American Scripture: Making the Declaration of Independence* (1997). Meticulous and fascinating scholarship showing the context of and precursors to the famous document of 1776.

David McCullough, *1776* (2005). A highly readable, near cinematic account of one crucial year of the war.

Gary B. Nash, *The Unknown American Revolution: The Unruly Birth of Democracy and the Struggle to Create America* (2005). The Revolution not as a "glorious cause" by unified patriots but as a complex and turbulent struggle involving civil war, ethnic massacres, and keen suffering.

Alfred F. Young, *Masquerade: The Life and Times of Deborah Sampson, Continental Soldier* (2004). An ingeniously researched recovery of the full story of the cross-dressing soldier and her bid for recognition.

FOR MORE BOOKS ABOUT TOPICS IN THIS CHAPTER, see the Online Bibliography at **bedfordstmartins.com/roarkcompact**.

FOR ADDITIONAL FIRSTHAND ACCOUNTS OF THIS PERIOD, see Chapter 7 in Michael Johnson, ed., *Reading the American Past*, Fourth Edition.

FOR WEB SITES, IMAGES, AND DOCUMENTS RELATED TO TOPICS AND PLACES IN THIS CHAPTER, visit Make History at **bedfordstmartins.com/roarkcompact**.

★ TIMELINE

1775
- Second Continental Congress convenes.
- British win battle of Bunker Hill.
- King George rejects Olive Branch Petition.
- Americans lose battle of Quebec.

1776
- *Common Sense* published.
- British evacuate Boston.
- **July 4**. Congress adopts Declaration of Independence.
- British take Manhattan.

1777
- British take Fort Ticonderoga.
- Ambush at Oriskany.
- Americans hold Fort Stanwix.
- British occupy Philadelphia.
- British surrender at Saratoga.
- Continental army endures winter at Valley Forge.

1778
- France enters war on American side.
- American militiamen destroy Mohawk chief Joseph Brant's village.
- White Eyes negotiates treaty with Americans; later mysteriously dies.

1779
- Militias attack Cherokee settlements in far western North Carolina.
- Americans destroy forty Iroquois villages in New York.
- Americans take Forts Kaskaskia and Vincennes.

1780
- Philadelphia Ladies Association raises money for soldiers.
- British take Charleston, South Carolina.
- French army arrives in Newport, Rhode Island.
- British win battle of Camden.
- Benedict Arnold exposed as traitor.
- Americans win battle of King's Mountain.

1781
- British forces invade Virginia.
- French fleet blockades Chesapeake Bay.
- Cornwallis surrenders at Yorktown; concedes British defeat.

1783
- Treaty of Paris ends war; United States gains all land to Mississippi River.

A CHAIR FOR THE NEW NATION

George Washington sat in this splendid and unique chair for three hot months in the summer of 1787, presiding over a convention of fifty-five delegates engaged in writing a document that would define the government of the United States. Made of mahogany and topped with a carved sun painted in gold, the chair signaled dignity and respect for Washington's role. Mercifully, a padded leather seat provided him with some comfort as he sat for long hours. At just over six feet, Washington was a tall man by the standards of his day. Even so, this chair was sufficiently tall (five feet) that his head did not obscure the gold embellishment. After weeks of serious debate and heated disagreement, most of the delegates lined up on the last day of the convention to sign the new Constitution of the United States. Among them was the ever-observant Benjamin Franklin. James Madison took note of Franklin's words during the signing: "Whilst the last members were signing it Doctr. FRANKLIN looking towards the Presidents Chair, at the back of which a rising sun happened to be painted, observed to a few members near him, that Painters had found it difficult to distinguish in their art a rising from a setting sun. I have, said he, often and often in the course of the Session, and the vicissitudes of my hopes and fears as to its issue, looked at that behind the President without being able to tell whether it was rising or setting: But now at length I have the happiness to know that it is a rising and not a setting Sun." Independence National Historic Park.

Building a Republic
1775–1789

JAMES MADISON GRADUATED from Princeton College in New Jersey in 1771, not knowing what to do next with his life. Certainly, the twenty-year-old had an easy fallback position. As the firstborn son of a wealthy plantation owner, he could return home to the foothills of Virginia and wait to inherit substantial land and a large force of slaves. But **James Madison** was an intensely studious young man, uninterested in farming and reluctant to leave the collegiate environment. Five years at boarding school had given him fluency in Greek, Latin, French, and mathematics; and three years at Princeton had acquainted him with the great thinkers, both ancient and modern. Driven by a thirst for learning, young Madison slept only five hours a night, perhaps undermining his health. Protesting that he was too ill to travel, he hung around Princeton for six months after graduation.

In 1772, he returned home, still adrift. He tried studying law, but his unimpressive oratorical talents discouraged him. Instead, he swapped reading lists and ideas about political theory by letter with a Princeton classmate, prolonging his student life. While Madison struggled for direction, the powerful winds before the storm of the American Revolution swirled through the colonies. In May 1774, Madison traveled north to deliver his brother to boarding school and was in Philadelphia when the startling news broke that Britain had closed the port of Boston in retaliation for the destruction of the tea. Turbulent protests over the Coercive Acts turned him into a committed revolutionary.

Back in Virginia, Madison joined his father on the newly formed committee of public safety. For a few days in early 1775, the twenty-four-year-old took up musket practice, but his continued poor health ruled out the soldier's life. His special talent lay in the science of politics, and in the spring of 1776, he gained election to the Virginia Convention, a Revolutionary assembly replacing the defunct royal government. The convention's main task was to hammer out a state constitution with innovations such as frequent elections and limited executive power. Shy, self-effacing, and still learning the ropes, Madison mostly stayed on the sidelines, but Virginia's elder statesmen noted the young man's logical, thoughtful contributions. When his county failed to return him to the assembly in the next election, he was appointed to the governor's council, where he spent two years gaining experience in a wartime government.

Previewing the Chapter

The Articles of Confederation 183
Q: *Why was the confederation government's authority so limited?*

The Sovereign States 185
Q: *How did states determine who would be allowed to vote?*

The Confederation's Problems 190
Q: *Why did farmers in western Massachusetts revolt against the state legislature?*

The United States Constitution 195
Q: *Why did the government proposed by the constitutional convention employ multiple checks on each branch?*

Ratification of the Constitution 197
Q: *Why did Antifederalists oppose the Constitution?*

Conclusion: The "Republican Remedy" 201

James Madison, **by Charles Willson Peale** A short and slight man, Madison appeared younger than he was. This miniature portrait, made in 1783 when he was thirty-two, shows him with natural hair (no wig) and a boyishly smooth face. Madison commissioned the portrait on the occasion of his first serious romance. The Philadelphia artist Charles Willson Peale painted matching miniatures of Madison and his fiancée, Kitty Floyd, the sixteen-year-old daughter of a New York delegate to the Continental Congress. Madison and his Virginia friend Thomas Jefferson both boarded with the Floyd family while the congress met in Philadelphia. Jefferson, a very recent widower, encouraged the shy Madison and assured him that Kitty "will render you happier than you can possibly be in a single state." Madison's portrait was mounted in a brooch (note the pin sticking out on the right) so that his lady love might wear it on her person; the back of the brooch held a neatly plaited lock of Madison's hair. The companion miniature of Kitty no longer holds a lock of her hair, if it ever did, for Kitty soon jilted Madison for a suave younger man and returned the Madison miniature to the grieving bachelor. Eleven years later, Madison tried romance again when New York congressman Aaron Burr introduced him to a Virginia widow named Dolley Payne Todd, seventeen years his junior. Madison was forty-three, and Todd was twenty-six; they married four months after meeting. Library of Congress.

In early 1780, Madison represented Virginia in the Continental Congress. Not quite twenty-nine, unmarried, and supported by his father's money, he was free of the burdens that made distant political service difficult for so many others. He stayed in the North for three years, working with men such as Alexander Hamilton of New York and Robert Morris of Pennsylvania as the congress wrestled with the chaotic economy and the ever-precarious war effort. In one crisis, Madison's negotiating skills proved crucial: He broke the deadlock over the ratification of the Articles of Confederation by arranging for the cession of Virginia's vast western lands. Those lands would soon appear on maps as the Northwest Territory, calling forth a series of western land ordinances, planned out by Madison's friend Thomas Jefferson, that exemplified the promise of and high hopes for the future of the new confederation government. But more often, service in the congress proved frustrating to Madison because the confederation government seemed to lack essential powers, chief among them the power to tax.

Madison resumed a seat in the Virginia assembly in 1784. But he did not retreat to a local point of view as so many other state politicians of the decade did. The difficult economic hardships created by heavy state taxation programs — which in Massachusetts led to a full-fledged rebellion against state government — spurred Madison to pursue means to strengthen the government of the thirteen new states. In this, he was in the minority: It was by no means clear to many Americans that the Articles of Confederation needed major revamping.

Madison thought it did. He worked hard to bring about an all-state convention in Philadelphia in the late spring of 1787, where he took the lead in steering the delegates to a complete rewrite of the structure of the national government, investing it with considerably greater powers. True to form, Madison spent the months before the convention in feverish study of the great thinkers he had read in college, seeking the best way to constitute a government on republican principles. His lifelong passion for scholarly study, seasoned by a dozen years of energetic political experience, paid off handsomely. The United States Constitution was the result.

By the end of the 1780s, James Madison had had his finger in every kind of political pie on the local, state, confederation, and finally national level. He had transformed himself from a directionless and solitary youth into one of the leading political thinkers of the Revolutionary period. His personal history over the 1780s was deeply entwined with the path of the emerging United States. ★

The Articles of Confederation

Beginning in 1775 and continuing for five years after declaring independence, the Second Continental Congress met in Philadelphia and other cities without any formal constitutional basis. Delegates first had to work out a plan of government that embodied Revolutionary principles. With monarchy gone, where would sovereignty lie? What would be the nature of representation? Who would hold the power of taxation? Who should vote; who should rule? The resulting plan, called the **Articles of Confederation**, proved to be surprisingly difficult to implement, mainly because the thirteen states had serious disagreements about how to manage areas to the west whose political ownership was contested. Once the Articles were finally ratified and the confederation was formally constituted, that arena of government seemed to many to be far less relevant or interesting than the state governments.

Congress, Confederation, and the Problem of Western Lands

Only after declaring independence did the Continental Congress turn its attention to creating a written document that would specify what powers the congress had and by what authority it existed. There was widespread agreement on key government powers: pursuing war and peace, conducting foreign relations, regulating trade, and running a postal service. But there was serious disagreement about the powers of the congress over the western boundaries of the states. Virginia and Connecticut, for example, had old colonial charters that located their western boundaries at the Mississippi River. States without extensive land claims insisted on redrawing those colonial boundaries.

This was no mere quarrel over lines on a map. In the 1780s, more than 100,000 Americans had moved west of the Appalachian Mountains, and another 100,000 were moving from eastern towns to newly opened land in northern Vermont and western New York and Pennsylvania, as well as to Kentucky, Georgia, and beyond. Who owned the land, who protected it, who governed it? These were major and pressing questions.

For over a year, the congress tinkered with drafts of the Articles of Confederation, reaching agreement only in November 1777. The Articles defined the union as a loose confederation of states, characterized as "a firm league of friendship" existing mainly to foster a common defense. The structure of the government paralleled that of the existing Continental Congress. There was no national executive (that is, no president) and no national judiciary. The congress was composed of two to seven delegates from each state, selected annually by the state legislatures and prohibited from serving more than three years out of any six. The actual number of delegates was not critical, since each state delegation cast a single vote.

Routine decisions in the congress required a simple majority of seven states; for momentous decisions, such as declaring war, nine states needed to agree. To approve or amend the Articles required the unanimous consent both of the thirteen state delegations and of the thirteen state legislatures. This plan protected any single state from coercion by the other twelve in fundamental matters. But it also crippled politics, giving a single state veto power.

On the delicate question of taxes, necessary to finance the war, the Articles provided an ingenious but troublesome solution. Each state was to contribute in proportion to the property value of the state's land. Large and populous states would give more than small or sparsely populated states. The actual taxes would be levied by the state legislatures, not by the congress, to preserve the Revolution's principle of taxation only by direct representation. However, no mechanism compelled states to pay.

The lack of centralized authority in the confederation government was exactly what many state leaders wanted in the late 1770s. A league of states with rotating personnel, no executive branch, no power of taxation, and a requirement of unanimity for any major change seemed to be a good way to keep government in check. Yet there were problems. The requirement for unanimous approval stalled the acceptance of the Articles for four additional years. The key dispute involved lands west of the existing states (Map 8.1). Five states, all lacking land claims, insisted that the congress preserve western lands as a national domain that would eventually constitute new states. The other eight states refused to yield their colonial-era claims and opposed giving the congress power to alter boundaries. In all the heated debates, few seemed to remember that those same western lands were inhabited by many thousands of Indians not party to the disputes.

The eight land-claiming states were ready to sign the Articles of Confederation in 1777. Three states without claims—Rhode Island, Pennsylvania, and New Jersey—eventually capitulated and signed, "not from a Conviction of the Equality and Justness of it," said a New Jersey delegate, "but merely from an absolute Necessity there was of complying to save the Continent." But Delaware and Maryland continued to hold out, insisting on a national domain policy. In 1779, the disputants finally compromised: Any land a state volunteered to relinquish would become the national domain. When James

Madison and Thomas Jefferson ceded Virginia's huge land claim in 1781, the Articles were at last unanimously approved.

The western lands issue demonstrated that powerful interests divided the thirteen new states. The apparent unity of purpose inspired by fighting the war against Britain papered over sizable cracks in the new confederation.

Running the New Government No fanfare greeted the long-awaited inauguration of the new government. The congress continued to sputter along, its problems far from solved by the signing of the Articles. Lack of a quorum often hampered day-to-day activities. The Articles required representation from seven states to conduct business and a minimum of two men from each state's delegation. But some days, fewer than fourteen men in total showed up. State legislatures were slow to select delegates, and many of those appointed were reluctant to attend, especially if they had wives and children at home. Consequently, some of the most committed delegates were young bachelors, such as James Madison, and men in their fifties and sixties whose families were grown, such as Samuel Adams.

MAP 8.1 **Cession of Western Lands, 1782–1802**

The thirteen new states found it hard to ratify the Articles of Confederation without settling their conflicting land claims in the West, an area larger than the original states and occupied by Indian tribes. The five states objecting to the Articles' silence over western lands policy were Maryland, Delaware, New Jersey, Rhode Island, and Pennsylvania.

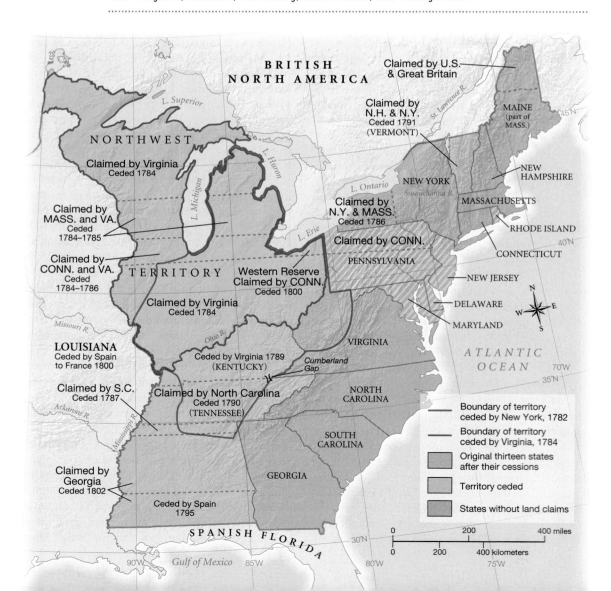

Many politicians preferred to devote their energies to state governments, especially when the congress seemed deadlocked or, worse, irrelevant. It also did not help that the congress had no permanent home. During the war, when the British army threatened Philadelphia, the congress relocated to small Pennsylvania towns such as Lancaster and York and then to Baltimore. After hostilities ceased, the congress moved from Trenton to Princeton to Annapolis to New York City.

To address the difficulties of an inefficient congress, executive departments of war, finance, and foreign affairs were created in 1781 to handle purely administrative functions. When the department heads were ambitious—as was Robert Morris, a wealthy Philadelphia merchant who served as superintendent of finance—they could exercise considerable executive power. The Articles of Confederation had deliberately refrained from setting up an executive branch, but a modest one was being invented by necessity.

Q: Why was the confederation government's authority so limited?

The Sovereign States

In the first decade of independence, the states were sovereign and all-powerful. Relatively few functions, such as declaring war and peace, had been transferred to the confederation government. As Americans discarded their British identity, they thought of themselves instead as Virginians or New Yorkers or Rhode Islanders. Familiar and close to home, state governments claimed the allegiance of citizens and became the arena in which the Revolution's innovations would first be tried. States defined who was a voter, and they also defined who would be free. Squaring slavery with revolutionary ideals became a front-burner issue everywhere; northern states had more success ending inconsistency than did southern states, where slavery was deeply entrenched in the economy.

The State Constitutions In May 1776, the congress recommended that all states draw up constitutions based on "the authority of the people." By 1778, ten states had done so, and three more (Connecticut, Massachusetts, and Rhode Island) had adopted and updated their original colonial charters. Having been denied unwritten British liberties, Americans wanted written contracts that guaranteed basic principles.

A shared feature of all the state constitutions was the conviction that government ultimately rests on the consent of the governed. Political writers in the late 1770s embraced the concept of **republicanism** as the underpinning of the new governments. Republicanism meant more than popular elections and representative institutions. For some, republicanism invoked a way of thinking about who leaders should be: autonomous, virtuous citizens who placed civic values above private interests. For others, it suggested direct democracy, with nothing standing in the way of the will of the people. For all, it meant government that promoted the people's welfare.

Widespread agreement about the virtues of republicanism went hand in hand with the idea that republics could succeed only in relatively small units, so the people could make sure their interests were being served. Nearly every state continued the colonial practice of a two-chamber assembly but greatly augmented the powers of the lower house. Two states, Pennsylvania and Georgia, abolished the more elite upper house altogether, and most states severely limited the term and powers of the governor. Instead, real power resided with the lower houses, constituted to be responsive to popular majorities, with annual elections and guaranteed rotation in office. If a representative displeased his constituents, he could be out of office in a matter of months.

Six of the state constitutions included **bills of rights**—lists of basic individual liberties that government could not abridge. Virginia debated and passed the first bill of rights in June 1776, and many of the other states borrowed from it. Its language bears a close resemblance to the wording of the Declaration of Independence, which Thomas Jefferson was drafting that same June in Philadelphia: "That all men are by nature equally free and independent, and have certain inherent rights, of which, when they enter into a state of society, they cannot by any compact deprive or divest their posterity; namely, the enjoyment of life and liberty, with the means of acquiring and possessing property, and pursuing and obtaining happiness and safety." Along with these inherent rights went more specific rights to freedom of speech, freedom of the press, and trial by jury.

Who Are "the People"? When the Continental Congress called for state constitutions based on "the authority of the people," and when the Virginia bill of rights granted "all men" certain rights, who was meant by "the people"? Who exactly were the citizens of this new country, and how far would the principle of democratic government extend? Different people answered these questions differently, but in the 1770s certain limits to full political participation by all Americans were widely agreed upon.

One limit was defined by property. In nearly every state, candidates for the highest offices had to meet substantial property qualifications. In Maryland, a candidate for governor had to be worth £5,000, a large sum of money. Voters in Maryland had to own fifty acres of land or £30, a barrier to one-third

A Possible Voter in Essex County, New Jersey
Mrs. Elizabeth Alexander Stevens was married to John Stevens, a New Jersey delegate to the Continental Congress in 1783. Widowed in 1792, she would have then been eligible to vote in state elections according to New Jersey's unique enfranchisement of property-holding women. Mrs. Stevens's family was a prominent one. Her father had been surveyor general of New Jersey and New York; her husband was active in politics and was secretary to the governor of New York. Her son John was the inventor of steamboat and locomotive innovations; her daughter Mary married Robert R. Livingston of New York, also a delegate to the Continental Congress and a man who later built a fortune in steamboating. Essex County, where Elizabeth Stevens lived, was said to be the place where female suffrage was exercised most actively. This portrait, done around 1793–1794, represents the most likely face of that rare bird, the eighteenth-century female voter. The widow Stevens died in 1799, before suffrage was redefined to be the exclusive right of males. New Jersey Historical Society.

of adult white males. In the most democratic state, Pennsylvania, voters and candidates needed to be taxpayers, owning enough property to owe taxes. Only property owners were presumed to possess the necessary independence of mind to make wise political choices. Are not propertyless men, asked John Adams, "too little acquainted with public affairs to form a right judgment, and too dependent upon other men to have a will of their own?"

Property qualifications probably disfranchised from one-quarter to one-half of adult white males in all the states. Not all of them took their nonvoter status quietly. One Maryland man wondered what was so special about being worth £30: "Every poor man has a life, a personal liberty, and a right to his earnings; and is in danger of being injured by government in a variety of ways." Why then restrict such a man from voting? Others pointed out that propertyless men were fighting and dying in the Revolutionary War; surely they were expressing an active concern about politics. Finally, a few radical voices challenged the notion that owning property transformed men into good citizens. Perhaps it did the opposite: The richest men might well be greedy and selfish and therefore bad citizens. But ideas like this were outside the mainstream. The writers of the new constitutions, themselves men of property, viewed the right to own and preserve property as a central principle of the Revolution.

Another exclusion from voting — women — was so ingrained that few stopped to question it. Yet the logic of allowing propertied females to vote did occur to a handful of well-placed women. Abigail Adams wrote to her husband, John, in 1782, "Even in the freest countrys our property is subject to the controul and disposal of our partners, to whom the Laws have given a sovereign Authority. Deprived of a voice in Legislation, obliged to submit to those Laws which are imposed upon us, is it not sufficient to make us indifferent to the publick Welfare?"

Only three states specified that voters had to be male, so powerful was the unspoken assumption that only men could vote. Still, in one state, small numbers of women began to turn out at the polls in the 1780s. New Jersey's constitution of 1776 enfranchised all free inhabitants worth more than £50, language that in theory opened the door to free blacks as well as unmarried women who met the property requirement. (Married women owned no property, for by law their husbands held title to everything.) Little fanfare accompanied this radical shift, and some historians have inferred that the inclusion of unmarried women and blacks was an oversight. Yet other parts of the suffrage clause pertaining to residency and property were extensively debated when the clause was put in the state constitution, and no objections were raised at that time to its gender- and race-free language. Thus other historians have concluded that the law was intentionally inclusive. In 1790, a revised election law used the words *he or she* in reference to voters, making woman suffrage explicit. As one New Jersey legislator declared, "Our Constitution gives this right to maids or widows *black* or *white*." However, that legislator was complaining, not bragging, so his expansive words do not mean that egalitarian suffrage was an accepted fact.

In 1790, only about 1,000 free black adults of both sexes lived in New Jersey, a state with a population of 184,000. The number of unmarried adult white women was probably also small and comprised mainly widows. In view of the property requirement, the voter blocs enfranchised under this law were miniscule. Still, this highly unusual situation lasted until 1807, when a new state law specifically disfranchised both blacks and women. Henceforth, independence of mind, that essential precondition of voting, was redefined to be sex- and race-specific.

In the 1780s, voting everywhere was class-specific due to the property restrictions. John Adams urged the framers of the Massachusetts constitution not even to discuss the scope of suffrage but simply to adopt the traditional colonial property qualifications. If suffrage is brought up for debate, he warned, "there will be no end of it. New claims will arise; women will demand a vote; lads from twelve to twenty-one will think their rights not enough attended to; and every man who has not a farthing, will demand an equal voice with any other." Adams was astute enough to anticipate complaints about excluding women, youths, and poor men from political life, but it did not even occur to him to worry about another group: slaves.

Equality and Slavery Restrictions on political participation did not mean that propertyless people enjoyed no civil rights and liberties. The various state bills of rights applied to all individuals who had, as the Virginia bill so carefully phrased it, "enter[ed] into a state of society." No matter how poor, a free person was entitled to life, liberty, property, and freedom of conscience. Unfree people, however, were another matter.

The author of the Virginia bill of rights was George Mason, a plantation owner with 118 slaves. When he penned the sentence "All men are by nature equally free and independent," he did not have slaves in mind; he instead was asserting that white Americans were the equals of the British and could not be denied the liberties of British citizens. Other Virginia legislators, worried about misinterpretations, added the phrase specifying that rights belonged only to people who had entered civil society. As one wrote, with relief, "Slaves, not being

constituent members of our society, could never pretend to any benefit from such a maxim."

One month later, the Declaration of Independence used essentially the same phrase about equality, this time without the modifying clause about entering society. Two state constitutions, for Pennsylvania and Massachusetts, also picked it up. In Massachusetts, one town suggested rewording the draft constitution to read "All men, whites and blacks, are born free and equal." The suggestion was not implemented.

Nevertheless, after 1776, the ideals of the Revolution about natural equality and liberty began to erode the institution of slavery. Often, enslaved blacks led the challenge. In 1777, several Massachusetts slaves petitioned the state legislature, claiming a "natural & unalienable right to that freedom which the great Parent of the Universe hath bestowed equally on all mankind." They modestly asked for freedom for their children at age twenty-one and were turned down. In 1779, similar petitions in Connecticut and New Hampshire met with no success. Seven Massachusetts freemen, including the mariner brothers Paul and John Cuffe, refused to pay taxes for three years on the grounds that they could not vote and so were not represented. The Cuffe brothers landed in jail in 1780 for tax evasion, but their petition to the Massachusetts legislature spurred the extension of suffrage to taxpaying free blacks in 1783.

Another way to bring the issue before lawmakers was to sue in court. In 1781, a woman called **Elizabeth Freeman (Mum Bett)** was the first to win freedom in a Massachusetts court, basing her case on the just-passed state constitution that declared "all men are born free and equal." (See "Seeking the American Promise," page 188.) Later that year, another Massachusetts slave, Quok Walker, charged his master with assault and battery, arguing that he was a free man under that same constitutional phrase. Walker won and was set free, a decision confirmed in an appeal to the state's superior court in 1783. Several similar cases followed, and by 1789 slavery had been effectively abolished by a series of judicial decisions in Massachusetts.

State legislatures acted more slowly. Pennsylvania enacted a **gradual emancipation** law in 1780. Only infants born to a slave mother on or after March 1, 1780, would be freed, but not until age twenty-eight. Thus no current slave in Pennsylvania could

Legal Changes to Slavery, 1777–1804

A Slave Sues for Her Freedom

The stirring language about liberty, equality, and freedom that inspired American revolutionaries in the 1770s was written into many state constitutions in the 1780s. Yet unfree people, held as property, had little recourse to challenge their status.

Massachusetts law presented an unusual opportunity because it recognized slaves as persons with legal standing to bring lawsuits against whites. Less than 2 percent of the state's population consisted of slaves, who numbered well under four thousand and lived preponderantly in the coastal cities. Before 1780, some thirty Massachusetts slaves had sued for their freedom, but their cases had turned on particular circumstances, such as an owner's unfulfilled promise to emancipate or a dispute over a slave's parentage. In 1780, a new Massachusetts state constitution boldly declared that "all men are born free and equal," opening the door to lawsuits based on a broad right to freedom. The first to bring suit under the new constitution was Bett, a thirty-year-old slave living in the western Massachusetts town of Sheffield.

Born of African parents in the early 1740s, Bett and her sister Lizzie grew up as slaves in Claverack, New York, in the wealthy Dutch American family of Pieter Hogeboom. When Hogeboom died in 1758, Bett and Lizzie were transported twenty-four miles east into Massachusetts, where Hogeboom's daughter Hannah lived with her husband, Colonel John Ashley. A town tax list of 1771 shows that Colonel Ashley owned five slaves. Clusters of slaves appeared in western Massachusetts towns such as Sheffield and Stockbridge because of a pattern of eastward migration of both whites and blacks from the relatively slave-dense Hudson River region of New York. Sheffield, a town with two hundred to three hundred families, probably had three dozen to four dozen unfree blacks. Bett was not an isolated slave.

Colonel Ashley was the richest man in Sheffield, and among the oldest, having been born in 1709. His title derived from militia service; he was also a judge and a respected leader in the patriot cause. He was known as a kind and gentle man, but as one account suggests, his wife was "a shrew untamable" and "the most despotic of mistresses." One day, Hannah Ashley became enraged with Lizzie and heaved a hot kitchen shovel at her. Bett interceded to protect her sister, sustaining a burn on her arm that left a lifetime scar.

On another occasion, in 1773, Bett was, in her own words, "keepin' still and mindin' things" while she served refreshments to a dozen white men gathered at her master's house to draw up a protest petition against the British. Colonel Ashley took the lead in drafting a set of resolutions, the first of which read "Resolved, That mankind in a state of nature are equal, free, and independent of each other, and have a right to the undisturbed enjoyment of their lives, their liberty and property." The import of their discussion was well noted by Bett.

In the fall of 1780, Bett overheard conversations at the Ashleys' house about the new Massachusetts state constitution. Bett pondered the words proclaiming equality and reasonably concluded that they applied to her. She sought out a young lawyer named Theodore Sedgwick who had been present at the petition meeting in 1773. Sedgwick, Sheffield's representative in the new Massachusetts legislature, filed a writ in April 1781 requesting the recovery of unlawfully held property—in this case, the human property of Bett and a second plaintiff owned by Ashley, a man identified only as Brom, "a Negro man" and a "labourer." (Brom, a common Dutch nickname for Abraham, probably also came from Claverack.) Ashley contested the writ, and the case, officially called *Brom and Bett v. J. Ashley, Esq.*, went to court.

When the case came to trial, a jury agreed that Bett and Brom were entitled to freedom and ordered Ashley to pay each plaintiff thirty shillings in damages as well as all the court costs. The brief court records do not reveal the legal arguments or evidence presented, but the later boast among Sedgwick descendants was that Theodore Sedgwick had invoked the Massachusetts constitution to argue that slavery could not exist in the state.

gain freedom until 1808, while those born before 1780 remained slaves. Not until 1847 did Pennsylvania fully abolish slavery. But slaves did not wait for such slow implementation. Untold numbers in Pennsylvania simply ran away and asserted their freedom, sometimes with the help of sympathetic whites. One estimate holds that more than half of young slave men in Philadelphia joined the ranks of free blacks, and by 1790, free blacks outnumbered slaves in Pennsylvania two to one.

Rhode Island and Connecticut adopted gradual emancipation laws in 1784. In 1785, New York expanded the terms under which individual owners could free slaves, but only in 1799 did the state adopt a gradual emancipation law; New Jersey followed suit in 1804. These were the two northern

Bett chose a new name to go with her new status: Elizabeth Freeman. She left Colonel Ashley's employ and became a paid housekeeper in the Sedgwick family, virtually raising the children when their mother became incapacitated by mental illness. "Her spirit spurned slavery," a Sedgwick daughter wrote, offering this quotation from Bett as evidence: "Anytime, anytime while I was a slave, if one minute's freedom had been offered to me, and I had been told I must die at the end of that minute, I would have taken it—just to stand one minute, I would have taken it just to stand one minute on God's earth a free woman—I would."

The Sedgwicks were especially grateful to Freeman for her commanding presence of mind during Shays's Rebellion in 1786 (see page 194). Because Sedgwick represented the legal elite of the county, he was the target of hostile crowd action. Freeman was home alone when insurgents, searching for Sedgwick and for valuables to plunder, demanded entry. Unable to prevent their entry, Freeman let the dissidents in but followed the men around with a large shovel and threatened to flatten anyone who damaged any property.

Freeman died in 1829 and was buried in the Sedgwick family plot. Her will, signed with an *X*, indicates that she had children and grandchildren. A Sedgwick son paid her this tribute: "If there could be a practical refutation of the imagined superiority of our race to hers, the life and character of this woman would afford that refutation. . . . Even in her humble station, she had, when occasion required it, an air of command which conferred a degree of dignity." Freeman's lawsuit of 1781 inspired others to sue, and in a case in 1783, the judge of the Massachusetts Supreme Court declared that "slavery is in my judgment as effectively abolished as it can be by the granting of rights and privileges" in the state constitution. It took several more legal challenges and additional time for that news to trickle out—no newspaper reported the change—but the erosion of slavery in Massachusetts gradually picked up speed as blacks demanded manumission or wages for work, or simply walked away from their masters. In 1790, the federal census listed 5,369 "other free persons" (that is, nonwhites) in the state and not a single slave.

★ **Elizabeth Freeman** Solo portraits of African American women in the early Republic are incredibly rare. This 1811 watercolor of Mum Bett was the work of Susan Ridley Sedgwick, wife of one of the Sedgwick sons. It indicates the importance of Freeman to the Sedgwick household. Upon her death, one of the Sedgwick sons wrote: "She was born a slave and remained a slave for nearly thirty years. She could neither read nor write, yet in her own sphere she had no superior nor equal. . . . She was the most efficient helper, and the tenderest friend." The blue dress, gathered at the bustline and topped by a white neckerchief, was standard dress for an older woman of the late eighteenth century but out-of-date in 1811. (Compare the earlier portrait of Mrs. Stevens on page 186.) Freeman very likely lacks a corset, an essential undergarment surely worn by the white women in the Sedgwick household. In this she was fortunate. Massachusetts Historical Society.

states with the largest number of slaves: New York in 1800 with 20,000, New Jersey with more than 12,000. In contrast, slaves in Pennsylvania numbered just 1,700. Gradual emancipation illustrates the tension between radical and conservative implications of republican ideology. Republican government protected people's liberties and property, yet slaves were both people and property. Gradual emancipation balanced the civil rights of blacks and the property rights of their owners by delaying the promise of freedom.

South of Pennsylvania, in Delaware, Maryland, and Virginia, where slavery was so important to the economy, emancipation bills were rejected. All three states, however, eased legal restrictions and allowed individual acts of emancipation for

Black Loyalists in Canada: Passport to Freedom This rare sketch from 1788 portrays a black woodcutter who resided in Nova Scotia along with three thousand other black loyalists who had escaped to northeastern Canada between 1783 and 1785. The inset is a passport issued by the British high command to Cato Rammsay, permitting him to leave New York in 1783. Very few of the Nova Scotia refugees were able to acquire land, and after 1786 the British authorities stopped provisioning them. Most, like the man pictured here, were forced to become servants or day laborers for whites. Low wages created dissatisfaction, and racial tensions mounted. In 1791–1792, nearly a third of the black refugees in Nova Scotia left for Sierra Leone in West Africa, where British officials promised them land and opportunities for self-rule. Sketch: William Booth, National Archives of Canada C-401621; Passport: Nova Scotia Archives & Records Management.

adult slaves below the age of forty-five under new manumission laws passed in 1782 (Virginia), 1787 (Delaware), and 1790 (Maryland). By 1790, close to 10,000 newly freed Virginia slaves had formed local free black communities complete with schools and churches.

In the deep South—the Carolinas and Georgia—freedom for slaves was unthinkable among whites. Yet several thousand slaves had defected to the British during the war, and between 3,000 and 4,000 shipped out of Savannah and Charleston, destined for freedom. Adding northern blacks evacuated from New York City in 1783, the probable total of emancipated blacks who left the United States was between 8,000 and 10,000. Some went to Canada, some to England, and some to Sierra Leone on the west coast of Africa. Many hundreds took refuge with the Seminole and Creek Indians, becoming permanent members of their communities in Spanish Florida and western Georgia.

Although all these instances of emancipation were gradual, small, and certainly incomplete,

their symbolic importance was enormous. Every state from Pennsylvania north acknowledged that slavery was fundamentally inconsistent with Revolutionary ideology; "all men are created equal" was beginning to acquire real force as a basic principle.

Q: How did states determine who would be allowed to vote?

The Confederation's Problems

In 1783, the confederation government faced three interrelated concerns: paying down the large war debt, making formal peace with the Indians, and dealing with western settlement. The federal debt remained a vexing problem, since the Articles of Confederation lacked the power to tax. Western lands suggested a promising source of income, but competing land claims made it difficult for states to use the proceeds of land sales to retire state debts. The Indian inhabitants of those same lands had different ideas, of course.

From 1784 to 1786, the congress struggled mightily with these three issues. Some leaders were gripped by a sense of crisis, fearing that the Articles of Confederation were too weak. Others defended the Articles as the best guarantee of liberty because real governance occurred at the state level, closer to the people. A major outbreak of civil disorder in western Massachusetts quickly crystallized the debate and propelled the critics of the Articles into decisive and far-reaching action.

Financial Chaos and Paper Money Seven years of war produced a chaotic economy in the 1780s. The confederation and the individual states had run up huge war debts financed by printing paper money and borrowing from private sources. Some $400 million to $500 million in paper currency had been injected into the economy, and prices and wages fluctuated wildly. Private debt and rapid expenditure flourished, and as Massachusetts laborer William Manning described, "jails were crowded with debtors." A serious postwar depression settled in by the mid-1780s and did not lift until the 1790s.

The confederation government itself was in a terrible financial fix. Continental dollars had lost almost all value; in 1781, it took 146 of them to buy what one dollar had bought in 1775. Desperate times required desperate measures. The congress chose Robert Morris, Philadelphia merchant and newly reelected delegate, to be superintendent of finance. Morris had a gift for financial dealings but had resigned from the congress in 1778 amid accusations that he had unfairly profited from public service. Now his talents were again needed, and from 1781 to 1784, he took charge of the confederation's economic problems.

To augment the government's revenue, Morris first proposed a 5 percent **impost** (an import tax). Since the Articles of Confederation did not authorize taxation, an amendment was needed, but unanimous agreement proved impossible. Rhode Island and New York, whose bustling ports provided ample state revenue, preferred to keep their money and simply refused to agree to a national impost.

Morris's next idea was the creation of the Bank of North America. This private bank would enjoy a special relationship with the confederation, holding the government's hard money (gold and silver coins) as well as private deposits, and providing it

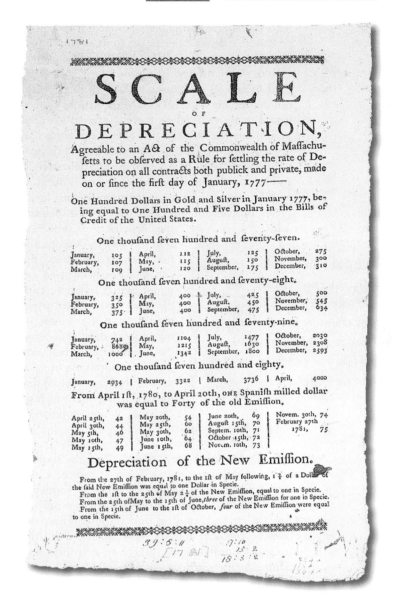

Scale of Depreciation This chart shows the declining monthly value of two emissions of paper dollars from January 1777 to October 1781 as stipulated by the government of Massachusetts. From early in 1777 to April 1780, the paper dollar dropped to a fortieth of its value, requiring 4,000 paper dollars to equal the buying power of $100 in gold or silver. Starting in April 1780, the chart pegged the paper dollar against the Spanish dollar coin, at a 1:40 ratio, and by the end of February 1781, the ratio fell to 1:75. Then a new emission of paper money in February tried to restore the U.S. dollar to the value of the Spanish dollar, and it too fell in four months to a 1:4 ratio. Such a chart was needed when debtors and creditors settled accounts contracted at one time and paid off later in greatly depreciated dollars. Courtesy, American Antiquarian Society.

FOR MORE HELP ANALYZING THIS IMAGE, see the visual activity for this chapter in the Online Study Guide at bedfordstmartins.com/roarkcompact.

with short-term loans. The bank's contribution to economic stability came in the form of banknotes, pieces of paper inscribed with a dollar value. Unlike paper money, banknotes were backed by hard money in the bank's vaults and thus would not depreciate. Morris hoped this form of money would retain value; the congress agreed and voted to approve the bank in 1781. But the bank had limited success curing the confederation's economic woes because it issued very little currency, and its charter was allowed to expire in 1786.

If Morris could not resuscitate the economy in the 1780s, probably no one could have done it. Because the Articles of Confederation reserved most economic functions to the states, the congress was helpless to tax trade, control inflation, curb the flow of state-issued paper money, or pay the mounting public debt. However, the confederation had one source of enormous potential wealth: the huge western territories, attractive to the fast-growing white population but inhabited by Indians.

> When tribal leaders balked, one of the commissioners replied, "You are mistaken in supposing that . . . you are become a free and independent nation and may make what terms you please. It is not so. You are a subdued people."

The Treaty of Fort Stanwix Since the Indians had not participated in the Treaty of Paris of 1783, the confederation government hoped to formalize treaties ending ongoing hostilities between Indians and settlers and securing land cessions. The most pressing problem was the land inhabited by the **Iroquois Confederacy**, a league of six tribes, now claimed by the states of New York and Massachusetts based on their colonial charters (see Map 8.1). The Massachusetts charter was older by four decades, but New York felt entitled because the disputed land bordered its territory.

At issue was the revenue stream that land sales would generate for both states and the confederation government. The congress summoned the Iroquois to a meeting in October 1784 at Fort Stanwix, on the upper reaches of the Mohawk River. The Articles of Confederation gave the congress (as opposed to individual states) the right to manage diplomacy, war, and "all affairs with the Indians, not members of any of the States." But New York's governor seized on this ambiguous language to claim that the Iroquois were in fact "members" of his state, giving New York sole rights

to negotiate. He called his own meeting with the Iroquois at Fort Stanwix in September. Suspecting that New York might be superseded by the congress, the most important chiefs declined to come and instead sent deputies without authority to negotiate. The Mohawk leader Joseph Brant shrewdly identified the problem of divided authority that afflicted the confederation government: "Here lies some Difficulty in our Minds, that there should be two separate bodies to manage these Affairs." No deal was struck with New York.

Three weeks later, U.S. commissioners opened proceedings at Fort Stanwix with the Seneca chief Cornplanter and Captain Aaron Hill, a Mohawk leader, accompanied by six hundred Indians from the six tribes. The U.S. commissioners arrived with a security detail of one hundred New Jersey militiamen.

The Americans demanded a return of prisoners of war; recognition of the confederation's authority to negotiate, rather than that of individual states; and an all-important cession of a strip of land from Fort Niagara due south, which established U.S.-held territory adjacent to the border with Canada. This crucial change enclosed the Iroquois land within the United States and made it impossible for the Indians to claim to be *between* the United States and Canada. When the tribal leaders balked, one of the commissioners sternly replied, "You are mistaken in supposing that, having been excluded from the treaty between the United States and the King of England, you are become a free and independent nation and may make what terms you please. It is not so. You are a subdued people."

In the end, the treaty was signed, gifts were given, and six high-level Indian hostages were kept at the fort awaiting the release of the American prisoners taken during the Revolutionary War, mostly women and children. In addition, a significant side deal sealed the release of much of the Seneca tribe's claim to the Ohio Valley to the United States. This move was a major surprise and disappointment to the Delaware, Mingo, and Shawnee Indians who lived there. In the months to come, tribes not at the meeting tried to disavow the **Treaty of Fort Stanwix** as a document signed under coercion by virtual hostages. But the confederation government ignored those complaints and made plans to survey and develop the Ohio Territory.

New York's governor shrewdly figured that the congress's power to implement the treaty terms was

Treaty of Fort Stanwix

limited. The confederation's financial coffers were nearly empty, and its leadership was stretched. So New York quietly began surveying and then selling the very land it had failed to secure by individual treaty with the Iroquois. As that fact became generally known, it pointed up the weakness of the confederation government. One Connecticut leader wondered, "What is to defend us from the ambition and rapacity of New-York, when she has spread over that vast territory, which she claims and holds? Do we not already see in her the seeds of an over-bearing ambition?"

Land Ordinances and the Northwest Territory The congress ignored western New York and turned instead to the Ohio Valley to make good on the promise of western expansion. Delegate Thomas Jefferson, charged with drafting a policy, proposed dividing the territory north of the Ohio River and east of the Mississippi—called the **Northwest Territory**—into nine new states with evenly spaced east-west boundaries and townships ten miles square. He at first advocated giving the land to settlers, rather than selling it, arguing that future property taxes on the improved land would be payment enough. Jefferson's aim was to encourage rapid and democratic settlement, to build a nation of freeholders (as opposed to renters), and to discourage land speculation. Jefferson also insisted on representative governments in the new states; they would not become colonies of the older states. Finally, Jefferson's draft prohibited slavery in the ten new states.

The congress adopted parts of Jefferson's plan in the Ordinance of 1784: the rectangular grid, the ten states, and the guarantee of self-government and eventual statehood. What the congress found

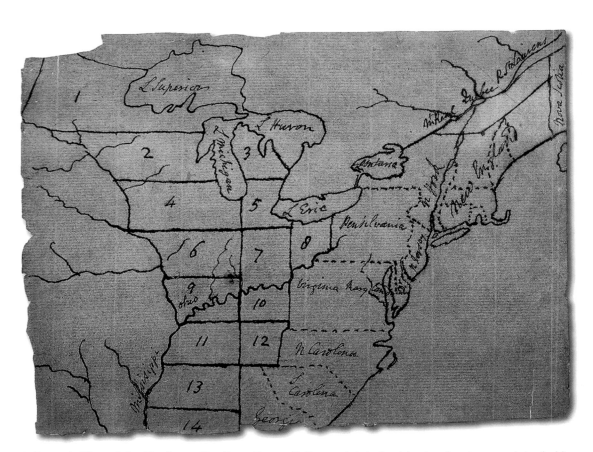

Jefferson's Map of the Northwest Territory Thomas Jefferson sketched out borders for nine new states in his initial plan for the Northwest Territory in 1784 and additional anticipated states below the Ohio River. Straight lines and right angles held a strong appeal for him. But such regularity ignored inconvenient geographic features such as rivers and even more inconvenient political features such as Indian territorial claims most unlikely to be ceded by treaty in orderly blocks. Jefferson also submitted ten distinctive names for the states. Number 9, for example, was Polypotamia, "land of many rivers" in Greek. Other proposed names were Sylvania, Michigania, Assenisipia, and Metropotamia. William L. Clements Library.

FOR MORE HELP ANALYZING THIS IMAGE, see the visual activity for this chapter in the Online Study Guide at bedfordstmartins.com/roarkcompact.

too radical was the proposal to give away the land; the national domain was the confederation's only source of independent wealth. The slavery prohibition also failed, by a vote of seven to six states.

A year later, the congress revised the legislation with procedures for mapping and selling the land. The Ordinance of 1785 called for three to five states, divided into townships six miles square, further divided into thirty-six sections of 640 acres, each section enough for four family farms. Property was thus reduced to easily mappable squares. Land would be sold by public auction at a minimum price of one dollar an acre, with highly desirable land bid up for more. Two further restrictions applied: The minimum purchase was 640 acres, and payment must be in hard money or in certificates of debt from Revolutionary days. This effectively meant that the land's first owners would be prosperous speculators. The grid of invariant squares further enhanced speculation, allowing buyers and sellers to operate without ever setting foot on the acreage. The commodification of land had been taken to a new level.

Speculators usually held the land for resale rather than inhabiting it. Thus they avoided direct contact with the most serious obstacle to settlement: the dozens of Indian tribes that claimed the land as their own. The treaty signed at Fort Stanwix in 1784 was followed by the Treaty of Fort McIntosh in 1785, which similarly coerced partial cessions of land from the Delaware, Huron, and Miami tribes. Finally, in 1786, a united Indian meeting near Detroit issued an ultimatum: No cession would be valid without unanimous consent of the tribes. The Indians advised the United States to "prevent your surveyors and other people from coming upon our side of the Ohio river." For two more decades, violent Indian wars in Ohio and Indiana would continue to impede white settlement (see chapter 9).

In 1787, a third land act, called the **Northwest Ordinance**, set forth a three-stage process by which settled territories would advance to statehood. First, the congress would appoint officials for a sparsely populated territory who would adopt a legal code and appoint local magistrates to administer justice. When the free male population of voting age and landowning status (fifty acres) reached 5,000, the territory could elect its own legislature and send a nonvoting delegate to the congress. When the population of voting citizens reached 60,000, the territory could write a state constitution and apply for full admission to the Union. At all three territorial stages, the inhabitants were subject to taxation to support the Union, in the same manner as were the original states.

The Northwest Ordinance of 1787 was perhaps the most important legislation passed by the confederation government. It ensured that the new United States, so recently released from colonial dependency, would not itself become a colonial power—at least not with respect to white citizens. The mechanism it established allowed for the successful and orderly expansion of the United States across the continent in the next century.

Nonwhites were not forgotten or neglected in the 1787 ordinance. The brief document acknowledged the Indian presence in the Northwest Territory and promised that "the utmost good faith shall always be observed towards the Indians; their lands and property shall never be taken from them without their consent; and, in their property, rights, and liberty, they shall never be invaded or disturbed, unless in just and lawful wars authorized by Congress." The 1787 ordinance further pledged that "laws founded in justice and humanity, shall from time to time be made for preventing wrongs being done to them, and for preserving peace and friendship with them." Such promises were full of noble intentions, but they were not generally honored in the decades to come.

Jefferson's original and remarkable suggestion to prohibit slavery in the Northwest Territory resurfaced in the 1787 ordinance, passing this time without any debate. Probably the addition of a fugitive slave provision in the act set southern congressmen at ease: Escaped slaves caught north of the Ohio River would be returned south. The ordinance thus acknowledged and supported slavery even as it prohibited it in one region. Further, abundant territory south of the Ohio remained available for the spread of slavery. Still, the prohibition of slavery in the Northwest Territory perpetuated the dynamic of gradual emancipation in the North. North-South sectionalism based on slavery was slowly taking shape.

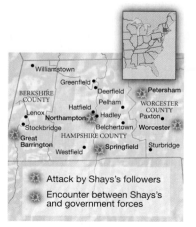

Shays's Rebellion, 1786–1787

Shays's Rebellion, 1786–1787

Without an impost amendment, and with public land sales projected but not yet realized, the confederation turned to the states in the 1780s to contribute revenue voluntarily. Struggling with their own war debts, most state legislatures were reluctant to tax their constituents too heavily. Massachusetts, however, had a fiscally conservative legislature dominated by the coastal commercial centers. For four years, the legislature passed tough tax laws that called for payment in hard money, not cheap paper. Farmers in the western two-thirds of the state found it increasingly difficult to comply and repeatedly petitioned against what they called oppressive taxation. In July 1786, when the legislature adjourned, having yet again ignored their complaints, dissidents held a series of conventions and called for revisions to the state constitution to promote democracy, eliminate the elite upper house, and move the capital farther west in the state.

Still unheard in Boston, the dissidents targeted the county courts, the local symbol of state authority. In the fall of 1786, several thousand armed men marched on courthouses in six Massachusetts counties and forced bewildered judges to close their courts until the state constitution was revised. Sympathetic local militias did not intervene. The insurgents were not predominantly poor or debt-ridden farmers; they included veteran soldiers and officers in the Continental army as well as town leaders. One was a farmer and onetime army captain, **Daniel Shays**.

The governor of Massachusetts, James Bowdoin, once a protester against British taxes, now characterized the western dissidents as illegal rebels. He vilified Shays as the chief leader, and a Boston newspaper claimed Shays planned to burn Boston to the ground and overthrow the government, clearly an overreaction. Another former radical, Samuel Adams, took the extreme position that "the man who dares rebel against the laws of a republic ought to suffer death." Those aging revolutionaries had little considered that popular majorities embodied in a state legislature could seem to be as oppressive as monarchs. The dissidents challenged the assumption that popularly elected governments would always be fair and just.

Members of the Continental Congress worried that the Massachusetts insurgency was spinning out of control. In October, the congress attempted to triple the size of the federal army, but fewer than 100 men enlisted. So Governor Bowdoin raised a private army, gaining the services of some 3,000 with pay provided by wealthy and fearful Boston merchants.

In January 1787, the insurgents learned of the private army marching their way, and 1,500 of them moved swiftly to capture a federal armory in Springfield to gain weapons. But a militia band loyal to the state government beat them to the weapons facility and met their attack with gunfire; 4 rebels were killed and another 20 wounded. The final and bloodless encounter came at Petersham, where Bowdoin's army surprised the rebels on a freezing February morning and took 150 prisoners; the others fled into the woods but were soon rounded up and jailed.

In the end, 2 men were executed for rebellion; 16 more sentenced to hang were reprieved at the last moment on the gallows. Some 4,000 men gained leniency by confessing their misconduct and swearing an oath of allegiance to the state. A special Disqualification Act prohibited the penitent rebels from voting, holding public office, serving on juries, working as schoolmasters, or operating taverns for up to three years.

Shays's Rebellion caused leaders throughout the country to worry about the confederation's ability to handle civil disorder. Inflammatory Massachusetts newspapers wrote about bloody mob rule; perhaps, some feared, similar "combustibles" in other states were awaiting the spark that would set off a dreadful political conflagration. New York lawyer John Jay wrote to George Washington, "Our affairs seem to lead to some crisis, some revolution—something I cannot foresee or conjecture. I am uneasy and apprehensive; more so than during the war." Benjamin Franklin, in his eighties, shrewdly observed that in 1776, Americans had feared "an excess of power in the rulers" but now the problem was perhaps "a defect of obedience" in the subjects. Among such leaders, the sense of crisis in the confederation had greatly deepened.

Q: Why did farmers in western Massachusetts revolt against the state legislature?

The United States Constitution

Shays's Rebellion provoked an odd mixture of fear and hope that the government under the Articles of Confederation was losing its grip on power. A small circle of Virginians decided to try one last time to augment the powers granted to the government by the Articles. Their call for a meeting to discuss trade regulation led, more quickly than they could have imagined in 1786, to a total reworking of the national government.

Silver Bowl for an Anti-Shays General Members of the Springfield militia presented their leader, General William Shepard, with this silver bowl to honor his victory over the Shays insurgents. Presentational silver conveyed a double message: It announced gratitude and praise in engraved words, and the silver itself transmitted considerable monetary value. General Shepard could display his trophy on a shelf, use it as a punch bowl, will it to descendants to keep his moment of fame alive, or melt it down in hard times. Yale University Art Gallery, Mabel Brady Garvan Collection.

From Annapolis to Philadelphia The Virginians, led by James Madison, convinced the confederation congress to allow a meeting of delegates at Annapolis, Maryland, in September 1786, to try again to revise the trade regulation powers of the Articles. Only five states participated, and they rescheduled the meeting for Philadelphia in May 1787. The congress reluctantly endorsed the Philadelphia meeting and limited its scope to "the sole and express purpose of revising the Articles of Confederation." But at least one representative at the Annapolis meeting had more ambitious plans. Alexander Hamilton of New York hoped the Philadelphia meeting would do whatever was necessary to strengthen the federal government.

The fifty-five men who assembled at Philadelphia in May 1787 for the **constitutional convention** were generally those who had already concluded that there were weaknesses in the Articles of Confederation. Few attended who were opposed to revising the Articles. Patrick Henry, author of the Virginia Resolves in 1765 and more recently state governor, refused to go to the convention, saying he "smelled a rat." Rhode Island refused to send delegates. Two New York representatives left in dismay in the middle of the convention, leaving Alexander Hamilton as the sole delegate from New York.

The Pennsylvania Statehouse The constitutional convention assembled at the Pennsylvania statehouse to sweat out the summer of 1787. Despite the heat, the delegates nailed the windows shut to eliminate the chance of being heard by eavesdroppers, so intent were they on secrecy. The statehouse, built in the 1740s to house the colony's assembly, accommodated the Continental Congress at various times in the 1770s and 1780s. The building is now called Independence Hall in honor of the signing of the Declaration of Independence there in 1776. Historical Society of Pennsylvania.

This gathering of white men included no artisans or day laborers or even farmers of middling wealth. Two-thirds of the delegates were lawyers. The majority had served in the confederation congress and knew its strengths and weaknesses; half had been officers in the Continental army. Seven men had been governors of their states and knew firsthand the frustrations of thwarted executive power. A few elder statesmen attended, such as Benjamin Franklin and George Washington, but on the whole, the delegates were young, like Madison and Hamilton.

The Virginia and New Jersey Plans The convention worked in secrecy so the men could freely explore alternatives without fear that their honest opinions would come back to haunt them. The Virginia delegation first laid out a fifteen-point plan for a complete restructuring of the government. This **Virginia Plan** was a total repudiation of the principle of a confederation of states. Largely the work of Madison, the plan set out a three-branch government composed of a two-chamber legislature, a powerful executive, and a judiciary. It practically eliminated the voices of the smaller states by pegging representation in both houses of the congress to population. The theory was that government operated directly on people, not on states. Among the breathtaking powers assigned to the congress were the rights to veto state legislation and to coerce states militarily to obey national laws. To prevent the congress from having absolute power, the executive and judiciary could jointly veto its actions.

In mid-June, a delegate from New Jersey, after caucusing with delegates from other small states, unveiled an alternative proposal. The **New Jersey Plan**, as it was called, maintained the existing single-house congress of the Articles of Confederation in which each state had one vote. Acknowledging the need for an executive, it created a plural presidency to be shared by three men elected by the congress from among its membership. Where it sharply departed from the existing government was in the sweeping powers it gave to the new congress: the right to tax, regulate trade, and use force on unruly state governments. In favoring national power over states' rights, it aligned itself with the Virginia Plan. But the New Jersey Plan retained the confederation principle that the national government was to be an assembly of states, not of people.

For two weeks, delegates debated the two plans, focusing on the key issue of representation. The small-state delegates conceded that one house in a two-house legislature could be apportioned by population, but they would never agree that both houses could be. Madison was equally vehement about bypassing representation by state, which he viewed as the fundamental flaw in the Articles.

The debate seemed deadlocked, and for a while the convention was "on the verge of dissolution, scarce held together by the strength of a hair," according to one delegate. Only in mid-July did the so-called Great Compromise break the stalemate and produce the basic structural features of the emerging United States Constitution. Proponents of the competing plans agreed on a bicameral legislature.

Representation in the lower house, the House of Representatives, would be apportioned by population, and representation in the upper house, the Senate, would come from all the states equally. Instead of one vote per state in the upper house, as in the New Jersey Plan, the compromise provided two senators who voted independently. Representation by population turned out to be an ambiguous concept once it was subjected to rigorous discussion. Who counted? Were slaves, for example, people or property? As people, they would add weight to the southern delegations in the House of Representatives, but as property they would add to the tax burdens of those states. What emerged was the compromise known as the **three-fifths clause**: All free persons plus "three-fifths of all other Persons" constituted the numerical base for the apportionment of representatives.

Using "all other Persons" as a substitute for "slaves" indicates the discomfort delegates felt in acknowledging in the Constitution the existence of slavery. But though slavery was nowhere named, nonetheless it was recognized, protected, and thereby perpetuated by the U.S. Constitution.

Democracy versus Republicanism The delegates in Philadelphia made a distinction between *democracy* and *republicanism* new to the American political vocabulary. Pure democracy was now taken to be a dangerous thing. As a Massachusetts delegate put it, "The evils we experience flow from the excess of democracy." The delegates still favored republican institutions, but they created a government that gave direct voice to the people only in the House and that granted a check on that voice to the Senate, a body of men elected not by direct popular vote but by the state legislatures. Senators served for six years, with no limit on reelection; they were protected from the whims of democratic majorities, and their long terms fostered experience and maturity in office.

Similarly, the presidency evolved into a powerful office out of the reach of direct democracy. The delegates devised an electoral college whose only function was to elect the president and vice president. Each state's legislature would choose the electors, whose number was the sum of representatives and senators for the state, an interesting blending of the two principles of representation. The president thus would owe his office not to the Congress,

the states, or the people, but to a temporary assemblage of distinguished citizens who could vote their own judgment on the candidates.

The framers had developed a far more complex form of federal government than that provided by the Articles of Confederation. To curb the excesses of democracy, they devised a government with limits and checks on all three of its branches. They set forth a powerful president who could veto legislation passed in Congress, but they gave Congress power to override presidential vetoes. They set up a national judiciary to settle disputes between states and citizens of different states. They separated branches of government not only by functions and by reciprocal checks but also by deliberately basing the election of each branch on different universes of voters—voting citizens (the House), state legislators (the Senate), and the electoral college (the presidency). The convention carefully listed the powers of the president and of Congress. The president could initiate policy, propose legislation, and veto acts of Congress; he could command the military and direct foreign policy; and he could appoint the entire judiciary, subject to Senate approval. Congress held the purse strings: the power to levy taxes, to regulate trade, and to coin money and control the currency. States were expressly forbidden to issue paper money. Two more powers of Congress—to "provide for the common defence and general Welfare" of the country and "to make all laws which shall be necessary and proper" for carrying out its powers—provided elastic language that came closest to Madison's wish to grant sweeping powers to the new government.

While no one was entirely satisfied with every line of the Constitution, only three dissenters refused to sign the document. The Constitution specified a mechanism for ratification that avoided the dilemma faced earlier by the confederation government: Nine states, not all thirteen, had to ratify it, and special ratifying conventions elected only for that purpose, not state legislatures, would make the crucial decision.

Q: Why did the government proposed by the constitutional convention employ multiple checks on each branch?

Ratification of the Constitution

Had a popular vote been taken on the Constitution in the fall of 1787, it would probably have been rejected. In the three most populous states—Virginia, Massachusetts, and New York—substantial majorities opposed a powerful new national government.

North Carolina and Rhode Island refused to call ratifying conventions. Seven of the eight remaining states were easy victories for the Constitution, but securing the approval of the ninth proved difficult. Pro-Constitution forces, called Federalists, had to strategize very shrewdly to defeat anti-Constitution forces, called Antifederalists.

The Federalists Proponents of the Constitution moved into action swiftly. To silence the criticism that they had gone beyond their charge, they sent the document to the congress. The congress withheld explicit approval but resolved to send the Constitution to the states for their consideration. The pro-Constitution forces shrewdly secured another advantage by calling themselves **Federalists**. By all logic, this label was more suitable for the backers of the confederation concept, because the Latin root of the word *federal* means "league." Their opponents became known as **Antifederalists**, a label that made them sound defensive and negative, lacking a program of their own.

To gain momentum, the Federalists targeted the states most likely to ratify quickly. Delaware provided unanimous ratification by early December, before the Antifederalists had even begun to campaign. Pennsylvania, New Jersey, and Georgia followed within a month (Map 8.2). Delaware and New Jersey were small states surrounded by more powerful neighbors; a government that would regulate trade and set taxes according to population was an attractive proposition. Georgia sought the protection that a stronger national government would afford against hostile Indians and Spanish Florida to the south. "If a weak State with the Indians on its back and the Spaniards on its flank does not see the necessity of a General Government there must I think be wickedness or insanity in the way," said Federalist George Washington.

Another three easy victories came in Connecticut, Maryland, and South Carolina. As in Pennsylvania, merchants, lawyers, and urban artisans in general favored the new Constitution, as did large landowners and slaveholders. This tendency for the established political elite to be Federalist enhanced the prospects of victory, for Federalists already had power and influence disproportionate to their number. Antifederalists in these states tended to be rural, western, and noncommercial, men whose access to news was limited and whose participation in state government was tenuous.

Massachusetts was the only early state that gave the Federalists difficulty. The vote to select the ratification delegates decidedly favored the Antifederalists, whose strength lay in the western areas of the state, home to Shays's Rebellion. One rural delegate from Worcester County voiced widely shared suspicions: "These lawyers and men of learning and money men that talk so finely, and gloss over matters so smoothly, to make us poor illiterate people swallow down the pill, expect to get into Congress themselves; they expect to be the managers of the Constitution and get all the power and all the money into their own hands, and then they will swallow up all us little folks." Nevertheless, the Antifederalists' lead was slowly eroded by a vigorous newspaper campaign. In the end, the Federalists won by a very slim margin and only with promises that amendments to the Constitution would be taken up in the first Congress.

By May 1788, eight states had ratified; only one more was needed. North Carolina and Rhode Island were hopeless for the Federalist cause, and New Hampshire seemed nearly as bleak. More worrisome was the failure to win over the largest and most important states, Virginia and New York.

The Antifederalists The Antifederalists were a composite group, united mainly in their desire to block the Constitution. Although much of their strength came from backcountry areas long suspicious of eastern elites, many Antifederalist leaders came from the same social background as Federalist leaders; economic class alone did not differentiate them. The Antifederalists also drew strength in states already on sure economic footing, such as New York, that could afford to remain independent. Probably the biggest appeal of the Antifederalists' position lay in the long-nurtured fear that distant power might infringe on people's liberties. The language of the earlier Revolutionary movement was not easily forgotten.

But by the time eight states had ratified the Constitution, the Antifederalists faced a far harder task than they had once imagined. First, they were no longer defending the status quo now that the momentum lay with the Federalists. Second, it was difficult to defend the confederation government with its admitted flaws. Even so, they remained genuinely fearful that the new government would be too distant from the people and could thus become corrupt or tyrannical. "The difficulty, if not impracticability, of exercising the equal and equitable powers of government by a single legislature over an extent of territory that reaches from the Mississippi to the western lakes, and

> One rural delegate voiced widely shared suspicions: "These lawyers and men of learning . . . expect to . . . be the managers of the Constitution and get all the power and all the money into their own hands, and then they will swallow up all us little folks."

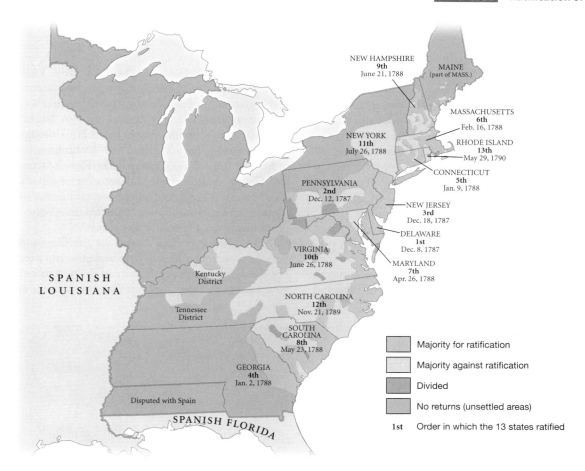

MAP 8.2 Ratification of the Constitution, 1788–1790
Populated areas cast votes for delegates to state ratification conventions. This map shows Antifederalist strength generally concentrated in backcountry, noncoastal, and non-urban areas, but with significant exceptions (for example, Rhode Island).

READING THE MAP: Where was Federalist strength concentrated? How did the distribution of Federalist and Antifederalist sentiment affect the order of state ratifications of the Constitution?

CONNECTIONS: What objections did Antifederalists have to the new United States Constitution? How did their locations affect their views of the Federalist argument?

FOR MORE HELP ANALYZING THIS MAP, see the map activity for this chapter in the Online Study Guide at bedfordstmartins.com/roarkcompact.

from them to the Atlantic ocean, is an insuperable objection to the adoption of the new system," wrote Mercy Otis Warren, an Antifederalist woman writing under the alias "A Columbia Patriot."

The new government was indeed distant. In the proposed House of Representatives, the only directly democratic element of the Constitution, one member represented some 30,000 people. How could that member really know or communicate with his whole constituency, Antifederalists worried. They also feared that representatives would always be elites and thus "ignorant of the sentiments of the middling and much more of the lower class of citizens, strangers to their ability, unacquainted with their wants, difficulties, and distress," a Maryland

man worried. None of this would be a problem under a confederation system, according to the Antifederalists, because real power would continue to reside in the state governments.

The Federalists generally agreed that the elite would be favored for national elections. Indeed, Federalists wanted power to reside with intelligent, virtuous leaders like themselves. They did not envision a government constituted of every class of people. "Fools and knaves have voice enough in government already," argued one Federalist, without being guaranteed representation in proportion to their total population. Alexander Hamilton claimed that mechanics and laborers preferred to have their social betters represent them.

Antifederalists disagreed: "In reality, there will be no part of the people represented, but the rich. . . . It will literally be a government in the hands of the few to oppress and plunder the many."

Antifederalists fretted over many specific features of the Constitution. It prohibited state-issued paper money. It regulated the time and place of congressional elections, leading to fears that only one inconvenient polling place might be authorized, disfranchising rural voters. The most widespread objection was the Constitution's glaring omission of any guarantees of individual liberties in a bill of rights like those contained in many state constitutions.

Despite Federalist campaigns in the large states, it was a small state—New Hampshire—that provided the decisive ninth vote for ratification on June 21, 1788. Federalists there succeeded in getting the convention postponed from February to June and conducted an intense and successful lobbying effort on specific delegates in the interim.

The Big Holdouts: Virginia and New York

Four states still remained outside the new union, and a glance at a map demonstrated the necessity of pressing the Federalist case in the two largest, Virginia and New York (see Map 8.2). Although Virginia was home to Madison and Washington, an influential Antifederalist group led by Patrick Henry and George Mason made the outcome uncertain. The Federalists finally but barely won ratification by proposing twenty specific amendments that the new government would promise to consider.

New York voters tilted toward the Antifederalists out of a sense that a state so large and powerful need not relinquish so much authority to the new federal government. But New York was also home to some of

Silk Banner of the New York Society of Pewterers As soon as nine states ratified the Constitution, the Federalists held spectacular victory celebrations meant to demonstrate national unity behind the new government. New York City's parade, coming three days before the state's own ratification vote in July 1788, involved five thousand participants marching under seventy-six occupational banners. Foresters and farmers headed the procession; coopers, tanners, cutlers, brewers, wig makers, tobacconists, chocolate makers, lawyers, and other tradesmen, artisans, professionals, and workers followed. This banner was carried by the Society of Pewterers, men who made household utensils from an alloy of tin, copper, and lead. Despite the broad spectrum of male workers represented in the parade, many of whom could not vote, no working women—milliners, dressmakers, or household servants—participated. Why? Note that the pewterers jumped the gun a bit with their thirteen-star flag. © Collection of the New-York Historical Society.

the most persuasive Federalists. Starting in October 1787, Alexander Hamilton collaborated with James Madison and New York lawyer John Jay on a series of eighty-five essays on the political philosophy of the new Constitution published in New York newspapers and later republished as ***The Federalist Papers***. The essays brilliantly set out the failures of the Articles of Confederation and offered an analysis of the complex nature of the Federalist position. In one of the most compelling essays, number 10, Madison challenged the Antifederalists' heartfelt conviction that republican government had to be small-scale. Madison argued that a large and diverse population was itself a guarantee of liberty. In a national government, no single faction could ever be large enough to subvert the freedom of other groups. "Extend the sphere, and you take in a greater variety of parties and interests; you make it less probable that a majority of the whole will have a common motive to invade the rights of other citizens," Madison asserted. He called it "a republican remedy for the diseases most incident to republican government."

At New York's ratifying convention, Antifederalists predominated, but impassioned debate and lobbying—plus the dramatic news of Virginia's ratification—finally tipped the balance to the Federalists. New York's ratification ensured the legitimacy of the new government. It took another year and a half for Antifederalists in North Carolina to come around. Fiercely independent Rhode Island held out until May 1790, and even then it ratified by only a two-vote margin.

In less than twelve months, the U.S. Constitution was both written and ratified. (See appendix I, page A-3.) An amazingly short time by twenty-first-century standards, it is even more remarkable for the late eighteenth century, with its horse-powered transportation and hand-printed communications. The Federalists had faced a formidable task, but by building momentum and ensuring consideration of a bill of rights, they did indeed carry the day.

Q: Why did Antifederalists oppose the Constitution?

Conclusion: The "Republican Remedy"

Thus ended one of the most intellectually tumultuous and creative periods in American history. American leaders experimented with ideas and drew up plans to embody their evolving and conflicting notions of how a society and a government ought to be formulated. There was widespread agreement that government should derive its power and authority from the people, but a narrow vision of "the people" prevailed. With limited exceptions—New Jersey, for example—free blacks and women were excluded from government. Indians, even when dubiously called "members" of a state, were outside the sovereign people authorizing government, as were all slaves. Even taking free white males as "the people," men disagreed fiercely over the degree of democracy—the amount of direct control of government by the people—that would be workable in American society.

The period began in 1775 with a confederation government that could barely be ratified because of its requirement of unanimity, but there was no reaching unanimity on the western lands, an impost, or the proper way to respond to unfair taxation in a republican state. The new Constitution offered a different approach to these problems by loosening the grip of impossible unanimity and by embracing the ideas of a heterogeneous public life and a carefully balanced government that together would prevent any one part of the public from tyrannizing another. The genius of James Madison was to anticipate that diversity of opinion was not only an unavoidable reality but a hidden strength of the new society beginning to take shape. This is what he meant in his tenth *Federalist* essay when he spoke of the "republican remedy" for the troubles most likely to befall a government where the people are the source of authority.

Despite Madison's optimism, political differences remained keen and worrisome to many. The Federalists still hoped for a society in which leaders of exceptional wisdom would discern the best path for public policy. They looked backward to a society of hierarchy, rank, and benevolent rule by an aristocracy of talent, but they created a government with forward-looking checks and balances as a guard against corruption, which they figured would most likely emanate from the people. The Antifederalists also looked backward, but to an old order of small-scale direct democracy and local control, where virtuous people kept a close eye on potentially corruptible rulers. The Antifederalists feared a national government led by distant, self-interested leaders who needed to be held in check. In the 1790s, these two conceptions of republicanism and of leadership would be tested in real life.

Reviewing the Chapter

★ KEY TERMS

Explain each term's significance

WHO

James Madison (p. 181)

Elizabeth Freeman (Mum Bett) (p. 187)

Iroquois Confederacy (p. 192)

Daniel Shays (p. 195)

Federalists (p. 198)

Antifederalists (p. 198)

WHAT

Articles of Confederation (p. 183)

republicanism (p. 185)

bills of rights (p. 185)

gradual emancipation (p. 187)

impost (p. 191)

Treaty of Fort Stanwix (p. 192)

Northwest Territory (p. 193)

Northwest Ordinance (p. 194)

constitutional convention (p. 196)

Virginia Plan (p. 196)

New Jersey Plan (p. 196)

three-fifths clause (p. 197)

The Federalist Papers (p. 201)

★ REVIEW QUESTIONS Q:

Use key terms and dates to support your answer

1. Why was the confederation government's authority so limited? (pp. 183–85)

2. How did states determine who would be allowed to vote? (pp. 185–90)

3. Why did farmers in western Massachusetts revolt against the state legislature? (pp. 190–95)

4. Why did the government proposed by the constitutional convention employ multiple checks on each branch? (pp. 195–97)

5. Why did Antifederalists oppose the Constitution? (pp. 197–201)

★ MAKING CONNECTIONS

Draw on key terms, timeline, and review questions

1. Leaders in the new nation held that voting should be restricted to citizens who possessed independence of mind. Why? What did they mean by independence of mind? How did this principle limit voters in the early Republic?

2. Why did many Revolutionary leaders shaping the government of the new nation begin to find the principle of democracy troubling? How did they attempt to balance democracy with other concerns in the new government?

3. Twenty-first-century Americans see a profound tension between the Revolutionary ideals of liberty and equality and the persistence of American slavery. Did Americans in the late eighteenth century see a tension? In your answer, be sure to discuss factors that might have shaped varied responses, such as region, race, and class.

4. The Northwest Territory was the confederation's greatest asset. Discuss the proposals to manage settlement of the new territory. How did they shape the nation's expansion? Which proposals succeeded and which failed?

FOR PRACTICE QUIZZES AND OTHER STUDY TOOLS, see the Online Study Guide at **bedfordstmartins.com/roarkcompact**.

★ SUGGESTED READINGS

Lance Banning, *The Sacred Fire of Liberty: James Madison and the Founding of the Federal Republic* (1995). An eloquent biography detailing Madison's passionate involvement in the politics of the 1780s.

Woody Holton, *Unruly Americans and the Origins of the Constitution* (2007). A study that credits ordinary Americans of the 1780s for pushing elite political leaders further than they intended toward democracy and personal liberty.

Joanne Pope Melish, *Disowning Slavery: Gradual Emancipation and "Race" in New England, 1780–1860* (1998). A fine-grained study of gradual emancipation in New England.

Leonard L. Richards, *Shays's Rebellion: The American Revolution's Final Battle* (2002). A new interpretation of the Massachusetts insurgency based on a social profile of the arrested men.

Alan Taylor, *The Divided Ground: Indians, Settlers, and the Northern Borderland of the American Revolution* (2006). A masterful study of the borderlands between New York and Canada including the Native Americans' point of view.

Rosemarie Zagarri, *A Woman's Dilemma: Mercy Otis Warren and the American Revolution* (1995). A short, highly readable account of the life of the foremost political woman of the 1780s.

FOR MORE BOOKS ABOUT TOPICS IN THIS CHAPTER, see the Online Bibliography at **bedfordstmartins.com/roarkcompact.**

FOR ADDITIONAL FIRSTHAND ACCOUNTS OF THIS PERIOD, see Chapter 8 in Michael Johnson, ed., *Reading the American Past,* Fourth Edition.

FOR WEB SITES, IMAGES, AND DOCUMENTS RELATED TO TOPICS AND PLACES IN THIS CHAPTER, visit Make History at **bedfordstmartins.com/roarkcompact.**

★ TIMELINE

1775	• Second Continental Congress begins to meet.
1776	• Virginia adopts state bill of rights.
1777	• Articles of Confederation sent to states.
1778	• State constitutions completed.
1780	• Pennsylvania institutes gradual emancipation.
1781	• Articles of Confederation ratified. • Creation of executive departments. • Bank of North America chartered. • Slaves Mum Bett and Quok Walker successfully sue for freedom in Massachusetts.
1782	• Virginia relaxes state manumission law.
1783	• Treaty of Paris signed, ending the Revolutionary War. • Massachusetts extends suffrage to taxpaying free blacks.
1784	• Gradual emancipation laws passed in Rhode Island and Connecticut. • Treaty of Fort Stanwix.
1786	• Shays's Rebellion begins.
1787	• Shays's Rebellion crushed. • Northwest Ordinance. • Delaware provides manumission law. • Constitutional convention meets in Philadelphia.
1788	• U.S. Constitution ratified.
1789	• Slavery ended in Massachusetts by judicial decision.
1790	• Maryland provides manumission law.
1799	• Gradual emancipation law passed in New York.
1804	• Gradual emancipation law passed in New Jersey.

WASHINGTON STANDS OUTSIDE OF TIME A French clockmaker and artist produced this piece of Washington memorabilia after the death of the president. Washington's trim figure, rendered in gilt bronze, sports a spiffy uniform complete with fringed epaulets. One gloved hand rests on a sword; the other holds a rolled parchment, offered up in front of an eagle, the symbol of America's strength. Below the eagle a familiar motto is inscribed: "E Pluribus Unum"— "Out of many, one"—a reference to the political unity of the sovereign states. Below the clock is a motto about Washington that was first uttered in his funeral eulogy: "First in War, First in Peace, and First in the Hearts of his Countrymen." Death elevated Washington to celebrity status, and Americans immortalized him by purchasing souvenirs, many of them European-made.

The Warner Collection of Gulf States Paper Corporation.

The New Nation Takes Form

1789–1800

ALEXANDER HAMILTON was thirty-four years old when President George Washington appointed him secretary of the treasury, a job with vast influence over the economic and domestic policy of the new nation. Acknowledged as a brilliant leader during the 1788 ratification of the Constitution, **Alexander Hamilton** soon proved to be the most polarizing figure of the 1790s.

Determination marked his disadvantaged childhood. Hamilton grew up on the small West Indies island of Nevis. His parents never married. His father, the impoverished fourth son of a Scottish lord, disappeared when Alexander was nine, and his mother, a woman with a checkered past, died two years later. Jeered as a "whore child," Hamilton developed a fierce ambition to make good. After serving an apprenticeship to a merchant, he made his way to New York City. In a mere six months, he sufficiently mastered Greek and Latin to gain admission to King's College (now Columbia University). Articles he wrote for a New York newspaper brought him to the attention of General Washington, who made the twenty-year-old an officer in the Continental army and hired him as a close aide. After the war, Hamilton practiced law in New York and then played a central role at the constitutional convention in Philadelphia. His astute *Federalist* essays — more than fifty drafted in just six months — helped secure the ratification of the Constitution.

Hamilton's private life was similarly upwardly mobile. Handsome and now well connected, he married Betsey Schuyler, whose father was one of the richest men in New York. He had a magnetic personality that attracted both men and women eager to experience the charm that was fully on display at dinner parties and friendly gatherings. Late-night socializing, however, never interfered with his prodigious capacity for work.

As secretary of the treasury, Hamilton quickly moved into high gear. "If a Government appears to be confident of its own powers, it is the surest way to inspire the same confidence in others," he once remarked. He immediately secured big loans from two banks and started to track tax revenues from trade, the government's main source of income. Most trade was with Britain, so Hamilton sought ways to protect Anglo-American relations. Next he tackled the country's unpaid **Revolutionary War debt**, writing in three months a forty-thousand-word report for Congress laying out a plan that

Previewing the Chapter

The Search for Stability 206
Q: *How did political leaders in the 1790s attempt to overcome the divisions of the 1780s?*

Hamilton's Economic Policies 209
Q: *Why were Hamilton's economic policies controversial?*

Conflicts West, East, and South 215
Q: *Why did the United States feel vulnerable to international threats in the 1790s?*

Federalists and Republicans 220
Q: *Why did Congress pass the Alien and Sedition Acts in 1798?*

Conclusion: Parties Nonetheless 223

Alexander Hamilton, **by John Trumbull** Hamilton was confident, handsome, audacious, brilliant, and very hardworking. Ever slender, in marked contrast to the more corpulent leaders of his day, he posed for this portrait in 1792, at the age of thirty-seven and at the height of his power. Yale University Art Gallery/Art Resource, NY.

both funded the debt and pumped millions of dollars into the U.S. economy. In short order, he drafted a bold plan for a national banking system to enhance and control the money supply. Finally, he turned his attention to industrial development, writing a richly detailed analysis of ways to promote manufacturing via government subsidies and tariff policies.

Hamilton was both visionary and practical. No one could doubt that he was a gifted man with remarkable political intuitions. It is strange, then, that this magnetic man made enemies in the 1790s, as the "founding fathers" of the Revolution and Constitution became competitors and even bitter rivals. To some extent, jealousy over Hamilton's talents and his access to President Washington explains the chill, but serious differences in political philosophy drove the divisions deeper.

Personalities clashed. Hamilton's charm no longer worked with James Madison, now a representative in Congress and at odds with Hamilton on all his plans. His charm had never worked with John Adams, the new vice president, who privately called him "the bastard brat of a Scotch pedlar" motivated by "disappointed Ambition and unbridled malice and revenge." Years later, when asked why he deserted Hamilton, Madison replied, "Colonel Hamilton deserted me." Hamilton assumed that government was safest when in the hands of "the rich, the wise, and the good" — in other words, America's commercial elite. For Hamilton, economic and political power naturally belonged together, creating an energetic force for economic growth. In contrast, Jefferson and Madison trusted most those whose livelihood was tied to the land. Agrarian values ran deep with them, and they were suspicious of get-rich-quick speculators, financiers, and manufacturing development. Differing views of European powers also loomed large in the rivalries. Whereas Hamilton was an unabashed admirer of everything British, Jefferson was enchanted by France, his residence in the 1780s. These loyalties governed foreign relations in the late 1790s, when the United States tangled with both overseas rivals.

The personal and political antagonisms of this first generation of American leaders left their mark on the young country. No one was prepared for the intense and passionate polarization that emerged over economic and foreign policy. The disagreements were articulated around particular events and policies: taxation and the public debt, a new farmers' rebellion in a western region, policies favoring commercial development, a treaty with Britain, a rebellion in Haiti, and the Quasi-War with France that led to severe strictures on sedition and free speech. But at their heart, these disagreements arose out of opposing ideological stances on the value of democracy, the nature of leadership, and the limits of federal power. About the only major policy development that did not replicate or intensify these antagonisms among political leaders was Indian policy in the new republic. Out in war-torn western Ohio, three forts named for Washington, Hamilton, and Jefferson symbolized the government's unified stance on Indians.

By 1800, the opposing politics ripening between Hamiltonian and Jeffersonian politicians would begin to crystallize into political parties, the Federalists and the Republicans. To the men of that day, this was an unhappy development. ★

The Search for Stability

After the struggles of the 1780s, the most urgent task in establishing the new government was to secure stability. Leaders sought ways to heal old divisions, and the first presidential election offered the means to do that in the person of George Washington, who enjoyed widespread veneration. People trusted him to exercise the untested and perhaps elastic powers of the presidency.

Congress had important work as well in initiating the new government. Congress quickly agreed on the Bill of Rights, which answered concerns of many Antifederalists. Beyond politics, cultural change in the area of gender also enhanced political stability. The private virtue of women was mobilized to bolster the public virtue of male citizens; republicanism was forcing a rethinking of women's relation to the state.

Washington Inaugurates the Government

The election of George Washington in February 1789 was quick work, the tallying of the unanimous votes by the electoral college a mere formality. Washington perfectly embodied the republican ideal of disinterested, public-spirited leadership. Indeed, he cultivated that image through astute ceremonies such as the dramatic surrender of his sword to the Continental Congress at the end of the war, symbolizing the subservience of military power to the law.

Once in office, Washington calculated his moves, knowing that every step set a precedent and any misstep could be dangerous for the fragile government. Congress debated a title for Washington, such as "His Highness, the President of the United States of America and Protector of Their Liberties" and "His Majesty, the President"; Washington favored "His High Mightiness." But in the end, republican simplicity prevailed. The final title was simply "President of the United States of America," and the established form of address became "Mr. President," a subdued yet dignified title in a society where only property-owning adult white males could presume to be called "Mister."

Washington's genius in establishing the presidency lay in his capacity for implanting his own reputation for integrity into the office itself. He was not a brilliant thinker or a shrewd political strategist. He was not even a particularly congenial man. In the political language of the day, he was "virtuous," meaning that he took pains to elevate the public good over private interest and projected honesty and honor over ambition. He remained aloof, resolute, and dignified, to the point of appearing wooden at times. He encouraged pomp and ceremony to create respect for the office, traveling with six horses to pull his coach, hosting formal balls, and surrounding himself with uniformed servants. He even held weekly "levees," as European monarchs did, hour-long audiences granted to distinguished visitors (including women), at which Washington appeared attired in black velvet, with a feathered hat and a polished sword. The president and his guests bowed, avoiding the egalitarian familiarity of a handshake. But he always managed, perhaps just barely, to avoid the extreme of royal splendor.

Washington chose talented and experienced men to preside over the newly created Departments of War, Treasury, and State. For the Department of War, Washington chose General Henry Knox, former secretary of war in the confederation government. For the Treasury — an especially tough job in view of revenue conflicts during the Confederation (see chapter 8) — the president picked Alexander Hamilton, known for his general brilliance and financial astuteness. To lead the Department of State, the foreign policy arm of the executive branch, Washington chose Thomas Jefferson, a master of diplomatic relations and the current minister to France. For attorney general, Washington picked Edmund Randolph, a Virginian who had attended the constitutional convention but had turned Antifederalist during ratification. For chief justice of the Supreme Court, Washington designated John Jay, a New York lawyer who, along with Madison and Hamilton, had vigorously defended the Constitution in *The Federalist Papers*.

Soon Washington began to hold regular meetings with these men, thereby establishing the precedent of a presidential cabinet. (Vice President John Adams was not included; his only official duty, to preside over the Senate, he found "a punishment."

Liverpool Souvenir Pitcher, 1789 A British pottery manufacturer produced this commemorative pitcher for the American market to capture sales at the time of George Washington's inauguration in 1789. The design shows Liberty as a woman dressed in a golden gown, her liberty cap on a pole. She is holding a laurel wreath (signifying classical honors) over Washington's head. Fifteen labeled links encircle the scene, representing the states, although in 1789, Rhode Island and North Carolina had not yet ratified the Constitution, and Vermont and Kentucky were merely anticipated states. The Liverpool manufacturer was looking ahead; commemorative pitchers, jugs, and mugs were commonplace articles of consumer culture produced in Britain for the American market. Smithsonian Institution, Washington, D.C.

To his wife he complained, "My country has in its wisdom contrived for me the most insignificant office.") No one anticipated that two decades of party turbulence would emerge from the brilliant but explosive mix of Washington's first cabinet.

The Bill of Rights An important piece of business for the First Congress, meeting in 1789, was the passage of the **Bill of Rights**. Seven states had ratified the Constitution on the condition that guarantees of individual liberties and limitations to federal power be swiftly incorporated. The Federalists of 1787 had thought an enumeration of rights unnecessary, but in 1789 Congressman James Madison understood that healing the divisions of the 1780s was of prime importance. "It will be a desirable thing to extinguish from the bosom of every member of the community, any apprehensions that there are those among his countrymen who wish to deprive them of the liberty for which they valiantly fought and honorably bled."

Madison pulled much of his wording of rights directly from various state constitutions with bills of rights. He enumerated guarantees of freedom of speech, press, and religion; the right to petition and assemble; and the right to be free from unwarranted searches and seizures. One amendment asserted the right to keep and bear arms in support of a "well-regulated militia," to which Madison added, "but no person religiously scrupulous of bearing arms, shall be compelled to render military service in person." That provision for what a later century would call "conscientious objector" status failed to gain acceptance in Congress.

In September 1789, Congress approved a set of twelve amendments and sent them to the states for approval; by 1791, ten were eventually ratified. The First through Eighth Amendments dealt with individual liberties, and the Ninth and Tenth concerned the boundary between federal and state authority. (See the amendments to the U.S. Constitution in appendix I, page A-7.) The process of state ratification took another two years, but there was no serious doubt about the outcome.

Still, not everyone was entirely satisfied. State ratifying conventions had submitted some eighty proposed amendments. Congress never considered proposals to change structural features of the new government, and Madison had no intention of reopening debates about the length of the president's term or the power to levy excise taxes.

Significantly, no one complained about one striking omission in the Bill of Rights: the right to vote. Only much later was voting seen as a fundamental liberty requiring protection by constitutional amendment—indeed, by four amendments. The Constitution deliberately left the definition of voters to the states because of the existing wide variation in local voting practices. Most of these practices were based on property qualifications, but some touched on religion and, in one unusual case (New Jersey), on sex and race (see chapter 8, page 186).

The Republican Wife and Mother The exclusion of women from political activity did not mean they had no civic role or responsibility. A flood of periodical articles in the 1790s by both male and female writers reevaluated courtship, marriage, and motherhood in light of republican ideals. Tyrannical power in the ruler, whether king or husband, was declared a thing of the past. Affection, not duty, bound wives to their husbands and citizens to their government. In republican marriages, the writers claimed, women had the capacity to reform the morals and manners of men. One male author promised women that "the solidity and stability of the liberties of your country rest with you; since Liberty is never sure, 'till Virtue reigns triumphant. . . . While you thus keep our country virtuous, you maintain its independence." (For the relatively few American voices that raised questions about what rights women might have, see "Beyond America's Borders," page 210.)

Until the 1790s, public virtue was strictly a masculine quality. But another sort of virtue enlarged in importance: sexual chastity, a private asset prized as a feminine quality. Essayists of the 1790s explicitly advised young women to use sexual virtue to increase public virtue in men. "Love and courtship . . . invest a lady with more authority than in any other situation that falls to the lot of human beings," one male essayist proclaimed. If women spurned selfish suitors, they could promote good morals more than any social institution could, essayists promised.

Republican ideals also cast motherhood in a new light. Throughout the 1790s, advocates for female education, still a controversial proposition, argued that education would produce better mothers, who in turn would produce better citizens, a concept historians call **republican motherhood**. Benjamin Rush, a Pennsylvania physician and educator, called for female education because "our ladies should be qualified . . . in instructing their sons in the principles of liberty and government." A series of essays by **Judith Sargent Murray** of Massachusetts favored education that would remake women into self-confident, rational beings. Her first essay, published in 1790, was boldly titled "On the Equality of the Sexes." In a subsequent essay on education, she reassured readers that educated women "will not be assuming; the characteristic trait [sweetness] will still remain." Even Murray had to justify female education in the context of family duty.

Republican Womanhood: Judith Sargent Murray The twenty-one-year-old in this portrait, completed in 1772, became known eighteen years later as America's foremost spokeswoman for woman's equality. Judith Sargent Murray frequently wrote essays for the *Massachusetts Magazine* under the pen name "Constantia." In "On the Equality of the Sexes," published in 1790, she confidently asserted that women had "natural powers" of mind fully the equal of men's. Murray, the wife of a Universalist minister, also wrote plays that were performed on the Boston stage. In 1798, she published her collected "Constantia" essays in a book titled *The Gleaner*; George Washington and John Adams each bought a copy. Murray was the only woman of the era to keep an indexed letter book, which contains copies of nearly two thousand letters that she wrote during her lifetime. John Singleton Copley, Portrait of Mrs. John Stevens (Judith Sargent, later Mrs. John Murray), 1770–1772, oil on canvas, 50 × 40 inches, Terra Foundation for America, Chicago/Art Resource, NY.

Although women's obligations as wives and mothers were now infused with political meaning, traditional gender relations remained unaltered. The analogy between marriage and civil society worked precisely because of the self-subordination inherent in the term *virtue*. Men should put the public good first, before selfish desires, just as women must put their husbands and families first, before themselves. Women might gain literacy and knowledge, but only in the service of improved domestic duty. In Federalist America, wives and citizens alike should feel affection for and trust in their rulers; neither should ever rebel.

Q: How did political leaders in the 1790s attempt to overcome the divisions of the 1780s?

Hamilton's Economic Policies

The new government had the luck to be launched in flush economic times. Compared to the severe financial instability of the 1780s, the 1790s brimmed with opportunity, as seen in increased agricultural trade and improvements in transportation and banking. In 1790, the federal government moved from New York City to Philadelphia, a more central location with a substantial mercantile class. There, Alexander Hamilton, secretary of the treasury, embarked on his innovative plan to solidify the government's economic base. But controversy arose at every turn. Hamilton's plan to combine the large national debt with unpaid state debts produced a crisis in the first Congress. And his plan to raise revenues via taxation on whiskey brought on the country's first domestic rebellion.

Agriculture, Transportation, and Banking

Dramatic increases in international grain prices motivated American farmers to boost agricultural production for the export trade. Europe's rising population needed grain, and the French Revolutionary and Napoleonic Wars that engulfed Europe for a dozen years after 1793 severely compromised production there. From the Connecticut River valley to the Chesapeake, farmers planted more wheat, generating new jobs for millers, coopers, dockworkers, and ship and wagon builders.

Cotton production also underwent a boom, spurred by market demand and a mechanical invention. Limited amounts of smooth-seed cotton had long been grown in the coastal areas of the South, but this variety of cotton did not prosper in the drier inland regions. Greenseed cotton grew well inland, but its rough seeds stuck to the cotton fibers and were labor-intensive to remove. In 1793, Yale graduate Eli Whitney devised a machine called a gin that easily separated out the seeds; cotton production soared.

France, Britain, and Woman's Rights in the 1790s

During the 1770s and 1780s, only rarely did anyone in America wonder about rights for women. Abigail Adams's letter to her husband, John, in 1776, asking him to "Remember the Ladies" when writing new laws, stayed a private document for a century. Boycotts by the Daughters of Liberty before the Revolution did not challenge gender hierarchy, nor did New Jersey's handful of women voters (see chapter 8). Simply replacing a monarchy with a republic did not lead to an immediate or substantial challenge to women's subordinate status. Instead, it was influence from abroad that initially sparked new ideas about women's place in American society.

In France between 1789 and 1793, the revolution against monarchy enlarged ideas about citizenship and led some women to argue for the concept of the *citoyenne*, the female citizen. Women's political clubs, such as the Society of Republican Revolutionary Women in Paris, sent petitions and gave speeches to the National Assembly, demanding education, voting rights, and a curbing of the paternal and marital powers of men over women. In 1791, Frenchwoman Olympe de Gouges rewrote the male revolutionaries' document *The Rights of Man* into *The Rights of Woman*, asserting that "all women are born free and remain equal to men in rights." Another prominent woman, Théroigne de Méricourt, held a feminist salon, marched around Paris in masculine riding attire, and took part in an attack on a palace. Her vision went beyond political rights to the social customs that dictated women's subordination: "It is time for women to break out of the shameful incompetence in which men's ignorance, pride, and injustice have so long held us captive."

Although the male National Assembly never approved voting rights for French women in that era, it did reform French civil and family law in the early 1790s. Marriage was removed from the control of the church, divorce was legalized, and the age of majority for women was lowered. A far-reaching advance in inheritance law required division of a patriarch's estate among all his children, regardless of age, sex, and even legitimacy. Henceforth,

daughters could inherit along with sons; no longer did a woman from a family of means need to marry money — or, indeed, to marry at all. In contrast, most American states adopted traditional English family law virtually unchanged.

French feminism traveled across the Channel to England and directly inspired a talented woman named Mary Wollstonecraft. In 1792, she published *A Vindication of the Rights of Woman*, arguing for the intellectual equality of the sexes, economic independence for women, and women's participation in representative government. Most radically, she called marriage legalized prostitution.

Wollstonecraft's book created a sensation in America. Excerpts appeared immediately in Philadelphia and Boston periodicals, bookstores stocked the London edition, and by 1795 there were three American reprints. Some women readers were cautious. A sixty-year-old Philadelphian, Elizabeth Drinker, reflected in her diary, "In very many of her sentiments, she, as some of our friends say, speaks my mind; in some others, I do not altogether coincide with her. I am not for quite so much independence." Other women embraced Wollstonecraft's ideas. In 1794, a woman much younger than Drinker, Priscilla Mason, gave a biting commencement address at the new Young Ladies' Academy in Philadelphia, using Wollstonecraft as the inspiration for her rousing speech condemning "the high and mighty lords" (men) who denied women education and professional opportunities in church, law, and politics. "Happily, a more liberal way of thinking begins to prevail. . . . Let us by suitable education, qualify ourselves for those high departments," Mason said. She concluded with unwarranted optimism, "They will open before us." Many women's letters report lively debates stimulated by *A Vindication of the Rights of Woman*.

Male readers' responses were varied as well. Aaron Burr, a senator from New York, called the book "a work of genius." A Fourth of July speaker in New Jersey in 1793 proclaimed that "the Rights of Woman are no longer strange sounds to an American ear," and he hoped they would soon be embedded in state law codes. A more negative orator on that same holiday in New York argued that woman's rights really meant a woman's duty "to submit to the control of that government she has voluntarily chosen"—namely, the government of a husband. And a New Hampshire orator advanced this tart joke: "Every man, by the Constitution, is born with an equal right to be elected to the highest office. And every woman is born with an equal right to be the wife of the most eminent man." For some, it was clearly hard to think seriously about gender equality.

The notion of equal rights for women had a long incubation period in the United States. In the 1790s, ideas of equality were too closely associated with the radicalism of the French Revolution, a divisive topic in America; the unhappy fate of de Gouges, guillotined in France in 1794 for her feminist polemic, was widely reported in the American press. Soon revelations of Wollstonecraft's unconventional personal life as an unwed mother dampened enthusiasm for her pioneering book. Not until the 1830s and 1840s would a new generation of women, led by Sarah Grimké, raise new and insistent questions about woman's equality (see chapter 11, page 269, and chapter 12, page 301). Most Americans of the 1790s preferred a moderate stance, praising women's contributions to civil society through their influence on the family—the "republican motherhood" concept, as historians have called it. Although this fell far short of

an egalitarian claim to rights, it did justify—and this was no small gain—women's formal education. A young woman speaker at a Fourth of July picnic in Connecticut in 1799 summed it up perfectly for her all-female audience: "As mothers, wives, sisters, and daughters, we may all be important, [and] teach our little boys, the inestimable value of Freedom, how to blend and harmonize the natural and social rights of man, and as early impressions are indelible, thus assist our dear country, to be as glorious in maintaining, as it was great in gaining her immortal independence."

FRONTISPIECE.

Publish'd at Philad.ª Dec.ʳ 1.ˢᵗ 1792.

★ **Woman's Rights in the *Lady's Magazine*, 1792** This frontispiece appeared in the first volume of the Philadelphia periodical *Lady's Magazine and Repository of Entertaining Knowledge*, published in December 1792. Excerpts from Mary Wollstonecraft's *A Vindication of the Rights of Woman* also appeared in that issue. (The editor was a literary man, Charles Brockden Brown.) The caption identified the kneeling figure as "the Genius of the *Lady's Magazine*." She is accompanied by "the Genius of Emulation," carrying a trumpet and a laurel wreath. (*Genius* here meant a spirit; *emulation* meant ambition to excel. Thus, the genius of emulation was the spirit of ambition—women's ambition in this case.) The spirit representing the *Lady's Magazine* kneels before Liberty, identified by her liberty cap on a pole, and presents a paper titled "Rights of Woman." Study the objects arranged below Liberty: a book, a musical instrument, an artist's palette, a globe, and a page of geometrical shapes. The kneeling figure seems to gesture toward them. What do they suggest about the nature of the "rights of woman" that this picture endorses? Library Company of Philadelphia.

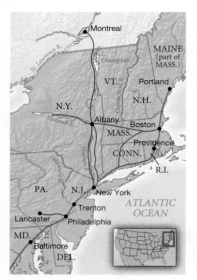

Major Roads in the 1790s

A surge of road building also stimulated the economy. Before 1790, one bumpy road connected Maine to Georgia, but with the establishment of the U.S. Post Office in 1792, road mileage sextupled to facilitate the transport of mail. Private companies also built toll roads, the first of which was the Lancaster Turnpike of 1794, connecting Philadelphia with Lancaster, Pennsylvania. Another turnpike linked Boston with Albany, New York. Farther inland, a major road extended southwest down the Shenandoah Valley, while another joined Richmond, Virginia, with the Tennessee towns of Knoxville and Nashville.

By 1800, a dense network of dirt, gravel, and plank roadways connected towns in southern New England and the Middle Atlantic states, spurring commercial stage companies to regularize and speed up passenger traffic. A trip from New York to Boston took four days; from New York to Philadelphia, less than two (Map 9.1). In 1790, Boston had only three stagecoach companies; by 1800, there were twenty-four.

A third development signaling economic resurgence was the growth of commercial banking. During the 1790s, the number of banks nationwide multiplied tenfold, from three to twenty-nine in 1800. Banks drew in money chiefly through the sale of stock. They then made loans in the form of banknotes, paper currency backed by the gold and silver that stockholders paid in. Because banks issued two or three times as much money in banknotes as they held in hard money, they were creating new money for the economy.

The U.S. population expanded along with economic development, propelled by large average family size and better than adequate food and land resources. As measured by the first two federal censuses in 1790 and 1800, population grew from 3.9 million to 5.3 million, an increase of 35 percent.

The Public Debt and Taxes The upturn in the economy, plus the new taxation powers of the government, suggested that the government might soon repay its wartime debt, amounting to more than $52 million owed to foreign and domestic creditors. But Hamilton had a different plan. He issued a *Report on Public Credit* in January 1790, recommending that the debt be funded—but not repaid immediately—at full value. This meant that old certificates of debt would be rolled over into new bonds, which would earn interest until they were retired several years later. There would

1790 Census Page This page provides a published tally of the final results of the first federal census in 1790, mandated by the U.S. Constitution as the means by which representation in Congress and proportional taxation on the states would be determined. Notice the choice of five classifications for the count: free white males age sixteen or older, free white males under age sixteen, free white females, all other free persons, and slaves. To implement the Constitution's three-fifths clause (counting slaves as three-fifths of a person), slaves had to be counted separately from all free persons. Separating white males into two broad age groups at sixteen provides a measure of military strength, something important for the government to gauge at a time of continuing and threatened Indian wars. U.S. Census Bureau.

FOR MORE HELP ANALYZING THIS IMAGE, see the visual activity for this chapter in the Online Study Guide at bedfordstmartins.com/roarkcompact.

still be a public debt, but it would be secure, giving its holders a direct financial stake in the new government. The bonds would circulate, injecting millions of dollars of new money into the economy. "A national debt if not excessive will be to us a national blessing; it will be a powerfull cement of our union," Hamilton wrote to a financier. Hamilton's goal was to make the new country creditworthy, not debt-free.

Funding the debt in full was controversial because speculators had already bought up debt certificates cheaply, and Hamilton's report touched off further speculation. (Hamilton himself held no certificates, but his father-in-law held some with a face value of $60,000.) Philadelphia and New York speculators sent agents into backcountry regions looking for certificates of debt whose unwary owners were ignorant about the proposed face-value funding.

Hamilton compounded controversy with his proposal to add to the federal debt another $25 million that some state governments still owed to individuals. During the war, states had obtained supplies by issuing IOUs to farmers, merchants, and moneylenders. Some states, such as Virginia and New York, had paid off these debts entirely. Others, such as Massachusetts, had partially paid them off through heavy taxation of the people. About half the states had made little headway. Hamilton called for the federal government to assume these state debts and combine them with the federal debt, in effect consolidating federal power over the states.

Congressman James Madison strenuously objected to putting windfall profits in the pockets of speculators. He instead proposed a complex scheme to pay both the original holders of the federal debt and the speculators, each at fair fractions of the face value. He also strongly objected to assumption of all the states' debts. A large debt was dangerous, Madison warned, especially because it would lead to high taxation. Secretary of State Jefferson also was fearful of Hamilton's proposals. "No man is more ardently intent to see the public debt soon and sacredly paid off than I am. This exactly marks the difference between Colonel Hamilton's views and mine, that I would wish the debt paid tomorrow; he wishes it never to be paid, but always to be a thing where with to corrupt and manage the legislature." A solution to this impasse arrived when Jefferson invited Hamilton and Madison to dinner. Over good food and wine, Hamilton secured the reluctant Madison's promise to restrain his opposition. In return, Hamilton pledged to back efforts to locate the nation's new capital city in the South, along the Potomac River, an outcome that was sure to please Virginians. In early July 1790, Congress voted for the Potomac site, and in late July, Congress passed the debt package, assumption and all.

The First Bank of the United States and the *Report on Manufactures*

The second and third major elements of Hamilton's economic plan were his proposal to create a national Bank of the United States and his program to encourage

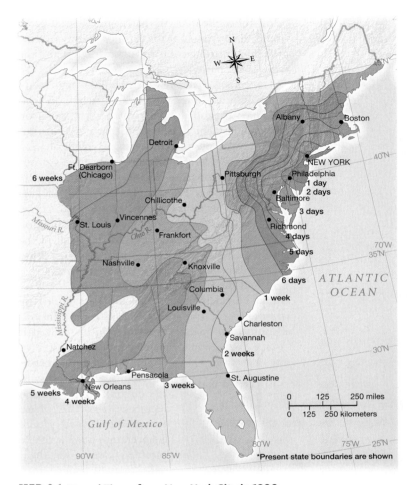

MAP 9.1 Travel Times from New York City in 1800

Notice that travel out of New York extends over a much greater distance in the first week than in subsequent weeks. In one week, a traveler could get to Pittsburgh, but it would take another four weeks to go a comparable distance west of that city. River corridors in the west and east speeded up travel—but only if one were going downriver. Also notice that travel by sea (north and south along the coast) was much faster than land travel.

domestic manufacturing. Arguing that banks were the "nurseries of national wealth," Hamilton modeled his bank plan on European central banks, such as the Bank of England, a private corporation that used its government's money to invigorate the British economy. According to Hamilton's plan, the central bank was to be capitalized at $10 million, a sum larger than all the hard money in the entire nation. The federal government would hold 20 percent of the bank's stock, making the bank in effect the government's fiscal agent, holding its revenues derived from import duties, land sales, and various other taxes. The other 80 percent of the bank's capital would come from private investors, who could buy stock in the bank with either hard money (silver or gold) or federal securities. Because of its size and the privilege of being the only national bank, the central bank would help stabilize the economy by exerting prudent control over credit, interest rates, and the value of the currency.

Concerned that a few rich bankers might have undue influence over the economy, Madison tried but failed to stop the plan in Congress. Jefferson advised President Washington that the Constitution did not permit Congress to charter banks. Hamilton, however, pointed out that the Constitution gave Congress specific powers to regulate commerce and a broad right "to make all laws which shall be necessary and proper for carrying into execution the foregoing powers." Washington sided with Hamilton and signed the Bank of the United States into law in February 1791, with a charter allowing it to operate for twenty years.

When the bank's privately held stock went on sale in Philadelphia, Boston, and New York City in July, it sold out in a few hours, touching off an immediate mania of speculation in resale that lasted a month and drew in many hundreds of urban merchants and artisans. A discouraged Madison reported that in New York, "the Coffee House is an eternal buzz with the gamblers," some of them self-interested congressmen intent on "public plunder." Stock prices shot upward, then crashed in mid-August. Hamilton shrewdly managed to cushion the crash to an extent, but Jefferson worried about the risk to morality inherent in gambling in stocks: "The spirit of gaming, once it has seized a subject, is incurable. The tailor who has made thousands in one day, tho' he has lost them the next, can never again be content with the slow and moderate earnings of his needle."

The third component of Hamilton's plan was issued in December 1791 in the **_Report on Manufactures_**, a proposal to encourage the production of American-made goods. Domestic manufacturing was in its infancy, and Hamilton aimed to mobilize the new powers of the federal government to grant subsidies to manufacturers and to impose moderate tariffs on those same products from overseas. Hamilton's plan targeted manufacturing of iron goods, arms and ammunition, coal, textiles, wood products, and glass. Among the blessings of manufacturing, he counted the new employment opportunities that would open to children and unmarried young women, who he assumed were underutilized in agricultural societies. The _Report on Manufactures_, however, was never approved by Congress. Many

> A discouraged Madison reported that in New York, "the Coffee House is an eternal buzz with the gamblers," some of them self-interested congressmen intent on "public plunder."

confirmed agriculturalists in Congress feared that manufacturing was a curse rather than a blessing. Madison and Jefferson in particular were alarmed by stretching the "general welfare" clause of the Constitution to include public subsidies to private businesses.

The Whiskey Rebellion Hamilton's plan to restore public credit required new taxation to pay the interest on the large national debt. In deference to the merchant class, Hamilton did not propose a general increase in import duties, nor did he propose land taxes, which would have fallen hardest on the nation's wealthiest landowners. Instead, he convinced Congress in 1791 to pass a 25 percent excise tax on whiskey, to be paid by farmers when they brought their grain to the distillery, then passed on to individual whiskey consumers in the form of higher prices. Members of Congress from eastern areas favored the tax — especially those from New England, where the favorite drink was rum. A New Hampshire representative cheerfully observed that the country would be "drinking down the national debt," an idea he evidently found acceptable. Virginia representative James Madison took a different but approving view of the tax, which he hoped might promote "sobriety and thereby prevent disease and untimely deaths."

Not surprisingly, the new excise tax proved unpopular with grain farmers in the western regions and whiskey drinkers everywhere. In 1791, farmers in Kentucky and the western parts of Pennsylvania, Virginia, Maryland, and the Carolinas forcefully conveyed to Congress their resentment of Hamilton's tax. One farmer complained that he already paid half his grain to the local distillery for distilling his rye, and now the distiller was taking the new whiskey tax out of the farmer's remaining half. This "reduces the balance to less than one-third of the original quantity. If this is not an oppressive tax, I am at a loss to describe what is so," the farmer wrote. Congress responded with modest modifications to the tax in 1792, but even so, discontent was rampant. Simple evasion of the law was the most common response. In some places, crowds threatened to tar and feather federal tax collectors, and distilleries underreported their production. Four counties in Pennsylvania established committees of correspondence and held assemblies to carry their message to Congress. Hamilton admitted to Congress that the revenue was far less than anticipated. But rather than abandon the law, he tightened up the prosecution of tax evaders.

In western Pennsylvania, Hamilton had one ally, a stubborn tax collector named John Neville who refused to quit even after a group of spirited farmers burned him in effigy. In May 1794, Neville filed charges against seventy-five farmers and distillers for tax evasion. His action touched off the **Whiskey Rebellion**. In July, he and a federal marshal were ambushed in Allegheny County by a group of forty men. Neville's house was then burned to the ground by a crowd estimated at five hundred, and one man in the crowd was killed. At the end of July, seven thousand Pennsylvania farmers planned a march — or perhaps an attack, some thought — on Pittsburgh to protest the hated tax.

In response, President Washington nationalized the Pennsylvania militia and set out, with Hamilton at his side, at the head of thirteen thousand soldiers. A worried Philadelphia newspaper criticized the show of force: "Shall Pennsylvania be converted into a human slaughter house because the dignity of the United States will not admit of conciliatory measures? Shall torrents of blood be spilled to support an odious excise system?" But in the end, no blood was spilled. By the time the army arrived in late September, the demonstrators had dispersed. No battles were fought, and no shots were exchanged. Twenty men were rounded up as rebels and charged with high treason, but only two were convicted, and both were soon pardoned by Washington.

Had the federal government overreacted? Thomas Jefferson thought so; he saw the event as a replay of Shays's Rebellion of 1786, when a protest against government taxation had been met with unreasonable government force (see chapter 8). The rebel farmers agreed; they felt entitled to protest oppressive taxation. Hamilton and Washington, however, thought that laws passed by a republican government must be obeyed. The Whiskey Rebellion presented an opportunity for the new federal government to flex its muscles and stand up to civil disorder.

Q: **Why were Hamilton's economic policies controversial?**

Conflicts West, East, and South

While the whiskey rebels challenged federal leadership from within the country, disorder threatened the United States from external sources as well. From 1790 onward, serious trouble brewed in three directions. To the west, a powerful confederation of Indian tribes in the Ohio Country resisted white encroachment, resulting in a brutal war. At the same time, conflicts between the major European powers forced Americans to take sides and nearly thrust the country into another war, this time across the Atlantic. And to the south, a Caribbean slave rebellion raised fears that racial war would be imported to the United States. Despite these conflicts and the grave threats they posed to the young country, Washington won reelection to the presidency unanimously in the fall of 1792.

To the West: The Indians In the 1783 Treaty of Paris, Britain had yielded all land east of the Mississippi River to the United States without regard to the resident Indian population. The 1784 Treaty of Fort Stanwix (see chapter 8) had attempted to solve that omission by establishing terms between the new confederation government and native peoples, but the key tribes of the Ohio Valley — the Shawnee, Delaware, and Miami — had not been involved in those negotiations. To confuse matters further, British troops still occupied a half dozen forts in the northwest, protecting an ongoing fur trade between British traders and Indians and thereby sustaining Indians' claims to that land.

The doubling of the American population from two million in 1770 to nearly four million in 1790 greatly intensified the pressure for western land. Several thousand settlers a year moved down the Ohio River in the mid-1780s. Most headed for Kentucky on the south bank of the river, but some eyed the forests to the north, in Indian country. By the late 1780s, government land sales in eastern Ohio had commenced, although actual settlement lagged.

Meanwhile, the U.S. army entered the western half of Ohio, where white settlers did not dare to go. Fort Washington, built on the Ohio River in 1789 at the site of present-day Cincinnati, became the command post for three major invasions of Indian country (Map 9.2). General Josiah Harmar, under orders to subdue the Indians of western Ohio, marched with 1,400 men into Ohio's northwest region in the fall of 1790, burning Indian villages. His inexperienced troops were ambushed by Miami and Shawnee Indians led by their chiefs, **Little Turtle** and **Blue Jacket**. Harmar lost one-eighth of his soldiers.

Harmar's defeat — so humiliating that he was court-martialed — spurred efforts to clear Ohio for permanent American settlement. General **Arthur St. Clair**, the military governor of the Northwest Territory, had pursued peaceful tactics in the 1780s, signing treaties with Indians for land in eastern Ohio — dubious treaties, as it happened, since the Indian negotiators were not authorized to

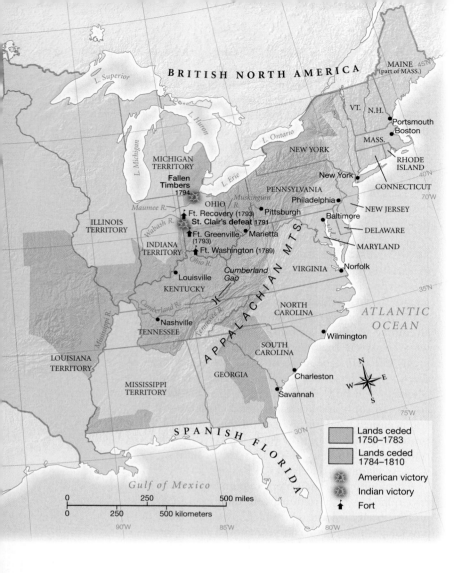

MAP 9.2 Western Expansion and Indian Land Cessions to 1810

By the first decade of the nineteenth century, intense Indian wars had resulted in significant cessions of land to the U.S. government by treaty.

READING THE MAP: Locate the Appalachians. The Proclamation Line of 1763 that ran along these mountains forbade colonists to settle west of the line. How well was that purpose met?

CONNECTIONS: How much did the population of the United States grow between 1750 and 1790? How did this growth affect western settlement?

FOR MORE HELP ANALYZING THIS MAP, see the map activity for this chapter in the Online Study Guide at bedfordstmartins.com/roarkcompact.

yield land. In the wake of Harmar's bungled operation, St. Clair geared up for military action, and in the fall of 1791, he led two thousand men (accompanied by two hundred women camp followers) north from Fort Washington to claim Ohio territory from the Miami and Shawnee tribes. Along the route, St. Clair's men quickly built two forts, named for Hamilton and Jefferson. However, when the Indians attacked at daybreak on November 4 at the headwaters of the Wabash River, St. Clair's army was not protected by fortifications.

Before noon, 55 percent of the Americans were dead or wounded; only three of the women escaped alive. "The savages seemed not to fear anything we could do," wrote an officer afterward. "The ground was literally covered with the dead." The Indians captured valuable weaponry, scalped and dismembered the dying, and pursued fleeing survivors for miles. With more than nine hundred lives lost, this was the most stunning American loss in the history of the U.S.-Indian wars. Grisly tales of St. Clair's

defeat became instantly infamous, increasing the level of terror that Americans brought to their confrontations with the Indians.

Washington doubled the U.S. military presence in Ohio and appointed a new commander, General Anthony Wayne of Pennsylvania, nicknamed "Mad Anthony" for his headstrong, hard-drinking style of leadership. About the Ohio natives, Wayne wrote, "I have always been of the opinion that we never should have a permanent peace with those Indians until they were made to experience our superiority." Throughout 1794, Wayne's army engaged in skirmishes with Shawnee, Delaware, and Miami Indians. Chief Little Turtle of the Miami tribe advised negotiation; in his view, Wayne's large army looked overpowering. But Blue Jacket of the Shawnees counseled continued warfare, and his view prevailed. The decisive action came in August 1794 at the **battle of Fallen Timbers**, near the Maumee River where a recent tornado had felled many trees. The confederated Indians—mainly

Ottawas, Potawatomis, Shawnees, and Delawares numbering around eight hundred—ambushed the Americans but were underarmed, and Wayne's troops made effective use of their guns and bayonets. The Indians withdrew and sought refuge at nearby Fort Miami, still held by the British. Their former allies locked the gate and refused protection. The surviving Indians fled to the woods, their ranks decimated.

Fallen Timbers was a major defeat for the Indians. The Americans had destroyed cornfields and villages on the march north, and with winter approaching, the Indians' confidence was sapped. They reentered negotiations in a much less powerful bargaining position. In 1795, about a thousand Indians representing nearly a dozen tribes met with Wayne and other American emissaries to work out the **Treaty of Greenville**. The Americans offered treaty goods (calico shirts, axes, knives, blankets, kettles, mirrors, ribbons, thimbles, and abundant wine and liquor casks) worth $25,000 and promised additional shipments every year. The government's idea was to create a dependency on American goods to keep the Indians friendly. In exchange, the Indians ceded most of Ohio to the Americans; only the northwest part of the territory was reserved solely for the Indians.

The treaty brought temporary peace to the region, but it did not restore a peaceful life to the Indians. The annual allowance from the United States too often came in the form of liquor. "More

Treaty of Greenville, 1795 This painting by an unknown artist of the 1790s purports to depict the signing of the Treaty of Greenville in 1795. The treaty was signed by General Anthony Wayne, Chief Little Turtle of the Miami tribe, and Chief Tarhe the Crane of the Wyandot tribe. An American officer kneels in front of a group of other officers, apparently writing something down—not a likely posture in which to draft a formal treaty. One Indian of the three pictured seems to be gesturing with emphasis, as if to dictate terms to the Americans, but in fact the treaty was most favorable to the United States. Although many Indians from a dozen Ohio tribes congregated at the signing of the treaty, this picture shows unrealistically open spaces and very few Indians. The treaty medal commemorates the event. It is one of probably dozens distributed to Indian participants by U.S. officials. Why might "E Pluribus Unum"—"Out of many, one"—appear on the medal? Painting: Chicago Historical Society; Medal: Indiana Historical Society.

> "This liquor that they introduce into our country is more to be feared than the gun and tomahawk," said Chief Little Turtle in 1800.

of us have died since the Treaty of Greenville than we lost by the years of war before, and it is all owing to the introduction of liquor among us," said Chief Little Turtle in 1800. "This liquor that they introduce into our country is more to be feared than the gun and tomahawk."

Across the Atlantic: France and Britain

While Indian battles engaged the American military in the west, another war overseas to the east was also closely watched. Since 1789, revolution had been raging in France. At first, the general American reaction was positive, for it was flattering to think that the American Revolution had inspired imitation in France. As monarchy and privilege were overthrown in France, towns throughout America celebrated the victory of the French

people with civic feasts and public festivities. Dozens of pro-French political clubs, called democratic or republican societies, sprang up around the country.

Many American women exhibited solidarity with revolutionary France by donning sashes and cockades made with ribbons of red, white, and blue. Pro-French headgear for committed women included an elaborate turban, leading one horrified Federalist newspaper editor to chastise the "fiery frenchified dames" thronging Philadelphia's streets. In Charleston, South Carolina, a pro-French pageant in 1793 united two women as partners, one representing France and the other America. The women repudiated their husbands "on account of ill treatment" and pledged mutual "union and friendship," while a gun salute sealed the pledge. Most likely, this ceremony was not the country's first civil union but instead a richly metaphorical piece of street theater in which the spurned husbands represented Britain.

Revolutionary Solidarity In the early 1790s, some Americans showed enthusiasm for the French Revolution by wearing a tricolor cockade — a distinctive bow made from red, white, and blue ribbons. A woman seeking the full pro-French look could copy Parisian revolutionary outfits, as in this style described in a Philadelphia newspaper in 1790: a black beaver hat with cockade and feathers; a dark blue jacket with a white collar, red cuffs, and yellow buttons; a white blouse; a blue skirt with white trim; and black shoes. Another pro-French statement appeared in several marriage announcements in Boston, Hartford, and Philadelphia newspapers in the early months of 1793. In these announcements, men often adopted *Citizen* as their title of address, with the corresponding term *Citess* for women. (*Citess* was invented on the spot and spelled eighteenth-century style with a character shaped like the letter *f*.) In France, *Citoyen* and *Citoyenne* enjoyed widespread use as egalitarian titles of address. Outfit: Bibliothèque Nationale de France; Announcement: Courtesy, American Antiquarian Society.

Anti–French Revolution sentiments also ran deep. Vice President John Adams, who lived in France in the 1780s, trembled to think of radicals in France or America. "Too many Frenchmen, after the example of too many Americans, pant for the equality of persons and property," Adams said. "The impracticability of this, God Almighty has decreed, and the advocates for liberty, who attempt it, will surely suffer for it."

Support for the French Revolution remained a matter of personal conviction until 1793, when Britain and France went to war and French versus British loyalty became a critical foreign policy debate. France had helped America substantially during the American Revolution, and the confederation government had signed an alliance in 1778 promising aid if France were ever under attack. Americans optimistic about the eventual outcome of the French Revolution wanted to deliver on that promise. Others, including those shaken by the report of the guillotining of thousands of French people, as well as those with strong commercial ties to Britain, sought ways to stay neutral.

In May 1793, President Washington issued the Neutrality Proclamation, which contained friendly assurances to both sides, in an effort to stay out of European wars. Yet American ships continued to trade between the French West Indies and France. In late 1793 and early 1794, the British expressed their displeasure by capturing more than three hundred of these vessels near the West Indies. Clearly, something had to be done to assert American power.

President Washington sent John Jay, the chief justice of the Supreme Court and a man of strong pro-British sentiments, to England to negotiate commercial relations in the British West Indies and secure compensation for the seizure of American ships. In addition, Jay was supposed to resolve several long-standing problems. Southern planters wanted reimbursement for the slaves lured away by the British army during the war, and western settlers wanted Britain to vacate the frontier forts still occupied because of their proximity to the Indian fur trade.

Jay returned from his diplomatic mission in 1795 with a treaty that no one could love. First, the **Jay Treaty** failed to address the captured cargoes or the lost property in slaves. Second, it granted the British a lenient eighteen months to withdraw from the frontier forts, as well as continued rights in the fur trade. (The provision disheartened the Indians just then negotiating the Treaty of Greenville in Ohio. It was a significant factor in their decision to make peace.) Finally,

the treaty called for repayment with interest of the debts that some American planters still owed to British firms dating from the Revolutionary War. In exchange for such generous terms, Jay secured limited trading rights in the West Indies and agreement that some issues—boundary disputes with Canada and the damage and loss claims of shipowners—would be decided later by arbitration commissions.

When newspapers published the terms of the treaty, powerful opposition emerged from Maine to Georgia. In Massachusetts, this graffiti appeared on a wall: "Damn John Jay! Damn everyone who won't damn John Jay! Damn everyone who won't stay up all night damning John Jay!" Bonfires in many places burned effigies of Jay and copies of the treaty. Nevertheless, the treaty passed the Senate in 1795 by a vote of 20 to 10. Some representatives in the House, led by Madison, tried to undermine the Senate's approval by insisting on a separate vote on the funding provisions of the treaty, on the grounds that the House controlled all money bills. Finally, in 1796, the House approved funds to implement the various commissions mandated by the treaty, but by only a three-vote margin. The bitter vote in both houses of Congress divided along the same lines as the Hamilton-Jefferson split on economic policy.

To the South: The Haitian Revolution In addition to the Indian wars in Ohio and the European wars across the Atlantic, a third bloody conflict to the south polarized and even terrorized many Americans in the 1790s. The western third of the large Caribbean island of Hispaniola, just to the east of Cuba, became engulfed in revolution starting in 1791. The eastern portion of the island was a Spanish colony called Santo Domingo; the western part, in bloody conflagration, was the French Saint Domingue. War raged in Saint Domingue for more than a decade, resulting in 1804 in the birth of the Republic of Haiti, the first and only independent black state to arise out of a successful slave revolution.

The **Haitian Revolution** was a complex event involving many participants, including the diverse local population and, eventually, three European countries. Some 30,000 whites ruled the island in 1790, running sugar and coffee plantations with close to half a million enslaved blacks, two-thirds of them of African birth. The white French colonists were

Haitian Revolution, 1791–1804

CUBA (Sp.)

HISPANIOLA *ATLANTIC OCEAN*

Le Cap • • Fort Dauphin
SAINT DOMINGUE (France)
Port-au-Prince
SANTO DOMINGO (Spain)

Caribbean Sea

Beginning of slave revolt, 1791
Border of Saint Domingue/ Santo Domingo, 1790
Border of Haiti/ Santo Domingo, 1820

not the only plantation owners, however. About 28,000 free mixed-race people (*gens de couleur*) also lived in Saint Domingue; they owned one-third of the island's plantations and nearly a quarter of the slave labor force. Despite their economic status, these mixed-race planters were barred from political power, but they aspired to it.

The French Revolution of 1789 was the immediate catalyst for rebellion in this already tense society. First, white colonists challenged the white royalist government in an effort to link Saint Domingue with the new revolutionary government in France. Next, the mixed-race planters rebelled in 1791, demanding equal civil rights with the whites. No sooner was this revolt viciously suppressed than another part of the island exploded as thousands of enslaved blacks armed with machetes and torches wreaked devastation and slaughter. In 1793, the civil war escalated to include French, Spanish, and British troops fighting the inhabitants and also each other. Slaves led by Toussaint L'Ouverture in alliance with Spain occupied the northern regions of the island, leaving a thousand plantations in ruins and tens of thousands of people dead. Thousands of white and mixed-race planters, along with some of their slaves, fled to Spanish Louisiana and southern cities in the United States.

White Americans followed the revolution in fascinated horror through newspapers and refugees' accounts. A few sympathized with the impulse for liberty, but many more feared that violent black insurrection might spread to the United States. Many black American slaves also followed the revolution, for the amazing news of the success of a first-ever massive revolution by slaves traveled quickly in this oral culture. Whites complained of behaviors that might prefigure plots and conspiracies, such as increased insolence and higher runaway rates among slaves.

The Haitian Revolution provoked naked fear of a race war in white southerners. Jefferson, agonizing over the contagion of liberty in 1797, wrote another Virginia slaveholder that "if something is not done, and soon done, we shall be the murderers of our own children . . . ; the revolutionary storm, now sweeping the globe, will be upon us, and happy if we make timely provision to give it an easy passage over our land. From the present state of things in Europe and America, the day which brings our combustion must be near at hand; and only a single spark is wanting to make that day to-morrow."

Q: Why did the United States feel vulnerable to international threats in the 1790s?

Federalists and Republicans

By the mid-1790s, polarization over the French Revolution, Haiti, the Jay Treaty, and Hamilton's economic plans had led to two distinct and consistent rival political groups: **Federalists** and **Republicans**. Politicians and newspapers adopted these labels, words that summarized conflicting political positions. Federalist leaders supported Britain in foreign policy and commercial interests at home, while Republicans rooted for liberty in France and worried about monarchical Federalists at home. The labels did not yet describe full-fledged political parties, which were still thought to be a sign of failure of the experiment in government. Washington's decision not to seek a third term led to serious partisan electioneering in the presidential and congressional elections of 1796. Federalist John Adams won the presidency, but party strife accelerated over failed diplomacy in France, bringing the United States to the brink of war. Pro-war and antiwar antagonism created a major crisis over political free speech, militarism, and fears of sedition and treason.

The Election of 1796 Washington struggled to appear to be above party politics, and in his farewell address, he stressed the need to maintain a "unity of government" reflecting a unified body politic. He also urged the country to "steer clear of permanent alliances with any portion of the foreign world." The leading contenders for his position, John Adams of Massachusetts and Thomas Jefferson of Virginia, in theory agreed with him, but around them raged a party contest split along pro-British versus pro-French lines.

Adams and Jefferson were not adept politicians in the modern sense, skilled in the arts of persuasion and intrigue. Bruised by his conflicts with Hamilton, Jefferson had resigned as secretary of state in 1793 and retreated to Monticello, his home in Virginia. Adams's job as vice president kept him closer to the political action, but his personality often put people off. He was temperamental, thin-skinned, and quick to take offense. A friend once listed Adams's shortcomings as a politician: "He can't dance, drink, game, flatter, promise, dress, swear with gentlemen, and small talk and flirt with the ladies."

The leading Federalists informally caucused and chose Adams as their candidate, with Thomas Pinckney of South Carolina to run with him. The Republicans settled on Aaron Burr of New York to pair with Jefferson. The Constitution did not anticipate parties and tickets. Instead, each electoral college voter could cast two votes for any two candidates, but on only one ballot. The top vote-getter became president, and the next-highest assumed the vice presidency. (This procedural flaw was corrected by the Twelfth Amendment, adopted

Washington's Farewell Address Printed on a Textile, 1806 This small square of fabric, suitable for framing or tacking to the wall, was one of many items that served to immortalize Washington as the benevolent savior of the young Republic. Known well by close associates as a man with ordinary human failings — one Federalist member of his last cabinet complained that he was "vain and weak and ignorant" — Washington in death became a demigod, a genius of inspired leadership and faultless integrity. This 1806 textile features the final paragraph of Washington's 1796 farewell address, one highlighting his modesty and self-deprecation. At the bottom, the American eagle and the British lion flank two sailing ships (one close, one far-off) under the words *Commercial Union*. This textile picture was in fact an implicit criticism of President Thomas Jefferson (1801–1809), whose leadership was producing deteriorating relations with Britain that would finally result in the War of 1812. Collection of Janice L. and David J. Frent.

in 1804.) With only one ballot, careful maneuvering was required to make sure the chief rivals for the presidency did not land in the top two spots.

Into that maneuverable moment stepped Alexander Hamilton. No longer in the cabinet, Hamilton had returned to his law practice in 1795, but he kept a firm hand on political developments. Hamilton did not trust Adams; he preferred Pinckney, and he tried to influence electors to throw their support to the South Carolinian. But his plan backfired: Adams was elected president with 71 electoral votes; Jefferson came in second with 68 and thus became vice president. Pinckney got 59 votes, while Burr trailed with 30.

Adams's inaugural speech pledged neutrality in foreign affairs and respect for the French people, which made Republicans hopeful. To please Federalists, Adams retained three cabinet members from Washington's administration — the secretaries of state, treasury, and war. But the three were Hamilton loyalists, passing off Hamilton's judgments and advice as their own to the unwitting Adams. Vice President Jefferson extended a conciliatory hand to Adams and the two took temporary lodging in the same boardinghouse. But the Hamiltonian cabinet ruined the honeymoon. Jefferson's advice was spurned, and he withdrew from active counsel of the president.

The XYZ Affair From the start, Adams's presidency was in crisis. France retaliated for the British-friendly Jay Treaty by abandoning its 1778 alliance with the United States. French privateers — armed private vessels — started detaining American ships carrying British goods; by March 1797, more than three hundred American vessels had been seized. To avenge these insults, Federalists started murmuring openly about war with France. Adams preferred negotiations and dispatched a three-man commission to France in the fall of 1797. When the three commissioners arrived in Paris, French officials would not receive them. Finally, the French minister of foreign affairs, Talleyrand, sent three French agents — unnamed and later known to the American public as X, Y, and Z — to the American commissioners with the information that $250,000 might grease the wheels of diplomacy and a $12 million loan to the French government would be the price of a peace treaty. Incensed, the commissioners brought news of the bribery attempt to the president.

Americans reacted to the **XYZ affair** with shock and anger. Even staunch pro-French Republicans began to reevaluate their allegiance. The Federalist-dominated Congress appropriated money for an army of ten thousand soldiers and repealed all prior treaties with France. In 1798, twenty naval warships launched the United States into its first undeclared war, called the **Quasi-War** by historians to underscore its uncertain legal status. The main scene of action was the Caribbean, where more than one hundred French ships were captured.

There was no home-front unity in this time of undeclared war; antagonism only intensified between Federalists and Republicans. Republican newspapers heaped abuse on Adams. Pro-French mobs roamed the capital, and Adams, fearing for his personal safety, stocked weapons in his presidential quarters. Federalists, too, went on the offensive. In Newburyport, Massachusetts, they lit a huge bonfire and burned issues of the state's Republican newspapers. One Federalist editor ominously declared that "he who is not for us is against us."

The Alien and Sedition Acts With tempers so dangerously high and fears that political dissent was perhaps akin to treason, Federalist leaders moved to muffle the opposition. In mid-1798, Congress hammered out the Sedition Act, which not only made conspiracy and revolt illegal but also penalized speaking or writing anything that defamed the president or Congress. Criticizing government leaders became a criminal offense. One Federalist warned of the threat that existed "to overturn and ruin the government by publishing the most shameless falsehoods against the representatives of the people." In all, twenty-five men, almost all Republican newspaper editors, were charged with sedition; twelve were convicted.

Congress also passed two Alien Acts. The first extended the waiting period for an alien to achieve citizenship from five to fourteen years and required all aliens to register with the federal government. The second empowered the president in time of war to deport or imprison without trial any foreigner suspected of being a danger to the United States. The clear intent of these laws was to harass French immigrants already in the United States and to discourage others from coming.

Republicans strongly opposed the **Alien and Sedition Acts** on the grounds that they were in conflict

Cartoon of the Matthew Lyon Fight in Congress The political tensions of 1798 were not merely intellectual. A February session in Congress degenerated from name-calling to a brawl. Roger Griswold, a Connecticut Federalist, called Matthew Lyon, a Vermont Republican, a coward. Lyon responded with some well-aimed spit, the first departure from the gentleman's code of honor. Griswold responded by raising his cane to Lyon, whereupon Lyon grabbed nearby fire tongs to beat back his assailant. Madison wrote to Jefferson that the two should have dueled: "No man ought to reproach another with cowardice, who is not ready to give proof of his own courage" by negotiating a duel, the honorable way to avenge insults in Virginia's planter class. But Lyon, a Scots-Irish immigrant, did not come from a class or culture that cultivated the art of the duel. Rough-and-tumble fighting was his first response to insult. Library of Congress.

FOR MORE HELP ANALYZING THIS IMAGE, see the visual activity for this chapter in the Online Study Guide at bedfordstmartins.com/roarkcompact.

with the Bill of Rights, but they did not have the votes to revoke the acts in Congress, nor could the federal judiciary, dominated by Federalist judges, be counted on to challenge them. Jefferson and Madison turned to the state legislatures, the only other competing political arena, to press their opposition. Each man drafted a set of resolutions condemning the acts and had the legislatures of Virginia and Kentucky present them to the federal government in late fall 1798. The Virginia and Kentucky Resolutions tested the novel argument that state legislatures have the right to judge the constitutionality of federal laws and to nullify laws that infringe on the liberties of the people as defined in the Bill of Rights. The resolutions made little dent in the Alien and Sedition Acts, but the idea of a state's right to nullify federal law did not disappear. It would resurface several times in decades to come, most notably in a major tariff dispute in 1832 and in the sectional arguments that led to the Civil War.

Amid all the war hysteria and sedition fears in 1798, President Adams regained his balance. He was uncharacteristically restrained in pursuing opponents under the Sedition Act, and he finally refused to declare war on France, as extreme Federalists wished. No doubt he was beginning to realize how much he had been the dupe of Hamilton. He also shrewdly realized that France was not eager for war and that a peaceful settlement might be close at hand. In January 1799, a peace initiative from France arrived in the form of a letter assuring Adams that diplomatic channels were open again and that new commissioners would be welcomed in France.

Adams accepted this overture and appointed new negotiators. By late 1799, the Quasi-War with France had subsided, and in 1800 the negotiations resulted in a treaty declaring "a true and sincere friendship" between the United States and France. But Federalists were not pleased; Adams lost the support of a significant part of his own party and sealed his fate as the first one-term president of the United States.

The election of 1800 was openly organized along party lines. The self-designated national leaders of each group met to handpick their candidates for president and vice president. Adams's chief opponent was Thomas Jefferson. When the election was finally over, President Jefferson mounted the inaugural platform to announce, "We are all republicans, we are all federalists," an appealing rhetoric of harmony appropriate to an inaugural address. But his formulation perpetuated a denial of the validity of party politics, a denial that ran deep in the founding generation of political leaders.

Q: **Why did Congress pass the Alien and Sedition Acts in 1798?**

Conclusion: Parties Nonetheless

American political leaders began operating the new government in 1789 with great hopes of unifying the country and overcoming selfish factionalism. The enormous trust in President Washington was the central foundation for those hopes, and Washington did not disappoint, becoming a model Mr. President with a blend of integrity and authority. Stability was further aided by easy passage of the Bill of Rights (to appease Antifederalists) and by attention to cultivating a virtuous citizenry of upright men supported and rewarded by republican womanhood. Yet the hopes of the honeymoon period soon turned to worries and then fears as major political disagreements flared up.

At the core of the conflict was a group of talented men—Hamilton, Madison, Jefferson, and Adams—so recently allies but now opponents. They diverged over Hamilton's economic program, over relations with the British and the Jay Treaty, over the French and Haitian revolutions, and over preparedness for war abroad and free speech at home. Hamilton was perhaps the driving force in these conflicts, but the antagonism was not about mere personality. Parties were taking shape not around individuals, but around principles, such as ideas about what constituted enlightened leadership, how powerful the federal government should be, who was the best ally in Europe, and when oppositional political speech turned into treason. The Federalists were pro-British, pro-commerce, and ever alarmed about the potential excesses of democracy. The Republicans celebrated, up to a point, the radical republicanism of France and opposed the Sedition Act as an alarming example of an overbearing government cutting off freedom of speech.

When Jefferson in his inaugural address of 1800 offered his conciliatory assurance that Americans were at the same time "all republicans" and "all federalists," he probably mystified some listeners. Possibly, he meant to suggest that both groups shared two basic ideas—the value of republican government, in which power derived from the people, and the value of the unique federal system of shared governance structured by the Constitution. But by 1800, *Federalist* and *Republican* defined competing philosophies of government. To at least some of his listeners, Jefferson's assertion of harmony across budding party lines could only have seemed bizarre. For the next two decades, these two groups would battle each other, each fearing that the success of the other might bring the demise of the country. And for the next two decades, leaders continued to worry that partisan spirit itself was a bad thing.

Reviewing the Chapter

★ KEY TERMS

Explain each term's significance

WHO

Alexander Hamilton (p. 205)

Judith Sargent Murray (p. 208)

Little Turtle (p. 215)

Blue Jacket (p. 215)

Arthur St. Clair (p. 215)

WHAT

Revolutionary War debt (p. 205)

Bill of Rights (p. 208)

republican motherhood (p. 208)

Report on Public Credit (p. 212)

Report on Manufactures (p. 214)

Whiskey Rebellion (p. 215)

battle of Fallen Timbers (p. 216)

Treaty of Greenville (p. 217)

Jay Treaty (p. 219)

Haitian Revolution (p. 219)

Federalists (p. 220)

Republicans (p. 220)

XYZ affair (p. 221)

Quasi-War (p. 221)

Alien and Sedition Acts (p. 222)

★ REVIEW QUESTIONS Q:

Use key terms and dates to support your answer

1. How did political leaders in the 1790s attempt to overcome the divisions of the 1780s? (pp. 206–09)

2. Why were Hamilton's economic policies controversial? (pp. 209–15)

3. Why did the United States feel vulnerable to international threats in the 1790s? (pp. 215–20)

4. Why did Congress pass the Alien and Sedition Acts in 1798? (pp. 220–23)

★ MAKING CONNECTIONS

Draw on key terms, timeline, and review questions

1. Why did the Federalist alliance fracture in the 1790s? Why was this development troubling to the nation? In your answer, cite specific ideological and political developments that compromised cooperation.

2. What provoked the Whiskey Rebellion? How did the government respond? In your answer, discuss the foundations and precedents of the conflict, as well as the significance of the government's response.

3. Americans held that virtue was pivotal to the success of their new nation. What did they mean by *virtue*? How did they hope to ensure that their citizens and their leaders possessed virtue?

4. The domestic politics of the new nation were profoundly influenced by conflicts beyond the nation's borders. Discuss how conflicts abroad contributed to domestic political developments in the 1790s.

FOR PRACTICE QUIZZES AND OTHER STUDY TOOLS, see the Online Study Guide at **bedfordstmartins.com/roarkcompact**.

★ SUGGESTED READINGS

Ron Chernow, *Alexander Hamilton* (2004). An intimate biography of the financial genius of the 1790s.

Joseph J. Ellis, *Founding Brothers: The Revolutionary Generation* (2000). Captivating chapters illuminate the complex rivalries of the 1790s leaders.

David McCullough, *John Adams* (2001). John Adams glorified *and* humanized by a superb storyteller.

Jeffrey L. Pasley, *The Tyranny of Printers: Newspaper Politics in the Early American Republic* (2001). How journalism in the 1790s helped to create partisan politics.

Henry Wiencek, *An Imperfect God: George Washington, His Slaves, and the Creation of America* (2003). A close exploration of Washington's words and actions regarding slavery.

Rosemarie Zagarri, *Revolutionary Backlash: Women and Politics in the Early American Republic* (2007). A book that shows how the potential for women's political advancement in the 1790s was dramatically cut off after 1800.

FOR MORE BOOKS ABOUT TOPICS IN THIS CHAPTER, see the Online Bibliography at **bedfordstmartins.com/roarkcompact**.

FOR ADDITIONAL FIRSTHAND ACCOUNTS OF THIS PERIOD, see Chapter 9 in Michael Johnson, ed., *Reading the American Past*, Fourth Edition.

FOR WEB SITES, IMAGES, AND DOCUMENTS RELATED TO TOPICS AND PLACES IN THIS CHAPTER, visit Make History at **bedfordstmartins.com/roarkcompact**.

★ TIMELINE

1789
- George Washington inaugurated first president.
- French Revolution begins.
- First Congress meets.
- Fort Washington erected in western Ohio.

1790
- Congress approves Hamilton's debt plan.
- Judith Sargent Murray publishes "On the Equality of the Sexes."
- Shawnee and Miami Indians in Ohio defeat General Josiah Harmar.

1791
- States ratify Bill of Rights.
- Congress and president charter Bank of the United States.
- Ohio Indians defeat General Arthur St. Clair.
- Congress passes whiskey tax.
- Haitian Revolution begins.
- Hamilton issues *Report on Manufactures*.

1793
- Napoleonic Wars break out between France and Britain.
- Washington issues Neutrality Proclamation.
- Eli Whitney invents cotton gin.

1794
- Whiskey Rebellion.
- Battle of Fallen Timbers.

1795
- Treaty of Greenville.
- Jay Treaty.

1796
- Federalist John Adams elected second president.

1797
- XYZ affair.

1798
- Quasi-War with France erupts.
- Alien and Sedition Acts.
- Virginia and Kentucky Resolutions.

1800
- Republican Thomas Jefferson elected third president.

PATRIOTIC PITCHER, 1800 This pitcher, a humble piece of everyday tableware, celebrates American military readiness. A militia officer strikes a springy pose, ready for action. Two naval ships lie offshore; a cannon juts out aggressively. Banners proclaim "Success to America Whose Militia Is Better Than Standing Armies" and "May Its Citizens Emulate Soldiers, and Its Soldiers Heroes." The picture's swagger implies a military preparedness that was woefully off the mark. In 1800, the U.S. navy had only a dozen frigates. Serious trouble was brewing in the Mediterranean, where North African privateers attacked American ships with impunity. In 1801, President Jefferson received the first official declaration of war against the United States, from the leader of Tripoli. Marines, not militiamen, were needed. Earthenware pitchers emblazoned with patriotic messages all came from English manufacturers in Liverpool, with its good clay and ready supply of coal for high-temperature firing. Thousands of American-themed pitchers — with eagles and flags, Miss Liberty and George Washington — were made and sold. Pitchers saw daily use in the early Republic wherever people gathered to eat or drink. Water or milk, ale or apple juice, hot rum toddies or mulled cider — early Americans' beverage choices were more limited than ours today, and everyone gathered around the table typically drank the same beverage from the shared pitcher. Kahn Fine Antiques/photo courtesy of Antiques and Fine Arts.

Republicans in Power

1800–1824

THE NAME TECUMSEH translates as "Shooting Star," a fitting name for the Shawnee chief who reached meteoric heights of fame among Indians during Thomas Jefferson's presidency. From Canada to Georgia and west to the Mississippi, **Tecumseh** was accounted a charismatic leader, for which white Americans praised (and feared) him. Graceful, eloquent, compelling, astute: Tecumseh was all these and more, a gifted natural commander, equal parts politician and warrior.

The Ohio Country, where Tecumseh was born in 1768, was home to some dozen Indian tribes, including the Shawnee, recently displaced from the South. During the Revolutionary War, the region became a battleground with the "Big Knives," as the Shawnee people called the Americans. The Revolution's end in 1783 brought no peace to Indian country. American settlers pushed west, and the youthful Tecumseh honed his warrior skills by ambushing pioneers flatboating down the Ohio River. He fought at the battle of Fallen Timbers, a major Indian defeat, but avoided the 1795 negotiations of the Treaty of Greenville in which half a dozen dispirited tribes ceded much of Ohio to the Big Knives. In frustration, he watched as seven treaties between 1802 and 1805 whittled away more Indian land.

Some Indians, resigned and tired, looked for ways to accommodate, taking up farming, trade, and even intermarriage with the Big Knives. Others spent their treaty payments on alcohol. Tecumseh's younger brother Tenskwatawa led an embittered life of idleness and drink. But Tecumseh rejected accommodation and instead campaigned for a return to ancient ways. Donning traditional animal-skin garb, he traveled around the Great Lakes region after 1805 persuading tribes to join his pan-Indian confederacy. The territorial governor of Indiana, William Henry Harrison, reported, "For four years he has been in constant motion. You see him today on the Wabash, and in a short time hear of him on the shores of Lake Erie or Michigan, or on the banks of the Mississippi, and wherever he goes he makes an impression favorable to his purpose."

Even his dissolute brother was born anew. After a near-death experience in 1805, Tenskwatawa revived and recounted a startling vision of meeting the Master of Life. Renaming himself the Prophet, he urged Indians everywhere to regard whites as children of the Evil Spirit, destined to be destroyed.

Previewing the Chapter

Jefferson's Presidency 228
Q: *How did Jefferson attempt to undo the Federalist innovations of earlier administrations?*

The Madisons in the White House 235
Q: *Why did Congress declare war on Great Britain in 1812?*

Women's Status in the Early Republic 239
Q: *How did the civil status of American women and men differ in the early Republic?*

Monroe and Adams 242
Q: *How did the collapse of the Federalist Party influence the administrations of James Monroe and John Quincy Adams?*

Conclusion: Republican Simplicity Becomes Complex 247

Tecumseh Several portraits of Tecumseh exist, but they all present a different visage, and none of them enjoys verified authenticity. This one perhaps comes closest to how Tecumseh actually looked. It is an 1848 engraving adapted from an earlier drawing that no longer exists, sketched by a French trader in Indiana named Pierre Le Dru in a live sitting with the Indian leader in 1808. The engraver has given Tecumseh a British army officer's uniform, showing that he fought on the British side in the War of 1812. Notice the head covering and the medallion around Tecumseh's neck, marking his Indian identity. Library of Congress.

Tecumseh and the Prophet established a new village called Prophetstown, located in present-day Indiana, offering a potent blend of spiritual regeneration and political unity that attracted thousands of followers. Governor Harrison admired and feared Tecumseh, calling him "one of those uncommon geniuses which spring up occasionally to produce revolutions."

President Thomas Jefferson worried about an organized Indian confederacy and its potential for a renewed alliance with the British in Canada. Those worries became a reality during Jefferson's second term in office (1805–1809). Although his first term (1801–1805) brought notable successes, such as the Louisiana Purchase and the Lewis and Clark expedition, his second term was consumed by the threat of war with either Britain or France, in a replay of the late-1790s tensions. When war came in 1812, the enemy was Britain, bolstered by a reenergized Indian-British alliance. Among the causes of the war were insults over international shipping rights and the capture of U.S. vessels. But the war also derived compelling strength from Tecumseh's confederacy. Significant battles pitted U.S. soldiers against Indians in the Great Lakes, Tennessee, and Florida.

In the end, the War of 1812 settled little between the United States and Britain, but it was tragically conclusive for the Indians. Eight hundred warriors led by Tecumseh helped defend Canada against U.S. attacks, but the British did not reciprocate when the Indians were under threat. Tecumseh died on Canadian soil at the battle of the Thames in the fall of 1813. No Indian leader with his star power would emerge again east of the Mississippi.

The briefly unified Indian confederacy under Tecumseh had no counterpart in the young Republic's confederation of states, where widespread unity behind a single leader proved impossible to achieve. Republicans did battle with Federalists during the Jefferson and Madison administrations, but then Federalists doomed their party by opposing the War of 1812 and after 1815 ceased to be a major force in political life. The next two presidents, James Monroe and John Quincy Adams, congratulated themselves on the Federalists' demise and Republican unity, but in fact divisions within their own party were extensive. Wives of politicians increasingly inserted themselves into this dissonant mix, managing their husbands' politicking and enabling them to appear above the fray and maintain the fiction of a nonpartisan state. That it was a fiction became sharply apparent in the most serious political crisis of this period, the Missouri Compromise of 1820.   ★

Jefferson's Presidency

The nerve-wracking election of 1800, decided in the House of Representatives, stoked fears that party divisions would ruin the country. A panicky Federalist newspaper in Connecticut predicted that Jefferson's victory would produce a bloody civil war and usher in an immoral reign of "murder, robbery, rape, adultery and incest." Similar fears were expressed in the South,

where a frightful slave uprising seemed a possible outcome of Jefferson's victory. But nothing nearly so dramatic occurred. Jefferson later called his election the "revolution of 1800," referring to his repudiation of Federalist practices and his cutbacks in military spending and taxes.

Jefferson did radically transform the presidency, away from the Federalists' vision of a powerful executive branch and toward republican simplicity and limited government. Yet even Jefferson found that circumstances sometimes required him to draw on the expansive powers of the presidency. The rise of Napoleon in France brought France and Britain into open warfare again in 1803, creating unexpected opportunities and challenges for Jefferson. One major opportunity arrived in the spectacular purchase from France of the Louisiana Territory; a significant challenge arose when pirates threatened American ships off the north coast of Africa and when British and French naval forces nipped at American ships—and American honor—in the Atlantic Ocean.

Turbulent Times: Election and Rebellion The result of the election of 1800 remained uncertain from polling time in November to repeated roll call votes in the House of Representatives in February 1801. Federalist John Adams, never secure in his leadership of the Federalist Party, was no longer in the presidential race once it got to the House. Instead, the contest was between Jefferson and his running mate, Senator **Aaron Burr** of New York. Republican voters in the electoral college slipped up, giving Jefferson and Burr an equal number of votes, an outcome possible because of the single balloting to choose both president and vice president. (To fix this problem, the Twelfth Amendment to the Constitution, adopted in 1804, provided for distinct ballots for the two offices.) The vain and ambitious Burr declined to concede, so the sitting Federalist-dominated House of Representatives got to choose the president.

Each state delegation had one vote, and nine were needed to win. Some Federalists preferred Burr, believing that his character flaws made him susceptible to Federalist pressure. But the influential Alexander Hamilton, though no friend of Jefferson, recognized that the high-strung Burr would be more dangerous in the presidency. Jefferson was a "contemptible hypocrite" in Hamilton's opinion, but at least he was not corrupt. (In 1804, Burr shot and killed Hamilton in a formal but illegal duel. See "Historical Question," page 230.) Jefferson received the votes of eight states on the first ballot. Thirty-six ballots and six days later, he got the critical ninth vote, as well as a tenth. This election demonstrated a remarkable feature of the new government: No matter how hard fought the campaign, the leadership of the nation could shift from one group to its rivals in a peaceful transfer of power effected by ballots, not bullets.

As the country struggled over its white leadership crisis, a twenty-four-year-old blacksmith named Gabriel, the slave of Thomas Prossor, plotted rebellion in Virginia. Inspired by the Haitian Revolution (see chapter 9), and perhaps directly informed of it by French slaves new to the Richmond area, Gabriel was said to be organizing a thousand slaves to march on the state capital of Richmond and take the governor, James Monroe, hostage. On the appointed day, however, a few nervous slaves went to the authorities with news of **Gabriel's rebellion**, and within days, scores of implicated conspirators were jailed and brought to trial.

One of the jailed rebels compared himself to the most venerated icon of the early Republic: "I have nothing more to offer than what General Washington would have had to offer, had he been taken by the British and put to trial by them." Such talk invoking the specter of a black George Washington worried white Virginians, and in the fall of 1800, twenty-seven black men were hanged for allegedly contemplating rebellion. Finally, Jefferson advised Governor Monroe to halt the hangings. "The world at large will forever condemn us if we indulge a principle of revenge," Jefferson wrote.

The Jeffersonian Vision of Republican Simplicity Once elected, **Thomas Jefferson** turned his attention to establishing his administration in clear contrast to the Federalists. For his inauguration, held in the village called Washington City, he dressed in everyday clothing to strike a tone of republican simplicity, and he walked to the Capitol for the modest swearing-in ceremony. As president, he scaled back Federalist building plans for Washington and cut the government budget.

> For his inauguration, held in the village called Washington City, Jefferson dressed in everyday clothing to strike a tone of republican simplicity.

Martha Washington and Abigail Adams had received the wives of government officials at weekly teas, thereby cementing social relations in the governing class. But Jefferson, a longtime widower, disdained female gatherings and avoided the women of Washington City. He abandoned George Washington's practice of holding weekly formal receptions. His preferred social event was the small dinner party with carefully chosen politicos, either all Republicans or all Federalists (and all male). At these intimate dinners, the president exercised influence and strengthened informal relationships that would help him govern.

Jefferson was no Antifederalist. He had supported the Constitution in 1788, despite his concern about the unrestricted reelection allowed to the president. But events of the 1790s had caused him to worry about the stretching of powers in the executive branch. Jefferson had watched with distrust as Hamiltonian policies refinanced the public debt, established a national bank, and secured commercial ties with Britain (see chapter 9). These policies seemed to Jefferson to promote the interests of greedy

How Could a Vice President Get Away with Murder?

On July 11, 1804, the vice president of the United States, Aaron Burr, shot Alexander Hamilton, the architect of the Federalist Party, in a duel on a narrow ledge below the cliffs of Weehawken, New Jersey, across the Hudson River from New York City. The pistol blast tore through a rib, demolished Hamilton's liver, and splintered his spine. The forty-nine-year-old Hamilton died the next day in agonizing pain.

How could it happen that a sitting vice president and a prominent political leader could put themselves at such risk? Why did men who made their living by the legal system go outside the law and turn to the centuries-old ritual of the duel? Here were two eminent attorneys, skilled in the legalistic negotiations meant to substitute for violent resolution of disputes, firing .54-caliber hair-trigger weapons at ten paces. Did anyone try to stop them? How did the public react? Was Hamilton's death a criminal act? How could Burr continue to fulfill his federal office as vice president and preside over the U.S. Senate?

Burr challenged Hamilton in late June after learning about a newspaper report that Hamilton "looked upon Mr. Burr to be a dangerous man, and one who ought not be trusted with the reins of government." Burr knew that Hamilton had long held a very low opinion of him and had never hesitated to say so in private, but now his disparagement had made its way into print. Compounding the insult were political consequences: Burr was sure that Hamilton's remark cost him election to the governorship of New York.

Quite possibly he was right. Knowing that Jefferson planned to dump him from the federal ticket in the 1804 election, Burr had chosen to run for New York's highest office. His opponent was an obscure Republican judge; Burr's success depended on the support of the old Federalist leadership in the state. Up to the eve of the election, he appeared to have it—until Hamilton's remark was circulated.

So on June 18, Burr challenged Hamilton to a duel if he did not disavow his comment. Over the next three weeks, the men exchanged several letters clarifying the nature of the insult that had aggrieved Burr. Hamilton the lawyer evasively quibbled over words, causing Burr finally to rail against his focus on syntax and grammar. At heart, Hamilton could not deny the insult, nor could he spurn the challenge without injury to his reputation for integrity

and bravery. Both Burr and Hamilton were locked in a highly ritualized procedure meant to uphold a gentleman's code of honor.

Each man had a trusted "second," in accord with the code of dueling, who helped frame and deliver the letters and finally assisted at the duel site. Only a handful of close friends knew of the challenge, and no one tried to stop it. Hamilton did not tell his wife. He wrote her a tender farewell letter the night before, to be opened in the event of his death. He knew full well the pain dueling

★ *Aaron Burr, by John Vanderlyn* Aaron Burr was fifty-three years old at the time of this portrait, painted in 1809 by the New York artist John Vanderlyn. Collection of The New-York Historical Society.

brought to loved ones, for his nineteen-year-old son Philip had been killed in a duel three years earlier, on the same Weehawken ledge, as a result of heated words exchanged at a New York theater. Even when Hamilton's wife was called to her husband's deathbed, she was first told he had terrible spasms from an illness. Women were completely shut out of the masculine world of dueling.

News of Hamilton's death spread quickly in New York and then throughout the nation. On the day of the funeral, church bells tolled continuously, and New York merchants shut down their businesses. Thousands joined the procession, and the city council declared a six-week mourning period. Burr fled to Philadelphia, fearing retribution by the crowd.

While northern newspapers expressed indignation over the illegal duel and the tragic death of so prominent a man, response in the South was more subdued. Dueling was fully accepted there as an extralegal remedy for insult, and Burr's grievance fit perfectly the sense of violated honor that legitimated duels. In addition, southerners had never been particularly fond of the Federalist Hamilton. Many northern states, in contrast, had criminalized dueling recently, treating a challenge as a misdemeanor and a dueling death as a homicide. Even after death, the loser of an illegal duel could endure one final penalty—being buried without a coffin, having a stake driven through the body, being strung up in public until the body rotted, or, more horrible still for the time, being donated to medical students for dissection. By dishonoring the corpse, northern lawmakers hoped to discourage dueling. Hamilton's body was spared such a fate. But two ministers in succession refused to administer Holy Communion to him in his dying hours because he was a duelist; one finally relented.

The public demanded to know the reasons for the duel, so the seconds prepared the correspondence between the principals for publication. A coroner's jury in New York soon indicted Burr on misdemeanor charges for issuing a challenge; a grand jury in New Jersey indicted him for murder. By that time, Burr was a fugitive from justice hiding out with sympathetic friends in South Carolina.

But not for long. Amazingly, he returned to Washington, D.C., in November 1804 to resume presiding over sessions of the Senate, a role he continued to perform until his term ended in March 1805. Federalists snubbed him, but eleven Republican senators petitioned New Jersey to drop its indictment on the grounds that "civilized nations" do not treat dueling deaths as "common murders." New Jersey did not pursue the murder charge. Burr freely visited New Jersey and New York for three more decades, paying no penalty for killing Hamilton.

Few would doubt that Burr was a scoundrel, albeit a brilliant one. A few years later, he was indicted for treason against the U.S. government in a presumed plot to break off part of the United States and start his own country in the Southwest. (He dodged that bullet, too, in a spectacular trial presided over by John Marshall, chief justice of the Supreme Court.) Hamilton certainly thought Burr a scoundrel, and when that opinion reached print, Burr had cause to defend his honor under the etiquette of dueling. The accuracy of Hamilton's charge was of absolutely no account.

Dueling redressed questions of honor, not questions of fact. Dueling continued to be a feature of southern society for many more decades, but in the North the custom became extremely rare by the 1820s, discouraged by the tragedy of Hamilton's death and by the rise of a legalistic society that now preferred evidence, interrogation, and monetary judgments to avenge injury.

★ **Pistols from the Burr-Hamilton Duel** Alexander Hamilton's brother-in-law John B. Church purchased this pair of dueling pistols in London in 1797. Church used them once in a duel with Aaron Burr occasioned by Church's calling Burr a scoundrel in public; neither man was hurt. Hamilton's son Philip had borrowed them for his own fatal duel three years before. When Burr challenged Hamilton, the latter also turned to Church for the weapons. The guns stayed in the Church family until 1930, when they were given to the Chase Manhattan Bank in New York City, chartered in 1799 as the Manhattan Company. (Burr, Church, and Hamilton all served on the bank's board of directors.) When the pistols were cleaned in 1874, a hidden hair trigger came to light. It could be cocked by moving the trigger forward one-eighth inch. It then required only a half-pound pull, instead of a ten-pound pull, to fire the gun. If Hamilton knew about the hair trigger, he gained no advantage from it. Courtesy of Chase Manhattan Archives.

***Thomas Jefferson*, by John Trumbull** When the young widower Thomas Jefferson lived in Paris in the late 1780s, he distributed three copies of this miniature portrait as affectionate gifts, one to his daughter Martha, another to a very attractive (but married) American woman in London, and the third to a British woman, also married, who had won his heart but not his head. A much younger fourth woman in Paris shared his residence: his slave Sally Hemings, attendant to Jefferson's two daughters. Early in Jefferson's presidency, a scandal erupted when a journalist charged that Jefferson had fathered several children by Sally Hemings. In 1998, a careful DNA study concluded that uniquely marked Jefferson Y chromosomes were common to male descendants in both the Hemings and Jefferson lines. The DNA evidence, when combined with historical evidence about Jefferson's whereabouts at the start of each of Hemings's six pregnancies, makes a powerful case that Jefferson fathered some and possibly all of her children. What cannot be known is the nature of the relationship between the two. Was it coerced or voluntary, or somewhere in between? Was a voluntary relationship even possible, given the power differential between master and slave? In all his voluminous writings, Jefferson left no comment about Sally Hemings, and the record on her side is entirely mute. Two of her four surviving children were allowed to slip away to freedom in the 1820s; the other two were freed in Jefferson's will. Monticello/Thomas Jefferson Memorial Foundation, Inc.

speculators and profiteers at the expense of the rest of the country. In Jefferson's vision, the source of true liberty in America was the independent farmer, someone who owned and worked his land both for himself and for the market.

Jefferson set out to dismantle Federalist innovations. He reduced the size of the army by a third, preferring "a well-disciplined militia" for defense, and he cut back the navy to just a half-dozen ships. With the consent of Congress, he abolished all federal taxes based on population or whiskey. Government revenue would now derive solely from customs duties and the sale of western land. This strategy benefited the South, where three-fifths of the slaves counted for representation but not for taxation now. By the end of his first term, Jefferson had deeply reduced Hamilton's cherished national debt.

Faced with 217 last-minute appointments of Federalists to various judicial and military posts made by John Adams, Jefferson refused to honor those not yet fully processed. One disappointed job seeker, William Marbury, sued the new secretary of state, James Madison, for failure to make good on the appointment. This action gave rise to a landmark Supreme Court case, *Marbury v. Madison*, decided in 1803. The Court ruled that although Marbury's commission was valid and the new president should have delivered it, the Court could not compel him to do so. What made the case significant was little noted at the time: The Court found that the grounds of Marbury's suit, resting in the Judiciary Act of 1789, were in conflict with the Constitution. For the first time, the Court acted to disallow a law on the grounds that it was unconstitutional.

A properly limited federal government, according to Jefferson, was responsible merely for running a postal system, maintaining the federal courts, staffing lighthouses, collecting customs duties, and conducting a census once every ten years. Government jobs were kept to a minimum. The president had one private secretary, a young man named Meriwether Lewis, to help with his correspondence, and Jefferson paid him out of his own pocket. The Department of State employed only 8 people: Secretary James Madison, 6 clerks, and a messenger. The Treasury Department was by far the largest unit, with 73 revenue commissioners, auditors, and clerks, plus 2 watchmen. The entire payroll of the executive branch amounted to a mere 130 people in 1801.

The Promise of the West: The Louisiana Purchase and the Lewis and Clark Expedition Jefferson's government was small, but his ambitions for the trans-Mississippi West were great. A large expanse of the Great Plains had been transferred from France to Spain under the 1763 Treaty of Paris. Spain never controlled or settled it, due to Indian habitation, especially the powerful and expansionist Comanche nation. Spanish power

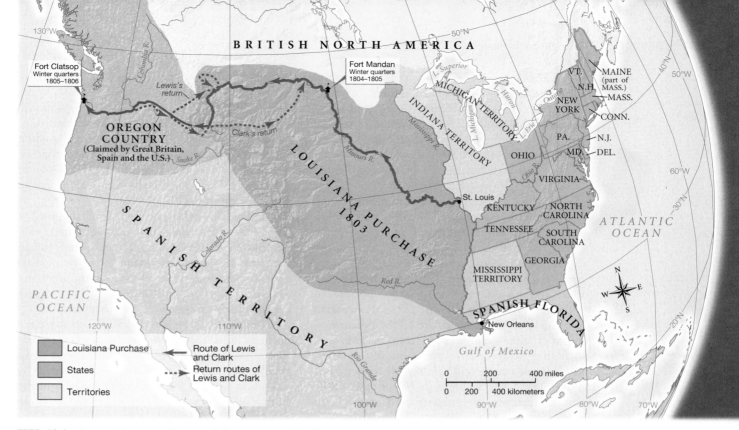

MAP 10.1 **The Louisiana Purchase and the Lewis and Clark Expedition**

Robert Livingston's bargain buy of 1803 far exceeded his initial assignment to acquire the city of New Orleans. New England Federalists, worried that their geographically based power in the federal government would someday be eclipsed by the West, voted against the purchase. The Indians who inhabited the vast region, unaware that their land had been claimed by either the French or the Americans, got their first look at Anglo-American and African American men when the Lewis and Clark expedition explored the territory in 1804–1806.

READING THE MAP: What natural boundaries defined the Louisiana Purchase? How did the size of the newly acquired territory compare to the land area of the existing American states and territories?

CONNECTIONS: What political events in Europe created the opportunity for the Jefferson administration to purchase Louisiana? What constitutional obstacles to expansion did Jefferson have to contend with? How did the acquisition of Louisiana affect Spain's hold on North America?

FOR MORE HELP ANALYZING THIS MAP, see the map activity for this chapter in the Online Study Guide at bedfordstmartins.com/roarkcompact.

in North America remained precarious everywhere outside New Orleans. In an effort to augment population, Spain encouraged American farmers to move west across the Mississippi River, and by 1801, Americans made up a sizable minority of the population around New Orleans. Publicly, Jefferson protested the luring of Americans to Spanish territory, but privately he welcomed it: "I wish a hundred thousand of our inhabitants would accept the invitation; it will be the means of delivering to us peaceably, what may otherwise cost us a war."

In 1802, rumors reached Jefferson that Spain had struck a secret bargain with France to transfer all of Spain's trans-Mississippi territory to Napoleon in exchange for land in Italy. Spain had proved a weak western neighbor, but France was another story. Jefferson was so alarmed that he instructed Robert R. Livingston, America's minister in France, to try to buy New Orleans. At first, the French denied they owned the city. But when Livingston hinted that the United States might seize it if buying was not an option, the French negotiator asked him to name his price for the entire Louisiana Territory from the Gulf of Mexico north to Canada. Livingston stalled, and the Frenchman made suggestions: $125 million? $60 million? Livingston shrewdly stalled some more and within days accepted the bargain price of $15 million (Map 10.1). In late 1803, the American army

233

took formal control of the Louisiana Territory, and the United States nearly doubled in size.

Even before the **Louisiana Purchase**, Jefferson had eyed the trans-Mississippi West with intense curiosity. In early 1803, he had arranged congressional funding for a secret scientific and military mission into Indian territory. Jefferson appointed twenty-eight-year-old Meriwether Lewis, his secretary, to head the expedition, instructing him to investigate Indian cultures, to collect plant and animal specimens, and to chart the geography of the West. Congress wanted the expedition to scout locations for military posts, negotiate fur trade agreements, and identify river routes to the West.

For his co-leader, Lewis chose Kentuckian William Clark, a veteran of the 1790s Indian wars. Together, they handpicked a crew of forty-five, including expert rivermen, gunsmiths, hunters, interpreters, a cook, and Clark's slave named York. The explorers left St. Louis in the spring of 1804, working their way northwest up the Missouri River. They camped for the winter at a Mandan village in what is now central North Dakota.

The following spring, they headed west, accompanied by a sixteen-year-old Shoshoni woman named **Sacajawea**. Kidnapped by Mandans at about age ten, she had been sold to a French trapper as a slave/wife. Hers was not a unique story among Indian women; such women knew several languages, making them valuable translators and mediators. Further, Sacajawea and her new baby allowed the American expedition to appear peaceful to suspicious tribes. As Lewis wrote in his journal, "No woman ever accompanies a war party of Indians in this quarter."

The **Lewis and Clark expedition** reached the Pacific Ocean at the mouth of the Columbia River in November 1805. When Lewis and Clark returned home the following year, they were greeted as national heroes. They had established favorable relations with dozens of Indian tribes; they had collected invaluable information on the peoples, soils, plants, animals, and geography of the West; and they had inspired a nation of restless explorers and solitary imitators.

Challenges Overseas: The Barbary Wars The inspiring story of westward exploration was matched at the same time by a frustrating challenge from the Middle East, leading to the first declaration of war against the United States by a foreign power. For well over a century, four Muslim states on the northern coast of Africa—Morocco, Algiers, Tunis, and Tripoli, called the Barbary States by Americans—controlled all Mediterranean shipping traffic by demanding large annual payments (called "tribute") for safe passage. Countries electing not to pay found their ships at risk for seizure. By the mid-1790s the United States was paying $50,000 a year. About a hundred American merchant ships annually traversed the Mediterranean, trading lumber, tobacco, sugar, and rum for regional delicacies such as raisins, figs, capers, and opium for medicinal use. Some 20 percent of all American exports went to the Middle East.

In May 1801, when the pasha (military head) of Tripoli failed to secure a large increase in his tribute, he declared war on the United States. Jefferson had long considered such payments extortion, and he sent four warships to the Mediterranean to protect U.S. shipping. From 1801 to 1803, U.S. frigates engaged in skirmishes with Barbary privateers.

Then, in late 1803, the USS *Philadelphia* ran aground near Tripoli harbor. Its three-hundred-man crew was captured along with the ship. In retaliation, a U.S. naval ship commanded by navy lieutenant Stephen Decatur sailed into the harbor after dark, guided by an Arabic-speaking pilot to fool harbor sentries. Decatur's crew set the *Philadelphia* on fire, making Decatur an instant hero in America. A later foray into the harbor to try to blow up the entire Tripoli fleet with a bomb-laden boat failed when the explosives detonated prematurely, killing eleven Americans.

In 1804, William Eaton, an American officer stationed in Tunis, felt the humiliation of his country's ineffectiveness. He wrote to Secretary of State James Madison to ask for a thousand Marines to invade Tripoli. Madison rejected the plan and another scheme to ally with the pasha's exiled brother to effect a regime change. On his own, Eaton contacted the brother, assembled a force of four hundred men (more than three hundred Egyptian mercenaries and a handful of Marines), and marched them over five hundred miles of desert for a surprise attack on Tripoli's second-largest city. Amazingly, he succeeded. The pasha of Tripoli yielded, released the prisoners taken from the *Philadelphia*, and negotiated a treaty with the United States. Peace with the other Barbary States came in a second treaty in 1812.

The Barbary Wars of 1801–1805 cost Jefferson's government more money than the tribute demanded. But the honor of the young country was thought to be at stake. At political gatherings, the slogan "Millions for defense, but not a cent for tribute" became a popular toast.

More Transatlantic Troubles: Impressment and Embargo Jefferson easily retained the presidency in the election of 1804, with his 162 electoral votes trouncing the 14 won by Federalist Charles Cotesworth Pinckney of South Carolina. But governing in his second term was not easy, due to seriously escalating tensions between the United States and both France and Britain. Beginning in 1803, both European rivals, embroiled in a war with each other, repeatedly warned the United States not to ship arms to the other. Britain acted on these threats in 1806, stopping U.S. ships to inspect cargoes for military aid to France and seizing suspected deserters from the British navy, along with many Americans. Ultimately, 2,500 U.S. sailors were "impressed" (taken by force) by the British. In retaliation against the **impressment** of U.S. sailors, Jefferson convinced Congress to pass nonimportation laws banning certain British-made goods.

One incident made the usually cautious Jefferson nearly belligerent. In June 1807, the American ship *Chesapeake*, harboring some British deserters, was ordered to stop by the British frigate *Leopard*. The *Chesapeake* refused, and the *Leopard* opened fire, killing three Americans—right at the mouth of the Chesapeake Bay, well within U.S. territory. In response, Congress passed the **Embargo Act of 1807**, banning all importation of British goods into the country. Though a drastic measure, the embargo was meant to forestall war. The goal was to make Britain suffer. All foreign ports were declared off-limits to American merchants to discourage illegal trading through secondary ports. Jefferson was convinced that Britain needed America's agricultural products far more than America needed British goods.

The Embargo Act of 1807 was a disaster. From 1790 to 1807, U.S. exports had increased fivefold, but the embargo brought commerce to a standstill. In New England, the heart of the shipping industry, unemployment rose. Grain plummeted in value, river traffic halted, tobacco rotted in the South, and cotton went unpicked. Protest petitions flooded Washington. The federal government suffered, too, for import duties were a significant source of revenue. Jefferson paid political costs as well. The Federalist Party, in danger of fading away after its weak showing in the election of 1804, began to revive.

> **Q:** How did Jefferson attempt to undo the Federalist innovations of earlier administrations?

The Madisons in the White House

In mid-1808, Jefferson indicated that he would not run for a third term. Secretary of State James Madison was chosen by the Republican caucuses—informal political groups that orchestrated the selection of candidates. The Federalist caucuses again

chose Charles Cotesworth Pinckney. Madison won, but Pinckney received 47 electoral votes, nearly half of Madison's total. Support for the Federalists remained centered in New England, and Republicans still held the balance of power nationwide.

As president, Madison continued Jefferson's policy of economic pressure on Britain and France with a modified embargo, but he broke new ground in the domestic management of the executive office with the aid of his talented wife, Dolley Madison. Under her leadership, the president's house was designated the White House—something close to a palace, but a palace many Americans were welcome to visit. Under his leadership, the country went to war in 1812 with Britain and with Tecumseh's Indian confederacy. In 1814, British forces burned the White House and the Capitol to the ground.

The *Chesapeake* Incident, June 22, 1807

Women in Washington City Although women could not vote and supposedly left politics to men, the female relatives of Washington politicians took on several overtly political functions that greased the wheels of the affairs of state. They networked through dinners, balls, receptions, and the intricate custom of "calling," in which men and women paid brief visits at each other's homes. Webs of friendship and influence in turn facilitated female political lobbying. It was not uncommon for women in this social set to write letters of recommendation for men seeking government work. Hostessing was no trivial or leisured business; it significantly influenced the federal government's patronage system.

When James Madison became president, **Dolley Madison**, called by some the "presidentress," struck a balance between queenliness and republican openness. She dressed the part in resplendent clothes, choosing a plumed velvet turban for her headdress at her husband's inauguration. She opened three elegant rooms in the executive mansion for a weekly party called "Mrs. Madison's crush" or "squeeze." In contrast to George and Martha Washington's stiff, brief receptions, the Madisons' parties went on for hours, with scores or even hundreds of guests milling about, talking, and eating. Members of Congress, cabinet officers, distinguished guests, envoys from foreign countries, and their womenfolk attended with regularity. Mrs. Madison's squeeze was an essential event for gaining political access, trading information, and establishing informal channels that would smooth the governing process.

Dolley Madison, by Gilbert Stuart The "presidentress" of the Madison administration sat for this official portrait in 1804. She wears an empire-style dress, at the height of French fashion in 1804 and a style worn by many women at the coronation of the emperor Napoleon in Paris. The hallmarks of such a dress were a light fabric (muslin or chiffon), short sleeves, a high waistline from which the fabric fell straight to the ground, and usually a low, open neckline, as shown here. © White House Historical Association.

In 1810–1811, the Madisons' house acquired its present name, the White House. The many guests at the weekly parties experienced simultaneously the splendor of the executive mansion and the atmosphere of republicanism that made it accessible to so many. Dolley Madison, ever an enormous political asset to her rather shy husband, understood well the symbolic function of the White House to enhance the power and legitimacy of the presidency.

Indian Troubles in the West While the Madisons cemented alliances at home, difficulties with Britain and France overseas and with Indians in the old Northwest continued to increase. The Shawnee chief Tecumseh actively solidified his confederacy, while the more northern tribes renewed their ties with supportive British agents and fur traders in Canada, a potential source of food and weapons. If the United States went to war with Britain, there would clearly be serious repercussions on the frontier.

Shifting demographics raised the stakes for both sides. The 1810 census counted some 230,000 Americans in Ohio only seven years after it achieved statehood. Another 40,000 Americans inhabited the territories of Indiana, Illinois, and Michigan.

The Indian population of the entire region (the old Northwest Territory) was much smaller, probably about 70,000.

Up to 1805, Indiana's territorial governor, William Henry Harrison, had negotiated a series of treaties in a divide-and-conquer strategy aimed at extracting Indian lands for paltry payments. But with the rise to power of Tecumseh and his brother Tenskwatawa, the Prophet, Harrison's strategy faltered. A fundamental part of Tecumseh's message was the assertion that all Indian lands were held in common by all the tribes. "No tribe has the right to sell [these lands], even to each other, much less to strangers . . . ," Tecumseh said. "Sell a country! Why not sell the air, the great sea, as well as the earth? Didn't the Great Spirit make them all for the use of his children?" In 1809, while Tecumseh was away on a recruiting trip, Harrison assembled the leaders of the Potawatomi, Miami, and Delaware tribes to negotiate the Treaty of Fort Wayne. After promising (falsely) that this was the last cession of land the United States would seek, Harrison secured three million acres at about two cents per acre.

When he returned, Tecumseh was furious with both Harrison and the tribal leaders. Leaving his

Tenskwatawa, by George Catlin Tenskwatawa, the Prophet, and his brother Tecumseh led the spiritual and political efforts of a number of Indian tribes to resist land-hungry Americans moving west in the decade before the War of 1812. Artist George Catlin portrays the Prophet wearing beaded necklaces, metal arm- and wristbands, and earrings. Compare the metal gorget here with the one worn by Joseph Brant (page 165). National Museum of American Art, Washington, D.C./Art Resource, NY.

brother in charge at Prophetstown on Tippecanoe River, the Shawnee chief left to seek alliances with tribes in the South. In November 1811, Harrison decided to attack Prophetstown with a thousand men. The two-hour battle resulted in the deaths of sixty-two Americans and forty Indians before the Prophet's forces fled the town, which Harrison's men set on fire. The **battle of Tippecanoe** was heralded as a glorious victory for the Americans, but Tecumseh was now more ready than ever to make war on the United States.

The War of 1812 The Indian conflicts in the old Northwest soon merged into the wider conflict with Britain now known as the War of 1812. Between 1809 and 1812, President Madison teetered between declaring either Britain or France America's primary enemy, as attacks by both countries on U.S. ships continued. In 1809, Congress replaced Jefferson's stringent embargo with the Non-Intercourse Act, which prohibited trade only with Britain and France and their colonies, thus opening up other trade routes to alleviate somewhat the anguish of shippers, farmers, and planters. By 1811, the country was seriously divided and on the verge of war.

The new Congress seated in March 1811 contained several dozen young Republicans eager to avenge the insults from abroad. Thirty-four-year-old **Henry Clay** from Kentucky and twenty-nine-year-old John C. Calhoun from South Carolina became the center of a group informally known as the **War Hawks**. Mostly lawyers by profession, they came from the West and South and welcomed a war with Britain both to justify attacks on the Indians and to bring an end to impressment. Many were also expansionists, looking to occupy Florida and threaten Canada. Clay was elected Speaker of the House, an extraordinary honor for a newcomer. Calhoun won a seat on the Foreign Relations Committee. The War Hawks approved major defense expenditures, and the army soon quadrupled in size.

In June 1812, Congress declared war on Great Britain in a vote divided along sectional lines: New England and some Middle Atlantic states opposed the war, fearing its effect on commerce, while the South and West were strongly for it. Ironically, Britain had just announced that it would stop the search and seizure of American ships, but the war momentum would not be slowed. The Foreign Relations Committee issued an elaborate justification titled *Report on the Causes and Reasons for War*, written mainly by Cal-

Battle of Tippecanoe, 1811

houn and containing extravagant language about Britain's "lust for power," "unbounded tyranny," and "mad ambition." These were fighting words in a war that was in large measure about insult and honor.

The War Hawks proposed an invasion of Canada, confidently predicting victory in four weeks. Instead, the war lasted two and a half years, and Canada never fell. The northern invasion turned out to be a series of blunders that revealed America's grave unpreparedness for war against the unexpectedly powerful British and Indian forces. Detroit quickly fell, as did Fort Dearborn, site of the future Chicago (Map 10.2). By the fall of 1812, the outlook was grim.

Worse, the New England states dragged their feet in raising troops, and some New England merchants carried on illegal trade with Britain. While President Madison fumed about Federalist disloyalty, Bostonians drank India tea in Liverpool cups. The fall presidential election pitted Madison against DeWitt Clinton of New York, nominally a Republican but able to attract the Federalist vote. Clinton picked up all of New England's electoral votes, with the exception of Vermont's, and also took New York, New Jersey, and part of Maryland. Madison won in the electoral college, 128 to 89, but his margin of victory was considerably smaller than in 1808.

In late 1812 and early 1813, the tide began to turn in the Americans' favor. First came some reassuring victories at sea. Then the Americans attacked York (now Toronto), and burned it in April 1813. A few months later, Commodore Oliver Hazard Perry defeated the British fleet at the western end of Lake Erie. Emboldened, General Harrison drove an army into Canada from Detroit and in October 1813 defeated the British and Indians at the battle of the Thames, where Tecumseh was killed.

Creek Indians in the South who had allied with Tecumseh's confederacy were also plunged into all-out war. Some 10,000 living in the Mississippi Territory put up a spirited fight against U.S. forces for ten months, using guns obtained from Spanish Florida. But the **Creek War** ended suddenly in March 1814 when a general named Andrew Jackson led 2,500 Tennessee militiamen in a bloody attack called the Battle of Horseshoe Bend. More than 550 Indians were killed, and several hundred more died trying to escape across a river. Later that year, General Jackson extracted from the defeated tribe a treaty relinquishing thousands of square miles of their land to the United States.

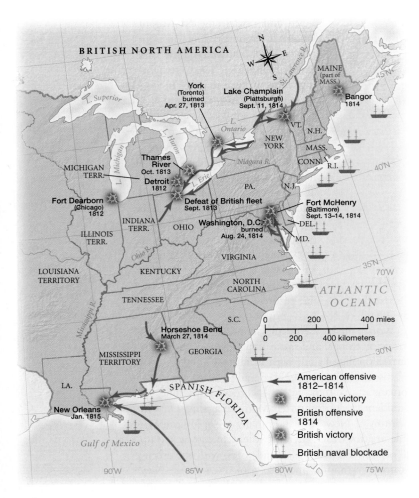

MAP 10.2 The War of 1812

During the War of 1812, battles were fought along the Canadian border and in the Chesapeake region. The most important American victory came in New Orleans two weeks after a peace agreement had been signed in Europe.

Washington City Burns: The British Offensive

In August 1814, British ships sailed into the Chesapeake Bay, landing 5,000 troops and throwing the capital into a panic. Families evacuated, banks hid their money, and government clerks carted away boxes of important papers. Dolley Madison fled with her husband's papers and a portrait of George Washington. All 5,000 British troops entered the city and burned the White House, the Capitol, a newspaper office, and a well-stocked arsenal. Instead of trying to hold the city, the British headed north and attacked Baltimore, but a fierce defense by the Maryland militia thwarted that effort.

In another powerful offensive that same month, British troops marched from Canada into New York State, but a series of mistakes cost them a naval skirmish at Plattsburgh on Lake Champlain, and they retreated to Canada. Five months later, another large British army landed in lower Louisiana and, in early January 1815, encountered General Andrew Jackson and his militia just outside New Orleans. Jackson's forces dramatically carried the day. The British suffered between 2,000 and 3,000 casualties, the Americans fewer than 80. Jackson became an instant hero. The **battle of New Orleans** was the most glorious victory the Americans had experienced, allowing some Americans to boast that the United States had won a second war of independence from Britain. No one in the United States knew that negotiators in Europe had signed a peace agreement two weeks earlier.

The Treaty of Ghent, signed in December 1814, settled few of the surface issues that had led to war. Neither country could claim victory, and no land changed hands. Instead, the treaty reflected a mutual agreement to give up certain goals. The Americans dropped their plea for an end to impressments, which in any case subsided as soon as Britain and France ended their war in 1815. They also gave up any claim to Canada. The British agreed to stop all aid to the Indians. Nothing was said about shipping rights. The most concrete result was a plan for a commission to determine the exact boundary between the United States and Canada.

Antiwar Federalists in New England could not gloat over the war's ambiguous conclusion because of an ill-timed and seemingly unpatriotic move on their part. The region's leaders had convened a secret meeting in Hartford, Connecticut, in December 1814 to discuss dramatic measures to curb the South's power. They proposed abolishing the Constitution's three-fifths clause as a basis of representation; requiring a two-thirds vote instead of a simple majority for imposing embargoes, admitting states, or declaring war; limiting the president to one term; and prohibiting the election of successive presidents from the same state. The cumulative aim of these proposals was to reduce the South's political power and break Virginia's lock on the presidency. The Federalists at Hartford even discussed secession from the Union but rejected that path. Coming just as peace was achieved, however, the **Hartford Convention** looked very unpatriotic. The Federalist Party never recovered its grip, and within a few years, it was reduced to a shadow of its former self, even in New England.

No one really won the War of 1812. Americans celebrated as though they had, however, with parades and fireworks. The war gave rise to a new spirit of nationalism. The paranoia over British tyranny evident in the 1812 declaration of war was laid to rest, replaced by pride in a more equal relationship with the old mother country. Indeed, in 1817 the two countries signed the Rush-Bagot disarmament treaty (named after its two negotiators), which limited each country to a total of four naval vessels, each with just a single cannon, to patrol the vast watery border between them. The Rush-Bagot treaty was perhaps the most successful disarmament treaty for a century to come.

The biggest winners in the War of 1812 were the young men, once called War Hawks, who took up the banner of the Republican Party and carried it in new, expansive directions. These young politicians favored trade, western expansion, internal improvements, and the energetic development of new economic markets. The biggest losers of the war were the Indians. Tecumseh was dead, his brother the Prophet was discredited, the prospects of an Indian confederacy were dashed, the Creeks' large homeland was seized, and the British protectors were gone.

Q: Why did Congress declare war on Great Britain in 1812?

Women's Status in the Early Republic

Dolley Madison's pioneering role as "presidentress" showed that at the pinnacles of power, elite women could assume an active presence in civic affairs. But, as with the 1790s cultural compromise that endorsed female education to make women into better wives and mothers (see chapter 9), Mrs. Madison and her female circle practiced politics to further their husbands' careers. There was little talk of the "rights of woman."

From 1800 to 1825, key institutions central to the shaping of women's lives — the legal system, marriage, and religion — proved fairly resistant to change. State legislatures and the courts maintained the legal dependency of married white women in a country whose defining characteristic for men was independence. Marriage laws for whites continued to support unequal power between men and women, while religious organizations reconsidered the role of women in church governance in the face

THE PROMISE OF TECHNOLOGY

The Cookstove In this 1820s remodeled kitchen we see the most underrated technological achievement of household life of the day, the cast-iron stove. It changed the way men and women labored to put food on the table. Men had once chopped and hauled immense quantities of wood, while women sweated by open fires to cook one-pot meals. But eastern forest depletion doubled the price of wood fuel between 1800 and 1815, and Jefferson's embargo stimulated an industry of iron forging. Inventors got to work creating a cast-iron gizmo in which a single, contained charcoal fire could heat both an oven chamber and a multi-pot cooktop surface. A key challenge was the design of a damper system of movable iron plates that regulated airflow to the fire and hence controlled the rate of combustion. Another challenge was the exit strategy for sooty and dangerous air filled with combustion pollutants. In this scene, the new stove sits on the hearth of the old fireplace, now bricked up, and the stovepipe runs the smoke into the old chimney. Women appreciated the safety features of stoves and the waist-high workspace; men were glad to find the work of carrying wood sharply curtailed. Old Sturbridge Village.

of rising church membership rates for women. The most dramatic opportunity for women came with the flowering of female academies whose rigorous curricula fostered high-level literacy and rational thought. Even when advertised as institutions to prepare girls to be intelligent mothers, many academies built up their students' self-confidence and implanted expectations that their mental training would find a use beyond the kitchen and nursery.

Women and the Law The Anglo-American view of women, embedded in English common law, was that wives had no independent legal or political personhood. The legal doctrine of **feme covert** (covered woman) held that a wife's civic life was completely subsumed by her husband's. A wife was obligated to obey her husband; her property was his, her domestic and sexual services were his, and even their children were legally his. Women had no right to keep their wages, to make contracts, or to sue or be sued. State legislatures generally passed up the opportunity to rewrite the laws of domestic relations even though they redrafted other British laws in light of republican principles. Lawyers never paused to defend, much less to challenge, the assumption that unequal power relations lay at the heart of marriage.

The one aspect of family law that changed in the early Republic was divorce. Before the Revolution, only New England jurisdictions recognized a limited right to divorce; by 1820, every state except South Carolina did so. However, divorce was uncommon and in many states could be obtained only by petition to the state's legislature, a daunting obstacle for many ordinary people. A mutual wish to terminate a marriage was never sufficient grounds for a legal divorce. A New York judge affirmed that "it would be aiming a deadly blow at public morals to decree a dissolution of the marriage contract merely because the parties requested it. Divorces should never be allowed, except for the protection of the innocent party, and for the punishment of the guilty." States upheld the institution of marriage both to protect persons they thought of as naturally dependent (women and children) and to regulate the use and inheritance of property. (Unofficial self-divorce, desertion, and bigamy were remedies that ordinary people sometimes chose to get around the law, but all were socially unacceptable.) Legal enforcement of marriage as an unequal relationship played a major role in maintaining gender inequality in the nineteenth century.

Single adult women could own and convey property, make contracts, initiate lawsuits, and pay taxes. They could not vote (except in New Jersey before 1807), serve on juries, or practice law, so their civil status was limited. Single women's economic status was often limited as well, by custom as much as by law. Unless they had inherited adequate property or could live with married siblings, single adult women in the early Republic were very often poor.

None of the legal institutions that structured white gender relations applied to black slaves. As property themselves, under the jurisdiction of slave owners, they could not freely consent to any contractual obligations, including marriage. The protective features of state-sponsored unions were thus denied to black men and women in slavery. But this also meant that slave unions did not establish unequal power relations between partners backed by the force of law, as did marriages among the free.

Women and Church Governance In most Protestant denominations around 1800, white women made up the majority of congregants. Yet church leadership of most denominations rested in men's hands. There were some exceptions, however. In Baptist congregations in New England, women served along with men on church governance committees, deciding on the admission of new members, voting on hiring ministers, and even debating doctrinal points. Quakers, too, had a history of recognizing women's spiritual talents. Some were accorded the status of minister, capable of leading and speaking in Quaker meetings.

Between 1790 and 1820, a small and highly unusual set of women actively engaged in open preaching. Most were from Freewill Baptist groups centered in New England and upstate New York. Others came from small Methodist sects, and yet others rejected any formal religious affiliation. Probably fewer than a hundred such women existed, but several dozen traveled beyond their local communities, creating converts and controversy. They spoke from the heart, without prepared speeches, often exhibiting trances and claiming to exhort (counsel or warn) rather than to preach.

The best-known exhorting woman was **Jemima Wilkinson**, who called herself "the Publick Universal Friend." After a near-death experience from a high fever, Wilkinson proclaimed her body no longer female or male but the incarnation of the "Spirit of Light." She dressed in men's clothes, wore her hair in a masculine style, shunned gender-specific pronouns, and preached openly in Rhode Island and Philadelphia. In the early nineteenth century, Wilkinson established a town called New Jerusalem in western New York with some 250 followers. Her fame was sustained by periodic newspaper articles that fed public curiosity about her lifelong transvestism and her unfeminine forcefulness.

The decades from 1790 to the 1820s marked a period of unusual confusion, ferment, and creativity in American religion. New denominations blossomed, new styles of religiosity gripped adherents, and an extensive periodical press devoted to religion popularized all manner of theological and institutional innovations. Congregations increasingly attracted vibrant female participation, often eclipsing the number of male congregants. In such a climate, the age-old tradition of gender subordination came into question here and there among the most radically democratic of the churches. But the presumption of male authority over women was deeply entrenched in American culture. Even denominations that had allowed women to participate in church governance began to pull back, and most churches reinstated patterns of hierarchy along gender lines.

Female Education First in the North and then in the South, states and localities began investing in public schools to foster an educated citizenry deemed essential to the healthy functioning of a republic. Young girls attended district schools, sometimes along with boys or, in rural areas, more often in separate summer sessions. Basic literacy and numeracy formed the curriculum taught to white children aged roughly six to eleven. By 1830, girls had made rapid gains, in many places approaching male literacy rates. (Far fewer schools addressed the needs of free black children, whether male or female.)

More advanced female education came from a growing number of private academies. Judith Sargent Murray, the Massachusetts author who had called for equality of the sexes around 1790 (see chapter 9), predicted in 1800 that "a new era in female history" would emerge because "**female academies** are everywhere establishing." Some dozen female academies were established in the 1790s, and by 1830 that number had grown to nearly two hundred.

The three-year curriculum included both ornamental arts and solid academics. The former strengthened female gentility: drawing, needlework, music, and French conversation. The academic subjects included English grammar, literature, history, the natural sciences, geography, and elocution (the art of effective public speaking). Academy catalogs show that, by the 1820s, the courses and reading lists at the top female academies equaled those at male colleges such as Harvard, Yale, Dartmouth, and Princeton. The girls at these academies studied Latin, rhetoric, logic, theology, moral philosophy, algebra, geometry, and even chemistry and physics.

Two of the best-known female academies were the Troy Female Seminary in New York, founded by Emma Willard in 1821, and the Hartford Seminary in Connecticut, founded by Catharine Beecher in 1822. Both prepared their students to teach, on the grounds that women made better teachers than men. Author Harriet Beecher Stowe, educated at her sister's school and then a teacher there, agreed: "If men have more knowledge they have less talent

Home and Away: The New Boarding School These two engravings show "before" and "after" pictures of a young woman around 1820 whose family enrolled her in one of the new female academies. The artist, Philadelphia painter John Lewis Krimmel, worked as a drawing master at such an academy. Library Company of Philadelphia.

FOR MORE HELP ANALYZING THIS IMAGE, see the visual activity for this chapter in the Online Study Guide at bedfordstmartins.com/roarkcompact.

at communicating it. Nor have they the patience, the long-suffering, and gentleness necessary to superintend the formation of character."

The most immediate value of advanced female education lay in the self-cultivation and confidence it provided. Following the model of male colleges, female graduation exercises showcased speeches and recitations performed in front of a mixed-sex audience

of family, friends, and local notables. Here, the young women's elocution studies paid off; they had learned the art of persuasion along with correct pronunciation and the skill of fluent speaking. Academies also took care to promote a pleasing female modesty. Female pedantry or intellectual immodesty triggered the stereotype of the "bluestocking," a British term of hostility for a too-learned woman doomed to fail in the marriage market.

By the mid-1820s, the total annual enrollment at the female academies and seminaries equaled male enrollment at the five dozen male colleges in the United States. Both groups accounted for only about 1 percent of their age cohorts in the country at large, indicating that advanced education was clearly limited to a privileged few. Among the men, this group disproportionately filled the future rosters of ministers, lawyers, judges, and political leaders. Most female graduates in time married and raised families, but first many of them became teachers at academies and district schools. A large number also became authors, contributing essays and poetry to newspapers, editing periodicals, and publishing novels. The new attention to the training of female minds laid the foundation for major changes in the gender system as girl students of the 1810s matured into adult women of the 1830s.

Q: How did the civil status of American women and men differ in the early Republic?

Monroe and Adams

With the elections of 1816 and 1820, Virginians continued their hold on the presidency. In 1816, **James Monroe** beat Federalist Rufus King of New York, garnering 183 electoral votes to King's 34. In 1820, Republican Monroe was reelected with all but one electoral vote. The collapse of the Federalist Party ushered in an apparent period of one-party rule, but politics remained highly contentious. At the state level, increasing voter engagement sparked a drive for universal white male suffrage.

Many factors promoted increased partisanship. Monroe and his aloof wife, Elizabeth, sharply curtailed social gatherings at the White House, driving the hard work of social networking into competing channels. Ill feelings were stirred by a sectional crisis over the admission of Missouri to

One delegate to New York's constitutional convention said, "More integrity and more patriotism are generally found in the labouring class of the community than in the higher orders."

the Union, and foreign policy questions involving European claims to Latin America animated sharp disagreements as well. The election of 1824 brought forth an abundance of candidates, all claiming to be Republicans. The winner was John Quincy Adams in an election decided by the House of Representatives and, many believed, a backroom bargain. Put to the test of practical circumstances, the one-party political system failed and then fractured.

From Property to Democracy Up to 1820, presidential elections occurred in the electoral college, at a remove from ordinary voters. The excitement generated by state elections, however, created an insistent pressure for greater democratization of presidential elections.

In the 1780s, twelve of the original thirteen states enacted property qualifications based on the time-honored theory that only male freeholders—landowners, as distinct from tenants or servants—had sufficient independence of mind to be entrusted with the vote. Of course, not everyone accepted that restricted idea of the people's role in government (see chapter 8). In the 1790s, Vermont became the first state to enfranchise all adult males, and four other states soon broadened suffrage considerably by allowing all taxpayers to vote. Between 1800 and 1830, greater democratization became a lively issue both in established states and in new states emerging in the West.

In new states, small populations together with yet smaller numbers of large property owners meant that few men could vote under typical restrictive property qualifications. Congress initially set a fifty-acre freehold as the threshold for voting, but in Illinois, fewer than three hundred men met that test at the time of statehood. When Indiana, Illinois, and Mississippi became states, their constitutions granted suffrage to all taxpayers. Five additional new western states abandoned property and taxpayer qualifications altogether.

The most heated battles over suffrage occurred in eastern states, where expanding numbers of commercial men, renters, and mortgage holders of all classes contended with entrenched landed elites who, not surprisingly, favored the status quo. Still, by 1820, a half dozen states passed suffrage reform. Some stopped short of complete manhood suffrage, instead tying the vote to tax status or militia service. In the remainder of the states, the defenders of landed property qualifications managed to delay expanded suffrage for two more decades. But it was increasingly hard to persuade the disfranchised that landowners alone had a stake in government. Proponents of the status quo began to argue instead that the "industry and good habits" necessary to achieve a propertied status in life were what gave landowners the right character to vote. Opponents fired back blistering attacks. One delegate to New York's constitutional convention said, "More integrity and more patriotism are generally found in the labouring class of the community than in the higher orders." Owning land was no more predictive of wisdom and good character than it was of a person's height or strength, said another.

Both sides of the debate generally agreed that character mattered, and many ideas for ensuring an electorate of proper wisdom came up for discussion. The exclusion of paupers and felons convicted of "infamous crimes" found favor in legislation in many states. Literacy tests and raising the voting age to a figure in the thirties were debated but ultimately discarded. The exclusion of women required no discussion in the constitutional conventions, so firm was the legal power of feme covert. But in one exceptional moment, at the Virginia convention in 1829, a delegate wondered aloud why unmarried women over the age of twenty-one could not vote; he was quickly silenced with the argument that all women lacked the "free agency and intelligence" necessary for wise voting.

Free black men's enfranchisement was another story, generating much discussion at all the conventions. Under existing freehold qualifications, a small number of propertied black men could vote; universal or taxpayer suffrage would inevitably enfranchise many more. Many delegates at the various state conventions spoke against that extension, claiming that blacks as a race lacked prudence, independence, and knowledge. With the exception of New York, which retained the existing property qualification for black voters as it removed it for whites, the general pattern was one of expanded suffrage for whites and a total eclipse of suffrage for blacks.

The Missouri Compromise The politics of race produced perhaps the most divisive issue during Monroe's term. In February 1819, Missouri applied for statehood. Since 1815, four other states had joined the Union (Indiana, Mississippi, Illinois, and Alabama) following the blueprint laid out by the Northwest Ordinance of 1787. But Missouri posed a problem. Although much of its area was

A View of St. Louis from an Illinois Town, 1835 Just fifteen years after the Missouri Compromise, St. Louis was already a booming city, having gotten its start in the eighteenth century as a French fur-trading village. It was incorporated as a town in 1809 and chartered as a city in 1822. In this 1835 view, commercial buildings and steamships line the riverfront; a ferry on the Illinois shore prepares to transport travelers across the Mississippi River. Black laborers (in the foreground) handle loading tasks. Illinois was a free state; Missouri, where the ferry will land, was a slave state. Private collection.

FOR MORE HELP ANALYZING THIS IMAGE, see the visual activity for this chapter in the Online Study Guide at bedfordstmartins.com/roarkcompact.

on the same latitude as the free state of Illinois, its territorial population included ten thousand slaves brought there by southern planters.

Missouri's unusual combination of geography and demography led a New York congressman, James Tallmadge Jr., to propose two amendments to the statehood bill. The first stipulated that slaves born in Missouri after statehood would be free at age twenty-five, and the second declared that no new slaves could be imported into the state. Tallmadge's model was New York's gradual emancipation law of 1799. It did not strip slave owners of their current property, and it allowed them full use of the labor of newborn slaves well into their prime productive years. Still, southern congressmen objected because in the long run the amendments would make Missouri a free state, presumably no longer allied with southern economic and political interests. Just as southern economic power rested on slave labor, southern political power drew extra strength from the slave population because of the three-fifths rule. In 1820, the South owed seventeen of its seats in the House of Representatives to its slave population.

Tallmadge's amendments passed in the House by a close and sharply sectional vote of North against South. The ferocious debate led a Georgia representative to observe that the question had started "a fire which all the waters of the ocean could not extinguish. It can be extinguished only in blood." The Senate, with an even number of slave and free states, voted down the amendments, and Missouri statehood was postponed until the next congressional term.

In 1820, a compromise emerged. Maine, once part of Massachusetts, applied for statehood as a free state, balancing against Missouri as a slave state. The Senate further agreed that the southern boundary of Missouri—latitude 36°30′—extended west, would become the permanent line dividing slave from free states, guaranteeing the North a large area where slavery was banned (Map 10.3). The House also approved the **Missouri Compromise**, thanks to expert deal brokering by Kentucky's Henry Clay, who earned the nickname "the Great Pacificator" for his superb negotiating skills. The whole package passed because seventeen northern congressmen decided that minimizing sectional conflict was the best course and voted with the South.

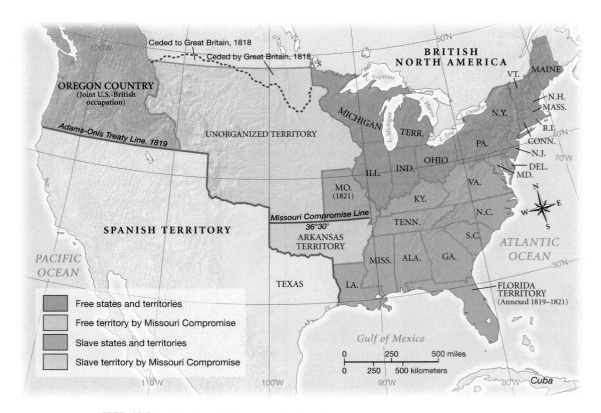

MAP 10.3 The Missouri Compromise, 1820

After a difficult battle in Congress, Missouri entered the Union in 1821 as part of a package of compromises. Maine was admitted as a free state to balance slavery in Missouri, and a line drawn at latitude 36°30′ put most of the rest of the Louisiana Territory off-limits to slavery in the future.

President Monroe and former president Jefferson at first worried that the Missouri crisis would reinvigorate the Federalist Party as the party of the North. But even ex-Federalists agreed that the split between free and slave states was too dangerous a fault line to be permitted to become a shaper of national politics. When new parties did develop in the 1830s, they took pains to bridge geography, each party developing a presence in both North and South. Monroe and Jefferson also worried about the future of slavery. Both understood slavery to be deeply problematic, but, as Jefferson said, "we have the wolf by the ears, and we can neither hold him, nor safely let him go. Justice is in one scale, and self-preservation in the other."

The Monroe Doctrine New foreign policy challenges arose even as Congress struggled with the slavery issue. In 1816, U.S. troops led by General Andrew Jackson invaded Spanish Florida in search of Seminole Indians harboring escaped slaves. Once there, Jackson declared himself the commander of northern Florida, demonstrating his power in 1818 by executing two British men who he claimed were dangerous enemies. In asserting rule over the territory, and surely in executing the two British subjects on Spanish land, Jackson had gone too far. Privately, President Monroe was distressed and pondered court-martialing Jackson, prevented only by Jackson's immense popularity as the hero of the battle of New Orleans. Instead, John Quincy Adams, the secretary of state, negotiated with Spain the Adams-Onís Treaty, which delivered Florida to the United States in 1819. In exchange, the Americans agreed to abandon any claim to Texas or Cuba. Southerners viewed this as a large concession, having eyed both places as potential acquisitions for future slave states.

Spain at that moment was preoccupied with its colonies in South America. One after another, Chile, Colombia, Peru, and finally Mexico declared themselves independent in the early 1820s. To discourage Spain or France from reconquering these colonies, Monroe in 1823 formulated a declaration of principles on South America, known in later years as the **Monroe Doctrine**. The president warned that "the American Continents, by the free and independent condition which they have assumed and maintain, are henceforth not to be considered as subjects for future colonization by any European power." Any attempt to interfere in the Western Hemisphere would be regarded as "the manifestation of an unfriendly disposition towards the United States." In exchange for noninterference by Europeans, Monroe pledged that the United States would stay out of European struggles. At that time, Monroe did not intend his statement to lay a

foundation for U.S. intervention in South America. Indeed, the small American navy could not realistically defend Chile or Peru against Spain or France. The doctrine was Monroe's idea of sound foreign policy, but it did not have the force of law.

The Election of 1824 Monroe's nonpartisan administration was the last of its kind, a throwback to eighteenth-century ideals, as was Monroe, with his powdered wig and knee breeches. Monroe's cabinet contained men of sharply different philosophies, all calling themselves Republicans. Secretary of State John Quincy Adams represented the urban Northeast; South Carolinian John C. Calhoun spoke for the planter aristocracy as secretary of war; and William H. Crawford of Georgia, secretary of the treasury, was a proponent of Jeffersonian states' rights and limited federal power. Even before the end of Monroe's first term, these men and others began to maneuver for the election of 1824.

Crucially helping them to maneuver were their wives, who accomplished some of the work of modern campaign managers by courting men — and women — of influence. The parties not thrown by Elizabeth Monroe were now given all over

Election Sewing Box Everyday household objects could become vehicles for the expression of political partisanship. Here a sewing box sporting John Quincy Adams's face allowed its owner — almost certainly a woman — to proclaim her sympathy for the Adams Republicans. A new lithographic process, just coming into widespread use in the 1820s, made possible the production of thousands of pictures from a single master stone plate. (Wood and copper plates, the earlier technology, produced prints numbering only in the hundreds before deteriorating under pressure.) The top of the Adams box (not visible here) has a velvet pincushion printed with the slogan "Be Firm for Adams." Collection of Janice L. and David J. Frent.

town by women whose husbands were jockeying for political favor. Louisa Catherine Adams had a weekly party for guests numbering in the hundreds. The somber Adams lacked charm—"I am a man of reserved, cold, austere, and forbidding manners," he once wrote—but his abundantly charming (and hardworking) wife made up for that. She attended to the etiquette of social calls, sometimes making two dozen in a morning, and counted sixty-eight members of Congress as her regular guests. This was smart politics, in case the House of Representatives wound up deciding the 1824 election—which it did.

John Quincy Adams (and Louisa Catherine) were ambitious for the presidency, but so were others. Candidate Henry Clay, Speaker of the House and negotiator of the Treaty of Ghent with Britain in 1814, promoted a new "American System," a package of protective tariffs to encourage manufacturing and federal expenditures for internal improvements such as roads and canals. Treasurer William Crawford was a favorite of Republicans from Virginia and New York, even after he suffered an incapacitating stroke in mid-1824. Calhoun was another serious contender, having served in Congress and in several cabinets. A southern planter, he attracted northern support for his backing of internal improvements and protective tariffs.

The final candidate was an outsider and a latecomer: General Andrew Jackson of Tennessee. Jackson had far less national political experience than the others, but he enjoyed great celebrity from his military career. In 1824, on the anniversary of the battle of New Orleans, the Adamses threw a spectacular ball in his honor, hoping that some of Jackson's charisma would rub off on Adams. Not long after, Jackson's supporters put his name forward for the presidency, and voters in the West and South reacted with enthusiasm. Adams was dismayed, while Calhoun dropped out of the race.

Along with democratizing the vote, eighteen states had put the power to choose members of the electoral college directly in the hands of voters, making the 1824 election the first one to have a popular vote tally for the presidency. Jackson proved by far to be the most popular candidate, winning 153,544 votes. Adams was second with 108,740, Clay won 47,136 votes, and the debilitated Crawford garnered 46,618. This was not a large turnout, probably amounting to just over a quarter of adult white males. Nevertheless, the election of 1824 marked a new departure in choosing presidents. Partisanship energized the electorate; apathy and a low voter turnout would not recur until the twentieth century.

In the electoral college, Jackson received 99 votes, Adams 84, Crawford 41, and Clay 37 (Map 10.4). Jackson lacked a majority, so the House of Representatives stepped in for the second time in U.S. history.

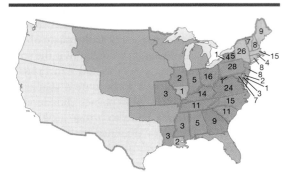

Candidate*	Electoral Vote	Popular Vote	Percent of Popular Vote
John Q. Adams	84	108,740	30.5
Andrew Jackson	99	153,544	43.1
Henry Clay	37	47,136	13.2
W. H. Crawford	41	46,618	13.1

*No distinct political parties

Note: Because no candidate garnered a majority in the electoral college, the election was decided in the House of Representatives. Although Clay was eliminated from the running, as Speaker of the House he influenced the final decision in favor of Adams.

MAP 10.4 The Election of 1824

Each congressional delegation had one vote; according to the Constitution's Twelfth Amendment, only the top three candidates joined the runoff. Thus Henry Clay was out of the race and in a position to bestow his support on another candidate.

Jackson's supporters later characterized the election of 1824 as the "corrupt bargain." Clay backed Adams, and Adams won by one vote in the House in February 1825. Clay's support made sense on several levels. Despite strong mutual dislike, he and Adams agreed on issues such as federal support to build roads and canals, and Clay was uneasy with Jackson's volatile temperament and unstated political views and with Crawford's diminished capacity. What made Clay's decision look "corrupt" was that immediately after the election, Adams offered to appoint Clay secretary of state—and Clay accepted.

In fact, there probably was no concrete bargain; Adams's subsequent cabinet appointments demonstrated his lack of political astuteness. But Andrew Jackson felt that the election had been stolen from him, and he wrote bitterly that "the Judas of the West [Clay] has closed the contract and will receive the thirty pieces of silver."

The Adams Administration John Quincy Adams, like his father, was a one-term president. His career had been built on diplomacy, not electoral politics, and despite his wife's deftness in the art of political influence, his own political horse sense was not well developed. With his cabinet choices, he welcomed his opposition into his inner circle. He asked Crawford to stay on in the Treasury. He retained an openly pro-Jackson postmaster general even though that position controlled thousands of nationwide patronage appointments. He even asked Jackson to become secretary of war. With Calhoun as vice president (elected without opposition by the electoral college) and Clay at the State Department, the whole argumentative crew would have been thrust into the executive branch. Crawford and Jackson had the good sense to decline the appointments.

Adams had lofty ideas for federal action during his presidency, and the plan he put before Congress was sweeping. Adams called for federally built roads, canals, and harbors. He proposed a national university in Washington as well as government-sponsored scientific research. He wanted to build observatories to advance astronomical knowledge and to promote precision in timekeeping, and he backed a decimal-based system of weights and measures. In all these endeavors, Adams believed he was continuing the Jefferson and Madison legacy, using the powers of government to advance knowledge. But his opponents feared he was too Hamiltonian, using federal power inappropriately to advance commercial interests.

Whether he was more truly Federalist or Republican was a moot point. Lacking the give-and-take political skills required to gain congressional support, Adams was unable to implement much of his program. He scorned the idea of courting voters to gain support and using the patronage system to enhance his power. He often made appointments to placate enemies rather than reward friends. A story of a toast offered to the president may well have been mythical, but as humorous folklore it made the rounds during his term and came to summarize Adams's precarious hold on leadership. A dignitary raised a glass and said, "May he strike confusion to his foes," to which another voice scornfully chimed in, "as he has already done to his friends."

Q: How did the collapse of the Federalist Party influence the administrations of James Monroe and John Quincy Adams?

Conclusion: Republican Simplicity Becomes Complex

The Jeffersonian Republicans tried at first to undo much of what the Federalists had created in the 1790s, but their promise of a simpler government gave way to the complexities of domestic and foreign issues. The sudden acquisition of the Louisiana Purchase promised land and opportunity to settlers but also complicated the country's political future with the issues central to the Missouri Compromise. Antagonism from both foreign and Indian nations led to complex and costly policies such as embargoes, treaties, and military action, culminating in the War of 1812, a war motivated less by concrete economic or political issues than by questions of honor. Its conclusion at the battle of New Orleans allowed Americans to foster the illusion that they had fought a second war of independence.

The War of 1812 was the Indians' second lost war for independence. Tecumseh's vision of an unprecedentedly large confederacy of Indian tribes that would halt westward expansion by white Americans was cut short by the war and by his death. Without British support, the Indians probably could not have successfully challenged the westward dynamic of American settlement for long. But when Canada was under attack, the British valued its defense more than they valued their promises to help the Indians.

The war elevated to national prominence General Andrew Jackson, whose popularity with voters in the 1824 election surprised traditional politicians—and their politically astute wives—and threw the one-party rule of Republicans into a tailspin. John Quincy Adams had barely assumed office in 1825 before the election campaign of 1828 was off and running. Appeals to the people—the mass of white male voters—would be the hallmark of all elections after 1824. It was a game Adams could not easily play.

Politics in this entire period was a game that women could not play either. Except for the political wives of Washington, women, whether white or free black, had no place in government. Male legislatures maintained women's feme covert status, keeping wives dependent on husbands. A few women found a pathway to greater personal autonomy through religion. Meanwhile, the routine inclusion of girls in public schools and the steady spread of female academies planted seeds that would blossom into a major transformation of gender in the 1830s and 1840s.

The War of 1812 started another chain of events that would prove momentous in later decades. Jefferson's long embargo and Madison's wartime trade stoppages gave strong encouragement to American manufacturing, momentarily protected from competition with British factories. When peace returned in 1815, the years of independent development burst forth into a period of sustained economic growth that continued nearly unabated into the mid-nineteenth century.

Reviewing the Chapter

★ KEY TERMS

Explain each term's significance

WHO

Tecumseh (p. 227)

Aaron Burr (p. 229)

Thomas Jefferson (p. 229)

Sacajawea (p. 234)

Dolley Madison (p. 235)

Henry Clay (p. 237)

Jemima Wilkinson (p. 240)

James Monroe (p. 242)

John Quincy Adams (p. 246)

WHAT

Gabriel's rebellion (p. 229)

Louisiana Purchase (p. 234)

Lewis and Clark Expedition (p. 234)

impressment (p. 235)

Embargo Act of 1807 (p. 235)

battle of Tippecanoe (p. 237)

War Hawks (p. 237)

Creek War (p. 237)

battle of New Orleans (p. 238)

Hartford Convention (p. 238)

feme covert (p. 240)

female academies (p. 241)

Missouri Compromise (p. 244)

Monroe Doctrine (p. 245)

★ REVIEW QUESTIONS Q:

Use key terms and dates to support your answer

1. How did Jefferson attempt to undo the Federalist innovations of earlier administrations? (pp. 228–35)

2. Why did Congress declare war on Great Britain in 1812? (pp. 235–39)

3. How did the civil status of American women and men differ in the early Republic? (pp. 239–42)

4. How did the collapse of the Federalist Party influence the administrations of James Monroe and John Quincy Adams? (pp. 242–47)

★ MAKING CONNECTIONS

Draw on key terms, timeline, and review questions

1. When Jefferson assumed the presidency following the election of 1800, he expected to transform the national government. Describe his republican vision and his successes and failures in implementing it. Did subsequent Republican presidents advance the same objectives?

2. How did the United States expand and strengthen its control of territory in North America in the early nineteenth century? In your answer, discuss the roles of diplomacy, military action, and political leadership in contributing to this development.

3. Regional tensions emerged as a serious danger to the American political system in the early nineteenth century. Discuss specific conflicts that had regional dimensions. How did Americans resolve, or fail to resolve, these tensions?

4. Although the United States denied its female citizens equality in public life, some women were able to exert considerable influence. How did they do so? In your answer, discuss the legal, political, and educational status of women in the early Republic.

FOR PRACTICE QUIZZES AND OTHER STUDY TOOLS, see the Online Study Guide at **bedfordstmartins.com/roarkcompact**.

★ SUGGESTED READINGS

Joanne B. Freeman, *Affairs of Honor: National Politics in the New Republic* (2001). A study of honor in the new nation that situates slander and dueling in the culture of politics.

Annette Gordon-Reed, *The Hemingses of Monticello: An American Family* (2008). A vivid prize-winning book that brings to life the entire Hemings family and explores its complex relationship to Thomas Jefferson.

Mary Kelley, *Learning to Stand and Speak: Women, Education, and Public Life in America's Republic* (2006). A pivotal study that shows the far-reaching consequences of ladies' academies on advances for women in the early national period.

Jon Kukla, *A Wilderness So Immense: The Louisiana Purchase and the Destiny of America* (2003). A gripping story of the country's greatest real estate purchase, rich with colorful characters on the national and international scene.

John Sugden, *Tecumseh: A Life* (1997). A detailed biography of the legendary Shawnee leader of a pan-Indian resistance and his brother Tenskwatawa.

Sean Wilentz, *The Rise of American Democracy: Jefferson to Lincoln* (2005). Prize-winning definitive synthesis of the masculine realm of politics and the roots of democracy in the early Republic.

FOR MORE BOOKS ABOUT TOPICS IN THIS CHAPTER, see the Online Bibliography at **bedfordstmartins.com/roarkcompact**.

FOR ADDITIONAL FIRSTHAND ACCOUNTS OF THIS PERIOD, see Chapter 10 in Michael Johnson, ed., *Reading the American Past*, Fourth Edition.

FOR WEB SITES, IMAGES, AND DOCUMENTS RELATED TO TOPICS AND PLACES IN THIS CHAPTER, visit Make History at **bedfordstmartins.com/roarkcompact**.

★ TIMELINE

1800	• Republicans Thomas Jefferson and Aaron Burr tie in electoral college.
	• Fears of slave rebellion led by Gabriel in Virginia result in twenty-seven executions.
	• House of Representatives elects Thomas Jefferson president after thirty-six ballots.
1801	• Pasha of Tripoli declares war on United States.
1803	• *Marbury v. Madison.*
	• Britain and France warn United States not to ship war-related goods to each other.
	• United States purchases Louisiana Territory.
1804	• U.S. Marines under William Eaton take Tripoli.
1804–1806	• Lewis and Clark expedition goes to Pacific Ocean.
1807	• British attack and search *Chesapeake.*
	• Embargo Act.
1808	• Republican James Madison elected president; Dolley Madison soon dubbed "presidentress."
1809	• Treaty of Fort Wayne.
	• Non-Intercourse Act.
1811	• Battle of Tippecanoe.
1812	• United States declares war on Great Britain.
1813	• Tecumseh dies at battle of the Thames.
1814	• British attack Washington, D.C.
	• Treaty of Ghent.
	• New England Federalists meet at Hartford Convention.
1815	• Battle of New Orleans.
1816	• Republican James Monroe elected president.
1819	• Adams-Onís Treaty.
1820	• Missouri Compromise.
1823	• Monroe Doctrine asserted.
1825	• John Quincy Adams elected president by House of Representatives.

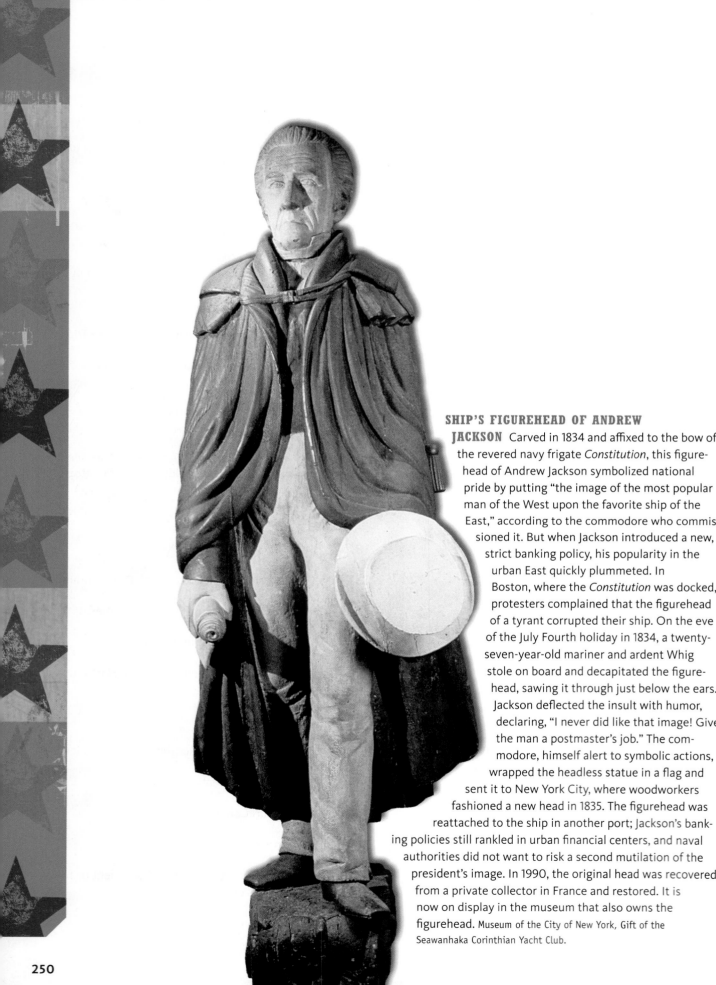

SHIP'S FIGUREHEAD OF ANDREW JACKSON Carved in 1834 and affixed to the bow of the revered navy frigate *Constitution*, this figurehead of Andrew Jackson symbolized national pride by putting "the image of the most popular man of the West upon the favorite ship of the East," according to the commodore who commissioned it. But when Jackson introduced a new, strict banking policy, his popularity in the urban East quickly plummeted. In Boston, where the *Constitution* was docked, protesters complained that the figurehead of a tyrant corrupted their ship. On the eve of the July Fourth holiday in 1834, a twenty-seven-year-old mariner and ardent Whig stole on board and decapitated the figurehead, sawing it through just below the ears. Jackson deflected the insult with humor, declaring, "I never did like that image! Give the man a postmaster's job." The commodore, himself alert to symbolic actions, wrapped the headless statue in a flag and sent it to New York City, where woodworkers fashioned a new head in 1835. The figurehead was reattached to the ship in another port; Jackson's banking policies still rankled in urban financial centers, and naval authorities did not want to risk a second mutilation of the president's image. In 1990, the original head was recovered from a private collector in France and restored. It is now on display in the museum that also owns the figurehead. Museum of the City of New York, Gift of the Seawanhaka Corinthian Yacht Club.

The Expanding Republic

1815–1840

PRESIDENT ANDREW JACKSON was the dominant figure of his age, yet his precarious childhood little foretold the fame, fortune, and influence he would enjoy in the years after 1815. **Andrew Jackson** was born in the Carolina backcountry in 1767. His Scots-Irish father had recently died, leaving a poor, struggling mother to support three small boys. During the Revolution, Andrew followed his brothers into the militia, where both died of disease, as did his mother. Orphaned at fourteen, Jackson drifted around, drinking, gambling, and brawling.

Then at seventeen, his prospects began to improve. He studied under a lawyer for three years and moved to Nashville, a frontier community full of opportunities for a young man with legal training and an aggressive temperament. He became a public prosecutor, married into a leading family, and acquired land and slaves. When Tennessee became a state in 1796, Jackson, then twenty-nine, was elected to Congress and served a single term. But his real calling was the military. Jackson captured national attention in 1815 by leading the United States to victory at the battle of New Orleans. Songs, broadsides, and an admiring biography set him up as the original self-made man — the parentless child magically responsible for his own destiny. Jackson seemed to have created himself — a gritty, forceful personality extracting opportunities from the dynamic, turbulent frontier.

Jackson was more than a man of action, however. He was also strong-willed, reckless, and quick to anger, impulsively challenging men to duels, sometimes on slight pretexts. In one legendary fight in 1806, Jackson deliberately let his opponent, an expert marksman, shoot first. The bullet hit him in a rib, but Jackson masked all sign of injury under a loose cloak and an immobile face. He then took careful aim at the astonished man and killed him. Such steely courage chilled his political opponents.

Jackson's image as a tough frontier hero set him apart from the learned and privileged gentlemen from Virginia and Massachusetts who had occupied the presidency up to 1828. When he lost the 1824 election to John Quincy Adams, an infuriated Jackson vowed to fight a rematch. He won in 1828 and again in 1832, capturing large majorities. His appeal stretched across the urban working classes of the East, frontier voters of the West, and

Previewing the Chapter

The Market Revolution 252
Q: *Why did the United States experience a market revolution after 1815?*

The Spread of Democracy 258
Q: *Why did Andrew Jackson defeat John Quincy Adams so dramatically in the 1828 election?*

Jackson Defines the Democratic Party 260
Q: *Why did Jackson promote Indian removal?*

Cultural Shifts, Religion, and Reform 264
Q: *How did evangelical Protestantism contribute to the social reform movements of the 1830s?*

Van Buren's One-Term Presidency 272
Q: *How did slavery figure as a campaign issue in the election of 1836?*

Conclusion: The Age of Jackson or the Era of Reform? 274

President Andrew Jackson Boston painter Ralph E. W. Earl traveled to Nashville, Tennessee, in 1817 to paint the hero of the battle of New Orleans. There, Earl met and married Mrs. Jackson's niece. When the niece died a year later in childbirth, Earl moved into the Hermitage, the Jacksons' plantation home. He stayed ten years and then moved with Andrew Jackson to the White House. The two men were fast friends. Earl was Jackson's "court painter," producing three dozen portraits of him, hundreds of which were sold as lithographic copies to Jackson's supporters. Earl was a shrewd publicist, manufacturing a kindly, subdued, gentle Jackson to counteract the many satirical cartoons that generally portrayed him as a villain (see page 260). Earl stayed with Jackson throughout his presidency. He died in 1838. North Carolina Museum of Art, purchased with funds from the State of North Carolina.

slaveholders in the South, who all saw something of themselves in Jackson. In office, his combative style helped him enlarge the powers of the presidency.

The confidence and even recklessness of Jackson's personality mirrored the new confidence of American society in the years after 1815. An entrepreneurial spirit gripped the country, producing a market revolution of unprecedented scale. Old social hierarchies eroded; ordinary men dreamed of moving high up the ladder of success, just as Jackson had done. Stunning advances in transportation and economic productivity fueled such dreams and propelled thousands to move west or to cities. Urban growth and technological change fostered the diffusion of a distinctive and vibrant public culture, spread mainly through the increased circulation of newspapers, which allowed popular opinions to coalesce and intensify.

Expanded communication transformed politics dramatically. Sharp disagreements over the best way to promote individual liberty, economic opportunity, and national prosperity in the new market economy defined key differences between Jackson and Adams and the parties they gave rise to in the 1830s. The process of party formation brought new habits of political participation and party loyalty to many thousands more adult white males. Religion became democratized as well. A nationwide evangelical revival brought its adherents the certainty that salvation and perfection were now available to all.

As president from 1829 to 1837, Jackson presided over all these changes, fighting some and supporting others in his vigorous and volatile way. As with his stubborn personality, there was a dark underside to the confidence and expansiveness of American society. Steamboats blew up, banks and businesses periodically collapsed, alcoholism rates soared, Indians were killed or relocated farther west, and slavery continued to expand. The brash confidence that turned some people into rugged, self-promoting, Jackson-like individuals inspired others to think about the human costs of rapid economic expansion and thus about reforming society in dramatic ways. The common denominator was a faith that people and societies could shape their own destinies.   ★

The Market Revolution

The return of peace in 1815 unleashed powerful forces that revolutionized the organization of the economy. Spectacular changes in transportation facilitated the movement of commodities, information, and people, while textile mills and other factories created many new jobs, especially for young unmarried women. Innovations in banking, legal practices, and tariff policies promoted swift economic growth.

This was not yet an industrial revolution, as was beginning in Britain, but rather a market revolution fueled by traditional sources — water, wood,

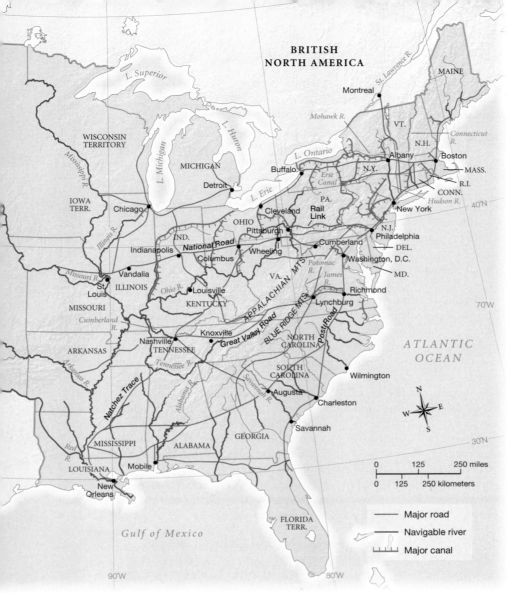

MAP 11.1 Routes of Transportation in 1840

By the 1830s, transportation advances had cut travel times significantly. By way of the Erie Canal, goods and people could move from New York City to Buffalo in four days, a trip that had taken two weeks by road in 1800. Similarly, the trip from New York to New Orleans, which had taken four weeks in 1800, could now be accomplished in less than half that time on steamboats plying the western rivers.

beasts of burden, and human muscle. What was new was the accelerated pace of economic activity and the scale of the distribution of goods. Men and women were drawn out of old patterns of rural self-sufficiency into the wider realm of national market relations. At the same time, the nation's money supply enlarged considerably, leading to speculative investments in commerce, manufacturing, transportation, and land. The new nature and scale of production and consumption changed Americans' economic behavior, attitudes, and expectations. But in 1819 and again in 1837 and 1839, serious crashes of the economy punctured those optimistic expectations.

Improvements in Transportation Before 1815, transportation in the United States was slow and expensive; it cost as much to ship a crate

over thirty miles of domestic roads as it did to send it across the Atlantic Ocean. A stagecoach trip from Boston to New York took four days. But between 1815 and 1840, networks of roads, canals, steamboats, and finally railroads dramatically raised the speed and lowered the cost of travel (Map 11.1). The young Andrew Jackson spent weeks riding to Nashville along old Indian trails in the 1790s, but his journey east to assume the presidency in 1829 took only days by steamboat and turnpike.

Improved transportation moved goods into wider markets. It moved passengers, too, broadening their horizons and allowing young people as well as adults to take up new employment in cities or factory towns. Transportation also facilitated the flow of political information via the U.S. mail with its bargain postal rates for newspapers, periodicals, and books. Enhanced public transport was expensive and produced uneven economic benefits, so presidents from Jefferson to Monroe were reluctant to fund it with federal dollars. Only the National Road, begun in 1806, was government sponsored. By 1818, it linked Baltimore with Wheeling, in western Virginia. In all other cases, private investors pooled resources and chartered transport companies, receiving significant subsidies and monopoly rights from state governments. Turnpike and roadway mileage increased dramatically after 1815, reducing shipping costs. Stagecoach companies proliferated, and travel time on main routes was cut in half.

Water travel was similarly transformed. In 1807, Robert Fulton's steam-propelled boat, the *Clermont*, churned up the Hudson River from New York City to Albany, touching off a steamboat craze. By 1820, a dozen boats left New York City daily, and scores more operated on midwestern rivers and the Great Lakes. A voyager on one of the first steamboats to go down the Mississippi reported that the Chickasaw Indians called the vessel a "fire canoe" and considered it "an omen of evil." By the early 1830s, more than seven hundred steamboats were in operation on the Ohio and Mississippi rivers.

Steamboats were not benign advances, however. The urgency to cut travel time led to overstoked furnaces, sudden boiler explosions, and terrible mass fatalities. Another huge cost, to the environment, was the deforestation brought by steamboats, which had to load fuel—"wood up"—every twenty miles or so. By the 1830s, the banks of many main rivers were denuded of trees, and forests miles back from the rivers fell to the ax. Wood combustion transferred the carbon stored in trees into the atmosphere, creating America's first significant air pollution.

Canals were another major innovation of the transportation revolution. These shallow highways of water allowed passage for boats pulled by mules. Travel was slow—under five miles per hour—but the low-friction water enabled one mule to pull a fifty-ton barge. Pennsylvania in 1815 and New York in 1817 commenced major state-sponsored canal enterprises. Pennsylvania's Schuylkill Canal stretched 108 miles west from Philadelphia when it was completed in 1826. Much more impressive was the **Erie Canal**, finished in 1825, covering 350

THE PROMISE OF TECHNOLOGY

Awful Conflagration of the Steam Boat **LEXINGTON** *In Long Island Sound on Monday Eve*. *Jan*. *13th 1840, by which melancholy occurrence; over* 100 PERSONS PERISHED.

Early Steamboats The American traveling public fell in love with steamboats for their speed and power. People and products could now go upriver, against the current, under the enthralling and modern power of steam. On every boat, a furnace heated water under pressure in a boiler to produce that steam, powering an engine that drove large paddlewheels. The technology was far from safe. Between 1811 and 1851, accidents destroyed nearly a thousand boats, a third of all steam vessels built in that period, and killed a total of several thousand travelers. Fires and boiler explosions made for horrifying spectacles, as this lithograph by the famed printmakers Currier and Ives attests. In 1840, the *Lexington* caught fire in Long Island Sound. Despite having the latest safety features, only 4 people survived; many of the 139 victims froze to death in the icy winter waters. The Mariners Museum, Newport News, Va.

miles between Albany and Buffalo and linking the port of New York City with the entire Great Lakes region. Wheat and flour moved east, household goods and tools moved west, and passengers went in both directions. By the 1830s, the cost of shipping by canal fell to less than a tenth of the cost of overland transport, and New York City quickly blossomed into the premier commercial city in the United States.

In the 1830s, private railroad companies began to give canals competition. The nation's first railroad, the Baltimore and Ohio, laid thirteen miles of track in 1829. During the 1830s, three thousand more miles of track materialized nationwide, the result of a speculative fever in railroad construction masterminded by bankers, locomotive manufacturers, and state legislators who provided subsidies, charters, and land rights-of-way. Rail lines in the 1830s were generally short, on the order of twenty to one hundred miles. They did not yet provide an efficient distribution system for goods, but passengers flocked to experience the marvelous speeds of fifteen to twenty miles per hour. Railroads and other advances in transportation made possible enormous change by unifying the country culturally and economically.

Factories, Workingwomen, and Wage Labor

Transportation advances promoted the expansion of manufacturing after 1815, creating an ever-expanding market for goods. The two leading industries, textiles and shoes, altered methods of production and labor relations. Textile production was greatly spurred by the development of water-driven machinery built near fast-coursing rivers. Shoe manufacturing, still using the power and skill of human hands, involved only a reorganization of production. Shoes and textiles pulled young women into wage-earning labor for the first time.

The earliest factory was built by English immigrant Samuel Slater in Pawtucket, Rhode Island, in the 1790s. It featured a mechanical spinning machine that produced thread and yarn. By 1815, nearly 170 spinning mills had been built along New England rivers. In British manufacturing cities, entire families worked in low-wage, health-threatening factories. In contrast, American factories targeted young women as employees; they were cheap to hire because of their limited employment options. Mill girls would "retire" to marriage, replaced by fresh recruits earning beginners' wages.

In 1821, a group of Boston entrepreneurs founded the town of Lowell on the Merrimack River, centralizing all aspects of cloth production:

combing, shrinking, spinning, weaving, and dyeing. By 1836, the eight mills in Lowell employed more than five thousand young women, who lived in carefully managed company-owned boardinghouses. Corporation rules at the **Lowell mills** required church attendance and prohibited drinking and unsupervised courtship; dorms were locked at 10 p.m. A typical mill worker earned $2 to $3 for a seventy-hour week, more than a seamstress or domestic servant could earn but less than a young man's wages. The job consisted of tending noisy power looms in rooms kept hot and humid, ideal for thread but not for people.

Despite the discomforts, young women embraced factory work as a means to earn spending money and build savings before marriage. Also welcome was the unprecedented, though still limited, personal freedom of living in an all-female social space, away from parents and domestic tasks. In the evening, the women could engage in self-improvement activities, such as attending lectures or writing for the company's periodical, the *Lowell Offering*.

In the mid-1830s, worldwide changes in the cotton market impelled mill owners to speed up work and decrease wages. The workers protested, emboldened by their communal living arrangement and by their relative independence as temporary employees. In 1834 and again in 1836, hundreds of women at Lowell went out on strike. All over New England, female mill workers led strikes and formed unions. In 1834, mill women in Dover, New Hampshire, denounced their owners for trying to turn them into "slaves": "However freely the epithet of 'factory slaves' may be bestowed upon us, we will never deserve it by a base and cringing submission to proud wealth or haughty insolence." Their assertiveness surprised many, but ultimately the ease of replacing them undermined their bargaining power, and owners in the 1840s began to shift to immigrant families as their primary labor source.

The shoe manufacturing industry centered in eastern New England reorganized production and hired women, including wives, as shoebinders. Male shoemakers still cut the leather and made the soles in shops, but female shoebinders working from home now stitched the upper parts of the shoes. Working from home meant that wives could still perform their domestic chores. But they earned money to contribute to family income, which was unusual for most wives in that period.

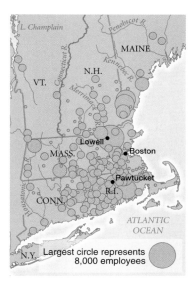

Cotton Textile Industry, ca. 1840

Mill Worker Tending a Power Loom, 1850 This daguerreotype (the earliest form of photograph) shows a young woman tending a power loom in a textile mill. Her main task was to replace the spindle when it ran out of thread and load a new spindle into the shuttle. Spindles carried the woof — the crosswise threading — that was woven into the warp already mounted on the loom. The close-up shows spindles of pink and blue thread next to a shuttle. Factory workers had to be constantly alert for sudden breaks in the warp, which required a fast shutdown of the loom and a quick repair of the thread. In the 1830s, women weavers generally tended two machines at a time. In the 1840s, some companies increased the workload to four. Mill worker: American Textile History Museum; Shuttle with spindles: Picture Research Consultants & Archives.

In the economically turbulent 1830s, shoebinder wages fell. Unlike mill workers, female shoebinders worked in isolation, a serious hindrance to organized protest. In Lynn, Massachusetts, a major shoemaking center, women used female church networks to organize resistance, communicating via religious newspapers. The Lynn shoebinders who demanded higher wages in 1834 built on a collective sense of themselves as women even though they did not work together daily. "Equal rights should be extended to all — to the weaker sex as well as the stronger," they wrote in a document establishing the Female Society of Lynn.

In the end, the Lynn shoebinders' protests failed to achieve wage increases. At-home workers all over New England continued to accept low wages, and even in Lynn, many women shied away from organized protest, preferring to situate their work in the context of family duty (helping their husbands to finish the shoes) instead of market relations.

Bankers and Lawyers Entrepreneurs like the Lowell factory owners relied on innovations in the banking system to finance their ventures. Between 1814 and 1816, the number of state-chartered banks in the United States more than doubled from fewer than 90 to 208. By 1830, there were 330, and by 1840 hundreds more. Banks stimulated the economy by making loans to merchants and manufacturers and by enlarging the money supply. Borrowers were issued loans in the form of bank-notes — certificates unique to each bank — that were used as money for all transactions. Neither federal nor state governments issued paper money, so banknotes became the country's currency.

In theory, a note could always be traded in at a bank for its hard-money equivalent in gold or silver, a transaction known as a "specie payment." A note from a solid local bank might be worth exactly what it was written for, but the face value of a note from a distant or questionable bank would be discounted. Buying and selling banknotes in this era required knowledge and caution. Not surprisingly, counterfeiting flourished.

Bankers exercised great power over the economy, and the most powerful bankers sat on the board of directors for the second Bank of the United States, headquartered in Philadelphia. The twenty-year charter of the first Bank of the United States had expired in 1811. The **second Bank of the United States**, with eighteen branches throughout the country, opened for business in 1816 under another twenty-year charter. The rechartering of this bank would become a major issue in Andrew Jackson's reelection campaign in 1832.

Lawyer-politicians too exercised economic power, by refashioning commercial law to enhance the prospects of private investment. In 1811, states started to rewrite their laws of incorporation (allowing the chartering of businesses by states), and the number of corporations expanded rapidly, from about twenty in 1800 to eighteen hundred by 1817. Incorporation protected individual investors from being held liable for corporate debts. State lawmakers also wrote laws of eminent domain, empowering states to buy land for roads and canals even from unwilling sellers. In such ways, entrepreneurial lawyers of the 1820s and 1830s created the legal foundation for an economy that favored ambitious individuals interested in maximizing their own wealth.

Not everyone applauded these developments. Andrew Jackson, himself a skillful lawyer turned politician, spoke for a large and mistrustful segment of the population when he warned about the potential abuses of power "which the moneyed interest derives from a paper currency which they are able to control, from the multitude of corporations with exclusive privileges which they have succeeded in obtaining in the different states, and which are employed altogether for their benefit." Jacksonians believed that ending government-granted privileges was the way to maximize individual liberty and economic opportunity.

Booms and Busts One aspect of the economy that the lawyer-politicians could not control was the threat of financial collapse. In 1819 and again in the 1830s, boom times of high inflation and speculative investment were punctured by sharp economic recessions called "panics." In the first, the overnight rich suddenly became the overnight poor. Some blamed the **panic of 1819** on the second Bank of the United States for failing to control state banks that had suspended specie payments — the exchange of gold or silver for banknotes — in their eagerness to expand the economic bubble. By mid-1818, when the Bank of the United States called in its loans and insisted that the state banks do likewise, the contracting of the money supply sent tremors throughout the economy. The crunch was made worse by a financial crisis in Europe in the spring of 1819. Overseas, prices for American cotton, tobacco, and wheat plummeted by more than 50 percent. Thus, when the banks began to call in their outstanding loans, American debtors involved in the commodities trade could not come up with the money. Business and personal bankruptcies skyrocketed. The intricate web of credit and debt relationships meant that almost everyone with even a toehold in the new commercial economy was affected by the panic. Thousands of Americans lost their savings and property, and unemployment estimates suggest that half a million people lost their jobs.

Recovery took several years. Unemployment declined, but bitterness lingered, ready to be stirred up by politicians in the decades to come. The dangers of a system dependent on extensive credit were now clear. In one folksy formulation that circulated around 1820, a farmer compared credit to "a man pissing in his breeches on a cold day to keep his arse warm — very comfortable at first but I dare say . . . you know how it feels afterwards."

By the mid-1820s, the economy was back on track, driven by increases in productivity, consumer demand for goods, and international trade. Despite the panic of 1819, credit financing continued to fuel the system. With the growth of manufacturing and transportation networks, buyers and sellers operated in a much larger arena, using credit transactions on paper instead of moving actual (and scarce) hard money around. A network of credit and debt relations grew dense by the 1830s in a system that encouraged speculation and risk taking. A pervasive optimism about continued growth supported the elaborate system, but a single business failure could produce many innocent victims. Well after

> "A farmer compared credit to "a man pissing in his breeches on a cold day to keep his arse warm — very comfortable at first but I dare say . . . you know how it feels afterwards."

the panic of 1819, an undercurrent of anxiety about rapid economic change continued to shape the political views of many Americans.

Q: Why did the United States experience a market revolution after 1815?

The Spread of Democracy

Just as the market revolution held out the promise, if not the reality, of economic opportunity for all who worked, the political transformation of the 1830s held out the promise of political opportunity for hundreds of thousands of new voters. During Andrew Jackson's presidency (1829–1837), the second American party system took shape. Not until 1836, however, would the parties have distinct names and consistent programs transcending the particular personalities running for office. Over those years, more men could and did vote, responding to new methods of arousing voter interest. In 1828, Jackson's charismatic personality defined his party, and his victory over incumbent president John Quincy Adams turned on questions of character. Once in office, Jackson championed ordinary citizens against the power elite—democracy versus aristocracy in Jackson's terminology. A lasting contribution of the Jackson years was the notion that politicians needed to have the common touch in their dealings with voters.

Popular Politics and Partisan Identity The election of 1828 was the first presidential contest in which the popular vote determined the outcome. In twenty-two out of twenty-four states, voters—not state legislatures—designated the number of electors committed to a particular candidate. More than a million voters participated, three times the number in 1824 and nearly half the free male population, reflecting the high stakes that voters perceived in the Adams-Jackson rematch. Throughout the 1830s, voter turnout continued to rise and reached 70 percent in some localities, partly due to the disappearance of property qualifications in all but three states and partly due to heightened political interest.

The 1828 election inaugurated new campaign styles. State-level candidates routinely gave speeches at rallies, picnics, and banquets. Adams and Jackson still declined such appearances as undignified, but **Henry Clay** of Kentucky, campaigning for Adams, earned the nickname "the Barbecue Orator." Campaign rhetoric became more informal and even blunt. The Jackson camp established many Hickory Clubs, trading on Jackson's popular nickname, "Old Hickory," from a common Tennessee tree suggesting resilience and toughness. (Jackson was the first presidential candidate to have an affectionate and widely used nickname.)

Partisan newspapers in ever-larger numbers defined issues and publicized political personalities as never before. Improved printing technology and rising literacy rates fueled a great expansion of newspapers of all kinds (Table 11.1). Party leaders dispensed subsidies and other favors to secure the support of papers, even in remote towns and villages. In New York State, where party development was most advanced, a pro-Jackson group called the Bucktails controlled fifty weekly publications. Stories from the leading Jacksonian paper in Washington, D.C., were reprinted two days later in a Boston or Cincinnati paper, for example, as fast as the mail stage could carry them. Presidential campaigns were now coordinated in a national arena.

Politicians at first identified themselves as Jackson or Adams men, honoring the fiction of Republican Party unity. By 1832, however, the terminology had evolved to National Republicans, favoring federal action to promote commercial development, and Democratic Republicans, who promised to be responsive to the will of the majority. Between 1834 and 1836, National Republicans came to be called Whigs, while Jackson's party became simply the Democrats.

The Election of 1828 and the Character Issue The campaign of 1828 was the first national election in which scandal and character questions reigned supreme. They became central issues because voters used them to comprehend the kind of public official each man would make. Character issues conveyed in shorthand larger questions about morality, honor, and discipline. Jackson and Adams presented two radically different styles of manhood.

John Quincy Adams was vilified by his opponents as an elitist, a bookish academic, and even a monarchist. They attacked his "corrupt bargain" of 1824—the alleged election deal between Adams and Henry Clay (see chapter 10). Adams's supporters returned fire with fire. They played on Jackson's fatherless childhood to portray him as the bastard son of a prostitute. Worse, the cloudy

★ **TABLE 11.1   Growth of Newspapers, 1820–1840**

	1820	1830	1835	1840
U.S. population (in millions)	9.6	12.8	15.0	17.1
Number of newspapers published	500	800	1,200	1,400
Daily newspapers	42	65	—	138

circumstances around his marriage to Rachel Donelson Robards in 1791 gave rise to the story that Jackson was a seducer and an adulterer, having married a woman whose divorce from her first husband was not entirely legal. Pro-Adams newspapers howled that Jackson was sinful and impulsive, while portraying Adams as pious, learned, and virtuous.

Editors in favor of Adams played up Jackson's violent temper, as evidenced by his participation in many duels, brawls, and canings. Jackson's supporters used the same stories to project Old Hickory as a tough frontier hero who knew how to command obedience. As for learning, Jackson's rough frontier education gave him a "natural sense," wrote a Boston editor, that "can never be acquired by reading books—it can only be acquired, in perfection, by reading men."

Jackson won a sweeping victory, 56 percent of the popular vote and 178 electoral votes to Adams's 83 (Map 11.2). Old Hickory took most of the South and West and carried Pennsylvania and New York as well; Adams carried the remainder of the East. Jackson's vice president was **John C. Calhoun**, who had just served as vice president under Adams but had broken with Adams's policies.

After 1828, national politicians no longer deplored the existence of political parties. They were coming to see that parties mobilized and delivered voters, sharpened candidates' differences, and created party loyalty that surpassed loyalty to individual candidates and elections. Adams and Jackson clearly symbolized the competing ideas of the emerging parties: a moralistic, top-down party (the **Whigs**) ready to make major decisions to promote economic growth competing against a contentious, energetic party (the **Democrats**) ready to embrace liberty-loving individualism.

Jackson's Democratic Agenda

Before the inauguration in March 1829, Jackson's wife Rachel died, and the president went into deep mourning, his depression worsened by constant pain from the bullet still lodged in his chest from the 1806 duel. Aged sixty-two, Jackson carried only 140 pounds on his six-foot-one frame. His adversaries doubted that he would make it to a second term. His supporters, however, went wild at the inauguration. Thousands cheered his ten-minute inaugural address, the shortest in history. An open reception at the White House turned into a near riot as well-wishers jammed the premises, used windows as doors, stood on furniture for a better view of the great man, and broke thousands of dollars' worth of china and glasses.

During his presidency, Jackson continued to offer unprecedented hospitality to the public.

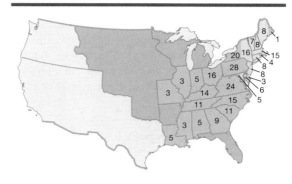

Candidate	Electoral Vote	Popular Vote	Percent of Popular Vote
Andrew Jackson (Democratic Republican)	178	647,286	56
John Q. Adams (National Republican)	83	508,064	44

MAP 11.2 The Election of 1828

Twenty spittoons newly installed in the East Room of the White House accommodated the tobacco chewers among the throngs that arrived daily to see the president. The courteous Jackson, committed to his image as president of the "common man," held audiences with unannounced visitors throughout his two terms.

Past presidents had tried to lessen party conflict by including men of different factions in their cabinets, but Jackson would have only loyalists. For secretary of state, the key job, he tapped New Yorker Martin Van Buren, one of the shrewdest politicians of the day. Throughout the federal government, from postal clerks to ambassadors, Jackson replaced competent civil servants with party loyalists. "To the victor belong the spoils," said a Democratic senator from New York, expressing approval of patronage-driven appointments. Jackson's appointment practices got tagged the spoils system; it was a concept the president strenuously defended.

Jackson's agenda quickly emerged. He favored a Jeffersonian limited federal government, fearing that intervention in the economy inevitably favored some groups at the expense of others. He therefore opposed federal support of transportation and grants of monopolies and charters that privileged wealthy investors. Like Jefferson, he anticipated the rapid settlement of the country's interior, where land sales would spread economic democracy to settlers. Thus, establishing a federal policy to remove the Indians had high priority. Unlike Jefferson, Jackson exercised his presidential veto power over Congress. In 1830, he vetoed a Congress-backed highway project in Maysville,

Kentucky, Henry Clay's home state. The Maysville Road veto articulated Jackson's principled stand that citizens' tax dollars could be spent only on projects of a "general, not local" character. In all, Jackson used the veto twelve times; all previous presidents had exercised that right a total of nine times.

Q: Why did Andrew Jackson defeat John Quincy Adams so dramatically in the 1828 election?

Jackson Defines the Democratic Party

In his two terms as president, Andrew Jackson worked to implement his vision of a politics of opportunity for all white men. To open land for white settlement, he favored the relocation of all eastern Indian tribes. He dramatically confronted John C. Calhoun and South Carolina when that state tried to nullify the tariff of 1828. Disapproving of all government-granted privilege, Jackson challenged what he called the "monster" Bank of the United States and took it down to defeat. In all this, he greatly enhanced the power of the presidency.

Indian Policy and the Trail of Tears Probably nothing defined Jackson's presidency more than his efforts to solve what he saw as the Indian problem. Thousands of Indians lived in the South and the old Northwest, and many remained in New England and New York. Jackson, who rose to fame fighting the Creek and Seminole tribes in the 1810s, declared, in his first message to Congress in 1829, that removing the Indians to territory west of the Mississippi was the only way to save them. White civilization destroyed Indian resources and thus doomed the Indians, he claimed: "That this fate surely awaits them if they remain within the limits of the states does not admit of a doubt. Humanity and national honor demand that every effort should be made to avert so great a calamity." Jackson never publicly wavered from this seemingly noble theme, returning to it in his next seven annual messages.

Prior administrations had experimented with different Indian policies. Starting in 1819, Congress funded missionary associations eager to "civilize" native peoples by converting them to Christianity and to whites' agricultural practices. Missionaries also promoted white gender customs, but with little success. The federal government had pursued aggressive treaty making with many tribes, dealing with the Indians as foreign nations

Andrew Jackson as "the Great Father" In 1828, a new process of cheap commercial lithography found immediate application in a colorful presidential campaign aimed at capturing popular votes, and with it, a rich tradition of political cartoons was born. Jackson inspired at least five dozen satirical cartoons centering on caricatures of him. Strikingly, only one of them featured his Indian policy, controversial as it was, and only a single copy still exists. At some point, this cartoon was cropped at the bottom and top, and thus we do not have the cartoonist's caption or signature, both important for more fully understanding the artist's intent. Still, the sarcastic visual humor of Jackson cradling miniaturized Indians packs an immediate punch. William L. Clements Library.

FOR MORE HELP ANALYZING THIS IMAGE, see the visual activity for this chapter in the Online Study Guide at bedfordstmartins.com/roarkcompact.

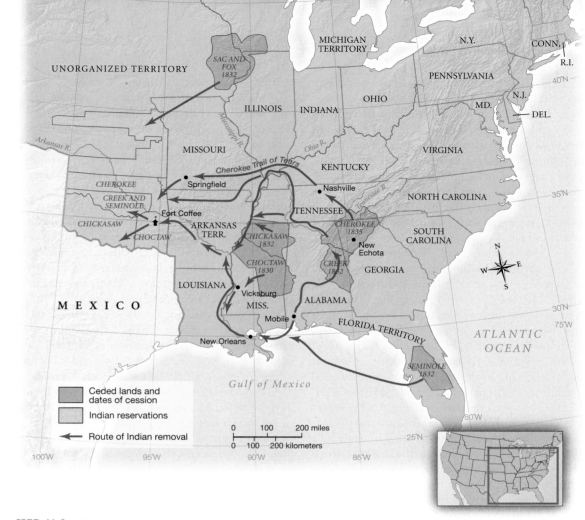

MAP 11.3 **Indian Removal and the Trail of Tears**

The federal government under President Andrew Jackson pursued a vigorous policy of Indian removal in the 1830s. Tribes were forcibly moved west to land known as Indian Territory (present-day Oklahoma). As many as a quarter of the Cherokee Indians died on the route known as the Trail of Tears in 1838.

READING THE MAP: From which states were most of the Native Americans removed? Through which states did the Trail of Tears go?

CONNECTIONS: Before Jackson's presidency, how did the federal government view Native Americans, and what policy initiatives were undertaken by the government and private groups? How did Jackson change the government's policy toward Native Americans?

FOR MORE HELP ANALYZING THIS MAP, see the map activity for this chapter in the Online Study Guide at bedfordstmartins.com/roarkcompact.

(see chapter 10, page 236). In contrast, Jackson saw Indians as subjects of the United States, and he did not approve of assimilation. In his 1833 message to Congress, he wrote, "They have neither the intelligence, the industry, the moral habits, nor the desire of improvement which are essential. . . . Established in the midst of a superior race . . . they must necessarily yield to the force of circumstances and ere long disappear." Congress backed Jackson's goal and passed the **Indian Removal Act of 1830**, appropriating $500,000 to relocate eastern tribes west of the Mississippi. About 100 million acres of

eastern land would be vacated for eventual white settlement under this act authorizing ethnic expulsion (Map 11.3).

Jackson's frequent claim that removal would save the Indians from extinction was in part formulated in response to the widespread controversy generated by the Indian Removal Act. Newspapers, public lecturers, and local clubs debated the expulsion law, and in an unprecedented move, thousands of northern white women signed anti-removal petitions. The right to petition for redress of grievances, part of the Constitution's First Amendment, had long been used by individual women acting on personal cause — say, a military widow requesting her husband's pension. But mass petitioning by women was something new; it directly challenged the prevailing assumption that women could not be political actors. Between 1830 and 1832, women's petitions rolled into Washington, arguing specifically that the Cherokee Indians of Georgia were a sovereign people on the road to Christianity and entitled to stay on their land. Jackson ignored the petitions.

For the northern tribes, their numbers diminished by years of war, gradual removal was already well under way. But not all the Indians went quietly. In 1832 in western Illinois, Black Hawk, a leader of the Sauk and Fox Indians who had fought in alliance with Tecumseh in the War of 1812 (see chapter 10, page 237), resisted removal. Volunteer militias attacked and chased the Indians into southern Wisconsin, where, after several skirmishes and a deadly battle (later called the Black Hawk War), Black Hawk was captured and four hundred of his people were massacred.

The large southern tribes — the Creek, Chickasaw, Choctaw, and Cherokee — proved even more resistant to removal. The tribal leadership of the Cherokee in Georgia chose a unique path of resistance by taking their case to the U.S. Supreme Court. Georgia Cherokees had already taken several assimilationist steps. Aided by dedicated missionaries, these leaders had incorporated written laws, including, in 1827, a constitution modeled on the U.S. Constitution. Two hundred of the wealthiest Cherokee men had intermarried with whites, adopting white styles of housing, dress, and cotton agriculture, including the ownership of slaves. They developed a written alphabet and published a newspaper and Christian prayer books in their language. These features helped make their cause attractive to the northern white women who petitioned the government on their behalf. Yet most of the seventeen thousand Cherokees maintained cultural continuity with past traditions.

In 1831, when Georgia announced its plans to seize all Cherokee property, the tribal leaders asked the U.S. Supreme Court to restrain Georgia. The Court held that the Cherokee were not citizens and lacked standing to sue. A year later they brought suit again, this time using an ally, a white missionary, as their stand-in plaintiff. In *Worcester v. Georgia* (1832), the Supreme Court upheld the territorial sovereignty of the Cherokee people, recognizing their existence as "a distinct community, occupying its own territory, in which the laws of Georgia can have no force." An angry President Jackson ignored the Court and pressed the Cherokee

tribe to move west: "If they now refuse to accept the liberal terms offered, they can only be liable for whatever evils and difficulties may arise. I feel conscious of having done my duty to my red children."

The Cherokee tribe remained in Georgia for two more years without significant violence. Then, in 1835, a small, unauthorized faction of the acculturated leaders signed a treaty selling all the tribal lands to the state, which rapidly resold the land to whites. Most Cherokees refused to move, so in May 1838, the deadline for voluntary evacuation, federal troops sent by Jackson's successor, Martin Van Buren, arrived to remove them. Under armed guard, the Cherokees embarked on a 1,200-mile journey west that came to be called the **Trail of Tears**. Nearly a quarter of the Cherokees died en route from the hardship. Survivors joined the fifteen thousand Creek, twelve thousand Choctaw, five thousand Chickasaw, and several thousand Seminole Indians also forcibly relocated to Indian Territory (which became the state of Oklahoma in 1907).

In his farewell address to the nation in 1837, Jackson professed his belief in the benefit of Indian removal: "This unhappy race . . . are now placed in a situation where we may well hope that they will share in the blessings of civilization and be saved from the degradation and destruction to which they were rapidly hastening while they remained in the states." Perhaps Jackson genuinely believed that exile to the West was necessary to save Indian cultures from destruction. But for the forcibly removed tribes, the costs of relocation were high.

The Tariff of Abominations and Nullification

Jackson's Indian policy happened to harmonize with the principle of states' rights; the president supported Georgia's right to ignore the Supreme Court's decision in *Worcester v. Georgia*. But in another pressing question of states' rights, Jackson contested South Carolina's attempt to ignore federal tariff policy.

Federal tariffs as high as 33 percent on imports such as textiles and iron goods had been passed in 1816 and again in 1824 in an effort to shelter new American manufacturers from foreign competition. Some southern congressmen opposed the steep tariffs, fearing they would decrease overseas shipping and thereby hurt cotton exports. In 1828, Congress passed a revised tariff that came to be known as the Tariff of Abominations. A bundle of conflicting duties, some as high as 50 percent, the legislation contained provisions that pleased and angered every economic and sectional interest.

South Carolina in particular suffered from the Tariff of Abominations. Worldwide prices for cotton had declined in the late 1820s, and the falloff in shipping caused by the high tariffs further hurt the South. In 1828, a group of South Carolina politicians headed by John C. Calhoun advanced a doctrine called **nullification**. The Union, they argued, was a confederation of states that had yielded some but not all power to the federal government. When Congress overstepped its powers, states had the right to nullify Congress's acts. As precedents, they pointed to the Virginia and Kentucky Resolutions of 1798, intended to invalidate the Alien and Sedition Acts (see chapter 9). Congress had erred in using tariff policy to benefit specific industries, they claimed; tariffs should be used only to raise revenue.

On assuming the presidency in 1829, Jackson ignored the South Carolina statement of nullification and shut out Calhoun, his new vice president, from influence or power. Tariff revisions in early 1832 brought little relief to the South. Sensing futility, Calhoun resigned the vice presidency and became a senator to better serve his state. Finally, strained to their limit, South Carolina leaders declared federal tariffs null and void in their state as of February 1, 1833. The constitutional crisis was out in the open.

Opting for a dramatic confrontation, Jackson sent armed ships to Charleston harbor and threatened to invade the state. He pushed through Congress the Force Bill, defining the Carolina stance as treason and authorizing military action to collect federal tariffs. At the same time, Congress moved quickly to pass a revised tariff that was more acceptable to the South. The conciliating Senator Henry Clay rallied support for a moderate bill that gradually reduced tariffs down to the 1816 level. On March 1, 1833, Congress passed both the new tariff and the Force Bill. South Carolina then withdrew its nullification of the old tariff—and then nullified the Force Bill. It was a symbolic gesture, since Jackson's show of muscle was no longer necessary. Both sides were satisfied: Federal power had prevailed over an assertion of states' rights, and South Carolina got the lower tariff it wanted.

Yet the question of federal power versus states' rights was far from settled. The implied threat behind nullification was secession, a position articulated in 1832 by some South Carolinians whose concerns went beyond tariff policy. In the 1830s, the political moratorium on discussions of slavery agreed on at the time of the Missouri Compromise (see chapter 10) was coming unglued, and new northern voices opposed to slavery gained increasing attention. If and when a northern-dominated federal government decided to end slavery, the South Carolinians thought, the South should nullify such laws, or remove itself from the Union.

The Bank War and Economic Boom Along with the tariff and nullification, President Jackson fought another political battle, over the Bank of the United States. After riding out the panic of 1819, the bank finally prospered. With twenty-nine branches, it handled the federal government's deposits, extended credit and loans, and issued banknotes—by 1830, the most stable currency in the country. Jackson, however, did not find the bank's functions sufficiently valuable to offset his criticism of the concept of a national bank: that it concentrated undue economic power in the hands of a few.

National Republican (Whig) senators Daniel Webster and Henry Clay decided to force the issue. They convinced the bank to apply for charter renewal in 1832, well before the fall election, even though the existing charter ran until 1836. They fully expected that Congress's renewal would force Jackson to follow through on his rhetoric with a veto, that the unpopular veto would cause Jackson to lose the election, and that the bank would survive on an override vote by a new Congress swept into power on the anti-Jackson tide.

At first, the plan seemed to work. The bank applied for rechartering, Congress voted to renew, and Jackson, angry over being manipulated, issued his veto. But it was a brilliantly written veto, full of fierce language about the privileges of the moneyed elite who oppress the democratic masses in order to enrich themselves. "Many of our rich men have not been content with equal protection and equal benefits, but have besought us to make them richer by act of Congress," Jackson wrote.

Clay and his supporters found Jackson's economic ideas and his language of class antagonism so absurd that they distributed thousands of copies of the bank veto as campaign material for their own party. A confident Henry Clay headed his party's ticket for the presidency. But the plan backfired. Jackson's translation of the bank controversy into a language of class antagonism and egalitarian ideals resonated with many Americans. Old Hickory won the election easily, gaining 55 percent of the popular vote and 219 electoral votes to Clay's 49. Jackson's party still controlled Congress, so no override was possible. The second Bank of the United States would cease to exist after 1836.

Jackson, however, wanted to destroy the bank sooner. Calling it a "monster," he ordered the sizable federal deposits to be removed from its vaults and redeposited into Democratic-inclined state banks. In retaliation, the Bank of the United States raised interest rates and called in loans. This action caused a brief decline in the economy in 1833 and actually enhanced Jackson's claim that the bank was too powerful for the good of the country.

Unleashed and unregulated, the economy went into high gear in 1834. Just at this moment, an excess of silver from Mexican mines made its way into American banks, giving bankers license to print ever more banknotes. From 1834 to 1837, inflation soared; prices of basic goods rose more than 50 percent. States quickly chartered hundreds of new private banks, each issuing its own banknotes. Entrepreneurs borrowed and invested money, and the webs of credit and debt relationships that were the hallmark of the American economy grew denser yet.

The market in western land sales also heated up. In 1834, about 4.5 million acres of the public domain had been sold, the highest annual volume since 1818. By 1836, the total reached an astonishing 20 million acres. Some of this was southern land in Mississippi and Louisiana, which slave owners rushed to bring under cultivation, but much more was in the North, where land offices were deluged with buyers. The Jackson administration worried that the purchasers were overwhelmingly eastern capitalist land speculators instead of independent farmers intending to settle on the land.

In one respect, the economy attained an admirable goal: The national debt disappeared, and from 1835 to 1837, for the only time in American history, the government had a monetary surplus. But much of that surplus consisted of questionable bank currencies—"bloated, diseased" currencies, in Jackson's vivid terminology. While the boom was on, however, few stopped to worry about the consequences if and when the bubble burst.

Q: **Why did Jackson promote Indian removal?**

Cultural Shifts, Religion, and Reform

The growing economy, booming by the mid-1830s, transformed social and cultural life. For many families, especially in the commercialized Northeast, standards of living rose, consumption patterns changed, and the nature and location of work were altered. All this had a direct impact on the duties of men and women and on the training of youths for the economy of the future.

Along with economic change came an unprecedented revival of evangelical religion known as the **Second Great Awakening**. Just as universal male suffrage allowed all white men to vote, democratized religion offered salvation to all who embraced it. Among the most serious adherents of evangelical Protestantism were men and women of the new merchant classes, whose self-discipline in pursuing market ambitions meshed well with the message of self-discipline in pursuit of spiritual perfection. Not content with individual perfection, many of these people sought to perfect society as well, by defining excessive alcohol consumption, nonmarital sex, and slavery as three major evils of modern life in need of correction.

The Family and Separate Spheres The centerpiece of new ideas about gender relations was the notion that husbands found their status and authority in the new world of work, leaving wives to tend the hearth and home. Sermons, advice books, periodicals, and novels reinforced the idea that men and women inhabited **separate spheres** and had separate duties. "To woman it belongs . . . to elevate the intellectual character of her household [and] to kindle the fires of mental activity in childhood," wrote Mrs. A. J. Graves in a popular book titled *Advice to American Women*. For men, in contrast, "the absorbing passion for gain, and the pressing demands of business, engross their whole attention." In particular, the home, now the exclusive domain of women, was sentimentalized as the source of intimacy, love, and safety, a refuge from the cruel and competitive world of market relations.

Some new aspects of society gave substance to this formulation of separate spheres. Men's work was undergoing profound change after 1815 and increasingly brought cash to the household, especially in the manufacturing and urban Northeast. Farmers and tradesmen sold products in a market, and bankers, bookkeepers, shoemakers, and canal diggers got pay envelopes. Furthermore, many men now worked away from the home, at an office or store.

A woman's domestic role was more complicated than the cultural prescriptions indicated. (See "Global Comparison.") Although the vast majority of married white women did not hold paying jobs, their homes required time-consuming labor. But the advice books treated housework as a loving familial duty, thus rendering it invisible in an economy that evaluated work by how much cash it

Changing Trends in Age at First Marriage for Women

	Nineteenth Century		Twentieth Century		
	1800	*1850*	*1900*	*1960*	*2000*
United States	21	23	23	20	25
England	20	24	24	22	28
Netherlands	—	28	26	25	28
Russia	—	19	—	25	22

Note: Dates are approximate. Dashes indicate a lack of reliable information.

Average age at first marriage is a remarkably complex indicator of social, economic, and cultural factors in all societies. It is also a number that is dauntingly hard to determine for historical populations because marriage registration before the twentieth century rarely included age data. Historical demographers have developed techniques to link brides' birth and marriage records in small community studies. For larger populations, sophisticated quantitative methods can generate data on mean age at marriage based on reported age and marital status in a census. In general, conditions favoring a low age at marriage for women are those that provide young couples with early financial support: abundant affordable farmland, coresidence with parents, or steady employment for men at a wage that can support a family. Factors that postpone marriage include a lack of farmland, deterioration in male employment prospects, a changed economy requiring more years of prejob education and training, or enhanced employment for women that makes the job market more attractive than the marriage market. The low mean ages in this table reflect abundant farmland (1800, United States), factory wage labor (1800, England), and serfdom (1850, Russia). In Europe and the United States, age at marriage for women rose steeply in the nineteenth century. The northeastern United States led the way in the 1820s and 1830s. Can you suggest reasons why? One immediate consequence of later marriage was a decline in completed family size, since brides shaved two years off their exposure to the risk of pregnancy. Finally, demographers note that in some cases, rising age at first marriage is accompanied by rising rates of nonmarriage, sometimes as high as 20 percent. How might these two trends be connected?

generated. In reality, wives contributed directly to family income in many ways. Some took in boarders; others earned pay for shoebinding or needlework done at home. Wives in the poorest classes, including most free black wives, did not have the luxury of husbands earning adequate wages; for them, work as servants or laundresses helped augment family income.

Idealized notions about the feminine home and the masculine workplace gained acceptance in the 1830s (and well beyond) because of the cultural ascendancy of the commercialized Northeast, with its domination of book and periodical publication. Beyond white families of the middle and upper classes, however, these new gender ideals had limited applicability. Despite their apparent authority in printed material of the period, they were never all-pervasive.

The Education and Training of Youths The market economy required expanded opportunities for training youths of both sexes. By the 1830s, in both the North and South, state-supported public school systems were the norm, designed to produce

Women Graduates of Oberlin College, Class of 1855 Oberlin College, founded in Ohio by evangelical and abolitionist activists in the 1830s, admitted men and women, both white and black. In the early years, the black students were all male, and the women students were all white. Instruction was not coeducational; the women attended classes in the separate Ladies' Department. By 1855, as this daguerreotype shows, black women had integrated the Ladies' Department. The two older women wearing bonnets are the principal and a member of the board. Each student is dressed in the latest fashion: a dark taffeta dress with sloping shoulders, a tight bodice, and a detachable white lace collar. Hairstyles were similarly uniform for women of all ages throughout the 1850s: hair parted down the middle, dressed with oil, and lustrously coiled over the ears. Compare these women with the mill worker pictured on page 256. What differences do you see? Oberlin College Archives, Oberlin, Ohio.

pupils of both sexes able, by age twelve to fourteen, to read, write, and participate in marketplace calculations. Literacy rates for white females climbed dramatically, rivaling the rates for white males for the first time. The fact that taxpayers paid for children's education created an incentive to seek an inexpensive teaching force. By the 1830s, school districts replaced male teachers with young females, for, as a Massachusetts report on education put it, "females can be educated cheaper, quicker, and better, and will teach cheaper after they are qualified." Many were trained in private female academies, now numbering in the hundreds (see chapter 10).

Advanced education continued to expand in the 1830s, with an additional two dozen colleges for men and several more female seminaries offering education on a par with the male colleges. Mount Holyoke Seminary in western Massachusetts, founded by educator Mary Lyon in 1837, developed a rigorous scientific curriculum,

and Oberlin College in Ohio, founded by Presbyterians in 1835, became the first coeducational college when it opened its doors to women in 1837. Oberlin's goal was to train young men for the ministry and to prepare young women to be ministers' wives.

Still, only a very small percentage of young people attended institutions of higher learning. The vast majority of male youths left public school at age fourteen to apprentice in specific trades or to embark on business careers by seeking entry-level clerkships, abundant in the growing urban centers. Young girls headed for mill towns or cities in unprecedented numbers, seeking work in the expanding service sector as seamstresses and domestic servants. Changes in patterns of youth employment meant that large numbers of youngsters escaped the watchful eyes of their parents. Moralists fretted about the dangers of unsupervised youths, and following the lead of the Lowell

Charles G. Finney and His Broadway Tabernacle The Reverend Charles Grandison Finney (shown here in a portrait done in 1834) took his evangelical movement to New York City in the early 1830s, operating first out of a renovated theater. In 1836, the Broadway Tabernacle was built for his pastorate. In its use of space, the tabernacle resembled a theater more than a traditional church, but it departed radically from one very theaterlike tradition of churches — the custom of charging pew rents. In effect, most churches required worshippers to purchase their seats. Finney insisted that all the seats in his house were free, unreserved, and open to anyone. Oberlin College Archives, Oberlin, Ohio.

FOR MORE HELP ANALYZING THIS IMAGE, see the visual activity for this chapter in the Online Study Guide at bedfordstmartins.com/roarkcompact.

mill owners, some established apprentices' libraries and uplifting lecture series to keep young people honorably occupied. Advice books published by the hundreds instructed youths in the virtues of hard work and delayed gratification.

The Second Great Awakening A newly invigorated version of Protestantism gained momentum in the 1820s and 1830s as the economy reshaped gender and age relations. The earliest manifestations of this fervent piety appeared in 1801 in Kentucky, when a crowd of ten thousand people camped out on a hillside at Cane Ridge for a revival meeting that lasted several weeks. By the 1810s and 1820s, "camp meetings" had spread to the Atlantic seaboard states. The outdoor settings permitted huge attendance, intensifying the emotional impact of the revival.

The gatherings attracted women and men hungry for a more immediate access to spiritual peace, one not requiring years of soul-searching. One eyewitness reported that "some of the people were singing, others praying, some crying for mercy. . . . At one time I saw at least five hundred swept down in a moment as if a battery of a thousand guns had been opened upon them, and then immediately followed shrieks and shouts that rent the very heavens."

From 1800 to 1820, church membership doubled in the United States, much of it among the evangelical groups. Methodists, Baptists, and Presbyterians formed the core of the new movement; Episcopalians, Congregationalists, Unitarians, Dutch Reformed, Lutherans, and Catholics maintained strong skepticism about the emotional enthusiasm. Women more than men were attracted to the evangelical movement, and wives and mothers typically recruited husbands and sons to join them.

The leading exemplar of the Second Great Awakening was a lawyer turned minister named **Charles Grandison Finney**. Finney lived in western New

> One eyewitness at a revival reported that "at one time I saw at least five hundred swept down in a moment as if a battery of a thousand guns had been opened upon them, and then immediately followed shrieks and shouts that rent the very heavens."

York, where the completion of the Erie Canal in 1825 fundamentally altered the social and economic landscape overnight. Towns swelled with new inhabitants who brought remarkable prosperity along with other, less admirable side effects, such as prostitution, drinking, and gaming. Finney saw New York canal towns as especially ripe for evangelical awakening. In Rochester, he sustained a six-month revival through the winter of 1830–31, generating thousands of converts.

Finney's message was directed primarily at the business classes. He argued that a reign of Christian perfection loomed, one that required public-spirited outreach to the less-than-perfect to foster their salvation. Evangelicals promoted Sunday schools to bring piety to children; they battled to end mail delivery, stop public transport, and close shops on Sundays to honor the Sabbath. Many women formed missionary societies that distributed millions of Bibles and religious tracts. Through such avenues, evangelical religion offered women expanded spheres of influence. Finney adopted the tactics of Jacksonian-era politicians — publicity, argumentation, rallies, and speeches — to sell his cause. His object, he said, was to get Americans to "vote in the Lord Jesus Christ as the governor of the Universe."

The Temperance Movement and the Campaign for Moral Reform

The evangelical disposition — a combination of faith, energy, self-discipline, and righteousness — animated vigorous campaigns to eliminate alcohol abuse and eradicate sexual sin. Millions of Americans took the temperance pledge to abstain from strong drink, and thousands became involved in efforts to end prostitution.

Alcohol consumption had risen steadily in the decades up to 1830, when the average person over age thirteen annually consumed an astonishing nine gallons of hard liquor plus thirty gallons of hard cider, beer, and wine. All classes imbibed. A lively saloon culture fostered masculine camaraderie along with extensive alcohol consumption among laborers, while in elite homes, the after-dinner whiskey or sherry was commonplace. Colleges before 1820 routinely served students a pint of ale with meals, and the military included rum in the daily ration.

Organized opposition to drinking first surfaced in the 1810s among health and religious reformers. In 1826, Lyman Beecher, a Connecticut minister of an "awakened" church, founded the **American Temperance Society**, which warned that drinking led to poverty, idleness, crime, and family violence. Adopting the methods of evangelical ministers,

temperance lecturers traveled the country expounding the damage of drink. By 1833, some six thousand local affiliates of the American Temperance Society boasted more than a million members. Middle-class drinking began a steep decline. One powerful tool of persuasion was the temperance pledge, which many business owners began to require of employees.

In 1836, leaders of the temperance movement regrouped into a new society, the American Temperance Union, which demanded total abstinence from its adherents. The intensified war against alcohol moved beyond individual moral suasion into the realm of politics as reformers sought to deny taverns liquor licenses. By 1845, temperance advocates had put an impressive dent in alcohol consumption, which diminished to one-quarter of the per capita consumption of 1830. In 1851, Maine became the first state to ban entirely the manufacture and sale of all alcoholic beverages.

More controversial than temperance was a social movement called "moral reform," which first aimed at public morals in general but quickly narrowed to a campaign to eradicate sexual sin. In 1833, a group of Finneyite women started the New York Female Moral Reform Society. Its members insisted that uncontrolled male sexual expression posed a serious threat to society in general and to women in particular. The society's nationally distributed newspaper, the *Advocate of Moral Reform*, was the first major paper in the country that was written, edited, and typeset by women. In it, they condemned men who visited brothels or seduced innocent women. Within five years, more than four thousand auxiliary groups of women had sprung up, mostly in New England, New York, Pennsylvania, and Ohio.

In its analysis of the causes of licentiousness and its conviction that women had a duty to speak out about unspeakable things, the Moral Reform Society pushed the limits of what even the men in the evangelical movement could tolerate. Yet these women did not regard themselves as radicals. They were simply pursuing the logic of a gender system that defined home protection and morality as women's special sphere and a religious conviction that called for the eradication of sin.

Organizing against Slavery

More radical still was the movement in the 1830s to abolish the sin of slavery. The abolitionist movement had its roots in Great Britain in the late 1700s. (See "Beyond America's Borders," page 270.) Previously, the American Colonization Society, founded in 1817 by Maryland and Virginia planters, aimed to promote gradual individual emancipation of slaves followed by colonization in Africa. By the early 1820s, several thousand ex-slaves had been transported to Liberia on the West African coast. But not surprisingly, newly freed men and women were often not eager to emigrate; their African roots were three or more generations in the past. Colonization was too gradual (and expensive) to have much impact on American slavery.

Around 1830, northern challenges to slavery surfaced with increasing frequency and resolve, beginning in free black communities. In 1829, a Boston printer named **David Walker** published *An Appeal . . . to the Coloured Citizens of the World*, which condemned racism, invoked the egalitarian language of the Declaration of Independence, and hinted at racial violence if whites did not change their prejudiced ways. In 1830, at the inaugural National Negro Convention meeting in Philadelphia, forty blacks from nine states discussed the racism of American society and proposed emigration to Canada. In 1832 and 1833, a twenty-eight-year-old black woman named Maria Stewart delivered public lectures on slavery and racial prejudice to black audiences in Boston. Her lectures gained wider circulation when published in a national publication called the *Liberator*.

The *Liberator*, founded in 1831 in Boston, took antislavery agitation to new heights. Its founder and editor, an uncompromising twenty-six-year-old white printer named **William Lloyd Garrison**, advocated immediate abolition: "On this subject, I do not wish to think, or speak, or write, with moderation. No! No! Tell a man whose house is on fire to give a moderate alarm; tell him to moderately rescue his wife from the hands of the ravisher; tell the mother to gradually extricate her babe from the fire into which it has fallen;—but urge me not to use moderation in a cause like the present." In 1832, Garrison's supporters started the New England Anti-Slavery Society.

Similar groups were organized in Philadelphia and New York in 1833. Soon a dozen antislavery newspapers and scores of antislavery lecturers were spreading the word and inspiring the formation of new local societies, which numbered thirteen hundred by 1837. Entirely confined to the North, their membership totaled a quarter of a million men and women.

Many white northerners, even those who opposed slavery as a blot on the country's ideals, were not prepared to embrace the abolitionist call for emancipation. From 1834 to 1838, there were more than a hundred eruptions of serious mob violence against abolitionists and free blacks. In one incident, Illinois abolitionist editor Elijah Lovejoy was killed by a rioting crowd attempting to destroy his printing press.

Women played a prominent role in abolition, just as they did in moral reform and evangelical religion. They formed women's auxiliaries and held fairs to sell handmade crafts to support male lecturers in the field. They circulated antislavery petitions, presented to the U.S. Congress with tens of thousands of signatures. Up to 1835, women's petitions were framed as respectful memorials to Congress about the evils of slavery, but by mid-decade these petitions used urgent language to call for political action, instructing Congress to outlaw slavery in the District of Columbia (the only area under Congress's sole power).

Garrison particularly welcomed women's activity. When a southern plantation daughter named Angelina Grimké wrote to him about her personal repugnance for slavery, Garrison published the letter in the *Liberator* and brought her overnight fame. In 1837, Grimké and her older sister, Sarah, became antislavery lecturers targeting women, but their powerful eyewitness speeches attracted men as well, causing leaders of the Congregational Church in Massachusetts to warn all ministers not to let the Grimké sisters use their pulpits.

In the late 1830s, the cause of abolition divided the nation as no other issue did. Even among abolitionists, significant divisions emerged. **Angelina and Sarah Grimké**, radicalized by the public reaction to their speaking tour, began to write and speak about woman's rights. They were opposed by moderate abolitionists who were unwilling to mix the new and controversial issue of woman's rights with their first cause, the rights of blacks. A few radical men, such as Garrison, embraced woman's rights fully, working to get women leadership positions in the national antislavery group.

The many men and women active in reform movements in the 1830s found their initial inspiration in evangelical Protestantism's dual message: Salvation was open to all, and society needed to be perfected. Their activist mentality squared well with the interventionist tendencies of the party forming in opposition to Andrew Jackson's Democrats. Generally, reformers gravitated toward the Whig Party, the males as voters and the females as rallying supporters in the 1830s campaigns.

Q: **How did evangelical Protestantism contribute to the social reform movements of the 1830s?**

Transatlantic Abolition

Abolitionism blossomed in the United States in the 1830s, but its roots stretched back to the 1780s in both Britain and America. Developments on both sides of the Atlantic reinforced each other, leading to a transatlantic antislavery movement with shared ideas, strategies, activists, songs, and, eventually, victories.

An important source of antislavery sentiment derived from the Quaker religion, with its deep convictions regarding human equality. But moral sentiment alone does not make a political movement; something needs to galvanize it. English Quakers, customarily an apolitical group, awoke to sudden antislavery zeal in 1783, triggered in part by the loss of the imperial war for America and the debate it spurred about citizenship and slavery. The end of the war also brought a delegation of Philadelphia Quakers to meet with the London group, and an immediate result was the first petition, signed by 273 Quaker men in 1783, requesting that Parliament abolish the slave trade.

The English Quakers, now joined by a scattering of evangelical Anglicans and Methodists, formed the Society for Effecting the Abolition of the Slave Trade in 1787 and in just five years became a force to be reckoned with. They amassed thousands of signatures on petitions to Parliament. They organized a boycott of slave-produced sugar from the British West Indies—a boycott said to have involved 300,000 Britons. (Women, the traditional cooks of English families, were essential to the effort.) In 1789, the society scored a publicity coup by publishing two chilling illustrations of slave ships stacked with human cargo. These images, reprinted by the thousands, created a sensation. The society's Reverend Thomas Clarkson distributed them in Paris and in northern U.S. cities along with a book he wrote detailing the shipboard tortures inflicted on slaves by the use of shackles, handcuffs, whips, and branding irons. The society mobilized the resulting groundswell of antislavery sentiment to pressure Parliament once again. A sympathetic member of that body, the Methodist William Wilberforce, brought the anti–slave trade issue to a debate and vote in 1791; it lost.

Meanwhile, Pennsylvania Quakers in 1784 launched their own Society for Promoting the Abolition of Slavery, which non-Quakers Benjamin Franklin and Thomas Paine joined. It worked to end slavery in that state and petitioned the confederation congress—unsuccessfully—to put an end to American participation in the international slave trade. A French group, the Société des Amis des Noirs (Society of the Friends of Blacks), sprang up in Paris in 1788. All three groups, in close communication, agreed that ending the slave trade was the critical first step in abolishing slavery.

★ **International Abolitionists** George Thompson (middle), a leading figure in the British antislavery campaign, brought his lecture tour to the United States in 1834 and 1835. Although he had some success in converting audiences to abolition, some newspapers called him the "imported incendiary" and claimed that he had proposed that all slave owners' throats be cut, a charge he denied. William Lloyd Garrison (left) promoted Thompson's speaking tour in his antislavery newspaper, the *Liberator*. Wendell Phillips (right), a young Boston lawyer, heard Thompson speak and was inspired to make abolition his lifework. All three attended the World Anti-Slavery Convention in 1840. They met again in 1850 when Thompson returned to the United States, providing the occasion for this historic picture. Historical Library of Swarthmore College.

DESCRIPTION OF A SLAVE SHIP.

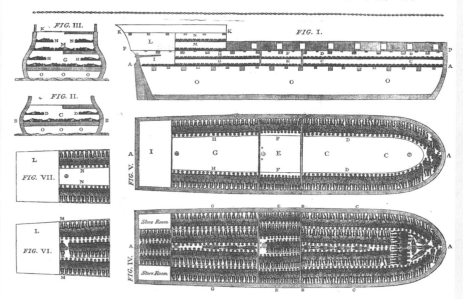

★ **Description of a Slave Ship** This powerful and often-reprinted image combines a precise technical rendering of a British ship (normally evoking pride in Britons) with the horrors of a crowded mass of dark human flesh. Peabody Essex Museum, Salem, Mass.

In lockstep with the British campaign, American Quakers petitioned the U.S. Congress in 1790 to end the slave trade immediately. Congress tabled the petition, pointing to the U.S. Constitution's clause that prohibited federal regulation of the trade before 1808. In response, a bolder appeal came the next day, calling for an end not only to the slave trade but to slavery itself. The petitioners suggested that the constitutional power to make laws "necessary and proper" to ensure the "general welfare" of the country could include "Liberty for all Negroes" as crucial to the country's general welfare. Congress debated slavery for the first time, and by a close vote (29 to 25) rejected the petition. It also set an important precedent by resolving that slavery was under the sole control of the states where it existed.

Over the next three decades, the antislavery cause in Britain and America moved forward in piecemeal fashion. In 1807, Parliament finally made it illegal for British ships to transport Africans into slavery. A year later, in 1808, the United States also banned the slave trade. The rapid natural increase of the African American population made passage of this law relatively easy. Older slave states along the coast supported the ban because it actually increased the value of their native-born slaves sold and transported west in the domestic slave trade.

British antislavery forces took a new tack in the 1820s, when women became active and pushed beyond the ban on trade. Quaker widow Elizabeth Heyrick authored *Immediate Not Gradual Abolition* in 1824, prompting the formation of scores of all-women societies. American women abolitionists soon followed suit. Abolitionists again bombarded Parliament with a massive petition campaign, and 30 percent of the 1.3 million signatures submitted in 1833 were women's. That year, Parliament finally passed the Abolition of Slavery Act, which freed all slave children under age six and gradually phased out slavery for everyone older during a four-year apprenticeship. The act also provided financial compensation for owners (£20 million), a key proviso made possible by the relatively small number of slave owners in the British slaveholding colonies.

The success of the British movement generated even greater transatlantic communication. In 1840, British and American abolitionists came together in full force at the World Anti-Slavery Convention in London. Among the 409 delegates to the convention were Reverend Clarkson, who presided; William Lloyd Garrison of Boston; and Philadelphia Quaker Lucretia Mott, a lifelong antislavery activist. Most of the delegates were from Britain and the West Indies, although 53 Americans and a half dozen French delegates also attended. Only about a quarter of the attendees were Quakers. Ten days of meetings produced speeches and reports on the worldwide practice of slavery, along with debates over various economic and religious strategies to end it. A key plan was to publicize throughout America the British movement's success in achieving emancipation. The delegates closed their meeting fully energized by their international congress, called to propose international solutions to an international problem.

Van Buren's One-Term Presidency

By the mid-1830s, a vibrant and tumultuous political culture occupied center stage of American life. Andrew Jackson's vice president and handpicked successor, the northerner Martin Van Buren, inherited a strong Democratic organization, but he faced doubts from slave-owning Jacksonians and outright opposition from increasingly combative Whigs. Abolitionist tactics had pushed slavery into the political debate, but Van Buren managed to defuse that conflict somewhat and even use it to his advantage. What could not be forestalled, however, was the collapse of the economic boom so celebrated by both Democrats and Whigs. The shattering panic of 1837, followed by another panic in 1839, brought the country its worst economic depression yet.

The Politics of Slavery Sophisticated party organization was the specialty of **Martin Van Buren**. Nicknamed "the Little Magician" for his consummate political skills, the New Yorker had built his career by pioneering many of the loyalty-enhancing techniques the Democrats used in the 1830s. First a senator and then governor, he became Jackson's secretary of state and then his running mate in 1832. His eight years in the volatile Jackson administration required the full measure of his political deftness as he sought repeatedly to save Jackson from both his enemies and his own obstinacy.

Jackson clearly favored Van Buren for the nomination in 1836, but starting in 1832, the major political parties had developed nominating conventions to choose their candidates. In 1835, Van Buren got the convention nod unanimously, to the dismay of his archrival, Calhoun, who then worked to discredit Van Buren among southern proslavery Democrats. Van Buren spent months assuring them that he was a "northern man with southern principles." This was not hard, since his Dutch family hailed from the Hudson River counties where New York slavery had once flourished, and his own family had owned at least one slave as late as the 1810s, although he chose not to broadcast that fact. (Slavery was only gradually phased out in New York starting in 1799; see chapter 8, page 188.) Calhoun's partisans whipped up controversy over Van Buren's support of suffrage for New York's propertied free blacks at the 1821 state convention on suffrage. Van

Buren's partisans countered by emphasizing that the Little Magician had argued that the mass of "poor, degraded blacks" were incapable of voting; he had merely favored retaining the existing stiff property qualifications for the handful of elite blacks who had always voted in New York, while simultaneously removing all such qualifications for white men.

Calhoun was able to stir up trouble for Van Buren because, in 1835, southerners were increasingly alarmed by the rise of northern antislavery sentiment. When, in late 1835, abolitionists prepared to circulate in the South a million pamphlets condemning slavery, a mailbag of their literature was hijacked at the post office in Charleston, South Carolina, and ceremoniously burned along with effigies of leading abolitionists. President Jackson condemned the theft but issued approval for individual postmasters to exercise their own judgment about whether to allow incendiary materials to reach their destination. Abolitionists saw this as censorship of the mail.

The petitioning tactics of abolitionists escalated sectional tensions. As petitions demanding Congress to "purify" the District of Columbia by outlawing slavery grew into the hundreds, proslavery congressmen sought to short-circuit the appeals by passing a "gag rule" in 1836. The gag rule prohibited entering the documents into the public record on the grounds that what the abolitionists prayed for was unconstitutional and, further, an assault on the rights of white southerners, as one South Carolina representative put it.

Van Buren shrewdly seized on both mail censorship and the gag rule to express his prosouthern sympathies. Abolitionists were "fanatics," he repeatedly claimed, possibly under the influence of "foreign agents" (British abolitionists). He dismissed the issue of abolition in the District of Columbia as "inexpedient" and promised that if he was elected president, he would not allow any interference in southern "domestic institutions."

Elections and Panics Although the elections of 1824, 1828, and 1832 clearly bore the stamp of Jackson's personality, by 1836 the party apparatus was sufficiently developed to give Van Buren, a backroom politician, a shot at the presidency. Local and state committees existed throughout the country. Democratic candidates ran in every state election, succeeding even in the old Federalist stronghold of New England. More than four hundred newspapers were Democratic partisans.

The Whigs had also built state-level organizations and newspaper loyalty. They had no top contender with nationwide support, so three regional candidates opposed Van Buren. Senator Daniel Webster of Massachusetts could deliver New England, home to reformers, merchants, and manufacturers; Senator Hugh Lawson White of Tennessee attracted proslavery voters still suspicious of the northern Magician; and the aging General William Henry Harrison, now residing in Ohio and memorable for his Indian war heroics in 1811, pulled in the western anti-Indian vote. Not one of the three candidates had the ability to win the presidency, but together they came close to denying Van Buren a majority vote. Van Burenites called the three-Whig strategy a deliberate plot to derail the election and move it to the House of Representatives.

In the end, Van Buren won by 170 electoral votes, while the other three received a total of 113. The popular vote told a somewhat different story. Van Buren's narrow majorities, where he won, were far below those Jackson had commanded. Although Van Buren had pulled together a national Democratic Party with wins in both the North and the South, he had done it at the cost of committing northern Democrats to the proslavery agenda. And running three candidates had maximized the Whigs' success by drawing Whigs into office at the state level.

When Van Buren took office in March 1837, the financial markets were already quaking; by April, the country was plunged into crisis. The causes of the **panic of 1837** were multiple and far-ranging. Bad harvests in Europe and a large trade imbalance between Britain and the United States caused the Bank of England to start calling in loans to American merchants. Failures in various crop markets and a 30 percent downturn in international cotton prices fed the growing disaster. Cotton merchants in the South could no longer meet their obligations to New York creditors, whose firms began to fail—ninety-eight of them in March and April 1837 alone. Frightened citizens thronged the banks to try to get their money out, and businesses rushed to liquefy their remaining assets to pay off debts. Prices of stocks, bonds,

The Panic of 1837 A sad family with an unemployed father faces sudden privation in this cartoon showing the consequences of the panic of 1837. The wife and children complain of hunger, the house is nearly stripped bare, and rent collectors loom in the doorway. Faint pictures on the wall show Andrew Jackson and Martin Van Buren presiding over the economic devastation of the family. The only support system for the unemployed in 1837 was the local almshouse, where families were split up and living conditions were harsh. Library of Congress.

and real estate fell 30 to 40 percent. The familiar events of the panic of 1819 unfolded again, with terrifying rapidity, and the credit market tumbled like a house of cards.

Some Whig leaders were certain that Jackson's antibank and hard-money policies were responsible for the ruin. New Yorker Philip Hone, a wealthy Whig, called the Jackson administration "the most disastrous in the annals of the country" for its "wicked interference" in banking and monetary matters. Others framed the devastation as retribution for an immoral frenzy of speculation that had gripped the nation. A religious periodical in Boston hoped that Americans would now moderate their greed: "We were getting to think that there was no end to the wealth, and could be no check to the progress of our country; that economy was not needed, that prudence was weakness." In this view, the panic was a wakeup call, a blessing in disguise. Others identified the competitive, profit-maximizing capitalist system as the cause and looked to Britain and France for new socialist ideas calling for the common ownership of the means of production. American socialists, though few in number, were vocal and imaginative, and in the early 1840s, several thousand developed utopian alternative communities (see chapter 12, page 300).

The panic of 1837 subsided by 1838, but in 1839, another run on the banks and ripples of business failures deflated the economy, creating a second panic. President Van Buren called a special session of Congress to consider creating an independent treasury system to perform some of the functions of the defunct Bank of the United States. Such a system, funded by government deposits, would deal only in hard money and would exert a powerful moderating influence on inflation and the credit market. But Van Buren encountered strong resistance in Congress, even among Democrats. The treasury system finally won approval in 1840, but by then Van Buren's chances of winning a second term in office were virtually nil.

In 1840, the Whigs settled on **William Henry Harrison** to oppose Van Buren. The campaign drew on voter involvement as no presidential campaign ever had. The Whigs borrowed tricks from the Democrats: Harrison was touted as a common man born in a log cabin (in reality, he was born on a Virginia plantation), and raucous campaign parades featured toy log cabins held aloft. His Indian-fighting days, now thirty years behind him, were played up to give him a Jacksonian aura. Whigs staged

festive rallies around the country, drumming up mass appeal with candlelight parades and song shows, and women participated in rallies as never before. Some 78 percent of eligible voters cast ballots — the highest percentage ever in American history. Harrison took 53 percent of the popular vote and won a resounding 234 electoral college votes to Van Buren's 60. A Democratic editor lamented, "We have taught them how to conquer us!"

Q: **How did slavery figure as a campaign issue in the election of 1836?**

Conclusion: The Age of Jackson or the Era of Reform?

Harrison's election closed a decade that had brought the common man and democracy to the forefront of American politics. Economic transformations loom large in explaining the fast-paced changes of the 1830s. Transportation advances put goods and people in circulation, augmenting urban growth and helping to create a national culture, and water-powered manufacturing began to change the face of wage labor. Trade and banking mushroomed, and western land once occupied by Indians was auctioned off in a landslide of sales. Two periods of economic downturn — including the panic of 1819 and the panics of 1837 and 1839 — offered sobering lessons about speculative fever.

Andrew Jackson symbolized this age of opportunity for many. His fame as an aggressive general, Indian fighter, champion of the common man, and defender of slavery attracted growing numbers of voters to the emergent Democratic Party, which championed personal liberty, free competition, and egalitarian opportunity for all white men.

Jackson's constituency was challenged by a small but vocal segment of the population troubled by serious moral problems that Jacksonians preferred to ignore. Reformers drew sustenance from the message of the Second Great Awakening: that all men and women were free to choose salvation and that personal and societal sins could be overcome. Reformers targeted personal vices (illicit sex and intemperance) and social problems (prostitution, poverty, and slavery), and joined forces with evangelicals and wealthy lawyers and merchants (North and South) who appreciated a national bank and protective tariffs. The Whig Party was the party of activist moralism and state-sponsored entrepreneurship. Whig voters were, of course, male, but thousands of reform-minded women broke new ground by signing political petitions on the issues of Indian removal and slavery.

National politics in the 1830s were more divisive than at any time since the 1790s. The new party system of Democrats and Whigs reached far deeper into the electorate than had the Federalists and Republicans. Stagecoaches and steamboats carried newspapers from the cities to the backwoods, politicizing voters and creating party loyalty. Politics acquired immediacy and excitement, causing nearly four out of five white men to cast ballots in 1840.

High rates of voter participation would continue into the 1840s and 1850s. Unprecedented urban growth, westward expansion, and early industrialism marked those decades, sustaining the Democrat-Whig split in the electorate. But critiques of slavery, concerns for free labor, and an emerging protest against women's second-class citizenship complicated the political scene of the 1840s, leading to third-party political movements. One of these third parties, called the Republican Party, would achieve dominance in 1860 with the election of an Illinois lawyer, Abraham Lincoln, to the presidency.

Reviewing the Chapter

★ KEY TERMS

Explain each term's significance

WHO

Andrew Jackson (p. 251)

Henry Clay (p. 258)

John C. Calhoun (p. 259)

Charles Grandison Finney (p. 267)

David Walker (p. 269)

William Lloyd Garrison (p. 269)

Angelina and Sarah Grimké (p. 269)

Martin Van Buren (p. 272)

William Henry Harrison (p. 274)

WHAT

Erie Canal (p. 254)

Lowell mills (p. 255)

second Bank of the United States (p. 257)

panic of 1819 (p. 257)

Whigs (p. 259)

Democrats (p. 259)

Indian Removal Act of 1830 (p. 261)

Trail of Tears (p. 262)

nullification (p. 263)

Second Great Awakening (p. 264)

separate spheres (p. 264)

American Temperance Society (p. 268)

panic of 1837 (p. 273)

★ REVIEW QUESTIONS Q:

Use key terms and dates to support your answer

1. Why did the United States experience a market revolution after 1815? (pp. 252–58)

2. Why did Andrew Jackson defeat John Quincy Adams so dramatically in the 1828 election? (pp. 258–60)

3. Why did Jackson promote Indian removal? (pp. 260–64)

4. How did evangelical Protestantism contribute to the social reform movements of the 1830s? (pp. 264–69)

5. How did slavery figure as a campaign issue in the election of 1836? (pp. 272–74)

★ MAKING CONNECTIONS

Draw on key terms, timeline, and review questions

1. Describe the market revolution that began in the 1810s. How did it affect Americans' work and domestic lives? In your answer, be sure to consider how gender contributed to these developments.

2. Andrew Jackson's presidency coincided with important changes in American politics. Discuss how Jackson benefited from, and contributed to, the vibrant political culture of the 1830s. Cite specific national developments in your answer.

3. Describe Andrew Jackson's response to the "Indian problem" during his presidency. How did his policies revise or continue earlier federal policies toward Native Americans? How did Native Americans respond to Jackson's actions?

4. While a volatile economy buffeted the United States in the 1830s, some Americans looked to reform the nation. Discuss the objectives and strategies of two reform movements. What was the relationship of these reform movements to larger political and economic trends of the 1830s?

FOR PRACTICE QUIZZES AND OTHER STUDY TOOLS, see the Online Study Guide at **bedfordstmartins.com/roarkcompact**.

★ SUGGESTED READINGS

Edward J. Balleisen, *Navigating Failure: Bankruptcy and Commercial Society in Antebellum America* (2001). An absorbing study of the culture of American capitalism showing how 1840s personal bankruptcy laws developed in the wake of the antebellum economic panics.

Bruce Dorsey, *Reforming Men and Women: Gender in the Antebellum City* (2002). An intricate gender analysis of the benevolent reformers who took on problems of poverty, drink, slavery, and immigration in antebellum Philadelphia.

Richard S. Newman, *The Transformation of American Abolitionism: Fighting Slavery in the Early Republic* (2002). A study demonstrating the importance of black abolitionists in radicalizing the U.S. antislavery movement in the 1830s.

Theda Perdue, *Cherokee Women: Gender and Culture Change, 1700–1835* (1998). An innovative ethnohistorical account of the Cherokee gender system showing how Cherokee women resisted acculturation to white society and maintained cultural traditions.

Carol Sheriff, *The Artificial River: The Erie Canal and the Paradox of Progress, 1817–1862* (1996). An illuminating study of central antebellum ideas about progress, technology, the landscape, and the market revolution, as refracted in the gripping story of the Erie Canal.

Sean Wilentz, *The Rise of American Democracy: Jefferson to Lincoln* (2005). A prize-winning synthesis of six decades of political history, with the history of democracy as the main thread braided through it.

FOR MORE BOOKS ABOUT TOPICS IN THIS CHAPTER, see the Online Bibliography at **bedfordstmartins.com/roarkcompact**.

FOR ADDITIONAL FIRSTHAND ACCOUNTS OF THIS PERIOD, see Chapter 11 in Michael Johnson, ed., *Reading the American Past*, Fourth Edition.

FOR WEB SITES, IMAGES, AND DOCUMENTS RELATED TO TOPICS AND PLACES IN THIS CHAPTER, visit Make History at **bedfordstmartins.com/roarkcompact**.

★ TIMELINE

1807	• Robert Fulton's *Clermont* sets off steamboat craze.
1816	• Second Bank of the United States chartered.
1817	• American Colonization Society founded.
1818	• National Road links Baltimore to western Virginia.
1819	• Economic panic.
1821	• Mill town of Lowell, Massachusetts, founded.
1825	• Erie Canal completed in New York.
1826	• American Temperance Society founded. • Schuylkill Canal completed in Pennsylvania.
1828	• Congress passes Tariff of Abominations. • Democrat Andrew Jackson elected president.
1829	• David Walker's *Appeal . . . to the Coloured Citizens of the World* published. • Baltimore and Ohio Railroad begun.
1830	• Indian Removal Act. • Women's petitions for Indian rights begin.
1830–1831	• Charles Grandison Finney preaches in Rochester, New York.
1831	• William Lloyd Garrison starts *Liberator*.
1832	• Massacre of Sauk and Fox Indians led by Chief Black Hawk. • *Worcester v. Georgia*. • Jackson vetoes charter renewal of Bank of the United States. • New England Anti-Slavery Society founded.
1833	• Nullification of federal tariffs declared in South Carolina. • New York and Philadelphia antislavery societies founded. • New York Female Moral Reform Society founded.
1834	• Female mill workers strike in Lowell, Massachusetts, and again in 1836.
1836	• Democrat Martin Van Buren elected president. • American Temperance Union founded.
1837	• Economic panic.
1838	• Trail of Tears: Cherokees forced to relocate west.
1839	• Economic panic.
1840	• Whig William Henry Harrison elected president.

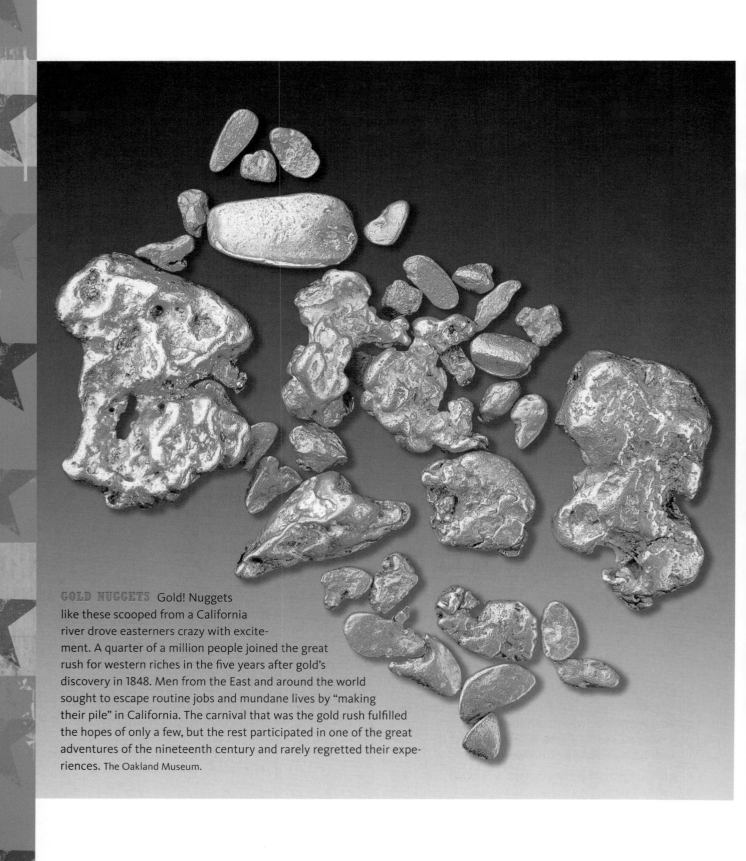

GOLD NUGGETS Gold! Nuggets like these scooped from a California river drove easterners crazy with excitement. A quarter of a million people joined the great rush for western riches in the five years after gold's discovery in 1848. Men from the East and around the world sought to escape routine jobs and mundane lives by "making their pile" in California. The carnival that was the gold rush fulfilled the hopes of only a few, but the rest participated in one of the great adventures of the nineteenth century and rarely regretted their experiences. The Oakland Museum.

The New West and Free North

1840–1860

EARLY IN NOVEMBER 1842, Abraham Lincoln and his new wife, Mary, moved into their first home in Springfield, Illinois, a rented room measuring eight by fourteen feet on the second floor of the Globe Tavern. The small, noisy room above the tavern was the nicest place that Abraham Lincoln had ever lived; it was the worst place that Mary Todd Lincoln had ever inhabited. She had grown up in Lexington, Kentucky, attended by slaves in the elegant home of her father, a prosperous merchant, banker, and politician. Less than twenty years after their marriage, in March 1861, the Lincolns moved into what would prove to be their last home, the presidential mansion in Washington, D.C.

Abraham Lincoln climbed from the Globe Tavern to the White House by relentless work, unslaked ambition, and immense talent—traits he had honed since boyhood. Lincoln and many others celebrated his rise from humble origins as an example of the opportunities that beckoned in the free-labor economy of the North and West. They attributed his spectacular ascent to his individual qualities and tended to ignore the help he received from Mary and many others.

Born in a Kentucky log cabin in 1809, Lincoln grew up on small, struggling farms as his family migrated west. His father, Thomas, left Virginia, where he had been born, and settled in Kentucky. Thomas Lincoln never learned to read and, as his son recalled, "never did more in the way of writing than to bunglingly sign his own name." Lincoln's mother, Nancy, could neither read nor write. In December 1816, Thomas Lincoln moved his young family from Kentucky to the Indiana wilderness. On the Indiana farmstead, Abraham learned the arts of agriculture practiced by families throughout the nation. Although only eight years old, he "had an axe put into his hands at once" and used it "almost constantly" for the next fifteen years, as he recalled later. When he could be spared from work, the boy attended school, less than a year in all. "There was absolutely nothing to excite ambition for education," Lincoln recollected. In contrast, Mary Todd received ten years of schooling in Lexington's best private academies for young women.

In 1830, Thomas Lincoln decided to move farther west. The Lincolns hitched up the family oxen and headed to central Illinois. The next spring,

Previewing the Chapter

Economic and Industrial Evolution 280
Q: *Why did the United States become a leading industrial power in the nineteenth century?*

Free Labor: Promise and Reality 284
Q: *How did the free-labor ideal account for economic inequality?*

The Westward Movement 287
Q: *Why did westward migration expand dramatically in the mid-nineteenth century?*

Expansion and the Mexican-American War 293
Q: *Why was the annexation of Texas such a controversial policy?*

Reforming Self and Society 300
Q: *Why were women especially prominent in many nineteenth-century reform efforts?*

Conclusion: Free Labor, Free Men 303

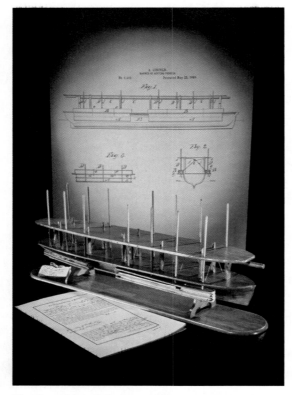

Abraham Lincoln's Patent In 1849, lawyer Abraham Lincoln applied for a patent based on this model illustrating his idea of using inflatable rubberized bags (the long white objects under the lower deck) to lift riverboats over stretches of shallow water. Lincoln knew firsthand the difficulties of transporting goods on the nation's rivers, having rafted two loads of farm products all the way from the Midwest to New Orleans as a young man. His desire to solve practical problems grew out of his firm belief "that heads and hands should cooperate as friends," a key ingredient of the widespread free-labor ideology. Lincoln received his patent, becoming the only patent holder ever to serve as president. Although his patented idea never caught on, tens of thousands of other Americans sought to bring together knowledge and ingenuity in their quest for progress and to patent their schemes to profit from their inventiveness. Smithsonian Institution, National Museum of American History.

Thomas moved yet again, but this time Abraham stayed behind and set out on his own, a "friend-less, uneducated, penniless boy," as he described himself.

By dogged striving, Abraham Lincoln gained an education and the respect of his Illinois neighbors, although a steady income eluded him for years. Mary Todd had many suitors, including Stephen A. Douglas, Lincoln's eventual political rival. After she married Lincoln, she said, "Intellectually my husband towers above Douglas . . . [and he] has no equal in the United States." The newlyweds received help from Mary's father, including eighty acres of land and a yearly allowance of about $1,100 for six years that helped them move out of their room above the Globe Tavern and into their own home. Abraham eventually built a thriving law practice in Springfield, Illinois, and served in the state legislature and then in Congress. Mary helped him in many ways, rearing their sons, tending their household, and integrating him into her wealthy and influential extended family in Illinois and Kentucky. Mary also shared Abraham's keen interest in politics and ambition for power. With Mary's support, Abraham's striving ultimately propelled them into the White House, where he became the first president born west of the Appalachian Mountains.

Like Lincoln, millions of Americans believed they could make something of themselves, whatever their origins, so long as they were willing to work. Individuals who refused to work — who were lazy, undisciplined, or foolish — had only themselves to blame if they failed. Work was a prerequisite for success, not a guarantee. This emphasis on work highlighted the individual efforts of men and tended to slight the many crucial contributions of women, family members, neighbors, and friends to the successes of men like Lincoln. In addition, the rewards of work were skewed toward white men and away from women and free African Americans. Nonetheless, the promise of rewards from hard work spurred efforts that shaped the contours of America, pushing the boundaries of the nation ever westward to the Pacific Ocean. The nation's economic, political, and geographic expansion raised anew the question of whether slavery should also move west, the question that Lincoln and other Americans confronted again and again following the Mexican-American War, yet another outgrowth of the nation's ceaseless westward movement. ★

Economic and Industrial Evolution

During the 1840s and 1850s, Americans experienced a profound economic transformation that had been under way since the start of the nineteenth century. Since 1800, the total output of the U.S. economy had multiplied twelvefold. Four fundamental changes in American society fueled this remarkable economic growth.

First, millions of Americans — Abraham Lincoln among them — moved from farms to towns and cities. Even so, 80 percent of the nation's 31 million people remained in rural areas in 1860. Second, the number of Americans who worked in factories, mainly in urban centers, grew to about 20 percent of the labor force by 1860. This trend contributed to the nation's economic growth because, in general, factory workers produced twice as much (per unit of labor) as agricultural workers.

Third, a shift from water power to steam as a source of energy raised productivity, especially in factories and transportation. In the 1840s, mines in Pennsylvania, Ohio, and elsewhere began to excavate millions of tons of coal for industrial fuel, accelerating the shift to steam power. Between 1840 and 1860, coal production multiplied eightfold, cutting prices in half and permitting coal-fired steam engines to power ever more factories, railroads, and ships. Nonetheless, by 1860, coal supplied less than a fifth of the nation's energy consumption, and the muscles of people and work animals still provided thirty times more energy for manufacturing than did steam.

A fourth fundamental change propelling America's economic development was the rise in agricultural productivity, which nearly doubled during Lincoln's lifetime. More than any other single factor, agricultural productivity spurred the nation's economic growth. While cities, factories, and steam engines multiplied throughout the nation—particularly in the North and West—the roots of the United States' economic growth lay in agriculture.

Historians often refer to this cascade of changes in farms, cities, factories, power, and transportation as an industrial revolution. However, these changes did not cause an abrupt discontinuity in America's economy or society. The United States remained overwhelmingly agricultural. Old methods of production continued alongside the new. The changes in the American economy during the 1840s and 1850s might better be termed "industrial evolution."

Agriculture and Land Policy As farmers pushed westward in a quest for cheap land, they encountered the Midwest's comparatively treeless prairie, where they could spend less time with an ax and more time with a plow and hoe. Rich prairie soils yielded bumper crops, enticing farmers such as the Lincolns to migrate to the Midwest by the tens of thousands between 1830 and 1860. The populations of Indiana, Illinois, Michigan, Wisconsin, and Iowa exploded tenfold between 1830 and 1860, four times faster than the growth of the nation as a whole.

Laborsaving improvements in farm implements also hiked agricultural productivity. In 1837, John Deere patented a strong, smooth steel plow that sliced through prairie soil so cleanly that farmers called it the "singing plow." Deere's company became the

leading plow manufacturer in the Midwest, turning out more than ten thousand plows a year by the late 1850s. Energy for plowing still came from human and animal muscles, but better plows permitted farmers to break more ground and plant more crops.

Improvements in wheat harvesting also multiplied farmers' productivity. In 1850, most farmers harvested wheat by hand, cutting two or three acres a day with backbreaking labor. In the 1840s, Cyrus McCormick and others experimented with designs for **mechanical reapers**, and by the 1850s, a McCormick reaper that cost between $100 and $150 allowed a farmer to harvest twelve acres a day. Most continued to cut their grain by hand, but improved reapers and plows, usually powered by horses or oxen, allowed farmers to cultivate more land, doubling the corn and wheat harvests between 1840 and 1860.

Federal land policy made possible the agricultural productivity that fueled the nation's economy. Up to 1860, the United States continued to be land-rich and labor-poor. Territorial acquisitions made the nation a great deal richer in land, adding more than a billion acres with the Louisiana Purchase (see chapter 10) and the annexation of Florida, Oregon, and vast territories following the Mexican-American War (see page 293). The federal government made most of this land available for purchase to attract settlers and to generate revenue. Wily speculators found ways to claim large tracts of the most desirable plots and sell them to settlers at a generous markup. But millions of ordinary farmers bought federal land for just $1.25 an acre, or $50 for a forty-acre farm that could support a family. Millions of other farmers squatted on unclaimed federal land, carved out farms, and, if they still lacked funds to buy the land after a few years, usually moved farther west to squat on federal land elsewhere. By making land available to millions of Americans on relatively easy terms, the federal government achieved the goal of attracting settlers to the new territories in the West, which in due course joined the Union as new states. Above all, federal land policy facilitated the increase in agricultural productivity that underlay the nation's impressive economic growth.

Manufacturing and Mechanization Changes in manufacturing arose from the nation's land-rich, labor-poor economy. Britain and other European countries had land-poor, labor-rich economies; there, meager opportunities in agriculture kept factory laborers plentiful and wages low. In the United States, western expansion and government land policies buoyed agriculture, keeping millions of people on the farm and thereby limiting the supply of workers for manufacturing and elevating wages. Because of this relative shortage of workers, manufacturers searched constantly for ways to save labor.

Mechanization allowed manufacturers to produce more with less labor. The practice of manufacturing and then assembling interchangeable parts spread from gun making to other industries and became known as the **American system**. Standardized parts produced by machine allowed manufacturers to employ unskilled workers who were much cheaper and more readily available than highly trained craftsmen. A visitor to a Springfield, Massachusetts, gun factory in 1842 noted, for example, that standardized parts made the trained gunsmith's "skill of the eye and the hand, [previously] acquired by practice alone . . . no longer indispensable." Even in heavily mechanized industries, factories remained fairly small; few had more than twenty or thirty employees.

Manufacturing and agriculture meshed into a dynamic national economy. New England led the nation in manufacturing, shipping goods such as guns, clocks, plows, and axes west and south, while southern and western states sent commodities such as wheat, pork, whiskey, tobacco, and cotton north and east. Manufacturers specialized in producing for the gigantic domestic market rather than for export. British goods dominated the international market and, on the whole, were cheaper and better than American-made products. U.S.

manufacturers supported tariffs to minimize British competition, but their best protection from British competitors was to strive harder to please their American customers, most of them farmers. The burgeoning national economy was further fueled by the growth of the railroads, which served to link farmers and factories in new ways.

Railroads: Breaking the Bonds of Nature

Railroads seemed to break the bonds of nature. When canals and rivers froze in winter or became impassable during summer droughts, trains steamed ahead. When becalmed sailing ships went nowhere, locomotives kept on chugging, averaging over twenty miles an hour during the 1850s. Above all, railroads gave cities not blessed with canals or navigable rivers a way to compete for rural trade.

By 1850, trains steamed along 9,000 miles of track, almost two-thirds of it in New England and the Middle Atlantic states. By 1860, several railroads spanned the Mississippi River, connecting frontier farmers to the nation's 30,000 miles of track, approximately as much as in all of the rest of the world combined (Map 12.1). The massive expansion of American railroads helped catapult the nation into position as the world's second-greatest industrial power, after Great Britain.

In addition to speeding transportation, railroads propelled the growth of other industries, such as iron and communications. Iron production

THE PROMISE OF TECHNOLOGY

The Telegraph Samuel F. B. Morse is credited with inventing the telegraph because of his patent in June 1840, but, as one contemporary observed, Morse's talent consisted of "combining and applying the discoveries of others in the invention of a particular instrument and process for telegraphic purposes." Morse sent the first message in 1844 on this telegraph using a code he devised that represented each letter and number with dots and dashes. With a series of taps on a telegraph key, operators sent short and long pulses of electricity. By 1846, most eastern cities were connected by telegraph. By 1850, of the states east of the Mississippi River, only Florida remained without it. More than fifty thousand miles of wires webbed the nation by 1861, when the telegraph reached California. The telegraph obliterated distance, and cheap, efficient, and fast communication changed American businesses, newspapers, government, and everyday life. The telegraph made it possible to synchronize clocks, which in turn allowed railroads to run safely according to precise schedules. Newspapers could gather information from around the country and have it in the headlines within hours. On a personal level, families across the continent could communicate more quickly than letter writing allowed. The telegraph met the needs of the vigorous, sprawling nation.
Division of Political History, Smithsonian Institution, Washington, D.C.

MAP 12.1 Railroads in 1860

Railroads were a crucial component of the revolutions in transportation and communications that transformed nineteenth-century America. The railroad system reflected the differences in the economies of the North and South.

grew five times faster than the population during the decades up to 1860, in part to meet railroads' demand. Railroads also stimulated the fledgling telegraph industry. In 1844, **Samuel F. B. Morse** persuasively demonstrated the potential of his telegraph by transmitting a series of dots and dashes that instantly conveyed an electronic message along forty miles of wire strung between Washington, D.C., and Baltimore. By 1861, more than fifty thousand miles of wire stretched across the continent to the Pacific Ocean, often alongside railroad tracks, making trains safer and more efficient and accelerating communications of all sorts.

Private corporations built and owned almost all railroads, in contrast to government ownership of railroads common in other industrial nations. But privately owned American railroads received massive government aid, especially federal land grants. Up to 1850, the federal government had granted a total of seven million acres of federal land to various

turnpike, highway, and canal projects. In 1850, Congress approved a precedent-setting grant to railroads of six square miles of federal land for each mile of track laid. By 1860, Congress had granted railroads more than twenty million acres of federal land, thereby underwriting construction costs and promoting the expansion of the rail network, the settlement of federal land, and the integration of the domestic market.

The railroad boom of the 1850s signaled the growing industrial might of the American economy. But railroads, like other industries, succeeded because they served both farms and cities. Despite this growth, in 1860, most Americans were far more familiar with horses than with locomotives.

The economy of the 1840s and 1850s linked an expanding, westward-moving population in farms and cities with muscles, animals, machines, steam, and railroads. Abraham Lincoln cut trees, planted corn, and split rails as a young man before he moved to Springfield, Illinois, and became a successful attorney

Westward the Star of Empire Takes Its Way—near Council Bluffs, Iowa This painting by Andrew Melrose depicts the mid-nineteenth-century landscape of agricultural and technological progress. On the right, the dark forest is boldly transformed by railroad tracks that interrupt the irregularity of nature with a level roadbed and straight iron rails. A hard-charging locomotive illuminates the path of progress and bears down on a group of innocent deer frightened by the unstoppable industrial power so alien to their familiar natural world. On the left, a frontier homestead, with grazing milk cows, a laundry line, and smoke rising from the chimney, is linked to the urban and industrial world beyond by the cinder-spouting locomotive that passes along the edge of freshly cleared land. Museum of the American West, Autry National Center, 92.147.1.

FOR MORE HELP ANALYZING THIS IMAGE, see the visual activity for this chapter in the Online Study Guide at bedfordstmartins.com/roarkcompact.

who defended, among others, railroad corporations. His mobility—westward, from farm to city, from manual to mental labor, and upward—illustrated the direction of economic change and the opportunities that beckoned enterprising individuals.

Q: **Why did the United States become a leading industrial power in the nineteenth century?**

Free Labor: Promise and Reality

The nation's impressive economic performance did not reward all Americans equally. Native-born white men tended to do better than immigrants. With few exceptions, women were excluded from opportunities open to men. Tens of thousands of women worked as seamstresses, laundresses, domestic servants, factory hands, and teachers but had little opportunity to aspire to higher-paying jobs. In the North and West, slavery was slowly eliminated in the half century after the American Revolution, but most free African Americans were relegated to dead-end jobs as laborers and servants. Discrimination against immigrants, women, and free blacks did not trouble most white men. With certain notable exceptions, they considered it proper and just.

The Free-Labor Ideal: Freedom plus Labor
During the 1840s and 1850s, leaders throughout the North and West emphasized a set of ideas that seemed to explain why the changes under way in their society benefited some people more than others. They referred again and again to the advantages of what they termed *free labor*. (The word *free* referred to laborers who were not slaves. It did not mean laborers who worked for nothing.) By the 1850s, free-labor ideas described a social and economic ideal that accounted for both the successes and the shortcomings of the economy and society taking shape in the North and West.

Spokesmen for the **free-labor ideal** celebrated hard work, self-reliance, and independence. They proclaimed that the door to success was open not just to those who inherited wealth or status but also to self-made men such as Abraham Lincoln. Free labor, Lincoln argued, was "the just and generous, and prosperous system, which opens the way for all—gives hope to all, and energy, and progress, and improvement of condition to all." Free labor permitted farmers and artisans to enjoy the products of their own labor, and it also benefited wageworkers. "The prudent, penniless beginner in the world," Lincoln asserted, "labors for wages awhile, saves a surplus with which to buy tools or land, for himself; then labors on his own account another while, and at length hires another new beginner to help him."

The free-labor ideal affirmed an egalitarian vision of human potential. Lincoln and other spokesmen stressed the importance of universal education to permit "heads and hands [to] cooperate as friends." (See "Global Comparison.") By 1860, many cities and towns had public schools that boasted that up to 80 percent of children ages seven to thirteen attended school at least for a few weeks each year. In rural areas, where the labor of children was more difficult to spare, schools typically enrolled no more than half the school-age children. Lessons included more than arithmetic, penmanship, and a smattering of other subjects. Textbooks and teachers—most of whom were young women—drummed into students the lessons of the free-labor system: self-reliance, discipline, and, above all else, hard work. "Remember that all the ignorance, degradation, and misery in the world is the result of indolence and vice," one textbook intoned. In school and out, free-labor ideology emphasized labor as much as freedom.

Economic Inequality The free-labor ideal made sense to many Americans, especially in the North and West, because it seemed to describe their own experiences. Lincoln frequently referred to his humble beginnings as a hired laborer and implicitly invited his listeners to consider how far he had come. In 1860, his wealth of $17,000 easily placed him in the top 5 percent of the population. The opportunities presented by the expanding economy made a few men much, much richer. Most Americans, however, measured success in more modest terms. The average wealth of adult white men in the North in 1860 barely topped $2,000. Nearly half of American men had no wealth at all; about 60 percent owned no land. Because property possessed by married women was normally considered to belong to their husbands, women had less wealth than men. Free African Americans had still

less; 90 percent of them were propertyless.

Free-labor spokesmen considered these economic inequalities a natural outgrowth of freedom—the inevitable result of some individuals being more able and willing to work and luckier. These inequalities also demonstrate the gap between the promise and the performance of the free-labor ideal. Economic growth permitted many men to move from being landless squatters to landowning farmers and from being hired laborers to independent, self-employed producers. But many more Americans remained behind, landless and working for wages. Even those who realized their aspirations often had a precarious hold on their independence. Bad debts, market volatility, crop

> Free labor, Abraham Lincoln argued, was "the just and generous, and prosperous system, which opens the way for all."

Miner with Pick, Pan, and Shovel This young man exhibits the spirit of individual effort that was the foundation of free-labor ideals. Posing with a pick and shovel to loosen gold-bearing deposits and a pan to wash away debris, the man appears determined to succeed as a miner by his own muscles and sweat. Hard work with these tools, the picture suggests, promised rewards and maybe riches. Collection of Matthew Isenburg.

Nineteenth-Century School Enrollment and Literacy Rates

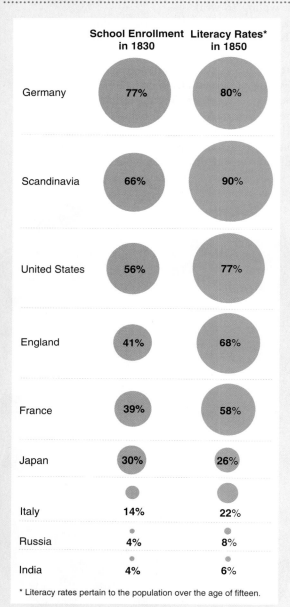

	School Enrollment in 1830	Literacy Rates* in 1850
Germany	77%	80%
Scandinavia	66%	90%
United States	56%	77%
England	41%	68%
France	39%	58%
Japan	30%	26%
Italy	14%	22%
Russia	4%	8%
India	4%	6%

* Literacy rates pertain to the population over the age of fifteen.

In the first half of the nineteenth century, school enrollment and literacy rates in northern and western Europe and the United States were high compared to those in the rest of the world. U.S. figures would be even higher but for the South, where fewer than 10 percent of black slaves were literate and whites were less likely to attend school than in the North. The ability to read and write facilitates communication, business transactions, acquisition of skills, and perhaps even greater openness to change, all building blocks of rapid economic growth. But mass literacy has not always been a prerequisite for economic development. When England underwent industrialization between 1780 and 1830, fewer than half of the nation's children attended school. By 1850, England was the world's greatest industrial power, but where did it rank in literacy? Literacy levels may actually have fallen in Lancashire, a region of England that experienced great industrial growth, as children went to work in factories rather than attend school.

failure, sickness, or death could quickly eliminate a family's gains.

Seeking out new opportunities in pursuit of free-labor ideals created restless social and geographic mobility. While fortunate people such as Abraham Lincoln rose far beyond their social origins, others shared the misfortune of a merchant who, an observer noted, "has been on the sinking list all his life." In search of better prospects, roughly two-thirds of the rural population moved every decade, and population turnover in cities was even greater. This constant coming and going weakened community ties to neighbors and friends and threw individuals even more on their own resources in times of trouble.

Immigrants and the Free-Labor Ladder The risks and uncertainties of free labor did not deter millions of immigrants from entering the United States during the 1840s and 1850s. Almost 4.5 million immigrants arrived between 1840 and 1860, six times more than had come during the previous two decades. By 1860, foreign-born residents made up about one-eighth of the U.S. population.

Nearly three out of four immigrants who arrived in the United States between 1840 and 1860 came from Germany and Ireland. The vast majority of the 1.4 million Germans who entered during these years were skilled tradesmen and their families. German butchers, bakers, beer makers, carpenters, shopkeepers, and machinists settled mostly in the Midwest, often congregating in cities. Roughly a quarter of German immigrants were farmers, some of whom settled in Texas. On the whole, German Americans occupied the middle stratum of independent producers celebrated by free-labor spokesmen. Relatively few Germans occupied the bottom rung of the free-labor ladder as wage laborers or domestic servants.

Irish immigrants, in contrast, entered at the bottom of the free-labor ladder and struggled to climb up. Nearly 1.7 million Irish immigrants arrived between 1840 and 1860, nearly all of them desperately poor and often weakened by hunger and disease. Potato blight struck Ireland in 1845 and returned repeatedly in subsequent years, spreading a catastrophic famine throughout the island. Many of the lucky ones crowded into the holds of ships and set out for America, where they congregated in northeastern cities. As one immigrant group declared, "All we want is to get out of Ireland; we must be better anywhere than here." Roughly three out of four Irish immigrants worked as laborers or domestic servants. Irish men dug canals, loaded ships, laid railroad track, and did odd jobs while Irish women hired out to cook, wash and iron, mind children, and clean house. Almost all Irish immigrants were Catholic, a fact that set them apart from the overwhelmingly Protestant native-born residents. Many natives regarded the Irish as hard-drinking, obstreperous, half-civilized folk. Such views lay behind the discrimination reflected in job announcements that commonly stated, "No Irish need apply." Despite such prejudices, native residents hired Irish immigrants because they accepted low pay and worked hard.

In America's labor-poor economy, Irish laborers could earn more in one day than in several weeks in Ireland, if they could find work there. In America, one immigrant explained in 1853, there was "plenty of work and plenty of wages plenty to eat and no land lords thats enough what more does a man want." But some immigrants wanted more, especially respect and decent working conditions. One immigrant complained that he was "a slave for the Americans as the generality of the Irish . . . are."

Such testimony illustrates that the free-labor system, whether for immigrants or native-born laborers, often did not live up to the optimistic vision outlined by Abraham Lincoln and others. Many wage laborers could not realistically aspire to become independent, self-sufficient property holders, despite the claims of free-labor proponents.

Q: How did the free-labor ideal account for economic inequality?

The Westward Movement

In the 1840s, the nation's swelling population, booming economy, and boundless confidence propelled a new era of rapid westward migration. Until then, the overwhelming majority of Americans lived east of the Mississippi River. Native Americans inhabited the plains, deserts, and rugged coasts to the west. The British claimed the Oregon Country, and the Mexican flag flew over the vast expanse of the Southwest. But by 1850, the boundaries of the United States stretched to the Pacific, and the nation had more than doubled in size. By 1860, the great migration had carried four million Americans west of the Mississippi River.

Frontier settlers took the land and then, with the exception of the Mormons, lobbied their government to acquire the territory they had settled. The human cost of aggressive expansionism was high. The young Mexican nation lost a war and half of its territory. Two centuries of Indian wars east of the Mississippi ended during the 1830s, but the fierce struggle between native inhabitants and invaders continued for another half century in the West. Americans believed it was their destiny to conquer the continent.

Manifest Destiny Most Americans believed that the superiority of their institutions and white culture bestowed on them a God-given right to spread their civilization across the continent. They imagined the West as a howling wilderness, empty and undeveloped. If they recognized Indians and Mexicans at all, they dismissed them as primitive drags on progress who would have to be redeemed, shoved aside, or exterminated. The West provided young men especially an arena in which to "show their manhood." The sense of uniqueness and mission was as old as the Puritans, but by the 1840s, the conviction of superiority had been bolstered by the United States' amazing success. Most Americans believed that the West needed the civilizing power of the hammer and the plow, the ballot box and the pulpit, which had transformed the East.

In 1845, a New York political journal edited by John L. O'Sullivan coined the term **manifest destiny** as the latest justification for white settlers to take the land they coveted. O'Sullivan called on Americans to resist any foreign power — British, French, or Mexican — that attempted to thwart "the fulfillment of our manifest destiny to overspread the continent allotted by Providence for the free development of our yearly multiplying millions . . . [and] for the development of the great experiment of liberty and federative self-government entrusted to us." Almost overnight, the magic phrase *manifest destiny* swept the nation and provided an ideological shield for conquering the West.

As important as national pride and racial arrogance were to manifest destiny, economic gain made up its core. Land hunger drew hundreds of thousands of average Americans westward. Some politicians, moreover, had become convinced that national prosperity depended on capturing the rich trade of the Far East. To trade with Asia, the United States needed the Pacific coast ports that stretched from San Diego to Puget Sound. "The sun of civilization must shine across the sea: socially and commercially," Missouri senator Thomas Hart Benton declared. The United States and Asia must "talk together, and trade together. Commerce is a great civilizer." In the 1840s, American economic expansion came wrapped in the rhetoric of uplift and civilization.

Oregon and the Overland Trail The Oregon Country — a vast region bounded on the west by the Pacific Ocean, on the east by the Rocky Mountains, on the south by the forty-second parallel, and on the north by Russian Alaska — caused the pulse of American expansionists to race. But the British also coveted the area. They argued their claim lay with Sir Francis Drake's discovery of the Oregon coast in 1579. Americans countered with historic claims of their own. Unable to agree, the United States and Great Britain decided in 1818 on "joint occupation" that would leave Oregon "free and open" to settlement by both countries. A handful of American fur traders and "mountain men" roamed the region in the 1820s.

By the late 1830s, settlers began to trickle along the **Oregon Trail** (Map 12.2). The first wagon trains headed west in 1841, and by 1843 about 1,000 emigrants a year set out from Independence, Missouri. By 1869, when the first transcontinental railroad was completed, approximately 350,000 migrants had traveled west to the Pacific in wagon trains.

Emigrants encountered a quarter of a million Plains Indians. Some Native Americans were farmers who lived peaceful, sedentary lives, but a majority — the Sioux, Cheyenne, Shoshoni, and Arapaho of the central plains and the Kiowa, Wichita, and Comanche of the southern plains — were horse-mounted, nomadic, nonagricultural peoples whose warriors symbolized the "savage Indian" in the minds of whites.

Plains Indians and Trails West in the 1840s and 1850s

Horses, which had been brought to North America by Spaniards in the sixteenth century, permitted the Plains tribes to become highly mobile hunters of buffalo. They came to depend on buffalo for nearly everything — food, clothing, shelter, and fuel. Competition for buffalo led to war between the tribes. Young men were introduced to warfare early, learning to ride ponies at breakneck speed while firing off arrows and, later, rifles with astounding accuracy. "A Comanche on his feet is out of his element," observed western artist George Catlin, "but the moment he lays his hands upon his horse, his *face* even becomes handsome, and he gracefully flies away like a different being."

The Plains Indians struck fear in the hearts of whites on the wagon trains. But Native Americans had far more to fear from whites. Indians killed fewer than four hundred emigrants on the trail between 1840 and 1860, while whites brought alcohol and deadly epidemics of smallpox, measles, cholera, and scarlet fever. Moreover, whites killed the buffalo, often slaughtering them for sport. The buffalo still numbered some twelve million in 1860, but the herds were shrinking rapidly, intensifying conflict among the Plains tribes.

Emigrants insisted that the federal government provide them with more protection. The government constructed a chain of forts along the Oregon Trail (see Map 12.2). More important, it adopted a new Indian policy: "concentration." In 1851, the government called the Plains tribes to a conference at **Fort Laramie**, Wyoming. Government negotiators persuaded the chiefs to sign agreements that cleared a wide corridor for wagon trains by restricting Native Americans to specific areas that whites promised they would never violate. This policy of concentration became the seedbed for the subsequent policy of reservations. But whites would not keep out of Indian territory, and Indians would not easily give up their traditional ways of life. Struggle for control of the West meant warfare for decades to come.

Still, Indians threatened emigrants less than life on the trail did. The men, women, and children who headed west each spring could count on at least six months of grueling travel. With nearly two thousand miles to go and traveling no more than fifteen miles a day, the pioneers endured parching heat, drought, treacherous rivers, disease, physical and emotional exhaustion, and, if the snows closed the mountain passes before they got through, freezing and starvation. Women sometimes faced the dangers of trailside childbirth. It was said that a person could walk from Missouri to the Pacific stepping only on the graves of those who had died heading west. Such

MAP 12.2 Major Trails West

In the 1830s, wagon trains began snaking their way to the Southwest and the Pacific coast. Deep ruts, some of which can still be seen today, soon marked the most popular routes.

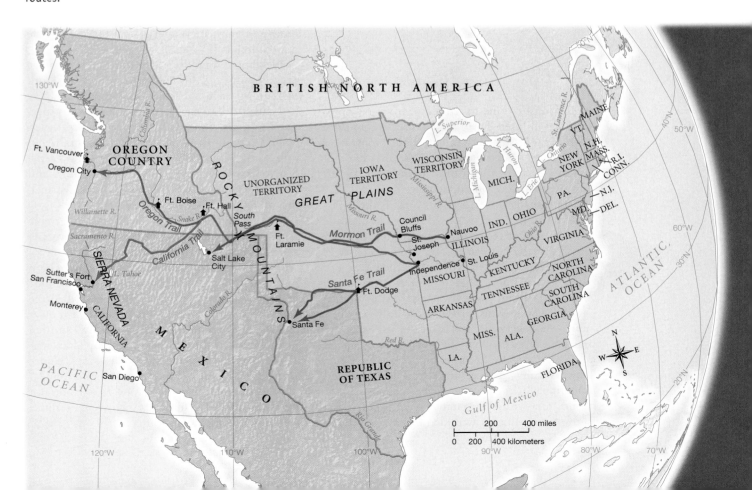

Kee-O-Kuk, the Watchful Fox, Chief of the Tribe, by George Catlin, 1835
In the 1830s, Pennsylvania-born artist George Catlin traveled the West painting Native American portraits, rituals, and landscapes. Though not the first artist to paint Indians, he was the first to portray them in their own environments and one of the few to present them as human beings, not savages. Convinced that western Indian cultures would soon disappear, Catlin sought to document Indian life through hundreds of paintings and prints. Keokuk, chief of the Sauk and Fox, struggled with the warrior Black Hawk (see chapter 11) about the proper strategy for dealing with whites. Black Hawk fought American expansion; Keokuk believed that war was fruitless and signed over land in Illinois, Missouri, and Wisconsin. Smithsonian American Art Institution, Washington, D.C. Gift of Mrs. Joseph Harrison Jr.

tribulations led one miserable woman, trying to keep her children dry in a rainstorm and to calm them as they listened to Indian shouts, to wonder "what had possessed my husband, anyway, that he should have thought of bringing us away out through this God forsaken country."

Men usually found Oregon "one of the greatest countries in the world." From "the Cascade mountains to the Pacific, the whole country can be cultivated," exclaimed one eager settler. When women reached Oregon, they found that neighbors were scarce and things were in a "primitive state." One young wife arrived with only her husband, one stew kettle, and three knives. Necessity blurred the traditional division between men's and women's work. "I am maid of all traids," one busy woman remarked in 1853. Work seemed unending. "I am a very old woman," declared twenty-nine-year-old Sarah Everett. "My face is thin sunken and wrinkled, my hands bony

withered and hard." Another settler observed, "A woman that can not endure almost as much as a horse has no business here." Yet despite the ordeal of the trail and the difficulties of starting from scratch, emigrants kept coming.

The Mormon Exodus Not every wagon train heading west was bound for the Pacific Slope. One remarkable group of religious emigrants halted near the Great Salt Lake in what was then Mexican territory. The **Mormons** deliberately chose the remote site as a refuge. After years of persecution in the East, they fled west to find religious freedom and communal security.

In 1830, Joseph Smith Jr., who was only twenty-four, published *The Book of Mormon* and founded the Church of Jesus Christ of Latter-Day Saints (the Mormons). A decade earlier, the upstate New York farm boy had begun to experience revelations that were followed, he said, by a visit from an angel who led him to golden tablets buried near his home. With the aid of magic stones, Smith translated the mysterious language on the tablets to produce *The Book of Mormon*. It told the story of an ancient Hebrew civilization in the New World and predicted the appearance of an American prophet who would reestablish Jesus Christ's undefiled kingdom in America. Converts, attracted to the promise of a pure faith in the midst of antebellum America's social turmoil and rampant materialism, flocked to the new church.

Neighbors branded Mormons heretics and drove Smith and his followers from New York to Ohio, then to Missouri, and finally in 1839 to Nauvoo, Illinois, where they built a prosperous community. But a rift in the church developed after Smith sanctioned "plural marriage" (polygamy). Non-Mormons caught wind of the controversy and eventually arrested Smith and his brother. On June 27, 1844, a mob stormed the jail and shot both men dead.

The embattled church turned to an extraordinary new leader, Brigham Young, who oversaw a great exodus. In 1846, traveling in 3,700 wagons, 12,000 Mormons made their way to eastern Iowa, then the following year to their new home beside the Great Salt Lake. Young described the region as a barren waste, "the paradise of the lizard, the cricket and the rattlesnake." Within ten years, however, the Mormons developed an irrigation system that made the desert bloom. Under Young's stern leadership, the Mormons built a thriving community using cooperative labor, not the individualistic and competitive enterprise common among most emigrants.

Pioneer Family on the Trail West In 1860, W. G. Chamberlain photographed these unidentified travelers momentarily at rest by the upper Arkansas River in Colorado. We do not know their fates, and we can only hope that they fared better than the Sager family. Henry and Naomi Sager and their six children set out from St. Joseph, Missouri, in 1844. "Father," one of Henry and Naomi's daughters remembered, "was one of those restless men who are not content to remain in one place long at a time. [He] had been talking of going to Texas. But mother, hearing much said about the healthfulness of Oregon, preferred to go there." Still far from Oregon, Henry Sager died of fever. Twenty-six days later, Naomi died, leaving seven children, the last delivered on the trail. The Sager children, under the care of other families in the wagon train, pressed on. After traveling two thousand miles in seven months, the migrants arrived in Oregon, where Marcus and Narcissa Whitman, whose own daughter had drowned, adopted all seven of the Sager children. Denver Public Library, Western History Division # F3226.

FOR MORE HELP ANALYZING THIS IMAGE, see the visual activity for this chapter in the Online Study Guide at bedfordstmartins.com/roarkcompact.

In 1850, the Mormon kingdom was annexed to the United States as Utah Territory. The nation's attention focused on Utah in 1852 when Brigham Young announced that many Mormons practiced polygamy. Although only one Mormon man in five had more than one wife (Young had twenty-three), Young's statement caused a popular outcry that forced the U.S. government to establish its authority in Utah. In 1857, 2,500 U.S. troops invaded Salt Lake City in what was known as the Mormon War. The bloodless occupation illustrates that most Americans viewed the Mormons as a threat to American morality, law, and institutions. The invasion did not dislodge the Mormon Church from its central place in Utah, however, and for years to come, most Americans perceived the Mormon settlement as strange and suitably isolated.

The Mexican Borderlands In the Mexican Southwest, westward-moving Anglo-American pioneers confronted northern-moving Spanish-speaking frontiersmen. On this frontier as elsewhere, national cultures, interests, and aspirations collided. Since 1821, when Mexico won its independence from Spain, the Mexican flag had flown over the vast expanse that stretched from the Gulf of Mexico to the Pacific and from the Oregon Country to Guatemala (Map 12.3). But Mexico's northern provinces were sparsely populated, and the young nation was plagued by civil wars, economic crises, quarrels with the Roman Catholic Church, and devastating raids by the Comanche, Apache, and Kiowa. Mexico found it increasingly difficult to defend its borderlands, especially when faced with a northern neighbor convinced of its superiority and bent on territorial acquisition.

MAP 12.3 **Texas and Mexico in the 1830s**
As Americans spilled into lightly populated and loosely governed northern Mexico, Texas and then other Mexican provinces became contested territory.

By the 1830s, the settlers had established a thriving plantation economy in Texas. Americans numbered 35,000, while the *Tejano* (Spanish-speaking) population was less than 8,000. Few Anglo-American settlers were Roman Catholic, spoke Spanish, or cared about assimilating into Mexican culture. Afraid of losing Texas to the new arrivals, the Mexican government in 1830 banned further immigration to Texas from the United States and outlawed the introduction of additional slaves. The Anglo-Americans made it clear that they wanted to be rid of the "despotism of the sword and the priesthood" and to govern themselves. In Mexico City, however, General **Antonio López de Santa Anna** seized political power and set about restoring order to the northern frontier.

When the Texan settlers rebelled, Santa Anna ordered the Mexican army northward. In February 1836, the army arrived at the outskirts of San Antonio. Commanded by Colonel William B. Travis from Alabama, the rebels included the Tennessee frontiersman David Crockett and the Louisiana adventurer James Bowie, as well as a handful of Tejanos. They took refuge in a former Franciscan mission known as the **Alamo**. Santa Anna sent wave after wave of his 2,000-man army crashing against the walls until the attackers finally broke through and killed all 187 rebels. A few weeks later, outside the small town of Goliad, Mexican forces captured a garrison of Texans. Mexican firing squads executed almost 400 of the men as "pirates and outlaws." In April 1836, at San Jacinto, General Sam Houston's army adopted the massacre of Goliad as a battle cry and crushed Santa Anna's troops. The Texans had succeeded in establishing the Lone Star Republic, and the following year, the United States recognized the independence of Texas from Mexico.

The American assault began quietly. In the 1820s, Anglo-American trappers, traders, and settlers drifted into Mexico's far northern provinces. Santa Fe, a remote outpost in the province of New Mexico, became a magnet for American enterprise. Each spring, American traders gathered at Independence, Missouri, for the long trek southwest along the Santa Fe Trail (see Map 12.2). They crammed their wagons with inexpensive American manufactured goods and returned home with Mexican silver, furs, and mules.

The Mexican province of Texas attracted a flood of Americans who had settlement, not long-distance trade, on their minds (see Map 12.3). Wanting to populate and develop its northern territory, the Mexican government granted the American **Stephen F. Austin** a huge tract of land along the Brazos River. In the 1820s, Austin became the first Anglo-American *empresario* (colonization agent) in Texas, offering land at only ten cents an acre. Thousands of Americans poured across the border. Most were Southerners who brought cotton and slaves with them.

Texas War for Independence, 1836

Earlier, in 1824, in an effort to increase Mexican migration to the province of California, the Mexican government granted *ranchos*—huge estates devoted to cattle raising—to new settlers. *Rancheros* ruled over near-feudal empires worked by Indians whose condition sometimes approached that of slaves. Not satisfied, the rancheros coveted the vast lands controlled by the Franciscan missions. In 1834, they persuaded the Mexican government to confiscate the missions and make their lands available to new settlement, a development that accelerated the decline of the California Indians. Devastated by disease, the Indians, who had numbered approximately 300,000 when the Spanish arrived in 1769, had declined to half that number by 1846.

Despite the efforts of the Mexican government, California in 1840 had a population of only 7,000 Mexican settlers. Non-Mexican settlers numbered only 380, but among them were Americans who championed manifest destiny. They sought to woo American emigrants to California. In the 1840s, wagon after wagon left the Oregon Trail to head southwest on the California Trail (see Map 12.2). As the trickle of Americans became a river, Mexican officials grew alarmed. As a New York newspaper put it in 1845, "Let the tide of emigration flow toward California and the American population will soon be sufficiently numerous to play the Texas game." Only a few Americans in California wanted a war for independence, but many dreamed of living again under the U.S. flag.

The U.S. government made no secret of its desire to acquire California. In 1835, President Andrew Jackson tried unsuccessfully to purchase it. In 1846, American settlers in the Sacramento Valley took matters into their own hands. Prodded by John C. Frémont, a former army captain and explorer who had arrived with a party of sixty buckskin-clad frontiersmen spoiling for a fight, the Californians raised an independence movement known as the Bear Flag Revolt. By then, James K. Polk, a champion of aggressive expansion, sat in the White House.

> **Q:** Why did westward migration expand dramatically in the mid-nineteenth century?

Expansion and the Mexican-American War

Although emigrants acted as the advance guard of American empire, there was nothing automatic about the U.S. annexation of territory in the West. Acquiring territory required political action. In the 1840s, the politics of expansion became entangled with sectionalism and the slavery question. Texas, Oregon, and the Mexican borderlands thrust the United States into dangerous diplomatic crises with Great Britain and Mexico.

Aggravation between Mexico and the United States escalated to open antagonism in 1845 when the United States annexed Texas. Absorbing territory still claimed by Mexico ruptured diplomatic relations between the two countries and set the stage for war. But it was President James K. Polk's insistence on having Mexico's other northern provinces that made war certain. The war was not as easy as Polk anticipated, but it ended in American victory and the acquisition of a new American West.

The Politics of Expansion Texans had sought admission to the Union almost since winning their independence from Mexico in 1836. But any suggestion of adding another slave state to the Union outraged most Northerners. Moreover, annexing Texas risked precipitating war, because Mexico had never relinquished its claim to its lost province.

President John Tyler, who became president in April 1841 when William Henry Harrison died one month after taking office, understood that Texas was a dangerous issue. Adding to the danger, Great Britain began sniffing around Texas, apparently contemplating adding the young republic to its growing empire. Tyler, an ardent expansionist, decided to risk annexing the Lone Star Republic. In April 1844, when he laid an annexation treaty before the Senate, howls of protest erupted across the North. Future Massachusetts senator Charles Sumner deplored the "insidious" plan to annex Texas and carve from it "great slaveholding states." The Senate soundly rejected the treaty, and it appeared that Tyler had succeeded only in inflaming sectional conflict.

The issue of Texas had not died down by the 1844 election. In an effort to appeal to northern voters, the Whig nominee for president, **Henry Clay**, came out against annexation of Texas. "Annexation and war with Mexico are identical," he declared. The Democrats chose Tennessean **James K. Polk**, who was strongly in favor of annexation. To make annexation palatable to Northerners, the Democrats shrewdly yoked Texas to Oregon, thus tapping the desire for expansion in the free states of the North as well as in the slave states of the South. The Democratic platform called for the "reannexation of Texas" and the "reoccupation of Oregon." The suggestion that the United States was merely reasserting existing rights was poor history but good politics.

When Clay finally recognized the popularity of expansion, he waffled, hinting that he might accept the annexation of Texas. His retreat succeeded only in alienating antislavery opinion in the North. James G. Birney, the candidate of the fledgling Liberty

Polk and Dallas Banner, 1844 In 1844, Democratic presidential nominee James K. Polk and vice presidential nominee George M. Dallas campaigned under this cotton banner. The extra star spilling over into the red and white stripes symbolizes Polk's vigorous support for annexing the huge slave republic of Texas, which had declared its independence from Mexico eight years earlier. Henry Clay, Polk's Whig opponent, ran under a banner that was similar but conspicuously lacked the additional star. Collection of Janice L. and David J. Frent.

up California, Nevada, Utah, most of New Mexico and Arizona, and parts of Wyoming and Colorado. Polk hoped to buy the territory, but when the Mexicans refused to sell, he concluded that military force would be needed to realize the United States' manifest destiny.

Polk had already ordered General **Zachary Taylor** to march his 4,000-man army 150 miles south from its position on the Nueces River, the southern boundary of Texas according to the Mexicans, to the banks of the Rio Grande, the boundary claimed by Texans (Map 12.4). Viewing the American advance as aggression, the Mexican general in Matamoros ordered Taylor back to the Nueces. Taylor refused, and on April 25, Mexican cavalry attacked a party of American soldiers, killing or wounding sixteen and capturing the rest. Even before news of the battle arrived in Washington, Polk had obtained his cabinet's approval of a war message.

On May 11, 1846, the president told Congress, "Mexico has passed the boundary of the United States, has invaded our territory, and shed American blood upon American soil." Thus "war exists, and, notwithstanding all our efforts to avoid it, exists by the act of Mexico herself." Congress passed a declaration of war and began raising an army. The U.S. army was pitifully small, only 8,600 soldiers. Faced with the nation's first foreign war, against a Mexican army that numbered more than 30,000, Polk called for volunteers. Eventually, more than 112,000 white Americans (blacks were banned) joined the army to fight in Mexico.

Despite the flood of volunteers, the war divided the nation. Northern Whigs in particular condemned the war. The Massachusetts legislature claimed that the war was being fought for the "triple object of extending slavery, of strengthening the slave power, and of obtaining control of the free states." On January 12, 1848, a gangly freshman Whig representative from Illinois rose in the House of Representatives to deliver his first important speech in Congress. Before Abraham Lincoln sat down, he had questioned Polk's intelligence, honesty, and sanity. The president ignored the upstart representative, but antislavery, antiwar Whigs kept up the attack throughout the conflict. In their effort to undercut national support, they labeled it "Mr. Polk's War."

Since most Americans backed the war, it was not really Polk's war, but the president acted as if it were and directed the war personally. He planned a short war in which U.S. armies would occupy Mexico's northern provinces and defeat the Mexican army in a decisive battle or two, after which Mexico would sue for peace and the United States would keep the territory its armies occupied.

Party, picked up the votes of thousands of disillusioned Clay supporters. In the November election, Polk received 170 electoral votes and Clay 105.

The nation did not have to wait for Polk's inauguration in March 1845 to see results from his victory. One month after the election, President Tyler announced that the triumph of the Democratic Party provided a mandate for the annexation of Texas "promptly and immediately." In February 1845, after a fierce debate between antislavery and proslavery forces, Congress approved a joint resolution offering the **Republic of Texas** admission to the United States. Texas entered as the fifteenth slave state.

Tyler delivered Texas, but Polk had promised Oregon, too. Westerners particularly demanded that the new president make good on the Democrats' pledge "Fifty-four Forty or Fight"—that is, all of Oregon, right up to Alaska (54°40′ was the southern latitude of Russian Alaska). But Polk was close to war with Mexico and could not afford a war with Britain over U.S. claims in Canada. He renewed an old offer to divide Oregon along the forty-ninth parallel. When Britain accepted the compromise, some Americans cried betrayal, but most celebrated the agreement that gave the nation an enormous territory peacefully. When the Senate finally approved the treaty in June 1846, the United States and Mexico were already at war.

The Mexican-American War, 1846–1848

From the day he entered the White House, Polk craved Mexico's remaining northern provinces: California and New Mexico, land that today makes

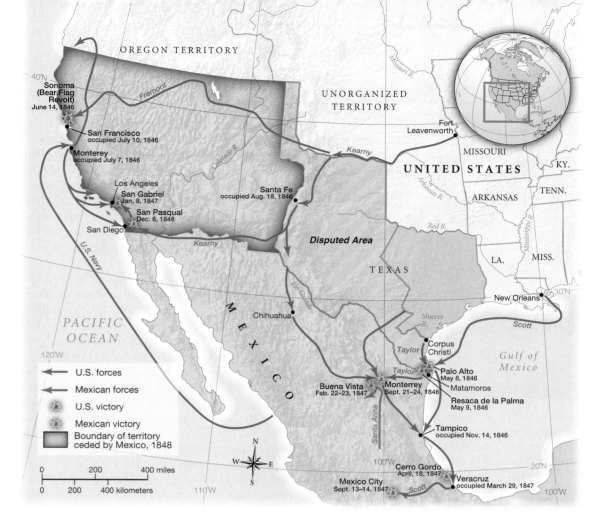

MAP 12.4 **The Mexican-American War, 1846–1848**
American and Mexican soldiers skirmished across much of northern Mexico, but the major battles took place between the Rio Grande and Mexico City.

At first, Polk's strategy seemed to work. In May 1846, Zachary Taylor's troops drove south from the Rio Grande and routed the Mexican army, first at Palo Alto, then at Resaca de la Palma (see Map 12.4). "Old Rough and Ready," as Taylor was affectionately known among his adoring troops, became an instant war hero. Polk rewarded Taylor for his victories by making him commander of the Mexican campaign.

A second prong of the campaign centered on Colonel Stephen Watts Kearny, who led a 1,700-man army from Missouri into New Mexico. Without firing a shot, U.S. forces took Santa Fe in August 1846. Kearny then marched into San Diego three months later, encountering a major Mexican rebellion against American rule. In January 1847, after several clashes and severe losses, the U.S. forces occupied Los Angeles. California and New Mexico were in American hands.

By then, Taylor had driven deep into the interior of Mexico. In September 1846, after house-to-house fighting, he took the city of Monterrey. Taylor then pushed his 5,000 troops southwest, where the Mexican hero of the Alamo, General Antonio López de Santa Anna, was concentrating an army of 21,000. On February 23, 1847, Santa Anna's troops attacked Taylor at Buena Vista. Superior American artillery and accurate musket fire won the day, but the Americans suffered heavy casualties. The Mexicans suffered even greater losses (some 3,400 dead, wounded, and missing, compared with 650 Americans). During the night, Santa Anna withdrew his battered army, much to the "profound disgust of the troops," one Mexican officer remembered. "They are filled with grief that they were going to lose the benefit of all the sacrifices

> On **May 11, 1846, President Polk told Congress, "War exists, and, notwithstanding all our efforts to avoid it, exists by the act of Mexico herself."**

Mexican Family This family had its portrait taken in 1847, in the middle of the war. Where were the adult males? Mexican civilians were vulnerable to atrocities committed by the invading army. Volunteers, a large portion of the American troops, received little training and resisted discipline. The "lawless Volunteers stop at no outrage," Brigadier General William Worth declared. "Innocent blood has been basely, cowardly, and barbarously shed in cold blood." Generals Zachary Taylor and Winfield Scott gradually tamed the volunteers with stern military justice. Mexican Family, unknown, ca. 1847, Daguerreotype, Amon Carter Museum, Fort Worth, Texas.

that they had made; that the conquered field would be abandoned, and that the victory would be given to the enemy."

The series of uninterrupted victories in northern Mexico fed the American troops' sense of superiority. "No American force has ever thought of being defeated by any amount of Mexican troops," one soldier declared. The Americans worried about other hazards, however. "I can assure you that fighting is the least dangerous & arduous part of a soldier's life," one young man declared. Letters home told of torturous marches across arid wastes alive with tarantulas, scorpions, and rattlesnakes. Others recounted dysentery, malaria, smallpox, cholera, and yellow fever. Of the 13,000 American soldiers who died (some 50,000 Mexicans perished), fewer than 2,000 fell to Mexican bullets and shells. Disease killed most of the others. Medicine was so primitive that, as one Tennessee man observed, "nearly all who take sick die."

Victory in Mexico Although the Americans won battle after battle, President Polk's strategy misfired. Despite heavy losses on the battlefield, Mexico refused to trade land for peace. One American soldier captured the Mexican mood: "They cannot submit to be deprived of California after the loss of Texas, and nothing but the conquest of their Capital will force them to such a humiliation." Polk had arrived at the same conclusion. While Taylor occupied the north, General **Winfield Scott** would land an army on the Gulf coast of Mexico and march 250 miles inland to Mexico City. Polk's plan entailed enormous risk because Scott would have to cut himself off from supplies and lead his men deep into enemy country against a much larger army.

An amphibious landing on March 9, 1847, near Veracruz put some 10,000 American troops ashore. After a siege of two weeks and furious shelling, Veracruz surrendered. In early April 1847, the U.S. army moved westward. After the defeat at Buena Vista, Santa Anna had returned to Mexico City, where he rallied his ragged troops and marched them east to set a trap for Scott in the mountain pass at Cerro Gordo. Knifing through Mexican lines, the Americans almost captured Santa Anna, who fled the field on foot. So complete was the victory that Scott gloated to Taylor, "Mexico no longer has an army." But Santa Anna, ever resilient, again rallied the Mexican army. Some 30,000 troops took up defensive positions on the outskirts of Mexico City and began melting down church bells to cast new cannons.

In August, Scott began his assault on the Mexican capital. The fighting proved the most brutal of the war. Santa Anna backed his army into the city, fighting each step of the way. At the battle of Churubusco, the Mexicans took 4,000 casualties in a single day and the Americans more than 1,000. At the castle of Chapultepec, American troops scaled the walls and fought the Mexican defenders hand to hand. After Chapultepec, Mexico City officials persuaded Santa Anna to evacuate the city to save it from destruction, and on September 14, 1847, General Winfield Scott rode in triumphantly.

On February 2, 1848, American and Mexican officials signed the **Treaty of Guadalupe Hidalgo** in Mexico City. Mexico agreed to give up all claims to Texas north of the Rio Grande and to cede the provinces of New Mexico and California—more than 500,000 square miles—to the United States (see Map 12.4). The United States agreed to pay Mexico $15 million and to assume $3.25 million in claims that American citizens had against Mexico. In March 1848, the Senate ratified the treaty. Polk had his Rio Grande border, his Pacific ports, and all the land that lay between.

The American triumph had enormous consequences. Less than three-quarters of a century after

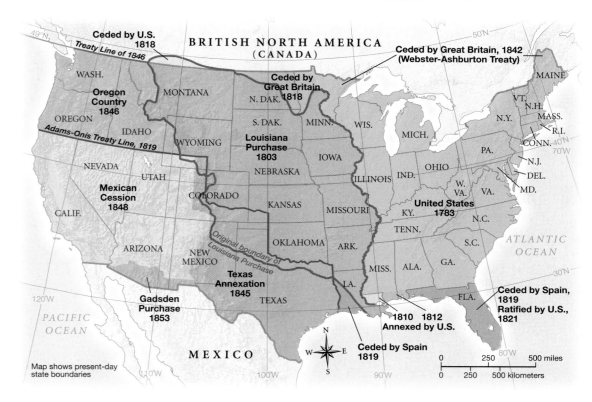

MAP 12.5 **Territorial Expansion by 1860**

Less than a century after its founding, the United States spread from the Atlantic seaboard to the Pacific coast. War, purchase, and diplomacy had gained a continent.

READING THE MAP: List the countries from which the United States acquired land. Which nation lost the most land because of U.S. expansion?

CONNECTIONS: Who coined the phrase *manifest destiny*? When? What does it mean? What areas targeted for expansion were the subjects of debate during the presidential campaign of 1844?

FOR MORE HELP ANALYZING THIS MAP, see the map activity for this chapter in the Online Study Guide at bedfordstmartins.com/roarkcompact.

its founding, the United States had achieved its self-proclaimed manifest destiny to stretch from the Atlantic to the Pacific (Map 12.5). It would enter the industrial age with vast new natural resources and a two-ocean economy, while Mexico faced a sharply diminished economic future.

Golden California Another consequence of the Mexican defeat was that California gold poured into American, not Mexican, pockets. In January 1848, just weeks before the formal transfer of territory, James Marshall discovered gold in the American River in the foothills of the Sierra Nevada. Marshall's discovery set off the **California gold rush**, one of the wildest mining stampedes in the world's history. Between 1849 and 1852, more than 250,000 "forty-niners," as

the would-be miners were known, descended on the Golden State. In less than two years, Marshall's discovery transformed California from foreign territory to statehood.

News of gold quickly spread around the world. Soon, a stream of men of various races and nationalities, all bent on getting rich, arrived in California, where they remade the quiet world of Mexican ranches into a raucous, roaring mining and town economy. (See "Historical Question," page 298.) Only a few struck it rich, and life in the goldfields was nasty, brutish, and often short. Men faced miserable living conditions, sometimes sheltering in holes and brush lean-tos. They also faced cholera and scurvy, exorbitant prices for food (eggs cost a dollar apiece), deadly encounters with claim jumpers, and

Who Rushed for California Gold?

When news of James Marshall's discovery reached the East in the fall of 1848, gold proved irresistible. Newspapers went crazy with stories about prospectors who extracted half a pan of gold from every pan of gravel they scooped from western streams. Soon, cities reverberated with men singing:

> Oh Susannah, don't you cry for me;
> I'm gone to California with
> my wash-bowl on my knee.

Scores of ships sailed from East Coast ports, headed either around South America to San Francisco or across the Gulf of Mexico to Panama, where the passengers made their way by foot and canoe to the Pacific and waited for a ship to carry them north. Even larger numbers of gold seekers took riverboats to the Missouri River and then set out in wagons, on horseback, or by foot for the West.

Young men everywhere contracted gold fever. As stories of California gold circled the globe, Chinese and Germans, Mexicans and Irish, Australians and French, Chileans and Italians, and people of dozens of other nationalities set out to strike it rich. Louisa Knapp Clappe, wife of a minister and one of the few women in gold country, remarked that when she walked through Indian Bar, the little mining town where she lived, she heard English, French, Spanish, German, Italian, Kanaka (Hawaiian), Asian Indian, and American Indian languages. Hangtown, Hell's Delight, Gouge Eye, and a hundred other crude mining camps became temporary homes to a diverse throng of nationalities and peoples.

One of the largest groups of new arrivals was the Chinese. Between 1848 and 1854, Chinese men numbering 45,000 (but almost no Chinese women) arrived in California. Most considered themselves "sojourners,"

temporary residents who planned to return home as soon as their savings allowed. The majority came under a Chinese-controlled contract labor system in which each immigrant worked out the cost of his transportation. In the early years, most became wage laborers in mining. By the 1860s, they dominated railroad construction in the West. Ninety percent of the Central Pacific Railroad's 10,000 workers were Chinese. The Chinese also made up nearly half of San Francisco's labor force, working in the shoe, tobacco, woolen, laundry, and sewing trades. By 1870, the Chinese population in California had grown to 63,200, including 4,500 women. They constituted nearly 10 percent of the state's people and 25 percent of its wage-earning force.

The presence of peoples from around the world shattered the Anglo-American dream of a racially and ethnically homogeneous West, but ethnic diversity did nothing to increase the tolerance of Anglo-American prospectors. In their eyes, no "foreigner" had a right to dig for gold. In 1850, the California legislature passed the Foreign Miners' Tax Law, which levied high taxes on non-Americans to drive them from the goldfields, except as hired laborers working on claims owned by Americans. Stubborn foreign miners were sometimes hauled before "Judge Lynch." Among the earliest victims of lynching in the goldfields were a Frenchman and a Chilean.

Anglo-Americans considered the Chinese devious and unassimilable. They also feared that hardworking, self-denying Chinese labor would undercut white labor and drive it from the country. As a consequence, the Chinese were segregated residentially and occupationally and made ineligible for citizenship. Along with blacks and Indians, Chinese were denied public education and the right to testify in court. In addition

endless backbreaking labor. An individual with gold in his pocket could find only temporary relief in the saloons, card games, dogfights, gambling dens, and brothels that flourished in the mining camps.

By 1853, San Francisco had grown into a raw, booming city of 50,000 that depended as much on gold as did the mining camps inland. Like

all the towns that dotted the San Joaquin and Sacramento valleys, it suffered from overcrowding, fire, crime, and violence. But enterprising individuals had learned that there was money to be made tending to the needs of the miners. Hotels, saloons, restaurants, laundries, and stores of all kinds exchanged services and goods for miners' gold.

to exclusion, they suffered from violence. Mobs drove them from Eureka, Truckee, and other mining towns.

American prospectors swamped the *Californios*, Spanish and Mexican settlers who had lived in California for generations. Soon after the American takeover, raging prejudice and discriminatory laws pushed Hispanic rancheros, professionals, merchants, and artisans into the ranks of unskilled labor. Americans took their land even though the U.S. government had pledged to protect Mexican and Spanish land titles after the cession of 1848. Anglo forty-niners branded Spanish-speaking miners, even native-born Californios, "foreigners" and drove them from the diggings. Mariano Vallejo, a leading Californio, said of the forty-niners, "The good ones were few and the wicked many."

For Native Americans, the gold rush was a catastrophe. Numbering about 150,000 in 1848, the Indian population of California fell to 25,000 in 1856. The Californios had exploited the native peoples, but the forty-niners wanted to eradicate them. Starvation, disease, and a declining birthrate took a heavy toll. Indians also fell victim to wholesale murder. "That a war of extermination will continue to be waged between the two races until the Indian race becomes extinct must be expected," declared California governor Peter W. Burnett in 1851. The nineteenth-century historian Hubert Howe Bancroft described white behavior toward Indians during the gold rush as "one of the last human hunts of civilization, and the basest and most brutal of them all." To survive, Indians moved to the most remote areas of the state and tried to stay out of the way.

★ **Chinese Man** This daguerreotype of an unidentified Chinese man was made by Isaac Wallace Baker, a photographer who traveled through California's mining camps in his wagon studio. One of the earliest known portraits of an Asian in California, the portrait shows a proud man boldly displaying his queue (long braid). This was almost certainly an act of defiance, for Anglos ridiculed Chinese cultural traditions, and vigilantes chased down men who wore queues. Copyright the Dorothea Lange Collection, Oakland Museum of California, City of Oakland. Gift of Paul S. Taylor.

The forty-niners created dazzling wealth — in 1852, 81 million ounces of gold, nearly half of the world's production. Only a few prospectors struck it rich, however. The era of the prospector panning in streams quickly gave way to corporate-owned deep-shaft mining. The larger the mining operations became, the smaller individual miners' opportunities were. Most forty-niners eventually took up farming, opened small businesses, or worked for wages for the corporations that pushed them out. But because of gold, a flood of people had roared into California. Anglo-Americans were the most numerous, but the gold rush also brought a rainbow of other nationalities. Anglo dominance developed early, however, and not everyone shared equally in the bonanza. Both Anglo-American ascendancy and ethnic and racial diversity in the West were among the most significant legacies of the gold rush.

In 1851, the Committee of Vigilance determined to bring order to the city. Members pledged that "no thief, burglar, incendiary or assassin shall escape punishment, either by the quibbles of the law, the insecurity of prisons, the carelessness or corruption of the police, or a laxity of those who pretended to administer justice." Lynchings proved that the committee meant business. In time, merchants, artisans, and professionals made the city their home and brought their families from back east. Gunfights declined, but many years would pass before anyone pacified San Francisco.

Establishing civic order was made more difficult by California's diversity and Anglo bigotry. The Chinese attracted special scrutiny. By 1851, 25,000 Chinese lived in California, and their religion, language, dress, queues (long pigtails), eating habits, and opium convinced many Anglos that they were not fit citizens of the Golden State. As early as 1852, opponents demanded a halt to Chinese immigration. Chinese leaders in San Francisco fought back. Admitting deep cultural differences, they insisted that "in the important matters we are good men. We honor our parents; we take care of our children; we are industrious and peaceable; we trade much; we are trusted for small and large sums; we pay our debts; and are honest, and of course must tell the truth." Their protestations offered little protection, however, and racial violence persisted.

Westward expansion did not stop at the California shore. California's ports were connected to a vast trade network throughout the Pacific. Americans traded furs, hides and tallow, and lumber and engaged in whaling and the China trade. Still, as California's first congressional representative observed, the state was separated "by thousands of miles of plains, deserts, and almost impossible mountains" from the rest of the Union. Some dreamers imagined a railroad that would someday connect the Golden State with the booming agriculture and thriving industry of the East. Others imagined an America transformed not by transportation, but by progressive individual and institutional reform.

> **Q:** **Why was the annexation of Texas such a controversial policy?**

Reforming Self and Society

While manifest destiny, the Mexican-American War, and the California gold rush transformed the nation's geography, many Americans sought personal and social reform. The emphasis on self-discipline and individual effort at the core of the free-labor ideal led Americans to believe that insufficient self-control caused the major social problems of the era. Evangelical Protestants struggled to control individuals' propensity to sin. Temperance advocates exhorted drinkers to control their urge for alcohol. In the midst of the worldly disruptions of geographic expansion and economic change, evangelicals brought more Americans than ever before into churches. Historians estimate that church members accounted for about one-third of the American population by 1850. Most Americans remained outside churches, as did Abraham Lincoln. But the influence of evangelical religion reached far beyond those who belonged to churches. The evangelical temperament—a

conviction of righteousness coupled with energy, self-discipline, and faith that the world could be improved—animated most reformers.

A few activists pointed out that certain fundamental injustices lay beyond the reach of individual self-control. Transcendentalists and utopians believed that perfection could be attained only by rejecting the competitive, individualistic values of mainstream society. Woman's rights activists and abolitionists sought to reverse the subordination of women and to eliminate the enslavement of blacks by changing laws and social institutions as well as attitudes and customs. They confronted the daunting challenge of repudiating widespread assumptions about male supremacy and white supremacy and somehow subverting the entrenched institutions that reinforced those assumptions: the family and slavery.

The Pursuit of Perfection: Transcendentalists and Utopians

A group of New England writers who came to be known as transcendentalists believed that individuals should conform neither to the dictates of the materialistic world nor to the dogma of formal religion. Instead, people should look within themselves for truth and guidance. The leading transcendentalist, Ralph Waldo Emerson—an essayist, poet, and lecturer—proclaimed that the power of the solitary individual was nearly limitless. Henry David Thoreau, Margaret Fuller, and other transcendentalists agreed with Emerson that "if the single man plant himself indomitably on his instincts, and there abide, the huge world will come round to him." In many ways, the inward gaze and confident egoism of transcendentalism represented less an alternative to mainstream values than an exaggerated form of the rampant individualism of the age.

Unlike transcendentalists who sought to turn inward, a few reformers tried to change the world by organizing utopian communities as alternatives to prevailing social arrangements. Although these communities never attracted more than a few thousand people, the activities of their members demonstrated both dissatisfaction with the larger society and their efforts to realize their visions of perfection.

Some communities set out to become models of perfection whose success would point the way toward a better life for everyone. During the 1840s, more than two dozen communities organized around the ideas of Charles Fourier, a French critic of contemporary society. Members of **Fourierist phalanxes**, as these communities were called, believed that individualism and competition were evils that denied the basic truth that "men . . . are brothers and not competitors." Phalanxes aspired to replace competition with harmonious cooperation based on communal ownership of property. But Fourierist communities failed to realize their lofty goals, and few survived more than two or three years.

The **Oneida community** went beyond the Fourierist notion of communalism. John Humphrey Noyes, the charismatic leader of Oneida, believed that American society's commitment to private property made people greedy and selfish. Noyes claimed that the root of private property lay in marriage, in men's conviction that their wives were their exclusive property. Drawing from a substantial inheritance, Noyes organized the Oneida community in New York in 1848 to abolish marital property rights through the practice of what he called "complex marriage." Sexual intercourse was not restricted to married couples but was permitted between any consenting man and woman in the community. Noyes also required all members to relinquish their economic property to the community, which developed a lucrative business manufacturing animal traps. Oneida's sexual and economic communalism attracted several hundred members, but most of their neighbors considered Oneidans adulterers, blasphemers, and worse. Yet the practices that set Oneida apart from its mainstream neighbors strengthened the community, and it survived long after the Civil War.

Woman's Rights Activists

Women participated in the many reform activities that grew out of evangelical churches. Women church members outnumbered men two to one and worked to put their religious ideas into practice by joining peace, temperance, antislavery, and other societies. Involvement in reform organizations gave a few women activists practical experience in such political arts as speaking in public, running a meeting, drafting resolutions, and circulating petitions. Along with such experience came confidence. The abolitionist Lydia Maria Child pointed out in 1841 that "those who urged women to become missionaries and form tract societies . . . have changed the household utensil to a living energetic being and they have no spell to turn it into a broom again."

In 1848, about three hundred reformers led by **Elizabeth Cady Stanton** and Lucretia Mott gathered at Seneca Falls, New York, for the first national woman's rights convention in the United States. As Stanton recalled, "The general discontent I felt with women's portion as wife, mother, housekeeper, physician, and spiritual guide, [and] the wearied anxious look of the majority of women impressed me with a strong feeling that some active measure should be taken to right the wrongs of society in general, and of women in particular." The

Mary Cragin, Oneida Woman A founding member of the Oneida community, Mary Cragin had a passionate sexual relationship with John Humphrey Noyes even before the community was organized. Within the bounds of complex marriage as practiced by the Oneidans, Cragin's magnetic sexuality made her a favorite partner of many men. In her journal, she confessed that "every evil passion was very strong in me from my childhood, sexual desire, love of dress and admiration, deceit, anger, pride." Oneida, however, transformed evil passion to holy piety. Cragin wrote, "In view of [God's] goodness to me and of his desire that I should let him fill me with himself, I yield and offer myself, to be penetrated by his spirit, and desire that love and gratitude may inspire my heart so that I shall sympathize with his pleasure in the thing, before my personal pleasure begins, knowing that it will increase my capability for happiness." Oneida's sexual practices were considered outrageous and sinful by almost all other Americans. Even Oneidans did not agree with all of Noyes's ideas about sex. "There is no reason why [sex] should not be done in public as much as music and dancing," he declared. It would display the art of sex, he explained, and watching "would give pleasure to a great many of the older people who now have nothing to do with the matter." Nonetheless, public sex never caught on among Oneidans. Oneida Community Mansion House.

Seneca Falls Declaration of Sentiments set an ambitious agenda to right the wrongs of women and society. The declaration proclaimed that "the history of mankind is a history of repeated injuries and usurpations on the part of man toward woman, having in direct object the establishment of an absolute tyranny over her." In the style of the Declaration of Independence (see appendix I, page A-1), the Seneca Falls declaration demanded that women "have immediate admission to all the

Abolitionist Meeting This rare daguerreotype was made by Ezra Greenleaf Weld in August 1850 at an abolitionist meeting in Cazenovia, New York. Frederick Douglass, who had escaped from slavery in Maryland twelve years earlier, is seated on the platform next to the woman at the table. One of the nation's most brilliant and eloquent abolitionists, Douglass also supported equal rights for women. The man immediately behind Douglass gesturing with his outstretched arm is Gerrit Smith, a wealthy New Yorker and militant abolitionist whose funds supported many reform activities. Notice the two black women in similar clothing on either side of Smith and the white woman next to Douglass. Most white Americans considered such voluntary racial proximity scandalous and promiscuous. What messages did abolitionists attempt to convey by attending such protest meetings? Collection of the J. Paul Getty Museum, Malibu, Calif.

Stanton and other activists sought fair pay and expanded employment opportunities for women by appealing to free-labor ideology. Woman's rights advocate Paula Wright Davis urged Americans to stop discriminating against able and enterprising women: "Let [women] . . . open a Store, . . . plant and tend an Orchard, . . . learn any of the lighter mechanical Trades, . . . study for a Profession, . . . be called to the lecture-room, [and] . . . the Temperance rostrum . . . [and] let her be appointed [to serve in the Post Office]." Some women pioneered in these and many other occupations during the 1840s and 1850s. Woman's rights activists also succeeded in protecting married women's rights to their own wages and property in New York in 1860. But discrimination against women persisted, as most men believed that free-labor ideology required no compromise of male supremacy.

Abolitionists and the American Ideal During the 1840s and 1850s, abolitionists continued to struggle to draw the nation's attention to the plight of slaves and the need for emancipation. Former slaves **Frederick Douglass**, Henry Bibb, and Sojourner Truth lectured to reform audiences throughout the North about the cruelties of slavery. Abolitionists published newspapers, held conventions, and petitioned Congress, but they never attracted a mass following among white Americans. Many white Northerners became convinced that slavery was wrong, but they still believed that blacks were inferior. Many other white Northerners shared the common view of white Southerners that slavery was necessary and even desirable. The geographic expansion of the nation during the 1840s offered abolitionists an opportunity to link their unpopular ideal to a goal that many white Northerners found much more attractive—limiting the geographic expansion of slavery, an issue that moved to the center of national politics during the 1850s (see chapter 14).

Black leaders rose to prominence in the abolitionist movement during the 1840s and 1850s. African Americans had actively opposed slavery for decades, but a new generation of leaders came to the forefront in these years. Frederick Douglass, Henry Highland Garnet, William Wells Brown, Martin R. Delany, and others became impatient with white abolitionists' appeals to the conscience of the white majority. In 1843, Garnet urged slaves to choose "Liberty or Death" and rise in insurrection against their masters, an idea that alienated almost all white people and carried little influence among slaves. To express their own uncompromising ideas, black abolitionists founded their own newspapers and held their own antislavery conventions, although they still cooperated with sympathetic whites.

rights and privileges which belong to them as citizens of the United States," particularly the "inalienable right to the elective franchise."

Nearly two dozen other woman's rights conventions assembled before 1860, repeatedly calling for suffrage and an end to discrimination against women. But women had difficulty receiving a respectful hearing, much less achieving legislative action. Even so, the Seneca Falls declaration served as a pathbreaking manifesto of dissent against male supremacy and of support for woman suffrage, and it inspired many women to challenge the barriers that limited their opportunities.

The commitment of black abolitionists to battling slavery grew out of their own experiences with white supremacy. The 250,000 free African Americans in the North and West constituted less than 2 percent of the total population in 1860. They confronted the humiliations of racial discrimination in nearly every arena of daily life. Only Maine, Massachusetts, New Hampshire, and Vermont permitted black men to vote; New York imposed a special property-holding requirement on black— but not white—voters, effectively excluding most black men from the franchise. The pervasive racial discrimination both handicapped and energized black abolitionists. Some cooperated with the efforts of the **American Colonization Society** to send freed slaves and other black Americans to Liberia in West Africa. Others sought to move to Canada, Haiti, or someplace else, convinced that, as an African American from Michigan wrote, "it is impracticable, not to say impossible, for the whites and blacks to live together, and upon terms of social and civil equality, under the same government." Most black American leaders refused to embrace emigration and worked against racial prejudice in their own communities, organizing campaigns against segregation, particularly in transportation and education. Their most notable success came in 1855 when Massachusetts integrated its public schools. Elsewhere, white supremacy continued unabated.

Outside the public spotlight, free African Americans in the North and West contributed to the antislavery cause by quietly aiding fugitive slaves. **Harriet Tubman** escaped from slavery in Maryland in 1849 and repeatedly risked her freedom and her life to return to the South to escort slaves to freedom. When the opportunity arose, free blacks in the North provided fugitive slaves with food, a safe place to rest, and a helping hand. An outgrowth of the antislavery sentiment and opposition to white supremacy that unified nearly all African Americans in the North, this "underground railroad" ran mainly through black neighborhoods, black churches, and black homes.

> **Q:** **Why were women especially prominent in many nineteenth-century reform efforts?**

Conclusion: Free Labor, Free Men

During the 1840s and 1850s, a cluster of interrelated developments—steam power, railroads, and the growing mechanization of agriculture and manufacturing—meant greater economic productivity, a burst of output from farms and factories, and prosperity for many. Diplomacy and war handed the United States 1.2 million square miles and more than 1,000 miles of Pacific coastline. One prize of manifest destiny, California, almost immediately rewarded its new owners with tons of gold. To most Americans, new territory and vast riches were appropriate accompaniments to the nation's stunning economic progress.

To Northerners, industrial evolution confirmed the choice they had made to eliminate slavery and promote free labor as the key to independence, equality, and prosperity. Like Abraham Lincoln, millions of Americans could point to their personal experiences as evidence of the practical truth of the free-labor ideal. But millions of others had different stories to tell. They knew that in the free-labor system, poverty and wealth continued to rub shoulders. By 1860, more than half of the nation's free-labor workforce still toiled for someone else. Free-labor enthusiasts denied that the problems were inherent in the country's social and economic systems. Instead, they argued, most social ills— including poverty and dependency—sprang from individual deficiencies. Consequently, many reformers focused on self-control and discipline, on avoiding sin and alcohol. Other reformers focused on woman's rights and slavery. They challenged widespread conceptions of male supremacy and black inferiority, but neither group managed to overcome the prevailing free-labor ideology based on individualism, racial prejudice, and notions of male superiority.

By midcentury, the nation was half slave and half free, and each region was animated by different economic interests, cultural values, and political aims. Not even the victory over Mexico could bridge the deepening divide between North and South.

Reviewing the Chapter

★ KEY TERMS

Explain each term's significance

WHO

Samuel F. B. Morse (p. 283)

Stephen F. Austin (p. 292)

Antonio López de Santa Anna (p. 292)

Henry Clay (p. 293)

James K. Polk (p. 293)

Zachary Taylor (p. 294)

Winfield Scott (p. 296)

Elizabeth Cady Stanton (p. 301)

Frederick Douglass (p. 302)

Harriet Tubman (p. 303)

WHAT

mechanical reapers (p. 281)

American system (p. 282)

free-labor ideal (p. 285)

manifest destiny (p. 288)

Oregon Trail (p. 288)

Fort Laramie conference (p. 289)

Mormons (p. 290)

Alamo (p. 292)

Republic of Texas (p. 294)

Treaty of Guadalupe Hidalgo (p. 296)

California gold rush (p. 297)

Fourierist phalanxes (p. 300)

Oneida community (p. 301)

Seneca Falls Declaration of Sentiments (p. 301)

American Colonization Society (p. 303)

> **FOR PRACTICE QUIZZES AND OTHER STUDY TOOLS**, see the Online Study Guide at **bedfordstmartins.com/roarkcompact**.

★ REVIEW QUESTIONS Q:

Use key terms and dates to support your answer

1. Why did the United States become a leading industrial power in the nineteenth century? (pp. 280–84)

2. How did the free-labor ideal account for economic inequality? (pp. 284–87)

3. Why did westward migration expand dramatically in the mid-nineteenth century? (pp. 287–93)

4. Why was the annexation of Texas such a controversial policy? (pp. 293–300)

5. Why were women especially prominent in many nineteenth-century reform efforts? (pp. 300–03)

★ MAKING CONNECTIONS

Draw on key terms, timeline, and review questions

1. Varied political, economic, and technological factors promoted westward migration in the mid-nineteenth century. Considering these factors, discuss migration to two different regions (for instance, Texas, Oregon, Utah, or California). What drew migrants to the regions? How did the U.S. government contribute to their efforts?

2. How did the ideology of manifest destiny contribute to the mid-nineteenth-century drive for expansion? Discuss its implications for individual migrants and the nation. In your answer, consider how manifest destiny built on, or revised, earlier understandings of the nation's history and racial politics.

3. The Mexican-American War reshaped U.S. borders and more. Discuss the consequences of the war for national political and economic developments in subsequent decades. What resources did the new territory give the United States? How did debate over annexation revive older political disputes?

4. Some nineteenth-century reform movements drew on the free-labor ideal, while others challenged it. Discuss the free-labor ideal in relation to two reform movements (such as abolitionism and utopian communalism). How did the reform movements draw on the ideal to pursue specific reforms? How did these minority movements try to influence national developments?

★ SUGGESTED READINGS

H. W. Brands, *The Age of Gold: The California Gold Rush and the New American Dream* (2002). The rollicking story of the fortune-seekers who flocked to California and the way western gold transformed American values.

Pekka Hämäläinen, *The Comanche Empire* (2008). A thoughtful reconsideration of the power of the Comanche in the struggle for control of the southern Great Plains.

Timothy Patrick McCarthy and John Stauffer, eds., *Prophets of Protest: Reconsidering the History of American Abolitionism* (2006). Recent analyses of the complex history of abolitionism.

Sally McMillen, *Seneca Falls and the Origins of the Women's Rights Movement* (2008). A compelling account of the Seneca Falls convention and the struggle for women's rights.

Richard Bruce Winders, *Mr. Polk's Army: The American Military Experience in the Mexican War* (1997). A careful account of the war from the U.S. soldier's perspective.

Kenneth J. Winkle, *The Young Eagle: The Rise of Abraham Lincoln* (2001). The surprising story of Lincoln's rise from log cabin to lawyer and politician.

FOR MORE BOOKS ABOUT TOPICS IN THIS CHAPTER, see the Online Bibliography at **bedfordstmartins.com/roarkcompact**.

FOR ADDITIONAL FIRSTHAND ACCOUNTS OF THIS PERIOD, see Chapter 12 in Michael Johnson, ed., *Reading the American Past*, Fourth Edition.

FOR WEB SITES, IMAGES, AND DOCUMENTS RELATED TO TOPICS AND PLACES IN THIS CHAPTER, visit Make History at **bedfordstmartins.com/roarkcompact**.

★ TIMELINE

1836
- Texas declares independence from Mexico.

1837
- John Deere patents steel plow.

1840s
- Practical mechanical reapers created.

1841
- First wagon trains head west on Oregon Trail.
- Vice President John Tyler becomes president when William Henry Harrison dies.

1844
- Democrat James K. Polk elected president.
- Samuel F. B. Morse demonstrates telegraph.

1845
- Term *manifest destiny* coined.
- United States annexes Texas, which enters Union as slave state.
- Potato blight in Ireland spurs immigration to United States.

1846
- Bear Flag Revolt in California.
- Congress declares war on Mexico.
- United States and Great Britain agree to divide Oregon Country.

1847
- Mormons settle in Utah.

1848
- Treaty of Guadalupe Hidalgo.
- Oneida community organized in New York.
- First U.S. woman's rights convention takes place at Seneca Falls, New York.

1849
- California gold rush begins.

1850
- Mormon community annexed to United States as Utah Territory.

1851
- Conference in Laramie, Wyoming, marks the beginning of government policy of concentration.

1855
- Massachusetts integrates public schools.

1857
- U.S. troops invade Salt Lake City in Mormon War.

CLAY JUG Enslaved African American potters created tens of thousands of ceramic pots to hold water and store food. Pottery sometimes went beyond the utilitarian and became art. The most renowned slave potter, Dave, worked in Edgefield District, South Carolina, an area with rich deposits of high-quality clay and a concentration of white-owned pottery shops. Many of Dave's vessels are huge. This pot, completed on August 24, 1857, is nearly three feet tall and holds more than twenty-five gallons. Beyond their extraordinary size, Dave's pots are unusual for their inscriptions. At a time when teaching slaves to read and write was illegal, Dave signed his work with a grand flourish: "Dave" or "Dave the potter." He also inscribed some of his pots with verse. His rhymes provide glimpses into his life. For example, "I wonder where is all my relations / Friendship to all and every nation" probably refers to the slave sales that sent some of his family to Louisiana. Collection of McKissick Museum, University of South Carolina.

CHAPTER

The Slave South

1820–1860

NAT TURNER WAS BORN A SLAVE in Southampton County, Virginia, in October 1800. People in his neighborhood claimed that he had always been different. His parents noticed special marks on his body, which they said were signs that he was "intended for some great purpose." His master said that he learned to read without being taught. As an adolescent, he adopted an austere lifestyle of Christian devotion and fasting. In his twenties, he received visits from the "Spirit," the same spirit, he believed, that had spoken to the ancient prophets. In time, **Nat Turner** began to interpret these things to mean that God had appointed him an instrument of divine vengeance for the sin of slaveholding.

In the early morning of August 22, 1831, he set out with six trusted friends — Hark, Henry, Sam, Nelson, Will, and Jack — to punish slave owners. Turner struck the first blow, an ax to the head of his master, Joseph Travis. The rebels killed all of the white men, women, and children they encountered. By noon, they had visited eleven farms and slaughtered fifty-seven whites. Along the way, they had added fifty or sixty men to their army. Word spread quickly, and soon the militia and hundreds of local whites gathered. By the next day, whites had captured or killed all of the rebels except Turner, who hid out for about ten weeks before being captured in nearby woods. Within a week, he was tried, convicted, and executed. By then, forty-five slaves had stood trial, twenty had been convicted and hanged, and another ten had been banished from Virginia. Frenzied whites had killed another hundred or more blacks — insurgents and innocent bystanders — in their counterattack against the rebellion.

White Virginians prided themselves on having the "mildest" slavery in the South, but sixty black rebels on a rampage challenged the comforting theory of the contented slave. Nonetheless, whites found explanations that allowed them to feel safer. They placed the blame on outside agitators. In 1829, **David Walker**, a freeborn black man living in Boston, had published his *Appeal ... to the Coloured Citizens of the World*, an invitation to slaves to rise up in bloody rebellion, and copies had fallen into the hands of Virginia slaves. Moreover, on January 1, 1831, in Boston, the Massachusetts abolitionist **William Lloyd Garrison** had published the first issue of the *Liberator*, his fiery newspaper. White Virginians

Previewing the Chapter

The Growing Distinctiveness of the South 308
Q: *Why did the nineteenth-century southern economy remain primarily agricultural?*

Masters, Mistresses, and the Big House 316
Q: *Why did the ideology of paternalism gain currency among planters in the nineteenth century?*

Slaves and the Quarter 319
Q: *What types of resistance did slaves participate in, and why did slave resistance rarely take the form of rebellion?*

Black and Free: On the Middle Ground 323
Q: *Why did many state legislatures pass laws restricting free blacks' rights in the 1820s and 1830s?*

The Plain Folk 324
Q: *Why did yeomen dominate the upcountry?*

The Politics of Slavery 327
Q: *How did planters benefit from their control of state legislatures?*

Conclusion: A Slave Society 328

Horrid Massacre in Virginia There are no known contemporary images of Nat Turner. This woodcut simply imagines the rebellion as a nightmare in which black brutes took the lives of innocent whites. Although there was never another rebellion as large as Turner's, images of black violence continued to haunt white imaginations. Library of Congress.

also dismissed the rebellion's leader, Nat Turner, as insane. "He is a complete fanatic, or plays his part admirably," wrote Thomas R. Gray, the lawyer who was assigned to defend Turner.

In the months following the insurrection, the Virginia legislature reaffirmed the state's determination to preserve black bondage by passing laws that strengthened the institution of slavery and further restricted free blacks. A professor at the College of William and Mary, **Thomas R. Dew**, published a vigorous defense of slavery that became the bible of Southerners' proslavery arguments. More than ever, the nation was divided along the **Mason-Dixon line**, the surveyors' mark that in colonial times had established the boundary between Maryland and Pennsylvania but half a century later divided the free North and the slave South.

Black slavery increasingly molded the South into a distinctive region. In the decades after 1820, Southerners, like Northerners, raced westward, but unlike Northerners who spread small farms and free labor, Southerners spread slavery, cotton, and plantations. Geographic expansion meant that slavery became more vigorous and profitable than ever, embraced more people, and increased the South's political power. Antebellum Southerners included diverse people who at times found themselves at odds with one another — not only slaves and free people but also women and men; Indians, Africans, and Europeans; and aristocrats and common folk. Nevertheless, beneath this diversity, a distinctively southern society and culture were forming. The South became a slave society, and most white Southerners were proud of it. ★

The Growing Distinctiveness of the South

From the earliest settlements, inhabitants of the southern colonies had shared a great deal with northern colonists. Most whites in both sections were British and Protestant, spoke a common language, and shared an exuberant pride in their victorious revolution against British rule. The creation of the new nation under the Constitution in 1789 forged political ties that bound all Americans. The beginnings of a national economy fostered economic interdependence and communication across regional boundaries. White Americans everywhere celebrated the achievements of the prosperous young nation, and they looked forward to its seemingly boundless future.

Despite these national similarities, Southerners and Northerners grew increasingly different. The French political observer Alexis de Tocqueville believed he knew why. "I could easily prove," he asserted in 1831, "that almost all the differences which may be noticed between the character of the Americans in the Southern and Northern states have originated in slavery." Slavery made the

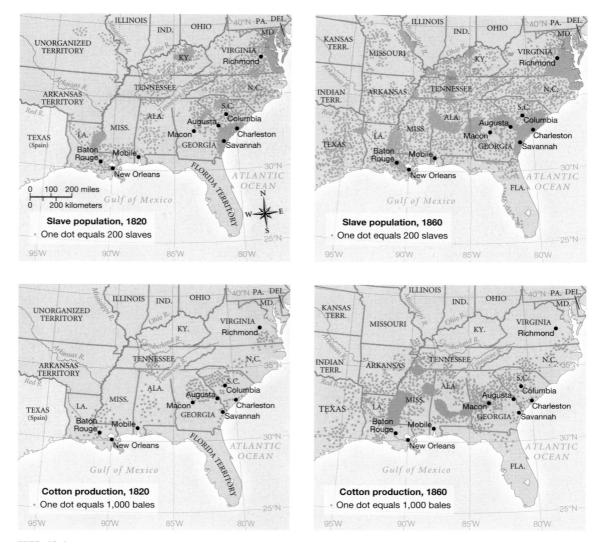

MAP 13.1 **Cotton Kingdom, Slave Empire: 1820 and 1860**
As the production of cotton soared, the slave population increased dramatically. Slaves continued to toil in tobacco and rice fields along the Atlantic seaboard, but increasingly they worked on cotton plantations in Alabama, Mississippi, and Louisiana.

South different, and it was the differences between the North and South, not the similarities, that increasingly shaped antebellum American history.

Cotton Kingdom, Slave Empire In the first half of the nineteenth century, millions of Americans migrated west. In the South, the stampede began after the Creek War of 1813–1814, which divested the Creek Indians of 24 million acres and initiated the government campaign to remove Indian people living east of the Mississippi River to the West (see chapters 10 and 11). Southerners—planters, small farmers, and herders and drovers—pushed westward relentlessly, until by midcentury the South encompassed nearly a million square miles. Contemporaries spoke of this vast region as the Lower

South, those states where cotton was dominant, and the Upper South, where cotton was less important.

The South's climate and geography were ideally suited for the cultivation of cotton. By the 1830s, cotton fields stretched from southern Virginia to central Texas. Heavy migration led to statehood for Arkansas in 1836 and for Texas and Florida in 1845. Production soared from 300,000 bales in 1830 to nearly 5 million in 1860, when the South produced three-fourths of the world's supply. The South—especially that tier of states from South Carolina west to Texas—had become the **cotton kingdom** (Map 13.1).

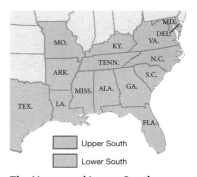

The Upper and Lower South

The cotton kingdom was also a slave empire. The South's cotton boom rested on the backs of slaves, who grew 75 percent of the crop on plantations, toiling in gangs under the direct supervision of whites. As cotton agriculture expanded westward, whites shipped more than 300,000 slaves out of the tobacco regions of the Chesapeake. Victims of this brutal domestic slave trade marched hundreds of miles southwest to new plantations in the Lower South. Cotton, slaves, and plantations moved west together.

The slave population grew enormously. Southern slaves numbered fewer than 700,000 in 1790, about 2 million in 1830, and almost 4 million by 1860. By 1860, the South contained more slaves than all the other slave societies in the New World combined. The extraordinary growth was not the result of the importation of slaves, which the federal government outlawed in 1808. Instead, the slave population grew through natural reproduction. By the nineteenth century, most slaves were native-born Southerners. In comparison, Cuba and Brazil, slave societies that kept their slave trades open until the mid-nineteenth century, had more African-born slaves and thus stronger ties to Africa.

The South in Black and White By 1860, one in every three Southerners was black (approximately 4 million blacks and 8 million whites). In the Lower South states of Mississippi and South Carolina, blacks were the majority (Figure 13.1). The contrast with the North was striking: In 1860, only one Northerner in seventy-six was black (about 250,000 blacks to 19 million whites).

The presence of large numbers of African Americans had profound consequences for the South. Southern culture—language, food, music, religion, and even accents—was in part shaped by blacks. But the most direct consequence of the South's biracialism was southern whites' commitment to white supremacy. Northern whites believed in racial superiority, too, but their

---

FIGURE 13.1 Black and White Populations in the South, 1860
Blacks represented a much larger fraction of the population in the South than in the North, but considerable variation existed from state to state. Only one Missourian in ten, for example, was black, while Mississippi and South Carolina had black majorities. States in the Upper South were "whiter" than states in the Lower South, despite the Upper South's greater number of free blacks.

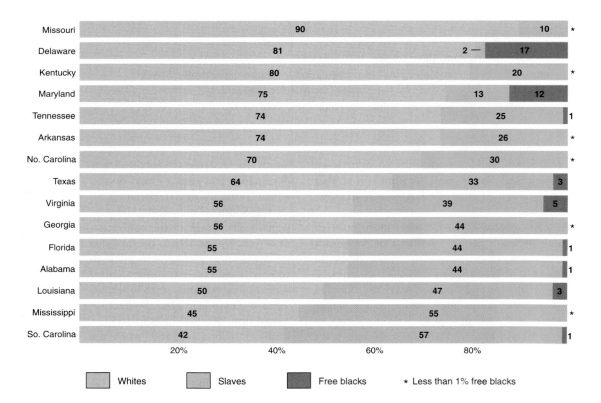

dedication to white supremacy lacked the intensity and urgency increasingly felt by white Southerners who lived among millions of blacks who had every reason to hate them and to strike back, as Nat Turner had.

Attacks on slavery after 1820 — from blacks and a handful of white antislavery advocates within the South and from abolitionists outside — jolted southern slaveholders into an awareness that they lived in a dangerous world. As the only slave society embedded in an egalitarian, democratic republic, the South made extraordinary efforts to strengthen slavery. State legislatures constructed **slave codes** (laws) that required the total submission of slaves. As the Louisiana code stated, a slave "owes his master . . . a respect without bounds, and an absolute obedience." The laws also underlined the authority of all whites, not just masters. Any white could "correct" slaves who did not stay "in their place."

Intellectuals joined legislators in the campaign to strengthen slavery and employed every imaginable defense. They argued that in the South slaves were legal property, and wasn't the protection of property the bedrock of American liberty? History also endorsed slavery, they claimed. Weren't the great civilizations — such as those of the Hebrews, Greeks, and Romans — slave societies? They claimed that the Bible, properly interpreted, also sanctioned slavery. Old Testament patriarchs owned slaves, they observed, and in the New Testament, Paul returned the runaway slave Onesimus to his master. Proslavery spokesmen played on the fears of Northerners and Southerners alike by charging that giving blacks equal rights would lead to the sexual mixing of the races, or **miscegenation**.

Others attacked the North's free-labor economy and society. George Fitzhugh of Virginia argued that behind the North's grand slogans lay a heartless philosophy: "Every man for himself, and the devil take the hindmost." Gouging capitalists exploited wageworkers unmercifully, Fitzhugh declared, and he contrasted the North's vicious free-labor system with the humane relations that he claimed prevailed between masters and slaves because slaves were valuable capital that masters sought to protect.

But at the heart of the defense of slavery lay the claim of black inferiority. Black enslavement was both necessary and proper, antebellum defenders argued, because Africans were lesser beings. Rather than exploitative, slavery was a mass civilizing effort that lifted lowly blacks from barbarism and savagery, taught them disciplined work, and converted them to soul-saving Christianity. According to Virginian Thomas R. Dew, most slaves were grateful. He declared that "the slaves of a good master are his warmest, most constant, and most devoted friends."

Whites gradually moved away from defending slavery as a "necessary evil" — the halfhearted argument popular in Jefferson's day — and toward an aggressive defense of slavery as a "positive good." John C. Calhoun, an influential southern politician, declared that in the states where slavery had been abolished, "the condition of the African, instead of being improved, has become worse," while in the slave states, the Africans "have improved greatly in every respect." (See "Documenting the American Promise," page 312.)

Black slavery encouraged southern whites to unify around race rather than to divide by class. The grubbiest, most tobacco-stained white man could proudly proclaim his superiority to all blacks and his equality with the most refined southern patrician. Because of racial slavery, Georgia attorney Thomas R. R. Cobb observed, every white Southerner "feels that he belongs to an elevated class. It matters not that he is no slaveholder; he is not of the inferior race; he is a freeborn citizen." Consequently, the "poorest meets the richest as an equal; sits at his table with him; salutes him as a neighbor; meets him in every public assembly, and stands on the same social platform." In the South, Cobb boasted, "there is no war of classes."

In reality, slavery did not create perfect harmony among whites or ease every strain along class lines. But by providing every white Southerner membership in the ruling race, slavery helped whites bridge differences in wealth, education, and culture.

The Plantation Economy
As important as slavery was in unifying white Southerners, only about a quarter of the white population lived in slaveholding families. Most slaveholders owned fewer than five slaves. Only about 12 percent of slave owners owned twenty or more, the number of slaves that historians consider necessary to distinguish a **planter** from a farmer. Nevertheless, planters dominated the southern economy. In 1860, 52 percent of the South's slaves lived and worked on **plantations**. Plantation slaves produced more than 75 percent of the South's export crops, the backbone of the region's economy. Slavery was dying elsewhere in the New World (only Brazil and Cuba still defended slavery at

Defending Slavery

White Southerners who defended slavery were rationalizing their economic interests and racial privileges, of course, but they also believed what they said about slavery being just, necessary, and godly. Politicians, planters, clergymen, and academics wrote essays on economics, religion, morality, science, political theory, and law to defend the southern way of life and justify slavery. Whatever their specific arguments, they agreed with the Charleston Mercury *that without slavery, the South would become a "most magnificent jungle."*

DOCUMENT 1
John C. Calhoun, Speech before the U.S. Senate, 1837

When abolitionists began to flood Congress with petitions that denounced slavery as sinful and odious, John C. Calhoun, the South's leading proslavery politician, rose to defend the institution as "a positive good." Calhoun devoted part of his speech to the argument that enslavement benefited the slaves themselves.

Be it good or bad, it [slavery] has grown up with our society and institutions, and is so interwoven with them, that to destroy it would be to destroy us as a people. But let me not be understood as admitting, even by implication, that the existing relations between the two races in the slaveholding States is an evil: far otherwise; I hold it to be a good, as it has thus far proved to be to both, and will continue to prove so if not disturbed by the fell spirit of abolition. I appeal to facts. Never before has the black race of Central Africa, from the dawn of history to the present day, attained a condition so civilized and so improved, not only physically, but morally and intellectually. It came to us in a low, degraded, and savage condition, and in the course of a few generations, it has grown up under the fostering care of our institutions,

reviled they have been, to its present comparatively civilized condition. This, with the rapid increase of numbers, is conclusive proof of the general happiness of the race, in spite of all the exaggerated tales to the contrary. . . .

I hold that in the present state of civilization, where two races of different origin, and distinguished by color, and other physical differences, as well as intellectual, are brought together, the relation now existing in the slaveholding States between the two, is, instead of an evil, a good—a positive good. . . .

I may say with truth, that in few countries so much is left to the share of the laborer, and so little exacted from him, or where there is more kind attention paid to him in sickness or infirmities of age. Compare his condition with the tenants of the poor houses in the more civilized portions of Europe—look at the sick, and the old and infirm slave, on one hand, in the midst of his family and friends, under the kind superintending care of his master and mistress, and compare it with the forlorn and wretched condition of the pauper in the poor house.

SOURCE: John C. Calhoun, "Speech on the Reception of Abolition Petitions, Delivered in the Senate, February 6th, 1837," in *Speeches of John C. Calhoun, Delivered in the House of Representatives and in the Senate of the United States.* Edited by Richard K. Cralle (Appleton, 1853), 625–33.

DOCUMENT 2
William Harper, *Memoir on Slavery*, 1837

Unlike Calhoun, who defended slavery by pointing to what he considered slavery's concrete benefits for blacks, William Harper—judge, politician, and academic—defended slavery by denouncing abolitionists, particularly the "atrocious philosophy" of "natural equality and inalienable rights" that they used to support their attacks on slavery.

All men are born free and equal. Is it not palpably nearer the truth to say that no man was ever born free,

midcentury), but slave plantations increasingly dominated southern agriculture.

The South's major cash crops—tobacco, sugar, rice, and cotton—grew on plantations

(Map 13.2). Tobacco, the original plantation crop in North America, had shifted westward in the nineteenth century from the Chesapeake to Tennessee and Kentucky. Large-scale sugar

and that no two men were ever born equal? . . . Wealth and poverty, fame or obscurity, strength or weakness, knowledge or ignorance, ease or labor, power or subjection, mark the endless diversity in the condition of men. . . .

It is the order of nature and of God, that the being of superior faculties and knowledge, and therefore of superior power, should control and dispose of those who are inferior. It is as much in the order of nature, that men should enslave each other, as that other animals should prey upon each other. I admit that he does this under the highest moral responsibility, and is most guilty if he wantonly inflicts misery or privation on beings more capable of enjoyment or suffering than brutes, without necessity or any view to the great good which is to result. . . .

Moralists have denounced the injustice and cruelty which have been practiced towards our aboriginal Indians, by which they have been driven from their native seats and exterminated.

. . . No doubt, much fraud and injustice has been practiced in the circumstances and manner of their removal. Yet who has contended that civilized man had no moral right to possess himself of the country? That he was bound to leave this wide and fertile continent, which is capable of sustaining uncounted myriads of a civilized race, to a few roving and ignorant barbarians? Yet if any thing is certain, it is certain that there were no means by which he could possess the country, without exterminating or enslaving them. Slave and civilized man cannot live together, and the savage can only be tamed by being enslaved or by having slaves.

SOURCE: William Harper, *Memoir of Slavery* (J.S. Burges, 1838).

DOCUMENT 3
Thornton Stringfellow, "The Bible Argument: or, Slavery in the Light of Divine Revelation," 1856

Reverend Thornton Stringfellow, a Baptist minister from Virginia, offered a defense of human bondage based on his reading of the Bible. In these passages, he makes a case that Jesus himself approved of the relationship between master and slave.

Jesus Christ recognized this institution [slavery] as one that was lawful among men, and regulated its relative duties.

. . . I affirm then, first, (and no man denies,) that Jesus Christ has not abolished slavery by a prohibitory command: and second, I affirm, he has introduced no new moral principle which can work its destruction, under the gospel dispensation; and that the principle relied on for this purpose, is a fundamental principle of the Mosaic law, under which slavery was instituted by Jehovah himself. . . .

To the church at Colosse, a city of Phrygia, in the lesser Asia, Paul in his letter to them, recognizes the three relations of wives and husbands, parents and children, servants and masters, as relations existing among the members . . . and to the servants and masters he thus writes: "Servants obey in all things your masters, according to the flesh: not with eye service, as men pleasers, but in singleness of heart, fearing God: and whatsoever you do, do it heartily, as to the Lord and not unto men; knowing that of the Lord ye shall receive the reward of the inheritance, for ye serve the Lord Christ. . . . Masters give unto your servants that which is just and equal, knowing that you also have a master in heaven."

SOURCES: *Slavery Defended: The Views of the Old South* by Eric L. McKitrick, editor. Published by Prentice-Hall, 1963. Reprinted with permission. *Cotton Is King and Pro-Slavery Arguments* by Thornton Stringfellow (Pritchard, Abbott & Loomis, 1860), 459–546.

Questions for Analysis and Debate

1. According to John C. Calhoun, what were slavery's chief benefits for blacks? How did his proslavery convictions shape his argument?

2. Why do you suppose William Harper interjected Americans' treatment of Indians into his defense of slavery?

3. According to Thornton Stringfellow, the Bible instructs both masters and slaves about their duties. What are their respective obligations?

production began in 1795, when Étienne de Boré built a modern sugar mill in what is today New Orleans, and sugar plantations were confined almost entirely to Louisiana. Commercial rice

production began in the seventeenth century, and like sugar, rice was confined to a small geographic area, a narrow strip of coast stretching from the Carolinas into Georgia.

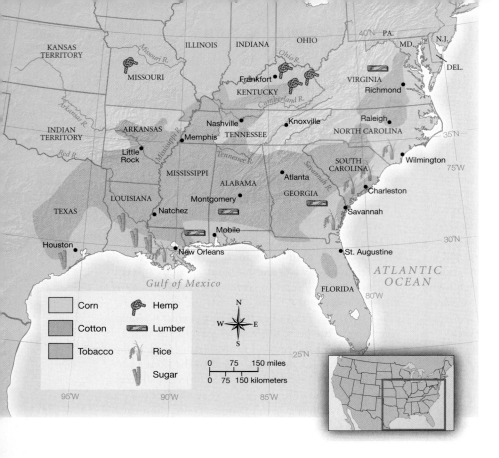

MAP 13.2 **The Agricultural Economy of the South, 1860**

Cotton dominated the South's agricultural economy, but the region grew a variety of crops and was largely self-sufficient in foodstuffs.

READING THE MAP: In what type of geographical areas were rice and sugar grown? After cotton, what crop commanded the greatest agricultural area in the South? In which region of the South was this crop predominantly found?

CONNECTIONS: What role did the South play in the U.S. economy in 1860? How did the economy of the South differ from that of the North?

FOR MORE HELP ANALYZING THIS MAP, see the map activity for this chapter in the Online Study Guide at bedfordstmartins .com/roarkcompact.

But by the nineteenth century, cotton was king of the South's plantation crops. Cotton became commercially significant in the 1790s after the invention of a new cotton gin by **Eli Whitney** dramatically increased the production of raw cotton. Cotton was relatively easy to grow and took little capital to get started — just enough to purchase land, seed, and simple tools. Thus, small farmers as well as planters grew cotton. But planters, whose fields were worked by slaves, produced three-quarters of the South's cotton, and cotton made planters rich.

Plantation slavery also enriched the nation. By 1840, cotton accounted for more than 60 percent of American exports. Much of the profit from the sale of cotton overseas returned to planters, but some went to northern middlemen who bought, sold, insured, warehoused, and shipped cotton to the mills in Great Britain and elsewhere. As one New York merchant observed, "Cotton has enriched all through whose hands it has passed." As middlemen invested their profits in the booming northern economy, industrial development received a burst of much-

> One New York merchant observed, "Cotton has enriched all through whose hands it has passed."

needed capital. Furthermore, southern plantations benefited northern industry by providing an important market for textiles, agricultural tools, and other manufactured goods.

The economies of the North and South steadily diverged. While the North developed a mixed economy — agriculture, commerce, and manufacturing — the South remained overwhelmingly agricultural. Year after year, planters funneled the profits they earned from land and slaves back into more land and slaves. With its capital flowing into agriculture, the South did not develop many factories. By 1860, only 10 percent of the nation's industrial workers lived in the South. Some cotton mills sprang up, but the region that produced 100 percent of the nation's cotton manufactured less than 7 percent of its cotton textiles.

Without significant economic diversification, the South developed fewer cities than the North and West. In 1860, it was the least urban region in the country. Whereas nearly 37 percent of New England's population lived in cities, less than 12 percent of Southerners were urban dwellers. Southern cities were mostly port cities and busy principally with exporting the agricultural products of plantations in the interior. Urban

THE PROMISE OF TECHNOLOGY

The Cotton Gin Machines for separating cotton fibers from seeds that clung to the fiber — cotton gins (the word *gin* is short for *engine*) — had been around for centuries, but none cleaned cotton quickly and efficiently. In 1793, Eli Whitney, a young New Englander living on a Georgia plantation, succeeded in building a simple little device for separating the fibers from the seeds. It was crude, but news of the invention spread like wildfire. The invention enabled southern cotton growers to supply huge quantities of clean cotton for the world market. The commercial production of cotton eventually bound millions of African Americans to slavery. Smithsonian Institution, Washington, D.C.

merchants provided agriculture with indispensable services, such as hauling, insuring, and selling cotton, rice, and sugar, but they were the tail on the plantation dog.

Because the South had so few cities and industrial jobs, it attracted small numbers of European immigrants. Seeking economic opportunity, not competition with slaves, immigrants steered northward. In 1860, 13 percent of all Americans were born abroad. But in nine of the fifteen slave states, only 2 percent or less of the population was foreign-born.

Not every Southerner celebrated the region's commitment to cotton and slaves. Diversification, reformers promised, would make the South economically independent and more prosperous. State governments encouraged economic development by helping to create banking systems that supplied credit

Less than 10%

10–19%

20–29%

More than 30%

Immigrants as a Percentage of State Populations, 1860

for a wide range of projects and by constructing railroads, but they also failed to create some of the essential services modern economies required. By the mid-nineteenth century, for example, no southern legislature had created a statewide public school system.

Northerners claimed that slavery was a backward labor system, and compared with Northerners, Southerners invested less of their capital in industry, transportation, and public education. But planters' pockets were never fuller than in the 1850s. Planters' decisions to reinvest in agriculture ensured the momentum of the plantation economy and the political and social relationships rooted in it.

Q: Why did the nineteenth-century southern economy remain primarily agricultural?

***The Henry Frank*, New Orleans** The steamboat *Henry Frank* sits dangerously overloaded with cotton bales at the New Orleans levee in 1854. The banner flying from the flagstaff indicates that captains boasted about the number of bales their boats carried. The crowd on hand to greet the *Henry Frank* suggests that it might have carried a record-breaking load. The magnitude of the cotton trade in the South's largest city and major port is difficult to capture. Six years earlier, a visitor, Solon Robinson, had expressed awe: "It must be seen to be believed; and even then, it will require an active mind to comprehend acres of cotton bales standing upon the levee, while miles of drays [carts] are constantly taking it off to the cotton presses. . . . Boats are constantly arriving, so piled up with cotton, that the lower tier of bales on deck are in the water." Amid the mountains of cotton, few Southerners doubted that cotton was king. Historic New Orleans Collection.

FOR MORE HELP ANALYZING THIS IMAGE, see the visual activity for this chapter in the Online Study Guide at bedfordstmartins.com/roarkcompact.

Masters, Mistresses, and the Big House

Nowhere was the contrast between northern and southern life more vivid than on the plantations of the South. Located on a patchwork of cleared fields and dense forests, a plantation typically included a "big house" and a slave quarter. Scattered about were numerous outbuildings, each with a special function. Near the big house were the kitchen, storehouse, smokehouse (for curing and preserving meat), and hen coop. More distant were the barns, toolsheds, artisans' workshops, and overseer's house. Large plantations sometimes had an infirmary and a chapel for slaves. Depending on the crop, there was a tobacco shed, a rice mill, a

sugar refinery, or a cotton gin house. Lavish or plain, plantations everywhere had an underlying similarity.

The plantation was the home of masters, mistresses, and slaves. Slavery shaped the lives of all the plantation's inhabitants, from work to leisure activities, but it affected each differently. A hierarchy of rigid roles and duties governed relationships. Presiding was the master, who ruled his wife, children, and slaves, none of whom had many legal rights and all of whom were designated by the state as dependents under his dominion and protection.

Plantation Masters Whereas smaller planters supervised the labor of their slaves themselves, larger planters hired **overseers** who went to the fields with the slaves, leaving the planters free to concentrate on marketing, finance, and general affairs of the plantation. Planters also found time to escape to town to discuss cotton prices, to the courthouse and legislature to debate politics, and to the woods to hunt and fish.

Increasingly, planters characterized their mastery in terms of what they called "Christian guardianship" and what historians have called **paternalism**. The concept of paternalism denied that the form of slavery practiced in the South was brutal and exploitative. As owners of blacks, masters argued, they had the responsibility of caring for a childlike, dependent people. In 1814, Thomas Jefferson captured the essence of the advancing ideal: "We should endeavor, with those whom fortune has thrown on our hands, to feed & clothe them well, protect them from ill usage, require such reasonable labor only as is performed voluntarily by freemen, and be led by no repugnancies to abdicate them, and our duties to them." A South Carolina rice planter insisted, "I manage them as my children."

Paternalism was part propaganda and part self-delusion. But it was also economically shrewd. Masters increasingly recognized slaves as valuable assets, particularly after the nation closed its external slave trade in 1808. They realized that the expansion of the slave labor force could come only from natural reproduction. As one planter declared in 1849, "It behooves those who own them to make them last as long as possible." One consequence of this paternalism and economic self-interest was a small improvement in slaves' welfare. Diet improved, although nineteenth-century slaves still ate mainly fatty pork and cornmeal. Housing improved, although the cabins still had cracks large enough, slaves said, for cats to slip through. Clothing improved, although slaves seldom received much more than two crude outfits a year and perhaps a pair of cheap shoes. In the fields, workdays remained sunup to sundown, but planters often provided a rest period in the heat of the day. And most owners ceased the colonial practice of punishing slaves by branding and mutilation.

Paternalism should not be mistaken for kindness and goodwill. It encouraged better treatment because it made economic sense to provide at least minimal care for valuable slaves. Nor did paternalism require that planters put aside their whips. State laws gave masters nearly "uncontrolled authority over the body" of the slave, according to one North Carolina judge. Paternalism offered slaves some informal protection against the most brutal punishments, but whipping remained the planters' essential form of coercion.

With its notion that slavery imposed on masters a burden and a duty, paternalism provided slaveholders with a means of rationalizing their rule. But it also provided some slaves with leverage in controlling the conditions of their lives. Slaves learned to manipulate the slaveholder's need to see himself as a good master. To avoid a reputation as a cruel tyrant, planters sometimes negotiated with slaves, rather than just resorting to the whip. Masters sometimes granted slaves small garden plots in which they could work for themselves after working all day in the fields, or they gave slaves a few days off and a dance when they had gathered the last of the cotton.

Virginia statesman Edmund Randolph argued that slavery created in white southern men a "quick and acute sense of personal liberty" and a "disdain for every abridgement of personal independence." Indeed, prickly individualism and aggressive independence became crucial features of the southern concept of honor. Social standing, political advancement, and even self-esteem rested on an honorable reputation. Defending honor became a male passion. Andrew Jackson's mother reportedly told her son, "Never tell a lie, nor take what is not your own, nor sue anybody for slander or assault and battery. *Always settle them cases yourself.*"

Southerners also expected an honorable gentleman to be a proper patriarch. Nowhere in America

Southern Man with Children and Their Mammy Obviously prosperous and looking like a man accustomed to giving orders and being obeyed, this patriarch poses around 1848 with his young daughters and their nurse. The black woman is clearly a servant, a status indicated by her race and her attire. Why does she appear in the daguerreotype? The absent mother may be dead. Her death might account for the inclusion of the African American woman in the family circle. In any case, her presence signals her importance in the household. Fathers left the raising of daughters to mothers and nurses. Collection of the J. Paul Getty Museum, Malibu, Calif.

was masculine power more accentuated. Planters brooked no opposition from any of their dependents, black or white. The master's absolute dominion sometimes led to miscegenation. Laws prohibited interracial sex, but how many trips masters and their sons made to slave cabins is impossible to tell. As long as slavery gave white men extraordinary power, however, slave women were forced to submit to the sexual appetites of the men who owned them.

In time, as the children of one elite family married the children of another, ties of blood and kinship, as well as economic interest and ideology, linked planters to one another. Conscious of what they shared as slaveholders, planters worked together to defend their common interests. The values of the big house — slavery, honor, male domination — washed over the boundaries of plantations and flooded all of southern life.

Plantation Mistresses Like their northern counterparts, southern ladies were expected to possess the feminine virtues of piety, purity, chastity, and obedience within the context of marriage, motherhood, and domesticity. Countless toasts praised the southern lady as the perfect complement to her husband, the commanding patriarch. For women, this image of the southern lady was no blessing. <u>Chivalry</u>—the South's romantic ideal of male-female relationships—glorified the lady while it subordinated her. Chivalry's underlying assumptions about the weakness of women and the protective authority of men resembled the paternalistic defense of slavery.

Indeed, the most articulate spokesmen for slavery also vigorously defended the subordination of women. George Fitzhugh insisted that "a woman, like children, has but one right and that is the right to protection. The right to protection involves the obligation to obey. A husband, a lord and master,

nature designed for every woman. . . . If she be obedient she stands little danger of maltreatment." Just as the slaveholder's mastery was written into law, so too were the paramount rights of husbands. Married women lost almost all their property rights to their husbands. Women throughout the nation found divorce difficult, but southern women found it almost impossible.

Daughters of planters confronted chivalry's demands at an early age. Their education aimed at fitting them to become southern ladies. At their private boarding schools, they read literature, learned languages, and studied the appropriate drawing-room arts. Elite women began courting at a young age and married early. Kate Carney exaggerated only slightly when she despaired in her diary: "Today, I am seventeen, getting quite

The Price of Blood This 1868 painting by T. S. Noble depicts a transaction between a slave trader and a rich planter. The trader nervously pretends to study the contract, while the planter waits impatiently for the completion of the sale. The planter's mulatto son, who is being sold, looks away. The children of white men and slave women were property and could be sold by the father/master. Morris Museum of Art, Augusta, Ga.

FOR MORE HELP ANALYZING THIS IMAGE, see the visual activity for this chapter in the Online Study Guide at bedfordstmartins.com/roarkcompact.

old, and am not married." Yet marriage meant turning their fates over to their husbands and making enormous efforts to live up to their region's lofty ideal.

Proslavery advocates claimed that slavery freed white women from drudgery. Surrounded "by her domestics," declared Thomas R. Dew, "she ceases to be a mere beast of burden" and "becomes the cheering and animating center of the family circle." In reality, however, having servants required the plantation mistress to work long hours. She managed the big house, directly supervising as many as a dozen slaves. But unlike her husband, the mistress had no overseer. All house servants answered directly to her. She assigned them tasks each morning, directed their work throughout the day, and punished them when she found fault.

Whereas masters used their status as slaveholders as a springboard into public affairs, mistresses' lives were circumscribed by the plantation. Masters left the plantation when they pleased, but mistresses needed chaperones to travel. When they could, they went to church, but women spent most days at home, where they often became lonely. In 1853, Mary Kendall wrote how much she enjoyed her sister's letter: "For about three weeks I did not have the pleasure of seeing one white female face, there being no white family except our own upon the plantation."

As members of slaveholding families, mistresses lived privileged lives. But they also had significant grounds for discontent. No feature of plantation life generated more anguish among mistresses than miscegenation. Mary Boykin Chesnut of Camden, South Carolina, confided in her diary, "Ours is a monstrous system, a wrong and iniquity. Like the patriarchs of old, our men live all in one house with their wives and their concubines; and the mulattos one sees in every family partly resemble the white children. Any lady is ready to tell you who is the father of all the mulatto children in everybody's household but her own. Those, she seems to think drop from the clouds."

Most planters' wives, including Chesnut, accepted slavery. After all, the mistress's world rested on slave labor, just as the master's did. By acknowledging the realities of male power, mistresses enjoyed the rewards of their class and race. But these rewards came at a price. Still, the heaviest burdens of slavery fell not on those who lived in the big house, but on those who toiled to support them.

Q: Why did the ideology of paternalism gain currency among planters in the nineteenth century?

Slaves and the Quarter

On most plantations, only a few hundred yards separated the big house and the slave quarter. But the distance was great enough to provide slaves with some privacy. Out of eyesight and earshot of the big house, slaves drew together and built lives of their own. They created families, worshipped God, and developed an African American community and culture. Individually and collectively, slaves found subtle and not so subtle ways to resist their bondage.

Despite the rise of plantations, a substantial minority of slaves lived and worked elsewhere. Most labored on small farms, where they wielded a hoe alongside another slave or two and perhaps their master. But by 1860, almost half a million slaves (one in eight) did not work in agriculture at all. Some were employed in towns and cities as domestics, day laborers, bakers, barbers, tailors, and more. Others, far from urban centers, toiled as fishermen, lumbermen, and railroad workers. Slaves could also be found in most of the South's factories. Nevertheless, a majority of slaves (52 percent) counted plantations as their workplaces and homes.

Work Ex-slave Albert Todd recalled, "Work was a religion that we were taught." Whites enslaved blacks for their labor, and all slaves who were capable of productive labor worked. Former slave Carrie Hudson recalled that children who were "knee high to a duck" were sent to the fields to carry water to thirsty workers or to protect ripening crops from hungry birds. Others helped in the slave nursery, caring for children even younger than themselves, or in the big house, where they swept floors or shooed flies in the dining room. When slave boys and girls reached the age of eleven or twelve, masters sent most of them to the fields, where they learned farmwork by laboring alongside their parents. After a lifetime of labor, old women left the fields to care for the small children and spin yarn, and old men moved on to mind livestock and clean stables.

The overwhelming majority of plantation slaves worked as field hands. Planters sometimes assigned men and women to separate gangs, the women working at lighter tasks and the men doing the heavy work of clearing and breaking the land. But women also did heavy work. "I had to work hard," Nancy Boudry remembered, and "plow and go and split wood just like a man." The backbreaking labor and the monotonous routines

> An ex-slave named Albert Todd recalled, "Work was a religion that we were taught."

Isaac Jefferson In this 1845 daguerreotype, seventy-year-old Isaac Jefferson proudly poses in the apron he wore while practicing his crafts as a tinsmith and nail maker. Slaves of Thomas Jefferson, he, his wife, and their two children were deeded to Jefferson's daughter Mary when she married in 1797. Isaac worked at Jefferson's home, Monticello, until 1820, when he moved to Petersburg, Virginia. When work was slow on the home plantation, slave owners often would hire out their skilled artisans to neighbors who needed a carpenter, blacksmith, mason, or tinsmith. Special Collections Department, University of Virginia Library.

caused one ex-slave to observe that the "history of one day is the history of every day."

A few slaves (about one in ten) became house servants. Nearly all of those (nine out of ten) were women. They cooked, cleaned, babysat, washed clothes, and did the dozens of other tasks the master and mistress required. House servants enjoyed somewhat less physically demanding work than field hands, but they were constantly on call, with no time that was entirely their own. Since no servant could please constantly, most bore the brunt of white frustration and rage. Ex-slave Jacob Branch of Texas remembered, "My poor mama! Every washday old Missy give her a beating."

Even rarer than house servants were skilled artisans. In the cotton South, no more than one slave in twenty (almost all men) worked in a skilled trade. Most were blacksmiths and carpenters, but slaves also worked as masons, mechanics, millers, and shoemakers. Slave craftsmen took pride in their skills and often exhibited the independence of spirit that caused slaveholder James H. Hammond of South Carolina to declare in disgust that when a slave became a skilled artisan, "he is more than half freed." Skilled slave fathers took pride in teaching their crafts to their sons. "My pappy was one of the black smiths and worked in the shop," John Mathews remembered. "I had to help my pappy in the shop when I was a child and I learnt how to beat out the iron and make wagon tires, and make plows."

Rarest of all slave occupations was that of **slave driver**. Probably no more than one male slave in a hundred worked in this capacity. These men were well named, for their primary task was driving other slaves to work harder in the fields. In some drivers' hands, the whip never rested. Ex-slave Jane Johnson of South Carolina called her driver the "meanest man, white or black, I ever see." But other drivers showed all the restraint they could. "Ole Gabe didn't like that whippin' business," West Turner of Virginia remembered. "When Marsa was there, he would lay it on 'cause he had to. But when old Marsa wasn't lookin', he never would beat them slaves."

Normally, slaves worked from what they called "can to can't," from "can see" in the morning to "can't see" at night. Even with a break at noon for a meal and rest, it made for a long day. For slaves, Lewis Young recalled, "work, work, work, 'twas all they do."

Family, Religion, and Community From dawn to dusk, slaves worked for the master, but at night, when the labor was done, and all day Sunday and usually Saturday afternoon, slaves were left largely to themselves. Bone tired perhaps, they nonetheless used the time to develop and enjoy what mattered most: family, religion, and community.

One of the most important consequences of slaves' limited autonomy was the preservation of the family. Though severely battered, the black family survived slavery. No laws recognized slave marriage, and therefore no master or slave was legally obligated to honor the bond. Nevertheless, plantation records show that slave marriages were often long-lasting. Young men and women in the quarter fell in love, married, and set up housekeeping in cabins of their own. The primary cause of the ending of slave marriages was death, just as it was in white families. But the second most frequent cause was the sale of the husband or wife, something no white family ever had to fear. Precise figures are unavailable, but in the years 1820 to 1860, research suggests that sales destroyed at least 300,000 slave marriages.

In 1858, a South Carolina slave named Abream Scriven wrote a letter to his wife, who lived on a neighboring plantation. "My dear wife," he began, "I take the pleasure of writing you . . . with much regret to inform you I am Sold to man by the name of Peterson, a Treader and Stays in New Orleans." Scriven promised to send some things when he got to his new home in Louisiana, but he admitted that he was not sure how he would "get them to you and my children." He asked his wife to "give my love to my father and mother and tell them good Bye for me. And if we do not meet in this world I hope to meet in heaven. . . . My dear wife for you and my children my pen cannot express the griffe I feel to be parted from you all." He closed with words no master would have permitted in a slave's marriage vows:

"I remain your truly husband until Death." The letter makes clear Scriven's love for his family; it also demonstrates slavery's massive assault on family life in the quarter.

Religion also provided slaves with a refuge and a reason for living. Evangelical Baptists and Methodists had great success in converting slaves from their African beliefs. By the mid-nineteenth century, perhaps as many as one-quarter of all slaves claimed church membership, and many of the rest would not have objected to being called Christians.

Planters promoted Christianity in the quarter because they believed that the slaves' salvation was part of their obligation and that religion made slaves more obedient. The *Catechism for Colored Persons*, published in 1834, instructed slaves "to count their Masters 'worthy of all honour,' as those whom God has placed over them in this world." But slaves laughed up their sleeves at such messages. "That old white preacher just was telling us slaves to be good to our masters," one ex-slave said with a chuckle. "We ain't cared a bit about that stuff he was telling us 'cause we wanted to sing, pray, and serve God in our own way."

Meeting in their cabins or secretly in the woods, slaves created an African American Christianity that served their needs, not the masters'. Laws prohibited teaching slaves to read, but a few could read enough to struggle with the Bible. They interpreted the Christian message themselves. Rather than obedience, their faith emphasized justice. Slaves believed that God kept score

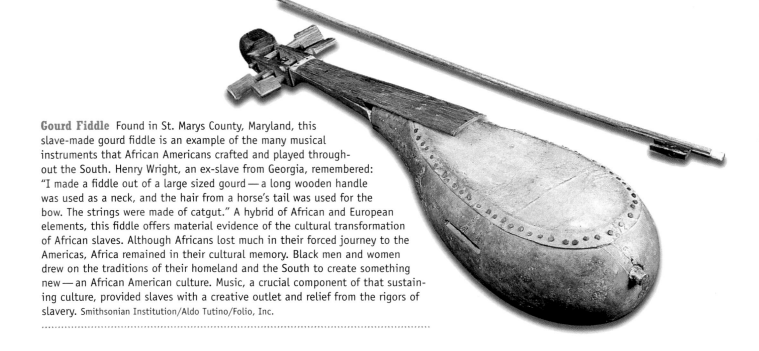

Gourd Fiddle Found in St. Marys County, Maryland, this slave-made gourd fiddle is an example of the many musical instruments that African Americans crafted and played throughout the South. Henry Wright, an ex-slave from Georgia, remembered: "I made a fiddle out of a large sized gourd — a long wooden handle was used as a neck, and the hair from a horse's tail was used for the bow. The strings were made of catgut." A hybrid of African and European elements, this fiddle offers material evidence of the cultural transformation of African slaves. Although Africans lost much in their forced journey to the Americas, Africa remained in their cultural memory. Black men and women drew on the traditions of their homeland and the South to create something new — an African American culture. Music, a crucial component of that sustaining culture, provided slaves with a creative outlet and relief from the rigors of slavery. Smithsonian Institution/Aldo Tutino/Folio, Inc.

and that the accounts of this world would be settled in the next. "The idea of a revolution in the conditions of the whites and blacks is the corner-stone" of the slaves' religion, recalled one ex-slave. But the slaves' faith also spoke to their experiences in this world. In the Old Testament, they discovered Moses, who delivered his people from slavery, and in the New Testament, they found Jesus, who offered salvation to all. Jesus' message of equality provided a potent antidote to the planters' claim that blacks were an inferior people whom God condemned to slavery.

Christianity did not entirely drive out traditional African beliefs. Even slaves who were Christians sometimes continued to believe that conjurers, witches, and spirits possessed the power to injure and protect. Moreover, slaves' Christian music, preaching, and rituals reflected the influence of Africa, as did many of their secular activities, such as wood carving, quilt making, and storytelling. But by the mid-nineteenth century, black Christianity had assumed a central place in slaves' quest for freedom. In the words of one spiritual, "O my Lord delivered Daniel / O why not deliver me too?"

Resistance and Rebellion Slaves did not suffer slavery passively. They were, as whites said, "troublesome property." Slaves understood that accommodation to what they could not change was the price of survival, but in a hundred ways, they protested their bondage. Theoretically, the master was all-powerful and the slave powerless. But sustained by their families, religion, and community, slaves engaged in day-to-day resistance against their enslavers.

The spectrum of slave resistance ranged from mild to extreme. Telling a pointed story by the fireside in a slave cabin was probably the mildest form of protest. But when the weak got the better of the strong, as they did in tales of Br'er Rabbit and Br'er Fox (*Br'er* is a contraction of *Brother*), listeners could enjoy the thrill of a vicarious victory over their masters. Protest in the fields was riskier and included putting rocks in their cotton bags before having them weighed and feigning illness. Slaves broke so many hoes that owners outfitted the tools with oversized handles. Slaves so mistreated the work animals that masters switched from horses to mules, which could absorb more abuse. Although slaves worked hard in the master's fields, they also sabotaged his interests.

Running away was a common form of protest. Except along the borders with northern states and with Mexico, escape to freedom was almost impossible. Most runaways could hope only to escape for a few days. Seeking temporary respite from hard labor or avoiding punishment, they usually stayed close to their plantations, keeping to the deep woods or swamps and slipping back into the quarter at night to get food. "Lying out," as it was known, usually ended when the runaway, worn-out and ragged, gave up or was finally chased down by slave-hunting dogs.

Although resistance was common, outright rebellion—a violent assault on slavery by large numbers of slaves—was very rare. The scarcity of revolts in the South is not evidence of the slaves' contentedness, however. Rather, conditions gave rebels almost no chance of success. By 1860, whites in the South outnumbered blacks two to one and were heavily armed. Moreover, communication between plantations was difficult, and the South provided little protective wilderness into which rebels could retreat and defend themselves. Rebellion, as Nat Turner's experience showed, was virtual suicide.

Despite the rarity of slave revolts, whites believed that they were surrounded by conspiracies to rebel. In 1822, whites in Charleston accused **Denmark Vesey**, a free black carpenter, of conspiring with plantation slaves to slaughter Charleston's white inhabitants. The authorities rounded up scores of suspects, who, prodded by torture and the threat of death, implicated others in the plot "to riot in blood, outrage, and rapine." Although the city fathers never found any weapons and Vesey and most of the accused steadfastly denied the charges of conspiracy, officials hanged thirty-five black men, including Vesey, and banished another thirty-seven blacks from the state.

Despite steady resistance and occasional rebellion, slaves did not have the power to end their bondage. Slavery thwarted their hopes and aspirations. It broke some and crippled others. But slavery's destructive power had to contend with the resiliency of the human spirit. Slaves fought back physically, culturally, and spiritually. They not only survived bondage, but they also created in the quarter a vibrant African American culture that buoyed them up during long hours in the fields and brought them joy and hope in the few hours they had to themselves.

Q: What types of resistance did slaves participate in, and why did slave resistance rarely take the form of rebellion?

Black and Free: On the Middle Ground

Not every black Southerner was a slave. In 1860, some 260,000 (approximately 6 percent) of the region's 4.1 million African Americans were free (see Figure 13.1, page 310). What is surprising is not that their numbers were small but that they existed at all. **Free black** seemed increasingly a contradiction to most white Southerners. According to the emerging racial thinking, blacks were supposed to be slaves. Blacks who were free stood out, and whites made them more and more targets of oppression. Free blacks stood precariously between slavery and full freedom, on what a free black artisan in Charleston characterized in 1848 as "a middle ground." But they made the most of their freedom, and a few found success despite the restrictions placed on them by white Southerners.

Precarious Freedom The population of free blacks swelled after the Revolution, when the natural rights philosophy of the Declaration of Independence and the egalitarian message of evangelical Protestantism joined to challenge slavery. A brief flurry of **emancipation**—the act of freeing from slavery—visited the Upper South, where the ideological assault on slavery coincided with a deep depression in the tobacco economy. By 1810, free blacks in the South numbered more than 100,000, a fact that worried white Southerners, who, because of the cotton boom, wanted more slaves, not more free blacks.

In the 1820s and 1830s, state legislatures acted to stem the growth of the free black population and to shrink the liberty of those blacks who had gained their freedom. Laws denied masters the right to free their slaves. Other laws humiliated and restricted free blacks by subjecting them to special taxes, prohibiting them from interstate travel, denying them the right to have schools and to participate in politics, and requiring them to carry "freedom papers" to prove they were not slaves. Increasingly, whites subjected free blacks to the same laws as slaves. They could not testify under oath in a court of law or serve on juries. Like slaves, they were liable to whipping. Free blacks were forbidden to strike whites, even to defend themselves. "Free negroes belong to a degraded caste of society," a South Carolina judge said in 1848. "They are in no respect on a perfect equality with the white man. . . . They ought, by law, to be compelled to demean themselves as inferiors."

Freedom Paper This legal document attests to the free status of the Reverend John F. Cook of Washington, D.C., his daughter Mary, and his son George. Cook was a free black man who kept his "freedom paper" in this watertight tin, which he probably carried with him at all times. Free blacks had to be prepared to prove their free status anytime a white man challenged them, for southern law presumed that a black person was a slave unless he or she could prove otherwise. Without such proof, free blacks risked enslavement. Moorland-Spingarn Research Center, Howard University, Washington, D.C.

Laws confined most free African Americans to a constricted life of poverty and dependence. Typically, free blacks were rural, uneducated, unskilled agricultural laborers and domestic servants. Opportunities of all kinds—for work, education, or community—were slim. Planters believed that free blacks set a bad example for slaves, subverting the racial subordination that was the essence of slavery.

Achievement despite Restrictions Despite increasingly harsh laws and stepped-up persecution, free African Americans made the most of the advantages their status offered. Unlike slaves, free blacks could legally marry. They could protect their families from arbitrary disruption and pass on their heritage of freedom to their children. Freedom also meant that they could choose occupations and own property. For most, however, these economic rights proved only theoretical, for a majority of the South's free blacks remained propertyless.

Still, some free blacks escaped the poverty and degradation whites thrust on them. Particularly in the cities of Charleston, Savannah, Mobile, and New Orleans, a small elite of free blacks emerged. Urban whites enforced restrictive laws only sporadically, allowing free blacks room to maneuver. The free black elite, which consisted overwhelmingly of light-skinned African Americans who worked at skilled trades, operated schools for their children and traveled in and out of their states, despite laws forbidding both activities. They worshipped with whites (in separate seating) in the finest churches and lived scattered about in white neighborhoods, not in ghettos. And like elite whites, some owned slaves. Blacks could own blacks because they had the right to own property, which in the South included human property. Of the 3,200 black slaveholders (barely 1 percent of the free black population), most owned only a few family members whom they could not legally free. Others owned slaves in large numbers and exploited them for labor.

Most free blacks neither became slaveholders nor sought to raise a slave rebellion, as whites accused Denmark Vesey of doing. Rather, most free blacks simply tried to preserve their freedom, which was under increasing attack. Unlike blacks in the North whose freedom was secure, free blacks in the South clung to a precarious freedom by seeking to impress whites with their reliability, economic contributions, and good behavior.

Q: Why did many state legislatures pass laws restricting free blacks' rights in the 1820s and 1830s?

The Plain Folk

Most whites in the South did not own slaves, not even one. In 1860, more than six million of the South's eight million whites lived in slaveless households. Some slaveless whites lived in cities and worked as artisans, mechanics, and traders. Others lived in the country and worked as

The Cotton Belt

storekeepers, parsons, and schoolteachers. But most "plain folk" were small farmers. Perhaps three out of four were **yeomen**, small farmers who owned their own land. As in the North, farm ownership provided a family with an economic foundation, social respectability, and political standing. Unlike their northern counterparts, however, southern yeomen lived in a region whose economy and society were increasingly dominated by unfree labor.

In an important sense, the South had more than one white yeomanry. The huge southern landscape provided space enough for two yeoman societies, separated roughly along geographical lines. Yeomen throughout the South had much in common, but the life of a small farm family in the cotton belt—the flatlands that spread from South Carolina to east Texas—differed from the life of a family in the upcountry—the area of hills and mountains. And some rural slaveless whites were not yeomen; they owned no land at all and were sometimes desperately poor.

Plantation Belt Yeomen Plantation belt yeomen lived within the orbit of the planter class. Small farms outnumbered plantations in the plantation belt, but they were dwarfed in importance. Small farmers grew mainly food crops, particularly corn, but they also devoted a portion of their land to cotton. With only family labor to draw upon, they produced only a few four-hundred-pound bales each year, whereas large planters measured their crop in hundreds of bales. The small farmers' cotton tied them to planters. Unable to afford cotton gins or baling presses of their own, they relied on slave owners to gin and bale their cotton. With no link to merchants in the port cities, plantation belt yeomen also turned to better-connected planters to ship and sell their cotton. A network of relationships laced small farmers and planters together. Planters hired out surplus slaves to ambitious yeomen who wanted to expand cotton production. They sometimes chose overseers from among the sons of local farm families. Plantation mistresses occasionally nursed ailing neighbors. Male yeomen helped police slaves by riding in slave patrols, which nightly scoured country roads to make certain that no slaves were moving about without permission. On Sundays, plantation dwellers and plain folk came together in church to worship and afterward lingered to gossip and to transact small business.

Plantation belt yeomen may have envied, and at times even resented, wealthy slaveholders, but small farmers learned to accommodate. Planters made accommodation easier by going out of their way to behave as good neighbors and avoid direct exploitation of slaveless whites in their community. As a consequence, rather than raging at the oppression of the planter regime, the typical plantation belt yeoman sought entry into it. He dreamed of adding acreage to his farm, buying a few slaves of his own, and retiring from exhausting field work.

Upcountry of the South

Even the hills had some plantations and slaves. The few upcountry folks who owned slaves usually had only two or three. As a result, slaveholders had much less social and economic power, and yeomen had more. But the upcountry did not oppose slavery. As long as upcountry plain folk were free to lead their own lives, they defended slavery and white supremacy just as staunchly as other white Southerners.

Upcountry Yeomen By contrast, the hills and mountains of the South resisted the spread of slavery and plantations. In the western parts of Virginia, North Carolina, and South Carolina; in northern Georgia and Alabama; and in eastern Tennessee and Kentucky, the higher elevation, colder climate, rugged terrain, and poor transportation made it difficult for commercial agriculture to make headway. As a result, yeomen dominated these isolated areas, and planters and slaves were scarce.

At the core of this upcountry society was the independent farm family working its own patch of land; raising hogs, cattle, and sheep; and seeking self-sufficiency and independence. Toward that end, all members of the family worked, their tasks depending on their sex and age. Husbands labored in the fields, and with their sons, they cleared, plowed, planted, and cultivated primarily food crops. Women and their daughters labored in and about the cabin most of the year. One upcountry farmer remembered that his mother "worked in the house cooking, spinning, weaving [and doing] patchwork." Women also tended the vegetable garden, kept a cow and some chickens, preserved food, cleaned their homes, fed their families, and cared for their children. Male and female tasks were equally crucial to the farm's success, but as in other white southern households, the domestic sphere was subordinated to the will of the male patriarch.

The typical upcountry yeoman also grew a little cotton or tobacco, but food production was more important than cash crops. Not much currency changed hands in the upcountry. Barter was common. A yeoman might trade his small cotton or tobacco crop to a country store owner for a little salt, lead shot, needles, and nails, or swap extra sweet potatoes for a plow from a blacksmith or for leather from a tanner. Farm families also joined together in logrolling, house and barn raising, and cornhusking.

Poor Whites Although hardworking, landholding small farmers made up the majority of white Southerners, Northerners had a different image of southern society. They believed that slavery had condemned most whites to poverty and backwardness. One antislavery advocate charged that the South harbored three classes: "the slaves on whom devolves all the regular industry, the slaveholders who reap all the fruits, and an idle and lawless rabble who live dispersed over vast plains little removed from absolute barbarism." Critics called this third class a variety of derogatory names: hillbillies, crackers, rednecks, and poor white trash. According to critics, poor whites were not just whites who were poor. They were also supposedly ignorant, diseased, and degenerate. Even slaves were known to chant, "I'd rather be a nigger an' plow ol' Beck / Than a white hillbilly with a long red neck."

Contrary to northern opinion, only about one in four nonslaveholding rural white men was landless and very poor. Some worked as tenants, renting land and struggling to make a go of it. Others survived by herding pigs and cattle. And still others worked for meager wages, ditching, mining, logging, and laying track for railroads. A Georgian remembered that his "father worked by the day when ever he could get work."

Some poor white men earned reputations for mayhem and violence. One visitor claimed that a "bowie-knife was a universal, and a pistol a not at all unusual companion." Edward Isham, an illiterate roustabout, spent about as much time fighting as he did working. When he wasn't engaged in ear-biting, eye-gouging free-for-alls, he was fighting with sticks, shovels, rocks, axes, tomahawks, knives, and guns. Working at what he could find, he took up with and abandoned many women, gambled, drank, stole, had run-ins with the law, and eventually murdered a respected slaveholder, for which he was hanged in 1860.

Unlike Isham, most poor white men did not engage in ferocious behavior but instead lived responsible lives. Although they sat at the bottom of the white pecking order, they were ambitious people eager to climb into the yeomanry. The Lipscomb family illustrates the possibility of upward mobility. In 1845, Smith and Sally Lipscomb and their children abandoned their worn-out land in South Carolina for Benton County, Alabama. "Benton is a mountainous country but ther is a heep of good levil land to tend in it," Smith wrote back to his brother. Alabama, Smith said, "will be better for the rising generation if not for ourselves but I think it will be the best for us all that live any length of time." Indeed, primitive living conditions made life precarious. All of the Lipscombs fell ill, but all recovered, and the entire family went to work.

Because they had no money to buy land, they squatted on seven unoccupied acres. With the help of neighbors, they built a 22-by-24-foot cabin, a detached kitchen, and two stables. From daylight to dark, Smith and his sons worked the land, and the first year they produced enough food for the table and several bales of cotton. Sally contributed to the family's income by selling homemade shirts and socks. In time, the Lipscombs bought land and joined the Baptist church, completing their transformation to respectable yeomen.

A Baptizing on the South Branch of the Potomac near Franklin, Virginia, **1844** In 1844, noted painter William Thompson Russell Smith undertook a geological expedition to Virginia, and there he encountered a rural baptism. Primarily a landscape painter, Smith portrayed the human figures as minor characters. If one of the participants had sketched the baptism, he or she might have emphasized the human drama, the emotional pitch of what was for evangelical Christians throughout the South a profound religious moment. The Charleston Renaissance Gallery, Robert M. Hicklin Jr., Inc., Charleston, South Carolina.

Many poor whites succeeded in climbing the economic ladder, but in the 1850s upward mobility slowed. The cotton boom of that decade caused planters to expand their operations, driving the price of land beyond the reach of poor families. Whether they gained their own land or not, however, poor whites shared common cultural traits with yeomen farmers.

The Culture of the Plain Folk Situated on scattered farms and in tiny villages, rural plain folk lived isolated lives. Life revolved around family, neighbors, the local church, and perhaps a country store. Work occupied most hours, but plain folk still found time for pleasure. "Dancing they are all fond of," a visitor to North Carolina discovered, "especially when they can get a fiddle, or bagpipe." They also loved their tobacco. Men smoked and chewed (and spat), while women dipped snuff. But the most popular pastimes of men and boys were fishing and hunting. A traveler in Mississippi recalled that his host sent "two of his sons, little fellows that looked almost too small to shoulder a gun," for food. "One went off towards the river and the other struck into the forest, and in a few hours we were feasting on delicious venison, trout and turtle."

Plain folk did not usually associate "book learning" with the basic needs of life. A northern woman visiting the South in the 1850s observed, "Education is not extended to the masses here as at the North." Private academies charged fees that yeomen could not afford, and public schools were scarce. Although most people managed to pick up the "three R's," approximately one southern white man in five was illiterate in 1860, and the rate for white women was even higher. "People here prefer talking to reading," a Virginian remarked. Telling stories, reciting ballads, and singing hymns were important activities in yeoman culture.

Plain folk spent more hours in revival tents than in classrooms. Not all rural whites were religious, but many were, and the most characteristic feature of their evangelical Christian faith was the revival. Preachers spoke day and night to save souls. Revivalism crossed denominational lines, but Baptists and Methodists adopted it most readily and by midcentury had become the South's largest religious groups. By emphasizing free choice and individual worth, the plain folk's religion was hopeful and affirming. Hymns and spirituals provided guides to right and wrong—praising humility and steadfastness, condemning drunkenness and profanity. Above all, hymns spoke of the eventual release from worldly sorrows and the assurance of eternal salvation.

 Why did yeomen dominate the upcountry?

The Politics of Slavery

By the mid-nineteenth century, all southern white men—planters and plain folk alike—had gained the vote. But even after the South's politics became democratic for the white male population, political power remained unevenly distributed. The nonslaveholding white majority wielded less political power than their numbers indicated. The slaveholding white minority wielded more. Self-conscious, cohesive, and with a well-developed sense of class interest, slaveholders busied themselves with party politics, campaigns, and officeholding and made demands of state governments. As a result, they received significant benefits. Nonslaveholding whites were concerned mainly with preserving their liberties and keeping their taxes low. Collectively, they asked government for little of an economic nature, and they received little.

Slaveholders sometimes worried about nonslaveholders' loyalty to slavery, but the majority of whites accepted the planters' argument that the existing social order served all Southerners' interests. Slavery rewarded every white man—no matter how poor—with membership in the South's white ruling race. It also provided the means by which nonslaveholders might someday advance into the ranks of the planters. White men in the South fought furiously about many things, but they agreed that they should take land from Indians, promote agriculture, uphold white supremacy and masculine privilege, and defend slavery from its enemies.

The Democratization of the Political Arena The political reforms that swept the nation in the first half of the nineteenth century reached deeply into the South. Southern politics became democratic politics—for white men. Southerners eliminated the wealth and property requirements that had once restricted political participation. Most southern states also removed the property requirements for holding state offices. To be sure, undemocratic features lingered. Plantation districts still wielded disproportionate power in several state legislatures. Nevertheless, southern politics took place within an increasingly democratic political structure.

White male suffrage ushered in an era of vigorous electoral competition in the South. Eager voters rushed to the polls to exercise their new rights. As politics became aggressively democratic, it also grew fiercely partisan. From the 1830s to the 1850s, Whigs and Democrats battled for the electorate's favor. Both parties presented themselves as the plain white folk's best friend. All candidates declared their commitment to republican equality and pledged to defend the people's liberty.

Planter Power Whether Whig or Democrat, southern officeholders were likely to be slave owners. By 1860, the percentage of slave owners in state legislatures ranged from 41 percent in Missouri to nearly 86 percent in North Carolina. Legislators not only tended to own slaves; they also often owned large numbers. The percentage of planters (individuals with twenty or more slaves) in southern legislatures in 1860 ranged from 5.3 percent in Missouri to 55.4 percent in South Carolina. The democratization of politics in the nineteenth century meant that more ordinary citizens participated in elections, but yeomen did not throw the planters out.

Upper-class dominance of southern politics reflected the elite's success in persuading the yeoman majority that what was good for slaveholders was also good for them. In reality, the South had, on the whole, done well by the plain folk. Most had farms of their own. They participated as equals in a democratic political system. They enjoyed an elevated social status, above all blacks and in theory equal to all other whites. They commanded patriarchal authority over their households. And as long as slavery existed, they could dream of joining the planter class. Slaveless white men found much to celebrate in the slave South.

Most slaveholders took pains to win the plain folk's trust and to nurture their respect. One South Carolinian told his wealthy neighbor that he had a bright political future because he never thought himself "too good to sit down & talk to a poor man." Mary Boykin Chesnut complained about the fawning attention her husband, U.S. senator from South Carolina, showed to poor men, including one who had "mud sticking up through his toes." Smart candidates found ways to convince wary plain folk of their democratic convictions and egalitarian sentiments, whether they were genuine or not.

Georgia politics illustrate how well planters protected their interests in state legislatures. In 1850, about half of the state's revenues came from taxes on slaves, the characteristic form of planter wealth.

However, the tax rate on slaves was trifling, only about one-fifth the rate on land. Moreover, planters benefited far more than other groups from public spending. Financing railroads—which carried cotton to market—was the largest state expenditure. The legislature also established low tax rates on land, the characteristic form of yeoman wealth, which meant that the typical yeoman's annual tax bill was small. Still, relative to their wealth, large slaveholders paid less than did other whites. Relative to their numbers, they got more in return. Slaveholding legislators protected planters' interests while giving the impression of protecting the small farmers' interests as well.

The South's elite defended slavery in other ways. In the 1830s, whites decided that slavery was too important to debate. "So interwoven is [slavery] with our interest, our manners, our climate and our very being," one man declared in 1833, "that no change can ever possibly be effected without a civil commotion from which the heart of a patriot must turn with horror." To end free speech on the slavery question, powerful whites dismissed slavery's critics from college faculties, drove them from pulpits, and hounded them from political life. Sometimes antislavery Southerners fell victim to vigilantes and mob violence. One could defend slavery; one could even delicately suggest mild reforms. But no Southerner could any longer safely call slavery evil or advocate its destruction.

In the South, therefore, the rise of the common man occurred alongside the continuing, even growing, power of the planter class. Rather than pitting slaveholders against nonslaveholders, elections remained an effective means of binding the region's whites together. Elections affirmed the sovereignty of white men, whether planter or plain folk, and the subordination of African Americans. Those twin themes played well among white women as well. Though unable to vote, white women supported equality for whites and slavery for blacks. In the antebellum South, the politics of slavery helped knit together all of white society.

Q: **How did planters benefit from their control of state legislatures?**

Conclusion: A Slave Society

By the early nineteenth century, northern states had either abolished slavery or put it on the road to extinction, while southern states were building the largest slave society in the New World. Regional differences increased over time, not merely because the South became more and more dominated by slavery, but also because developments in the North rapidly propelled it in a very different direction.

One-third of the South's population was enslaved by 1860. Bondage saddled blacks with enormous physical and spiritual burdens: hard labor, harsh treatment, broken families, and, most important, the denial of freedom itself. Although degraded and exploited, they were not defeated. Out of African memories and New World realities, blacks created a life-affirming African American culture that sustained and strengthened them. Their families, religion, and community provided defenses to white racism and power. Defined as property, they refused to be reduced to things. Perceived as inferior beings, they rejected the notion that they were natural slaves.

Slavery was crucial to the South's distinctiveness and to the loyalty and regional identification of its whites. The South was not merely a society with slaves; it had become a slave society. Slavery shaped the region's economy, culture, social structure, and politics. Whites south of the Mason-Dixon line believed that racial slavery was necessary and just. By making all blacks a pariah class, all whites gained a measure of equality and harmony.

Racism did not erase all stress along class lines, nor did the other features of southern life that helped confine class tensions: the wide availability of land, rapid economic mobility, the democratic nature of political life, and patriarchal power among all white men. Anxious slaveholders continued to worry that yeomen would defect from the proslavery consensus. But during the 1850s, a far more ominous division emerged—that between "slave states" and "free states."

Reviewing the Chapter

★ KEY TERMS

Explain each term's significance

WHO

Nat Turner (p. 307)

David Walker (p. 307)

William Lloyd Garrison (p. 307)

Thomas R. Dew (p. 308)

Eli Whitney (p. 314)

Denmark Vesey (p. 322)

WHAT

Mason-Dixon line (p. 308)

cotton kingdom (p. 309)

slave codes (p. 311)

miscegenation (p. 311)

planter (p. 311)

plantation (p. 311)

overseer (p. 316)

paternalism (p. 316)

chivalry (p. 318)

slave driver (p. 320)

free black (p. 323)

emancipation (p. 323)

yeomen (p. 324)

★ REVIEW QUESTIONS Q:

Use key terms and dates to support your answer

1. Why did the nineteenth-century southern economy remain primarily agricultural? (pp. 308–15)

2. Why did the ideology of paternalism gain currency among planters in the nineteenth century? (pp. 316–19)

3. What types of resistance did slaves participate in, and why did slave resistance rarely take the form of rebellion? (pp. 319–22)

4. Why did many state legislatures pass laws restricting free blacks' rights in the 1820s and 1830s? (pp. 323–24)

5. Why did yeomen dominate the upcountry? (pp. 324–27)

6. How did planters benefit from their control of state legislatures? (pp. 327–28)

★ MAKING CONNECTIONS

Draw on key terms, timeline, and review questions

1. By the mid-nineteenth century, the South had become a "cotton kingdom." How did cotton's profitability shape the region's antebellum development? In your answer, discuss the region's distinctive demographic and economic features.

2. How did southern white legislators and intellectuals attempt to strengthen the institution of slavery in the 1820s? What prompted them to undertake this work? In your answer, be sure to explore regional and national influences.

3. Although bondage restricted slaves' autonomy and left slaves vulnerable to extreme abuse, they resisted slavery. Discuss the variety of ways in which slaves attempted to lessen the harshness of slavery. What were the short- and long-term effects of their efforts?

4. Despite vigorous political competition in the South, by 1860 legislative power was largely concentrated in the hands of a regional minority — slaveholders. Why were slaveholders politically dominant? In your answer, be sure to consider how the region's biracialism contributed to its politics.

FOR PRACTICE QUIZZES AND OTHER STUDY TOOLS, see the Online Study Guide at **bedfordstmartins.com/roarkcompact**.

★ SUGGESTED READINGS

Ira Berlin, *Generations of Captivity: A History of African-American Slaves* (2003). A modern synthesis of the slave experience that emphasizes geographical diversity and change over time.

Steven Deyle, *Carry Me Back: The Domestic Slave Trade in American Life* (2005). An analysis of the internal slave trade after 1808 that demonstrates the centrality of the buying and selling of slaves to American slavery.

Drew G. Faust, *James Henry Hammond and the Old South: A Design for Mastery* (1982). A revealing biography of one of the South's most compelling planter-politicians.

Peter Kolchin, *American Slavery, 1619–1877* (1993). A masterful survey of slavery and reflection upon slavery's meaning for southern history.

Stephanie McCurry, *Masters of Small Worlds: Yeoman Households, Gender Relations, and the Political Culture of the Antebellum South* (1995). An insightful analysis of yeoman households that argues the importance of patriarchy to southern politics.

Willie Lee Rose, ed., *A Documentary History of Slavery in North America* (1976). A collection of contemporary documents that vividly illustrates slaves' responses to bondage.

FOR MORE BOOKS ABOUT TOPICS IN THIS CHAPTER, see the Online Bibliography at **bedfordstmartins.com/roarkcompact.**

FOR ADDITIONAL FIRSTHAND ACCOUNTS OF THIS PERIOD, see Chapter 13 in Michael Johnson, ed., *Reading the American Past,* Fourth Edition.

FOR WEB SITES, IMAGES, AND DOCUMENTS RELATED TO TOPICS AND PLACES IN THIS CHAPTER, visit Make History at **bedfordstmartins.com/roarkcompact.**

★ TIMELINE

1808	• External slave trade outlawed.
1810s–1850s	• Suffrage extended throughout South to all adult white males.
1813–1814	• Creek War opens Indian land to white settlement.
1820s–1830s	• Southern legislatures enact slave codes to strengthen slavery. • Southern legislatures enact laws to restrict growth of free black population. • Southern intellectuals fashion systematic defense of slavery.
1829	• *Appeal . . . to the Coloured Citizens of the World* published.
1830	• Southern slaves number approximately two million.
1831	• Nat Turner's slave rebellion. • First issue of the *Liberator* published.
1834	• *Catechism for Colored Persons* published.
1836	• Arkansas admitted to Union as slave state.
1840	• Cotton accounts for more than 60 percent of nation's exports.
1845	• Texas and Florida admitted to Union as slave states.
1860	• Southern slaves number nearly four million, one-third of South's population.

JOHN BROWN'S PIKES Scorning what he called "milk-and-water" abolitionists who only talked about slavery, John Brown favored "action!" In 1859, when he brought his abolitionist war to Harpers Ferry, Virginia, he carried with him 950 pikes, handsome but deadly spears made by a Connecticut blacksmith, which he expected to put into the hands of rebelling slaves. Bloody pikes, he thought, would end slavery in America. After Brown's failure at Harpers Ferry, townspeople sold many of the weapons as souvenirs. Chicago Historical Society.

CHAPTER 14

The House Divided
1846–1861

OTHER THAN TWENTY CHILDREN, John Brown did not have much to show for his life in 1859. Grizzled, gnarled, and fifty-nine years old, he had for decades lived like a nomad, hauling his large family back and forth across six states as he tried desperately to better himself. He turned his hand to farming, raising sheep, running a tannery, and selling wool, but failure dogged him. The world had given **John Brown** some hard licks, but it had not budged his conviction that slavery was wrong and ought to be destroyed. He had learned to hate slavery at his father's knee, and in the wake of the fighting that erupted over the issue in Kansas in the 1850s, his beliefs turned violent. On May 24, 1856, he led an eight-man antislavery posse in the midnight slaughter of five allegedly proslavery men at Pottawatomie, Kansas. He told Mahala Doyle, whose husband and two oldest sons he killed, that if a man stood between him and what he thought right, he would take that man's life as calmly as he would eat breakfast.

After the killings, Brown slipped out of Kansas and reemerged in the East. More than ever, he was a man on fire for abolition. He spent thirty months begging money to support his vague plan for military operations against slavery. He captivated the genteel easterners, particularly the Boston elite. They were awed by his iron-willed determination and courage, but most could not accept violence. "These men are all talk," Brown declared. "What is needed is action — action!" But enough donated to the hypnotic-eyed Brown that he was able to gather a small band of antislavery warriors.

On the night of October 16, 1859, Brown took his war against slavery into the South. With only twenty-one men, including five African Americans, he invaded Harpers Ferry, Virginia. His band seized the town's armory and rifle works, but the invaders were immediately surrounded, first by local militia and then by Colonel Robert E. Lee, who commanded the U.S. troops in the area. When Brown refused to surrender, federal soldiers charged with bayonets. Seventeen men, two of whom were slaves, lost their lives. Although a few of Brown's raiders escaped, federal forces killed ten (including two of his sons) and captured seven, among them Brown.

"When I strike, the bees will begin to swarm," Brown told Frederick Douglass a few months before the raid. As slaves rushed to Harpers Ferry, he said,

Previewing the Chapter

The Bitter Fruits of War   334

Q: *Why did response to the Wilmot Proviso split along sectional rather than party lines?*

The Sectional Balance Undone   338

Q: *Why did the Fugitive Slave Act provoke such strong opposition in the North?*

Realignment of the Party System   341

Q: *Why did the Whig Party disintegrate in the 1850s?*

Freedom under Siege   345

Q: *Why did the Dred Scott decision strengthen northern suspicions of a "Slave Power" conspiracy?*

The Union Collapses   349

Q: *Why did some southern states secede immediately after Lincoln's election?*

Conclusion: Slavery, Free Labor, and the Failure of Political Compromise   353

John Brown In this 1859 photograph, John Brown appears respectable, even statesmanlike, but contemporaries debated his mental state and moral character, and the debate still rages. Critics argue that he was a bloody terrorist, a religious fanatic who believed that he was touched by God for a great purpose, one for which he was willing to die. Admirers see a resolute and selfless hero, a rare white man who believed that black people were the equals of whites, and a shrewd political observer who recognized that only a full-scale revolt of the oppressed would end slavery in America. National Portrait Gallery, Smithsonian Institution/Art Resource, NY.

he would arm them with the pikes he carried with him and with weapons stolen from the armory. They would then fight a war of liberation. Brown, however, neglected to inform the slaves that he had arrived in Harpers Ferry, and the few who knew of his arrival wanted nothing to do with his enterprise. "It was not a slave insurrection," Abraham Lincoln observed. "It was an attempt by white men to get up a revolt among slaves, in which the slaves refused to participate. In fact, it was so absurd that the slaves, with all their ignorance, saw plainly enough it could not succeed."

Although Brown's raid ended in utter defeat, white Southerners viewed it as proof of their growing suspicion that Northerners actively sought to incite slaves in bloody rebellion. For more than a decade, Northerners and Southerners had accused one another of hostile intentions, and by 1859, emotions were raw. Sectional tension was as old as the Constitution, but hostility had escalated with the outbreak of war with Mexico in May 1846 (see chapter 12). Only three months after the war began, national expansion and the slavery issue intersected when Representative David Wilmot introduced a bill to prohibit slavery in any territory that might be acquired as a result of the war. After that, the problem of slavery in the territories became the principal wedge that divided the nation.

"Mexico is to us the forbidden fruit," South Carolina senator John C. Calhoun declared at the war's outset. "The penalty of eating it [is] to subject our institutions to political death." For a decade and a half, the slavery issue intertwined with the fate of former Mexican land, poisoning the national political debate. Slavery proved powerful enough to transform party politics into sectional politics. Rather than Whigs and Democrats confronting one another across party lines, Northerners and Southerners eyed one another hostilely across the Mason-Dixon line. Sectional politics encouraged the South's separatist impulses. Southern separatism, a fitful tendency before the Mexican-American War, gained strength with each confrontation. As the nation lurched from crisis to crisis, southern disaffection and alienation mounted, and support for compromise and conciliation eroded. The era began with a crisis of Union and ended with the Union in even graver peril. As Abraham Lincoln predicted in 1858, "A house divided against itself cannot stand." ★

The Bitter Fruits of War

Between 1846 and 1848, the nation grew by 1.2 million square miles, an incredible two-thirds. The gold rush of 1849 transformed the sleepy frontier of California into a booming, thriving economy (see chapter 12). The 1850s witnessed new "rushes," for gold in Colorado and silver in Nevada's Comstock Lode. People from around the world flocked to the West, where they produced a vibrant agriculture as well as tons of gold and silver. But it quickly became clear that Northerners and Southerners had very different visions of the West, particularly the place of slavery in its future.

History provided contradictory precedents for handling slavery in the territories. In 1787, the Northwest Ordinance banned slavery north of the Ohio River. In 1803, slavery was allowed to remain in the newly acquired Louisiana Territory. The Missouri Compromise of 1820 prohibited slavery in part of that territory but allowed it in the rest. In 1846, when the war with Mexico suggested new territory for the United States, politicians offered various plans. But when the war ended in 1848, Congress had made no headway in solving the issue of slavery in the land acquired from Mexico, called the Mexican cession. In 1850, Congress patched together a settlement, one that Americans hoped would be permanent.

The Wilmot Proviso and the Expansion of Slavery Most Americans agreed that the Constitution left the issue of slavery to the individual states to decide. Northern states had done away with slavery, while southern states had retained it. But what about slavery in the nation's territories? The Constitution states that "Congress shall have power to . . . make all needful rules and regulations respecting the territory . . . belonging to the United States." The debate about slavery, then, turned toward Congress.

The spark for the national debate was provided in August 1846 by a Democratic representative from Pennsylvania, David Wilmot, who proposed that Congress bar slavery from all lands acquired in the war with Mexico. The Mexicans had already abolished slavery in their country, and Wilmot declared, "God forbid that we should be the means of planting this institution upon it."

Regardless of party affiliation, Northerners lined up behind the **Wilmot Proviso**. Many supported free soil, by which they meant territory in which slavery would be prohibited, because they wanted to preserve the West for free labor, for hardworking, self-reliant free men, not for slave-holders and slaves. But support also came from those who were simply anti-South. New slave territories would eventually mean new slave states, and they opposed magnifying the political power of Southerners. Wilmot himself said his proposal would blunt "the *power* of slaveholders" in the national government.

Additional support for free soil came from Northerners who were hostile to blacks and wanted to reserve new land for whites. Wilmot himself blatantly encouraged racist support when he declared, "I would preserve for free white labor a fair country, a rich inheritance, where the sons of toil, of my own race and own color, can live without the disgrace which association with negro slavery brings upon free labor." It is no wonder that some called the Wilmot Proviso the "White Man's Proviso."

The thought that slavery might be excluded outraged white Southerners. Like Northerners, they regarded the West as a ladder for economic and social opportunity. They also believed that the exclusion of slavery was a slap in the face to veterans of the Mexican-American War, at least half of whom were Southerners. "When the war-worn soldier returns home," one Alabaman asked, "is he to be told that he cannot carry his property to the country won by his blood?"

Southern leaders also sought to maintain political parity with the North to protect the South's interests, especially slavery. The need seemed especially urgent in the 1840s, when the North's population and wealth were booming. James Henry Hammond of South Carolina predicted that ten new states would be carved from the acquired Mexican land. If free soil won, the North would

"ride over us roughshod" in Congress, he claimed. "Our only safety is in *equality* of POWER."

The two sides squared off in the nation's capital. Because Northerners had a majority in the House, they easily passed the Wilmot Proviso. In the Senate, however, where slave states outnumbered free states fifteen to fourteen, Southerners defeated it. Senator John C. Calhoun of South Carolina denied that Congress had the constitutional authority to exclude slavery from the nation's territories. He argued that the territories were the "joint and common property" of all the states and that Congress could not bar citizens of one state from migrating with their property (including slaves) to the territories. Whereas Wilmot demanded that Congress slam shut the door to slavery, Calhoun called on Congress to hold the door wide open.

In 1847, Senator **Lewis Cass** of Michigan offered a compromise through the doctrine of **popular sovereignty**, by which the people who settled the territories would decide for themselves slavery's fate. This solution, Cass argued, sat squarely in the American tradition of democracy and local self-government. It had the added attraction of removing the incendiary issue of the expansion of slavery from the nation's capital.

Popular sovereignty's most attractive feature was its ambiguity about the precise moment when settlers could determine slavery's fate. Northern advocates believed that the decision on slavery could be made as soon as the first territorial legislature assembled. With free-soil majorities likely because of the North's greater population, they would shut the door to slavery almost before the first slave arrived. Southern supporters believed that popular sovereignty guaranteed that slavery would be unrestricted throughout the entire territorial period. Only at the very end, when settlers in a territory drew up a constitution and applied for statehood, could they decide the issue of slavery. By then, slavery would have sunk deep roots. As long as the matter of timing remained vague, popular sovereignty gave hope to both sides.

When Congress ended its session in 1848, no plan had won a majority in both houses. Northerners who demanded no new slave territory anywhere, ever, and Southerners who demanded entry for their slave property into all territories, or else, staked out their extreme positions. Unresolved in Congress, the territorial question naturally became an issue in the presidential election of 1848.

Mexican Cession, 1848

The Election of 1848 When President Polk, worn-out and ailing, chose not to seek reelection, the Democratic convention nominated Lewis Cass of Michigan, the man most closely associated with popular sovereignty. The Whigs nominated a Mexican-American War hero, General Zachary Taylor. The Whigs declined to adopt a party platform, betting that the combination of a military hero and total silence on the slavery issue would unite their divided party. Taylor, who owned more than one hundred slaves on plantations in Mississippi and Louisiana, was hailed by Georgia politician Robert Toombs as a "Southern man, a slaveholder, a cotton planter."

Antislavery Whigs balked and looked for an alternative. Senator **Charles Sumner** called for a major political realignment, "one grand Northern party of Freedom." In the summer of 1848, antislavery Whigs and antislavery Democrats founded the **Free-Soil Party**, nominating a Democrat, Martin Van Buren, for president and a Whig, Charles Francis Adams, for vice president. The platform boldly proclaimed, "Free soil, free speech, free labor, and free men."

The November election dashed the hopes of the Free-Soilers. They did not carry a single state. The major parties went through contortions to present their candidates favorably in both North and South, and their evasions succeeded. Taylor won the all-important electoral vote 163 to 127, carrying eight of the fifteen slave states and seven of the fifteen free states (Map 14.1). (Wisconsin had entered the Union earlier in 1848 as the fifteenth

free state.) Northern voters were not yet ready for Sumner's "one grand Northern party of Freedom," but the struggle over slavery in the territories had shaken the major parties badly.

Debate and Compromise Believing that he could avoid further sectional strife if California and New Mexico skipped the territorial stage, new president Zachary Taylor in 1849 encouraged the settlers to apply for admission to the Union as states. Predominantly antislavery, the settlers began writing free-state constitutions. "For the first time," Mississippian Jefferson Davis lamented, "we are about permanently to destroy the balance of power between the sections."

Congress convened in December 1849, beginning one of the most contentious and most significant sessions in its history. President Taylor urged Congress to admit California as a free state immediately and to admit New Mexico, which lagged behind a few months, as soon as it applied. Southerners exploded. A North Carolinian declared that Southerners who would "consent to be thus degraded and enslaved, ought to be whipped through their fields by their own negroes."

In stepped Senator Henry Clay of Kentucky, the architect of Union-saving compromises in the Missouri and nullification crises (see chapters 10 and 11). Clay offered a series of resolutions meant to answer and balance "all questions in controversy between the free and slave states, growing out of the subject of slavery." Admit California as a free state, he proposed, but organize the rest of the Southwest without restrictions on slavery. Require Texas to abandon its claim to parts of New Mexico, but compensate it by assuming its preannexation debt. Abolish the domestic slave trade in Washington, D.C., but confirm slavery itself in the nation's capital. Reassert Congress's lack of authority to interfere with the interstate slave trade, and enact a more effective fugitive slave law.

Both antislavery advocates and "fire-eaters" (as radical Southerners who urged secession from the Union were called) savaged Clay's plan. Senator Salmon P. Chase of Ohio ridiculed it as "sentiment for the North, substance for the South." Senator Henry S. Foote of Mississippi denounced it as more offensive to the South than the speeches of abolitionists William Lloyd Garrison, Wendell Phillips, and Frederick Douglass combined. The most ominous response came from John C. Calhoun, who argued that the fragile political unity of North and South depended on continued equal representation in the Senate, which Clay's plan for a free California destroyed. "As things now stand," he said in February 1850, the South "cannot with safety remain in the Union."

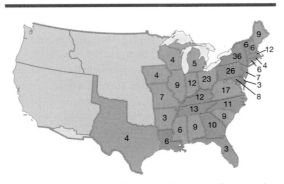

Candidate	Electoral Vote	Popular Vote	Percent of Popular Vote
Zachary Taylor (Whig)	163	1,360,099	47.4
Lewis Cass (Democrat)	127	1,220,544	42.5
Martin Van Buren (Free-Soil)	0	291,263	10.1

MAP 14.1 The Election of 1848

THE PROMISE OF TECHNOLOGY

Daguerreotypes In the late 1830s, Frenchman Louis Daguerre improved upon existing technology when he discovered how to keep photographic images from fading, a technique that arrived in New York City by 1839. The daguerreotype photographic process was cumbersome and complex, requiring several minutes of exposure, making candid shots impossible. Despite their shortcomings, daguerreotypes were an instant success, and by the 1850s Americans were buying millions of images each year.

No early American photographer was more important than Mathew Brady. In 1844, he opened his first gallery in New York City. Seeing himself as a historian of the nation, he shot portraits of distinguished citizens—presidents, congressmen, senators, and statesmen—as well as of everyday people who walked into his gallery. In 1850, Brady shot this hollow-cheeked and dark-eyed image of John C. Calhoun, who had only months to live. Brady hoped that the new technology of photography would serve as a moral agent furthering political reconciliation and peace. By 1860, however, daguerreotypes had all but disappeared from American life, replaced by more efficient photographic processes, and the Union remained imperiled. National Portrait Gallery, Smithsonian Institution/Art Resource, NY.

Senator Daniel Webster of Massachusetts then addressed the Senate. Like Clay, Webster defended compromise. He told Northerners that the South had legitimate complaints, but he told Southerners that secession from the Union would mean civil war. He appealed for an end to reckless proposals and, to the dismay of many Northerners, mentioned by name the Wilmot Proviso. A legal ban on slavery in the territories was unnecessary, he said, because the harsh climate effectively prohibited the expansion of cotton and slaves into the new American Southwest. "I would not take pains uselessly to reaffirm an ordinance of nature, nor to re-enact the will of God," Webster declared.

Free-Soil forces recoiled from what they saw as Webster's desertion. Senator William H. Seward of New York responded that Webster's and Clay's compromise with slavery was "radically wrong and essentially vicious." He flatly rejected Calhoun's argument that Congress lacked the constitutional authority to exclude slavery from the territories. In any case, Seward said, in the most sensational moment in his address, there was a "higher law than the Constitution"—the law of God—to ensure freedom in all the public domain. Claiming

that God was a Free-Soiler did nothing to cool the superheated political atmosphere.

In May, the Senate considered a bill that joined Clay's resolutions into a single comprehensive package, known as the Omnibus Bill because it was a vehicle on which "every sort of passenger" could ride. Clay bet that a majority of Congress wanted compromise and that the members would vote for the package. But the omnibus strategy backfired. Free-Soilers and proslavery Southerners voted down the comprehensive plan.

Fortunately for those who favored a settlement, Senator **Stephen A. Douglas**, a rising Democratic star from Illinois, broke the bill into its parts and skillfully ushered each through Congress. The agreement Douglas won in September 1850 was very much the one Clay had proposed in January. California entered the Union as a free state. New Mexico and Utah became territories where slavery would be decided by popular sovereignty. Texas accepted its boundary with New Mexico and received $10 million from the federal government. Congress ended the slave trade in the District of Columbia but enacted a more stringent fugitive slave law. In September, Millard Fillmore, who had

Free state or territory

Slave state

Opened to slavery by principle of popular sovereignty

● **Slave trade ended**

MAP 14.2 **The Compromise of 1850**
The patched-together sectional agreement was both clumsy and unstable. Few Americans — in either North or South — supported all five parts of the Compromise.

become president when Zachary Taylor died in July, signed into law each bill, collectively known as the **Compromise of 1850** (Map 14.2).

Actually, the Compromise of 1850 was not a true compromise at all. Douglas's parliamentary skill, not a spirit of conciliation, was responsible for the legislative success. Still, the nation breathed a sigh of relief, for the Compromise preserved the Union and peace for the moment.

Q: **Why did response to the Wilmot Proviso split along sectional rather than party lines?**

The Sectional Balance Undone

The Compromise of 1850 began to come apart almost immediately. The thread that unraveled it was not slavery in the Southwest, the crux of the disagreement, but runaway slaves in New England, a part of the settlement that had previously received little attention. Instead of restoring calm, the Compromise brought the horrors of slavery into the North.

Millions of Northerners who had never seen a runaway slave confronted slavery in the early 1850s. Harriet Beecher Stowe's ***Uncle Tom's Cabin***, a novel that vividly depicts the brutality of the South's "peculiar institution," aroused passions

so deep that many found goodwill toward white Southerners nearly impossible. But no groundswell of antislavery sentiment compelled Congress to reopen the slavery controversy. Politicians did it themselves. Four years after Congress stitched the sectional compromise together, it ripped the threads out. With the Kansas-Nebraska Act, it again posed the question of slavery in the territories, the deadliest of all sectional issues.

The Fugitive Slave Act The issue of runaway slaves was as old as the Constitution, which contained a provision for the return of any "person held to service or labor in one state" who escaped to another. In 1793, a federal law gave muscle to the provision by authorizing slave owners to enter other states to recapture their slave property. Proclaiming the 1793 law a license to kidnap free blacks, northern states in the 1830s began passing "personal liberty laws" that provided fugitives with some protection.

Some northern communities also formed vigilance committees to help runaways. Each year, a few hundred slaves escaped into free states and found friendly northern "conductors" who put them aboard the **underground railroad**, which was not a railroad at all but a series of secret "stations" (hideouts) on the way to Canada. Harriet Tubman, an escaped slave from Maryland, returned to the South more than a dozen times and guided more than three hundred slaves to freedom in this way.

Furious about northern interference, Southerners in 1850 insisted on the stricter fugitive slave law that was passed as part of the Compromise. According to the **Fugitive Slave Act**, to seize an alleged slave, a slaveholder simply had to appear before a commissioner and swear that the runaway was his. The commissioner earned $10 for every individual returned to slavery but only $5 for those set free. Most galling to Northerners, the law stipulated that all citizens were expected to assist officials in apprehending runaways.

In Boston in February 1851, an angry crowd overpowered federal marshals and snatched a runaway named Shadrach from a courtroom, put him on the underground railroad, and whisked him off to Canada. Three years later, when another Boston crowd rushed the courthouse in a failed attempt to rescue Anthony Burns, who had recently fled slavery in Richmond, a guard was shot dead. To white Southerners, it seemed that fanatics of the "higher law" creed had whipped Northerners into a frenzy of massive resistance.

Actually, the overwhelming majority of fugitives claimed by slaveholders were reenslaved peacefully. But brutal enforcement of the unpopular law had a radicalizing effect in the North, particularly in New

England. To Southerners it seemed that Northerners had betrayed the Compromise. "The continued existence of the United States as one nation," warned the *Southern Literary Messenger*, "depends upon the full and faithful execution of the Fugitive Slave Bill."

Uncle Tom's Cabin   The spectacle of shackled African Americans being herded south seared the conscience of every Northerner who witnessed such a scene. But even more Northerners were turned against slavery by a novel. Harriet Beecher Stowe, a Northerner who had never set foot on a plantation, made the South's slaves into flesh-and-blood human beings almost more real than life.

Uncle Tom's Cabin **Poster**   After Congress passed the Fugitive Slave Act in 1850, Harriet Beecher Stowe's outraged sister-in-law told her, "Now Hattie, if I could use a pen as you can, I would write something that will make this whole nation feel what an accursed thing slavery is." This poster advertising the novel Stowe wrote calls it "The Greatest Book of the Age." The novel's vivid characters gripped readers' imaginations and fueled the growing antislavery crusade. Granger Collection.

FOR MORE HELP ANALYZING THIS IMAGE, see the visual activity for this chapter in the Online Study Guide at bedfordstmartins.com/roarkcompact.

A member of a famous clan of preachers, teachers, and reformers, Stowe despised the slave catchers and wrote to expose the sin of slavery. Published as a book in 1852, *Uncle Tom's Cabin, or Life among the Lowly* became a blockbuster hit, selling 300,000 copies in its first year and more than 2 million copies within ten years. Stowe's characters leaped from the page. Here was the gentle slave Uncle Tom, a Christian saint who forgave those who beat him to death; the courageous slave Eliza, who fled with her child across the frozen Ohio River; and the fiendish overseer Simon Legree, whose Louisiana plantation was a nightmare of torture and death.

Northerners shed tears and sang praises to *Uncle Tom's Cabin.* What Northerners accepted as truth, Southerners denounced as slander. Virginian George F. Holmes proclaimed Stowe a member of the "Woman's Rights" and "Higher Law" schools and dismissed the novel as a work of "intense fanaticism." Although it is impossible to measure precisely the impact of a novel on public opinion, *Uncle Tom's Cabin* clearly helped to crystallize northern sentiment against slavery and to confirm white Southerners' suspicion that they no longer received any sympathy in the free states.

Other writers—ex-slaves who knew life in slave cabins firsthand—also produced stinging indictments of slavery. Solomon Northup's compelling *Twelve Years a Slave* (1853) sold 27,000 copies in two years, and the powerful *Narrative of the Life of Frederick Douglass, as Told by Himself* (1845) eventually sold more than 30,000 copies. But no work touched the North's conscience like the novel by a free white woman. A decade after its publication, when Stowe visited Abraham Lincoln at the White House, he reportedly said, "So you are the little woman who wrote the book that made this great war."

The Kansas-Nebraska Act   As the 1852 election approached, the Democrats and Whigs sought to close the sectional rifts that had opened within their parties. For their presidential nominee, the Democrats turned to Franklin Pierce of New Hampshire. Pierce's well-known sympathy with southern views on public issues caused his northern critics to include him among the "dough-faces," northern men malleable enough to champion southern causes. The Whigs were less successful in bridging differences. Adopting the formula that had worked in 1848, they chose another Mexican-American War hero, General Winfield Scott of Virginia. But the Whigs' northern and

> When Harriet Beecher Stowe visited Abraham Lincoln at the White House, he reportedly said, "So you are the little woman who wrote the book that made this great war."

Gadsden Purchase, 1853

southern factions were hopelessly divided, and the party suffered a humiliating defeat. The Democrat Pierce carried twenty-seven states to Scott's four and won the electoral college vote 254 to 42 (see Map 14.4, page 342). The Free-Soil Party lost almost half of the voters who had turned to it in the tumultuous political atmosphere of 1848.

Eager to leave the sectional controversy behind, the new president turned swiftly to foreign expansion. Manifest destiny remained robust. Pierce's major objective was Cuba, which was owned by Spain and in which slavery flourished, but antislavery Northerners blocked Cuba's acquisition to keep more slave territory from entering the Union. Pierce's fortunes improved in Mexico. In 1853, diplomat James Gadsden negotiated a $15 million purchase of some 30,000 square miles of land in present-day Arizona and New Mexico. The Gadsden Purchase stemmed from the dream of a transcontinental railroad to California and Pierce's desire for a southern route through Mexican territory. Talk of a railroad ignited rivalries in cities from New Orleans to Chicago as they maneuvered to become the eastern terminus. The desire for a transcontinental railroad evolved into a sectional

contest, which by the 1850s inevitably involved slavery.

Illinois's Democratic senator Stephen A. Douglas badly wanted the transcontinental railroad for Chicago, and his chairmanship of the Senate Committee on Territories provided him with an opportunity. Any railroad that ran west from Chicago would pass through a region that Congress in 1830 had designated a "permanent" Indian reserve. Douglas proposed giving this vast area between the Missouri River and the Rocky Mountains an Indian name, Nebraska, and then throwing the Indians out. Once the region achieved territorial status, whites could survey and sell the land, establish a civil government, and build a railroad.

Nebraska lay within the Louisiana Purchase and, according to the Missouri Compromise of 1820, was closed to slavery (see chapter 10). Douglas needed southern votes to pass his Nebraska legislation, but Southerners had no incentive to create another free territory or to help a northern city win the transcontinental railroad. Southerners, however, agreed to help if Congress organized Nebraska according to popular sovereignty. That meant giving slavery a chance in Nebraska Territory and reopening the dangerous issue of slavery expansion, which Douglas himself had helped to resolve only four years earlier.

In January 1854, Douglas introduced his bill to organize Nebraska Territory, leaving to the settlers themselves the decision about slavery. At southern insistence, and even though he knew it would "raise a hell of a storm," Douglas added an explicit repeal of the Missouri Compromise. Indeed, the Nebraska bill raised a storm of controversy. Free-Soilers branded Douglas's plan "a gross violation of a sacred pledge" and an "atrocious plot" to transform free land into a "dreary region of despotism, inhabited by masters and slaves."

Undaunted, Douglas skillfully shepherded the explosive bill through Congress in May 1854. Nine-tenths of the southern members (Whigs and Democrats) and half of the northern Democrats cast votes in favor of the bill. Like Douglas, most northern supporters believed that popular sovereignty would make Nebraska free territory. In its final form, the **Kansas-Nebraska Act** divided the huge territory in two: Nebraska and Kansas (Map 14.3). With this act, the government pushed the Plains Indians farther west, making way for farmers and railroads.

Free state or territory

Slave state or territory

Voters to decide on allowing slavery, Compromise of 1850

Voters to decide on allowing slavery, Kansas-Nebraska Act, 1854

MAP 14.3 The Kansas-Nebraska Act, 1854
Americans hardly thought twice about dispossessing the Indians of land guaranteed them by treaty, but many worried about the outcome of repealing the Missouri Compromise and opening up the region to slavery.

Q: Why did the Fugitive Slave Act provoke such strong opposition in the North?

Realignment of the Party System

The Kansas-Nebraska Act marked a fateful escalation of the sectional conflict. Douglas's measure had several consequences, none more crucial than the realignment of the nation's political parties. Since the rise of the Whig Party in the early 1830s, Whigs and Democrats had organized and channeled political conflict in the nation. This party system dampened sectionalism and strengthened the Union. To achieve national political power, the Whigs and Democrats had to retain their strength in both North and South. Strong northern and southern wings required that each party compromise and find positions acceptable to both wings.

The Kansas-Nebraska controversy shattered this stabilizing political system. In place of two national parties with bisectional strength, the mid-1850s witnessed the development of one party heavily dominated by one section and another party entirely limited to the other section. Rather than "national" parties, the country had what one critic disdainfully called "geographic" parties. Parties now sharpened ideological and policy differences between the sections and no longer muffled moral issues such as slavery. The new party system also thwarted political compromise and instead promoted political polarization that further jeopardized the Union.

The Old Parties: Whigs and Democrats

As early as the Mexican-American War, members of the Whig Party had clashed over the future of slavery in annexed Mexican lands. By 1852, the Whig Party could please its proslavery southern wing or its antislavery northern wing but not both. The Whigs' miserable showing in the election of 1852 made clear that they were no longer a strong national party. By 1856, after more than two decades of contesting the Democrats, they were hardly a party at all (Map 14.4).

The collapse of the Whig Party left the Democrats as the country's only national party. Although the Democrats were not immune to the disruptive pressures of the territorial question, they discovered in popular sovereignty a doctrine that many Democrats could support. Even so, popular sovereignty very nearly undid the party. When Stephen Douglas applied the doctrine to the part of the Louisiana Purchase where slavery had been barred, he divided northern Democrats and destroyed the dominance of the Democratic Party in the free states. After 1854, even though the Democrats were a southern-dominated party, they remained a national political organization. Gains in the South more than balanced Democratic losses in the North. During the 1850s, Democrats elected two presidents and won majorities in Congress in almost every election.

The breakup of the Whigs and the disaffection of significant numbers of northern Democrats set many Americans politically adrift. As they searched for new political harbors, Americans found that the death of the old party system created a multitude of fresh political alternatives.

The New Parties: Know-Nothings and Republicans

Dozens of new political organizations vied for voters' attention. Out of the confusion two emerged as true contenders. One grew out of the slavery controversy, a coalition of indignant antislavery Northerners. The other arose from an entirely different split in American society, between Roman Catholic immigrants and native Protestants.

The tidal wave of immigrants that broke over America from 1845 to 1855 produced a nasty backlash among Protestant Americans, who believed that the American Republic was about to drown in a sea of Roman Catholics from Ireland and Germany. Most immigrants became Democrats because they perceived that party as more tolerant of newcomers than were the Whigs. But in the 1850s, they met sharp political opposition when nativists (individuals who were anti-immigrant) began to organize, first into secret fraternal societies and then in 1854 into a political party. Recruits swore never to vote for either foreign-born or Roman Catholic candidates and not to reveal any information about the organization. When questioned, they said, "I know nothing." Officially, they were the American Party, but most Americans called them **Know-Nothings**.

The Know-Nothings exploded onto the political stage in 1854 and 1855 with a series of dazzling successes. They captured state legislatures in the Northeast, West, and South and claimed dozens of seats in Congress. Members of the Democratic and Whig parties described the phenomenal success of the Know-Nothings as a "tornado," a "hurricane," and "a freak of political insanity." By 1855, an observer might reasonably have concluded that the Know-Nothings had emerged as the successor to the Whigs.

The Know-Nothings were not the only new party making noise, however. One of the new antislavery organizations provoked by the Kansas-Nebraska Act called itself the **Republican Party**.

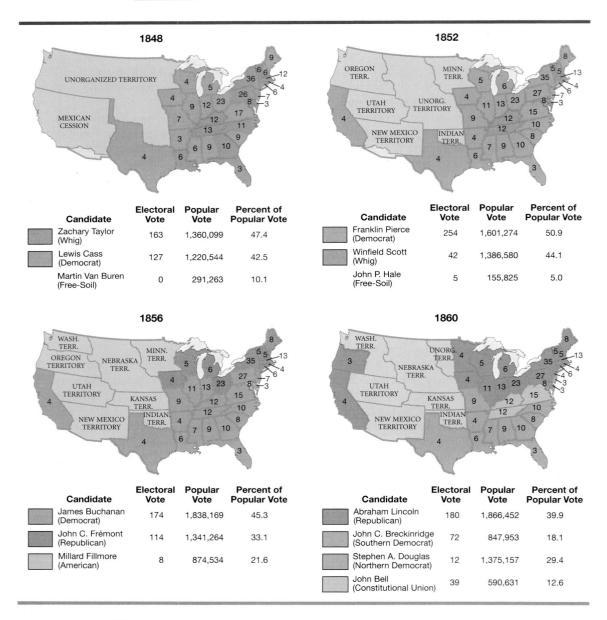

1848

Candidate	Electoral Vote	Popular Vote	Percent of Popular Vote
Zachary Taylor (Whig)	163	1,360,099	47.4
Lewis Cass (Democrat)	127	1,220,544	42.5
Martin Van Buren (Free-Soil)	0	291,263	10.1

1852

Candidate	Electoral Vote	Popular Vote	Percent of Popular Vote
Franklin Pierce (Democrat)	254	1,601,274	50.9
Winfield Scott (Whig)	42	1,386,580	44.1
John P. Hale (Free-Soil)	5	155,825	5.0

1856

Candidate	Electoral Vote	Popular Vote	Percent of Popular Vote
James Buchanan (Democrat)	174	1,838,169	45.3
John C. Frémont (Republican)	114	1,341,264	33.1
Millard Fillmore (American)	8	874,534	21.6

1860

Candidate	Electoral Vote	Popular Vote	Percent of Popular Vote
Abraham Lincoln (Republican)	180	1,866,452	39.9
John C. Breckinridge (Southern Democrat)	72	847,953	18.1
Stephen A. Douglas (Northern Democrat)	12	1,375,157	29.4
John Bell (Constitutional Union)	39	590,631	12.6

MAP 14.4 Political Realignment, 1848–1860

In 1848, slavery and sectionalism began taking their toll on the country's party system. The Whig Party was an early casualty. By 1860, national parties — those that contended for votes in both North and South — had been replaced by regional parties.

READING THE MAP: Which states did the Democrats pick up in 1852 compared to 1848? Which of these states did the Democrats lose in 1856? Compare the general geographical location of the states won by the Republicans in 1856 with those won in 1860.

CONNECTIONS: In the 1860 election, which party benefited the most from the western and midwestern states added to the Union since 1848? Why do you think these states chose to back the Republicans over the Democrats?

FOR MORE HELP ANALYZING THIS MAP, see the map activity for this chapter in the Online Study Guide at bedfordstmartins.com/roarkcompact.

The Republicans attempted to unite all those who opposed the extension of slavery into any territory of the United States.

The Republican creed tapped into the basic beliefs and values of the northern public. Slavery, the Republicans believed, degraded the dignity of white labor by associating work with blacks and servility. They warned that the insatiable slaveholders of the South, whom antislavery Northerners called the "Slave Power," were conspiring through their control of the Democratic Party to expand slavery, subvert liberty, and undermine the Constitution.

Only if slavery was restricted to the South, Republicans believed, could the system of free labor flourish elsewhere. In the North, one Republican declared in 1854, "every man holds his fortune in his own right arm; and his position in society, in life, is to be tested by his own individual character" (see chapter 12). Powerful images of liberty and opportunity attracted a wide range of Northerners to the Republican cause.

Women as well as men rushed to the new Republican Party. Indeed, three women helped found the party in Ripon, Wisconsin, in 1854. Although they could not vote before the Civil War and suffered from a raft of other legal handicaps, women nevertheless participated in partisan politics by writing campaign literature, marching in parades, giving speeches, and lobbying voters. Women's antislavery fervor attracted them to the Republican Party, and participation in party politics in turn nurtured the woman's rights movement. Susan B. Anthony, who attended Republican meetings throughout the 1850s, found that her political activity made her disfranchisement all the more galling. She and other women in the North worked on behalf of antislavery and to secure both woman suffrage and the right of married women to control their own property. (See "Seeking the American Promise," page 344.)

The Election of 1856

The election of 1856 revealed that the Republicans had become the Democrats' main challenger, and slavery in the territories, not nativism, was the election's principal issue. When the Know-Nothings insisted on a platform that endorsed the Kansas-Nebraska Act, most of the Northerners walked out, and the party came apart. The few Know-Nothings who remained nominated ex-president Millard Fillmore.

The Republicans adopted a platform that focused almost exclusively on "making every territory free." When they labeled slavery a "relic of barbarism," they signaled that they had written

Know-Nothing Banner Convinced that the incendiary issue of slavery had blinded Americans to the greater dangers of uncontrolled immigration and foreign influence, the Know-Nothings nominated Millard Fillmore for president in 1856. There is more than a little irony in this banner's appeal to "Native Americans" to stem the invasion from abroad. The Know-Nothings were referring to native-born Americans, but bona fide Native Americans — American Indians — also faced an invasion, and to them it made little difference whether the aggressors were fresh off the boat or born in the USA. Milwaukee County Historical Society.

off the South. For president, they nominated the dashing soldier and California adventurer **John C. Frémont**, "Pathfinder of the West." Frémont lacked political credentials, but his wife, **Jessie Frémont**, the daughter of Senator Thomas Hart Benton of Missouri, knew the political map as well as her husband knew the western trails. Though careful to maintain a proper public image, the vivacious young mother and antislavery zealot helped attract voters and draw women into politics.

The Democrats, successful in 1852 in bridging sectional differences by nominating a northern man with southern principles, chose another "doughface," James Buchanan of Pennsylvania. They took refuge in the ambiguity of popular sovereignty and portrayed the Republicans as extremists ("Black Republican Abolitionists") whose support for the Wilmot Proviso risked pushing the South out of the Union.

The Democratic strategy carried the day for Buchanan, but Frémont did astonishingly well. Buchanan won 174 electoral votes against Frémont's 114 and Fillmore's 8 (see Map 14.4). Campaigning under the banner "Free soil, Free men, Frémont," the Republican carried all but five of the states north of the Mason-Dixon line. The election made clear that the Whigs had disintegrated, the Know-Nothings would not ride nativism to national power, and the

"A Purse of Her Own": Petitioning for the Right to Own Property

In the early Republic, as today, having money and deciding how to spend it was a fundamental aspect of independent adulthood. Yet antebellum married women were denied this privilege, due to the laws of *coverture*, which placed wives under the full legal control of their husbands (see chapter 10). By law, husbands made all the financial decisions in a household. Even money that a wife earned or brought into a marriage from gifts or inheritance was not hers to control as long as she remained married. Ernestine Potowsky Rose of New York City thought that was wrong. She was not alone in thinking this, but being unusually plucky and enterprising, she became the first woman in the United States to take action to change the law.

Ernestine Potowsky, born in Poland in 1810, was a precocious child. Her mother died when she was young, and her father, a rabbi, homeschooled his daughter in religious texts as if she were a son. Yet as a daughter, her destiny was fixed: an arranged marriage, many children, and a life strictly governed by religious law. Ernestine rejected this fate and left home. At age nineteen, she arrived in London and joined a circle of radical intellectuals who proposed socialistic solutions to the problems of poverty and industrialization. She married William Rose, a like-minded intellectual, and at the age of twenty-six emigrated with him to the United States.

The couple settled in New York City, where William, a jeweler, started a business. Ernestine soon learned of a starkly egalitarian bill presented in 1837 in the New York assembly proposing that married women, "equally with males and unmarried females, possess the rights of *life*, *liberty*, and PROPERTY, and are equally entitled to be protected in all three." The bill's author was Thomas Herttell, a New York labor advocate, assembly member, and "freethinker" (one who rejects all formal religion). Rose, having abandoned Judaism and embraced English socialism, easily gravitated to Herttell's group. She went door-to-door soliciting women's support for the bill but met with indifference. Opponents feared that it would undermine a central pillar of marriage: the assumption that husband and wife shared identical interests. How could a wife not trust her husband to control the money? Herttell's utopian bill predictably failed to pass. The devastating panics of 1837 and 1839, and the resulting bankruptcies, soon changed some traditionalists' minds about wives and property. Men in several state legislatures crafted laws that shielded a wife's inherited property from creditors collecting debts from her husband. Mississippi led the way in 1839, and by 1848 eighteen states had modified property laws in the name of family protection.

In New York, support for a liberalized law grew in the late 1840s. Protecting family assets from creditors remained important for elite men married to women from wealthy families. Ernestine Rose broadened the debate to mobilize a new constituency of women activists around the far more egalitarian argument that married women should be able to own and control property, just as married men did. She circulated petitions and spoke from public platforms, often joined by Elizabeth Cady Stanton, a young wife from western New York. In April 1848, three months before the Seneca Falls woman's rights convention (see chapter 12), the New York assembly finally awarded married women sole authority over property they brought to a marriage.

Rose welcomed the new law but recognized its key shortcoming: It made no provision for wages earned by a married woman. It also did nothing to alter inheritance laws that limited a widow's share of her husband's estate. Speaking at every national woman's rights convention from 1850 to 1860, Rose argued for women's economic independence.

She challenged lawmakers with her well-honed debating skills and regaled audiences with her sharp sense of

---

Democrats were badly strained. But the big news was what the press called the "glorious defeat" of the Republicans. Despite being a brand-new party and purely sectional, the Republicans had seriously challenged the Democrats for national power. Sectionalism had fashioned a new party system, one that spelled danger for the Republic.

Indeed, war had already broken out between proslavery and antislavery forces in distant Kansas Territory.

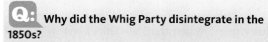

Why did the Whig Party disintegrate in the 1850s?

humor. In an 1853 speech, she itemized the limited belongings allowed to a widow if her husband died without a will: "As to the personal property, after all debts and liabilities are discharged, the widow receives one-half of it; and, in addition, the law allows her, her own wearing apparel, her own ornaments, proper to her station, one bed, with appurtenances for the same, a stove, the Bible, family pictures, and all the school-books; also all spinning wheels and weaving looms, one table, six chairs, ten cups and saucers, one tea-pot, one sugar dish, and six spoons." While her audience laughed appreciatively, Rose questioned whether the spoons would be teaspoons, "since a widow might live on tea only," and why no kettles or pots were included. Spinning wheels, long gone in 1853, needed no elaboration from her to make the law sound pathetically out-of-date.

Of particular concern to Rose was the plight of the many wives not from wealthy families. She and Susan B. Anthony traveled the state of New York and encountered women trapped in marriages with spendthrift or heartless husbands who drained family resources and failed to support their dependents. Anthony, herself a lifelong single woman, recalled that "as I passed from town to town I was made to feel the great evil of women's utter dependence on man. I never before took in so fully the grand idea of pecuniary independence. Woman must have a purse of her own." Rose's efforts paid off. In 1860, New York amended its law to include a wife's wages as her own, but only if she earned the money outside the household. Money earned selling eggs or butter or caring for boarders, even when fully the product of the wife's labor, still went directly into the husband's pocket. Perhaps the most significant beneficiaries of this law were women whose husbands were incompetent to support them or who had deserted them. These husbands now had no right to their wives' hard-earned nest eggs.

The revision of the New York law made other important changes to coverture. A wife could now sue (or be sued) and make legal contracts of her own. In addition, the wife was established as joint guardian of the children, "with equal powers, rights and duties in regard to them, with the husband." These changes, adopted in many states after 1860, began the long process of elevating married women to near equality with men, a process that still continues today.

★ **Ernestine Rose** Ernestine Rose, in her mid-forties when this photograph was taken, managed to hold a smile for the several minutes required to capture her image on a photographic plate. Schlesinger Library, Radcliffe Institute for Advanced Study, Harvard University.

Ever keen with sarcasm, Ernestine Rose produced great laughter at the 1860 woman's rights convention in New York City shortly after the passage of the revised law when she commented: "We 'woman's rights women' have redeemed our last legislature, by inducing them to give us one good act, among so many corrupt ones, and it strikes me that they owe us as many thanks as we owe them!"

Freedom under Siege

Events in Kansas Territory in the mid-1850s provided the young Republican organization with an enormous boost and help explain its strong showing in the election of 1856. Republicans organized around the premise that the slaveholding South provided a profound threat to "free soil, free labor, and free men," and now Kansas reeled with violence that Republicans argued was southern in origin. Kansas, Republicans claimed, opened a window to southern values and intentions. Republicans also pointed to the brutal beating by a Southerner of a respected

Armed Settlers near Lawrence, Kansas, and "Southern Rights" Flag Armed with rifles, knives, swords, and pistols, these tough antislavery men gathered for a photograph near Lawrence in 1856. Equally well-armed proslavery men marched under the red "Southern Rights" flag. This flag was adopted by the Palmetto Guards, a group formed by South Carolinians living in Kansas and named after the tree that symbolized their state. When proslavery forces attacked and occupied Lawrence in 1856, this flag flew briefly over the free-soil town. Kansas State Historical Society.

northern senator on the floor of Congress. Even the Supreme Court, in the Republicans' view, reflected the South's drive toward tyranny and minority rule. Then, in 1858, the issues dividing North and South received an extraordinary airing in a senatorial contest in Illinois, when the nation's foremost Democrat debated a resourceful Republican.

"Bleeding Kansas" Three days after the House of Representatives approved the Kansas-Nebraska Act in 1854, Senator William H. Seward of New York boldly challenged the South. "Come on then, Gentlemen of the Slave States," he cried, "since there is no escaping your challenge, I accept it in behalf of the cause of freedom. We will engage in competition for the virgin soil of Kansas, and God give the victory to the side which is stronger in numbers as it is in right." Because of Stephen Douglas, popular sovereignty would determine whether

"Bleeding Kansas," 1850s

Kansas became slave or free. Free-state and slave-state settlers each sought a majority at the ballot box, claimed God's blessing, and kept their rifles ready.

In both North and South, emigrant aid societies sprang up to promote settlement from free states or slave states. Missourians, already bordered on the east by the free state of Illinois and on the north by the free state of Iowa, especially thought it important to secure Kansas for slavery. Thousands of rough frontiersmen, egged on by Missouri senator David Rice Atchison, invaded Kansas. "There are eleven hundred coming over from Platte County to vote," Atchison reported, "and if that ain't enough we can send five thousand — enough to kill every God-damned abolitionist in the Territory." Not surprisingly, proslavery candidates swept the territorial elections in November 1854. When Kansas's first territorial legislature met, it enacted a raft of proslavery laws. Ever-pliant President Pierce endorsed the work of the fraudulently elected legislature. Free-soil Kansans did not. They elected their own legislature, which promptly banned both slaves and free blacks from the territory. Organized into two rival governments and armed to the teeth, Kansans verged on civil war.

Fighting broke out on the morning of May 21, 1856, when several hundred proslavery men raided the town of Lawrence, the center of free-state settlement. Only one man died, but the "Sack of Lawrence," as free-soil forces called it, inflamed northern opinion. Elsewhere in Kansas, news of events in Lawrence provoked John Brown, a free-soil settler, to announce that "it was better that a score of bad men should die than that one man who came here to make Kansas a Free State should be driven out" and to lead the posse that massacred five allegedly proslavery settlers along Pottawatomie Creek. After that, guerrilla war engulfed the territory.

Just as **"Bleeding Kansas"** gave the fledgling Republican Party fresh ammunition for its battle against the Slave Power, so too did an event that occurred in the national capital. In May 1856, Senator Charles Sumner of Massachusetts delivered a speech titled "The Crime against Kansas," which included a scalding personal attack on South Carolina senator Andrew P. Butler. Sumner described Butler as a "Don Quixote" who had taken as his mistress "the harlot, slavery."

Preston Brooks, a young South Carolina member of the House and a kinsman of Butler's, felt compelled to defend the honor of both his aged relative and his state. On May 22, Brooks entered the Senate, where he found Sumner working at his desk. He beat Sumner over the head with his cane until Sumner lay bleeding and unconscious on the floor. Brooks resigned his seat in the House, only to be promptly reelected. In the North, the southern hero became an arch-villain. Like "Bleeding Kansas," "Bleeding Sumner" provided the Republican Party with a potent symbol of the South's "twisted and violent civilization."

The Dred Scott Decision Political debate over slavery in the territories became so heated in part because the Constitution lacked precision on the issue. In 1857, in the case of *Dred Scott v. Sandford*, the Supreme Court announced its understanding of the meaning of the Constitution regarding slavery in the territories. The Court's decision demonstrated that it enjoyed no special immunity from the sectional and partisan passions that convulsed the land.

In 1833, an army doctor bought the slave Dred Scott in St. Louis, Missouri, and took him as his personal servant to Fort Armstrong, Illinois, and then to Fort Snelling in Wisconsin Territory. Back in St. Louis in 1846, Scott, with the help of white friends, sued to prove that he and his family were legally entitled to their freedom. Scott based his claim on his travels and residences. He argued that living in Illinois, a free state, and Wisconsin, a free territory, had made his family free, and that they remained free even after returning to Missouri, a slave state.

In 1857, the U.S. Supreme Court ruled in the case. Chief Justice **Roger B. Taney**, who hated Republicans and detested racial equality, wrote the Court's decision. First, the Court ruled in the ***Dred Scott* decision** that Scott could not legally claim violation of his constitutional rights because he was not a citizen of the United States. When the Constitution was written, Taney said, blacks "were regarded as beings of an inferior order . . . so far inferior, that they had no rights which the white man was bound to respect." Second, the laws of Dred Scott's home state, Missouri, determined his status, and thus his travels in free areas did not make him free. Third, Congress's power to make "all needful rules and regulations" for the territories

Dred Scott The *Dred Scott* case aroused enormous curiosity about the man suing for freedom. This portrait of Dred Scott was painted in 1857, the year of the Supreme Court's decision. A journalist who traveled to St. Louis to interview Scott "found him on examination to be a pure-blooded African, perhaps fifty years of age, with a shrewd, intelligent, good-natured face, of rather light frame, being not more than five feet six inches high." Although the Court rejected his suit, he gained his freedom in May 1857 when a white man purchased and freed Scott and his family. Collection of the New-York Historical Society.

did not include the right to prohibit slavery. The Court explicitly declared the Missouri Compromise unconstitutional, even though it had already been voided by the Kansas-Nebraska Act.

The Taney Court's extreme proslavery decision outraged Republicans. By denying the federal government the right to exclude slavery in the territories, it cut the legs out from under the Republican Party. Moreover, as the *New York Tribune* lamented, the decision cleared the way for "all our Territories . . . to be ripened into Slave States." Particularly frightening to African Americans in the North was the Court's declaration that free blacks were not citizens and had no rights.

The Republican rebuttal to the *Dred Scott* ruling relied heavily on the dissenting opinion of Justice Benjamin R. Curtis. Scott *was* a citizen of the United States, Curtis argued. At the time of the writing of the Constitution, free black men could vote in five states and participated in the ratification process. Scott *was* free. Because slavery was prohibited in Wisconsin, the "involuntary servitude of a slave, coming into the Territory with his master, should cease to exist." The Missouri Compromise *was* constitutional. The Founders had meant exactly what they said: Congress had the power to make "*all* needful rules and regulations" for the territories, including barring slavery.

In a seven-to-two decision, the Court rejected Curtis's arguments, thereby validating an extreme statement of the South's territorial rights. John C. Calhoun's claim that Congress had no authority to exclude slavery became the law of the land. White Southerners cheered, but the *Dred Scott* decision actually strengthened the young Republican Party. Indeed, that "outrageous" decision, one Republican argued, was "the best thing that could have happened." It provided dramatic evidence of the Republicans' claim that a hostile Slave Power conspired against northern liberties.

Prairie Republican: Abraham Lincoln By reigniting the sectional flames, the *Dred Scott* case provided Republican politicians with fresh challenges and fresh opportunities. **Abraham Lincoln** had long since put behind him his hardscrabble log-cabin beginnings in Kentucky and Indiana. He lived in a fine two-story house in Springfield, Illinois, and earned good money as a lawyer. The law provided Lincoln's living, but politics was his life. "His ambition was a little engine that knew no rest," observed his law partner William Herndon. Lincoln had served as a Whig in the Illinois state legislature and in the House of Representatives, but he had not held public office since 1849.

Convinced that slavery was a "great moral wrong" and an "unqualified evil to the negro, the white man,

and the State," Lincoln condemned Douglas's Kansas-Nebraska Act of 1854 for giving slavery a new life, and in 1856 he joined the Republican Party. He accepted that the Constitution permitted slavery in those states where it existed, but he believed that Congress could contain its spread. Penned in, Lincoln believed, plantation slavery would wither, and in time Southerners would end slavery themselves.

Lincoln held what were, for his times, moderate racial views. Although he denounced slavery and defended black humanity, he also viewed black equality as impractical and unachievable. "Negroes have natural rights . . . as other men have," he said, "although they cannot enjoy them here." Insurmountable white prejudice made it impossible to extend full citizenship to blacks in America, he believed. Freeing blacks and allowing them to remain in this country would lead to a race war. In Lincoln's mind, social stability and black progress required that slavery end and that blacks leave the country.

Lincoln envisioned the western territories as "places for poor people to go to, and better their conditions." But slavery's expansion threatened free men's basic right to succeed. The Kansas-Nebraska Act and the *Dred Scott* decision persuaded him that slaveholders were engaged in a dangerous conspiracy to nationalize slavery. The next step, Lincoln warned, would be "another Supreme Court decision, declaring that the Constitution of the United States does not permit a State to exclude slavery from its limits." Unless the citizens of Illinois woke up, he warned, the Supreme Court would make "Illinois a slave State."

In Lincoln's view, the nation could not "endure, permanently half slave and half free." Either opponents of slavery would arrest its spread and place it on the "course of ultimate extinction," or its advocates would see that it became legal in "*all* the States, *old* as well as *new—North* as well as *South*." Lincoln's convictions that slavery was wrong and that Congress must stop its spread formed the core of the Republican ideology. Lincoln so impressed his fellow Republicans in Illinois that in 1858, they chose him to challenge the nation's premier Democrat, who was seeking reelection to the U.S. Senate.

The Lincoln-Douglas Debates When Stephen Douglas learned that the Republican Abraham Lincoln would be his opponent for the Senate, he observed: "He is the strong man of the party—full of wit, facts, dates—and the best stump speaker, with his droll ways and dry jokes, in the West. He is as honest as he is shrewd, and if I beat him my victory will be hardly won."

Not only did Douglas have to contend with a formidable foe, but he also carried the weight of a burden not of his own making. The previous year, the nation's economy had experienced a sharp downturn. Prices had plummeted, thousands of businesses had failed, and many were unemployed. As a Democrat, Douglas had to go before the voters as a member of the party whose policies stood accused of causing the panic of 1857.

Douglas's response to another crisis in 1857, however, helped shore up his standing in Illinois. Proslavery forces in Kansas met in the town of Lecompton, drafted a proslavery constitution, and applied for statehood. Everyone knew that free-soilers outnumbered proslavery settlers, but President Buchanan instructed Congress to admit Kansas as the sixteenth slave state. Republicans denounced the "Lecompton swindle." Senator Douglas broke with the Democratic administration and denounced the Lecompton constitution; Congress killed the Lecompton bill. (When Kansans reconsidered the Lecompton constitution in an honest election, they rejected it six to one. Kansas entered the Union in 1861 as a free state.) By denouncing the fraudulent proslavery constitution, Douglas declared his independence from the South and, he hoped, made himself acceptable at home.

A relative unknown and a decided underdog in the Illinois election, Lincoln challenged Douglas to debate him face-to-face. The two met in seven communities for what would become a legendary series of debates. Thousands stood straining to see and hear as they debated the crucial issues of the age—slavery and freedom. They showed the citizens of Illinois (and much of the nation because of widespread press coverage) the difference between an anti-Lecompton Democrat and a true Republican.

Lincoln badgered Douglas with the question of whether he favored the spread of slavery. He tried to force Douglas into the damaging admission that the Supreme Court had repudiated Douglas's own territorial solution, popular sovereignty. At Freeport, Illinois, Douglas admitted that settlers could not now pass legislation barring slavery, but he argued that they could ban slavery just as effectively by not passing protective laws, such as those found in slave states. Southerners condemned Douglas's "Freeport Doctrine" and charged him with trying to steal the victory they had gained with the *Dred Scott* decision. Lincoln chastised his opponent for his "don't care" attitude about slavery, for "blowing out the moral lights around us."

Douglas worked the racial issue. He called Lincoln an abolitionist and an egalitarian enamored of "our colored brethren." Put on the defensive, Lincoln reaffirmed his faith in white rule: "I will say, then, that I am not, nor ever have been, in favor of bringing about in any way the social and political equality of the white and black race." But unlike Douglas, who told racist jokes, Lincoln was no negrophobe. He tried to steer the debate back to what he considered the true issue: the morality and future of slavery. "Slavery is wrong," Lincoln repeated, because "a man has the right to the fruits of his own labor."

As Douglas predicted, the election was hard-fought and closely contested. Until the adoption of the Seventeenth Amendment in 1911, citizens voted for state legislators, who in turn selected U.S. senators. Since Democrats won a slight majority in the Illinois legislature, the members returned Douglas to the Senate. But the **Lincoln-Douglas debates** thrust Lincoln, the prairie Republican, into the national spotlight.

Q: Why did the *Dred Scott* decision strengthen northern suspicions of a "Slave Power" conspiracy?

The Union Collapses

Lincoln's thesis that the "slavocracy" conspired to make slavery a national institution now seems exaggerated. But from the northern perspective, the Kansas-Nebraska Act, the Brooks-Sumner affair, the *Dred Scott* decision, and the Lecompton constitution amounted to irrefutable evidence of the South's aggressiveness. White Southerners, of course, saw things differently. They were the ones who were under siege, they declared. Signs were everywhere that the North planned to use its numerical advantage to attack slavery, and not just in the territories. Republicans had made it clear that they were unwilling to accept the *Dred Scott* ruling as the last word on the issue of slavery expansion. And John Brown's attempt to incite a slave insurrection in Virginia in 1859 proved that Northerners were unwilling to be bound by Christian decency and reverence for life.

Threats of secession increasingly laced the sectional debate. Talk of leaving the Union had been heard for years, but until the final crisis, Southerners had used secession as a ploy to gain concessions within the Union, not to destroy it. Then the 1850s delivered powerful blows to Southerners' confidence that they could remain Americans and protect slavery. When the Republican Party won the White House in 1860, many Southerners concluded that they would have to leave.

The Aftermath of John Brown's Raid For his attack on Harpers Ferry, John Brown stood trial for treason, murder, and incitement of slave insurrection. On December 2, 1859, Virginia executed

> In life, John Brown was a ne'er-do-well, but he died with courage and dignity. He told his wife that he was "determined to make the utmost possible out of a defeat."

Brown. In life, he was a ne'er-do-well, but he died with courage and dignity. He told his wife that he was "determined to make the utmost possible out of a defeat." He told the court: "If it is deemed necessary that I should forfeit my life for the furtherance of the ends of justice, and mingle my blood further with the blood of . . . millions in this slave country whose rights are disregarded by wicked, cruel, and unjust enactments, I say, let it be done."

After Brown's heroic death, northern denunciation of Brown as a dangerous fanatic gave way to grudging respect. Some even celebrated his "splendid martyrdom." Abolitionist Lydia Maria Child likened Brown to Christ and declared that he made "the scaffold . . . as glorious as the Cross of Calvary." Some abolitionists explicitly endorsed Brown's resort to violence. Abolitionist William Lloyd Garrison, who usually professed pacifism, announced, "I am prepared to say 'success to every slave insurrection at the South and in every country.'"

Most Northerners did not advocate bloody rebellion, however. Like Lincoln, they concluded that Brown's noble antislavery ideals could not "excuse violence, bloodshed, and treason." Still, when northern churches marked John Brown's execution with tolling bells, hymns, and prayer vigils, white Southerners contemplated what they had in common with people who "regard John Brown as a martyr and a Christian hero, rather than a murderer and robber." Georgia senator Robert Toombs

John Brown Going to His Hanging, **by Horace Pippin, 1942** The grandparents of Horace Pippin, a Pennsylvania artist, were slaves. His grandmother witnessed the hanging of John Brown, and this painting recalls the scene she so often described to him. Historically accurate, the painting depicts Brown tied and sitting erect on his coffin, passing resolutely before the silent, staring white men. The black woman in the lower right corner presumably is Pippin's grandmother. Pennsylvania Academy of Fine Arts, Philadelphia. John Lambert Fund.

FOR MORE HELP ANALYZING THIS IMAGE, see the visual activity for this chapter in the Online Study Guide at bedfordstmartins.com/roarkcompact.

announced solemnly that Southerners must "never permit this Federal government to pass into the traitorous hands of the black Republican party." At that moment, the presidential election was only months away.

Republican Victory in 1860 When the Democrats converged on Charleston for their convention in April 1860, fire-eating Southerners denounced Stephen Douglas and demanded a platform that included federal protection of slavery in the territories. But northern Democrats knew that northern voters would not stomach a federal slave code. When the delegates approved a platform with popular sovereignty, representatives from the entire Lower South and Arkansas stomped out of the convention. The remaining Democrats adjourned to meet a few weeks later in Baltimore, where they nominated Douglas for president.

When southern Democrats met, they nominated Vice President John C. Breckinridge of Kentucky and approved a platform with a federal slave code. Southern moderates, however, refused to support Breckinridge. They formed the Constitutional Union Party to provide voters with a Unionist choice. Instead of adopting a platform and confronting the slavery question, the Constitutional Union Party merely approved a vague resolution pledging "to recognize no political principle other than *the Constitution . . . the Union . . . and the Enforcement of the Laws.*" For president, they picked former senator John Bell of Tennessee.

The Republicans smelled victory, but they estimated that they needed to carry nearly all the free states to win. To make their party more appealing, they expanded their platform beyond antislavery. They hoped that free homesteads, a protective tariff, a transcontinental railroad, and a guarantee of immigrant political rights would provide an economic and social agenda broad enough to unify the North. While reasserting their commitment to stop the spread of slavery, they also denounced John Brown's raid as "among the gravest of crimes" and confirmed the security of slavery in the South.

Republicans cast about for a moderate candidate to go with their evenhanded platform. The foremost Republican, William H. Seward, had made enemies with his radical "higher law" doctrine and "irrepressible conflict" speech. Lincoln, however, since bursting onto the national scene in 1858 had demonstrated his clear purpose, good judgment, and solid Republican credentials. That, and his residence in Illinois, a crucial state, made him attractive to the party. On the third ballot, the delegates chose Lincoln. Defeated by Douglas in a state contest less than two years earlier, Lincoln now stood ready to take him on for the presidency.

Abraham Lincoln Lincoln actively sought the Republican presidential nomination in 1860. While in New York City to give a political address, he had his photograph taken by Mathew Brady. "While I was there I was taken to one of the places where they get up such things," Lincoln explained, sounding more innocent than he was, "and I suppose they got my shadow, and can multiply copies indefinitely." Multiply they did. Later, Lincoln credited his victory to his New York speech and to this dignified photograph by Brady. The Lincoln Museum, Fort Wayne, Indiana, #0–17.

The election of 1860 was like none other in American politics. It took place in the midst of the nation's severest crisis. Four major candidates crowded the presidential field. Rather than a four-cornered contest, however, the election broke into two contests, each with two candidates. In the North, Lincoln faced Douglas; in the South, Breckinridge confronted Bell. So outrageous did Southerners consider the Republican Party that they did not even permit Lincoln's name to appear on the ballot in ten of the fifteen slave states.

On November 6, 1860, Lincoln swept all of the eighteen free states except New Jersey, which split its electoral votes between him and Douglas. Although Lincoln received only 39 percent of the popular vote,

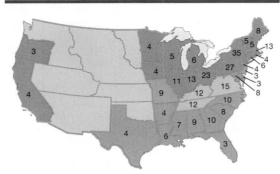

Candidate	Electoral Vote	Popular Vote	Percent of Popular Vote
Abraham Lincoln (Republican)	180	1,866,452	39.9
John C. Breckinridge (Southern Democrat)	72	847,953	18.1
Stephen A. Douglas (Northern Democrat)	12	1,375,157	29.4
John Bell (Constitutional Union)	39	590,631	12.6

MAP 14.5 **The Election of 1860**

he won easily in the electoral college with 180 votes, 28 more than he needed for victory (Map 14.5). Lincoln did not win because his opposition was splintered. Even if the votes of his three opponents had been combined, Lincoln would still have won. He won because his votes were concentrated in the free states, which contained a majority of electoral votes. Ominously, however, Breckinridge, running on a southern-rights platform, won the entire Lower South, plus Delaware, Maryland, and North Carolina.

Secession Winter The telegraphs had barely stopped tapping out the news of Lincoln's victory when anxious Southerners began debating what to do. Although Breckinridge had carried the South, a vote for "southern rights" was not necessarily a vote for secession. Besides, slightly more than half of the Southerners who had voted had cast ballots for Douglas and Bell, two stout defenders of the Union.

Southern Unionists tried to calm the fears that Lincoln's election triggered. Let the dust settle, they pleaded. Former congressman Alexander Stephens of Georgia asked what Lincoln had done to justify something as extreme as secession. Had he not promised to respect slavery where it existed? In Stephens's judgment, the fire-eater cure would be worse than the Republican disease. Secession might lead to war, which would loosen the hinges of southern society, possibly even open the door to slave

Secession of the Lower South, December 1860–February 1861

insurrection. "Revolutions are much easier started than controlled," he warned. "I consider slavery much more secure in the Union than out of it."

Secessionists emphasized the dangers of delay. "Mr. Lincoln and his party assert that this doctrine of equality applies to the negro," former Georgia governor Howell Cobb declared, "and necessarily there can exist no such thing as property in our equals." Lincoln's election without a single electoral vote from the South meant that Southerners were no longer able to defend themselves within the Union, Cobb argued. Why wait, he asked, for the abolitionists to attack? As for war, there would be none. The Union was a voluntary compact, and Lincoln would not coerce patriotism. If Northerners did resist with force, secessionists argued, one southern woodsman could whip five of Lincoln's greasy mechanics.

For all their differences, southern whites agreed that they had to defend slavery. John Smith Preston of South Carolina spoke for the overwhelming majority when he declared, "The South cannot exist without slavery." They disagreed about whether the mere presence of a Republican in the White House made it necessary to exercise what they considered a legitimate right to secede.

The debate about what to do was briefest in South Carolina; it seceded from the Union on December 20, 1860. By February 1861, the six other Lower South states marched in South Carolina's footsteps. In some states, the vote was close. In general, slaveholders spearheaded secession, while nonslaveholders in the Piedmont and mountain counties, where slaves were relatively few, displayed the greatest attachment to the Union. In February, representatives from South Carolina, Georgia, Florida, Alabama, Mississippi, Louisiana, and Texas met in Montgomery, Alabama, where they celebrated the birth of the Confederate States of America. **Jefferson Davis** became president, and Alexander Stephens, who had spoken so eloquently about the dangers of revolution, became vice president.

Lincoln's election had split the Union. Now secession split the South. Seven slave states seceded during the winter, but the eight slave states of the Upper South rejected secession, at least for the moment. The Upper South had a smaller stake in slavery. Barely half as many white families in the Upper South held slaves (21 percent) as in the Lower South (37 percent). Slaves represented twice as large a percentage of the population in the Lower South (48 percent) as in the Upper South (23 percent). Consequently, whites in the Upper South had fewer fears that Republican ascendancy meant economic catastrophe, social chaos, and racial war. Lincoln would need to do more than just be elected to provoke them into secession.

The nation had to wait until March 4, 1861, when Lincoln took office, to see what he would do. (Presidents-elect waited four months to take office until 1933, when the Twentieth Amendment to the Constitution shifted the inauguration to January 20.) After his election, Lincoln chose to stay in Springfield and to say nothing. "Lame-duck" president James Buchanan sat in Washington and did nothing. Buchanan demonstrated, William H. Seward said mockingly, that "it is the President's duty to enforce the laws, unless somebody opposes him." In Congress, efforts at cobbling together a peace-saving compromise came to nothing.

Lincoln began his inaugural address with reassurances to the South. He had "no lawful right" to interfere with slavery where it existed, he declared again, adding for emphasis that he had "no inclination to do so." Conciliatory about slavery, Lincoln proved inflexible about the Union. The Union, he declared, was "perpetual." Secession was "anarchy" and "legally void." The Constitution required him to execute the law "in all the States."

The decision for civil war or peace rested in the South's hands, Lincoln said. "You can have no conflict, without being yourselves the aggressors. *You* have no oath registered in Heaven to destroy the government, while *I* shall have the most solemn one to 'preserve, protect, and defend' it." What Confederates in Charleston held in their hands at that very moment were the cords for firing the cannons aimed at the federal garrison at Fort Sumter.

Q: Why did some southern states secede immediately after Lincoln's election?

Conclusion: Slavery, Free Labor, and the Failure of Political Compromise

As their economies, societies, and cultures diverged in the nineteenth century, Northerners and Southerners expressed different concepts of the American promise and the place of slavery within it. Their differences crystallized into political form in 1846 when David Wilmot proposed banning slavery in any territory won in the Mexican-American War. "As if by magic," a Boston newspaper observed, "it brought to a head the great question that is about to divide the American people." Discovery of gold and other precious metals in the West added urgency to the controversy over slavery in the territories. Although Congress addressed the issue with the Compromise of 1850, the consequences of the Fugitive Slave Act and the publication of *Uncle Tom's Cabin* hardened northern sentiments against slavery and confirmed southern suspicions of northern ill will. The bloody violence that erupted in Kansas in 1856 and the incendiary *Dred Scott* decision in 1857 further eroded hope for a solution to this momentous question.

During the extended crisis of the Union that stretched from 1846 to 1861, the slavery question braided with national politics. The traditional Whig and Democratic parties struggled to hold together, as new parties, most notably the Republican Party, emerged. Politicians fixed their attention on the expansion of slavery, but from the beginning, the nation recognized that the controversy had less to do with slavery in the territories than with the future of slavery in America.

For more than seventy years, statesmen had found compromises that accepted slavery and preserved the Union. But as each section grew increasingly committed to its labor system and the promise it offered, Americans discovered that accommodation had limits. In 1859, John Brown's militant antislavery pushed white Southerners to the edge. In 1860, Lincoln's election convinced whites in the Lower South that slavery and the society they had built on it were at risk in the Union, and they seceded. In his inaugural address, Lincoln pleaded, "We are not enemies but friends. We must not be enemies." By then, however, seven southern states had ceased to sing what he called "the chorus of the Union." It remained to be seen whether disunion would mean war.

Reviewing the Chapter

★ KEY TERMS

Explain each term's significance

WHO
John Brown (p. 333)

Lewis Cass (p. 335)

Charles Sumner (p. 336)

Stephen A. Douglas (p. 337)

John C. Frémont (p. 343)

Jessie Frémont (p. 343)

Roger B. Taney (p. 347)

Abraham Lincoln (p. 348)

Jefferson Davis (p. 352)

WHAT
Wilmot Proviso (p. 335)

popular sovereignty (p. 335)

Free-Soil Party (p. 336)

Compromise of 1850 (p. 338)

Uncle Tom's Cabin (p. 338)

underground railroad (p. 338)

Fugitive Slave Act (p. 338)

Kansas-Nebraska Act (p. 340)

Know-Nothings (p. 341)

Republican Party (p. 341)

free labor (p. 343)

"Bleeding Kansas" (p. 347)

Dred Scott decision (p. 347)

Lincoln-Douglas debates (p. 349)

FOR PRACTICE QUIZZES AND OTHER STUDY TOOLS, see the Online Study Guide at **bedfordstmartins.com/roarkcompact**.

★ REVIEW QUESTIONS Q:

Use key terms and dates to support your answer

1. Why did response to the Wilmot Proviso split along sectional rather than party lines? (pp. 334–38)

2. Why did the Fugitive Slave Act provoke such strong opposition in the North? (pp. 338–40)

3. Why did the Whig Party disintegrate in the 1850s? (pp. 341–44)

4. Why did the *Dred Scott* decision strengthen northern suspicions of a "Slave Power" conspiracy? (pp. 345–49)

5. Why did some southern states secede immediately after Lincoln's election? (pp. 349–53)

★ MAKING CONNECTIONS

Draw on key terms, timeline, and review questions

1. The process of compromise that had successfully contained tensions between slave and free states since the nation's founding collapsed with secession. Why did compromise fail at this moment? In your answer, address specific political conflicts and attempts to solve them between 1846 and 1861.

2. In the 1850s, many Americans supported popular sovereignty as the best solution to the explosive question of slavery in the western territories. Why was this solution so popular, and why did it ultimately prove inadequate? In your answer, be sure to address popular sovereignty's varied critics as well as its champions.

3. In the 1840s and 1850s, the United States witnessed the realignment of its long-standing two-party system. Why did the old system fall apart, what emerged to take its place, and how did this process contribute to the coming of the Civil War?

4. Abraham Lincoln believed that he had staked out a moderate position on the question of slavery, avoiding the extremes of immediate abolitionism and calls for unlimited protection of slavery. Why, then, did some southern states determine that his election necessitated the radical act of secession?

★ SUGGESTED READINGS

Charles B. Dew, *Apostles of Disunion: Southern Secession Commissioners and the Causes of the Civil War* (2001). An analysis that places slavery at the center of the decision to secede.

Don E. Fehrenbacher, *The Slaveholding Republic: An Account of the United States Government's Relations to Slavery* (2001). An insightful discussion of the federal government's changing relationship with slavery from the Constitution to the Civil War.

Eric Foner, *Free Labor, Free Soil, Free Men: The Ideology of the Republican Party before the Civil War* (1970). A probing analysis of the rise of the Republican Party.

Bruce C. Levine, *Half Slave and Half Free: The Roots of the Civil War* (1992). A vivid narrative that describes the growing divergence between North and South.

David S. Reynolds, *John Brown, Abolitionist: The Man Who Killed Slavery, Sparked the Civil War, and Seeded Civil Rights* (2005). A provocative biography of one of the era's most controversial figures.

Kenneth J. Winkle, *The Young Eagle: The Rise of Abraham Lincoln* (2001). An imaginative analysis of the young Lincoln that places him in the context of his times.

FOR MORE BOOKS ABOUT TOPICS IN THIS CHAPTER, see the Online Bibliography at **bedfordstmartins.com/roarkcompact**.

FOR ADDITIONAL FIRSTHAND ACCOUNTS OF THIS PERIOD, see Chapter 14 in Michael Johnson, ed., *Reading the American Past*, Fourth Edition.

FOR WEB SITES, IMAGES, AND DOCUMENTS RELATED TO TOPICS AND PLACES IN THIS CHAPTER, visit Make History at **bedfordstmartins.com/roarkcompact**.

★ TIMELINE

1820	• Missouri Compromise.
1846	• Wilmot Proviso introduced in Congress.
1847	• Wilmot Proviso defeated in Senate. • Compromise of "popular sovereignty" offered.
1848	• Free-Soil Party founded. • Whig Zachary Taylor elected president.
1849	• California gold rush.
1850	• Taylor dies; Vice President Millard Fillmore becomes president. • Compromise of 1850 becomes law.
1852	• *Uncle Tom's Cabin* published. • Democrat Franklin Pierce elected president.
1853	• Gadsden Purchase.
1854	• American (Know-Nothing) Party emerges. • Kansas-Nebraska Act. • Republican Party founded.
1856	• "Bleeding Kansas." • Preston Brooks canes Charles Sumner. • Pottawatomie massacre. • Democrat James Buchanan elected president.
1857	• *Dred Scott* decision. • Congress rejects Lecompton constitution. • Panic of 1857.
1858	• Abraham Lincoln and Stephen A. Douglas debate slavery; Douglas wins Senate seat.
1859	• John Brown raids Harpers Ferry, Virginia.
1860	• Republican Abraham Lincoln elected president. • South Carolina secedes from Union.
1861	• Six other deep South states secede. • Confederate States of America formed. • Lincoln takes office.

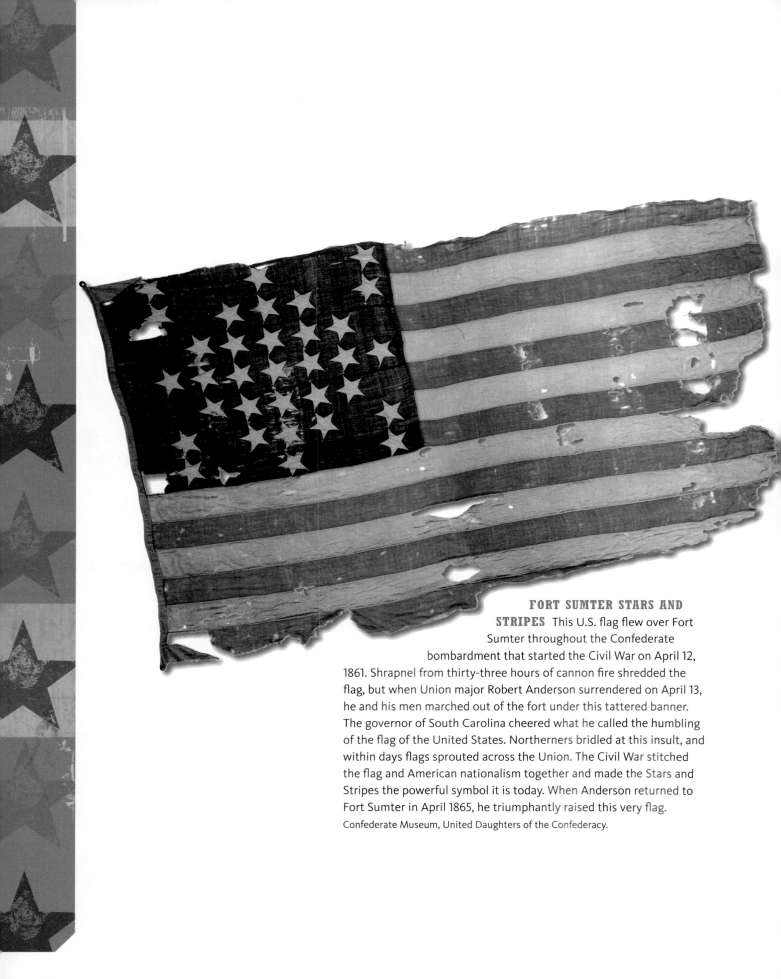

FORT SUMTER STARS AND STRIPES This U.S. flag flew over Fort Sumter throughout the Confederate bombardment that started the Civil War on April 12, 1861. Shrapnel from thirty-three hours of cannon fire shredded the flag, but when Union major Robert Anderson surrendered on April 13, he and his men marched out of the fort under this tattered banner. The governor of South Carolina cheered what he called the humbling of the flag of the United States. Northerners bridled at this insult, and within days flags sprouted across the Union. The Civil War stitched the flag and American nationalism together and made the Stars and Stripes the powerful symbol it is today. When Anderson returned to Fort Sumter in April 1865, he triumphantly raised this very flag. Confederate Museum, United Daughters of the Confederacy.

The Crucible of War

1861–1865

ON THE RAINY NIGHT OF SEPTEMBER 21, 1862, in Wilmington, North Carolina, twenty-four-year-old William Gould and seven other runaway slaves crowded into a small boat on the Cape Fear River and quietly pushed away from the dock. They rowed hard throughout the night, and by dawn they had reached the Atlantic Ocean. They plunged into the swells and made for the Union navy patrolling offshore to disrupt the flow of goods in and out of Wilmington, a major Confederate port. At 10:30 that morning, the USS *Cambridge* took the men aboard.

Astonishingly, on the same day that Gould reached the federal ship, President Abraham Lincoln revealed that he intended to issue a proclamation of emancipation freeing the slaves in the Confederate states. Because the proclamation would not take effect until January 1863, Gould was not legally free in the eyes of the U.S. government. But the U.S. navy, suffering from a shortage of sailors, cared little about the formal status of runaway slaves. Within days, all eight runaways became sailors "for three years," Gould said, "first taking the Oath of Allegiance to the Government of Uncle Samuel."

William Gould could read and write, and he began making almost daily entries in a remarkable diary. In some ways, Gould's naval experience looked like that of a white sailor. He found duty on a ship in the blockading squadron both boring and exhilarating. He often recorded comments such as "All hands painting, cleaning" and "Cruised as usual." But long days of tedious work were sometimes interrupted by a "period of daring exploit." When Gould's ship closed on a Confederate vessel, he declared that "we told them good morning in the shape of a shot." In a five-day period in 1862, his ship helped capture four blockade runners and ran another aground.

But Gould's Civil War experience was shaped by his race. Like most black men in the Union military, he saw service as an opportunity to fight slavery. From the beginning, Gould linked union and freedom, which he called "the holiest of all causes." But Gould witnessed a number of ugly racial incidents on federal ships. "There was A malee [melee] on Deck between the white and colard [colored] men," he observed. Later, when a black regiment came aboard, "they were treated verry rough by the crew," he

Previewing the Chapter

"And the War Came" 358
Q: *Why did both the Union and the Confederacy consider control of the border states crucial?*

The Combatants 360
Q: *Why did the South believe it could win the war despite numerical disadvantages?*

Battling It Out, 1861–1862 363
Q: *Why did the Confederacy's bid for international support fail?*

Union *and* Freedom 368
Q: *Why did the Union change policy in 1863 to allow black men to serve in the army?*

The South at War 371
Q: *How did wartime hardship in the South contribute to class animosity?*

The North at War 374
Q: *Why was the U.S. Congress able to pass such a bold legislative agenda during the war?*

Grinding Out Victory, 1863–1865 377
Q: *Why were the siege of Vicksburg and the battle of Gettysburg crucial to the outcome of the war?*

Conclusion: The Second American Revolution 381

The Crew of the USS *Hunchback* African Americans served as sailors in the federal military long before they were permitted to become soldiers. Blacks initially served only as coal heavers, cooks, and stewards, but within a year, some black sailors joined their ships' gun crews. The *Hunchback* was one of the Union's innovative ironclad ships. Although ironclads made wooden navies obsolete, they were far from invincible. During the assault on Charleston in 1863, five of the nine federal ironclads were partially or wholly disabled. National Archives.

said. The white sailors "refused to let them eat off the mess pans and called them all kinds of names[;] . . . in all they was treated shamefully."

Still, Gould was proud of his service in the navy and monitored the progress of racial equality during the war. On shore leave in 1863, he cheered the "20th Regmt of U.S. (collard) Volunteers, the first collard Regement raised in New York pronounce[d] by all to be A splendid Regement." In March 1865, he celebrated the "passage of an amendment of the Con[sti]-tution prohibiting slavery througho[ut] the United States." And a month later, he thrilled to the "Glad Tidings that the Stars and Stripe[s] had been planted over the Capital of the D—nd Confederacy by the invincible Grant." He added, we must not forget the "Mayrters to the cau[se] of Right and Equality."

Slaves like the eight runaways from Wilmington took the first steps toward making the war for union also a war for freedom. Early in the fighting, black abolitionist Frederick Douglass challenged the friends of freedom to "*be up and doing;—now is your time.*" But for the first eighteen months of the war, federal soldiers fought solely to uphold the Constitution and preserve the nation. With the Emancipation Proclamation, however, the northern war effort took on a dual purpose: to save the Union and to free the slaves.

Even if the Civil War had not touched slavery, the conflict still would have transformed America. As the world's first modern war, it mobilized the entire populations of North and South, harnessed the productive capacities of both economies, and produced battles that fielded 200,000 soldiers and created casualties in the tens of thousands. The carnage lasted four years and cost the nation an estimated 633,000 lives, nearly as many as in all of its other wars combined. The war helped mold the modern American nation-state, and the federal government emerged with new power and responsibility over national life. The war encouraged industrialization. It tore families apart and pushed women into new work and roles. But because the war for union also became a war against slavery, the northern victory had truly revolutionary meaning. Defeat and emancipation destroyed the slave society of the Old South and gave birth to a different southern society.

Recalling the Civil War years, Frederick Douglass said, "It is something to couple one's name with great occasions." It *was* something—for William Gould and millions of other Americans. Whether they fought for the Confederacy or the Union, whether they labored behind the lines to supply Yankee or rebel soldiers, whether they prayed for the safe return of Northerners or Southerners, all Americans experienced the crucible of war. But the war affected no group more than the 4 million African Americans who saw its beginning as slaves and emerged as free people.   ★

"And the War Came"

Abraham Lincoln faced the worst crisis in the history of the nation: disunion. He revealed his strategy on March 4, 1861, in his inaugural address, which was firm yet conciliatory. First, he sought to stop the contagion of secession by avoiding any act that would push the skittish Upper South (North Carolina, Virginia, Maryland, Delaware, Kentucky, Tennessee, Missouri, and Arkansas) out of the Union. Second, he sought to reassure the seceding Lower South (South Carolina, Georgia, Florida, Alabama, Mississippi, Louisiana, and Texas) that the Republicans would not abolish slavery. Lincoln believed that Unionists there would assert themselves and overturn the secession decision. Always, Lincoln denied the right of secession and upheld the Union.

His counterpart, Jefferson Davis, fully intended to establish the Confederate States of America as an independent republic. To achieve permanence, Davis had to sustain the secession fever that had carried the Lower South out of the Union. Even if the Lower South held firm, however, the Confederacy would remain weak without additional states. Davis watched for opportunities to add new stars to the Confederate flag.

Neither man sought war; both wanted to achieve their objectives peacefully. As Lincoln later observed, "Both parties deprecated war, but one of them would *make* war rather than let the nation survive, and the other would *accept* war rather than let it perish. And the war came."

Attack on Fort Sumter Major Robert Anderson and some eighty U.S. soldiers occupied **Fort Sumter**, which was perched on a tiny island at the entrance to Charleston harbor. The fort with its American flag became a hated symbol of the nation that Southerners had abandoned, and they wanted federal troops out. Sumter was also a symbol to Northerners, a beacon affirming federal sovereignty in the seceded states.

Lincoln decided to hold Fort Sumter, but to do so, he had to provision it, for Anderson was running dangerously short of food. In the first week of April 1861, Lincoln authorized a peaceful expedition to bring supplies, but not military reinforcements, to the fort. The president understood that he risked war, but his plan honored his inaugural promises to defend federal property and to avoid using military force unless first attacked. Masterfully, Lincoln had shifted the fateful decision of war or peace to Jefferson Davis.

On April 9, Davis and his cabinet met to consider the situation in Charleston harbor. The territorial integrity of the Confederacy demanded the end of the federal presence, Davis argued. But his secretary of state, Robert Toombs of Georgia, pleaded against military action. "Mr. President," he declared, "at this time it is suicide, murder, and will lose us every friend at the North. You will wantonly strike a hornet's nest which extends from mountain to ocean, and legions now quiet will swarm out and sting us to death." But Davis sent word to Confederate troops in Charleston to take the fort before the relief expedition arrived. Thirty-three hours of bombardment on April 12 and 13 reduced the fort to rubble. On April 14, with the fort ablaze, Major Anderson offered his surrender and lowered the U.S. flag. The Confederates had Fort Sumter, but they also had war.

On April 15, when Lincoln called for 75,000 militiamen to serve for ninety days to put down the rebellion, several times that number rushed to defend the flag. Democrats responded as fervently as Republicans. Stephen A. Douglas, the recently defeated Democratic candidate for president, pledged his support. "There are only two sides to the question," he said. "Every man must be for the United States or against it. There can be no neutrals in this war, *only patriots — or traitors*." But the people of the Upper South found themselves torn.

> "There are only two sides to the question," Stephen A. Douglas said. "Every man must be for the United States or against it. There can be no neutrals in this war, *only patriots — or traitors*."

The Upper South Chooses Sides The Upper South faced a horrendous choice: either to fight against the Lower South or to fight against the Union. Many who only months earlier had rejected secession now embraced the Confederacy. To vote against southern independence was one thing, to fight fellow Southerners another. Thousands felt betrayed, believing that Lincoln had promised to achieve a peaceful reunion by waiting patiently for Unionists to retake power in the seceding states. One man furiously denounced the conflict as a "politician's war," conceding that "this is no time now to discuss the causes, but it is the duty of all who regard Southern institutions of value to side with the South, make common cause with the Confederate States and sink or swim with them."

One by one, the states of the Upper South jumped off the fence. Virginia, Arkansas, Tennessee, and North Carolina joined the Confederacy (Map 15.1). But in the border states of Delaware, Maryland, Kentucky, and Missouri, Unionism triumphed. Only in Delaware, where slaves accounted for less than 2 percent of the population, was the victory easy. In Maryland, Unionism needed a helping hand. Rather than allow the state to secede and make Washington, D.C., a federal island in a Confederate sea, Lincoln suspended the writ of habeas corpus, essentially setting aside constitutional guarantees that protect citizens from arbitrary arrest and detention, and he ordered U.S. troops into Baltimore. Maryland's legislature rejected secession.

The struggle turned violent in the West. In Missouri, Unionists won a narrow victory, but southern-sympathizing guerrilla bands roamed the state for the duration of the war, terrorizing civilians and soldiers alike. In Kentucky, Unionists also narrowly defeated secession, but the prosouthern minority claimed otherwise. The Confederacy,

MAP 15.1 Secession, 1860–1861

After Lincoln's election, the fifteen slave states debated what to do. Seven states quickly left the Union, four left after the firing on Fort Sumter, and four remained loyal to the Union.

Map legend:
- Seceded before fall of Fort Sumter
- Seceded after fall of Fort Sumter
- Slave state loyal to Union
- Free state
- Territory
- 1 Order of secession

not especially careful about counting votes, eagerly made Missouri and Kentucky the twelfth and thirteenth stars on the Confederate flag.

Throughout the border states, but especially in Kentucky, the Civil War divided families. Seven of Henry Clay's grandsons fought: four for the Confederacy and three for the Union. Lincoln understood that the border states—particularly Kentucky—contained indispensable resources, population, and wealth and also controlled major rivers and railroads. "I think to lose Kentucky is nearly the same as to lose the whole game," Lincoln said. "Kentucky gone, we can not hold Missouri, nor, as I think, Maryland. These all against us, . . . we would as well consent to separation at once."

In the end, only eleven of the fifteen slave states joined the Confederate States of America. Moreover, the four seceding Upper South states contained significant numbers of people who felt little affection for the Confederacy. Dissatisfaction was so rife in the western counties of Virginia that in 1863, citizens there voted to create the separate state of West Virginia, loyal to the Union. Still, the acquisition of four new states greatly strengthened the Confederacy's drive for national independence.

Q: **Why did both the Union and the Confederacy consider control of the border states crucial?**

The Combatants

Only slaveholders had a direct economic stake in preserving slavery (estimated at some $3 billion in 1860), but most whites in the Confederacy defended the institution, the way of life built on it, and the Confederate nation. The degraded and subjugated status of blacks elevated the status of the poorest whites. "It matters not whether slaves be actually owned by many or by few," one Southerner declared. "It is enough that one simply belongs to the superior and ruling race, to secure consideration and respect." Moreover, Yankee "aggression" was no longer a mere threat; it was real and at the South's door.

For Northerners, rebel "treason" threatened to destroy the best government on earth. The South's failure to accept the democratic election of a president and its firing on the nation's flag challenged the rule of law, the authority of the Constitution, and the ability of the people to govern themselves. As an Indiana soldier told his wife, a "good government is the best thing on earth. Property is nothing without it, because it is not protected; a family is nothing without it, because they cannot be educated." Only a Union victory, Lincoln declared, would secure America's promise "to elevate the condition of man."

Northerners and Southerners rallied behind their separate flags, fully convinced that they were in the right and that God was on their side. But no one could argue that the South's resources and forces equaled the North's. Yankees took heart from their superior power, but the rebels believed they had advantages that nullified every northern strength. Both sides mobilized swiftly in 1861, and each devised what it believed would be a winning military and diplomatic strategy.

How They Expected to Win The balance sheet of northern and southern resources reveals enormous advantages for the Union (Figure 15.1). The twenty-three states remaining in the Union had a population of 22.3 million; the eleven Confederate states had a population of only 9.1 million, of whom 3.67 million (40 percent) were slaves. The North's economic advantages were even more overwhelming. Yet Southerners expected to win—for some good reasons—and they came very close to doing so.

Southerners knew they bucked the military odds, but hadn't the liberty-loving colonists in 1776 also done so? "Britain could not conquer three million," a Louisianan proclaimed, and "the world cannot conquer the South." How could anyone doubt the outcome of a contest between lean, hard, country-born rebel warriors defending family, property, and liberty, and soft, flabby, citified Yankee mechanics waging an unconstitutional war?

The South's confidence also rested on its belief that northern prosperity depended on the South's cotton. Without cotton, New England textile mills would stand idle. Without planters purchasing northern manufacturing goods, northern factories would drown in their own unsold surpluses. And without the foreign exchange earned by the overseas sales of cotton, the financial structure of the entire Yankee nation would collapse. A Virginian spoke for most Confederates when he declared that in the South's ability to "withhold the benefits of our trade, we hold a power over the North more powerful than a powerful army in the field."

Cotton would also make Europe a powerful ally of the Confederacy, Southerners reasoned. After all, they said, Britain's economy (and, to a lesser degree, France's) also depended on cotton. Of the 900 million pounds of cotton Britain imported annually, more than 700 million pounds came from the South. If the supply was interrupted, sheer economic need would make Britain (and perhaps France) a Confederate ally. And because the British navy ruled the seas, the North would find Britain a formidable foe.

Southerners' confidence may seem naive today, but even tough-minded European military observers picked the South to win. Offsetting the Union's power was the Confederacy's expanse. The North, Europeans predicted, could not conquer the vast territory (750,000 square miles) extending from the Potomac to the Rio Grande. To defeat the South, the Union would need to raise and equip a massive invading army and protect supply lines that would stretch farther than any in modern history.

Indeed, the South enjoyed major advantages, and the Confederacy devised a military strategy to exploit them. It recognized that a Union victory required the North to defeat and subjugate the South, but a Confederate victory required only that the South stay at home, blunt invasions, avoid battles that risked annihilating its army, and outlast the North's will to fight. When an opportunity presented itself, the South would strike the invaders. Like the American colonists, the South could win independence by not losing the war.

If the North did nothing, the South would by default establish itself as a sovereign nation. The Lincoln administration, therefore, adopted an

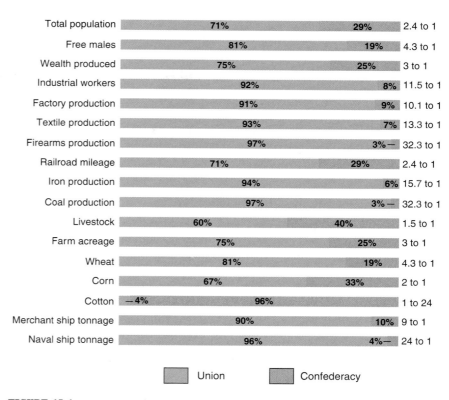

FIGURE 15.1 **Resources of the Union and Confederacy**
The Union's enormous statistical advantages failed to convince Confederates that their cause was doomed.

offensive strategy that applied pressure at many points. Lincoln declared a naval blockade of the Confederacy to deny it the ability to sell cotton abroad, giving the South far fewer dollars to pay for war goods. Even before the North could mount an effective blockade, however, Jefferson Davis decided voluntarily to cease exporting cotton. He wanted to create a cotton "famine" that would enfeeble the northern economy and precipitate European intervention. But the cotton famine Davis created devastated the South, not the North, and left Europe on the diplomatic sidelines. Lincoln also ordered the Union army into Virginia, at the same time planning a march through the Mississippi valley that would cut the Confederacy in two. This ambitious strategy took advantage of the Union's superior resources.

Neither side could foresee the magnitude and duration of the war. Americans thought of war in terms of the Mexican-American War of the 1840s, a conflict that had cost relatively few lives and had inflicted only light damage on the countryside. On the eve of the fighting, they could not know that four ghastly years of bloodletting lay ahead.

Lincoln and Davis Mobilize Mobilization required effective political leadership, and at first glance, the South appeared to have the advantage. Jefferson Davis brought to the Confederate presidency a distinguished political career, including experience in the U.S. Senate. He was also a West Point graduate, a combat veteran and authentic hero of the Mexican-American War, and a former secretary of war. Davis appeared to be everything a nation could want in a wartime leader.

In contrast, Abraham Lincoln brought to the White House one lackluster term in the House of Representatives and almost no administrative experience. His sole brush with anything military was as a captain in the militia in the Black Hawk War, a brief struggle in Illinois in 1832 in which whites expelled the last Indians from the state. Lincoln later joked about his service in the Black Hawk War as the time when he survived bloody encounters with mosquitoes and led raids on wild onion patches. Lincoln looked anything but military or presidential in his bearing.

Davis, however, proved to be less than he appeared. Although he worked hard, he had no gift for military strategy yet intervened often in military affairs. He was an even less able political leader. Quarrelsome and proud, he had an acid tongue that made enemies the Confederacy could ill afford. The Confederacy's intimidating problems might have defeated an even more talented leader, however. For example, state sovereignty, which was enshrined in the Confederate constitution, made Davis's task of organizing a new nation and fighting a war difficult in the extreme.

With Lincoln the North got far more than met the eye. He proved himself a master politician

and a superb leader. When forming his cabinet, Lincoln appointed the ablest men, no matter that they were often his chief rivals and critics. He appointed Salmon P. Chase secretary of the treasury knowing that Chase had presidential ambitions. As secretary of state, he chose his chief opponent for the Republican nomination in 1860, William H. Seward. Despite his civilian background, Lincoln displayed an innate understanding of military strategy. No one was more crucial in mapping the Union war plan.

Lincoln and Davis began gathering their armies. Confederates had to build almost everything from scratch, and Northerners had to channel their superior numbers and industrial resources to the purposes of war. On the eve of the war, the federal army numbered only 16,000 men, most of them scattered over the West subjugating Indians. One-third of the officers followed the example of the Virginian Robert E. Lee, resigning their commissions and heading south. The U.S. navy was in better shape. Forty-two ships were in service, and a large merchant marine would in time provide more ships and sailors for the Union cause. Possessing a much weaker navy, the South pinned its hopes on its armies.

The Confederacy made prodigious efforts to build new factories to produce tents, blankets, shoes, and its gray uniforms, but many rebel soldiers slept in the open air without blankets, and were sometimes without shoes. Even when factories managed to produce what the soldiers needed, southern railroads often could not deliver the goods. And each year, more railroads were captured, destroyed, or left in disrepair. Food production proved less of a problem, but food sometimes rotted before it reached the soldiers. The one bright spot was the Confederacy's Ordnance Bureau, headed by Josiah Gorgas, a near miracle worker when it came to manufacturing gunpowder, cannons, and rifles. In April 1864, Gorgas proudly observed: "Where three years ago we were not making a gun, a pistol nor a sabre, no shot nor shell . . . we now make all these in quantities to meet the demands of our large armies."

Recruiting and supplying huge armies required enormous new revenues. At first, the Union and the Confederacy sold war bonds, which essentially were loans from patriotic citizens. In addition, both sides turned to taxes. The North raised one-fifth of its wartime revenue from taxes; the South raised only one-twentieth. Eventually, both began printing paper money. Inflation soared, but the Confederacy suffered more because it financed a greater part of its wartime costs through the printing press. Prices in the Union rose by about

The Minié Ball The Union army was one of the best equipped armies in history, but none of its weaponry proved more vital than a French innovation by Captain Claude Minié. In 1848, Minié created an inch-long bullet that was rammed down a rifle barrel and would spin at great speed as it left the muzzle. The spin gave the bullet greater distance and accuracy than bullets fired from smoothbore weapons. When the war began, most soldiers carried smoothbore muskets, but by 1863 infantry on both sides fought with rifles. Bullets caused more than 90 percent of battle wounds, and minié balls proved extremely destructive to human bodies on impact. Picture Research Consultants & Archives.

80 percent during the war, while inflation in the Confederacy topped 9,000 percent.

Within months of the bombardment of Fort Sumter, both sides found men to fight and ways to supply them. But the underlying strength of the northern economy gave the Union the decided advantage. With their military and industrial muscles beginning to ripple, Northerners became itchy for action that would smash the rebellion. Horace Greeley's *New York Tribune* began to chant: "Forward to Richmond! Forward to Richmond!"

Q: Why did the South believe it could win the war despite numerical disadvantages?

Battling It Out, 1861–1862

During the first year and a half of the war, armies fought major campaigns in both East and West. Because the rival capitals—Richmond and Washington, D.C.—were only ninety miles apart and each was threatened more than once with capture, the eastern campaign was especially dramatic. But the battles in the West proved more decisive. As Yankee and rebel armies pounded each other on land, the navies fought on the seas and on the rivers of the South. In Europe, Confederate and U.S. diplomats competed for advantage in the corridors of power. All the while, casualty lists on both sides reached appalling lengths.

Stalemate in the Eastern Theater In the summer of 1861, Lincoln ordered the Union army assembling outside Washington to attack the Confederates defending Manassas, a railroad junction in Virginia about thirty miles southwest of Washington. On July 21, the army forded Bull Run, a branch of the Potomac River, and engaged the southern forces (Map 15.2). But fast-moving southern rein-forcements blunted the Union attack and then counterattacked. What began as

an orderly Union retreat turned into a panicky stampede. Demoralized federal troops ran over shocked civilians as the soldiers raced back to Washington.

By Civil War standards, the casualties (wounded and dead) at the **battle of Bull Run** (or **Manassas**, as Southerners called the battle) were light, about 2,000 Confederates and 1,600 Federals. The significance of the battle lay in the lessons Northerners and Southerners drew from it. For Southerners, it confirmed the superiority of rebel fighting men and the inevitability of Confederate nationhood. Manassas was *"one of the decisive battles of the world,"* a Georgian proclaimed. It *"has* secured our independence." While victory fed southern pride, defeat sobered Northerners. It was a major setback, admitted the *New York Tribune*, but "let us go to work, then, with a will." Bull Run taught Lincoln that victory would be neither quick nor easy. Within four days of the disaster, the president authorized the enlistment of 1 million men for three years.

The Battle of Savage's Station, by Robert Knox Sneden, 1862 In 1862, thirty-year-old Robert Sneden joined the Fortieth New York Volunteers and soon found himself in Virginia, part of George McClellan's peninsula campaign. A gifted artist in watercolors as well as an eloquent writer, Sneden captured an early Confederate assault in what became known as the Seven Days Battle. "The immense open space in front of Savage's [house] was densely thronged with wagon trains, artillery, caissons, ammunition trains, and moving troops," Sneden observed. The "storm of lead was continuous and deadly on the approaching lines of the Rebels. They bravely rushed up, however, to within twenty feet of our artillery, when bushels of grape and canister from the cannon laid them low in rows." Over the next three years, Sneden produced hundreds of vivid drawings and eventually thousands of pages of remembrance, providing one of the most complete accounts of a Union soldier's Civil War experience. 1996, Lora Robbins Collection of Virginia Art, Virginia Historical Society.

MAP 15.2 The Civil War, 1861–1862
While most eyes were focused on the eastern theater, especially the ninety-mile stretch of land between Washington, D.C., and the Confederate capital of Richmond, Virginia, Union troops were winning strategic victories in the West.

Lincoln also found a new general, the young **George B. McClellan**, whom he appointed commander of the newly named Army of the Potomac. Having graduated from West Point second in his class, the thirty-four-year-old McClellan believed that he was a great soldier and that Lincoln was a dunce, the "original Gorilla." A superb administrator and organizer, McClellan energetically whipped his dispirited soldiers into shape, but he was reluctant to send them into battle. For all his energy, McClellan lacked decisiveness. Lincoln wanted a general who would advance, take risks, and fight, but McClellan went into winter quarters. "If General McClellan does not want to use the army I would like to *borrow* it," Lincoln declared in frustration.

Finally, in May 1862, McClellan launched his long-awaited offensive. He transported his highly polished army, now 130,000 strong, to the mouth of the James River and began slowly moving up the Yorktown peninsula toward Richmond. When he was within six miles of the Confederate capital, General Joseph Johnston hit him like a hammer. In the assault, Johnston was wounded and was replaced by **Robert E. Lee**, who would become the South's most celebrated general. Lee named his command the Army of Northern Virginia.

The contrast between Lee and McClellan could hardly have been greater. McClellan brimmed with conceit and braggadocio; Lee was courteous and reserved. On the battlefield, McClellan grew timid and irresolute, and Lee became audaciously, even recklessly, aggressive. And Lee had at his side in the peninsula campaign military men of real talent: Thomas J. Jackson, nicknamed "Stonewall" for holding the line at Manassas, and James E. B. ("Jeb") Stuart, a dashing twenty-nine-year-old cavalry commander who rode circles around Yankee troops.

Lee's assault initiated the Seven Days Battle (June 25–July 1) and began McClellan's march back down the peninsula. By the time McClellan reached safety, 30,000 men from both sides had died or been wounded. Although Southerners suffered twice the casualties of Northerners, Lee had saved Richmond. Lincoln wired McClellan to abandon the peninsula campaign and replaced him with General John Pope.

In August, north of Richmond, at the second battle of Bull Run, Lee's smaller army battered Pope's forces and sent them scurrying back to Washington. Lincoln ordered Pope to Minnesota to pacify the Indians and restored McClellan to command. Lincoln had not changed his mind about McClellan's capacity as a warrior, but he reluctantly acknowledged that "if he can't fight himself, he excels in making others ready to fight."

Sensing that he had the enemy on the ropes, Lee pushed his army across the Potomac and invaded Maryland. A victory on northern soil would dislodge Maryland from the Union, Lee reasoned, and might even cause Lincoln to sue for peace. On September 17, 1862, McClellan's forces engaged Lee's army at Antietam Creek (see Map 15.2). With "solid shot . . . cracking skulls like eggshells," according to one observer, the armies went after each other. At Miller's Cornfield, the firing was so intense that "every stalk of corn in the . . . field was cut as closely as could have been done with a knife." By nightfall, 6,000 men lay dead or dying on the battlefield, and 17,000 more had been wounded. The **battle of Antietam** would be the bloodiest day of the war. Instead of being the war-winning fight Lee had anticipated when he came north, Antietam sent the battered Army of Northern Virginia limping back home. McClellan claimed to have saved the North, but Lincoln again removed him from command of the Army of the

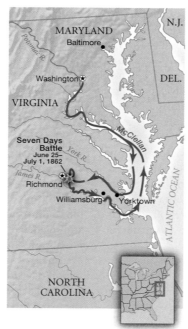

Peninsula Campaign, 1862

Potomac and appointed General Ambrose Burnside.

Though bloodied, Lee found an opportunity in December to punish the enemy at Fredericksburg, Virginia, where Burnside's 122,000 Union troops faced 78,500 Confederates dug in behind a stone wall on the heights above the Rappahannock River. Half a mile of open ground separated the armies. "A chicken could not live on that field when we open on it," a Confederate artillery officer predicted. Yet Burnside ordered a frontal assault. When the shooting ceased, the Federals counted nearly 13,000 casualties, the Confederates fewer than 5,000. The battle of Fredericksburg was one of the Union's worst defeats. As 1862 ended, the North seemed no nearer to ending the rebellion than it had been when the war began. Rather than checkmate, military struggle in the East had reached stalemate.

Union Victories in the Western Theater

While most eyes focused on events in the East, the decisive early encounters of the war were taking place between the Appalachian Mountains and the Ozarks (see Map 15.2). Confederates wanted Missouri and Kentucky, states they claimed but did not control. Federals wanted to split Arkansas, Louisiana, and Texas from the Confederacy by taking control of the Mississippi River and to occupy Tennessee, one of the Confederacy's main producers of food, mules, and iron—all vital resources.

Before Union forces could march on Tennessee, they needed to secure Missouri to the west. Union troops swept across Missouri to the border of Arkansas, where in March 1862, they encountered a 16,000-man Confederate army, which included three regiments of Indians from the Five Civilized Tribes in Indian Territory. Although Indians fought on both sides during the war, Native Americans who sided with the South hoped that the Confederacy would grant them more independence than had the United States. The Union victory at the battle of Pea Ridge left Missouri free of Confederate troops, but Missouri was not free of Confederate guerrillas. Guerrilla bands led by the notorious William Clarke Quantrill and "Bloody Bill" Anderson burned, tortured, scalped, and murdered Union civilians and soldiers until the final year of the war.

Battle of Glorieta Pass, 1862

Even farther west, Confederate armies sought to fulfill Jefferson Davis's vision of a slaveholding empire stretching all the way to the Pacific. Both sides recognized the immense value of the gold and silver mines of California, Nevada, and Colorado. A quick strike by Texas troops took Santa Fe, New Mexico, in the winter of 1861–62. Then in March 1862, a band of Colorado miners ambushed and crushed southern forces at Glorieta Pass, outside Santa Fe. Confederate military failures in the far West meant that there would be no Confederate empire beyond Texas.

The principal western battles took place in Tennessee, where General **Ulysses S. Grant** emerged as the key northern commander. Grant had graduated from West Point and served bravely in Mexico. When the Civil War began, he was a thirty-nine-year-old dry-goods clerk in Galena, Illinois. Gentle at home, he became pugnacious on the battlefield. "The art of war is simple," he said. "Find out where your enemy is, get at him as soon as you can and strike him as hard as you can, and keep moving on." Grant's philosophy of war as attrition would take a huge toll in human life, but it played to the North's superiority in manpower. In his private's uniform and slouch hat, Grant did not look much like a general. But Lincoln learned his worth. Later, to critics who wanted the president to sack Grant because of his drinking, Lincoln would say, *"I can't spare this man. He fights."*

In February 1862, operating in tandem with U.S. navy gunboats, Grant captured Fort Henry on the Tennessee River and Fort Donelson on the Cumberland (see Map 15.2). Defeat forced the Confederates to withdraw from all of Kentucky and most of Tennessee, but Grant followed.

On April 6, General Albert Sidney Johnston's army surprised him at Shiloh Church in Tennessee. Grant's troops were badly mauled the first day, but Grant remained cool and brought up reinforcements throughout the night. The next morning, the Union army counterattacked, driving the Confederates before it. The **battle of Shiloh** was terribly costly to both sides; there were 20,000 casualties, among them General Johnston. Grant later said that after Shiloh, he "gave up all idea of saving the Union except by complete conquest."

Although no one knew it at the time, Shiloh ruined the Confederacy's bid to control the theater of operations in the West. The Yankees quickly captured the strategic town of Corinth, Mississippi;

the river city of Memphis; and the South's largest city, New Orleans. By the end of 1862, the far West and most—but not all—of the Mississippi valley lay in Union hands. At the same time, the outcome of the struggle in another theater of war was also becoming clearer.

The Atlantic Theater When the war began, the U.S. navy's blockade fleet consisted of about three dozen ships to patrol more than 3,500 miles of southern coastline, and rebel merchant ships were able to slip in and out of southern ports nearly at will. Taking on cargoes in the Caribbean, sleek Confederate blockade runners brought in vital supplies—guns and medicine. But with the U.S. navy commissioning a new blockader almost weekly, the naval fleet eventually numbered 150 ships on duty, and the Union navy dramatically improved its score.

Unable to build a conventional navy equal to the expanding U.S. fleet, the Confederates experimented with a radical new maritime design: the ironclad warship. At Norfolk, Virginia, they layered the wooden hull of the frigate *Merrimack* with two-inch-thick armor plate. Rechristened *Virginia*, the ship steamed out in March 1862 and sank two wooden federal ships, killing at least 240 Union sailors (see Map 15.2). When the *Virginia* returned to finish off the federal blockaders the next morning, it was challenged by the *Monitor*, a federal ironclad of even more radical design, topped with a revolving turret holding two eleven-inch guns. On March 9, the two ships hurled shells at each other for two hours, but when neither could penetrate the other's armor, the battle ended in a draw.

The Confederacy never found a way to break the **Union blockade** despite exploring many naval innovations, including a new underwater vessel—the submarine. Each month, the Union fleet tightened its noose. The growing effectiveness of the federal blockade, a southern naval officer observed, "shut the Confederacy out from the world, deprived it of supplies, weakened its military and naval strength." By 1865, the blockaders were intercepting about half of the southern ships attempting to break through. The Confederacy was sealed off, with devastating results.

International Diplomacy What the Confederates could not achieve on the seas, they sought to achieve through international diplomacy. The world was watching the struggle in North America, and nationalists everywhere understood that the American Civil War engaged issues central to their own nation-building efforts. The Confederates rested their claims to separate nationhood on the principles of self-determination and rightful rebellion against tyrannical power, and they desperately

THE PROMISE OF TECHNOLOGY

The World's First Successful Submarine As the federal blockade of southern ports gradually began to strangle Confederate shipping, Southerners were forced to innovate in naval technology: the ironclad, floating mines (called

torpedoes), and, most spectacular of all, the submarine. Three years of trial and error, experimentation, and wartime innovation produced the CSS *H. L. Hunley*. A sleek, forty-foot, nine-man vessel, the *Hunley* was an engineering marvel that exhibited both sophisticated technology and primitive features. General P. G. T. Beauregard felt compelled to explain to men who were considering volunteering for its crew the "desperately hazardous nature of the service required." On the night of February 17, 1864, the *Hunley* sank the Union blockader USS *Housatonic* and then itself sank with its entire crew. No other submarine would sink an enemy ship until World War I, more than half a century later. The *Hunley* is shown here at Charleston in 1863 in a painting by Conrad Wise Chapman. U.S. Naval Historical Center.

wanted Europe to intervene. The Lincoln administration explained why the Union had to be preserved and Europe had to remain neutral. "The question," Lincoln explained, is "whether a constitutional republic, or a democracy—a government of the people, by the same people—can or cannot, maintain its territorial integrity, against its own domestic foes."

More practically, the Confederates based their hope for European support on King Cotton. In theory, cotton-starved European nations would have no choice but to break the Union blockade and recognize the Confederacy. Southern hopes were not unreasonable, for at the height of the "cotton famine" in 1862, when 2 million British workers were unemployed, Britain tilted toward recognition. Along with several other European nations, Britain granted the Confederacy "belligerent" status, which enabled it to buy goods and build ships in European ports. But no country challenged the blockade or recognized the Confederate States of America as a nation, a bold act that probably would have drawn that country into war.

King Cotton diplomacy failed for several reasons. A bumper cotton crop in 1860 meant that the warehouses of British textile manufacturers

bulged with surplus cotton throughout 1861. In 1862, when a cotton shortage did occur, European manufacturers found new sources in India, Egypt, and elsewhere. (See "Global Comparison.") In addition, the development of a brisk trade between the Union and Britain—British war materiel for American grain and flour—helped offset the decline in textiles and encouraged Britain to remain neutral.

Europe's temptation to intervene disappeared for good in 1862. Union military successes in the West made Britain and France think twice about linking their fates to the struggling Confederacy. Moreover, in September 1862, Lincoln announced a new policy that made an alliance with the Confederacy an alliance with slavery—a commitment the French and British, who had outlawed slavery in their empires and looked forward to its eradication worldwide, were not willing to make. After 1862, the South's cause was linked irrevocably with slavery and reaction, and the Union's cause was linked with freedom and democracy.

Q: Why did the Confederacy's bid for international support fail?

European Cotton Imports, 1860–1870

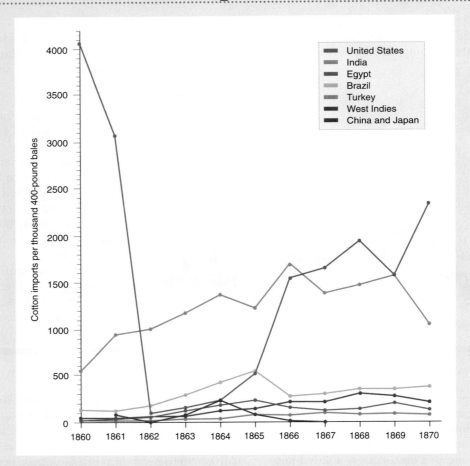

Cotton imports per thousand 400-pound bales

Legend:
- United States
- India
- Egypt
- Brazil
- Turkey
- West Indies
- China and Japan

In 1860, the South enjoyed a near monopoly in supplying cotton to Europe's textile mills, but the Civil War almost entirely halted its exports. Figures for Europe's importation of cotton for 1861 to 1865 reveal one of the reasons the Confederacy's King Cotton diplomacy failed: Europeans found other sources of cotton. Which countries were most important in filling the void? When the war ended in 1865, cotton production resumed in the South, and exports to Europe again soared. Did the South regain its near monopoly? How would you characterize the United States' competitive position five years after the war?

Union *and* Freedom

For a year and a half, Lincoln insisted that the North fought strictly to save the Union and not to abolish slavery. Despite Lincoln's repeated pronouncements, however, the war for union became a war for African American freedom. Each month the conflict dragged on, it became clearer that the Confederate war machine depended heavily on slavery. Rebel armies used slaves to build fortifications, haul materiel, tend horses, and perform camp chores. On the home front, slaves labored in ironworks and shipyards, and

they grew the food that fed both soldiers and civilians. Slavery undergirded the Confederacy as certainly as it had the Old South. Union military commanders and politicians alike gradually realized that to defeat the Confederacy, the North would have to destroy slavery. "I am a slow walker," Lincoln said, "but I never walk back."

From Slaves to Contraband Lincoln detested human bondage, but as president he felt compelled to act prudently in the interests of the Union. He doubted his right under the Constitution to tamper with the "domestic institutions" of any state, even states in rebellion. An astute politician, Lincoln worked within the tight limits of public opinion. The issue of black freedom was particularly explosive in the loyal border states, where slaveholders threatened to jump into the arms of the Confederacy at even the hint of emancipation.

Black freedom also raised alarms in the free states. The Democratic Party gave notice that emancipation would make the war strictly a Republican affair. Moreover, many white Northerners were not about to risk their lives to satisfy what they considered abolitionist "fanaticism." "We Won't Fight to Free the Nigger," one popular banner read. They feared that emancipation would propel "two or three million semi-savages" northward, where they would crowd into white neighborhoods, compete for white jobs, and mix with white "sons and daughters." Thus, emancipation threatened to dislodge the loyal slave states from the Union, alienate the Democratic Party, deplete the armies, and perhaps even spark race warfare.

Yet proponents of emancipation pressed Lincoln as relentlessly as the anti-emancipation forces. Abolitionists argued that by seceding, Southerners had forfeited their right to the protection of the Constitution, and that Lincoln could—as the price of their treason—legally confiscate their property in slaves. When Lincoln refused, abolitionists scalded him. Frederick Douglass labeled him "the miserable tool of traitors and rebels."

The Republican-dominated Congress declined to leave slavery policy entirely in President Lincoln's hands. In August 1861, Congress approved the Confiscation Act, which allowed the seizure of any slave employed directly by the Confederate military. It also fulfilled the free-soil dream of prohibiting slavery in the territories and abolished slavery in Washington, D.C. Democrats and border-state representatives voted against even these mild measures, but Congress's attitude was clearly stiffening against slavery.

Slaves, not politicians, became the most insistent force for emancipation. By escaping their masters by the tens of thousands and running away to Union lines, they forced slavery on the North's wartime agenda. Runaways forced Northerners to answer a crucial question: Were the runaways now free, or were they still slaves who, according to the fugitive slave law, had to be returned to their masters? At first, Yankee military officers sent the fugitives back. But Union armies needed laborers, and some officers accepted the runaways and put them to work. At Fort Monroe, Virginia, General Benjamin F. Butler refused to turn them over to their owners, calling them **contraband of war**, meaning "confiscated property." Congress made Butler's practice national policy in March 1862 when it forbade returning fugitive slaves

to their masters. Slaves were still not legally free, but there was a tilt toward emancipation.

Lincoln's policy of noninterference with slavery gradually crumbled. To calm Northerners' racial fears, Lincoln offered colonization, the deportation of African Americans from the United States to Haiti, Panama, or elsewhere. Congress voted a small amount of money to underwrite colonization, but after one miserable experiment on a small island in the Caribbean, practical limitations and stiff black opposition sank further efforts.

While Lincoln was developing his own antislavery initiatives, he snuffed out actions that he believed would jeopardize northern unity. He was particularly alert to Union commanders who tried to dictate slavery policy from the field. In August 1861, when John C. Frémont, former Republican presidential nominee and now commander of federal troops in Missouri, freed the slaves belonging to Missouri rebels, Lincoln forced the general to revoke his edict. The following May, when General David Hunter freed the slaves in Georgia, South Carolina, and Florida, Lincoln countermanded his order. Events moved so rapidly, however, that Lincoln found it impossible to control federal policy on slavery.

From Contraband to Free People On August 22, 1862, Lincoln replied to an angry abolitionist who demanded that he attack slavery. "My paramount objective in this struggle *is* to save the Union," Lincoln said deliberately, "and is *not* either to save or destroy slavery. If I could save the Union without freeing *any* slave I would do it, and if I could save it by freeing *all* the slaves I would do it; and if I could save it by freeing some and leaving others alone I would also do that." Instead of simply restating his old position that union was the North's sole objective, Lincoln announced that slavery was no longer untouchable and that he would emancipate every slave if doing so would preserve the Union.

By the summer of 1862, events were tumbling rapidly toward emancipation. On July 17, Congress adopted the second Confiscation Act. The first had confiscated slaves employed by the Confederate military; the second declared all slaves of rebel masters "forever free of their servitude." In theory, this breathtaking measure freed most Confederate slaves, for slaveholders formed the backbone of the rebellion. Congress had traveled far since the war began.

Lincoln had, too. In July 1862, the president informed his cabinet that he was ready "to take some definitive steps in respect to military action and slavery" and read a draft of a preliminary emancipation proclamation that promised to free *all* the slaves in the seceding states on January 1, 1863. Lincoln described emancipation as an "act of justice," but it was the lengthening casualty lists that finally brought

Confederate Soldiers and Their Slaves Soldiers of the Seventh Tennessee Cavalry pose with their slaves. Many slaveholders took "body servants" with them to war. These slaves cooked, washed, and cleaned for the white soldiers. In 1861, James H. Langhorne reported to his sister: "Peter . . . is charmed with being with me & 'being a soldier.' I gave him my old uniform overcoat & he says he is going to have his picture taken . . . to send to the servants." Do you think Peter was "puttin' on ol' massa" or just glad to be free of plantation labor? Daguerreotype courtesy of Tom Farish. Photographed by Michael Latil.

FOR MORE HELP ANALYZING THIS IMAGE, see the visual activity for this chapter in the Online Study Guide at bedfordstmartins.com/roarkcompact.

him around. Emancipation, he declared, was "a military necessity, absolutely essential to the preservation of the Union." Only freeing the slaves would "strike at the heart of the rebellion." On September 22, Lincoln issued his preliminary **Emancipation Proclamation** promising freedom to slaves in areas still in rebellion on January 1, 1863.

The limitations of the proclamation—it exempted the loyal border states and the Union-occupied areas of the Confederacy—caused some to ridicule the act. The *Times* (London) observed cynically, "Where he has no power Mr. Lincoln will set the negroes free, where he retains power he will consider them as slaves." But Lincoln had no power to free slaves in loyal states, and invading Union armies would liberate slaves in the Confederacy as they advanced.

By presenting emancipation as a "military necessity," Lincoln hoped he had disarmed his conservative critics. Emancipation would deprive the Confederacy of valuable slave laborers, shorten the war, and thus save lives. Democrats, however, fumed that the "shrieking and howling abolitionist faction" had captured the White House and made it "a nigger war." Democrats made political hay out of Lincoln's action in the November 1862 elections, gaining thirty-four congressional seats. House Democrats quickly proposed a resolution branding emancipation "a high crime against the Constitution." The Republicans, who maintained narrow majorities in both houses of Congress, barely beat it back.

As promised, on New Year's Day 1863, Lincoln issued the final Emancipation Proclamation. In addition to freeing the slaves in the rebel states, the edict also committed the federal government to the fullest use of African Americans to defeat the Confederate enemy.

War of Black Liberation Even before Lincoln proclaimed emancipation a Union war aim, African Americans in the North had volunteered to fight. But the War Department, doubtful of their abilities and fearful of white reaction to serving side by side with them, refused to make black men soldiers. Instead, the army employed black men as manual laborers; black women sometimes found employment as laundresses and cooks. The navy, however, accepted blacks from the outset, including runaway slaves such as William Gould.

As Union casualty lists lengthened, Northerners gradually and reluctantly turned to African Americans to fill the army's blue uniforms. With the Militia Act of July 1862, Congress authorized enrolling blacks in "any military or naval service for which they may be found competent." After the Emancipation Proclamation, whites—like it or not—were fighting and dying for black freedom, and few insisted that blacks remain out of harm's way behind the lines. Indeed, whites insisted that blacks share the danger, especially after March 1863, when Congress resorted to the draft to fill the Union army.

The military was far from color-blind. The Union army established segregated black regiments, paid black soldiers $10 per month rather than the $13 it paid whites, refused blacks the opportunity to become commissioned officers, punished blacks as if they were slaves, and assigned blacks to labor battalions rather than to combat units. Still, when the war ended, 179,000 African American men had served in the Union army, approximately 10 percent of all soldiers. An astounding 71 percent of black men ages eighteen to forty-five in the free states wore Union blue, a participation rate that was substantially higher than that of white men. More than 130,000 black soldiers came from the slave states, perhaps 100,000 of them ex-slaves.

In time, whites allowed blacks to put down their shovels and to shoulder rifles. At the battles of Port Hudson and Milliken's Bend on the Mississippi River and at Fort Wagner in Charleston harbor, black courage under fire finally dispelled notions that African Americans could not fight. More than 38,000 black soldiers died in the Civil War, a mortality rate that was higher than that of white troops. Blacks played a crucial role in the triumph of the Union and the destruction of slavery in the South. (See "Seeking the American Promise," page 372.)

Q: Why did the Union change policy in 1863 to allow black men to serve in the army?

The South at War

By seceding, Southerners brought on themselves a firestorm of unimaginable fury. Monstrous losses on the battlefield nearly bled the Confederacy to death. White Southerners on the home front also suffered, even at the hands of their own government. Efforts by the Davis administration in Richmond to centralize power in order to fight the war effectively convinced some men and women that the Confederacy had betrayed them. Wartime economic changes hurt everyone, some more than others. By 1863, planters and yeomen who had stood together began to drift apart. Most disturbing of all, slaves became open participants in the destruction of slavery and the Confederacy.

Revolution from Above As a Confederate general observed, Southerners were engaged in a total war "in which the whole population and the whole production . . . are to be put on a war footing, where every institution is to be made auxiliary to war." Jefferson Davis faced the task of building an army and navy from almost nothing, supplying them from factories that were scarce and anemic, and paying for it all from a treasury that did not exist. Finding eager soldiers proved easiest. Hundreds of officers defected from the U.S. army, and hundreds of thousands of eager young rebels volunteered to follow them. Very quickly, the Confederacy developed formidable striking power.

The Confederacy's economy and finances proved tougher problems. Because of the Union blockade, the government had no choice but to build an industrial sector itself. Government-owned clothing and shoe factories, mines, arsenals, and powder works sprang up. The government also harnessed private companies, such as the huge Tredegar Iron Works in Richmond, to the war effort. Paying for the war became the most difficult task. A flood of paper money caused debilitating inflation. By 1863, people in Charleston paid ten times more for food than they had paid at the start of the war. By Christmas 1864, a Confederate soldier's monthly pay no longer bought a pair of socks. The Confederacy manufactured much more than most people imagined possible, but it never produced all that the South needed.

Richmond's war-making effort brought unprecedented government intrusion into the private lives of Confederate citizens. In April 1862, the Confederate Congress passed the first conscription (draft) law in American history. All able-bodied white males between the ages of eighteen and thirty-five (later seventeen and fifty) were liable to serve in the rebel army. The government adopted a policy of impressment, which allowed officials to confiscate food, horses, wagons, and whatever else they wanted from private citizens and to pay for them at below-market rates. After March 1863, the Confederacy legally impressed slaves, employing them as military laborers.

Richmond's centralizing efforts ran head-on into the South's traditional values of states' rights and unfettered individualism. The states lashed out at what Georgia governor Joseph E. Brown denounced as the "dangerous usurpation by Congress of the reserved right of the States." Richmond and the states struggled for control of money, supplies, and soldiers, with damaging consequences for the war effort.

Hardship Below Hardships on the home front fell most heavily on the poor. Flour, which cost three or four cents a pound in 1861, cost thirty-five cents in 1863. The draft stripped yeoman farms of men, leaving the women and children to grow what they ate. Government agents took 10 percent of harvests as a "tax-in-kind" on agriculture. Like inflation, shortages afflicted the entire population, but the rich lost luxuries while the poor lost necessities. In the spring of 1863, bread riots broke out in a dozen cities and villages across the South. In Richmond, a mob of nearly a thousand hungry women broke into shops and took what they needed.

"Men cannot be expected to fight for the Government that permits their wives & children to starve," one Southerner observed. Although a few wealthy individuals shared their bounty and the Confederate and state governments made efforts at social welfare, every attempt fell short. In late 1864, one desperate farmwife told her husband, "I have always been proud of you, and since your connection with the Confederate army, I have been prouder of you than ever before. I would not have you do anything wrong for the world, but before God, Edward, unless you come home, we must die." When the war ended, one-third

The Right to Fight: Black Soldiers in the Civil War

When unprecedented bloodletting at Shiloh, Antietam, and elsewhere caused the flood of military volunteers to slow to a trickle, first the Confederacy and then the Union had to resort to the draft to force white men into their armies. But one group of Americans beat at the doors of the War Department, begging to enroll in the Union army. "A war undertaken and brazenly carried on for the perpetual enslavement of colored men, calls logically and loudly for colored men to help suppress it," black leader Frederick Douglass declared. Speaking for free blacks in the North and fugitive slaves in the South, he said, "Would to God you would let us do something. We lack nothing but your consent. We are ready and would go. . . . But you won't let us go."

The lengthening casualty lists gradually turned the Lincoln administration around. In 1863, the Union eagerly began recruiting black soldiers. In February of that year, four days after the 54th Massachusetts Colored Regiment opened its recruiting office, James Henry Gooding, a twenty-six-year-old seaman from New Bedford, enlisted. For the next year, Gooding documented his experiences in vivid letters published by his hometown newspaper, the *New Bedford Mercury*. He appealed for new recruits, but black soldiers earned even less than white soldiers, and he understood that many black men did not want to join the army and leave their families "destitute." Still, he said, "we are all determined to act like men, and fight, money or not." His heart filled with pride when he saw African Americans rush to the flag, refuting the notion that "the black race are incapable of patriotism, valor or ambition."

Like most black soldiers, Gooding viewed military service as a great opportunity to strike blows against slavery and white prejudice. Slavery in the South was vulnerable, Gooding observed, but "it depends on the free black men of the North, whether it will die or not—those who are in bonds must have some one to open the door; when the slave sees the white soldier approach, he dares not trust him and why? Because he has heard that *some* have treated him worse than their owners in rebellion. But if the slave sees a black soldier, he knows he has got a friend." Fighting for the Union also offered a chance to attack white prejudice. In military service lay "the germs of the elevation of a downtrodden and despised race," Gooding argued, the chance for African Americans "to make themselves a people." In the words of the 54th Massachusetts Colored Regiment, "We came to fight For Liberty justice & Equality."

Fighting, Gooding believed, offered blacks a chance to destroy the "foul aspersion that they were not men." According to the white commander of the 59th U.S. Colored Infantry, when an ex-slave put on a uniform of army blue, "he was completely metamorphosed, not only in appearance and dress, but in character and relations also." The change, he said, was dramatic: "Yesterday a filthy, repulsive 'nigger,' to-day a neatly-attired man; yesterday a slave, to-day a freeman; yesterday a civilian, to-day a soldier." Others noticed the same transformation: "Put a United States uniform on his back and the *chattel* is a *man*." Black veterans agreed. One black soldier remembered, "This was the biggest thing that ever happened in my life. I felt like a man with a uniform and a gun in my hand." Another said, "I felt freedom in my bones."

Black courage under fire ended skepticism about the capabilities of African American troops. As one white officer observed after a battle, "They seemed like men who were fighting to vindicate their manhood and they did it well." The truth is, another remarked, "they have fought their way into the respect of all the army." After the 54th fought courageously in South Carolina, Gooding reported: "It is not for us to blow our horn; but when a regiment of white men gave us three cheers as we were passing them, it shows that we did our duty as men should." Yet discrimination within the Union army continued. At first, blacks were assigned to manual labor rather than fighting. Even so, Gooding advised, "If it is to wield the shovel and pick, do it faithfully; if it is to haul siege guns, or load and unload transports, our motto is, work faithfully and willingly."

of the soldiers had already gone home. A Mississippi deserter explained, "We are poor men and are willing to defend our country but our families [come] first."

Yeomen perceived a profound inequality of sacrifice. They called it "a rich man's war and a poor man's fight." The draft law permitted a man who had money to hire a substitute to take his place. More- over, the "twenty-Negro law" exempted one white man on every plantation with twenty or more slaves. The government intended this law to provide protec- tion for white women and to see that slaves tended the crops, but yeomen perceived it as rich men evad- ing military service. A Mississippian complained that stay-at-home planters sent their slaves into the fields

Few issues disturbed Gooding and the 54th more than the government's refusal to pay blacks the same as whites. The 54th refused to accept unequal pay. Gooding wrote to President Lincoln himself to explain his regiment's decision: "Now the main question is, Are we Soldiers, or are we Labourers? . . . Now your Excellency, we have done a Soldier's Duty. Why Can't we have a Soldier's pay?" Gooding's eloquence and the 54th's principled stance helped reverse the government's position. In June 1864, Congress equalized the pay of black and white soldiers.

As Union troops advanced deeper into the collapsing Confederacy, countless former slaves greeted black soldiers as heroes. Gooding observed, "The contrabands did not believe we were coming; one [of] them said, 'I nebber bleeve black Yankee come here help culer men.' They think now the kingdom is coming sure enough." The white officer of a black regiment that occupied Wilmington, North Carolina, in March 1865 reported that black soldiers "stepped like lords & conquerors. The frantic demonstrations of the negro population will never die out of my memory. Their cheers & heartfelt 'God bress ye's' & cries of 'De chains is broke; De chains is broke,' mingled sublimely with the lusty shout of our brave soldiery." Hardened and disciplined by their military service, black soldiers drew tremendous strength from their participation in the Union effort. Although blacks remained second-class soldiers, army life proved to be a great counterweight to the degradation and dependency of slavery.

Black veterans emerged from the war with new confidence, proud of their contributions and convinced that their military service had earned them and their race full citizenship. Eager to shoulder the rights, privileges, and responsibilities of freedom, black veterans often took the lead in the hard struggle for equality after the war. Black soldiers made up a significant portion of the Union army that occupied the South after 1865, and they assumed a special obligation to protect the lives and property of former slaves. "The fact is," one black chaplain said, "when colored soldiers are about they [whites] are afraid to kick colored women and abuse colored people on the Streets, as they usually do." Black veterans fervently believed that their military service entitled African Americans not only to freedom but also to

civil and political rights. Black sergeant Henry Maxwell announced: "We want two more boxes besides the cartridge box—the ballot and the jury box." Having learned to read and write in the army, many veterans became schoolteachers. Others, having developed leadership skills, became politicians. Black soldiers had demonstrated what they could do if permitted to become warriors; they now demanded the chance to perform as citizens.

James Henry Gooding did not have a chance to participate in the postwar struggle for equal rights. Captured at the battle of Olustee in Florida, he was sent to the infamous Confederate prison Andersonville, where he died on July 19, 1864.

★ **Company E, 4th U.S. Colored Infantry, Fort Lincoln, Virginia** The Lincoln administration was slow to accept black soldiers into the Union army, in part because of lingering doubts about their ability to fight. But eventually, the battlefield valor of black troops eroded white skepticism. Colonel Thomas W. Higginson, the white commander of the Union's First South Carolina Infantry, which was made up of former slaves, celebrated the courage his men displayed in their first skirmish: "No officer in this regiment now doubts that the key to the successful prosecution of this war lies in the unlimited employment of black troops. . . . Instead of leaving their homes and families to fight they are fighting for their homes and families." Before the war was over, ex-slaves and free blacks filled 145 Union regiments. Library of Congress.

to grow cotton while in plain view "poor soldiers' wives are plowing with *their own* hands to make a subsistence for themselves and children—while their husbands are suffering, bleeding and dying for their country." In fact, most slaveholders went off to war, but the extreme suffering of common folk and the relative immunity of planters increased class friction.

The Richmond government hoped that the crucible of war would mold a region into a nation. Officials promoted a southern nationalism to "excite in our citizens an ardent and enduring attachment to our Government and its institutions." Clergymen assured their congregations that God had blessed slavery and the new nation. Patriotic songwriters, poets, authors, and artists extolled southern culture. Jefferson Davis asked citizens to observe national days of fasting and prayer. But these efforts failed to win over thousands of die-hard Unionists, and animosity between yeomen and planters increased rather than decreased. The war also threatened to rip the southern social fabric along its racial seam.

The Disintegration of Slavery The legal destruction of slavery was the product of presidential proclamation, congressional legislation, and eventually constitutional amendment, but the practical destruction of slavery was the product of war, what Lincoln called war's "friction and abrasion." Slaves took advantage of the upheaval to reach for freedom. Some half a million of the South's 4 million slaves ran away to Union military lines. More than 100,000 runaways took up arms as federal soldiers and sailors and attacked slavery directly. Other men and women stayed in the slave quarter, where they staked their claim to more freedom.

War disrupted slavery in a dozen ways. Almost immediately, it called the master away, leaving the mistress to assume responsibility for the plantation. But mistresses could not maintain traditional standards of slave discipline in wartime, and the balance of power shifted. Slaves got to the fields late, worked indifferently, and quit early. Some slaveholders responded violently; most saw no alternative but to strike bargains—offering gifts or part of the crop—to keep slaves at home and at work. An Alabama woman complained that she "begged . . . what little is done." Slaveholders had believed that they "knew" their slaves, but they learned that they did not. When the war began, a North Carolina woman praised her slaves as "diligent and respectful." When it ended, she said, "As to the idea of a *faithful servant, it is all a fiction.*"

As military action sliced through the southern countryside, some slaveholders fled, leaving their slaves behind. Many more took their slaves with them, but flight meant additional chaos and offered slaves new opportunities to resist bondage. Whites' greatest fear—retaliatory violence—rarely occurred, however. Slaves who stayed home steadily undermined white mastery and expanded control over their own lives.

Q: **How did wartime hardship in the South contribute to class animosity?**

The North at War

Although the North was largely untouched by the fighting, Northerners could not avoid being touched by the war. Almost every family had a son, husband, father, or brother in uniform. Moreover,

total war blurred the distinction between home front and battlefield. As in the South, men marched off to fight, but preserving the country was also women's work. For civilians as well as soldiers, for women as well as men, war was transforming.

The need to build and fuel the Union war machine boosted the economy. The Union sent nearly 2 million men into the military and still increased production in almost every area. But because the rewards and burdens of patriotism were distributed unevenly, the North experienced sharp, even violent, divisions. Workers confronted employers, whites confronted blacks, and Democrats confronted Republicans. Still, Northerners on the home front remained fervently attached to the Union.

The Government and the Economy When the war began, the United States had no national banking system, no national currency, and no federal income tax. But the secession of eleven slave states cut the Democrats' strength in Congress in half and destroyed their capacity to resist Republican economic programs. The Legal Tender Act of February 1862 created a national currency, paper money that Northerners called "greenbacks." With the passage of the National Banking Act in February 1863, Congress established a system of national banks that by the 1870s had largely replaced the antebellum system of decentralized state banks. Congress also enacted a series of sweeping tax laws. By revolutionizing the country's banking, monetary, and tax structures, the Republicans generated enormous economic power.

The Republicans' wartime legislation also aimed at integrating the West more thoroughly into the Union. In May 1862, Congress approved the Homestead Act, which offered 160 acres of public land to settlers who would live and labor on it. The Homestead Act bolstered western loyalty and in time resulted in more than a million new farms. The Pacific Railroad Act in July 1862 provided massive federal assistance for building a transcontinental railroad that ran from Omaha to San Francisco when completed in 1869. Congress further bound East and West by subsidizing the Pony Express mail service and a transcontinental telegraph.

Two additional initiatives had long-term economic consequences. Congress created the Department of Agriculture and passed the Land-Grant College Act (also known as the Morrill Act after its sponsor, Representative Justin Morrill of Vermont), which set aside public land to support universities that emphasized "agriculture and mechanical arts." The Lincoln administration immeasurably strengthened the North's effort to win the war, but its ideas also permanently changed the nation.

Union Ordnance, Yorktown, Virginia As the North successfully harnessed its enormous industrial capacity to meet the needs of the war, cannons, mortars, and shells poured out of its factories. A fraction of that abundance is seen here at Yorktown in 1862, ready for transportation to Union troops in the field. Two years later, Abraham Lincoln observed that the Union was "gaining strength, and may if need be maintain the contest indefinitely. . . . Material resources are now more complete and abundant than ever. . . . The national resources are unexhausted, and, as we believe, inexhaustible." Library of Congress.

FOR MORE HELP ANALYZING THIS IMAGE, see the visual activity for this chapter in the Online Study Guide at bedfordstmartins.com/roarkcompact.

Women and Work on the Home Front

More than a million farm men were called to the military, so farm women added men's chores to their own. "I met more women driving teams on the road and saw more at work in the fields than men," a visitor to Iowa reported in the fall of 1862. Rising production testified to their success in plowing, planting, and harvesting. Rapid mechanization assisted farm women in their new roles. Cyrus McCormick sold 165,000 of his reapers during the war years. The combination of high prices for farm products and increased production ensured that war and prosperity joined hands in the rural North.

A few industries, such as textiles (which depended on southern cotton), declined during the war, but many more grew. Huge profits prompted one Pennsylvania ironmaster to remark, "I am in no hurry for peace." With orders pouring in and a million nonfarmworkers at war, unemployment declined and wages often rose. The boom proved friendlier to owners than to workers, however. Inflation and taxes cut so deeply into workers' paychecks that their standard of living actually fell.

In cities, women stepped into jobs vacated by men, particularly in manufacturing, and also into essentially new occupations such as government secretaries and clerks. Women made up about one-quarter of the manufacturing workforce when the war began and one-third when it ended. As more and more women entered the workforce, employers cut wages. In 1864, New York seamstresses working fourteen-hour days earned only $1.54 a week. Urban workers resorted increasingly to strikes to wrench decent salaries from their employers, but their protests rarely succeeded. Nevertheless, tough times failed to undermine the patriotism of most workers.

Most middle-class white women stayed home and contributed to the war effort in traditional ways. They sewed, wrapped bandages, and sold homemade goods at local fairs to raise money to aid the soldiers. Other women expressed their patriotism in an untraditional way—as wartime nurses. Thousands of women on both sides defied prejudices about female delicacy and volunteered to nurse the wounded. Many northern female volunteers worked through the **U.S. Sanitary Commission**, a civilian organization that bought and distributed clothing, food, and medicine and recruited doctors and nurses.

Some volunteers went on to become paid military nurses. **Dorothea Dix**, well known for her efforts to reform insane asylums, was named superintendent of female nurses in April 1861. Eventually, some 3,000

> "I met more women driving teams on the road and saw more at work in the fields than men," a visitor to Iowa reported in the fall of 1862.

Women Doing Laundry for Federal Soldiers, ca. 1861 Northern women eagerly joined the Union war effort. Thousands aided in the work of the U.S. Christian Commission, the U.S. Sanitary Commission, and other philanthropic organizations to provide soldiers with Bibles, fresh food, and new socks. But some women were forced by their desperate financial circumstances to wash soldiers' dirty clothes to make a living. Army camps were difficult places for "respectable" women to work. One Union soldier discouraged his wife even from visiting, noting, "It is not a fit place for any woman, for there is all kinds of talk, songs and everything not good for them 2 hear." © Bettmann/Corbis.

women served under her. Most nurses worked in hospitals behind the battle lines, but some, like **Clara Barton**, who later founded the American Red Cross, worked in battlefield units. Women who served in the war went on to lead the postwar movement to establish training schools for female nurses.

Politics and Dissent At first, the bustle of economic and military mobilization seemed to silence politics, but bipartisan unity did not last. Within a year, Democrats were labeling the Republican administration a "reign of terror," and Republicans were calling Democrats the party of "Dixie, Davis, and the Devil." Democrats denounced Republican policies — emancipating the slaves, subsidizing private business, and expanding federal power — as unconstitutional, arguing that the "Constitution is as binding in war as in peace."

In September 1862, in an effort to stifle opposition to the war, Lincoln placed under military arrest any person who discouraged enlistments, resisted the draft, or engaged in "disloyal" practices. Before the war ended, his administration imprisoned nearly 14,000 individuals, most in the border states. The

campaign fell short of a reign of terror, for the majority of the prisoners were not northern Democratic opponents but Confederates, blockade runners, and citizens of foreign countries, and most of those arrested gained quick release. Still, the administration's heavy-handed tactics did suppress free speech.

When the Republican-dominated Congress enacted the draft law in March 1863, Democrats had another grievance. The law required that all men between the ages of twenty and forty-five enroll and make themselves available for a lottery that would decide who went to war. What poor men found particularly galling were provisions that allowed a draftee to hire a substitute or simply to pay a $300 fee and get out of his military obligation. As in the South, common folk could be heard chanting, "A rich man's war and a poor man's fight."

Linking the draft and emancipation, Democrats argued that Republicans employed an unconstitutional means (the draft) to achieve an unconstitutional end (emancipation). In the summer of 1863, antidraft, antiblack mobs went on rampages in northern cities. In New York City, Democratic Irish workingmen — crowded into filthy tenements, gouged by inflation, enraged by the draft, and dead set against fighting to free blacks—erupted in four days of rioting. The **New York City draft riots** killed at least 105 people, most of them black, and left the Colored Orphan Asylum a smoking ruin.

Racist mobs failed to subordinate African Americans, however. Free black leaders had lobbied aggressively for emancipation, and after Lincoln's proclamation, they fanned out over the North agitating for equality. They won a few small victories. Illinois and Iowa overturned laws that excluded blacks from entering those states. Illinois and Ohio began permitting blacks to testify in court. But significant progress toward black equality would have to wait until the war ended.

Q: Why was the U.S. Congress able to pass such a bold legislative agenda during the war?

Grinding Out Victory, 1863–1865

In the early months of 1863, the Union's prospects looked bleak, and the Confederate cause stood at high tide. Then, in July 1863, the tide began to turn. The military man most responsible for this shift was Ulysses S. Grant. Elevated to supreme command, Grant knit together a powerful war machine that integrated a sophisticated command structure, modern technology, and complex logistics and supply systems. But the arithmetic of this plain man remained unchanged: Killing more of the enemy than he kills of you equaled "the complete overthrow of the rebellion."

The North ground out the victory battle by bloody battle. The balance tipped in the Union's favor in 1863, but Southerners were not deterred. The fighting escalated in the last two years of the war. As national elections approached in the fall of 1864, Lincoln expected a war-weary North to reject him. Instead, northern voters declared their willingness to continue the war in the defense of the ideals of union and freedom.

Vicksburg and Gettysburg

Vicksburg, Mississippi, situated on the eastern bank of the Mississippi River, stood between Union forces and complete control of the river. Union forces under Grant lay siege to the city in an effort to starve out the enemy.

Vicksburg Campaign, 1863

Civilian residents moved into caves to escape the incessant Union bombardment, and as the **siege of Vicksburg** dragged on, they ate mules and rats to survive. After six weeks, on July 4, 1863, nearly 30,000 rebels marched out of Vicksburg, stacked their arms, and surrendered unconditionally. A Yankee captain wrote home to his wife: "The backbone of the Rebellion is this day broken. The Confederacy is divided. . . . Vicksburg is ours. The Mississippi River is opened, and Gen. Grant is to be our next President."

On the same Fourth of July, word arrived that Union forces had crushed General Lee at Gettysburg, Pennsylvania (Map 15.3). Emboldened by his victory at Chancellorsville in May, Lee and his 75,000-man army had invaded Pennsylvania. On June 28, Union forces under General George G. Meade intercepted the Confederates at the small town of Gettysburg, where Union soldiers occupied the high ground. Three days of furious fighting involving 165,000 troops could not dislodge the Federals from the hills. Lee ached for a decisive victory, and on July 3 he ordered a major assault against the Union center on Cemetery Ridge. The dug-in Yankees enjoyed three-quarters of a mile of clear vision, and they raked the line of Confederate soldiers under General George E. Pickett with cannon and rifle fire. The **battle of Gettysburg** cost Lee more than one-third of his army—28,000 casualties. "It's all my fault," he lamented. On the night of July 4, 1863, he marched his battered army back to Virginia.

The twin disasters at Vicksburg and Gettysburg proved to be the turning point of the war. The Confederacy could not replace the nearly 60,000 soldiers who were captured, wounded, or killed. Lee never launched another major offensive north of the Mason-Dixon line. It is hindsight, however, that permits us to see the pair of battles as decisive. At the time, the Confederacy still controlled the heartland of the South, and Lee still had a vicious sting. War-weariness threatened to erode the North's will to win before Union armies could destroy the Confederacy's ability to go on.

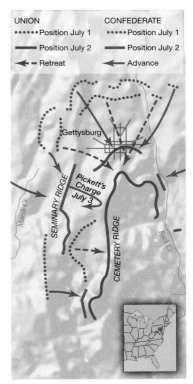

Battle of Gettysburg, July 1–3, 1863

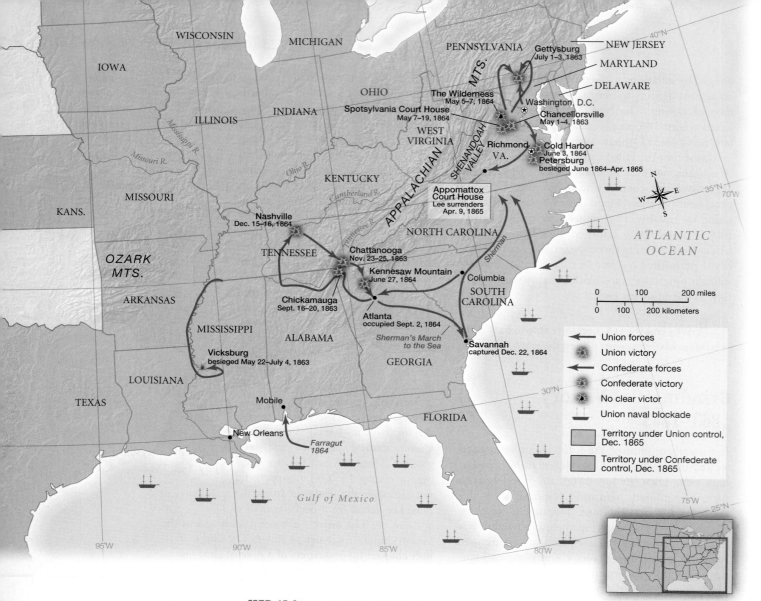

MAP 15.3 The Civil War, 1863–1865
Ulysses S. Grant's victory at Vicksburg divided the Confederacy at the Mississippi River. William Tecumseh Sherman's march from Chattanooga to Savannah divided it again. In northern Virginia, Robert E. Lee fought fiercely, but Grant's larger, better-supplied armies prevailed.

READING THE MAP: Describe the difference between Union and Confederate naval capacity. Were the battles shown on the map fought primarily in Union-controlled or Confederate-controlled territory? (Look at the land areas on the map.)

CONNECTIONS: Did former slaves serve in the Civil War? If so, on which side(s), and what did they do?

FOR MORE HELP ANALYZING THIS MAP, see the map activity for this chapter in the Online Study Guide at bedfordstmartins.com/roarkcompact.

Grant Takes Command In September 1863, Union general William Rosecrans placed his army in a dangerous situation in Chattanooga, Tennessee, where he had retreated after defeat at the battle of Chickamauga (see Map 15.3). Rebels surrounded the disorganized bluecoats and threatened to starve them into submission. Grant, now commander of Union forces between the Mississippi River and the Appalachians, arrived in Chattanooga in October. Within weeks, he opened an effective supply line, broke the siege, and routed the Confederate army. The victory at Chattanooga on November 25 opened the door to Georgia. It also confirmed Lincoln's estimation of Grant. In March 1864, the president asked Grant to come east to become the general in chief of all Union armies.

In Washington, General Grant implemented his grand strategy for a war of attrition. He ordered a series of simultaneous assaults from Virginia all the way to Louisiana. Two actions proved particularly significant. In one, General **William Tecumseh Sherman**, whom Grant appointed his successor to command the western armies, plunged southeast toward Atlanta. In the other, Grant, who took control of the Army of the Potomac, went head-to-head with Lee in Virginia for almost four straight weeks.

Grant and Lee met in the first week of May 1864 in a dense tangle of scrub oaks and small pines. Often unable to see more than ten paces, the armies pounded away at each other until approximately 18,000 Yankees and 11,000 rebels had fallen. The savagery of the **battle of the Wilderness** did not compare with that at Spotsylvania Court House a few days later. Frenzied men fought hand to hand for eighteen hours in the rain. One veteran remembered men "piled upon each other in some places four layers deep, exhibiting every ghastly phase of mutilation." Spotsylvania cost Grant another 18,000 casualties and Lee 10,000, but the Yankee bulldog would not let go. Grant kept moving and tangled with Lee again at Cold Harbor, where he suffered 13,000 additional casualties to Lee's 5,000.

Twice as many Union soldiers as rebel soldiers died in four weeks of fighting in Virginia in May and June, but because Lee had only half as many troops as Grant, his losses were equivalent to Grant's. Grant knew that the South could not replace the losses. Moreover, the campaign carried Grant to the outskirts of Petersburg, just south of Richmond, where he abandoned the costly tactic of the frontal assault and began a siege that immobilized both armies and dragged on for nine months.

Simultaneously, Sherman invaded Georgia. Grant instructed Sherman to "get into the interior of the enemy's country as far as you can, inflicting all the damage you can against their War resources." In May, Sherman moved 100,000 men south against 65,000 rebels. Skillful maneuvering, constant skirmishing, and one pitched battle, at Kennesaw Mountain, brought Sherman to Atlanta, which fell on September 2.

Intending to "make Georgia howl," Sherman marched out of Atlanta on November 15 with 62,000 battle-hardened veterans, heading for Savannah, 285 miles away on the Atlantic coast. One veteran remembered, "[We] destroyed all we could not eat, stole their niggers, burned their cotton & gins, spilled their sorghum, burned &

twisted their R. Roads and raised Hell generally." **Sherman's March to the Sea** aimed at destroying the will of the southern people. A few weeks earlier, General **Philip H. Sheridan** had carried out his own scorched-earth campaign in the Shenandoah Valley, complying with Grant's order to turn the valley into "a barren waste . . . so that crows flying over it for the balance of this season will have to carry their provender [food] with them." When Sherman's troops entered an undefended Savannah in mid-December, the general telegraphed Lincoln that he had "a Christmas gift" for him. A month earlier, Union voters had bestowed on the president an even greater gift.

The Election of 1864   In the summer of 1864, with Sherman temporarily checked outside Atlanta and Grant bogged down in the siege of Petersburg, the Democratic Party smelled victory in the fall elections. Rankled by a seemingly never-ending war, inflation, the draft, the attack on civil liberties, and the commitment to blacks, Northerners appeared ready for a change. Lincoln himself concluded, "It seems exceedingly probable that this administration will not be re-elected."

The Democrats were badly divided, however. "Peace" Democrats insisted on an armistice, while "war" Democrats supported the conflict but opposed Republican means of fighting it. The party tried to paper over the chasm by nominating a war candidate, General George McClellan, but adopting a peace platform that demanded that "immediate efforts be made for a cessation of hostilities." Republicans denounced the peace plank as a cut-and-run plan that "virtually proposed to surrender the country to the rebels in arms against us."

The capture of Atlanta in September turned the political tide in favor of the Republicans. Lincoln received 55 percent of the popular vote, but his electoral margin was a whopping 212 to McClellan's 21. Lincoln's party won a resounding victory, one that gave him a mandate to continue the war until slavery and the Confederacy were dead.

The Confederacy Collapses   As 1865 dawned, military disaster littered the Confederate landscape. With the destruction of John B. Hood's army at Nashville in December 1864, the interior of the Confederacy lay in Yankee hands (see Map 15.3). Sherman's troops, resting momentarily in Savannah, eyed South Carolina hungrily. Farther north, Grant had Lee's army pinned down in Petersburg, a few miles from Richmond.

Some Confederates turned their backs on the rebellion. News from the battlefield made it difficult not to conclude that the Yankees had beaten them. Soldiers' wives begged their husbands to

Richmond, Virginia, 1865 As the Confederate government evacuated Richmond during the evening of April 2, 1865, demolition squads set fire to everything that had military or industrial value. Huge explosions devastated the arsenal, the ruins of which are shown here. As one witness observed, "The old war-scarred city seemed to prefer annihilation to conquest." Library of Congress.

return home to keep their families from starving, and the stream of deserters grew dramatically. In most cases, when white Southerners lost the will to continue, it was not because they lost faith in independence but because they had been battered into submission. Despite the deep divisions within the Confederacy, white Southerners had demonstrated a remarkable endurance for their cause. Half of the 900,000 Confederate soldiers had been killed or wounded, and ragged, hungry women and children had sacrificed throughout one of the bloodiest wars then known to history.

The end came with a rush. On February 1, 1865, Sherman's troops stormed out of Savannah into South Carolina, the "cradle of the Confederacy." In Virginia, Lee abandoned Petersburg on April 2, and Richmond fell on April 3. Grant pur-

sued Lee until he surrendered on April 9, 1865, at Appomattox Court House, Virginia. Grant offered generous peace terms. He allowed Lee's men to return home and to keep their horses to help "put in a crop to carry themselves and their families through the next winter." With Lee gone, the remaining Confederate armies lost hope and gave up within two weeks. After four years, the war was over.

No one was more relieved than Lincoln, but his celebration was restrained. He told his cabinet that his postwar burdens would weigh almost as heavily as those of wartime. Seeking a distraction, Lincoln attended Ford's Theatre on the evening of Good Friday, April 14, 1865. John Wilkes Booth, an actor with southern sympathies, slipped into the president's box and shot Lincoln in the head.

He died at 7:22 the following morning. Vice President Andrew Johnson became president. The man who had led the nation through the war would not lead it during the postwar search for a just peace.

Q: **Why were the siege of Vicksburg and the battle of Gettysburg crucial to the outcome of the war?**

Conclusion: The Second American Revolution

A transformed nation emerged from the crucible of war. Antebellum America was decentralized politically and loosely integrated economically. To bend the resources of the country to a Union victory, Congress enacted legislation that reshaped the nation's political and economic character. It created a national currency and banking system and turned to free land, a transcontinental railroad, and miles of telegraph lines to bind the West to the rest of the nation. Congress also established the sovereignty of the federal government and permanently increased its power. To most citizens before the war, Washington meant the post office and little more. During the war, the federal government drafted, taxed, and judged Americans in unprecedented ways. The massive changes brought about by the war—the creation of a national government, a national economy, and a national spirit—led one historian to call the American Civil War the "Second American Revolution."

The Civil War also had a profound effect on individual lives. When the war began in 1861, millions of men dropped their hoes, hammers, and pencils; put on blue or gray uniforms; and fought and suffered for what they passionately believed was right. The war disrupted families, leaving women at home with additional responsibilities while offering new opportunities to others for wartime work in factories, offices, and hospitals. It offered blacks new and more effective ways to resist slavery and agitate for equality.

The war devastated the South. Three-fourths of southern white men of military age served in the Confederate army, and at least half of them were captured, wounded, or killed or died of disease. The war destroyed two-fifths of the South's livestock, wrecked half of the farm machinery, and blackened dozens of cities and towns. The immediate impact of the war on the North was more paradoxical. The struggle cost the North a heavy price: 373,000 lives. But rather than devastating the land, the war set the countryside and cities humming with business activity. The radical shift in power from South to North signaled a new direction in American development: the long decline of agriculture and the rise of industrial capitalism.

Most revolutionary of all, the war ended slavery. Ironically, the South's war to preserve slavery destroyed it. Nearly 200,000 black men, including ex-slave William Gould, dedicated their wartime service to its eradication. Because slavery was both a labor and a racial system, the institution was entangled in almost every aspect of southern life. Slavery's uprooting inevitably meant fundamental change. But the full meaning of abolition remained unclear in 1865. Determining the new economic, political, and social status of nearly 4 million ex-slaves would be the principal task of reconstruction.

Reviewing the Chapter

★ KEY TERMS

Explain each term's significance

WHO

George B. McClellan (p. 364)
Robert E. Lee (p. 364)
Ulysses S. Grant (p. 366)
Dorothea Dix (p. 375)
Clara Barton (p. 376)
William Tecumseh Sherman (p. 379)
Philip H. Sheridan (p. 379)

WHAT

Fort Sumter (p. 359)
battle of Bull Run/Manassas (p. 363)
battle of Antietam (p. 365)
battle of Shiloh (p. 366)
Union blockade (p. 366)
King Cotton diplomacy (p. 367)
contraband of war (p. 369)
Emancipation Proclamation (p. 370)
U.S. Sanitary Commission (p. 375)
New York City draft riots (p. 377)
siege of Vicksburg (p. 377)
battle of Gettysburg (p. 377)
battle of the Wilderness (p. 379)
Sherman's March to the Sea (p. 379)

FOR PRACTICE QUIZZES AND OTHER STUDY TOOLS, see the Online Study Guide at **bedfordstmartins.com/roarkcompact**.

★ REVIEW QUESTIONS Q:

Use key terms and dates to support your answer

1. Why did both the Union and the Confederacy consider control of the border states crucial? (pp. 358–60)

2. Why did the South believe it could win the war despite numerical disadvantages? (pp. 360–63)

3. Why did the Confederacy's bid for international support fail? (pp. 363–67)

4. Why did the Union change policy in 1863 to allow black men to serve in the army? (pp. 368–71)

5. How did wartime hardship in the South contribute to class animosity? (pp. 371–74)

6. Why was the U.S. Congress able to pass such a bold legislative agenda during the war? (pp. 374–77)

7. Why were the siege of Vicksburg and the battle of Gettysburg crucial to the outcome of the war? (pp. 377–81)

★ MAKING CONNECTIONS

Draw on key terms, timeline, and review questions

1. Despite loathing slavery, Lincoln embraced emancipation as a war objective late and with great caution. Why? In your answer, trace the progression of Lincoln's position, considering how legal, political, military, and moral concerns influenced his policies.

2. The Emancipation Proclamation did not accomplish the destruction of slavery on its own. How did a war over union bring about the end of slavery? In your answer, consider the direct actions of slaves and Union policymakers as well as indirect factors within the Confederacy.

3. In addition to restoring the Union and destroying slavery, what other significant changes did the war produce on the home front and in the nation's capital? In your answer, discuss economic, governmental, and social developments, being attentive to regional variations.

4. Brilliant military strategy alone did not determine the outcome of the war; victory also depended on generating revenue, materiel mobilization, diplomacy, and politics. In light of these considerations, explain why the Confederacy believed it would succeed and why it ultimately failed.

★ SUGGESTED READINGS

Ira Berlin et al., eds., *Freedom: A Documentary History of Emancipation, 1861–1867,* 5 vols. (1982–2008). A monumental collection of contemporary documents that recount the black experience in the war.

Richard J. Carwardine, *Lincoln* (2003). A fresh biography of Lincoln as war leader.

Drew Gilpin Faust, *This Republic of Suffering: Death and the American Civil War* (2008). A moving examination of how Americans coped with the unprecedented scale of death.

William B. Gould IV, ed., *Diary of a Contraband: The Civil War Passage of a Black Sailor* (2002). A remarkable account of an ex-slave's service in the Union navy.

Anne Sarah Rubin, *A Shattered Nation: The Rise and Fall of the Confederacy, 1861–1868* (2005). An investigation of how home front and battlefield contributed to the construction of Confederate identity.

Nina Silber, *Daughters of the Union: Northern Women Fight the Civil War* (2006). A reconsideration of the role of ordinary northern women in the Union war effort.

FOR MORE BOOKS ABOUT TOPICS IN THIS CHAPTER, see the Online Bibliography at **bedfordstmartins.com/roarkcompact.**

FOR ADDITIONAL FIRSTHAND ACCOUNTS OF THIS PERIOD, see Chapter 15 in Michael Johnson, ed., *Reading the American Past,* Fourth Edition.

FOR WEB SITES, IMAGES, AND DOCUMENTS RELATED TO TOPICS AND PLACES IN THIS CHAPTER, visit Make History at **bedfordstmartins.com/roarkcompact.**

★ TIMELINE

1861
- **April.** Attack on Fort Sumter.
- **April–May.** Four Upper South states join Confederacy.
- **July.** Union forces routed in first battle of Bull Run (Manassas).
- **August.** First Confiscation Act.

1862
- **February.** Grant captures Fort Henry and Fort Donelson.
- **March.** Confederates defeated at battle of Glorieta Pass. Union victory at battle of Pea Ridge.
- **April.** Battle of Shiloh in Tennessee ends Confederate bid to control Mississippi valley.
- **April.** Confederate Congress authorizes draft.
- **May.** Homestead Act.
- **May–July.** Union forces defeated during Virginia peninsula campaign.
- **July.** Second Confiscation Act. Militia Act.
- **September.** Battle of Antietam stops Lee's advance into Maryland.

1863
- **January.** Emancipation Proclamation becomes law.
- **February.** National Banking Act.
- **March.** Congress authorizes draft.
- **July.** Fall of Vicksburg to Union forces.
- **July.** Lee defeated at battle of Gettysburg.
- **July.** New York City draft riots.

1864
- **March.** Grant appointed Union general in chief.
- **May–June.** Wilderness campaign.
- **September.** Fall of Atlanta to Sherman.
- **November.** Lincoln reelected.
- **December.** Fall of Savannah to Sherman.

1865
- **April 2–3.** Fall of Petersburg and Richmond.
- **April 9.** Lee surrenders to Grant.
- **April 15.** Lincoln dies from bullet wound; Vice President Andrew Johnson becomes president.

CARPETBAG

A carpetbag was a nineteenth-century suitcase made from carpet, often brightly colored. Applied first to wildcat bankers on the western frontier, "carpetbagger" was a derogatory name for rootless and penniless adventurers who could carry everything they owned in a single bag. Critics of Republican administrations in the South hurled the name "carpetbaggers" at white Northerners who moved South during Reconstruction and became active in politics. According to white Southerners, carpetbaggers exploited gullible ex-slaves to gain power and wealth. In fact, many Northerners who came to the South joined with blacks and some southern whites to form Republican state and local governments that were among the most progressive anywhere in the nineteenth century. Private Collection/Picture Research Consultants & Archives.

CHAPTER

16

Reconstruction

1863–1877

IN 1856, JOHN RAPIER, a free black barber in Florence, Alabama, urged his four freeborn sons to flee the increasingly repressive and dangerous South. Searching for a color-blind society, the brothers scattered around the world. **James T. Rapier** chose Canada, where he went to live with his uncle in a largely black community and studied Greek and Latin in a log schoolhouse. After his conversion at a Methodist revival, James wrote to his father: "I have not thrown a card in 3 years[,] touched a woman in 2 years[,] smoked nor drunk any Liquor in going on 2 years." He vowed, "I will endeavor to do my part in solving the problems [of African Americans] in my native land."

The Union victory in the Civil War gave James Rapier the opportunity to redeem his pledge. In 1865, after more than eight years of exile, the twenty-seven-year-old Rapier returned to Alabama, where he presided over the first political gathering of former slaves in the state. Alabama freedmen produced a petition that called on the federal government to thoroughly reconstruct the South, to guarantee suffrage, free speech, free schools, and equal rights for all men, regardless of color.

Rapier soon discovered that Alabama's whites found it agonizingly difficult to accept defeat and black freedom. They responded to the revolutionary changes under the banner "White Man — Right or Wrong — Still the White Man!" In 1868, when Rapier and other Alabama blacks vigorously supported the Republican presidential candidate, former Union general Ulysses S. Grant, the recently organized Ku Klux Klan went on a bloody rampage of whipping, burning, and shooting. A mob of 150 outraged whites scoured Rapier's neighborhood seeking four black politicians they claimed were trying to "Africanize Alabama." They caught and hanged three, but the "nigger carpetbagger from Canada" escaped. Badly shaken, Rapier considered fleeing the state, but he decided to stay and fight.

Rapier emerged in the early 1870s as Alabama's most prominent black leader. He demanded that the federal government end the violence against ex-slaves, guarantee their civil rights, and give them land. In 1872, he won election to the House of Representatives and joined six other black congressmen in Washington, D.C. Even those who sought to destroy him and so-called Negro rule admitted that Rapier was "the best intellect under a

Previewing the Chapter

Wartime Reconstruction 386
Q: *Why did Congress object to Lincoln's wartime plan for reconstruction?*

Presidential Reconstruction 392
Q: *How did the North respond to the passage of black codes in the southern states?*

Congressional Reconstruction 395
Q: *Why did Johnson urge the southern states to reject the Fourteenth Amendment?*

The Struggle in the South 398
Q: *Why was the Republican Party in the South a coalition party?*

Reconstruction Collapses 402
Q: *How did the Supreme Court undermine the Fourteenth and Fifteenth Amendments?*

Conclusion: "A Revolution But Half Accomplished" 407

James T. Rapier Only two years after emancipation, ex-slaves in the United States gained full political rights and wielded far more political power than former bondsmen anywhere else in the New World. Black suffrage sent fourteen African American congressmen to Washington, D.C., during Reconstruction, among them James T. Rapier of Alabama. Temporarily at least, he and his black colleagues helped shape post-emancipation society. In 1874, when Rapier spoke on behalf of a civil rights bill, he described the humiliation of being denied service at inns all along his route from Montgomery to Washington. Elsewhere in the world, he said, class and religion were invoked to defend discrimination. In Europe, "they have princes, dukes, lords"; in India, "brahmans or priests, who rank above the sudras or laborers." But in America, "our distinction is color." Alabama Department of Archives and History.

colored skin in Alabama." Defeated for reelection in 1874 in a fraudulent campaign, Rapier turned to cotton farming, generously giving thousands of dollars of his profits to black schools and churches.

Embittered by persistent black poverty and demoralized by continuing racial violence, Rapier again chose exile. Rapier purchased land in Kansas and urged Alabama's blacks to escape with him. Buoyant and confident when he returned to Alabama in 1865, he had over the years grown to believe that blacks could never achieve equality and prosperity in the South. But in 1883, before he could leave Alabama, Rapier died of tuberculosis at the age of forty-five.

In 1865, Union general Carl Schurz had foreseen many of the troubles Rapier would encounter in the postwar South. Schurz concluded that the Civil War was "a revolution but half accomplished." Northern victory had freed the slaves, he observed, but it had not changed former slaveholders' minds about blacks' unfitness for freedom. Left to themselves, whites would "introduce some new system of forced labor, not perhaps exactly slavery in its old form but something similar to it." To defend their freedom, Schurz concluded, blacks would need federal protection, land of their own, and voting rights. Until whites "cut loose from the past, it will be a dangerous experiment to put Southern society upon its own legs."

As Schurz discovered, the end of the war did not mean peace. The United States was one of only two societies in the New World in which slavery ended in a bloody war. (The other was Haiti.) Not surprisingly, racial turmoil continued in the South after the armies quit fighting in 1865. The nation entered one of its most chaotic and conflicted eras — Reconstruction, a violent period that would define the defeated South's status within the Union and the meaning of freedom for ex-slaves.

The place of the South within the nation and the extent of black freedom were determined not only in Washington, D.C., where the federal government played an active role, but also in the state legislatures and county seats of the South, where blacks participated in the process. Moreover, on farms and plantations from Virginia to Texas, ex-slaves struggled to become free workers while exslaveholders clung to the Old South. A small band of white women joined in the struggle for racial equality, and soon their crusade broadened to include gender equality. Their attempts to secure voting rights for women as well as blacks were thwarted, however. Reconstruction witnessed a gigantic struggle to determine the consequences of Confederate defeat and emancipation. In the end, white Southerners prevailed. Their New South was a different South from the one to which most whites wished to return but also vastly unlike the one of which James Rapier dreamed.   ★

Wartime Reconstruction

Reconstruction did not wait for the end of war. As the odds of a northern victory increased, thinking about reunification quickened. Immediately, a question arose: Who had authority to devise a plan for reconstructing the Union?

President Abraham Lincoln believed firmly that reconstruction was a matter of executive responsibility. Congress just as firmly asserted its jurisdiction. Fueling the argument about who had the authority to set the terms of reconstruction were significant differences about the terms themselves.

In their eagerness to formulate a plan for political reunification, neither Lincoln nor Congress gave much attention to the South's land and labor problems. But as the war rapidly eroded slavery and traditional plantation agriculture, Yankee military commanders in the Union-occupied areas of the Confederacy had no choice but to oversee the emergence of a new labor system.

"To Bind Up the Nation's Wounds"

As early as 1863, Lincoln contemplated how "to bind up the nation's wounds" and achieve "a just, and a lasting peace." While deep compassion for the enemy guided his thinking, his plan for reconstruction aimed primarily at shortening the war and ending slavery.

Lincoln's Proclamation of Amnesty and Reconstruction in December 1863 set out his terms. He offered a full pardon, restoring property (except slaves) and political rights, to rebels willing to renounce secession and to accept emancipation. His offer excluded only high-ranking Confederate military and political officers and a few other groups. When 10 percent of a state's voting population had taken an oath of allegiance, the state could organize a new government. Lincoln's plan did not require ex-rebels to extend social or political rights to ex-slaves, nor did it anticipate a program of long-term federal assistance to freedmen. Clearly, the president looked forward to the speedy, forgiving restoration of the broken Union.

Lincoln's easy terms enraged abolitionists such as Wendell Phillips of Boston, who charged that the president "makes the negro's freedom a mere sham." He "is willing that the negro should be free but seeks nothing else for him." Phillips and other northern radicals called instead for a thorough overhaul of southern society. Their ideas proved to be too drastic for most Republicans during the war years, but Congress agreed that Lincoln's plan was inadequate. Congress feared that the president's program amounted to restoring the old southern ruling class to power. It wanted greater assurances of white loyalty and greater guarantees of black rights.

In July 1864 Congressman Henry Winter Davis of Maryland and Senator Benjamin Wade of Ohio jointly sponsored a bill that demanded that at least half of the voters in a conquered rebel state take the oath of allegiance before reconstruction could begin. The **Wade-Davis bill** also banned all ex-Confederates from participating in the drafting of new state constitutions. Finally, the bill guaranteed the equality of freedmen before the law. When Lincoln refused to sign the bill and let it die, Wade and Davis charged the president with usurpation of power. They warned Lincoln to confine himself to "his executive duties — to obey and execute, not make the laws — to suppress by arms armed rebellion, and leave political organization to Congress."

Undeterred, Lincoln continued to nurture the formation of loyal state governments under his own plan. Four states — Louisiana, Arkansas, Tennessee, and Virginia — fulfilled the president's requirements, but Congress refused to seat representatives from the "Lincoln states." In his last public address in April 1865, Lincoln defended his plan but for the first time expressed publicly his endorsement of suffrage for southern blacks, at least "the very intelligent, and . . . those who serve our cause as soldiers." The announcement demonstrated that Lincoln's thinking about reconstruction was still evolving. Four days later, he was dead.

Land and Labor

Of all the problems raised by the North's victory in the war, none proved more critical than the South's transition from slavery to free labor. As federal armies invaded and occupied the Confederacy, hundreds of thousands of slaves became free workers. In addition, Union armies controlled vast territories in the South where legal title to land had become unclear. The Confiscation Acts punished "traitors" by taking away their property. The question of what to do with federally occupied land and how to organize labor on it engaged former slaves, former slaveholders, Union military commanders, and federal government officials long before the war ended.

In the Mississippi valley, occupying federal troops announced a new labor code. It required slaveholders to sign contracts with ex-slaves and to pay wages. It obligated employers to provide food, housing, and medical care. It outlawed whipping, but it reserved to the army the right to discipline blacks who refused to work. The code required black laborers to enter into contracts, work diligently, and remain subordinate and obedient. Military leaders clearly had no intention of promoting a social or economic revolution. Instead, they sought to restore plantation agriculture with wage labor. The effort resulted in a hybrid system that one contemporary called "compulsory free labor," something that satisfied no one.

Planters complained because the new system fell short of slavery. Blacks could not be "transformed by proclamation," a Louisiana sugar planter declared. Yet under the new system, blacks "are expected to perform their new obligations without coercion, & without the fear of punishment which is essential to stimulate the idle and correct the vicious." Without the right to whip, he argued, the new labor system did not have a chance.

African Americans found the new regime too reminiscent of slavery to be called free labor. Its

Military Auction of Condemned Property, Beaufort, South Carolina, 1865 During the war, thousands of acres of land in the South came into federal hands as abandoned property or as a result of seizures due to nonpayment of taxes. The government authorized the sale of some of this land at public auction. This rare photograph shows expectant blacks (and a few whites) gathered in Beaufort, South Carolina, for a sale. Very few former slaves could raise enough money to purchase land, and even when they pooled their resources, they usually lost out to northern army officers, government officials, or speculators with deeper pockets. Several of the individuals here are wearing Union army caps, strong affirmation of their political loyalties. The Huntington Library, San Marino, California.

chief deficiency, they believed, was the failure to provide them with land of their own. Freedmen believed they had a moral right to land because they and their ancestors had worked it without compensation for more than two centuries. "What's the use of being free if you don't own land enough to be buried in?" one man asked. Several wartime developments led freedmen to believe that the federal government planned to undergird black freedom with landownership.

In January 1865, General William Tecumseh Sherman set aside part of the coast south of Charleston for black settlement. By June 1865, some 40,000 freedmen sat on 400,000 acres of "Sherman land." In March 1865, Congress passed a bill establishing the Bureau of Refugees, Freedmen, and Abandoned Lands. The **Freedmen's Bureau**, as it was called, distributed food and clothing to destitute Southerners and eased the transition of blacks from slaves to free persons. Congress also authorized the agency to divide abandoned and confiscated land into 40-acre plots, to rent them to freedmen, and eventually to sell them "with such title as the United States can convey." By June 1865, the bureau had situated nearly 10,000 black families on a half million acres abandoned by fleeing planters. Other ex-slaves eagerly anticipated farms of their own.

Despite the flurry of activity, wartime reconstruction failed to produce agreement about whether the president or Congress had the authority to devise policy or what proper policy should be.

The African American Quest for Autonomy

Ex-slaves never had any doubt about what they wanted from freedom. They had only to contemplate what they had been denied as slaves. (See "Documenting the American Promise," page 390.) Slaves had to remain on their plantations; freedom allowed blacks to see what was on the other side of the hill. Slaves had to be at work in the fields by dawn; freedom permitted blacks to sleep through a sunrise. Freedmen also tested the etiquette of racial subordination. "Lizzie's maid passed me today when I was coming from church *without speaking to me*," huffed one plantation mistress.

To whites, emancipation looked like pure anarchy. Blacks, they said, had reverted to their natural condition: lazy, irresponsible, and wild. Without the discipline of slavery, whites predicted, blacks would go the way of "the Indian and the

> "The way we can best take care of ourselves is to have land," one former slave declared in 1865, "and turn it and till it by our own labor."

Harry Stephens and Family, 1866, and Samuel Dove Ad, 1865 Dressed in their Sunday best, this Virginia family sits proudly for a photograph. Many black families were not as fortunate as the Stephens family. Separated by slavery or war, former slaves desperately sought news of missing family members through newspaper advertisements like the one posted by Samuel Dove in August 1865. We do not know whether he succeeded in locating his mother, brother, and sisters. Ad: Chicago Historical Society; Family: The Metropolitan Museum of Art, Gilman Collection, Purchase, The Horace W. Goldsmith Foundation Gift, 2005 (2005.100.277)

SAML. DOVE wishes to know of the whereabouts of his mother, Areno, his sisters Maria, Neziah, and Peggy, and his brother Edmond, who were owned by Geo. Dove, of Rockingham county, Shenandoah Valley, Va. Sold in Richmond, after which Saml. and Edmond were taken to Nashville, Tenn., by Joe Mick; Areno was left at the Eagle Tavern, Richmond

Respectfully yours,
SAML. DOVE.

Utica, New York, Aug. 5, 1865–3m

U. S. Christian Commission,
Nashville, Tenn., July 19, 1865.

buffalo." Actually, former slaves were experimenting with freedom, but they could not long afford to roam the countryside, neglect work, and casually provoke whites. Soon, most were back at work in whites' kitchens and fields.

But other items on ex-slaves' agenda of freedom endured. They continued to dream of land and economic independence. "The way we can best take care of ourselves is to have land," one former slave declared in 1865, "and turn it and till it by our own labor." Freedmen also wanted to learn to read and write. Many black soldiers had become literate in the Union army, and they understood the value of the pen and book. "I wishes the Childern all in School," one black veteran asserted. "It is beter for them then to be their Surveing a mistes [mistress]."

The restoration of broken families was another persistent black aspiration. Thousands of freedmen took to the roads in 1865 to look for kin who had been sold away or to free those who were being held illegally as slaves. A black soldier from Missouri wrote his daughters that he was coming for them. "I will have you if it cost me my life," he declared. "Your Miss Kitty said that I tried to steal you," he told them. "But I'll let her know that god never intended for a man to steal his own flesh and blood." And he swore that "if she meets me with ten thousand soldiers, she [will] meet her enemy."

Independent worship was another continuing aspiration. African Americans greeted freedom with a mass exodus from white churches, where they had been required to worship when slaves. Some joined the newly established southern branches of all-black northern churches, such as the African Methodist Episcopal Church. Others formed black versions of the major southern denominations, Baptists

The Meaning of Freedom

On New Year's Day 1863, President Abraham Lincoln issued the Emancipation Proclamation. It states that "all persons held as slaves" within the states still in rebellion "are, and henceforward shall be, free." Although the Proclamation in and of itself did not free any slaves, it transformed the character of the war. Despite often intolerable conditions, black people focused on the possibilities of freedom.

DOCUMENT 1
Letter from John Q. A. Dennis to Edwin M. Stanton, July 26, 1864

John Q. A. Dennis, formerly a slave in Maryland, wrote to ask Secretary of War Edwin M. Stanton for help in reuniting his family.

Boston
Dear Sir I am Glad that I have the Honour to Write you afew line I have been in troble for about four yars my Dear wife was taken from me Nov 19th 1859 and left me with three Children and I being a Slave At the time Could Not do Anny thing for the poor little Children for my master it was took me Carry me some forty mile from them So I Could Not do for them and the man that they live with half feed them and half Cloth them & beat them like dogs & when I was admitted to go to see them it use to brake my heart & Now I say again I am Glad to have the honour to write to you to see if you Can Do Anny thing for me or for my poor little Children I was keap in Slavy untell last Novr 1863. then the Good lord sent the Cornel borne [federal Colonel William Birney?] Down their in Marland in worsester Co So as I have been recently freed I have but letle to live on but I am Strieving Dear Sir but what I went too know of you Sir is it possible for me to go & take my Children from those men that keep them in Savery if it is possible will you pleas give me a permit from your hand then I think they would let them go. . . .

   Hon sir will you please excuse my Miserable writeing & answer me as soon as you can I want get the little Children out of Slavery, I being Criple would like to know of you also if I Cant be permited to rase a Shool Down there & on what turm I Could be admited to Do so No more At present Dear Hon Sir

SOURCE: *Freedom: A Documentary History of Emancipation, 1861–1867*, ser. 1, vol. 1, *The Destruction of Slavery*, 386, by Ira Berlin, Joseph P. Reidy, and Leslie S. Rowland, eds. Copyright © 1985. Reprinted with the permission of Cambridge University Press.

DOCUMENT 2
Report from Reverend A. B. Randall, February 28, 1865

Freedom prompted ex-slaves to seek legal marriages, which under slavery had been impossible. Writing from Little Rock, Arkansas, to the adjutant general of the Union army, A. B. Randall, the white chaplain of a black regiment, affirmed the importance of marriage to freed slaves and emphasized their conviction that emancipation was only the first step toward full freedom.

Weddings, just now, are very popular, and abundant among the Colored People. They have just learned, of the Special Order No. 15. of Gen Thomas [Adjutant General Lorenzo Thomas] by which, they may not only be lawfully married, but have their Marriage Certificates, Recorded; in a book furnished by the Government. This is most desirable. . . . Those who were captured . . . at Ivy's Ford, on the 17th of January, by Col Brooks, had their Marriage Certificates, taken from them; and destroyed; and then were roundly cursed, for having such papers in their posession. I have married, during the month, at this Post; Twenty five couples; mostly, those, who have families; & have been living together for years. I try to dissuade single men, who are soldiers, from marrying, till their time of enlistment is out: as that course seems to me, to be most judicious. The Colord People here, generally consider, this war not only; their exodus, from bondage; but the road, to Responsibility; Competency; and an honorable Citizenship — God grant that their hopes and expectations may be fully realized.

SOURCE: *Freedom: A Documentary History of Emancipation, 1861–1867*, ser. 2, vol. 1, *The Black Military Experience*, 712, by Ira Berlin, Joseph P. Reidy, and Leslie S. Rowland, eds. Copyright © 1982. Reprinted with the permission of Cambridge University Press.

DOCUMENT 3
Petition "to the Union Convention of Tennessee Assembled in the Capitol at Nashville," January 9, 1865

Early efforts at political reconstruction prompted petitions from former slaves and free blacks demanding civil and political rights. In January 1865, black Tennesseans petitioned a convention of white Unionists debating the reorganization of state government.

We the undersigned petitioners, American citizens of African descent, natives and residents of Tennessee, and devoted friends of the great National cause, do most respectfully ask a patient hearing of your honorable body in regard to matters deeply affecting the future condition of our unfortunate and long suffering race.

First of all, however, we would say that words are too weak to tell how profoundly grateful we are to the Federal Government for the good work of freedom which it is gradually carrying forward; and for the Emancipation Proclamation which has set free all the slaves in some of the rebellious States, as well as many of the slaves in Tennessee. . . .

We claim freedom, as our natural right, and ask that in harmony and co-operation with the nation at large, you should cut up by the roots the system of slavery, which is not only a wrong to us, but the source of all the evil which at present afflicts the State. For slavery, corrupt itself, corrupted nearly all, also, around it, so that it has influenced nearly all the slave States to rebel against the Federal Government, in order to set up a government of pirates under which slavery might be perpetrated.

In the contest between the nation and slavery, our unfortunate people have sided, by instinct, with the former. We have little fortune to devote to the national cause, for a hard fate has hitherto forced us to live in poverty, but we do devote to its success, our hopes, our toils, our whole heart, our sacred honor, and our lives. We will work, pray, live, and, if need be, die for the Union, as cheerfully as ever a white patriot died for his country. The color of our skin does not lessen in the least degree, our love either for God or for the land of our birth. . . .

We know the burdens of citizenship, and are ready to bear them. We know the duties of the good citizen, and are ready to perform them cheerfully, and would ask to be put in a position in which we can discharge them more effectually. . . .

This is a democracy — a government of the people. It should aim to make every man, without regard to the color of his skin, the amount of his wealth, or the character of his religious faith, feel personally interested in its welfare. Every man who lives under the Government should feel that it is his property, his treasure, the bulwark and defence of himself and his family, his pearl of great price, which he must preserve, protect, and defend faithfully at all times, on all occasions, in every possible manner.

This is not a Democratic Government if a numerous, law-abiding, industrious, and useful class of citizens, born and bred on the soil, are to be treated as aliens and enemies, as an inferior degraded class, who must have no voice in the Government which they support, protect and defend, with all their heart, soul, mind, and body, both in peace and war. . . .

The possibility that the negro suffrage proposition may shock popular prejudice at first sight, is not a conclusive argument against its wisdom and policy. No proposition ever met with more furious or general opposition than the one to enlist colored soldiers in the United States army. The opponents of the measure exclaimed on all hands that the negro was a coward; that he would not fight; that one white man, with a whip in his hand could put to flight a regiment of them; that the experiment would end in the utter rout and ruin of the Federal army. Yet the colored man has fought so well, on almost every occasion, that the rebel government is prevented, only by its fears and distrust of being able to force him to fight for slavery as well as he fights against it, from putting half a million of negroes into its ranks.

The Government has asked the colored man to fight for its preservation and gladly has he done it. It can afford to trust him with a vote as safely as it trusted him with a bayonet.

SOURCE: *Freedom: A Documentary History of Emancipation, 1861–1867*, ser. 2, vol. 1, *The Black Military Experience*, 811–16, by Ira Berlin, Joseph P. Reidy, and Leslie S. Rowland, eds. Copyright © 1982. Reprinted with the permission of Cambridge University Press.

Questions for Analysis and Debate

1. How does John Q. A. Dennis interpret his responsibility as a father?

2. Why do you think ex-slaves wanted their marriages legalized?

3. Why, according to petitioners to the Union Convention of Tennessee, did blacks deserve voting rights?

and Methodists. Freedmen interpreted the events of the Civil War and reconstruction as Christian people. One black woman thanked Lincoln for the Emancipation Proclamation, declaring, "When you are dead and in Heaven, in a thousand years that action of yours will make the Angels sing your praises I know it."

Q: Why did Congress object to Lincoln's wartime plan for reconstruction?

Presidential Reconstruction

Abraham Lincoln died on April 15, 1865, just hours after John Wilkes Booth shot him at a Washington, D.C., theater. Chief Justice Salmon P. Chase immediately administered the oath of office to Vice President **Andrew Johnson** of Tennessee. Congress had adjourned in March and would not reconvene until December. Throughout the summer and fall, the "accidental president" made critical decisions about the future of the South without congressional advice. With dizzying speed, he drew up and executed a plan of reconstruction.

Congress returned to the capital in December to find that, as far as the president and former Confederates were concerned, reconstruction was completed. Most Republicans, however, thought Johnson's puny demands of ex-rebels made a mockery of the sacrifice of Union soldiers. Instead of honoring the dead by insisting on "a new birth of freedom," as Lincoln had promised in his 1863 speech at Gettysburg, Johnson had acted as midwife to the rebirth of the Old South and the stillbirth of black liberty. They proceeded to dismantle Johnson's program and substitute a program of their own.

Johnson's Program of Reconciliation Born in 1808 in Raleigh, North Carolina, Andrew Johnson was the son of illiterate parents. Self-educated and ambitious, Johnson moved to Tennessee, where he worked as a tailor, accumulated a fortune in land, acquired five slaves, and built a career in politics championing the South's common white people and assailing its "illegitimate, swaggering, bastard, scrub aristocracy." The only senator from a Confederate state to remain loyal to the Union, Johnson held the planter class responsible for secession. Less than two weeks before he became president, he announced what he would do to planters if he ever had the chance: "I would arrest them — I would try them — I would convict them and I would hang them."

Despite such statements, Johnson was no friend of the Republicans. A Democrat all his life,

Johnson occupied the White House only because the Republican Party in 1864 had needed a vice presidential candidate who would appeal to loyal, Union-supporting Democrats. Johnson vigorously defended states' rights (but not secession) and opposed Republican efforts to expand the power of the federal government. A steadfast supporter of slavery, Johnson had owned slaves until 1862, when Tennessee rebels, angry at his Unionism, confiscated them. When he grudgingly accepted emancipation, it was more because he hated planters than sympathized with slaves. "Damn the negroes," he said. "I am fighting those traitorous aristocrats, their masters." At a time when the nation confronted the future of black Americans, the new president harbored unshakable racist convictions. Africans, Johnson said, were "inferior to the white man in point of intellect — better calculated in physical structure to undergo drudgery and hardship."

Like Lincoln, Johnson stressed the rapid restoration of civil government in the South. Like Lincoln, he promised to pardon most, but not all, ex-rebels. Johnson recognized the state governments created by Lincoln but set out his own requirements for restoring the other rebel states to the Union. All that the citizens of a state had to do was to renounce the right of secession, deny that the debts of the Confederacy were legal and binding, and ratify the Thirteenth Amendment abolishing slavery, which became part of the Constitution in December 1865.

Johnson's eagerness to restore relations with southern states and his lack of sympathy for blacks also led him to return to pardoned ex-Confederates all confiscated and abandoned land, even if it was in the hands of freedmen. Reformers were shocked. They had expected the president's hatred of planters to mean the permanent confiscation of the South's plantations and the distribution of the land to loyal freedmen. Instead, his instructions canceled the promising beginnings made by General Sherman and the Freedmen's Bureau to settle blacks on land of their own. As one freedman observed, "Things was hurt by Mr. Lincoln getting killed."

White Southern Resistance and Black Codes In the summer of 1865, delegates across the South gathered to draw up the new state constitutions required by Johnson's plan of reconstruction. Rather than take their medicine, delegates choked on even the president's mild requirements. Refusing to renounce secession, the South Carolina and Georgia conventions merely "repudiated" their secession ordinances, preserving in principle their right to secede. South Carolina and Mississippi refused to disown their Confederate

The Black Codes Titled "Selling a Freeman to Pay His Fine at Monticello, Florida," this 1867 drawing from a northern magazine equates black codes with the reinstitution of slavery. The laws stopped short of reenslavement but sharply restricted blacks' freedom. In Florida, as in other southern states, certain acts, such as breaking a labor contract, were made criminal offenses, the penalty for which could be involuntary plantation labor for a year. Granger Collection.

war debts. Mississippi rejected the Thirteenth Amendment outright, and Alabama rejected it in part. Despite these defiant acts, Johnson did nothing. White Southerners began to think that by standing up for themselves they—not victorious Northerners—would shape reconstruction.

State governments across the South adopted a series of laws known as **black codes**, which made a travesty of black freedom. The codes sought to keep ex-slaves subordinate to whites by subjecting them to every sort of discrimination. Several states made it illegal for blacks to own a gun. Mississippi made insulting gestures and language by blacks a criminal offense. The codes barred blacks from jury duty. Not a single southern state granted any black the right to vote.

At the core of the black codes, however, lay the matter of labor. Faced with the death of slavery, legislators sought to hustle freedmen back to the plantations. South Carolina attempted to limit

blacks to either farmwork or domestic service by requiring them to pay annual taxes of $10 to $100 to work in any other occupation. Mississippi declared that blacks who did not possess written evidence of employment could be declared vagrants and be subject to involuntary plantation labor. Under so-called apprenticeship laws, courts bound thousands of black children—orphans and others whose parents they deemed unable to support them—to work for planter "guardians."

Johnson refused to intervene. A staunch defender of states' rights, he believed that the citizens of every state should be free to write their own constitutions and laws. Moreover, Johnson was as eager as other white Southerners to restore white supremacy and black subordination.

But Johnson also followed the path that he believed offered him the greatest political return. A conservative Tennessee Democrat at the head of a northern Republican Party, he began to look southward for political allies. By pardoning powerful whites, by accepting governments even when they failed to satisfy his minimal demands, and by acquiescing in the black codes, he won useful southern friends.

In the fall elections of 1865, white Southerners dramatically expressed their mood. To represent them in Congress, they chose former Confederates. Of the eighty senators and representatives they sent to Washington, fifteen had served in the Confederate army, ten of them as generals. Another sixteen had served in civil and judicial posts in the Confederacy. Nine others had served in the Confederate Congress. One—Alexander Stephens—had been vice president of the Confederacy. As one Georgian remarked, "It looked as though Richmond had moved to Washington."

Expansion of Federal Authority and Black Rights Southerners had blundered monumentally. They had assumed that what Andrew Johnson was willing to accept, Republicans would accept as well. But southern intransigence compelled even moderates to conclude that ex-rebels were a "generation of vipers," still untrustworthy

and dangerous. So angry were Republicans with the rebels that the federal government refused to supply artificial limbs to disabled Southerners, as they did for Union veterans.

The black codes became a symbol of southern intentions to "restore all of slavery but its name." Northerners were hardly saints when it came to racial justice, but black freedom had become a hallowed war aim. "We tell the white men of Mississippi," the *Chicago Tribune* roared, "that the men of the North will convert the State of Mississippi into a frog pond before they will allow such laws to disgrace one foot of the soil in which the bones of our soldiers sleep and over which the flag of freedom waves."

The moderate majority of the Republican Party wanted only assurance that slavery and treason were dead. They did not champion black equality, the confiscation of plantations, or black voting, as did the radicals. But southern obstinacy had succeeded in forging unity (at least temporarily) among Republican factions. In December 1865, exercising Congress's right to determine the qualifications of its members, Republicans refused to seat the southern representatives elected in the fall elections. Rather than accept Johnson's claim that

THE PROMISE OF TECHNOLOGY

Artificial Limbs Approximately 45,000 of the 60,000 Civil War amputees survived. After the war, the great demand for artificial limbs prompted businesses to apply industrial manufacturing processes to limbs. The search for a functional, lightweight artificial limb drew on a number of advancing fields, including photography, physiology, physics, material science, mathematics, and psychology. Artificial limbs advanced quickly from crude peg legs to hollow willow legs with movable ankles that simulated the natural motions of the foot. Newly invented vulcanized rubber (called India rubber) increased strength and flexibility and allowed disabled veterans to dispense with metal bolts and springs in their new limbs. These "before and after" images of a veteran with and without his artificial legs from an A. A. Marks business card in about 1878 sent a clear message: Marks legs make maimed men whole again. Marks promised that, thus restored, the wounded man would be the "equal of his fellowmen in every employment of life." Warshaw Collection, National Museum of American History, Smithsonian Institution.

the "work of restoration" was done, Congress challenged his executive power.

Republican senator Lyman Trumbull declared that the president's policy meant that an ex-slave would "be tyrannized over, abused, and virtually reenslaved without some legislation by the nation for his protection." Early in 1866, the moderates produced two bills that strengthened the federal shield. The first, the Freedmen's Bureau bill, prolonged the life of the agency established by the previous Congress. It had distributed food, supervised labor contracts, and sponsored schools for freedmen. Arguing that the Constitution never contemplated a "system for the support of indigent persons," President Andrew Johnson vetoed the bill. Congress failed by a narrow margin to override the president's veto.

The moderates designed their second measure, the **Civil Rights Act**, to nullify the black codes by affirming African Americans' rights to "full and equal benefit of all laws and proceedings for the security of person and property as is enjoyed by white citizens." The act boldly required the end of racial discrimination in state laws and represented an extraordinary expansion of black rights and federal authority. The president argued that the civil rights bill amounted to "unconstitutional invasion of states' rights" and vetoed it. In essence, he denied that the federal government possessed the authority to protect the civil rights of blacks.

In April 1866, an incensed Republican Party again pushed the civil rights bill through Congress and overrode the presidential veto. In July, it passed another Freedmen's Bureau bill and overrode Johnson's veto. For the first time in American history, Congress had overridden presidential vetoes of major legislation. As a worried South Carolinian observed, Johnson had succeeded in uniting the Republicans and probably touched off "a fight this fall such as has never been seen."

Q: How did the North respond to the passage of black codes in the southern states?

Congressional Reconstruction

By the summer of 1866, President Andrew Johnson and Congress had dropped their gloves and stood toe-to-toe in a bare-knuckle contest unprecedented in American history. Johnson made it clear that he would not budge on either constitutional issues or policy. Moderate Republicans responded by amending the Constitution. But the obstinacy of Johnson and white Southerners pushed Republican moderates ever closer to the radicals and to

acceptance of additional federal intervention in the South. Congress also voted to impeach the president. In time, Congress debated whether to make voting rights color-blind, while women sought to make voting sex-blind as well.

The Fourteenth Amendment and Escalating Violence In June 1866, Congress passed the **Fourteenth Amendment** to the Constitution, and two years later it gained the necessary ratification of three-fourths of the states. The most important provisions of this complex amendment made all native-born or naturalized persons American citizens and prohibited states from abridging the "privileges and immunities" of citizens, depriving them of "life, liberty, or property without due process of law," and denying them "equal protection of the laws." By making blacks national citizens, the amendment provided a national guarantee of equality before the law. In essence, it protected blacks against violation by southern state governments.

The Fourteenth Amendment also dealt with voting rights. It gave Congress the right to reduce the congressional representation of states that withheld suffrage from some of its adult male population. In other words, white Southerners could either allow black men to vote or see their representation in Washington slashed. Whatever happened, Republicans stood to benefit from the Fourteenth Amendment. If southern whites granted voting rights to freedmen, Republicans would gain valuable black votes. If whites refused, representation of southern Democrats would plunge.

The Fourteenth Amendment's suffrage provisions ignored the small band of politicized women who had emerged from the war demanding "the ballot for the two disenfranchised classes, negroes and women." Founding the **American Equal Rights Association** in 1866, **Susan B. Anthony** and **Elizabeth Cady Stanton** lobbied for "a government by the people, and the whole people; for the people and the whole people." They felt betrayed when their old antislavery allies refused to work for their goals. "It was the Negro's hour," Frederick Douglass explained. Senator Charles Sumner suggested that woman suffrage could be "the great question of the future."

The Fourteenth Amendment provided for punishment of any state that excluded voters on the basis of race but not on the basis of sex. The amendment also introduced the word *male* into the Constitution when it referred to a citizen's right to vote. Stanton predicted that "if that word 'male' be inserted, it will take us a century at least to get it out."

Tennessee approved the Fourteenth Amendment in July, and Congress promptly welcomed

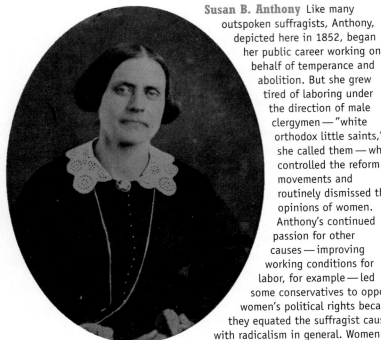

Susan B. Anthony Like many outspoken suffragists, Anthony, depicted here in 1852, began her public career working on behalf of temperance and abolition. But she grew tired of laboring under the direction of male clergymen—"white orthodox little saints," she called them—who controlled the reform movements and routinely dismissed the opinions of women. Anthony's continued passion for other causes—improving working conditions for labor, for example—led some conservatives to oppose women's political rights because they equated the suffragist cause with radicalism in general. Women could not easily overcome such views, and the long struggle for the vote eventually drew millions of women into public life. Susan B. Anthony House, Inc.

the state's representatives and senators back. Had President Johnson counseled other southern states to ratify this relatively mild amendment and warned them that they faced the fury of an outraged Republican Party if they refused, they might have listened. Instead, Johnson advised Southerners to reject the Fourteenth Amendment and to rely on him to trounce the Republicans in the fall congressional elections.

Johnson had decided to make the Fourteenth Amendment the overriding issue of the 1866 elections and to gather its white opponents into a new conservative party, the National Union Party. The president's strategy suffered a setback when whites in several southern cities went on rampages against blacks. When a mob in New Orleans assaulted delegates to a black suffrage convention, thirty-four blacks died. In Memphis, white mobs killed at least forty-six people. The slaughter shocked Northerners and renewed skepticism about Johnson's claim that southern whites could be trusted. "Who doubts that the Freedmen's Bureau ought to be abolished forthwith," a New Yorker observed sarcastically, "and the blacks remitted to the

Reconstruction Military Districts, 1867

paternal care of their old masters, who 'understand the nigger, you know, a great deal better than the Yankees can.'"

The 1866 elections resulted in an overwhelming Republican victory. Johnson had bet that Northerners would not support federal protection of black rights and that a racist backlash would blast the Republican Party. But the war was still fresh in northern minds, and as one Republican explained, southern whites "with all their intelligence were traitors, the blacks with all their ignorance were loyal."

Radical Reconstruction and Military Rule

When Johnson continued to urge Southerners to reject the Fourteenth Amendment, every southern state except Tennessee voted it down. "The last one of the sinful ten," thundered Representative James A. Garfield of Ohio, "has flung back into our teeth the magnanimous offer of a generous nation." After the South rejected the moderates' program, the radicals seized the initiative.

Each act of defiance by southern whites had boosted the standing of the radicals within the Republican Party. Except for freedmen themselves, no one did more to make freedom the "mighty moral question of the age." Radicals such as Massachusetts senator Charles Sumner and Pennsylvania representative Thaddeus Stevens did not speak with a single voice, but they united in demanding civil and political equality. Southern states were "like clay in the hands of the potter," Stevens declared in January 1867, and he called on Congress to begin reconstruction all over again.

In March 1867, Congress overturned the Johnson state governments and initiated military rule of the South. The **Military Reconstruction Act** (and three subsequent acts) divided the ten unreconstructed Confederate states into five military districts. Congress placed a Union general in charge of each district and instructed him to "suppress insurrection, disorder, and violence" and to begin political reform. After the military had completed voter registration, which would include black men, voters in each state would elect delegates to conventions that would draw up new state constitutions. Each constitution would guarantee black suffrage. When the voters of each state had approved the constitution and the state legislature had ratified the Fourteenth Amendment, the state could submit its work to Congress. If Congress approved, the state's senators and representatives could be seated, and political reunification would be accomplished.

Radicals proclaimed the provision for black suffrage "a prodigious triumph," for it extended far beyond the limited suffrage provisions of the Fourteenth Amendment. Republicans now believed that only the voting power of ex-slaves could bring about a permanent revolution in the South. When combined with the disfranchisement of thousands of ex-rebels, it promised to cripple any neo-Confederate resurgence and guarantee Republican state governments in the South.

Despite its bold suffrage provision, the Military Reconstruction Act of 1867 disappointed those who also advocated the confiscation and redistribution of southern plantations to ex-slaves. Thaddeus Stevens agreed with the freedman who said, "Give us our own land and we take care of ourselves, but without land, the old masters can hire us or starve us, as they please." But most Republicans believed they had provided blacks with what they needed: equal legal rights and the ballot. If blacks were to get land, they would have to gain it themselves.

Declaring that he would rather sever his right arm than sign such a formula for "anarchy and chaos," Andrew Johnson vetoed the Military Reconstruction Act. Congress overrode his veto,

dramatizing the shift in power from the executive to the legislative branch of government. With the passage of the Reconstruction Acts of 1867, congressional reconstruction was virtually completed. Congress left whites owning most of the South's land but, in a departure that justified the term "radical reconstruction," had given black men the ballot. In 1867, the nation began an unprecedented experiment in interracial democracy—at least in the South, for Congress's plan did not touch the North. But before the spotlight swung away from Washington to the South, the president and Congress had one more scene to play.

Impeaching a President Despite his defeats, Andrew Johnson had no intention of yielding control of reconstruction. In a dozen ways, he sabotaged Congress's will and encouraged southern whites to resist. He issued a flood of pardons, waged war against the Freedmen's Bureau, and replaced Union generals eager to enforce Congress's Reconstruction Acts with conservative men eager to defeat them. Johnson claimed that he was merely defending the "violated Constitution." At bottom, however, the president subverted congressional reconstruction to protect southern whites from what he considered the horrors of "Negro domination."

THIS LITTLE BOY WOULD PERSIST IN HANDLING BOOKS ABOVE HIS CAPACITY.

AND THIS WAS THE DISASTROUS RESULT.

Andrew Johnson Cartoon Appearing in 1868 during President Andrew Johnson's impeachment trial, this cartoon includes captions that read: "This little boy would persist in handling books above his capacity" and "And this was the disastrous result." The cartoonist's portrait of Johnson being crushed by the Constitution refers to the president's flouting of the Tenure of Office Act, which caused Republicans to vote for his impeachment. The cartoon's celebration of Johnson's destruction proved premature, however. Granger Collection.

According to the Constitution, the House of Representatives can impeach and the Senate can try any federal official for "treason, bribery, or other high crimes and misdemeanors." Radicals argued that Johnson's abuse of constitutional powers and his failure to fulfill constitutional obligations to enforce the law were impeachable offenses. But moderates interpreted the constitutional provision to mean violation of criminal statutes. As long as Johnson refrained from breaking the law, **impeachment** (the process of formal charges of wrongdoing against the president or other federal official) remained stalled.

Then in August 1867, Johnson suspended secretary of war Edwin M. Stanton from office. As required by the Tenure of Office Act, which demanded the approval of the Senate for the removal of any government official who had been appointed with Senate approval, the president requested the Senate to consent to the dismissal. When the Senate balked, Johnson removed Stanton anyway. "Is the President crazy, or only drunk?" asked a dumbfounded Republican moderate. "I'm afraid his doings will make us all favor impeachment."

News of Johnson's open defiance of the law convinced every Republican in the House to vote for a resolution impeaching the president. Supreme Court chief justice Salmon Chase presided over the Senate trial, which lasted from March until May 1868. Chase refused to allow Johnson's opponents to raise broad issues of misuse of power and forced them to argue their case exclusively on the narrow legal grounds of Johnson's removal of Stanton. Johnson's lawyers argued that the president had not committed a criminal offense, that the Tenure of Office Act was unconstitutional, and that in any case it did not apply to Stanton, who had been appointed by Lincoln. When the critical vote came, thirty-five senators voted guilty and nineteen not guilty. The impeachment forces fell one vote short of the two-thirds needed to convict.

After his trial, Johnson called a truce, and for the remaining ten months of his term, congressional reconstruction proceeded unhindered by presidential interference. Without interference from Johnson, Congress revisited the suffrage issue.

The Fifteenth Amendment and Women's Demands

In February 1869, Republicans passed the **Fifteenth Amendment** to the Constitution, which prohibited states from depriving any citizen of the right to vote because of "race, color, or previous condition of servitude." The Reconstruction Acts of 1867 already required black suffrage in the South; the Fifteenth Amendment extended black voting nationwide.

Some Republicans, however, found the final wording of the Fifteenth Amendment "lame and halting." Rather than absolutely guaranteeing the right to vote, the amendment merely prohibited exclusion on grounds of race. The distinction would prove to be significant. In time, white Southerners would devise tests of literacy and property and other apparently nonracial measures that would effectively disfranchise blacks yet not violate the Fifteenth Amendment. But an amendment that fully guaranteed the right to vote courted defeat outside the South. Rising antiforeign sentiment—against the Chinese in California and European immigrants in the Northeast—caused states to resist giving up total control of suffrage requirements. In March 1870, after three-fourths of the states had ratified it, the Fifteenth Amendment became part of the Constitution. Republicans generally breathed a sigh of relief, confident that black suffrage was "the last great point that remained to be settled of the issues of the war."

Woman suffrage advocates, however, were sorely disappointed with the Fifteenth Amendment's failure to extend voting rights to women. The amendment denied states the right to forbid suffrage only on the basis of race. Elizabeth Cady Stanton and Susan B. Anthony condemned the Republicans' "negro first" strategy and pointed out that women remained "the only class of citizens wholly unrepresented in the government." Stanton wondered aloud why ignorant black men should legislate for educated and cultured white women. Increasingly, activist women concluded that woman "must not put her trust in man." The Fifteenth Amendment severed the early feminist movement from its abolitionist roots. Over the next several decades, feminists established an independent suffrage crusade that drew millions of women into political life.

Republicans took enough satisfaction in the Fifteenth Amendment to promptly scratch the "Negro question" from the agenda of national politics. Even that steadfast crusader for equality Wendell Phillips concluded that the black man now held "sufficient shield in his own hands. . . . Whatever he suffers will be largely now, and in future, his own fault." Northerners had no idea of the violent struggles that lay ahead.

Q: **Why did Johnson urge the southern states to reject the Fourteenth Amendment?**

The Struggle in the South

Northerners believed they had discharged their responsibilities with the Reconstruction Acts and the amendments to the Constitution, but

Southerners knew that the battle had just begun. Black suffrage established the foundation for the rise of the Republican Party in the South. Gathering together outsiders and outcasts, southern Republicans won elections, wrote new state constitutions, and formed new state governments.

Challenging the established class for political control was dangerous business. Equally dangerous were the confrontations that took place on southern farms and plantations, where blacks sought to give economic meaning to their newly won legal and political equality. Ex-masters had their own ideas about the labor system that should replace slavery. Freedom remained contested territory, and Southerners fought pitched battles with one another to determine the contours of their new world.

Freedmen, Yankees, and Yeomen African Americans made up the majority of southern Republicans. After gaining voting rights in 1867, nearly all eligible black men registered to vote as Republicans, grateful to the party that had freed them and granted them the franchise. Southern blacks did not have identical political priorities, but they united in their desire for education and equal treatment before the law.

Northern whites who made the South their home after the war were a second element of the South's Republican Party. Conservative white Southerners called them **carpetbaggers**, men so poor that they could stuff all their earthly belongings in a single carpet-sided suitcase and swoop southward like buzzards to "fatten on our misfortunes." But most Northerners who moved south were young men who looked upon the South as they did the West—as a promising place to make a living. Northerners in the southern Republican Party consistently supported programs that encouraged vigorous economic development along the lines of the northern free-labor model.

Southern whites made up the third element of the South's Republican Party. Approximately one out of four white Southerners voted Republican. The other three condemned the one who did as a traitor to his region and his race and called him a **scalawag**, a term for runty horses and low-down, good-for-nothing rascals. Yeoman farmers accounted for the majority of southern white Republicans. Some were Unionists who emerged from the war with bitter memories of Confederate persecution. Others were small farmers who wanted to end state governments' favoritism toward plantation owners. Yeomen supported initiatives for public schools and for expanding economic opportunity in the South.

The South's Republican Party, then, was made up of freedmen, Yankees, and yeomen—an improbable coalition. The mix of races, regions, and classes inevitably meant friction as each group maneuvered to define the party. But Reconstruction represents an extraordinary moment in American politics: Blacks and whites joined together in the Republican Party to pursue political change. Formally, of course, only men participated in politics—casting ballots and holding offices—but white and black women also played a part in the political struggle by joining in parades and rallies, attending stump speeches, and even campaigning.

Reconstruction politics was not for cowards. Most whites in the South condemned southern Republicans as illegitimate and felt justified in doing whatever they could to stamp them out. Violence against blacks—the "white terror"—took brutal institutional form in 1866 with the formation in Tennessee of the **Ku Klux Klan**, a social club of Confederate veterans that quickly developed into a paramilitary organization supporting Democrats. The Klan went on a rampage of whipping, hanging, shooting, burning, and throat-cutting to defeat Republicans and restore white supremacy. Rapid demobilization of the Union army after the war left only twenty thousand troops to patrol the entire South. Without effective military protection, southern Republicans had to take care of themselves.

Republican Rule In the fall of 1867, southern states held elections for delegates to state constitutional conventions, as required by the Reconstruction Acts. About 40 percent of the white electorate stayed home because they had been disfranchised or because they had decided to boycott politics. Republicans won three-fourths of the seats. About 15 percent of the Republican delegates to the conventions were Northerners who had moved south, 25 percent were African Americans, and 60 percent were white Southerners. As a British visitor observed, the delegate elections reflected "the mighty revolution that had taken place in America."

The reconstruction constitutions introduced two broad categories of changes in the South: those that reduced aristocratic privilege and increased democratic equality and those that expanded the state's responsibility for the general welfare. In the first category, the constitutions adopted universal male suffrage, abolished property qualifications for holding office, and made more offices elective and fewer appointed. In the second category, they

> Conservative white Southerners called them "carpetbaggers," men so poor that they could stuff all their earthly belongings in a single carpet-sided suitcase and swoop southward like buzzards to "fatten on our misfortunes."

enacted prison reform; made the state responsible for caring for orphans, the insane, and the deaf and mute; and exempted debtors' homes from seizure.

To Democrats, however, these forward-looking state constitutions looked like wild revolution. They were blind to the fact that no constitution confiscated and redistributed land, as virtually every former slave wished, or disfranchised ex-rebels wholesale, as most southern Unionists advocated. And Democrats were convinced that the new constitutions initiated "Negro domination" in politics. In fact, although four out of five Republican voters were black men, more than four out of five Republican officeholders were white. Southerners sent fourteen black congressmen and two black senators to Washington, but only 6 percent of Southerners in Congress during Reconstruction were black (Figure 16.1). And no state legislature experienced "Negro rule," despite black majorities in the populations of some states.

Southern voters ratified the new constitutions and swept Republicans into power. When the former Confederate states ratified the Fourteenth Amendment, Congress readmitted them. Southern Republicans then turned to a staggering array of problems. Wartime destruction—burned cities, shattered bridges, broken levees—littered the landscape. Manufacturing limped along, and agricultural production remained anemic. The region's railroads lay devastated. Making matters worse, racial harassment and reactionary violence dogged Southerners who sought reform. In this desperate context, Republicans struggled to breathe life into the region.

Activity focused on three areas—education, civil rights, and economic development. Every state inaugurated a system of public education. Before the Civil War, whites had deliberately kept slaves illiterate, and planter-dominated governments rarely spent tax money to educate the children of yeomen. By 1875, half of Mississippi's and South Carolina's eligible children (the majority of whom were black) were attending school. Although schools were underfunded, literacy rates rose sharply. Public schools were racially segregated, but education remained for many blacks a tangible, deeply satisfying benefit of freedom and Republican rule.

State legislatures also attacked racial discrimination and defended civil rights. Republicans especially resisted efforts to segregate blacks from whites in public transportation. Mississippi levied fines of up to $1,000 and three years in jail for railroads and steamboats that pushed blacks into "smoking cars" or to lower decks. A Mississippian complained: "Money cannot buy for a colored man or woman decent treatment and the comforts that white people claim and can obtain." But passing color-blind laws was one thing; enforcing them was another. Despite the laws, segregation—later called Jim Crow—developed at white insistence and became a feature of southern life long before the end of the Reconstruction era.

Republican governments also launched ambitious programs of economic development. They envisioned a South of diversified agriculture, roaring factories, and booming towns. State legislatures chartered scores of banks and industrial companies, appropriated funds to fix ruined levees and drain swamps, and went on a railroad-building binge. These efforts fell far short of solving the South's economic troubles, however. Republican spending to stimulate economic growth also meant rising taxes and enormous debt that drained funds from schools and other programs.

The southern Republicans' record, then, was mixed. To their credit, the biracial party took up an ambitious agenda to change the South. Money was scarce, the Democrats continued their harassment, and factionalism threatened the Republican Party from within. However, corruption infected Republican governments in the South. Public morality reached new lows everywhere in the nation after the Civil War, and the chaos of the postwar South proved fertile soil for bribery, fraud, and influence peddling. Despite shortcomings, however, the Republican Party made headway in its efforts to purge the South of aristocratic privilege and racist oppression. Republican governments had less success in overthrowing the long-established white oppression of black farm laborers in the rural South.

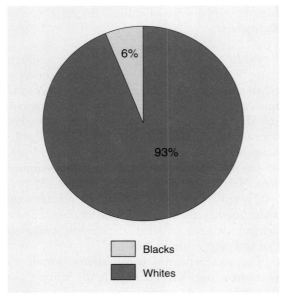

FIGURE 16.1 Southern Congressional Delegations, 1865–1877
The statistics contradict the myth of black domination of congressional representation during Reconstruction.

White Landlords, Black Sharecroppers

Ex-slaves who wished to escape slave labor and ex-masters who wanted to reinstitute old ways clashed repeatedly. Except for having to pay subsistence wages, planters had not been required to offer many concessions to emancipation. They continued to believe that African Americans would not work without coercion. Whites moved quickly to restore the antebellum world of work gangs, white overseers, field labor for black women and children, clustered cabins, minimal personal freedom, and even whipping whenever they could get away with it.

Ex-slaves resisted every effort to turn back the clock. They argued that if any class could be described as "lazy," it was the planters, who, as one ex-slave noted, "lived in idleness all their lives on stolen labor." Land of their own would anchor their economic independence, they believed, and end planters' interference in their personal lives. They could then, for example, make their own decisions about whether women and children would labor in the fields. Indeed, within months after the war, perhaps one-third of black women abandoned field labor to work on chores in their own cabins just as poor white women did. Hundreds of thousands of black children enrolled in school. But without their own land, ex-slaves had little choice but to work on plantations.

Although forced to return to the planters' fields, freedmen resisted efforts to restore slavelike conditions. Instead of working for wages, a South Carolinian observed, "the negroes all seem disposed to rent land," which increased their independence from whites. Out of this tug-of-war between white landlords and black laborers emerged a new system of southern agriculture.

Sharecropping was a compromise that offered both ex-masters and ex-slaves something but satisfied neither. Under the new system, planters divided their cotton plantations into small farms that freedmen rented, paying with a share of each year's crop, usually half. Sharecropping gave blacks more freedom than the system of wages and labor gangs and released them from the day-to-day supervision of whites. Black families abandoned the old slave quarters and scattered over plantations, building separate cabins for themselves on the patches of land they rented (Map 16.1). Black families now decided who would work, for how long, and how hard. Still, most blacks remained dependent on white landlords, who had the power to expel them at the end of each growing season. For planters, sharecropping offered a way to resume agricultural production, but it did not allow them to restore the old slave plantation.

Sharecropping introduced a new figure—the country merchant—into the agricultural equation. Landlords supplied sharecroppers with land, mules,

Black Woman in Cotton Fields, Thomasville, Georgia Few images of everyday black women during the Reconstruction era survive. This photograph was taken in 1895, but it nevertheless goes to the heart of the labor struggle after the Civil War. Before emancipation, black women worked in the fields; after emancipation, white landlords wanted them to continue working there. Freedom allowed some women to escape field labor, but not this Georgian, who probably worked to survive. The photograph reveals a strong person with a clear sense of who she is. Though worn to protect her head and body from the fierce heat, her intricately wrapped headdress dramatically expresses her individuality. Her bare feet also reveal something about her life. Courtesy, Georgia Department of Archives and History, Atlanta, Georgia.

seeds, and tools, but blacks also needed credit to obtain essential food and clothing before they harvested their crops. Thousands of small crossroads stores sprang up to offer credit. Under an arrangement called a crop lien, a merchant would advance goods to a sharecropper in exchange for a lien, or legal claim, on the farmer's future crop. Some merchants charged exorbitant rates of interest, as much as 60 percent, on the goods they sold. At the end

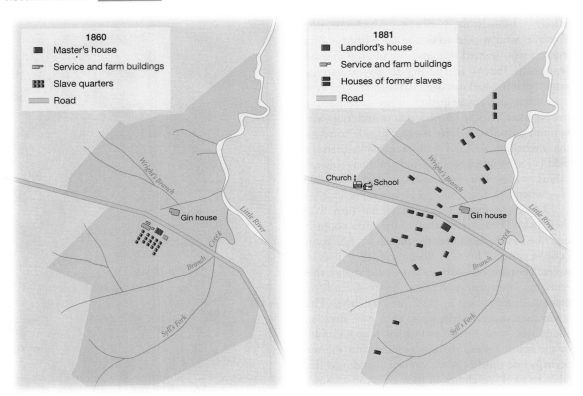

MAP 16.1 A Southern Plantation in 1860 and 1881

These maps of the Barrow plantation in Georgia illustrate some of the ways in which ex-slaves expressed their freedom. Freedmen and freedwomen deserted the clustered living quarters behind the master's house, scattered over the plantation, built family cabins, and farmed rented land. The former Barrow slaves also worked together to build a school and a church.

READING THE MAP: Compare the number and size of the slave quarters in 1860 with the homes of the former slaves in 1881. How do they differ? Which buildings were prominently located along the road in 1860, and which could be found along the road in 1881?

CONNECTIONS: How might the former master feel about the new configuration of buildings on the plantation in 1881? In what ways did the new system of sharecropping replicate the old system of plantation agriculture? In what ways was it different?

FOR MORE HELP ANALYZING THIS MAP, see the map activity for this chapter in the Online Study Guide at bedfordstmartins.com/roarkcompact.

of the growing season, after the landlord had taken half of the farmer's crop for rent, the merchant took most of the rest. Sometimes, the farmer's debt to the merchant exceeded the income he received from his remaining half of the crop, and the farmer would have no choice but to borrow more from the merchant and begin the cycle all over again.

An experiment at first, sharecropping spread quickly and soon dominated the cotton South. Lien merchants forced tenants to plant cotton, which was easy to sell, instead of food crops. The result was excessive production of cotton and falling cotton prices, developments that cost thousands of small white farmers their land and pushed them into the great army of sharecroppers. The new sharecropping system of agriculture took shape just as the political power of Republicans in the South began to buckle under Democratic pressure.

Q: Why was the Republican Party in the South a coalition party?

Reconstruction Collapses

By 1870, after a decade of war and reconstruction, Northerners wanted to put "the southern problem" behind them. Increasingly, practical, business-minded men came to the forefront of the Republican Party, replacing the band of reformers and idealists who had been prominent in the 1860s. While northern commitment to defend black freedom eroded, southern commitment to white supremacy intensified. Without northern protection, southern Republicans were no match for the Democrats' economic coercion, political corruption, and bloody violence. One by one, Republican state governments fell in the South. The election of 1876 both confirmed and completed the collapse of reconstruction.

Grant's Troubled Presidency In 1868, the Republican Party's presidential nomination went to Ulysses S. Grant, the North's favorite general. Hero of the Civil War and a supporter of congressional reconstruction, Grant was the obvious choice. His Democratic opponent, Horatio Seymour of New York, ran on a platform that blasted congressional reconstruction as "a flagrant usurpation of power . . . unconstitutional, revolutionary, and void." The Republicans answered by **waving the bloody shirt**—that is, they reminded voters that the Democrats were "the party of rebellion." During the campaign, the Ku Klux Klan erupted in a reign of terror across the South, murdering hundreds of Republicans. Violence cost Grant votes, but he gained a narrow 309,000-vote margin in the popular vote and a substantial victory (214 votes to 80) in the electoral college (Map 16.2).

Grant was not as good a president as he was a general. The talents he had demonstrated on the battlefield—decisiveness, clarity, and resolution—were less obvious in the White House. He surrounded himself with fumbling kinfolk

Grant and Scandal This anti-Grant cartoon by Thomas Nast, the nation's most celebrated political cartoonist, shows the president falling headfirst into the barrel of fraud and corruption that tainted his administration. During Grant's eight years in the White House, many members of his administration failed him. Sometimes duped, sometimes merely loyal, Grant stubbornly defended wrongdoers, even to the point of perjuring himself to keep an aide out of jail. Library of Congress.

FOR MORE HELP ANALYZING THIS IMAGE, see the visual activity for this chapter in the Online Study Guide at bedfordstmartins.com/roarkcompact.

Candidate	Electoral Vote	Popular Vote	Percent of Popular Vote
Ulysses S. Grant (Republican)	214	3,012,833	52.7
Horatio Seymour (Democrat)	80	2,703,249	47.3
Nonvoting states (Reconstruction)			

MAP 16.2 The Election of 1868

and old friends from his army days. He also made a string of dubious appointments that led to a series of damaging scandals. Charges of corruption tainted his vice president, Schuyler Colfax, and brought down two of his cabinet officers. Though never personally implicated in any scandal, Grant was aggravatingly naive and blind to the rot that filled his administration. Congressman James A. Garfield declared: "His imperturbability is amazing. I am in doubt whether to call it greatness or stupidity."

In 1872, anti-Grant Republicans bolted and launched the Liberal Party. To clean up the graft and corruption, Liberals proposed ending the spoils system, by which victorious parties rewarded loyal workers with public office, and replacing it with a nonpartisan civil service commission that would oversee competitive examinations for appointment to office. Liberals also demanded that the federal government remove its troops from the South and restore "home rule" (southern white control). Democrats liked the Liberals' southern policy and endorsed the Liberal presidential candidate, Horace Greeley, the longtime editor of the *New York Tribune*. The nation, however, still felt enormous affection for the man who had saved the Union and reelected Grant with 56 percent of the popular vote.

Grant's ambitions for his administration extended beyond reconstruction, but not even foreign affairs could escape the problems of the South. Grant coveted Santo Domingo in the Caribbean and argued that the acquisition of this tropical land would permit the United States to expand its trade and also provide a new home for the South's blacks, who were so desperately harassed by the Klan. Aggressive foreign policy had not originated with the Grant administration. Lincoln's and Johnson's secretary of state, William H. Seward, had thwarted French efforts to set up a puppet empire under Maximilian in Mexico, and his purchase of Alaska ("Seward's Ice Box") from Russia in 1867 for only $7 million fired Grant's imperialist ambition. But in the end, Grant could not convince Congress to approve the treaty annexing Santo Domingo. The South preoccupied Congress and undermined Grant's initiatives.

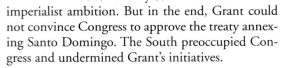

Grant's Proposed Annexation of the Dominican Republic

Northern Resolve Withers Although Grant genuinely wanted to see blacks' civil and political rights protected, he understood that most Northerners had grown weary of reconstruction and were increasingly willing to let southern whites manage their own affairs. Citizens wanted to shift their attention to other issues, especially after the nation slipped into a devastating economic depression in 1873. More than eighteen thousand businesses collapsed, leaving more than a million workers on the streets. Northern businessmen wanted to invest in the South but believed that recurrent federal intrusion was itself a major cause of instability in the region. Republican leaders began to question the wisdom of their party's alliance with the South's lower classes—its small farmers and sharecroppers. One member of Grant's administration proposed allying with the "thinking and influential native southerners . . . the intelligent, well-to-do, and controlling class."

Congress, too, wanted to leave reconstruction behind, but southern Republicans made that difficult. When the South's Republicans begged for federal protection from Klan violence, Congress enacted three laws in 1870 and 1871 that were intended to break the back of white terrorism. The severest of the three, the Ku Klux Klan Act (1871), made interference with voting rights a felony. Federal marshals arrested thousands of Klansmen and came close to

destroying the Klan, but they did not end all terrorism against blacks. Congress also passed the Civil Rights Act of 1875, which boldly outlawed racial discrimination in transportation, public accommodations, and juries. But federal authorities never enforced the law aggressively, and segregated facilities remained the rule throughout the South.

By the early 1870s, the Republican Party had lost its leading champions of African American rights to death or defeat at the polls. Other Republicans concluded that the quest for black equality was mistaken or hopelessly naive. In May 1872, Congress restored the right of officeholding to all but three hundred ex-rebels. Many Republicans had come to believe that traditional white leaders offered the best hope for honesty, order, and prosperity in the South.

Underlying the North's abandonment of reconstruction was unyielding racial prejudice. Northerners had learned to accept black freedom during the war, but deep-seated prejudice prevented many from accepting black equality. Even the actions they took on behalf of blacks often served partisan political advantage. Northerners generally supported Indiana senator Thomas A. Hendricks's harsh declaration that "this is a white man's Government, made by the white man for the white man."

The U.S. Supreme Court also did its part to undermine reconstruction. The Court issued a series of decisions that significantly weakened the federal government's ability to protect black Southerners. In the *Slaughterhouse* cases (1873), the Court distinguished between national and state citizenship and ruled that the Fourteenth Amendment protected only those rights that stemmed from the federal government, such as voting in federal elections and interstate travel. Since the Court decided that most rights derived from the states, it sharply curtailed the federal government's authority to defend black citizens. Even more devastating, the *United States v. Cruikshank* ruling (1876) said that the reconstruction amendments gave Congress the power to legislate against discrimination only by states, not by individuals. The "suppression of ordinary crime," such as assault, remained a state responsibility. The Supreme Court did not declare reconstruction unconstitutional but eroded its legal foundation.

The mood of the North found political expression in the election of 1874, when for the first time in eighteen years the Democrats gained control of the House of Representatives. As one Republican observed, the people had grown tired of the "negro question, with all its complications, and the reconstruction of Southern States, with all its interminable embroilments." Reconstruction had come apart. The people were tired of it. Grant grew increasingly unwilling to enforce it. Congress gradually abandoned it. And the Supreme Court denied the constitutionality of significant parts of it.

Rather than defend reconstruction from its southern enemies, Northerners steadily backed away from the challenge. By the early 1870s, southern Republicans faced the forces of reaction largely on their own.

White Supremacy Triumphs

Republican governments in the South attracted more hatred than any other political regimes in American history. To most whites, Republican rule meant intolerable insults: Black militiamen patrolled town streets, black laborers negotiated contracts with former masters, black maids stood up to former mistresses, black voters cast ballots, and black legislators such as James T. Rapier enacted laws. The northern retreat from reconstruction permitted southern Democrats to harness this white rage to politics.

Taking the name **Redeemers**, they promised to replace "bayonet rule" (a few federal troops continued to be stationed in the South) with "home rule." They branded Republican governments a carnival of extravagance, waste, and fraud and promised that honest, thrifty Democrats would supplant the irresponsible tax-and-spend Republicans. Above all, Redeemers swore to save southern civilization from a descent into "African barbarism." As one man put it, "We must render this either a white man's government, or convert the land into a Negro man's cemetery."

Southern Democrats adopted a multi-pronged strategy to overthrow Republican governments. First, they sought to polarize the parties around color. They went about gathering all the South's white voters into the Democratic Party, leaving the Republicans to depend on blacks, who made up a minority of population in almost every southern state. To dislodge whites from the Republican Party, Democrats fanned the flames of racial prejudice. A South Carolina Democrat crowed that his party appealed to the "proud Caucasian race, whose sovereignty on earth God has proclaimed." Local newspapers published the names of whites who kept company with blacks, and neighbors ostracized offenders.

Democrats also exploited the severe economic plight of small white farmers by blaming it on Republican financial policy. Government spending soared during reconstruction, and small farmers saw their tax burden skyrocket. "This is tax time," a South Carolinian reported. "We are nearly all on our head

"Of Course He Wants to Vote the Democratic Ticket" This Republican cartoon from the October 21, 1876, issue of *Harper's Weekly* comments sarcastically on the possibility of honest elections in the South. The caption reads, "You're free as air, ain't you? Say you are or I'll blow yer black head off." The cartoon demonstrates not only some Northerners' concern that violence would deliver the election to the Democrats but also the perception that white Southerners were crude, drunken, ignorant brutes. Granger Collection.

FOR MORE HELP ANALYZING THIS IMAGE, see the visual activity for this chapter in the Online Study Guide at bedfordstmartins.com/roarkcompact.

"White Man's Country" White supremacy emerged as a central tenet of the Democratic Party before the Civil War, and Democrats kept up a vicious racist attack on Republicans throughout Reconstruction. This silk ribbon from the 1868 presidential campaign between Republican Ulysses S. Grant and his Democratic opponent, New York governor Horatio Seymour, openly declares the Democrats' racial goal. During the campaign, Democratic vice presidential nominee Francis P. Blair Jr. promised that a Seymour victory would restore "white people" to power by declaring the reconstruction governments in the South "null and void." The Democrats' promotion of white supremacy reached new levels of shrillness in the 1870s, when northern support for reconstruction began to waver. Collection of Janice L. and David J. Frent.

about them. They are so high & so little money to pay with" that farmers were "selling every egg and chicken they can get." In 1871, Mississippi reported that one-seventh of the state's land—3.3 million acres—had been forfeited for nonpayment of taxes. The small farmers' economic distress had a racial dimension. Because few freedmen succeeded in acquiring land, they rarely paid taxes. In Georgia in 1874, blacks made up 45 percent of the population but paid only 2 percent of the taxes. From the perspective of a small white farmer, Republican rule meant that he was paying more taxes and paying them to aid blacks.

If racial pride, social isolation, and financial hardship proved insufficient to drive yeomen from the Republican Party, Democrats turned to terrorism. "Night riders" targeted white Republicans as well as blacks for murder and assassination. Whether white or black, a "dead Radical is very harmless," South Carolina Democratic leader Martin Gary told his followers.

But the primary victims of white violence were black Republicans. The object was to "kill out the leading men of the republican party," a black Republican from Florida declared. But violence targeted all black voters, not just leaders. And it escalated to unprecedented levels. In 1873, a clash between black militiamen and gun-toting whites in Louisiana killed two white men and an estimated seventy black men. The whites slaughtered half of the black men after they surrendered. Although the federal government indicted more than one hundred of the white men, local juries failed to convict even one.

Even before adopting the all-out white supremacist tactics of the 1870s, Democrats had taken control of the governments of Virginia, Tennessee, and North Carolina. The new campaign brought fresh gains. The Redeemers retook Georgia in 1871, Texas in 1873, and Arkansas and Alabama in 1874. Mississippi became a scene of open, unrelenting, and often savage intimidation of black voters and their few remaining white allies. As the state election approached in 1876, Governor Adelbert Ames appealed to Washington for federal troops to control the violence, only to hear from the attorney general that the "whole public are tired of these annual autumnal outbreaks in the South." Abandoned, Mississippi Republicans succumbed to the Democratic onslaught in the fall elections. By 1876, only three Republican state governments survived in the South (Map 16.3).

An Election and a Compromise The centennial year of 1876 witnessed one of the most tumultuous elections in American history. Its chaos and confusion provided a fitting conclusion to the experiment known as reconstruction. The election took place in November, but not until March 2 of the following year did the nation know who would be inaugurated president on March 4. The Democrats nominated New York's governor, **Samuel J. Tilden**, who immediately targeted the corruption of the Grant administration and the "despotism" of Republican reconstruction. The Republicans put forward **Rutherford B. Hayes**, governor of Ohio. Privately, Hayes considered "bayonet rule" a mistake but concluded that waving the bloody shirt—reminding voters that the Democrats were the "party of rebellion"—remained the Republicans' best political strategy.

On election day, Tilden tallied 4,288,590 votes to Hayes's 4,036,000. But in the all-important electoral college, Tilden fell one vote short of the majority required for victory. The electoral votes of three states—South Carolina, Louisiana, and Florida, the only remaining Republican governments in the South—remained in doubt because both Republicans and Democrats in those states claimed victory. To win, Tilden needed only one of the nineteen contested votes. Hayes had to have all of them.

Congress had to decide who had actually won the elections in the three southern states and thus who would be president. The Constitution provided no guidance for this situation. Moreover, Democrats controlled the House, and Republicans controlled the Senate. Congress created a special electoral commission to arbitrate the disputed returns. All of the commissioners voted their party affiliation, giving every state to the Republican Hayes and putting him over the top in electoral votes (Map 16.4).

Some outraged Democrats vowed to resist Hayes's victory. Rumors flew of an impending

MAP 16.3 The Reconstruction of the South Myth has it that Republican rule of the former Confederacy was not only harsh but long. In most states, however, conservative southern whites stormed back into power in months or just a few years. By the election of 1876, Republican governments could be found in only three states, and they soon fell.

COLORADO

KANSAS

ILLINOIS

IND.

OHIO

DEL.

MISSOURI

W. VA.

MD.

NEW MEXICO TERRITORY

INDIAN TERRITORY

KENTUCKY

VIRGINIA **1870**/1869

ARKANSAS **1868**/1874

TENNESSEE **1866**/1869

NORTH CAROLINA **1868**/1870

SOUTH CAROLINA **1868**/1876

MISS. **1870**/1876

ALABAMA **1868**/1874

GEORGIA **1870**/1871

TEXAS **1870**/1873

LOUISIANA **1868**/1877

FLA. **1868**/1877

Former Confederate states

1869 Date of readmission to the Union

1873 Date of reestablishment of conservative government

Candidate	Electoral Vote	Popular Vote	Percent of Popular Vote
Rutherford B. Hayes (Republican)	185*	4,036,298	47.9**
Samuel J. Tilden (Democrat)	184	4,288,590	51.0

*19 electoral votes were disputed.

**Percentages do not total 100 because some popular votes went to other parties.

MAP 16.4 The Election of 1876

coup and renewed civil war. But the impasse was broken when negotiations behind the scenes resulted in an informal understanding known as the **Compromise of 1877**. In exchange for a Democratic promise not to block Hayes's inauguration and to deal fairly with the freedmen, Hayes vowed to refrain from using the army to uphold the remaining Republican regimes in the South and to provide the South with substantial federal subsidies for internal improvements. Two days later, the nation celebrated Hayes's peaceful inauguration.

Stubborn Tilden supporters bemoaned the "stolen election" and damned "His Fraudulency," Rutherford B. Hayes. Old-guard radicals such as William Lloyd Garrison denounced Hayes's bargain as a "policy of compromise, of credulity, of weakness, of subserviency, of surrender." But the nation as a whole celebrated, for the country had weathered a grave crisis. The last three Republican state governments in the South fell quickly once Hayes abandoned them and withdrew the U.S. army. Reconstruction came to an end.

Q: **How did the Supreme Court undermine the Fourteenth and Fifteenth Amendments?**

Conclusion: "A Revolution But Half Accomplished"

In 1865, when General Carl Schurz visited the South, he discovered "a revolution but half accomplished." White Southerners resisted the passage from slavery to free labor, from white racial despotism to equal justice, and from white political monopoly to biracial democracy. The old elite wanted to get "things back as near to slavery as possible," Schurz reported, while African Americans such as James T. Rapier and some whites were eager to exploit the revolutionary implications of defeat and emancipation.

The northern-dominated Republican Congress pushed the revolution along. Although it refused to provide for blacks' economic welfare, Congress employed constitutional amendments to require ex-Confederates to accept legal equality and share political power with black men. Congress was not willing to extend such power to women, however. Conservative southern whites fought ferociously to recover their power and privilege. When Democrats regained control of politics, whites used both state power and private violence to wipe out many of the gains of Reconstruction, leading one observer to conclude that the North had won the war but the South had won the peace.

The Redeemer counterrevolution, however, did not mean a return to slavery. Northern victory in the Civil War ensured that ex-slaves no longer faced the auction block and could send their children to school, worship in their own churches, and work independently on their own rented farms. Sharecropping, with all its hardships, provided more autonomy and economic welfare than bondage had. It was limited freedom, to be sure, but it was not slavery.

The Civil War and emancipation set in motion the most profound upheaval in the nation's history, and nothing reactionary whites did entirely erased its revolutionary impact. War destroyed the largest slave society in the New World. The world of masters and slaves succumbed to that of landlords and sharecroppers, a world in which white racial dominance continued, though with greater freedom for blacks. War also gave birth to a modern nation-state, and Washington increased its role in national affairs. When the South returned to the Union, it did so as a junior partner. The victorious North set the nation's compass toward the expansion of industrial capitalism and the final conquest of the West.

Despite massive changes, however, the Civil War remained only a "half accomplished" revolution. By not fulfilling the promises the nation seemed to hold out to black Americans at war's end, Reconstruction represents a tragedy of enormous proportions. The failure to protect blacks and guarantee their rights had enduring consequences. Almost a century after Reconstruction, the nation would embark on what one observer called a "second reconstruction." The solid achievements of the Thirteenth, Fourteenth, and Fifteenth Amendments to the Constitution would provide a legal foundation for the renewed commitment. It is worth remembering, though, that it was only the failure of the first reconstruction that made the modern civil rights movement necessary.

Reviewing the Chapter

★ KEY TERMS

Explain each term's significance

WHO

James T. Rapier (p. 385)

Andrew Johnson (p. 392)

Susan B. Anthony (p. 395)

Elizabeth Cady Stanton (p. 395)

Samuel J. Tilden (p. 406)

Rutherford B. Hayes (p. 406)

WHAT

Wade-Davis bill (p. 387)

Freedmen's Bureau (p. 388)

black codes (p. 393)

Civil Rights Act of 1866 (p. 395)

Fourteenth Amendment (p. 395)

American Equal Rights Association (p. 395)

Military Reconstruction Act (p. 396)

impeachment (p. 398)

Fifteenth Amendment (p. 398)

carpetbagger (p. 399)

scalawag (p. 399)

Ku Klux Klan (p. 399)

sharecropping (p. 401)

waving the bloody shirt (p. 403)

Redeemers (p. 405)

Compromise of 1877 (p. 407)

FOR PRACTICE QUIZZES AND OTHER STUDY TOOLS, see the Online Study Guide at **bedfordstmartins.com/roarkcompact**.

★ REVIEW QUESTIONS Q:

Use key terms and dates to support your answer

1. Why did Congress object to Lincoln's wartime plan for reconstruction? (pp. 386–92)

2. How did the North respond to the passage of black codes in the southern states? (pp. 392–95)

3. Why did Johnson urge the southern states to reject the Fourteenth Amendment? (pp. 395–98)

4. Why was the Republican Party in the South a coalition party? (pp. 398–402)

5. How did the Supreme Court undermine the Fourteenth and Fifteenth Amendments? (pp. 402–07)

★ MAKING CONNECTIONS

Draw on key terms, timeline, and review questions

1. Reconstruction succeeded in advancing black civil rights but failed to secure them over the long term. Why and how did the federal government retreat from defending African Americans' civil rights in the 1870s? In your answer, cite specific actions by Congress and the Supreme Court.

2. Why was distributing plantation land to former slaves such a controversial policy? In your answer, discuss why landownership was important to freedmen and why Congress rejected redistribution as a general policy.

3. At the end of the Civil War, it remained to be seen exactly how emancipation would transform the South. How did emancipation change political and labor organization in the region? In your answer, discuss how ex-slaves exercised their new freedoms and how white Southerners attempted to limit them.

4. The Republican Party shaped Reconstruction through its control of Congress and state legislatures in the South. How did the identification of the Republican Party with Reconstruction policy affect the party's political fortunes in the 1870s? In your answer, be sure to address developments on the federal and state levels.

★ SUGGESTED READINGS

Jane Turner Censer, *The Reconstruction of White Southern Womanhood, 1865–1895* (2003). A lively investigation of the consequences of the Civil War for white southern women.

Eric Foner, *Reconstruction: America's Unfinished Revolution* (1988). A masterful synthesis that makes African Americans central actors in the Reconstruction era.

John Hope Franklin and Loren Schweninger, *In Search of the Promised Land: A Slave Family in the Old South* (2006). A careful retelling of the history of the Rapier family.

Stephen Kantrowitz, *Ben Tillman and the Reconstruction of White Supremacy* (2000). An eloquent biography of a leading white supremacist in South Carolina.

Hyman Rubin III, *South Carolina Scalawags* (2006). A probing analysis of white South Carolinians who became Republicans.

Brooks D. Simpson, *The Reconstruction Presidents* (1998). A thoughtful interpretation that emphasizes the differences between the policies and styles of Lincoln, Johnson, Grant, and Hayes.

FOR MORE BOOKS ABOUT TOPICS IN THIS CHAPTER, see the Online Bibliography at **bedfordstmartins.com/roarkcompact**.

FOR ADDITIONAL FIRSTHAND ACCOUNTS OF THIS PERIOD, see Chapter 16 in Michael Johnson, ed., *Reading the American Past*, Fourth Edition.

FOR WEB SITES, IMAGES, AND DOCUMENTS RELATED TO TOPICS AND PLACES IN THIS CHAPTER, visit Make History at **bedfordstmartins.com/roarkcompact**.

★ TIMELINE

1863	• Proclamation of Amnesty and Reconstruction.
1864	• Wade-Davis bill.
1865	• Freedmen's Bureau established. • President Abraham Lincoln shot; dies on April 15; succeeded by Andrew Johnson. • Black codes enacted. • Thirteenth Amendment becomes part of Constitution.
1866	• Congress approves Fourteenth Amendment. • Civil Rights Act. • American Equal Rights Association founded. • Ku Klux Klan founded.
1867	• Military Reconstruction Act. • Tenure of Office Act.
1868	• Impeachment trial of President Johnson. • Republican Ulysses S. Grant elected president.
1869	• Congress approves Fifteenth Amendment.
1871	• Ku Klux Klan Act.
1872	• Liberal Party formed; calls for end of government corruption. • President Grant reelected.
1873	• Economic depression sets in for remainder of decade. • *Slaughterhouse* cases.
1874	• Democrats win majority in House of Representatives.
1875	• Civil Rights Act.
1876	• *United States v. Cruikshank*.
1877	• Republican Rutherford B. Hayes assumes presidency; Reconstruction era ends.

Documents

For additional documents, see the DocLinks feature at Make History at bedfordstmartins.com/roarkcompact.

The Declaration of Independence

In Congress, July 4, 1776,

THE UNANIMOUS DECLARATION OF THE THIRTEEN UNITED STATES OF AMERICA

When in the course of human events, it becomes necessary for one people to dissolve the political bands which have connected them with another, and to assume, among the powers of the earth, the separate and equal station to which the laws of nature and of nature's God entitle them, a decent respect to the opinions of mankind requires that they should declare the causes which impel them to the separation.

We hold these truths to be self-evident, that all men are created equal; that they are endowed by their Creator with certain unalienable rights; that among these, are life, liberty, and the pursuit of happiness. That, to secure these rights, governments are instituted among men, deriving their just powers from the consent of the governed; that, whenever any form of government becomes destructive of these ends, it is the right of the people to alter or to abolish it, and to institute a new government, laying its foundation on such principles, and organizing its powers in such form, as to them shall seem most likely to effect their safety and happiness. Prudence, indeed, will dictate that governments long established, should not be changed for light and transient causes; and, accordingly, all experience hath shown, that mankind are more disposed to suffer, while evils are sufferable, than to right themselves by abolishing the forms to which they are accustomed. But, when a long train of abuses and usurpations, pursuing invariably the same object, evinces a design to reduce them under absolute despotism, it is their right, it is their duty, to throw off such government and to provide new guards for their future security. Such has been the patient sufferance of these colonies, and such is now the necessity which constrains them to alter their former systems of government. The history of the present King of Great Britain is a history of repeated injuries and usurpations, all having, in direct object, the establishment of an absolute tyranny over these States. To prove this, let facts be submitted to a candid world:

He has refused his assent to laws the most wholesome and necessary for the public good.

He has forbidden his governors to pass laws of immediate and pressing importance, unless suspended in their operation till his assent should be obtained; and, when so suspended, he has utterly neglected to attend to them.

He has refused to pass other laws for the accommodation of large districts of people, unless those people would relinquish the right of representation in the legislature; a right inestimable to them, and formidable to tyrants only.

He has called together legislative bodies at places unusual, uncomfortable, and distant from the depository of their public records, for the sole purpose of fatiguing them into compliance with his measures.

He has dissolved representative houses repeatedly for opposing, with manly firmness, his invasions on the rights of the people.

He has refused, for a long time after such dissolutions, to cause others to be elected; whereby the legislative powers, incapable of annihilation, have returned to the people at large for their exercise; the state remaining in the mean-time exposed to all the danger of invasion from without, and convulsions within.

He has endeavoured to prevent the population of these States; for that purpose, obstructing the laws for naturalization of foreigners, refusing to pass others to encourage their migration hither, and raising the conditions of new appropriations of lands.

He has obstructed the administration of justice, by refusing his assent to laws for establishing judiciary powers.

He has made judges dependent on his will alone, for the tenure of their offices, and the amount and payment of their salaries.

He has erected a multitude of new offices, and sent hither swarms of officers to harass our people, and eat out their substance.

He has kept among us, in times of peace, standing armies, without the consent of our legislature.

He has affected to render the military independent of, and superior to, the civil power.

He has combined, with others, to subject us to a jurisdiction foreign to our Constitution, and unacknowledged by our laws; giving his assent to their acts of pretended legislation:

For quartering large bodies of armed troops among us:

For protecting them by a mock trial, from punishment, for any murders which they should commit on the inhabitants of these States:

For cutting off our trade with all parts of the world:

For imposing taxes on us without our consent:

For depriving us, in many cases, of the benefit of trial by jury:

For transporting us beyond seas to be tried for pretended offences:

For abolishing the free system of English laws in a neighboring province, establishing therein an arbitrary government, and enlarging its boundaries, so as to render it at once an example and fit instrument for introducing the same absolute rule into these colonies:

For taking away our charters, abolishing our most valuable laws, and altering, fundamentally, the powers of our governments:

For suspending our own legislatures, and declaring themselves invested with power to legislate for us in all cases whatsoever.

He has abdicated government here, by declaring us out of his protection, and waging war against us.

He has plundered our seas, ravaged our coasts, burnt our towns, and destroyed the lives of our people.

He is, at this time, transporting large armies of foreign mercenaries to complete the works of death, desolation, and tyranny, already begun, with circumstances of cruelty and perfidy scarcely paralleled in the most barbarous ages, and totally unworthy the head of a civilized nation.

He has constrained our fellow citizens, taken captive on the high seas, to bear arms against their country, to become the executioners of their friends, and brethren, or to fall themselves by their hands.

He has excited domestic insurrections amongst us, and has endeavored to bring on the inhabitants of our frontiers, the merciless Indian savages, whose known rule of warfare is an undistinguished destruction of all ages, sexes, and conditions.

In every stage of these oppressions, we have petitioned for redress; in the most humble terms; our repeated petitions have been answered only by repeated injury. A prince, whose character is thus marked by every act which may define a tyrant, is unfit to be the ruler of a free people.

Nor have we been wanting in attention to our British brethren. We have warned them, from time to time, of attempts made by their legislature to extend an unwarrantable jurisdiction over us. We have reminded them of the circumstances of our emigration and settlement here. We have appealed to their native justice and magnanimity, and we have conjured them, by the ties of our common kindred, to disavow these usurpations, which would inevitably interrupt our connections and correspondence. They, too, have been deaf to the voice of justice and consanguinity. We must, therefore, acquiesce in the necessity which denounces our separation, and hold them as we hold the rest of mankind, enemies in war, in peace, friends.

We, therefore, the representatives of the United States of America, in general Congress assembled, appealing to the Supreme Judge of the world for the rectitude of our intentions, do, in the name, and by authority of the good people of these colonies, solemnly publish and declare, that these united colonies are, and of right ought to be, free and independent states: that they are absolved from all allegiance to the British Crown, and that all political connection between them and the state of Great Britain is, and ought to be, totally dissolved; and that, as free and independent states, they have full power to levy war, conclude peace, contract alliances, establish commerce, and to do all other acts and things which independent states may of right do. And, for the support of this declaration, with a firm reliance on the protection of Divine Providence, we mutually pledge to each other our lives, our fortunes, and our sacred honor.

The foregoing Declaration was, by order of Congress, engrossed, and signed by the following members:

JOHN HANCOCK

New Hampshire
Josiah Bartlett
William Whipple
Matthew Thornton

Massachusetts Bay
Samuel Adams
John Adams
Robert Treat Paine
Elbridge Gerry

Rhode Island
Stephen Hopkins
William Ellery

Connecticut
Roger Sherman
Samuel Huntington
William Williams
Oliver Wolcott

New York
William Floyd
Phillip Livingston
Francis Lewis
Lewis Morris

New Jersey
Richard Stockton
John Witherspoon
Francis Hopkinson
John Hart
Abraham Clark

Pennsylvania
Robert Morris
Benjamin Rush
Benjamin Franklin
John Morton
George Clymer
James Smith

George Taylor
James Wilson
George Ross

Delaware
Caesar Rodney
George Read
Thomas M'Kean

Maryland
Samuel Chase
William Paca
Thomas Stone
Charles Carroll, of
   Carrollton

North Carolina
William Hooper
Joseph Hewes
John Penn

South Carolina
Edward Rutledge
Thomas Heyward, Jr.
Thomas Lynch, Jr.
Arthur Middleton

Virginia
George Wythe
Richard Henry Lee
Thomas Jefferson
Benjamin Harrison
Thomas Nelson, Jr.
Francis Lightfoot Lee
Carter Braxton

Georgia
Button Gwinnett
Lyman Hall
George Walton

Resolved, That copies of the Declaration be sent to the several assemblies, conventions, and committees, or councils of safety, and to the several commanding officers of the continental

troops; that it be proclaimed in each of the United States, at the head of the army.

The Constitution of the United States

Agreed to by Philadelphia Convention, September 17, 1787. Implemented March 4, 1789.

Preamble

We the people of the United States, in order to form a more perfect union, establish justice, insure domestic tranquility, provide for the common defense, promote the general welfare, and secure the blessings of liberty to ourselves and our posterity, do ordain and establish this Constitution for the United States of America.

Article I

Section 1 All legislative powers herein granted shall be vested in a Congress of the United States, which shall consist of a Senate and a House of Representatives.

Section 2 The House of Representatives shall be composed of members chosen every second year by the people of the several States, and the electors in each State shall have the qualifications requisite for electors of the most numerous branch of the State Legislature.

No person shall be a Representative who shall not have attained to the age of twenty-five years, and been seven years a citizen of the United States, and who shall not, when elected, be an inhabitant of that State in which he shall be chosen.

Representatives and direct taxes shall be apportioned among the several States which may be included within this Union, according to their respective numbers, *which shall be determined by adding to the whole number of free persons, including those bound to service for a term of years and excluding Indians not taxed, three-fifths of all other persons.** The actual enumeration shall be made within three years after the first meeting of the Congress of the United States, and within every subsequent term of ten years, in such manner as they shall by law direct. The number of Representatives shall not exceed one for every thirty thousand, but each State shall have at least one Representative; *and until such enumeration shall be made, the State of New Hampshire shall be entitled to choose three, Massachusetts eight, Rhode Island and Providence Plantations one, Connecticut five, New York six, New Jersey four, Pennsylvania eight, Delaware one, Maryland six, Virginia ten, North Carolina five, South Carolina five, and Georgia three.*

When vacancies happen in the representation from any State, the Executive authority thereof shall issue writs of election to fill such vacancies.

The House of Representatives shall choose their Speaker and other officers; and shall have the sole power of impeachment.

Passages no longer in effect are in italic type.

Section 3 The Senate of the United States shall be composed of two Senators from each State, *chosen by the legislature thereof,* for six years; and each Senator shall have one vote.

Immediately after they shall be assembled in consequence of the first election, they shall be divided as equally as may be into three classes. The seats of the Senators of the first class shall be vacated at the expiration of the second year, of the second class at the expiration of the fourth year, and of the third class at the expiration of the sixth year, so that one-third may be chosen every second year; and if vacancies happen by resignation or otherwise, during the recess of the legislature of any State, the Executive thereof may make temporary appointments until the next meeting of the legislature, which shall then fill such vacancies.

No person shall be a Senator who shall not have attained to the age of thirty years, and been nine years a citizen of the United States, and who shall not, when elected, be an inhabitant of that State for which he shall be chosen.

The Vice-President of the United States shall be President of the Senate, but shall have no vote, unless they be equally divided.

The Senate shall choose their other officers, and also a President *pro tempore*, in the absence of the Vice-President, or when he shall exercise the office of President of the United States.

The Senate shall have the sole power to try all impeachments. When sitting for that purpose, they shall be on oath or affirmation. When the President of the United States is tried, the Chief Justice shall preside: and no person shall be convicted without the concurrence of two-thirds of the members present.

Judgment in cases of impeachment shall not extend further than to removal from the office, and disqualification to hold and enjoy any office of honor, trust or profit under the United States: but the party convicted shall nevertheless be liable and subject to indictment, trial, judgment and punishment, according to law.

Section 4 The times, places and manner of holding elections for Senators and Representatives shall be prescribed in each State by the legislature thereof; but the Congress may at any time by law make or alter such regulations, except as to the places of choosing Senators.

The Congress shall assemble at least once in every year, and such meeting *shall be on the first Monday in December, unless they shall by law appoint a different day.*

Section 5 Each house shall be the judge of the elections, returns and qualifications of its own members, and a majority of each shall constitute a quorum to do business; but a smaller number may adjourn from day to day, and may be authorized to compel the attendance of absent members, in such manner, and under such penalties, as each house may provide.

Each house may determine the rules of its proceedings, punish its members for disorderly behavior, and with the concurrence of two-thirds, expel a member.

Each house shall keep a journal of its proceedings, and from time to time publish the same, excepting such parts as may in their judgment require secrecy; and the yeas and nays of the members of either house on any question shall, at the desire of one-fifth of those present, be entered on the journal.

Neither house, during the session of Congress, shall, without the consent of the other, adjourn for more than three days, nor to any other place than that in which the two houses shall be sitting.

Section 6 The Senators and Representatives shall receive a compensation for their services, to be ascertained by law and paid out of the treasury of the United States. They shall in all cases except treason, felony and breach of the peace, be privileged from arrest during their attendance at the session of their respective houses, and in going to and returning from the same; and for any speech or debate in either house, they shall not be questioned in any other place.

No Senator or Representative shall, during the time for which he was elected, be appointed to any civil office under the authority of the United States, which shall have been created, or the emoluments whereof shall have been increased, during such time; and no person holding any office under the United States shall be a member of either house during his continuance in office.

Section 7 All bills for raising revenue shall originate in the House of Representatives; but the Senate may propose or concur with amendments as on other bills.

Every bill which shall have passed the House of Representatives and the Senate, shall, before it become a law, be presented to the President of the United States; if he approve he shall sign it, but if not he shall return it with objections to that house in which it shall have originated, who shall enter the objections at large on their journal, and proceed to reconsider it. If after such reconsideration two-thirds of that house shall agree to pass the bill, it shall be sent, together with the objections, to the other house, by which it shall likewise be reconsidered, and, if approved by two-thirds of that house, it shall become a law. But in all such cases the votes of both houses shall be determined by yeas and nays, and the names of the persons voting for and against the bill shall be entered on the journal of each house respectively. If any bill shall not be returned by the President within ten days (Sundays excepted) after it shall have been presented to him, the same shall be a law, in like manner as if he had signed it, unless the Congress by their adjournment prevent its return, in which case it shall not be a law.

Every order, resolution, or vote to which the concurrence of the Senate and House of Representatives may be necessary (except on a question of adjournment) shall be presented to the President of the United States; and before the same shall take effect, shall be approved by him, or being disapproved by him, shall be repassed by two-thirds of the Senate and House

of Representatives, according to the rules and limitations prescribed in the case of a bill.

Section 8 The Congress shall have power

To lay and collect taxes, duties, imposts, and excises, to pay the debts and provide for the common defense and general welfare of the United States; but all duties, imposts and excises shall be uniform throughout the United States;

To borrow money on the credit of the United States;

To regulate commerce with foreign nations, and among the several States, and with the Indian tribes;

To establish an uniform rule of naturalization, and uniform laws on the subject of bankruptcies throughout the United States;

To coin money, regulate the value thereof, and of foreign coin, and fix the standard of weights and measures;

To provide for the punishment of counterfeiting the securities and current coin of the United States;

To establish post offices and post roads;

To promote the progress of science and useful arts by securing for limited times to authors and inventors the exclusive right to their respective writings and discoveries;

To constitute tribunals inferior to the Supreme Court;

To define and punish piracies and felonies committed on the high seas and offences against the law of nations;

To declare war, grant letters of marque and reprisal, and make rules concerning captures on land and water;

To raise and support armies, but no appropriation of money to that use shall be for a longer term than two years;

To provide and maintain a navy;

To make rules for the government and regulation of the land and naval forces;

To provide for calling forth the militia to execute the laws of the Union, suppress insurrections and repel invasions;

To provide for organizing, arming, and disciplining the militia, and for governing such part of them as may be employed in the service of the United States, reserving to the States respectively the appointment of the officers, and the authority of training the militia according to the discipline prescribed by Congress;

To exercise exclusive legislation in all cases whatsoever, over such district (not exceeding ten miles square) as may, by cession of particular States, and the acceptance of Congress, become the seat of the government of the United States, and to exercise like authority over all places purchased by the consent of the legislature of the State, in which the same shall be, for erection of forts, magazines, arsenals, dock-yards, and other needful buildings; — and

To make all laws which shall be necessary and proper for carrying into execution the foregoing powers, and all other powers vested by this Constitution in the government of the United States, or in any department or officer thereof.

Section 9 *The migration or importation of such persons as any of the States now existing shall think proper to admit shall not be prohibited by the Congress prior to the year one thousand eight hundred and eight; but a tax or duty may be imposed on such importation, not exceeding ten dollars for each person.*

The privilege of the writ of habeas corpus shall not be suspended, unless when in cases of rebellion or invasion the public safety may require it.

No bill of attainder or ex post facto law shall be passed.

No capitation, or other direct, tax shall be laid, unless in proportion to the census or enumeration herein before directed to be taken.

No tax or duty shall be laid on articles exported from any State.

No preference shall be given by any regulation of commerce or revenue to the ports of one State over those of another; nor shall vessels bound to, or from, one State be obliged to enter, clear, or pay duties in another.

No money shall be drawn from the treasury, but in consequence of appropriations made by law; and a regular statement and account of the receipts and expenditures of all public money shall be published from time to time.

No title of nobility shall be granted by the United States: and no person holding any office of profit or trust under them, shall, without the consent of the Congress, accept of any present, emolument, office, or title, of any kind whatever, from any king, prince, or foreign state.

Section 10 No State shall enter into any treaty, alliance, or confederation; grant letters of marque and reprisal; coin money; emit bills of credit; make anything but gold and silver coin a tender in payment of debts; pass any bill of attainder, ex post facto law, or law impairing the obligation of contracts, or grant any title of nobility.

No State shall, without the consent of Congress, lay any imposts or duties on imports or exports, except what may be absolutely necessary for executing its inspection laws: and the net produce of all duties and imposts, laid by any State on imports or exports, shall be for the use of the treasury of the United States; and all such laws shall be subject to the revision and control of the Congress.

No State shall, without the consent of Congress, lay any duty of tonnage, keep troops, or ships of war in time of peace, enter into any agreement or compact with another State, or with a foreign power, or engage in war, unless actually invaded, or in such imminent danger as will not admit of delay.

Article II

Section 1 The executive power shall be vested in a President of the United States of America. He shall hold his office during the term of four years, and, together with the Vice-President, chosen for the same term, be elected as follows:

Each State shall appoint, in such manner as the legislature thereof may direct, a number of electors, equal to the whole number of Senators and Representatives to which the State may be entitled in the Congress; but no Senator or Representative, or person holding an office of trust or profit under the United States, shall be appointed an elector.

The electors shall meet in their respective States, and vote by ballot for two persons, of whom one at least shall not be an inhabitant of the same State with themselves. And they shall make a list of all the persons voted for, and of the number of votes for each; which list they shall sign and certify, and transmit sealed to the seat of government of the United States, directed to the President of the Senate. The President of the Senate shall, in the presence of the Senate and House of Representatives, open all the certificates, and the votes shall then be counted. The person having the greatest number of votes shall be the President, if such number be a majority of the whole number of electors appointed; and if there be more than one who have such majority, and have an equal number of votes, then the House of Representatives shall immediately choose by ballot one of them for President; and if no person have a majority, then from the five highest on the list said house shall in like manner choose the President. But in choosing the President the votes shall be taken by States, the representation from each State having one vote; a quorum for this purpose shall consist of a member or members from two-thirds of the States, and a majority of all the States shall be necessary to a choice. In every case, after the choice of the President, the person having the greatest number of votes of the electors shall be the Vice-President. But if there should remain two or more who have equal votes, the Senate shall choose from them by ballot the Vice-President.

The Congress may determine the time of choosing the electors, and the day on which they shall give their votes; which day shall be the same throughout the United States.

No person except a natural-born citizen, *or a citizen of the United States at the time of the adoption of this Constitution*, shall be eligible to the office of President; neither shall any person be eligible to that office who shall not have attained to the age of thirty-five years, and been fourteen years a resident within the United States.

In cases of the removal of the President from office or of his death, resignation, or inability to discharge the powers and duties of the said office, the same shall devolve on the Vice-President, and the Congress may by law provide for the case of removal, death, resignation, or inability, both of the President and Vice-President, declaring what officer shall then act as President, and such officer shall act accordingly, until the disability be removed, or a President shall be elected.

The President shall, at stated times, receive for his services a compensation, which shall neither be increased nor diminished during the period for which he shall have been elected, and he shall not receive within that period any other emolument from the United States, or any of them.

Before he enter on the execution of his office, he shall take the following oath or affirmation: — "I do solemnly swear (or affirm) that I will faithfully execute the office of the President of the United States, and will to the best of my ability preserve, protect and defend the Constitution of the United States."

Section 2 The President shall be commander in chief of the army and navy of the United States, and of the militia of the several States, when called into the actual service of the United States; he may require the opinion, in writing, of the principal officer in each of the executive departments, upon any subject relating to the duties of their respective offices, and he shall have power to grant reprieves and pardons for offenses against the United States, except in cases of impeachment.

He shall have power, by and with the advice and consent of the Senate, to make treaties, provided two-thirds of the Senators present concur; and he shall nominate, and by and with the advice and consent of the Senate, shall appoint ambassadors, other public ministers and consuls, judges of the Supreme Court, and all other officers of the United States, whose appointments are not herein otherwise provided for, and which shall be established by law: but Congress may by law vest the appointment of such inferior officers, as they think proper, in the President alone, in the courts of law, or in the heads of departments.

The President shall have power to fill up all vacancies that may happen during the recess of the Senate, by granting commissions which shall expire at the end of their next session.

Section 3 He shall from time to time give to the Congress information of the state of the Union, and recommend to their consideration such measures as he shall judge necessary and expedient; he may, on extraordinary occasions, convene both houses, or either of them, and in case of disagreement between them, with respect to the time of adjournment, he may adjourn them to such time as he shall think proper; he shall receive ambassadors and other public ministers; he shall take care that the laws be faithfully executed, and shall commission all the officers of the United States.

Section 4 The President, Vice-President and all civil officers of the United States shall be removed from office on impeachment for, and on conviction of, treason, bribery, or other high crimes and misdemeanors.

Article III

Section 1 The judicial power of the United States shall be vested in one Supreme Court, and in such inferior courts as the Congress may from time to time ordain and establish. The judges, both of the Supreme and inferior courts, shall hold their offices during good behavior, and shall, at stated times, receive for their services a compensation which shall not be diminished during their continuance in office.

Section 2 The judicial power shall extend to all cases, in law and equity, arising under this Constitution, the laws of the United States, and treaties made, or which shall be made, under their authority;—to all cases affecting ambassadors, other public ministers and consuls;—to all cases of admiralty and maritime jurisdiction;—to controversies to which the United States shall be a party;—to controversies between two or more States;—*between a State and citizens of another State;*—between citizens of different States;—between citizens of the same State claiming lands under grants of different States, and between a State, or the citizens thereof, and foreign states, citizens or subjects.

In all cases affecting ambassadors, other public ministers and consuls, and those in which a State shall be party, the Supreme Court shall have original jurisdiction. In all the other cases before mentioned, the Supreme Court shall have appellate jurisdiction, both as to law and fact, with such exceptions, and under such regulations, as the Congress shall make.

The trial of all crimes, except in cases of impeachment, shall be by jury; and such trial shall be held in the State where said crimes shall have been committed; but when not committed within any State, the trial shall be at such place or places as the Congress may by Law have directed.

Section 3 Treason against the United States shall consist only in levying war against them, or in adhering to their enemies, giving them aid and comfort. No person shall be convicted of treason unless on the testimony of two witnesses to the same overt act, or on confession in open court.

The Congress shall have power to declare the punishment of treason, but no attainder of treason shall work corruption of blood, or forfeiture except during the life of the person attainted.

Article IV

Section 1 Full faith and credit shall be given in each State to the public acts, records, and judicial proceedings of every other State. And the Congress may by general laws prescribe the manner in which such acts, records, and proceedings shall be proved, and the effect thereof.

Section 2 The citizens of each State shall be entitled to all privileges and immunities of citizens in the several States.

A person charged in any State with treason, felony, or other crime, who shall flee from justice, and be found in another State, shall on demand of the executive authority of the State from which he fled, be delivered up, to be removed to the State having jurisdiction of the crime.

No Person held to service or labor in one State, under the laws thereof, escaping into another, shall, in consequence of any law or regulation therein, be discharged from such service or labor, but shall be delivered up on claim of the party to whom such service or labor may be due.

Section 3 New States may be admitted by the Congress into this Union; but no new State shall be formed or erected within the jurisdiction of any other State; nor any State be formed by the junction of two or more States, or parts of States, without the consent of the legislatures of the States concerned as well as of the Congress.

The Congress shall have power to dispose of and make all needful rules and regulations respecting the territory or other property belonging to the United States; and nothing in this Constitution shall be so construed as to prejudice any claims of the United States, or of any particular State.

Section 4 The United States shall guarantee to every State in this Union a republican form of government, and shall protect each of them against invasion; and on application of the legislature, or of the executive (when the legislature cannot be convened), against domestic violence.

Article V

The Congress, whenever two-thirds of both houses shall deem it necessary, shall propose amendments to this Constitution, or, on the application of the legislatures of two-thirds of the several States, shall call a convention for proposing amendments, which, in either case, shall be valid to all intents and purposes, as part of this Constitution, when ratified by the legislatures of three-fourths of the several States, or by conventions in three-fourths thereof, as the one or the other mode of ratification may be proposed by the Congress; provided *that no amendments which may be made prior to the year one thousand eight hundred and eight shall in any manner affect the first and fourth clauses in the ninth section of the first article;* and that no State, without its consent, shall be deprived of its equal suffrage in the Senate.

Article VI

All debts contracted and engagements entered into, before the adoption of this Constitution, shall be as valid against the United States under this Constitution, as under the Confederation.

This Constitution, and the laws of the United States which shall be made in pursuance thereof; and all treaties made, or which shall be made, under the authority of the United States, shall be the supreme law of the land; and the judges in every State shall be bound thereby, anything in the Constitution or laws of any State to the contrary notwithstanding.

The Senators and Representatives before mentioned, and the members of the several State legislatures, and all executive and judicial officers, both of the United States and of the several States, shall be bound by oath or affirmation to support this Constitution; but no religious test shall ever be required as a qualification to any office or public trust under the United States.

Article VII

The ratification of the conventions of nine States shall be sufficient for the establishment of this Constitution between the States so ratifying the same.

Done in convention by the unanimous consent of the States present, the seventeenth day of September in the year of our Lord one thousand seven hundred and eighty-seven and of the Independence of the United States of America the twelfth. In witness whereof we have hereunto subscribed our names.

GEORGE WASHINGTON
PRESIDENT AND DEPUTY FROM VIRGINIA

New Hampshire
John Langdon
Nicholas Gilman

Massachusetts
Nathaniel Gorham
Rufus King

Connecticut
William Samuel Johnson
Roger Sherman

New York
Alexander Hamilton

New Jersey
William Livingston
David Brearley
William Paterson
Jonathan Dayton

Pennsylvania
Benjamin Franklin
Thomas Mifflin
Robert Morris
George Clymer
Thomas FitzSimons
Jared Ingersoll
James Wilson
Gouverneur Morris

Delaware
George Read
Gunning Bedford, Jr.
John Dickinson
Richard Bassett
Jacob Broom

Maryland
James McHenry
Daniel of St. Thomas Jenifer
Daniel Carroll

Virginia
John Blair
James Madison, Jr.

North Carolina
William Blount
Richard Dobbs
Spaight
Hugh Williamson

South Carolina
John Rutledge
Charles Cotesworth
Pinckney
Charles Pinckney
Pierce Butler

Georgia
William Few
Abraham Baldwin

Amendments to the Constitution (including the six unratified amendments)

(Although the first ten amendments to the Constitution are commonly known as the Bill of Rights, only Amendments 1–8 actually provide guarantees of individual rights. Amendments 9 and 10 deal with the structure of power within the constitutional system. The Bill of Rights was promised to appease Antifederalists who refused to ratify the Constitution without guarantees of individual liberties and limitations to federal power. After studying more than two hundred amendments recommended by the ratifying conventions of the states, Federalist James Madison presented a list of seventeen to Congress, which used Madison's list as the foundation for the twelve amendments that were sent to the states for ratification. Ten of the twelve were adopted in 1791. The first on the list of twelve, known as the Reapportionment Amendment, was never adopted [see the next column]. The second proposed amendment was adopted in 1992 as Amendment XXVII [see page A-12].   — Ed.)

Amendment I

Congress shall make no law respecting an establishment of religion, or prohibiting the free exercise thereof; or abridging the freedom of speech, or of the press; or the right of the people peaceably to assemble, and to petition the government for a redress of grievances.

Amendment II

A well-regulated militia being necessary to the security of a free State, the right of the people to keep and bear arms shall not be infringed.

Amendment III

No soldier shall, in time of peace, be quartered in any house without the consent of the owner, nor in time of war, but in a manner to be prescribed by law.

Amendment IV

The right of the people to be secure in their persons, houses, papers, and effects, against unreasonable searches and seizures, shall not be violated, and no warrants shall issue but upon probable cause, supported by oath or affirmation, and particularly describing the place to be searched, and the persons or things to be seized.

Amendment V

No person shall be held to answer for a capital, or otherwise infamous crime, unless on a presentment or indictment of a grand jury, except in cases arising in the land or naval forces, or in the militia, when in actual service in time of war or public danger; nor shall any person be subject for the same offence to be twice put in jeopardy of life or limb; nor shall be compelled in any criminal case to be a witness against himself, nor be deprived of life, liberty, or property, without due process of law; nor shall private property be taken for public use without just compensation.

Amendment VI

In all criminal prosecutions, the accused shall enjoy the right to a speedy and public trial, by an impartial jury of the State and district wherein the crime shall have been committed, which district shall have been previously ascertained by law, and to be informed of the nature and cause of the accusation; to be confronted with the witnesses against him; to have compulsory process for obtaining witnesses in his favor, and to have the assistance of counsel for his defence.

Amendment VII

In suits at common law, where the value in controversy shall exceed twenty dollars, the right of trial by jury shall be preserved, and no fact tried by a jury shall be otherwise reexamined in any court of the United States, than according to the rules of the common law.

Amendment VIII

Excessive bail shall not be required, nor excessive fines imposed, nor cruel and unusual punishments inflicted.

Amendment IX

The enumeration in the Constitution, of certain rights, shall not be construed to deny or disparage others retained by the people.

Amendment X

The powers not delegated to the United States by the Constitution, nor prohibited by it to the States, are reserved to the States respectively, or to the people.

Unratified Amendment

Reapportionment Amendment (proposed by Congress September 25, 1789, along with the Bill of Rights)

After the first enumeration required by the first article of the Constitution, there shall be one Representative for every thirty thousand, until the number shall amount to one hundred, after which the proportion shall be so regulated by Congress, that there shall be not less than one hundred Representatives, nor less than one Representative for every forty thousand persons, until the number of Representatives shall amount to two hundred; after which the proportion shall be so regulated by Congress, that there shall not be less than two hundred Representatives, nor more than one Representative for every fifty thousand persons.

Amendment XI

[Adopted 1798]

The judicial power of the United States shall not be construed to extend to any suit in law or equity, commenced or prosecuted against one of the United States by citizens of another State, or by citizens or subjects of any foreign state.

Amendment XII

[Adopted 1804]

The electors shall meet in their respective States, and vote by ballot for President and Vice-President, one of whom, at least, shall not be an inhabitant of the same State with themselves; they shall name in their ballots the person voted for as President, and in distinct ballots the person voted for as Vice-President, and they shall make distinct lists of all persons voted for as President, and of all persons voted for as Vice-President, and of the number of votes for each, which lists they shall sign and certify, and transmit sealed to the seat of government of the United States, directed to the President of the Senate;—the President of the Senate shall, in the presence of the Senate and House of Representatives, open all the certificates and the votes shall then be counted;—the person having the greatest number of votes for President shall be the President, if such number be a majority of the whole number of electors appointed; and if no person have such majority, then from the persons having the highest numbers not exceeding three on the list of those voted for as President, the House of Representatives shall choose immediately, by ballot, the President. But in choosing the President, the votes shall be taken by States, the representation from each State having one vote; a quorum for this purpose shall consist of a member or members from two-thirds of the States, and a majority of all the States shall be necessary to a choice. And if the House of Representatives shall not choose a President whenever the right of choice shall devolve upon them, before *the fourth day of March* next following, then the Vice-President shall act as President, as in the case of the death or other constitutional disability of the President.

The person having the greatest number of votes as Vice-President shall be the Vice-President, if such number be a majority of the whole number of electors appointed; and if no person have a majority, then from the two highest numbers on the list the Senate shall choose the Vice-President; a quorum for the purpose shall consist of two-thirds of the whole number of Senators, and a majority of the whole number shall be necessary to a choice. But no person constitutionally ineligible to the office of President shall be eligible to that of Vice-President of the United States.

Unratified Amendment

Titles of Nobility Amendment (proposed by Congress May 1, 1810)

If any citizen of the United States shall accept, claim, receive or retain any title of nobility or honor or shall, without the consent of Congress, accept and retain any present, pension, office or emolument of any kind whatever, from any emperor, king, prince or foreign power, such person shall cease to be a citizen of the United States, and shall be incapable of holding any office of trust or profit under them or either of them.

The Civil War and Reconstruction Amendments (Thirteenth, Fourteenth, and Fifteenth Amendments)

(In the four months between the election of Abraham Lincoln and his inauguration, more than 200 proposed constitutional amendments were presented to Congress as part of a desperate attempt to hold the rapidly dissolving Union together. Most of these were efforts to appease the southern states by protecting the right to own slaves or by disfranchising African Americans through constitutional amendment. None were able to win the votes required from Congress to send them to the states. The relatively innocuous Corwin Amendment seemed to be the only hope for preserving the Union by amending the Constitution.

The northern victors in the Civil War tried to restructure the Constitution just as the war had restructured the nation. Yet they were often divided in their goals. Some wanted to end slavery; others hoped for social and economic equality regardless of race; others hoped that extending the power of the ballot box to former slaves would help create a new political order. The debates over the Thirteenth, Fourteenth, and Fifteenth Amendments were bitter. Few of those who fought for these changes were satisfied with the amendments themselves; fewer still were satisfied with their interpretation. Although the amendments put an end to the legal status of slavery, it took nearly a hundred years after the amendments' passage before most of the descendants of former slaves could begin to experience the economic, social, and political equality the amendments had been intended to provide.   —Ed.)

Unratified Amendment

Corwin Amendment (proposed by Congress March 2, 1861)

No amendment shall be made to the Constitution which will authorize or give to Congress the power to abolish or interfere, within any State, with the domestic institutions thereof, including that of persons held to labor or service by the laws of said State.

Amendment XIII

[Adopted 1865]

Section 1 Neither slavery nor involuntary servitude, except as a punishment for crime whereof the party shall have been duly convicted, shall exist within the United States, or any place subject to their jurisdiction.

Section 2 Congress shall have power to enforce this article by appropriate legislation.

Amendment XIV

[Adopted 1868]

Section 1 All persons born or naturalized in the United States, and subject to the jurisdiction thereof, are citizens of the United States and of the State wherein they reside. No State shall make or enforce any law which shall abridge the privileges or immunities of citizens of the United States; nor shall any State deprive any person of life, liberty, or property, without due process of law; nor deny to any person within its jurisdiction the equal protection of the laws.

Section 2 Representatives shall be appointed among the several States according to their respective numbers, counting the whole number of persons in each State, excluding Indians not taxed. But when the right to vote at any election for the choice of Electors for President and Vice-President of the United States, Representatives in Congress, the executive and judicial officers of a State, or the members of the legislature thereof, is denied to any of the male inhabitants of such State, being twenty-one years of age and citizens of the United States, or in any way abridged, except for participation in rebellion, or other crime, the basis of representation therein shall be reduced in the proportion which the number of such male citizens shall bear to the whole number of male citizens twenty-one years of age in such State.

Section 3 No person shall be a Senator or Representative in Congress, or Elector of President and Vice-President, or hold any office, civil or military, under the United States, or under any State, who, having previously taken an oath, as a member of Congress, or as an officer of the United States, or as a member of any State legislature, or as an executive or judicial officer of any State, to support the Constitution of the United States, shall have engaged in insurrection or rebellion against the same, or given aid or comfort to the enemies thereof. Congress may, by a vote of two-thirds of each house, remove such disability.

Section 4 The validity of the public debt of the United States, authorized by law, including debts incurred for payment of pensions and bounties for services in suppressing insurrection or rebellion, shall not be questioned. But neither the United States nor any State shall assume or pay any debt or obligation incurred in aid of insurrection or rebellion against the United States, or any claim for the loss or emancipation of any slave; but all such debts, obligations, and claims shall be held illegal and void.

Section 5 The Congress shall have power to enforce, by appropriate legislation, the provisions of this article.

Amendment XV

[Adopted 1870]

Section 1 The right of citizens of the United States to vote shall not be denied or abridged by the United States or by any State on account of race, color, or previous condition of servitude.

Section 2 The Congress shall have power to enforce this article by appropriate legislation.

The Progressive Amendments (Sixteenth– Nineteenth Amendments)

(No amendments were added to the Constitution between the Civil War and the Progressive Era. America was changing, however, in fundamental ways. The rapid industrialization of the United States after the Civil War led to many social and economic problems. Hundreds of amendments were proposed, but none received enough support in Congress to be sent to the states. Some scholars believe that regional differences and rivalries were so strong during this period that it was almost impossible to gain a consensus on a constitutional amendment. During the Progressive Era, however, the Constitution was amended four times in seven years.   —Ed.)

Amendment XVI

[Adopted 1913]

The Congress shall have power to lay and collect taxes on incomes, from whatever source derived, without apportionment among the several States, and without regard to any census or enumeration.

Amendment XVII

[Adopted 1913]

Section 1 The Senate of the United States shall be composed of two Senators from each State, elected by the people thereof, for six years; and each Senator shall have one vote. The electors in each State shall have the qualifications requisite for electors of [voters for] the most numerous branch of the State legislatures.

Section 2 When vacancies happen in the representation of any State in the Senate, the executive authority of such State shall issue writs of election to fill such vacancies: Provided, that the Legislature of any State may empower the executive thereof to make temporary appointments until the people fill the vacancies by election as the Legislature may direct.

Section 3 This amendment shall not be so construed as to affect the election or term of any Senator chosen before it becomes valid as part of the Constitution.

Amendment XVIII

[Adopted 1919; repealed 1933 by Amendment XXI]

Section 1 After one year from the ratification of this article the manufacture, sale, or transportation of intoxicating liquors within, the importation thereof into, or the exportation thereof from the United States and all territory subject to the jurisdiction thereof, for beverage purposes, is hereby prohibited.

Section 2 The Congress and the several States shall have concurrent power to enforce this article by appropriate legislation.

Section 3 This article shall be inoperative unless it shall have been ratified as an amendment to the Constitution by the legislatures of the several States, as provided by the Constitution, within seven years from the date of the submission thereof to the States by the Congress.

Amendment XIX

[Adopted 1920]

Section 1 The right of citizens of the United States to vote shall not be denied or abridged by the United States or by any State on account of sex.

Section 2 Congress shall have the power to enforce this article by appropriate legislation.

Unratified Amendment

Child Labor Amendment (proposed by Congress June 2, 1924)

Section 1 The Congress shall have power to limit, regulate, and prohibit the labor of persons under eighteen years of age.

Section 2 The power of the several States is unimpaired by this article except that the operation of State laws shall be suspended to the extent necessary to give effect to legislation enacted by Congress.

Amendment XX

[Adopted 1933]

Section 1 The terms of the President and Vice-President shall end at noon on the 20th day of January, and the terms of Senators and Representatives at noon on the 3rd day of January, of the years in which such terms would have ended if this article had not been ratified; and the terms of their successors shall then begin.

Section 2 The Congress shall assemble at least once in every year, and such meeting shall begin at noon on the 3rd day of January, unless they shall by law appoint a different day.

Section 3 If, at the time fixed for the beginning of the term of the President, the President-elect shall have died, the Vice-President-elect shall become President. If a President shall not have been chosen before the time fixed for the beginning of his term, or if the President-elect shall have failed to qualify, then the Vice-President-elect shall act as President until a President shall have qualified; and the Congress may by law provide for the case wherein neither a President-elect nor a Vice-President-elect shall have qualified, declaring who shall then act as President, or the manner in which one who is to act shall be selected, and such person shall act accordingly until a President or Vice-President shall have qualified.

Section 4 The Congress may by law provide for the case of the death of any of the persons from whom the House of Representatives may choose a President whenever the right of choice shall have devolved upon them, and for the case of the death of any of the persons from whom the Senate may choose a Vice-President whenever the right of choice shall have devolved upon them.

Section 5 Sections 1 and 2 shall take effect on the 15th day of October following the ratification of this article.

Section 6 This article shall be inoperative unless it shall have been ratified as an amendment to the Constitution by the Legislatures of three-fourths of the several States within seven years from the date of its submission.

Amendment XXI

[Adopted 1933]

Section 1 The eighteenth article of amendment to the Constitution of the United States is hereby repealed.

Section 2 The transportation or importation into any State, Territory, or Possession of the United States for delivery or use therein of intoxicating liquors, in violation of the laws thereof, is hereby prohibited.

Section 3 This article shall be inoperative unless it shall have been ratified as an amendment to the Constitution by conventions in the several States, as provided in the Constitution, within seven years from the date of the submission thereof to the States by the Congress.

Amendment XXII

[Adopted 1951]

Section 1 No person shall be elected to the office of the President more than twice, and no person who has held the office of President, or acted as President, for more than two years of a term to which some other person was elected President shall be elected to the office of President more than once. But this article shall not apply to any person holding the office of President when this Article was proposed by the Congress, and shall not prevent any person who may be holding the office of President, or acting as President, during the term within which this Article becomes operative from holding the office of President or acting as President during the remainder of such term.

Section 2 This article shall be inoperative unless it shall have been ratified as an amendment to the Constitution by the legislatures of three-fourths of the several States within seven years from the date of its submission to the States by the Congress.

Amendment XXIII

[Adopted 1961]

Section 1 The District constituting the seat of Government of the United States shall appoint in such manner as the Congress may direct: A number of electors of President and Vice-President equal to the whole number of Senators and Representatives in Congress to which the District would be entitled if it were a State, but in no event more than the least populous State; they shall be in addition to those appointed by the States, but they shall be considered for the purposes of the election of President and Vice-President, to be electors appointed by a State; and they shall meet in the District and perform such duties as provided by the twelfth article of amendment.

Section 2 The Congress shall have the power to enforce this article by appropriate legislation.

Amendment XXIV

[Adopted 1964]

Section 1 The right of citizens of the United States to vote in any primary or other election for President or Vice-President, for electors for President or Vice-President, or for Senator or Representative in Congress, shall not be denied or abridged by the United States or any State by reason of failure to pay any poll tax or other tax.

Section 2 The Congress shall have the power to enforce this article by appropriate legislation.

Amendment XXV

[Adopted 1967]

Section 1 In case of the removal of the President from office or of his death or resignation, the Vice-President shall become President.

Section 2 Whenever there is a vacancy in the office of the Vice-President, the President shall nominate a Vice-President who shall take office upon confirmation by a majority vote of both Houses of Congress.

Section 3 Whenever the President transmits to the President pro tempore of the Senate and the Speaker of the House of Representatives his written declaration that he is unable to discharge the powers and duties of his office, and until he transmits to them a written declaration to the contrary, such powers and duties shall be discharged by the Vice-President as Acting President.

Section 4 Whenever the Vice-President and a majority of either the principal officers of the executive departments or of such other body as Congress may by law provide, transmit to the President pro tempore of the Senate and the Speaker of the House of Representatives their written declaration that the President is unable to discharge the powers and duties of his office, the Vice-President shall immediately assume the powers and duties of the office as Acting President.

Thereafter, when the President transmits to the President pro tempore of the Senate and the Speaker of the House of Representatives his written declaration that no inability exists, he shall resume the powers and duties of his office unless the Vice-President and a majority of either the principal officers of the executive department[s] or of such other body as Congress may by law provide, transmit within four days to the President pro tempore of the Senate and the Speaker of the House of Representatives their written declaration that the President is unable to discharge the powers and duties of his office. Thereupon Congress shall decide the issue, assembling within forty-eight hours for that purpose if not in session. If the Congress, within twenty-one days after receipt of the latter written declaration, or, if Congress is not in session, within twenty-one days after Congress is required to assemble, determines by two-thirds vote of both Houses that the President is unable to discharge the powers and duties of his office, the Vice-President shall continue to discharge the same as Acting President; otherwise, the President shall resume the powers and duties of his office.

Amendment XXVI

[Adopted 1971]

Section 1 The right of citizens of the United States, who are eighteen years of age or older, to vote shall not be denied or abridged by the United States or by any State on account of age.

Section 2 The Congress shall have power to enforce this article by appropriate legislation.

Unratified Amendment

Equal Rights Amendment (proposed by Congress March 22, 1972; seven-year deadline for ratification extended to June 30, 1982)

Section 1 Equality of rights under the law shall not be denied or abridged by the United States or by any State on account of sex.

Section 2 The Congress shall have the power to enforce, by appropriate legislation, the provisions of this article.

Section 3 This amendment shall take effect two years after the date of ratification.

Unratified Amendment

D.C. Statehood Amendment (proposed by Congress August 22, 1978)

Section 1 For purposes of representation in the Congress, election of the President and Vice-President, and article V of this Constitution, the District constituting the seat of government of the United States shall be treated as though it were a State.

Section 2 The exercise of the rights and powers conferred under this article shall be by the people of the District constituting the seat of government, and as shall be provided by Congress.

Section 3 The twenty-third article of amendment to the Constitution of the United States is hereby repealed.

Section 4 This article shall be inoperative, unless it shall have been ratified as an amendment to the Constitution by the legislatures of three-fourths of the several states within seven years from the date of its submission.

Amendment XXVII

[Adopted 1992]

No law, varying the compensation for the services of the Senators and Representatives, shall take effect, until an election of Representatives shall have intervened.

Facts and Figures: Government, Economy, and Demographics

PRESIDENTIAL ELECTIONS

Year	Candidates	Parties	Popular Vote	Percentage of Popular Vote	Electoral Vote	Percentage of Voter Participation
1789	**GEORGE WASHINGTON (Va.)***				69	
	John Adams				34	
	Others				35	
1792	**GEORGE WASHINGTON (Va.)**				132	
	John Adams				77	
	George Clinton				50	
	Others				5	
1796	**JOHN ADAMS (Mass.)**	Federalist			71	
	Thomas Jefferson	Democratic-Republican			68	
	Thomas Pinckney	Federalist			59	
	Aaron Burr	Dem.-Rep.			30	
	Others				48	
1800	**THOMAS JEFFERSON (Va.)**	Dem.-Rep.			73	
	Aaron Burr	Dem.-Rep.			73	
	John Adams	Federalist			65	
	C. C. Pinckney	Federalist			64	
	John Jay	Federalist			1	
1804	**THOMAS JEFFERSON (Va.)**	Dem.-Rep.			162	
	C. C. Pinckney	Federalist			14	
1808	**JAMES MADISON (Va.)**	Dem.-Rep.			122	
	C. C. Pinckney	Federalist			47	
	George Clinton	Dem.-Rep.			6	
1812	**JAMES MADISON (Va.)**	Dem.-Rep.			128	
	De Witt Clinton	Federalist			89	
1816	**JAMES MONROE (Va.)**	Dem.-Rep.			183	
	Rufus King	Federalist			34	
1820	**JAMES MONROE (Va.)**	Dem.-Rep.			231	
	John Quincy Adams	Dem.-Rep.			1	
1824	**JOHN Q. ADAMS (Mass.)**	Dem.-Rep.	108,740	30.5	84	26.9
	Andrew Jackson	Dem.-Rep.	153,544	43.1	99	
	William H. Crawford	Dem.-Rep.	46,618	13.1	41	
	Henry Clay	Dem.-Rep.	47,136	13.2	37	
1828	**ANDREW JACKSON (Tenn.)**	Democratic	647,286	56.0	178	57.6
	John Quincy Adams	National Republican	508,064	44.0	83	

*State of residence when elected president.

Year	Candidates	Parties	Popular Vote	Percentage of Popular Vote	Electoral Vote	Percentage of Voter Participation
1832	**ANDREW JACKSON (Tenn.)**	Democratic	687,502	55.0	219	55.4
	Henry Clay	National Republican	530,189	42.4	49	
	John Floyd	Independent			11	
	William Wirt	Anti-Mason	33,108	2.6	7	
1836	**MARTIN VAN BUREN (N.Y.)**	Democratic	765,483	50.9	170	57.8
	W. H. Harrison	Whig			73	
	Hugh L. White	Whig	739,795	49.1	26	
	Daniel Webster	Whig			14	
	W. P. Mangum	Independent			11	
1840	**WILLIAM H. HARRISON (Ohio)**	Whig	1,274,624	53.1	234	78.0
	Martin Van Buren	Democratic	1,127,781	46.9	60	
	J. G. Birney	Liberty	7,069		—	
1844	**JAMES K. POLK (Tenn.)**	Democratic	1,338,464	49.6	170	78.9
	Henry Clay	Whig	1,300,097	48.1	105	
	J. G. Birney	Liberty	62,300	2.3	—	
1848	**ZACHARY TAYLOR (La.)**	Whig	1,360,099	47.4	163	72.7
	Lewis Cass	Democratic	1,220,544	42.5	127	
	Martin Van Buren	Free-Soil	291,263	10.1	—	
1852	**FRANKLIN PIERCE (N.H.)**	Democratic	1,601,117	50.9	254	69.6
	Winfield Scott	Whig	1,385,453	44.1	42	
	John P. Hale	Free-Soil	155,825	5.0	—	
1856	**JAMES BUCHANAN (Pa.)**	Democratic	1,832,995	45.3	174	78.9
	John C. Frémont	Republican	1,339,932	33.1	114	
	Millard Fillmore	American	871,731	21.6	8	
1860	**ABRAHAM LINCOLN (Ill.)**	Republican	1,866,452	39.8	180	81.2
	Stephen A. Douglas	Democratic	1,375,157	29.4	12	
	John C. Breckinridge	Democratic	847,953	18.1	72	
	John Bell	Union	590,631	12.6	39	
1864	**ABRAHAM LINCOLN (Ill.)**	Republican	2,213,665	55.1	212	73.8
	George B. McClellan	Democratic	1,805,237	44.9	21	
1868	**ULYSSES S. GRANT (Ill.)**	Republican	3,012,833	52.7	214	78.1
	Horatio Seymour	Democratic	2,703,249	47.3	80	
1872	**ULYSSES S. GRANT (Ill.)**	Republican	3,597,132	55.6	286	71.3
	Horace Greeley	Democratic; Liberal Republican	2,834,125	43.9	66	
1876	**RUTHERFORD B. HAYES (Ohio)**	Republican	4,036,298	48.0	185	81.8
	Samuel J. Tilden	Democratic	4,288,590	51.0	184	
1880	**JAMES A. GARFIELD (Ohio)**	Republican	4,454,416	48.5	214	79.4
	Winfield S. Hancock	Democratic	4,444,952	48.1	155	
1884	**GROVER CLEVELAND (N.Y.)**	Democratic	4,874,986	48.5	219	77.5
	James G. Blaine	Republican	4,851,981	48.3	182	
1888	**BENJAMIN HARRISON (Ind.)**	Republican	5,439,853	47.9	233	79.3
	Grover Cleveland	Democratic	5,540,309	48.6	168	
1892	**GROVER CLEVELAND (N.Y.)**	Democratic	5,555,426	46.1	277	74.7
	Benjamin Harrison	Republican	5,182,690	43.0	145	
	James B. Weaver	People's	1,029,846	8.5	22	
1896	**WILLIAM McKINLEY (Ohio)**	Republican	7,104,779	51.1	271	79.3
	William J. Bryan	Democratic-People's	6,502,925	47.7	176	

Year	Candidates	Parties	Popular Vote	Percentage of Popular Vote	Electoral Vote	Percentage of Voter Participation
1900	**WILLIAM McKINLEY (Ohio)**	Republican	7,207,923	51.7	292	73.2
	William J. Bryan	Dem.-Populist	6,358,133	45.5	155	
1904	**THEODORE ROOSEVELT (N.Y.)**	Republican	7,623,486	57.9	336	65.2
	Alton B. Parker	Democratic	5,077,911	37.6	140	
	Eugene V. Debs	Socialist	402,283	3.0	—	
1908	**WILLIAM H. TAFT (Ohio)**	Republican	7,678,908	51.6	321	65.4
	William J. Bryan	Democratic	6,409,104	43.1	162	
	Eugene V. Debs	Socialist	420,793	2.8	—	
1912	**WOODROW WILSON (N.J.)**	Democratic	6,293,454	41.9	435	58.8
	Theodore Roosevelt	Progressive	4,119,538	27.4	88	
	William H. Taft	Republican	3,484,980	23.2	8	
	Eugene V. Debs	Socialist	900,672	6.1	—	
1916	**WOODROW WILSON (N.J.)**	Democratic	9,129,606	49.4	277	61.6
	Charles E. Hughes	Republican	8,538,221	46.2	254	
	A. L. Benson	Socialist	585,113	3.2	—	
1920	**WARREN G. HARDING (Ohio)**	Republican	16,143,407	60.5	404	49.2
	James M. Cox	Democratic	9,130,328	34.2	127	
	Eugene V. Debs	Socialist	919,799	3.4	—	
1924	**CALVIN COOLIDGE (Mass.)**	Republican	15,725,016	54.0	382	48.9
	John W. Davis	Democratic	8,386,503	28.8	136	
	Robert M. La Follette	Progressive	4,822,856	16.6	13	
1928	**HERBERT HOOVER (Calif.)**	Republican	21,391,381	57.4	444	56.9
	Alfred E. Smith	Democratic	15,016,443	40.3	87	
	Norman Thomas	Socialist	881,951	2.3	—	
	William Z. Foster	Communist	102,991	0.3	—	
1932	**FRANKLIN D. ROOSEVELT (N.Y.)**	Democratic	22,821,857	57.4	472	56.9
	Herbert Hoover	Republican	15,761,841	39.7	59	
	Norman Thomas	Socialist	881,951	2.2	—	
1936	**FRANKLIN D. ROOSEVELT (N.Y.)**	Democratic	27,751,597	60.8	523	61.0
	Alfred M. Landon	Republican	16,679,583	36.5	8	
	William Lemke	Union	882,479	1.9	—	
1940	**FRANKLIN D. ROOSEVELT (N.Y.)**	Democratic	27,244,160	54.8	449	62.5
	Wendell Willkie	Republican	22,305,198	44.8	82	
1944	**FRANKLIN D. ROOSEVELT (N.Y.)**	Democratic	25,602,504	53.5	432	55.9
	Thomas E. Dewey	Republican	22,006,285	46.0	99	
1948	**HARRY S. TRUMAN (Mo.)**	Democratic	24,105,695	49.5	303	53.0
	Thomas E. Dewey	Republican	21,969,170	45.1	189	
	J. Strom Thurmond	States'-Rights Democratic	1,169,021	2.4	38	
	Henry A. Wallace	Progressive	1,156,103	2.4	—	
1952	**DWIGHT D. EISENHOWER (N.Y.)**	Republican	33,936,252	55.1	442	63.3
	Adlai Stevenson	Democratic	27,314,992	44.4	89	
1956	**DWIGHT D. EISENHOWER (N.Y.)**	Republican	35,575,420	57.6	457	60.6
	Adlai Stevenson	Democratic	26,033,066	42.1	73	
	Other	—	—	—	1	
1960	**JOHN F. KENNEDY (Mass.)**	Democratic	34,227,096	49.9	303	62.8
	Richard M. Nixon	Republican	34,108,546	49.6	219	
	Other	—	—	—	15	
1964	**LYNDON B. JOHNSON (Texas)**	Democratic	43,126,506	61.1	486	61.7
	Barry M. Goldwater	Republican	27,176,799	38.5	52	

Year	Candidates	Parties	Popular Vote	Percentage of Popular Vote	Electoral Vote	Percentage of Voter Participation
1968	RICHARD M. NIXON (N.Y.)	Republican	31,770,237	43.4	301	60.9
	Hubert H. Humphrey	Democratic	31,270,533	42.7	191	
	George Wallace	American Indep.	9,906,141	13.5	46	
1972	RICHARD M. NIXON (N.Y.)	Republican	47,169,911	60.7	520	55.2
	George S. McGovern	Democratic	29,170,383	37.5	17	
	Other	—	—	—	1	
1976	JIMMY CARTER (Ga.)	Democratic	40,830,763	50.0	297	53.5
	Gerald R. Ford	Republican	39,147,793	48.0	240	
	Other	—	1,575,459	2.1	—	
1980	RONALD REAGAN (Calif.)	Republican	43,901,812	51.0	489	54.0
	Jimmy Carter	Democratic	35,483,820	41.0	49	
	John B. Anderson	Independent	5,719,722	7.0	—	
	Ed Clark	Libertarian	921,188	1.1	—	
1984	RONALD REAGAN (Calif.)	Republican	54,455,075	59.0	525	53.1
	Walter Mondale	Democratic	37,577,185	41.0	13	
1988	GEORGE H. W. BUSH (Texas)	Republican	47,946,422	54.0	426	50.2
	Michael S. Dukakis	Democratic	41,016,429	46.0	112	
1992	WILLIAM J. CLINTON (Ark.)	Democratic	44,908,254	43.0	370	55.9
	George H. W. Bush	Republican	39,102,282	38.0	168	
	H. Ross Perot	Independent	19,721,433	19.0	—	
1996	WILLIAM J. CLINTON (Ark.)	Democratic	47,401,185	49.2	379	49.0
	Robert Dole	Republican	39,197,469	40.7	159	
	H. Ross Perot	Independent	8,085,294	8.4	—	
2000	GEORGE W. BUSH (Texas)	Republican	50,456,062	47.8	271	51.2
	Al Gore	Democratic	50,996,862	48.4	267	
	Ralph Nader	Green Party	2,858,843	2.7	—	
	Patrick J. Buchanan	—	438,760	0.4	—	
2004	GEORGE W. BUSH (Texas)	Republican	61,872,711	50.7	286	60.3
	John F. Kerry	Democratic	58,894,584	48.3	252	
	Other	—	1,582,185	1.3	—	
2008	BARACK OBAMA (Ill.)	Democratic	69,456,897	52.9	365	56.8
	John McCain	Republican	59,934,814	45.7	173	

PRESIDENTS, VICE PRESIDENTS, AND SECRETARIES OF STATE

The Washington Administration (1789–1797)

Vice President	John Adams	1789–1797
Secretary of State	Thomas Jefferson	1789–1793
	Edmund Randolph	1794–1795
	Timothy Pickering	1795–1797

The John Adams Administration (1797–1801)

Vice President	Thomas Jefferson	1797–1801
Secretary of State	Timothy Pickering	1797–1800
	John Marshall	1800–1801

The Jefferson Administration (1801–1809)

Vice President	Aaron Burr	1801–1805
	George Clinton	1805–1809
Secretary of State	James Madison	1801–1809

The Madison Administration (1809–1817)

Vice President	George Clinton	1809–1813
	Elbridge Gerry	1813–1817
Secretary of State	Robert Smith	1809–1811
	James Monroe	1811–1817

The Monroe Administration (1817–1825)

Vice President	Daniel Tompkins	1817–1825
Secretary of State	John Quincy Adams	1817–1825

The John Quincy Adams Administration (1825–1829)

Vice President	John C. Calhoun	1825–1829
Secretary of State	Henry Clay	1825–1829

The Jackson Administration (1829–1837)

Vice President	John C. Calhoun	1829–1833
	Martin Van Buren	1833–1837
Secretary of State	Martin Van Buren	1829–1831
	Edward Livingston	1831–1833
	Louis McLane	1833–1834
	John Forsyth	1834–1837

The Van Buren Administration (1837–1841)

Vice President	Richard M. Johnson	1837–1841
Secretary of State	John Forsyth	1837–1841

The William Harrison Administration (1841)

Vice President	John Tyler	1841
Secretary of State	Daniel Webster	1841

The Tyler Administration (1841–1845)

Vice President	None	
Secretary of State	Daniel Webster	1841–1843
	Hugh S. Legaré	1843
	Abel P. Upshur	1843–1844
	John C. Calhoun	1844–1845

The Polk Administration (1845–1849)

Vice President	George M. Dallas	1845–1849
Secretary of State	James Buchanan	1845–1849

The Taylor Administration (1849–1850)

Vice President	Millard Fillmore	1849–1850
Secretary of State	John M. Clayton	1849–1850

The Fillmore Administration (1850–1853)

Vice President	None	
Secretary of State	Daniel Webster	1850–1852
	Edward Everett	1852–1853

The Pierce Administration (1853–1857)

Vice President	William R. King	1853–1857
Secretary of State	William L. Marcy	1853–1857

The Buchanan Administration (1857–1861)

Vice President	John C. Breckinridge	1857–1861
Secretary of State	Lewis Cass	1857–1860
	Jeremiah S. Black	1860–1861

The Lincoln Administration (1861–1865)

Vice President	Hannibal Hamlin	1861–1865
	Andrew Johnson	1865
Secretary of State	William H. Seward	1861–1865

The Andrew Johnson Administration (1865–1869)

Vice President	None	
Secretary of State	William H. Seward	1865–1869

The Grant Administration (1869–1877)

Vice President	Schuyler Colfax	1869–1873
	Henry Wilson	1873–1877
Secretary of State	Elihu B. Washburne	1869
	Hamilton Fish	1869–1877

The Hayes Administration (1877–1881)

Vice President	William A. Wheeler	1877–1881
Secretary of State	William M. Evarts	1877–1881

The Garfield Administration (1881)

Vice President	Chester A. Arthur	1881
Secretary of State	James G. Blaine	1881

The Arthur Administration (1881–1885)

Vice President	None	
Secretary of State	F. T. Frelinghuysen	1881–1885

The Cleveland Administration (1885–1889)

Vice President	Thomas A. Hendricks	1885–1889
Secretary of State	Thomas F. Bayard	1885–1889

The Benjamin Harrison Administration (1889–1893)

Vice President	Levi P. Morton	1889–1893
Secretary of State	James G. Blaine	1889–1892
	John W. Foster	1892–1893

The Cleveland Administration (1893–1897)

Vice President	Adlai E. Stevenson	1893–1897
Secretary of State	Walter Q. Gresham	1893–1895
	Richard Olney	1895–1897

The McKinley Administration (1897–1901)

Vice President	Garret A. Hobart	1897–1901
	Theodore Roosevelt	1901
Secretary of State	John Sherman	1897–1898
	William R. Day	1898
	John Hay	1898–1901

The Theodore Roosevelt Administration (1901–1909)

Vice President	Charles Fairbanks	1905–1909
Secretary of State	John Hay	1901–1905
	Elihu Root	1905–1909
	Robert Bacon	1909

The Taft Administration (1909–1913)

Vice President	James S. Sherman	1909–1913
Secretary of State	Philander C. Knox	1909–1913

The Wilson Administration (1913–1921)

Vice President	Thomas R. Marshall	1913–1921
Secretary of State	William J. Bryan	1913–1915
	Robert Lansing	1915–1920
	Bainbridge Colby	1920–1921

The Harding Administration (1921–1923)

Vice President	Calvin Coolidge	1921–1923
Secretary of State	Charles E. Hughes	1921–1923

The Coolidge Administration (1923–1929)

Vice President	Charles G. Dawes	1925–1929
Secretary of State	Charles E. Hughes	1923–1925
	Frank B. Kellogg	1925–1929

The Hoover Administration (1929–1933)

Vice President	Charles Curtis	1929–1933
Secretary of State	Henry L. Stimson	1929–1933

The Franklin D. Roosevelt Administration (1933–1945)

Vice President	John Nance Garner	1933–1941
	Henry A. Wallace	1941–1945
	Harry S. Truman	1945
Secretary of State	Cordell Hull	1933–1944
	Edward R. Stettinius Jr.	1944–1945

The Truman Administration (1945–1953)

Vice President	Alben W. Barkley	1949–1953
Secretary of State	Edward R. Stettinius Jr.	1945
	James F. Byrnes	1945–1947
	George C. Marshall	1947–1949
	Dean G. Acheson	1949–1953

The Eisenhower Administration (1953–1961)

Vice President	Richard M. Nixon	1953–1961
Secretary of State	John Foster Dulles	1953–1959
	Christian A. Herter	1959–1961

The Kennedy Administration (1961–1963)

Vice President	Lyndon B. Johnson	1961–1963
Secretary of State	Dean Rusk	1961–1963

The Lyndon Johnson Administration (1963–1969)

Vice President	Hubert H. Humphrey	1965–1969
Secretary of State	Dean Rusk	1963–1969

The Nixon Administration (1969–1974)

Vice President	Spiro T. Agnew	1969–1973
	Gerald R. Ford	1973–1974
Secretary of State	William P. Rogers	1969–1973
	Henry A. Kissinger	1973–1974

The Ford Administration (1974–1977)

Vice President	Nelson A. Rockefeller	1974–1977
Secretary of State	Henry A. Kissinger	1974–1977

The Carter Administration (1977–1981)

Vice President	Walter F. Mondale	1977–1981
Secretary of State	Cyrus R. Vance	1977–1980
	Edmund Muskie	1980–1981

The Reagan Administration (1981–1989)

Vice President	George H. W. Bush	1981–1989
Secretary of State	Alexander M. Haig	1981–1982
	George P. Shultz	1982–1989

The George H. W. Bush Administration (1989–1993)

Vice President	J. Danforth Quayle	1989–1993
Secretary of State	James A. Baker III	1989–1992
	Lawrence S. Eagleburger	1992–1993

The Clinton Administration (1993–2001)

Vice President	Albert Gore	1993–2001
Secretary of State	Warren M. Christopher	1993–1997
	Madeleine K. Albright	1997–2001

The George W. Bush Administration (2001–2009)

Vice President	Richard Cheney	2001–2009
Secretary of State	Colin Powell	2001–2005
	Condoleezza Rice	2005–2009

The Obama Administration (2009–)

Vice President	Joseph R. Biden	2009–
Secretary of State	Hillary Rodham Clinton	2009–

SUPREME COURT JUSTICES

NAME	SERVICE	APPOINTED BY	NAME	SERVICE	APPOINTED BY
John Jay*	1789–1795	Washington	Samuel Blatchford	1882–1893	Arthur
James Wilson	1789–1798	Washington	Lucius Q. C. Lamar	1888–1893	Cleveland
John Blair	1789–1796	Washington	**Melville W. Fuller**	1888–1910	Cleveland
John Rutledge	1790–1791	Washington	David J. Brewer	1889–1910	B. Harrison
William Cushing	1790–1810	Washington	Henry B. Brown	1890–1906	B. Harrison
James Iredell	1790–1799	Washington	George Shiras	1892–1903	B. Harrison
Thomas Johnson	1791–1793	Washington	Howell E. Jackson	1893–1895	B. Harrison
William Paterson	1793–1806	Washington	Edward D. White	1894–1910	Cleveland
John Rutledge†	1795	Washington	Rufus W. Peckham	1896–1909	Cleveland
Samuel Chase	1796–1811	Washington	Joseph McKenna	1898–1925	McKinley
Oliver Ellsworth	1796–1799	Washington	Oliver W. Holmes	1902–1932	T. Roosevelt
Bushrod Washington	1798–1829	J. Adams	William R. Day	1903–1922	T. Roosevelt
Alfred Moore	1799–1804	J. Adams	William H. Moody	1906–1910	T. Roosevelt
John Marshall	1801–1835	J. Adams	Horace H. Lurton	1910–1914	Taft
William Johnson	1804–1834	Jefferson	Charles E. Hughes	1910–1916	Taft
Henry B. Livingston	1806–1823	Jefferson	Willis Van Devanter	1910–1937	Taft
Thomas Todd	1807–1826	Jefferson	**Edward D. White**	1910–1921	Taft
Gabriel Duval	1811–1836	Madison	Joseph R. Lamar	1911–1916	Taft
Joseph Story	1811–1845	Madison	Mahlon Pitney	1912–1922	Taft
Smith Thompson	1823–1843	Monroe	James C. McReynolds	1914–1941	Wilson
Robert Trimble	1826–1828	J. Q. Adams	Louis D. Brandeis	1916–1939	Wilson
John McLean	1829–1861	Jackson	John H. Clarke	1916–1922	Wilson
Henry Baldwin	1830–1844	Jackson	**William H. Taft**	1921–1930	Harding
James M. Wayne	1835–1867	Jackson	George Sutherland	1922–1938	Harding
Roger B. Taney	1836–1864	Jackson	Pierce Butler	1923–1939	Harding
Philip P. Barbour	1836–1841	Jackson	Edward T. Sanford	1923–1930	Harding
John Catron	1837–1865	Van Buren	Harlan F. Stone	1925–1941	Coolidge
John McKinley	1837–1852	Van Buren	**Charles E. Hughes**	1930–1941	Hoover
Peter V. Daniel	1841–1860	Van Buren	Owen J. Roberts	1930–1945	Hoover
Samuel Nelson	1845–1872	Tyler	Benjamin N. Cardozo	1932–1938	Hoover
Levi Woodbury	1845–1851	Polk	Hugo L. Black	1937–1971	F. Roosevelt
Robert C. Grier	1846–1870	Polk	Stanley F. Reed	1938–1957	F. Roosevelt
Benjamin R. Curtis	1851–1857	Fillmore	Felix Frankfurter	1939–1962	F. Roosevelt
John A. Campbell	1853–1861	Pierce	William O. Douglas	1939–1975	F. Roosevelt
Nathan Clifford	1858–1881	Buchanan	Frank Murphy	1940–1949	F. Roosevelt
Noah H. Swayne	1862–1881	Lincoln	**Harlan F. Stone**	1941–1946	F. Roosevelt
Samuel F. Miller	1862–1890	Lincoln	James F. Byrnes	1941–1942	F. Roosevelt
David Davis	1862–1877	Lincoln	Robert H. Jackson	1941–1954	F. Roosevelt
Stephen J. Field	1863–1897	Lincoln	Wiley B. Rutledge	1943–1949	F. Roosevelt
Salmon P. Chase	1864–1873	Lincoln	Harold H. Burton	1945–1958	Truman
William Strong	1870–1880	Grant	**Frederick M. Vinson**	1946–1953	Truman
Joseph P. Bradley	1870–1892	Grant	Tom C. Clark	1949–1967	Truman
Ward Hunt	1873–1882	Grant	Sherman Minton	1949–1956	Truman
Morrison R. Waite	1874–1888	Grant	**Earl Warren**	1953–1969	Eisenhower
John M. Harlan	1877–1911	Hayes	John Marshall Harlan	1955–1971	Eisenhower
William B. Woods	1880–1887	Hayes	William J. Brennan Jr.	1956–1990	Eisenhower
Stanley Matthews	1881–1889	Garfield	Charles E. Whittaker	1957–1962	Eisenhower
Horace Gray	1882–1902	Arthur	Potter Stewart	1958–1981	Eisenhower

*Chief Justices appear in bold type.
†Acting Chief Justice; Senate refused to confirm appointment.

Name	Service	Appointed by
Byron R. White	1962–1993	Kennedy
Arthur J. Goldberg	1962–1965	Kennedy
Abe Fortas	1965–1969	L. Johnson
Thurgood Marshall	1967–1991	L. Johnson
Warren E. Burger	1969–1986	Nixon
Harry A. Blackmun	1970–1994	Nixon
Lewis F. Powell Jr.	1972–1988	Nixon
William H. Rehnquist	1972–1986	Nixon
John Paul Stevens	1975–	Ford
Sandra Day O'Connor	1981–2006	Reagan
William H. Rehnquist	1986–2005	Reagan

Name	Service	Appointed by
Antonin Scalia	1986–	Reagan
Anthony M. Kennedy	1988–	Reagan
David H. Souter	1990–2009	G. H. W. Bush
Clarence Thomas	1991–	G. H. W. Bush
Ruth Bader Ginsburg	1993–	Clinton
Stephen Breyer	1994–	Clinton
John G. Roberts Jr.	2005–	G. W. Bush
Samuel A. Alito Jr.	2006–	G. W. Bush
Sonia Sotomayor	2009–	B. Obama

FEDERAL SPENDING AND THE ECONOMY, 1790–2007

Year	Gross National Product (in billions)	Foreign Trade (in millions) Exports	Imports	Federal Budget (in billions)	Federal Surplus/Deficit (in billions)	Federal Debt (in billions)
1790	NA	20	23	0.004	0.00015	0.076
1800	NA	71	91	0.011	0.0006	0.083
1810	NA	67	85	0.008	0.0012	0.053
1820	NA	70	74	0.018	−0.0004	0.091
1830	NA	74	71	0.015	0.100	0.049
1840	NA	132	107	0.024	−0.005	0.004
1850	NA	152	178	0.040	0.004	0.064
1860	NA	400	362	0.063	−0.01	0.065
1870	7.4	451	462	0.310	0.10	2.4
1880	11.2	853	761	0.268	0.07	2.1
1890	13.1	910	823	0.318	0.09	1.2
1900	18.7	1,499	930	0.521	0.05	1.2
1910	35.3	1,919	1,646	0.694	−0.02	1.1
1920	91.5	8,664	5,784	6.357	0.3	24.3
1930	90.4	4,013	3,500	3.320	0.7	16.3
1940	99.7	4,030	7,433	9.6	−2.7	43.0
1950	284.8	10,816	9,125	43.1	−2.2	257.4
1960	503.7	19,600	15,046	92.2	0.3	286.3
1970	977.1	42,700	40,189	195.6	−2.8	371.0
1980	2,631.7	220,600	244,871	590.9	−73.8	907.7
1990	5,832.2	393,600	495,300	1,253.2	−221.2	3,266.1
2000	9,848.0	1,070,054	1,445,438	1,788.8	236.4	5,701.9
2005	12,520.8	1,283,753	1,995,320	2,153.9	−318.3	7,905.3
2007	13,937.0	1,645,726	2,345,983	2,568.2	−162.0	8,950.7

SOURCE: *Historical Statistics of the U.S., Colonial Times to 1970* (1975) and www.census.gov.

POPULATION GROWTH, 1630–2000

Year	Population	Percent Increase	Year	Population	Percent Increase
1630	4,600	—	1820	9,638,453	33.1
1640	26,600	473.3	1830	12,866,020	33.5
1650	50,400	89.1	1840	17,069,453	32.7
1660	75,100	49.0	1850	23,191,876	35.9
1670	111,900	49.1	1860	31,443,321	35.6
1680	151,500	35.4	1870	39,818,449	26.6
1690	210,400	38.9	1880	50,155,783	26.0
1700	250,900	19.3	1890	62,947,714	25.5
1710	331,700	32.2	1900	75,994,575	20.7
1720	466,200	40.5	1910	91,972,266	21.0
1730	629,400	35.0	1920	105,710,620	14.9
1740	905,600	43.9	1930	122,775,046	16.1
1750	1,170,800	30.0	1940	131,669,275	7.2
1760	1,593,600	36.1	1950	150,697,361	14.5
1770	2,148,100	34.8	1960	179,323,175	19.0
1780	2,780,400	29.4	1970	203,302,031	13.4
1790	3,929,214	41.3	1980	226,542,199	11.4
1800	5,308,483	35.1	1990	248,718,302	9.8
1810	7,239,881	36.4	2000	281,422,509	13.1

SOURCE: *Historical Statistics of the U.S., Colonial Times to 1970* (1975) and www.census.gov.

Birthrate, 1820–2000

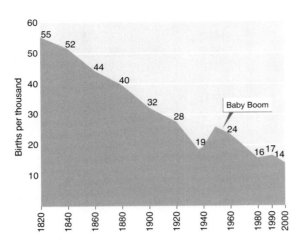

SOURCE: Data from *Historical Statistics of the U.S., Colonial Times to 1970* (1975) and www.census.gov.

Life Expectancy, 1900–2000

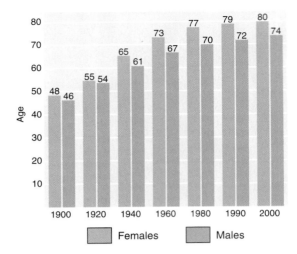

SOURCE: Data from *Historical Statistics of the U.S., Colonial Times to 1970* (1975) and www.census.gov.

Major Trends in Immigration, 1820–2000

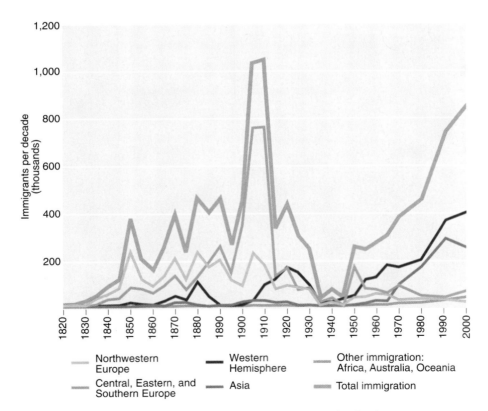

SOURCE: Data from *Historical Statistics of the U.S., Colonial Times to 1970* (1975) and www.census.gov.

Research Resources in U.S. History

For help refining your research skills, finding what you need on the Web, and using the Web effectively, see "Online Research and Reference Aids" at bedfordstmartins.com/roarkcompact.

While doing research in history, you will use the library to track down primary and secondary sources and to answer questions that arise as you learn more about your topic. This appendix suggests helpful indexes, references, periodicals, and sources of primary documents. It also offers an overview of electronic resources available through the Internet. The materials listed here are not carried at all libraries, but they will give you an idea of the range of sources available. Remember, too, that librarians are an extremely helpful resource. They can direct you to useful materials throughout your research process.

Bibliographies and Indexes

American Historical Association Guide to Historical Literature. 3rd ed. New York: Oxford University Press, 1995. Offers 27,000 citations to important historical literature arranged in forty-eight sections covering theory, international history, and regional history. An indispensable guide recently updated to include current trends in historical research.

American History and Life. Santa Barbara: ABC-Clio, 1964–. Covers publications of all sorts on U.S. and Canadian history and culture in a chronological and regional format, with abstracts and alphabetical indexes. Available in computerized format. The most complete ongoing bibliography for American history.

Primary Resources

There are many routes to finding contemporary material for historical research. You may search your library catalog using the name of a prominent historical figure as an author; you may also find anthologies covering particular themes or periods in history. Consider also the following special materials for your research.

THE PRESS

American Periodical Series, 1741–1900. Ann Arbor: University Microfilms, 1946–1979. Includes periodicals from the colonial period to 1900. Available in microfilm and as an online database.

Herstory Microfilm Collection. Berkeley: Women's History Research Center, 1973. A microfilm collection of alternative feminist periodicals published between 1960

and 1980. Provides an interesting documentary history of the women's movement.

New York Times Index. New York: New York Times, 1913–. Many libraries have this newspaper on microfilm going back to its beginning in 1851. An index is available to locate specific dates and pages of news stories. See also *ProQuest Historical Newspapers.*

ProQuest Historical Newspapers. Available at many libraries, a database of full-text articles from dozens of newspapers, including the *New York Times* for 1851–2001, the *Washington Post* for 1877–1988, and the *Los Angeles Times* for 1881–1984.

Readers' Guide to Periodical Literature. New York: Wilson, 1900–. This index to popular magazines started in 1900; an earlier index, *Poole's Index to Periodical Literature,* covers 1802–1906.

DIARIES, PAMPHLETS, BOOKS

The American Culture Series, 1493–1875. Ann Arbor: University Microfilms, 1941–1974. A microfilm set, with a useful index, featuring books and pamphlets published between 1493 and 1875.

American Women's Diaries. New Canaan: Readex, 1984–. A collection of reproductions of women's diaries. There are different series for different regions of the country.

The March of America Facsimile Series. Ann Arbor: University Microfilms, 1966. A collection of more than ninety facsimiles of travel accounts to the New World published in English or English translation from the fifteenth through the nineteenth centuries.

Women in America from Colonial Times to the Twentieth Century. New York: Arno, 1974. A collection of reprints of dozens of books written by women describing women's lives and experiences in their own words.

GOVERNMENT DOCUMENTS

Congressional Record. Washington, D.C.: Government Printing Office, 1874–. Covers daily debates and proceedings of Congress. Earlier series were called *Debates and Proceedings in the Congress of the United States* and *The Congressional Globe.*

Foreign Relations of the United States. Washington, D.C.: Department of State, 1861–. A collection of documents from 1861, including diplomatic papers, correspondence, and memoranda, that provides a documentary record of U.S. foreign policy.

Public Papers of the Presidents. Washington, D.C.: Office of the Federal Register, 1957–. Includes major documents issued by the executive branch from the Hoover administration to the present.

Serial Set. Washington, D.C.: Government Printing Office, 1789–1969. A huge collection of congressional documents, available in many libraries on microfiche, with a useful index.

LOCAL HISTORY COLLECTIONS

State and county historical societies often house a wealth of historical documents; consider their resources when planning your research. You may find yourself working with material that no one else has analyzed before.

Internet Resources

The following online sources are good places to find historical information. You can also search the Web using any of a number of search engines. Bear in mind that there is no board of editors screening Internet sites for accuracy or usefulness. Be critical of all sources, particularly those found on the Internet. When this book went to press, the sites listed below were active and maintained.

The American Civil War Homepage. **sunsite.utk.edu/civil-war.** A comprehensive resource bank on the American Civil War. Maintained by George Hoemann of the University of Tennessee, the site contains letters, documents, photographs, information about battles, links to other sites, and regiment rosters.

American Memory: Historical Collections for the National Digital Library. **memory.loc.gov/ammem/index.html.** A Web site that features digitized primary source materials from the Library of Congress, among them African American pamphlets, Civil War photographs, documents from the Constitutional Convention of 1774–1790, materials on woman suffrage, and oral histories.

Historical Text Archive. **historicaltextarchive.com.** One of the oldest and largest Internet archives of historical documents, articles, photographs, and more. Includes sections on Native American, African American, and U.S. history, in which can be found texts of the Declaration of Independence, the Constitution of Iroquois Nations, World War II surrender documents, and a great deal more.

Index of Native American Resources on the Internet. **hanksville.org/NAresources.** A vast index of Native American resources organized by category, including oral history, written history, geographical areas, timelines, and photographs. A central place to search for information on Native American history.

Internet Resources for Students of Afro-American History and Culture. **libraries.rutgers.edu/rul/rr_gateway/research_guides/history/afrores.shtml.** A good place to begin research on topics in African American history. The site is indexed and linked to a wide variety of sources, including primary documents, text collections, and archival sources on African American history.

Make History. **bedfordstmartins.com/makehistory.** Comprising the content of five online libraries—Map Central, the Bedford Image Library, DocLinks, HistoryLinks, and PlaceLinks—Make History provides access to relevant digital content including maps, documents, and Web links. Searchable by keyword, topic, date, or specific chapter of *The American Promise.*

NativeWeb. **nativeweb.org.** One of the best organized and most accessible sites on Native American issues, *NativeWeb* combines an events calendar and message board with history, statistics, a list of news sources, archives, new and related sites that are updated each week, and documents.

Perry-Castañeda Library Map Collection. **lib.utexas.edu/maps/.** The University of Texas at Austin library has put over seven hundred U.S. maps on the Web along with hundreds of other historical and contemporary maps from around the world.

Smithsonian Institution. **si.edu.** Organized by subject, such as military history or Hispanic/Latino American resources, this site offers selected links to sites hosted by Smithsonian museums and organizations. Content includes images, book suggestions, maps, and links.

Supreme Court Collection. **law.cornell.edu/supct/.** This database can be used to search for information on various Supreme Court cases. Although the site primarily covers cases that occurred after 1990, there is information on some earlier historic cases. The justices' opinions, as originally written, are included.

United States Holocaust Memorial Museum. **ushmm.org.** This site contains information about the Holocaust Museum in Washington, D.C., and the Holocaust in general, plus links to related sites.

Women and Social Movements in the United States, 1600–2000. **womhist.alexanderstreet.com.** Available at many libraries, this database brings together hundreds of documents, links, and bibliographies documenting women's activism in public life.

WWW-VL History Index. **vlib.iue.it/history.** A vast list of more than 1,700 links to sites of interest to historians, arranged by general topic and by continent and country. The United States history page includes links to online research tools as well as links arranged by topic and historical period.

A Note to Students: This list of terms is provided to help you build your historical vocabulary. Many of these terms refer to broad, enduring concepts that you may encounter not only in further studies of history but also when following current events. For definitions and discussions of words not included here, consult a dictionary and the book's index, which will point you to topics covered at greater length in the book.

affirmative action Policies established in the 1960s and 1970s by governments, businesses, universities, and other institutions to overcome the effects of past discrimination against specific groups such as racial and ethnic minorities and women. Measures to ensure equal opportunity include setting goals for admission, hiring, and promotion; considering minority status when allocating resources; and actively encouraging victims of past discrimination to apply for jobs and other resources.

agribusiness Farming on a large scale, using the production, processing, and distribution methods of modern business. Farming became a big business, not just a way to feed a family and make a living, in the late nineteenth century as farms got larger and more mechanized. In the 1940s and 1950s, specialized commercial farms replaced many family-run operations and grew to an enormous scale.

alliance system The military and diplomatic system formulated in an effort to create a balance of power in pre–World War I Europe. Nations were bound together by rigid and comprehensive treaties that promised mutual aid in the case of attack by specific nations. The system swung into action after the Austrian archduke Franz Ferdinand was assassinated in Sarajevo on June 28, 1914, dragging most of Europe into war.

anarchist A person who rebels against established order and authority. An anarchist believes that government of any kind is unnecessary and undesirable and should be replaced with voluntary cooperation and free association. Anarchists became increasingly visible in the United States in the late nineteenth and early twentieth centuries. They advocated revolution, and their numbers grew through appeals to discontented laborers. Anarchists frequently employed violence in an attempt to achieve their goals. In 1901, anarchist Leon Czolgosz assassinated President William McKinley.

antebellum A term that means "before a war" and commonly refers to the period prior to the Civil War.

antinomian A person who does not obey societal or religious laws. In colonial Massachusetts, Puritan authorities accused Anne Hutchinson of antinomianism because she believed that Christians could achieve salvation by faith alone. They further asserted, incorrectly, that Hutchinson also held the belief that it was not necessary to follow God's laws as set forth in the Bible.

archaeology A social science devoted to learning about people who lived in the past by studying physical artifacts created by humans. Most but not all archaeological study focuses on the history of people who lived before the use of the written word.

Archaic A term applied to various hunting and gathering cultures that descended from Paleo-Indians. The term also refers to the period of time when these cultures dominated ancient America, roughly 8000 BP to between 2000 and 1000 BP.

artifacts Material remains studied and used by archaeologists and historians to support their interpretations of human history. Examples of artifacts include bones, pots, baskets, jewelry, furniture, tools, clothing, and buildings.

artisan A term commonly used prior to 1900 to describe a skilled craftsperson, such as a cabinetmaker.

Bill of Rights The term commonly used to identify the first ten amendments to the U.S. Constitution (the last of which was ratified in 1791). The Bill of Rights guarantees individual liberties and defines limitations to federal power. Many states made the promise of the prompt addition of a bill of rights a precondition for their ratification of the Constitution.

black nationalism A term linked to several African American movements emphasizing racial pride, separation from whites and white institutions, and black autonomy. Black nationalism gained in popularity with the rise of Marcus Garvey and the Universal Negro Improvement Association (1917–1927) and later with the Black Panther Party, Malcolm X, and other participants in the black power movements of the 1960s.

bloody shirt A refrain used by Republicans in the late nineteenth century to remind the voting public that the Democratic Party, dominated by the South, was largely responsible for the Civil War and that the Republican Party had preserved the Union. Republicans urged their constituents to "vote the way you shot."

bracero program A policy begun during World War II to help with wartime agriculture in which Mexican laborers (*braceros*) were permitted to enter the United States and work for a limited period of time but not to gain citizenship or permanent residence. The program officially ended in 1964.

brinksmanship A Cold War practice of appearing willing and able to resort to nuclear war in order to make an enemy back down. Secretary of State John Foster Dulles was the foremost proponent of this policy.

Calvinism The religious doctrine of which the primary tenet is that salvation is predestined by God. Founded by John Calvin of Geneva during the Protestant Reformation, Calvinism required its adherents to live according to a strict religious and moral code. The Puritans who settled in colonial New England were devout Calvinists. *See also* predestination.

checks and balances A system in which the executive, legislative, and judicial branches of the government curb one other's power. Checks and balances were written into the U.S. Constitution during the Constitutional Convention of 1787.

civil disobedience The public and peaceful violation of certain laws or government orders by individuals or groups who act out of a profound conviction that the laws or directives are unjust or immoral and who are prepared to accept the consequences of their actions. Civil disobedience was practiced most famously in U.S. history in the black freedom struggle of the 1960s.

civil service The administrative service of a government. This term often applies to reforms following the passage of the Pendleton Act in 1883, which set qualifications for U.S. government jobs and sought to remove such jobs from political influence. *See also* spoils system.

closed shop An establishment in which every employee is required to join a union to be employed.

Cold War The hostile and tense relationship that existed between the Soviet Union on the one hand and the United States and other Western nations on the other from 1947 to 1989. This war was said to be "cold" because the hostility stopped short of armed (hot) conflict, which was warded off by the strategy of nuclear deterrence. *See also* deterrence.

collective bargaining Negotiation by a group of workers (usually through a union) with their employer concerning rates of pay and working conditions.

collective security An association of independent nations that agree to accept and implement decisions made by the group, including going to war in defense of one or more members. The United States resolutely avoided such alliances until after World War II, when it created the North Atlantic Treaty Organization (NATO) in response to the threat posed by the Soviet Union. *See also* North Atlantic Treaty Organization.

colonization The process by which a country or society gains control over another, primarily through settlement.

Columbian exchange The transatlantic exchange of goods, peoples, and ideas that began when Columbus arrived in the Caribbean in 1492, ending the age-old separation of the hemispheres.

communism (Communist Party) A system of government and political organization, based on Marxist-Leninist ideals, in which a single authoritarian party controls the economy through state ownership of production, as a step toward reaching the final stage of Marxist theory in which the state dissolves and economic goods are distributed evenly for the common good. Communists around the globe encouraged the spread of communism in other nations in the hope of fomenting worldwide revolution. At its peak in the 1930s, the Communist Party of the United States worked closely with labor unions and insisted that only the overthrow of the capitalist system by its workers could save the victims of the Great Depression. After World War II, the Communist Soviet Union was held to be a direct threat to American democracy, prompting the Cold War. *See also* Cold War.

conscription Compulsory military service. Americans were first subject to conscription during the Civil War. The Selective Service Act of 1940 marked its first peacetime use. *See also* draft.

conservatism A political and moral outlook dating back to Alexander Hamilton's belief in a strong central government resting on a solid banking foundation. Currently associated with the Republican Party, conservatism today places a high premium on military preparedness, free market economics, low taxes, and strong sexual morality.

consumer culture (consumerism) A society that places high value on, and devotes substantial resources to, the purchase and display of material goods. Elements of American consumerism were evident in the nineteenth century but really took hold in the twentieth century, with installment buying and advertising in the 1920s and with the postwar prosperity of the 1950s.

containment The U.S. foreign policy developed after World War II to hold in check the power and influence of the Soviet Union and other groups or nations espousing communism. The strategy was first fully articulated by diplomat George F. Kennan in 1946–1947.

covenant An agreement or pact; in American history, a religious agreement. The Pilgrims used this term in the Mayflower Compact to refer to the agreement they made with one another to establish a law-abiding community in which all members would work together for the common good. Later, New England Puritans used the term to refer to the agreement they made with God and one other to live according to God's will as revealed through Scripture. *See also* Halfway Covenant.

cult of domesticity The nineteenth-century belief that a woman's place was in the home, where she should create a haven for her husband, who was working in the outside world. This ideal was made possible by the separation of the workplace and the home and was used to sentimentalize the home and women's role in it. *See also* separate spheres.

culture A term that connotes what is commonly called "way of life." It refers not only to how a group of people supply themselves with food and shelter but also to their family relationships, social groupings, and religious ideas and to other features of their lives.

de-industrialization A long period of decline in the industrial sector. The term often refers specifically to the decline of manufacturing and the growth of the service sector of the economy in post–World War II America. This shift and the resulting loss of manufacturing were caused by more efficient and automated production techniques at home, increased competition from foreign-made goods, and the use of cheap labor abroad by U.S. manufacturers.

democracy A system of government in which the people have the power to rule, either directly or indirectly, through their elected representatives. Believing that direct democracy was dangerous, the framers of the Constitution created a government that gave direct voice to the people only in the House of Representatives. They placed a check on that voice in the Senate by offering unlimited six-year terms to senators, who were elected by the state legislatures to protect them from the whims of democratic majorities. The framers further curbed the perceived dangers of democracy by giving each of the three branches of government (legislative, executive, and judicial) the ability to check the power of the other two. *See also* checks and balances.

détente   French for "loosening." The term refers to the easing of tensions between the United States and the Soviet Union during the Nixon administration.

deterrence   The linchpin of U.S. military strategy during the Cold War. The strategy of deterrence dictated that the United States would maintain a nuclear arsenal so substantial that the Soviet Union would refrain from attacking the United States and its allies out of fear that the United States would retaliate in devastating proportions. The Soviets pursued a similar strategy.

disfranchisement   The denial of suffrage to a group or individual through legal or other means. Beginning in 1890, southern progressives preached the disfranchisement of black voters as a "reform" of the electoral system. The most common means of eliminating black voters were poll taxes and literary tests.

domino theory   The assumption underlying U.S. foreign policy from the early Cold War until the end of the Vietnam War that if one country fell to communism, neighboring countries also would fall under Communist control.

doves   Peace advocates, particularly during the Vietnam War.

draft (draftee)   A system for selecting individuals for compulsory military service. A draftee is an individual selected through this process. *See also* conscription.

emancipation   The act of freeing a person from slavery or bondage. The emancipation of American slaves, a goal shared by slaves and abolitionists alike, occurred with the passage of the Thirteenth Amendment in 1865.

English Reformation   *See* Reformation.

Enlightenment   An eighteenth-century philosophical movement that emphasized the use of reason to reevaluate previously accepted doctrines and traditions.

evangelicalism   The trend in Protestant Christianity stressing salvation through conversion, repentance of sin, and adherence to Scripture, and the importance of preaching over ritual. During the Second Great Awakening in the 1830s, evangelicals worshipped at camp meetings and religious revivals led by exuberant preachers. *See also* Second Great Awakening.

fascism   An authoritarian system of government characterized by dictatorial rule, disdain for international stability, and a conviction that warfare is the only means by which a nation can attain greatness. Nazi Germany and Mussolini's Italy are the prime examples of fascism.

federal budget deficit   The situation resulting when the government spends more money than it takes in.

feminism   The belief that men and women have the inherent right to equal social, political, and economic opportunities. The suffrage movement and second-wave feminism of the 1960s and 1970s were the most visible and successful manifestations of feminism, but feminist ideas were expressed in a variety of statements and movements as early as the late eighteenth century and continue to be expressed in the twenty-first.

finance capitalism   Refers to investment sponsored by banks and bankers and the profits garnered from the sale of financial assets such as stocks and bonds. The decades at the end of the twentieth century are known as a period of finance capitalism because banks and financiers increasingly took on the role of stabilizing markets and reorganizing industries.

flexible response   Military strategy employed by the Kennedy and Johnson administrations designed to match a wide range of military threats by complementing nuclear weapons with the buildup of conventional and special forces and using them all in a gradual and calibrated way as needed. Flexible response was a departure from the strategy of massive retaliation used by the Eisenhower administration.

franchise   The right to vote. The franchise was gradually widened in the United States to include groups such as women and African Americans, who had no vote when the Constitution was ratified. *See also* suffrage.

free labor   Work conducted free from constraint and in accordance with the laborer's personal inclinations and will. Prior to the Civil War, free labor was an ideal championed by Republicans (who were primarily northerners) to articulate individuals' right to work how and where they wished and to accumulate property in their own names. The ideal of free labor lay at the heart of the North's argument that slavery should not be extended into the western territories.

free silver   The late-nineteenth-century call by silver barons and poor American farmers for the widespread coinage of silver and for silver to be used as a base upon which to expand the paper money supply. The coinage of silver created a more inflationary monetary system that benefited debtors. *See also* gold standard.

free soil   The idea advanced in the 1840s that Congress should prohibit slavery within the western territories. "Free soil, free speech, free labor, and free men" became the rallying cry of the short-lived Free-Soil Party.

frontier   A borderland area. In U.S. history, the borderland between the areas primarily inhabited by Europeans or their descendants and the areas solely inhabited by Native Americans.

fundamentalism   Strict adherence to core, often religious, beliefs. The term has varying meanings for different religious groups. Protestant fundamentalists adhere to a literal interpretation of the Bible and thus deny the possibility of evolution. Muslim fundamentalists believe that traditional Islamic law should govern nations and that Western influences should be banned.

gag rule   A procedural rule invoked to prohibit discussion or debate on a particular subject in a legislative body. From 1836 to 1844, a series of gag rules prevented the House of Representatives from discussing the large number of anti-slavery petitions from abolitionist groups that flooded that chamber.

gender gap   An electoral phenomenon that became apparent in the 1980s when men and women began to display different preferences in voting. Women tended to favor liberal candidates, and men tended to support conservatives. The key voter groups contributing to the gender gap were single women and women who worked outside the home.

globalization   The spread of political, cultural, and economic influences and connections among countries, businesses, and individuals around the world through trade, immigration, communication, and other means. In the late twentieth century, globalization was intensified by new communications technology that connected individuals, corporations, and nations with greater speed at low prices. This led to an increase in political and economic interdependence and mutual influence among nations.

gold standard   A monetary system in which any circulating currency was exchangeable for a specific amount of gold. Advocates for the gold standard believed that gold alone should be used for coinage and that the total value of paper banknotes should never exceed the government's supply of gold. The triumph of gold standard supporter William McKinley in the 1896 presidential election was a big victory for supporters of this policy. *See also* free silver.

gospel of wealth   The idea that wealth garnered from earthly success should be used for good works. Andrew Carnegie promoted this view in an 1889 essay in which he maintained that the wealthy should serve as stewards and act in the best interests of society as a whole.

government bonds   Promissory notes issued by a government in order to borrow money from members of the public. Such bonds are redeemable at a set future date. Bondholders earn interest on their investments.

Great Awakening   The widespread movement of religious revitalization in the 1730s and 1740s that emphasized vital religious faith and personal choice. It was characterized by large open-air meetings at which emotional sermons were given by itinerant preachers.

Great Society   President Lyndon Johnson's domestic program, which included civil rights legislation, antipoverty programs, government subsidy of medical care, federal aid to education, consumer protection, and aid to the arts and humanities.

guerrilla warfare   Fighting carried out by an irregular military force usually organized into small, highly mobile groups. Guerrilla combat was common in the Vietnam War and during the American Revolution. Guerrilla warfare is often effective against opponents who have greater material resources.

Halfway Covenant   A Puritan compromise that allowed the unconverted children of the "visible saints" to become "halfway" members of the church and to baptize their own children, even though they were not full members of the church because they had not experienced full conversion. Massachusetts ministers accepted this compromise in 1662, but the compromise remained controversial throughout the seventeenth century.

hard currency (hard money)   Money coined directly from, or backed in full by, precious metals (particularly gold).

hawks   Advocates of aggressive military action or all-out war, particularly during the Vietnam War. *See also* War Hawks.

holding company   A system of business organization in which competing companies are combined under one central administration in order to curb competition and ensure profit. Pioneered in the late 1880s by John D. Rockefeller, holding companies, such as Standard Oil, exercised monopoly control even as the government threatened to outlaw trusts as a violation of free trade. *See also* monopoly; trust.

horizontal integration   A system in which a single person or corporation creates several subsidiary businesses to sell a product in different markets. John D. Rockefeller pioneered the use of horizontal integration in the 1880s to control the refining process, giving him a virtual monopoly on the oil-refining business. *See also* vertical integration; monopoly.

impeachment   The process by which formal charges of wrongdoing are brought against a president, a governor, or a federal judge.

imperialism   The system by which great powers gain control of overseas territories. The United States became an imperialist power by gaining control of Puerto Rico, Guam, the Philippines, and Cuba as a result of the Spanish-American War.

indentured servitude   A system that committed poor immigrants to four to seven years of labor in exchange for passage to the colonies and food and shelter after they arrived. An indenture is a type of contract.

iron curtain   A metaphor coined by Winston Churchill in his commencement address at Westminster College in Fulton, Missouri, in 1946 to refer to the political, ideological, and military barriers that separated Soviet-controlled Eastern Europe from the rest of Europe and the West following World War II.

isolationism   A foreign policy perspective characterized by a desire to have the United States withdraw from the conflicts of the world and enjoy the protection of two vast oceans.

Jim Crow   The system of racial segregation that developed in the post–Civil War South and extended well into the twentieth century; it replaced slavery as the chief instrument of white supremacy. Jim Crow laws segregated African Americans in public facilities such as trains and streetcars and denied them basic civil rights, including the right to vote. Jim Crow developed at the time that the doctrine of "separate but equal" became institutionalized.

Keynesian economics   A theory developed by economist John Maynard Keynes that guided U.S. economic policy from the New Deal to the 1970s. According to Keynesians, the federal government has a duty to stimulate and manage the economy by spending money on public works projects and by making general tax cuts in order to put more money into the hands of ordinary people, thus creating demand.

laissez-faire   The doctrine, based on economic theory, that government should not interfere in business or the economy. Laissez-faire ideas guided American government policy in the late nineteenth century and conservative politics in the twentieth century. Business interests that supported laissez-faire in the late nineteenth century accepted government interference when it took the form of tariffs or subsidies that worked to their benefit. A broader use of the term refers to the simple philosophy of abstaining from interference.

land grant   A gift of land from a government, usually intended to encourage settlement or development. The British government issued several land grants to encourage development in the American colonies. In the mid-nineteenth century, the U.S. government issued land grants to encourage railroad development and, through the passage of the Land-Grant College Act (also known as the Morrill Act) in 1862, set aside public land to support universities.

liberalism   The political doctrine that government rests on the consent of the governed and is duty-bound to protect the freedom and property of the individual. In the twentieth century, liberalism became associated with the idea that government should regulate the economy and ensure the material well-being and individual rights of all people.

liberty   The condition of being free or enjoying freedom from control. The term also refers to the possession of certain social, political, or economic rights, such as the right to own and control property. Eighteenth-century American colonists invoked the principle to argue for strict limitations on government's ability to tax its subjects.

manifest destiny   A term coined by journalist John O'Sullivan in 1845 to express the popular nineteenth-century belief that the United States was destined to expand westward to the Pacific Ocean and had an irrefutable right and God-given responsibility to do so. This idea provided an ideological shield for westward expansion and masked the economic and political motivations of many of those who championed it.

McCarthyism   The practice of searching out suspected Communists and others outside mainstream American society, discrediting them, and hounding them from government and other employment. The term derives from Senator Joseph McCarthy, who gained notoriety for leading such repressive activities from 1950 to 1954.

mercantilism   A set of policies that regulated colonial commerce and manufacturing for the enrichment of the mother country. Mercantilist policies ensured that the American colonies in the mid-seventeenth century produced agricultural goods and raw materials to be shipped to Britain, where they would increase wealth in the mother country through reexportation or manufacture into finished goods that would then be sold to the colonies and elsewhere.

Middle Passage   The crossing of the Atlantic (as a slave destined for auction) in the hold of a slave ship in the eighteenth and nineteenth centuries. Conditions were unimaginably bad, and many slaves died during these voyages.

military-industrial complex   A term first used by President Dwight D. Eisenhower to refer to the aggregate power and influence of the armed forces in conjunction with the aerospace, munitions, and other industries that produced supplies for the military in the post–World War II era.

miscegenation   The sexual mixing of races. In slave states, despite the social stigma and legal restrictions on interracial sex, masters' almost unlimited power over their female slaves meant that liaisons inevitably occurred. Many states maintained laws against miscegenation into the 1950s.

monopoly   Exclusive control and domination by a single business entity over an entire industry through ownership, command of supply, or other means. Gilded Age businesses monopolized their industries quite profitably, often organizing holding companies and trusts to do so. *See also* holding company; trust.

Monroe Doctrine   President James Monroe's 1823 declaration that the Western Hemisphere was closed to further colonization or interference by European powers. In exchange, Monroe pledged that the United States would not become involved in European struggles. Although Monroe could not back his policy with action, it was an important formulation of national goals.

nationalism   A strong feeling of devotion and loyalty toward one nation over others. Nationalism encourages the promotion of the nation's common culture, language, and customs.

nativism   Bias against immigrants and in favor of native-born inhabitants. American nativists especially favor persons who come from white, Anglo-Saxon, Protestant lines over those from other racial, ethnic, and religious heritages. Nativists may include former immigrants who view new immigrants as incapable of assimilation. Many nativists, such as members of the Know-Nothing Party in the nineteenth century and the Ku Klux Klan through the contemporary period, voice anti-immigrant, anti-Catholic, and anti-Semitic sentiments.

New Deal   The group of social and economic programs that President Franklin Roosevelt developed to provide relief for the needy, speed economic recovery, and reform economic and government institutions. The New Deal was a massive effort to bring the United States out of the Great Depression and ensure its future prosperity.

New Right   Politically active religious conservatives who became particularly vocal in the 1980s. The New Right criticized feminism, opposed abortion and homosexuality, and promoted "family values" and military preparedness.

New South   A vision of the South promoted after the Civil War by Henry Grady, editor of the *Atlanta Constitution*, that urged the South to abandon its dependence on agriculture and use its cheap labor and natural resources to compete with northern industry. Many southerners migrated from farms to cities in the late nineteenth century, and northerners and foreigners invested a significant amount of capital in railroads, cotton and textiles, mining, lumber, iron, steel, and tobacco in the region.

North Atlantic Treaty Organization (NATO)   A post–World War II alliance that joined the United States, Canada, and Western European nations into a military coalition designed to counter the Soviet Union's efforts to expand. Each NATO member pledged to go to war if any member was attacked. Since the end of the Cold War, NATO has been expanding to include the formerly Communist countries of Eastern Europe.

nullification   The idea that states can disregard federal laws when those laws represent an overstepping of congressional powers. The controversial idea was first proposed by opponents of the Alien and Sedition Acts of 1798 and later by South Carolina politicians in 1828 as a response to the Tariff of Abominations.

oligopoly   A competitive system in which several large corporations dominate an industry by dividing the market so each business has a share of it. More prevalent than outright monopolies during the late 1800s, the oligopolies of the Gilded Age successfully muted competition and benefited the participating corporations.

paternalism   The idea that slavery was a set of reciprocal obligations between masters and slaves, with slaves providing labor and obedience and masters providing basic care and direction. The concept of paternalism denied that the slave system was brutal and exploitative. Although paternalism did provide some protection against the worst brutality, it did not guarantee decent living conditions, reasonable work, or freedom from physical punishment.

planters Owners of large farms (or, more specifically, plantations) that were worked by twenty or more slaves. By 1860, planters had accrued a great deal of local, statewide, and national political power in the South despite the fact that they represented a minority of the white electorate. Planters' dominance of southern politics demonstrated both the power of tradition and stability among southern voters and the planters' success at convincing white voters that the slave system benefited all whites, even those without slaves.

plutocracy A society ruled by the richest members. The excesses of the Gilded Age and the fact that just 1 percent of the population owned more than half the real and personal property in the country led many to suggest that the United States was a plutocracy.

pogrom An organized and often officially encouraged massacre of an ethnic minority; usually used in reference to attacks on Jews.

popular sovereignty The idea that government is subject to the will of the people. Before the Civil War, this was the idea that the residents of a territory should determine, through their legislatures, whether to allow slavery.

Populism A political movement that led to the creation of the People's Party, primarily comprising southern and western farmers who railed against big business and advocated business and economic reforms, including government ownership of the railroads. The movement peaked in the late nineteenth century. The Populist ticket won more than 1 million votes in the presidential election of 1892 and 1.5 million in the congressional elections of 1894. The term *populism* has come to mean any political movement that advocates on behalf of the common person, particularly for government intervention against big business.

pragmatism A philosophical movement whose American proponents, William James and John Dewey, stated that there were no eternal truths and that the real worth of any idea lay in its consequences. Dewey tested his theories in the classroom, pioneering the role of process over content in American education and encouraging students to learn by doing. American pragmatists championed social experimentation, providing an important impetus for progressive reform in the early part of the twentieth century.

predestination The idea that individual salvation or damnation is determined by God at, or just prior to, a person's birth. The concept of predestination invalidated the idea that salvation could be obtained through either faith or good works. *See also* Calvinism.

progressivism (progressive movement) A wide-ranging twentieth-century reform movement that advocated government activism to mitigate the problems created by urban industrialism. Progressivism reached its peak in 1912 with the creation of the Progressive Party, which ran Theodore Roosevelt for president. The term *progressivism* has

come to mean any general effort advocating for social welfare programs.

Protestantism A powerful Christian reform movement that began in the sixteenth century with Martin Luther's critiques of the Roman Catholic Church. Over the centuries, Protestantism has taken many different forms, branching into numerous denominations with differing systems of worship.

Protestant Reformation *See* Reformation.

Puritanism The ideas and religious principles held by dissenters from the Church of England, including the belief that the church needed to be purified by eliminating elements of Catholicism from its practices.

Reformation The reform movement that began in 1517 with Martin Luther's critiques of the Roman Catholic Church, which led to the formation of Protestant Christian groups. The English Reformation began with Henry VIII's break with the Roman Catholic Church, which established the Protestant Church of England. Henry VIII's decision was politically motivated; he had no particular quarrel with Catholic theology and remained an orthodox Catholic in most matters of religious practice.

reform Darwinism A social theory, based on Charles Darwin's theory of evolution, that emphasized activism, arguing that humans could speed up evolution by altering the environment. A challenge to social Darwinism, reform Darwinism condemned laissez-faire and demanded that the government take a more active approach to solving social problems. It became the ideological basis for progressive reform in the late nineteenth and early twentieth centuries. *See also* laissez-faire; social Darwinism.

republicanism The belief that the unworkable model of European-style monarchy should be replaced with a form of government in which supreme power resides in the hands of citizens with the right to vote and is exercised by a representative government answerable to this electorate. In Revolutionary-era America, republicanism became a social philosophy that embodied a sense of community and called on individuals to act for the public good.

scientific management A system of organizing work, developed by Frederick Winslow Taylor in the late nineteenth century, to increase efficiency and productivity by breaking tasks into their component parts and training workers to perform specific parts. Labor resisted this effort because it de-skilled workers and led to the speedup of production lines. Taylor's ideas were most popular at the height of the Progressive Era.

Second Great Awakening A popular religious revival that preached that salvation was available to anybody who chose to take it. The revival peaked in the 1830s, and its focus on social perfection inspired many of the reform movements of the Jacksonian era. *See also* evangelicalism.

separate spheres A concept of gender relations, which developed in the Jacksonian era and continued well into the twentieth century, holding that women's proper place was in the home (the private sphere) and men's was in commerce and politics (the public sphere). The doctrine of separate spheres eroded slowly over the nineteenth and twentieth centuries as women became more and more involved in public activities. *See also* cult of domesticity.

social Darwinism A social theory, based on Charles Darwin's theory of evolution, that all progress in human society was the result of competition and natural selection. Gilded Age proponents such as William Graham Sumner and Herbert Spencer claimed that reform was useless because the rich and poor were precisely where nature intended them to be and intervention would retard the progress of humanity. *See also* reform Darwinism.

social gospel movement A religious movement in the late nineteenth and early twentieth centuries founded on the idea that Christians have a responsibility to reform society as well as individuals. Social gospel adherents encouraged people to put Christ's teachings to work in their daily lives by actively promoting social justice.

socialism A governing system in which the state owns and operates the largest and most important parts of the economy.

social purity movement A movement to end prostitution and eradicate venereal disease, often accompanied by the censorship of materials deemed "obscene."

spoils system An arrangement in which party leaders reward party loyalists with government jobs. This slang term for *patronage* comes from the saying "To the victor go the spoils." Widespread government corruption during the Gilded Age spurred reformers to curb the spoils system through the passage of the Pendleton Act in 1883, which created the Civil Service Commission to award government jobs on the basis of merit. *See also* civil service.

state sovereignty A state's autonomy or freedom from external control. The federal system adopted at the Constitutional Convention in 1787 struck a balance between state sovereignty and national control by creating a strong central government while leaving the states intact as political entities. The states remained in possession of many important powers on which the federal government cannot intrude.

states' rights A strict interpretation of the Constitution that holds that federal power over the states is limited and that the states hold ultimate sovereignty. First expressed in 1798 through the passage of the Virginia and Kentucky Resolutions, which were based on the assumption that the states have the right to judge the constitutionality of federal laws, the states' rights philosophy became a cornerstone of the South's resistance to federal control of slavery.

strict constructionism An approach to constitutional law that attempts to adhere to the original intent of the writers of the Constitution. Strict construction often produces Supreme Court decisions that defer to the legislative branch and to the states and restrict the power of the federal government. Opponents of strict construction argue that the Constitution is an organic document that must be interpreted to meet conditions unimagined when it was written.

suffrage The right to vote. The term *suffrage* is most often associated with the efforts of American women to secure voting rights. *See also* franchise.

Sun Belt The southern and southwestern regions of the United States, which grew tremendously in industry, population, and influence after World War II.

supply-side economics An economic theory based on the premise that tax cuts for the wealthy and for corporations encourage investment and production (supply), which in turn stimulate consumption. Embraced by the Reagan administration and other conservative Republicans, this theory reversed Keynesian economic policy, which assumes that the way to stimulate the economy is to create demand through federal spending on public works and general tax cuts that put more money into the hands of ordinary people. *See also* Keynesian economics.

temperance movement The reform movement to end drunkenness by urging people to abstain from the consumption of alcohol. Begun in the 1820s, this movement achieved its greatest political victory with the passage of a constitutional amendment in 1919 that prohibited the manufacture, sale, and transportation of alcohol. That amendment was repealed in 1933.

third world Originally a Cold War term linked to decolonization, *third world* was first used in the late 1950s to describe newly independent countries in Africa and Asia that were not aligned with either Communist nations (the second world) or non-Communist nations (the first world). Later, the term was applied to all poor, nonindustrialized countries in Latin America as well as in Africa and Asia. Many international experts see *third world* as a problematic category when applied to such a large and disparate group of nations, and they criticize the discriminatory hierarchy suggested by the term.

trickle-down economics The theory that financial benefits and incentives given to big businesses in the top tier of the economy will flow down to smaller businesses and individuals and thus benefit the entire nation. President Herbert Hoover unsuccessfully used the trickle-down strategy in his attempt to pull the nation out of the Great Depression, stimulating the economy through government investment in large economic enterprises and public works such as construction of the Hoover Dam. In the late twentieth century, conservatives used this economic theory to justify large tax cuts and other financial benefits for corporations and the wealthy.

Truman Doctrine President Harry S. Truman's assertion that American security depended on stopping any Communist government from taking over any non-Communist government—even nondemocratic and repressive dictatorships—anywhere in the world. Beginning in 1947 with American aid to help Greece and Turkey stave off Communist pressures, this approach became a cornerstone of American foreign policy during the Cold War.

trust A corporate system in which corporations give shares of their stock to trustees, who coordinate the industry to ensure profits to the participating corporations and curb competition. Pioneered by Standard Oil, such business practices were deemed unfair, were moderated by the Sherman Antitrust Act (1890), and were finally abolished by the combined efforts of Presidents Theodore Roosevelt and William Howard Taft and the sponsors of the 1914 Clayton Antitrust Act. The term *trust* is also loosely applied to all large business combinations. *See also* holding company.

vertical integration A system in which a single person or corporation controls all processes of an industry from start to finished product. Andrew Carnegie first used vertical integration in the 1870s, controlling every aspect of steel production from the mining of iron ore to the manufacturing of the final product, thereby maximizing profits by eliminating the use of outside suppliers or services. *See also* horizontal integration.

virtual representation The notion, propounded by the British Parliament in the eighteenth century, that the House of Commons represented all British subjects — wherever they lived and regardless of whether they had directly voted for their representatives. Prime Minister George Grenville used this idea to argue that the Stamp Act and other parliamentary taxes on British colonists did not constitute taxation without representation. The American colonists rejected the argument, insisting that political representatives derived authority only from explicit citizens' consent (indicated by elections), and that members of a distant government body were incapable of adequately representing their interests.

War Hawks Young Republicans elected to the U.S. Congress in the fall of 1810 who were eager for war with Britain in order to legitimize attacks on Indians, end impressment, and avenge foreign insults. *See also* hawks.

welfare capitalism The idea that a capitalistic industrial society can operate benevolently to improve the lives of workers. The notion of welfare capitalism became popular in the 1920s as industries extended the benefits of scientific management to improve safety and sanitation in the workplace as well as to institute paid vacations and pension plans. *See also* scientific management.

welfare state A nation or state in which the government assumes responsibility for some or all of the individual and social welfare of its citizens. Welfare states commonly provide education, health care, food programs for the poor, unemployment compensation, and other social benefits. The United States dramatically expanded its role as a welfare state with the provisions of the New Deal in the 1930s.

Yankee imperialism A cry raised in Latin American countries against the United States when it intervened militarily in the region without invitation or consent from those countries.

yeoman A farmer who owned a small plot of land that was sufficient to support a family and was tilled by family members and perhaps a few servants.

Spot Artifact Credits

A note about the index: Names of individuals appear in boldface. Letters in parentheses following page numbers refer to:

(i) illustrations, including photographs and artifacts

(f) figures, including charts and graphs

(m) maps

(t) tables

Abenaki Indians, 16
Abolition and abolitionism, 268–269
    black leaders in, 302–303, 302 *(i)*
    Brown's raid and, 350
    in England, 268, 270–271, 270 *(i)*
    feminist movement and, 398
    "gag rule" and, 272
    Lincoln and, 369, 387
    transatlantic, 270
    women and, 269, 271, 343
Abolition of Slavery Act (England, 1833), 271
Academies, for women, 240, 241–242, 241 *(i)*, 266
Acculturation, of slaves, 114–115
Acoma pueblo, 14, 42
Activism. *See* Protest(s); Revolts and rebellions
Act of Supremacy (England, 1534), 76–77
AD (date notation), 5
Adams, Abigail, 159–160, 159 *(i)*, 165, 186, 210, 229
Adams, Charles Francis, 336
Adams, John, 106–107, 145, 232
    cabinet of, 221
    election of 1796 and, 220–221
    election of 1800 and, 223
    at First Continental Congress, 148
    France and, 219, 221–222, 223
    at Second Continental Congress, 157
    as vice president, 207–208, 220
    on voting qualifications, 186, 187
Adams, John Quincy, 245
    cabinet of, 246–247
    election of 1824 and, 46 *(m)*, 242, 245–246, 245 *(i)*, 251
    election of 1828 and, 258–259
    presidency of, 246–247
Adams, Louisa Catherine, 246
Adams, Samuel, 140, 143, 145, 146, 194
    at First Continental Congress, 148
    at Second Continental Congress, 157
Adams-Onís Treaty (1819), 245
Adaptation, by Archaic Indians, 11
Advice to American Women (Graves), 264
Advocate of Moral Reform (newspaper), 268
Africa
    human emigration from, 5–6
    immigrants from, 69 *(f)*
    influence on slaves' Christianity, 321–322
    musicians from, 70 *(i)*
    Portugal and, 28–29, 28 *(m)*
    slaves and, 29, 42, 67, 68, 69 *(f)*, 113–114, 115, 115 *(i)*, 269
African American Christianity, 321–322

African Americans. *See also* Africa; Civil rights; Free blacks; Freedmen; Race and racism; Rights; Slaves and slavery
    as abolitionists, 302–303, 302 *(i)*
    antidraft riots and, 376–377
    in armed forces, 369, 370–371, 372–373
    black codes and, 393, 393 *(i)*, 394, 395
    in Boston Massacre, 144–145
    in Carolina colony, 68
    in Civil War, 357–358, 358 *(i)*, 369, 370–371, 372–373
    in colonies, 103, 104, 110
    in Continental army, 161
    culture of, 116, 321 *(i)*
    discrimination against, 284
    education for, 266 *(i)*
    elites of, 324
    emigration by, 151
    free, 323–324
    Haitian Revolution and, 219–220
    lineages of, 116
    migrations by, 101–102
    in New England, 108
    racism against, 303
    in Reconstruction, 385–386, 405–406
    in Republican Party, 399
    Revolution and, 150–151
    as slaveholders, 324
    in South, 112–116
    voting rights for, 187–190, 243
    wealth and, 285
    women and, 401, 401 *(i)*
    in workforce, 284
African Methodist Episcopal Church, 389
Africans, 57–58. *See also* African Americans; Slaves and slavery
Agencies. *See* Departments of government; Government (U.S.)
Agriculture. *See also* Crops; Farms and farming
    of ancient Americans, 12–16, 13 *(i)*, 19
    colonial, 117
    cotton, 310, 314
    decline of, 381
    of Eastern Woodland people, 12
    land policy and, 281
    in New England, 85
    plantation, 387
    productivity in, 281
    after Revolution, 209
    sharecropping system of, 401–402
    in South, 312–315, 314 *(m)*, 402
    tobacco, 56–57
Agriculture Department, creation of, 374
Air pollution, from steamboats, 254
Alabama, 352, 385, 393
Alamo, battle of the, 292
Alaska, 294, 404
    Indians from, 6, 123
Albany Congress, 133–134
Albany Plan of Union, 129, 133–134
Albuquerque, 42
Alcohol and alcoholism. *See also* Temperance
    consumption of, 268
Aleut language, 9

Algonquian Indians, 16–17, 44 *(i)*, 48 *(i)*, 49, 64, 131 *(m)*
Alien and Sedition Acts (1798), 222–223, 263
Allen, Noah, 169
Alliances
    with France, 160, 173, 175, 177, 221
    with Indians, 133, 134
    of Indian tribes, 136
    in Revolutionary War, 160, 175
Alphabet, Cherokee, 262
Amendments to Constitution. *See also* specific amendments
    Bill of Rights as, 208
    Tallmadge, 244
America(s). *See also* Central America; Exploration; North America; South America
    ancient (before 1492), 2–21
    Columbus and, 26, 26 *(i)*, 29–31
    European exploration of, 24, 25–42
    naming of, 32
    wealth from, 35, 43
American Colonization Society, 268–269, 303
American Equal Rights Association, 395
American Indians. *See* Native Americans
American Party. *See* Know-Nothing Party
American Red Cross, 376
American Revolution. *See* Revolutionary War
American System, of Clay, 246
American system, of manufacturing, 282
American Temperance Society, 268
American Temperance Union, 268
Amerind languages, 9
Ames, Adelbert, 406
Amherst, Jeffery, 136, 137
Amish, 109
Amistead, William, 175
Amusements. *See* Entertainment; Leisure
Anasazi people, 14
Ancestry, of colonial Americans, 103
Ancient Americans, 2 *(i)*, 3–16
Anderson, "Bloody Bill," 365
Anderson, Robert, 356 *(i)*, 359
Andersonville prison, 373
Andros, Edmund, 96
Anglican Church. *See* Church of England
Anglo-Americans
    in Mexican borderlands, 292
    in Ohio River region, 132
    in West, 298, 299
Angola, 70 *(i)*, 115
Animals
    in ancient Americas, 7, 11
    in Columbian Exchange, 33 *(i)*
Annexation(s)
    of Florida, 281
    after Mexican-American War, 281
    of Oregon, 281
    of Texas, 293–294
Antebellum era
    banking system in, 374
    Mormons in, 290
    property rights of married women in, 344–345
    southern society and culture in, 308

Anthony, Susan B., 343, 345, 395, 396 (i), 398
Antietam, battle of (1862), 364 (m), 365, 372
Antifederalists, 198–201
Antinomians, 84–85
Antislavery conventions, 302
Antislavery movement, 268–269, 336. *See also* Abolition and abolitionism
    free blacks in, 303
    in South, 328
    transatlantic, 270–271
Apache Indians, 17, 18, 291
Appalachian Mountains, movement west of, 183
Appeal . . . to the Coloured Citizens of the World, An (Walker), 269, 307
Appomattox Court House, Virginia, 378 (m), 380
Apprenticeship laws, in black codes, 393
Aragon, 25
Arbella (ship), 79, 81
Archaeology, 3, 4–5, 19
Archaic Indians, as hunters and gatherers, 8–12
Arctic region, native peoples of, 16
Aristocracy, vs. democracy, 258
Arizona, 14, 340
Ark (ship), 62
Arkansas, 309, 359, 387
Armed forces. *See* Military; Militia; Soldiers
Arminianism, 84
Army of Northern Virginia, 364, 365
Army of the Potomac, 364, 365, 379
Arnold, Benedict, 162–163, 174
Articles of Confederation (1781–1789), 183–185, 190–196
Artifacts, 3, 4, 5
    Clovis-era, 9
    from Folsom site, 3, 4
    of Spanish conquest, 36 (i)
    of Woodland Indians, 15
Artisans, 105
    in San Francisco, 299
    slaves as, 102 (i), 320, 320 (i)
Ashley Family, 188
Asia
    Columbus's search for, 29, 30
    human emigration from, 5–6
    trade with, 288
Asian people, Native American genes and, 9
Assassination, of Lincoln, 380–381, 392
Assemblies, 124, 143. *See also* Legislatures
    in Massachusetts, 147, 148
    in Pennsylvania, 91
    two-chamber, 185
Assimilation, of Indians, 261, 262
Assumption, of state debts, 213
Astrolabe, 27
Atahualpa (Incas), 35
Atchison, David Rice, 346
Athapascan Indians, 17–18
Atlanta, fall of (1864), 378 (m), 379
Atlantic Ocean region
    Civil War in, 366
    European exploration of, 29–32
    sailors in, 106–107, 107 (i)
    slave trade in, 112–113, 113 (m)
    Spanish exploration of, 42
    trade in, 105 (m), 118

Attucks, Crispus, 144–145, 145 (i)
Austin, Stephen F., 292
Australia, 8
Austria, 134
Ayllón, Lucas Vázquez de, 35
Aztecs. *See* Mexica people

Backcountry, immigrants in, 112
Bacon, Nathaniel, 64
Bacon's Laws (1676), 64, 65
Bacon's Rebellion, 64–65
Baker, Isaac Wallace, 299
Balance of power, in Revolutionary War, 176
Balboa, Vasco Núñez de, 32
Baltimore (Lord), 62, 96
Baltimore, Maryland, 351, 359
Baltimore and Ohio Railroad, 255
Bancroft, Hubert Howe, 299
Bank(s) and banking, 212, 256–257. *See also* Bank of the United States; Panics
    during Civil War, 374
    in South, 315
Banknotes, 192, 256–257, 263, 264
Bank of North America, 191–192
Bank of the United States
    First, 213–214, 257
    Jackson and, 260, 263–264
    Second, 257, 263–264
Bank War, 263–264
Baptists, 240, 321, 327, 389
Baptizing on the South Branch of the Potomac near Franklin, Virginia, 1844, A (Smith), 326 (i)
Barbados, 66–68, 80
Barbary Wars (1801–1805), 226 (i), 234
Barges, 254
Barter, among yeomen, 325
Barton, Clara, 376
Battle of Savage's Station, The (Sneden), 363 (i)
Battles. *See* Wars and warfare; specific battles and wars
Bayonet rule, in South, 405, 406
Bear Flag Revolt, 293
Beauregard, P. G. T., 367
Beaver furs, 132
Beecher, Lyman, 268. *See also* Stowe, Harriet Beecher
Bell, John, 351
Benton, Thomas Hart, 288, 343
Beringia (land bridge), 6
Berkeley, William, 63
Bernard, Francis, 141, 143, 144
Bethlehem, Pennsylvania, 110 (i)
Bett, Mum (Elizabeth Freeman), 187, 188–189, 189 (i)
Bett v. J. Ashley, Esq., 188–189
Bibb, Henry, 302
"Bible Argument, The: . . ." (Stringfellow), 313
Bight of Biafra, 101–102, 115
"Big Knives," 227
Bill of Rights (U.S.), 200, 207, 208. *See also* Amendments
Bills of rights, under Articles of Confederation, 185, 187
Birney, James G., 293–294
Bison (buffalo). *See* Buffalo
Black codes, 393, 393 (i), 394

Black Death, in Europe, 27
Blackfeet Indians, 17
Black Hawk (Sauk and Fox Indians), 262, 362
Black Hawk War (1832), 262
Black market, during Revolution, 169
Black people. *See* Africa; African Americans; Africans; Free blacks; Freedmen; Slaves and slavery
Black suffrage. *See also* African Americans; Voting and voting rights
    Fifteenth Amendment and, 398
    Radical Reconstruction and, 396–397
Blair, Francis P., Jr., 405 (i)
"Bleeding Kansas" (1850s), 346–347, 346 (m)
"Bleeding Sumner," 347
Blockade runners, 357, 366
Blockades, in Civil War, 357, 361, 366, 371
"Bloody shirt, waving the," 403, 406
Blue Jacket (Shawnee Indians), 215, 216
Boarding schools, 241 (i)
Board of Trade (England), 124
Bolivia, silver from, 40
Book of Mormon, The, 290
Books, in Americas, 74 (i)
Boom and bust cycles, 257
Boonesborough, Kentucky, 171
Booth, John Wilkes, 380, 392
Border(s). *See also* Boundaries
    with Canada, 219
    of Mexico, 291, 292 (m)
    of Oregon, 294
    Rio Grande as, 296
Borderlands
    Mexican, 291–293
    politics and, 121–124, 121 (m)
    Spanish, 65–66
Border states (Civil War), 376
    Emancipation Proclamation and, 370
    freedom for blacks and, 369
    secession and, 359–360, 360 (m)
Boré, Étienne de, 313
Boston, 104, 105, 107
    British military occupation of, 144–145
    nonconsumption in, 143–144
    Stamp Act protests in, 141–142
Boston Massacre, 144–145, 145 (i)
Boston Port Act (1774), 147
Boston Tea Party (173), 146
Boudry, Nancy, 319
Boundaries. *See also* Border(s)
    by 1850, 287
    Mason-Dixon line as, 308
    of slave and free states, 244
    of Texas, 294, 337
    western, of states, 183
    west of Appalachians, 138
Bouquet, Henry, 137
Bow and arrow, as Native American weapons, 11, 18–19
Bowdoin, James, 195
Bowen, Ashley, 106–107, 107 (i)
Bowie, James, 292
Boycotts
    anti-British, 143–144
    antislavery, 270
    of trade with Britain, 148
Boys. *See* Men
BP (years before the present, date notation), 5

Braddock, Edward, 134, 135
Bradford, William, 78
Brady, Mathew, 337, 351 *(i)*
Branch, Jacob, 320
Branches of government, in
    Constitution, 197
Brant, Joseph (Thayendanegea), 165–168,
    165 *(i)*, 171, 176, 192
Brazil, 32, 36, 37 *(m)*, 67 *(i)*, 310, 311
Brazos River, 292
Breckinridge, John C., 351, 352
Br'er Rabbit and Br'er Fox stories, 322
Britain. *See* England (Britain)
British East India Company, 146
British Empire, 91–96, 97. *See also*
    Colonies and colonization
British North America, 121 *(m)*. *See also*
    Colonies and colonization; England
    (Britain); Navigation Acts
    dual identity of colonists in, 124–125
    expansion of, 102–103
    taxation in, 117
    unifying elements in, 117–124
Broadway Tabernacle, 267 *(i)*
Brooks, Preston, 347
Brown, Charles Brockden, 211 *(i)*
Brown, John, 334 *(i)*, 353
    Harpers Ferry raid by, 332 *(i)*, 333–334, 351
    pikes of, 332 *(i)*
    Pottawatomie Creek killings by, 333, 347
    trial and execution of, 349–350, 350 *(i)*
Brown, Joseph E., 371
Brown, William Wells, 302
Bubonic plague. *See* Black Death
Buchanan, James, 343, 349, 353
Buena Vista, Mexico, battle at, 295, 296
Buffalo (bison), 288, 289
    Archaic Indian hunters of, 11
    fossils of, 3, 4
Bull Run (Manassas)
    first battle of (1861), 363, 364 *(m)*
    second battle of (1862), 364 *(m)*, 365
Bunker Hill, battle of (1775), 158, 158 *(m)*
Bureau of Refugees, Freedmen, and Abandoned
    Lands. *See* Freedmen's Bureau
Burgoyne, John, 158, 164 *(m)*, 169–171
Burial mounds, 12
    Mississippian, 15 *(m)*, 16
    of Woodland Indians, 12, 15–16
Burnett, Peter W., 299
Burns, Anthony, 338
Burnside, Ambrose, 365
Burr, Aaron, 182 *(i)*, 210–211, 220, 221
    duel with Hamilton, 229, 230–231, 230 *(i)*
    treason by, 231
Bute (Earl of), 135, 138
Butler, Andrew P., 347
Butler, Benjamin F., 369
Byles, Mather, 168

Cabot, John, 32, 44
Cabral, Pedro Álvars, 32
Cabrillo, Juan Rodríguez, 35–36
Cahokia, 2 *(i)*, 16
Caldwell, John, 133 *(i)*
Calhoun, John C., 237, 259, 272, 334, 337 *(i)*
    election of 1824 and, 245–246
    nullification and, 260, 263

on slavery, 311, 312, 335, 336, 348
as vice president, 247
California
    acquisition of, 296, 297 *(m)*
    Chinese in, 298–299, 299–300
    gold rush (1849–1852) in, 278 *(i)*, 297–298,
        298–299, 334
    Hispanics in, 299
    Mexican-American War in, 295
    Mexican migration to, 293
    missions in, 123–124, 123 *(i)*, 124 *(m)*
    Native Americans of, 11, 293, 299
    Russia and, 123
    Spanish exploration of, 35–36
    statehood for, 336, 337
California peoples, 11
California Trail, 289 *(m)*, 293
Californios, 299
Calusa Indians, 35
Calvinism, of Puritans, 82
Cambridge (ship), 357
Camden, battle of (1780), 174
Camp followers, 169
Camp meetings, 267
Canada
    boundaries of, 219
    England and, 44, 134, 219, 228
    France and, 43–44, 94, 96
    Indians in, 176
    loyalists in, 168–169
    in Revolutionary War, 162–163
    in Seven Years' War, 131 *(m)*
    War of 1812 and, 237, 238 *(m)*
Canals, 254–255
    Erie Canal, 254–255
Canary Islands, Columbus in, 29–30
Cane Ridge revival, 267
Cape Cod, 78
Cape Fear River, 357
Cape of Good Hope, 29
Cape Verde, 28, 29
Capital city, 209. *See also* Washington, D.C.
    under Articles of Confederation, 185
    location along Potomac, 213
Capitalism, industrial, 381
Capitol, British burning of, 235, 238
Caravel, 29
Caribbean region
    colonized African Americans in, 369
    Columbus in, 30, 32
    French in, 134
    Grant and, 404, 404 *(m)*
    in Seven Years' War, 134
    Spanish exploration in, 33
    sugar and slavery in, 66–67
Carmel, California, mission in, 123 *(i)*
Carney, Kate, 318–319
Carolina(s), 67–68, 68 *(m)*, 214. *See also* North
    Carolina; South Carolina
    settlement in, 111, 111 *(m)*
    slavery in, 190
Carpetbag, 384 *(i)*
Carpetbaggers, 384 *(i)*, 399
Cartier, Jacques, 43–44, 94
Cartographers, 32
Cash crops, in South, 312–315, 314 *(m)*
Cass, Lewis, 335, 336
Castile, 25

Casualties. *See also* specific wars
    in steamboat accidents, 254
Catechism for Colored Persons (Jones), 321
Cathay Company, 44
Catherine of Aragon (England), 77
Catholicism. *See also* Missions and missionaries
    in Canada, 94—95
    in colonies, 119
    in England, 76–77
    of Irish immigrants, 287
    in Maryland, 62, 96
    missionaries and, 37, 66
    vs. Protestantism, 43, 341
Catlin, George, 236 *(i)*, 288, 290 *(i)*
Cayuga Indians, 17, 165
Census
    of 1790 and 1800, 212, 212 *(i)*
    of 1810, 236
Central America, 37 *(m)*
    peoples of, 14 *(i)*
Central Pacific Railroad, 298
Cerro Gordo, Mexico, battle at (1847), 296
Cession, of Indian land. *See* Land; Native Americans
Chaco Canyon, 14, 15 *(i)*
Chamberlain, W. G., 291 *(i)*
Champlain, Lake, 134, 238
Chancellorsville, battle at (1863), 377, 378 *(m)*
Chapultepec, battle of (1847), 296
Charles I (England), 78, 85, 93
Charles II (England), 89, 90, 93, 96
Charles V (Charles I of Spain, Holy Roman
    Emperor), 32, 42–43
Charleston, South Carolina (Charles Town)
    Democratic convention in, 351
    Fort Sumter attack in, 359
    in Revolutionary War, 173 *(m)*, 174
Charlottesville, Virginia, 174
Charter of Privileges (Pennsylvania), 91
Charters
    for Bank of the United States, 214, 257, 263
    for banks, 256
    colonial, 93, 96
    of Virginia Company, 54
Chase, Salmon P., 336, 362, 398
Chattanooga, battle of (1863), 378, 378 *(m)*
Checks and balances, 197
Cherokee Indians, 261 *(m)*, 262
Chesapeake (ship), 235 *(m)*
Chesapeake region. *See also* Maryland; South;
    Tobacco and tobacco industry; Virginia
    Bacon's Rebellion in, 64
    English colonies in, 51–65
    labor in, 57–59
    landowners and landless in, 62–63
    population of, 64, 112
    Puritans in, 80
    religion in, 62
    in 17th century, 56 *(m)*
    slavery in, 68–70
    society in, 62–65
    tobacco in, 55–62
    Virginia colony in, 51–55
    War of 1812 in, 238, 238 *(m)*
    women in, 58, 59
    yeoman farmers in, 62–63
Chesnut, Mary Boykin, 319, 328
Cheyenne Indians, 17, 288
Chicago, 340

Chickamauga, battle of (1863), 378, 378 (m)
Chickasaw Indians, 17, 254, 262
Chiefdoms, 12, 15–16
Child, Lydia Maria, 301, 350
Childbearing, in New England, 103
Childbirth, 289
Children
    black codes, apprenticeship laws, and, 393
    education for, 285
    slave, 114, 115–116, 319
Chile, 245
China, European exploration and, 29
Chinese immigrants
    in California, 298–299, 299–300
    in mining, 298
    railroads and, 298
    work of, 298
Chino (racial category), 41 (i)
Chippewa Indians, 16–17, 136
Chivalry, in South, 318
Choctaw Indians, 17, 262
"Christian guardianship" (paternalism), 316
Christianity
    in colonies, 65–66, 119–121
    of Indians, 137
    in Jamestown, 53
    Protestant Reformation and, 43
    slaves and, 311, 313, 321–322
    in Spain, 25–26
    Spanish conquests and, 38–39
Chumash Indians, 11
Churches. *See also* Religion(s)
    black, 389–392
    Catholic, 66, 77
    colonial attendance at, 119–120
    membership in, 267, 300
    New England government and, 82–84, 83 (i)
    Puritan, 82–83, 84–85
    women and, 239–241
Church of England (Anglican), 62, 77, 78–81, 117
Church of Jesus Christ of Latter-Day Saints. *See* Mormons
Churubusco, battle of (1847), 296
Cincinnati, Ohio, 215
Circumnavigation of globe, 32
Cities and towns. *See also* specific locations
    free blacks in, 324
    in Massachusetts Bay colony, 80 (m)
    movement to, 280–281
    in New England, 81, 84
    railroads and, 282
    slaves employed in, 319
    in South, 314–315
Citizens and citizenship
    Articles of Confederation and, 185–187
    Asians and, 298
    black Civil War veterans and, 373
    Fourteenth Amendment and, 395
    for free blacks, 347, 348
    in Massachusetts, 96
    Supreme Court and, 404
City upon a hill, Massachusetts Bay colony as, 79, 80
Civil rights
    for African Americans, 373
    of freedmen, 395
    during Reconstruction, 400

Civil Rights Act
    of 1866, 395
    of 1875, 404
Civil service, 403
    as Jackson's "spoils system," 259
Civil war(s), in England, 85
Civil War (U.S., 1861–1865), 356–381
    African Americans in, 357–358, 370–371, 372–373
    battles in (1861–1862), 363–366, 364 (m)
    battles in (1863–1865), 377–380, 377 (m), 378 (m)
    casualties in, 358, 363, 365, 366, 371, 377, 379, 380, 381
    diplomacy in, 361, 366–367
    draft in, 370, 371, 372–373, 376–377
    in East, 363–365
    effects of, 381, 407
    emancipation and, 358, 369–370
    events leading to, 332–353
    financing of, 362–363, 371
    Fort Sumter attack and, 356 (i), 359
    home fronts during, 368, 371–374, 374–377
    Indians in, 365
    Lee's surrender and, 380
    navy in, 357–358, 362, 364 (m), 366, 367
    resources of North and South in, 360–361, 361 (f), 375 (i)
    secession and, 359–360, 360 (m)
    slavery and, 368–370, 374
    strategy in, 361, 379
    as total war, 371, 374
    weapons in, 362, 362 (i), 375 (i)
    in West, 364 (m), 365–366, 366 (m), 367
Clark, George Rogers, 171–172, 172 (m)
Clark, William, 234
Clarkson, Thomas, 270, 271
Classes, in South, 311, 327, 329
Clay, Henry, 237, 247, 258, 263, 360
    "corrupt bargain" and, 258
    election of 1824 and, 246, 246 (m)
    election of 1844 and, 293–294, 294 (i)
    Missouri Compromise and, 244
    on slavery in territories, 336
Clergy, in Chesapeake region, 62
Clermont (steamboat), 254
Cliff dwellings, Anasazi, 14
Climate
    of ancient Americas, 6
    of Carolina, 68
    warming of, 7
Clinton, DeWitt, 237
Clinton, Henry, 158, 173, 174
Clothing. *See also* Textiles and textile industry
    of Civil War soldiers, 362
    colonial, 111 (i)
    in 1850s, 266 (i)
    empire-style, 236 (i)
    homespun, 144
    of Revolutionary soldiers, 154 (i)
    of slaves, 317
Clovis culture, 7, 7 (i), 8, 9 (i)
Coal and coal industry, 281
Cobb, Howard, 352
Cobb, Thomas R. R., 311
Coeducational colleges, 266
Coercive (Intolerable) Acts (1774), 146–147, 149

Coins, 93 (i). *See also* Currency
Cold Harbor, battle of (1864), 378 (m), 379
Colombia, 245
Colonies and colonization, 16, 49. *See also* Native Americans; Revolutionary War
    in 16th century, 37 (m)
    in 17th century, 92 (m)
    in 18th century, 101–125
    African Americans and, 269, 303, 369
    British empire and, 91–96, 121–124
    British standing army in, 138
    in Chesapeake region, 51–65, 69–70
    consumption of goods in, 118–119
    economy in, 97, 103
    English, 49–50, 51–65, 66–71
    exports and, 70–71, 92, 118
    French, 94–95
    government of, 124
    Indian wars with, 122–123
    intercolonial defense in, 133–134
    Massachusetts and, 79–81
    mercantilism in, 64
    middle colonies, 108–112
    Monroe Doctrine and, 245
    New England, 103–108
    in New Spain, 36–42
    in North, 75–97
    population of English North America, 86 (f)
    Portuguese, 29
    Puritans and, 78–79
    religion in, 119–121
    rights in, 130
    at Roanoke, 44 (m), 45
    royal, 124
    in South, 112–117
    Spanish, 36–42
    taxation of, 138–148
    trade in, 91–93, 104–105, 105 (m)
    unifying elements in, 117–124
Colorado, 334
Colored Orphan Asylum, 377
Columbian exchange, 32, 33 (i)
Columbia University, as King's College, 205
Columbus, Christopher, 16, 24 (i), 25, 26, 26 (i), 29–31
Comanche Indians, 17, 232, 288, 291
Commerce. *See also* Trade
    colonial, 93, 111 (i), 118–119
    in New England, 104–105, 105 (m)
    treaty of (1785), 167
Commercial law, private investment and, 257
Committee of Vigilance, in San Francisco, 299
Committees of correspondence, 146, 147
Committees of public safety, 148, 181
Common Sense (Paine), 159
Commonwealth, New England families as, 81
Communication(s)
    national economy and, 308
    politics and, 252
    railroads and, 283
    telegraph and, 282
    transportation and, 253–254
Compass, 27
Complex marriage (Oneida community), 301, 301 (i)
Compromise of 1850, 336–338, 338 (m), 353
Compromise of 1877, 407
Comstock Lode (Nevada), 334

Concentration policy, 289
Concord, battle at, 149–150, 149 (m)
Conestoga Indians, 137
Confederacy, of Tecumseh, 228
Confederacy (Civil War South), 359
    "belligerent" status for, 367
    birth of, 352
    bread riots in, 371
    centralization in, 371
    collapse of, 379
    constitution of, 362
    Davis and, 362
    diplomacy and, 361, 366–367
    draft in, 371, 372–373
    emancipation of slaves and, 370
    industry in, 371
    inflation in, 362–363
    mobilization of, 362–363
    nationalism in, 373–374
    resources of, 360–361, 361 (f)
    secession and, 352–353, 359–360, 360 (m)
    slavery in, 368
Confederate Congress, 371
Confederation government. See Articles
        of Confederation
Confiscation Act
    of 1861, 369, 387
    of 1862, 369, 387
Congo, 115
Congregational Church, in colonies, 119
Congress (U.S.). See also Congressional
        Reconstruction; Continental Congress;
        Elections
    African Americans in, 385–386, 386 (i), 400
    under Articles of Confederation, 183–185,
        186
    Constitution on, 196
    ex-Confederates in, 394, 404
    representation in, 197
    slavery and, 271, 369
    southern congressional delegations
        (1865–1877), 400 (f)
    War of 1812 and, 237
    Wilmot Proviso and, 335
Congressional Reconstruction, 387, 395–398
Connecticut, 85, 104
    slavery in, 187, 188
Conquistadors, 34–36
    justification of actions, 38
Conscription. See Draft (military)
Conservatism and conservatives
    Johnson, Andrew, and, 393–394
    Lincoln and, 370
Constitution(s)
    of Cherokees, 262
    of Confederacy, 362
    Fundamental Orders of Connecticut as, 85
    Lecompton, 349
    reconstruction, in South, 392–393, 396,
        399–400
    state, 185
Constitution (frigate), 250 (i)
Constitution (U.S.), 195–197. See also
        Amendments; Bill of Rights; Supreme
        Court (U.S.)
    Congress in, 197
    Federalists, Antifederalists, and, 198–200
    Jefferson and, 229

nullification crisis and, 263
    ratification of, 197–201, 199 (m), 200 (i)
    slavery and, 334–335
    Washington and, 180 (i)
Constitutional convention (1787), 196
Constitutional Union Party, 351, 352 (m)
Consumer goods, 118–119
Consumers, economic cycles and, 257
Continental army, 154 (i), 157, 158. See also
        Revolutionary War
    African Americans in, 161
    campaigns of 1777–1779 and, 169–173
    southern strategy and, 173–175, 173 (m)
    at Valley Forge, 171
Continental Association, 148
Continental Congress, 154 (i), 156. See also
        Articles of Confederation; Congress
        (U.S.)
    First (1774), 148–149, 182
    Madison in, 182
    Second (1775), 149, 156–158, 160, 183
Continental dollars, 191
Continental drift, 5, 6 (m)
Contraband, runaway slaves as, 369, 373
Contract labor
    Chinese-controlled, 298
    freedmen and, 387–388
Conversion
    of Jews to Christianity, 26
    of Native Americans to Christianity, 53
    of Puritans, 87
Coode, John, 96
Cook, John F., George, and Mary, 323 (i)
Corinth, Mississippi, in Civil War, 364 (m), 366
Corn (maize), 12, 13, 30, 33 (i), 281
    in Jamestown, 52–53
Cornplanter (Seneca Indians), 192
Cornstalk (Shawnee Indians), 171
Cornwallis, Charles, 174–175
Coronado, Francisco Vásquez de, 35
Corporations, commercial law and, 257
"Corrupt bargain," 246, 258
Corruption
    under Grant, 403, 403 (i)
    during Revolution, 169
    in southern Republican governments, 400
Cortés, Hernán, 26 (i), 33–34, 35 (i), 36,
        36 (i)
Cotton, John, 84
Cotton and cotton industry, 209, 316 (i).
        See also Cotton gin
    Civil War and, 361
    climate and geography for, 309
    cotton famine in, 361, 367
    European imports and, 368, 368 (f)
    mills and, 255
    panic of 1837 and, 273
    production in, 309 (m)
    sharecropping and, 401–402
    slaves and, 309–310
    yeomen farmers in, 324
Cotton belt, 324 (m)
Cotton gin, 209, 314, 315
Cotton kingdom, 309, 309 (m)
Country-born slaves, 114
Courts. See also Supreme Court (U.S.)
    church, 62
Covenant

of grace, 84
    Puritan, 75–76, 79, 80, 82
    of works, 84
Covenant Chain, 133 (i), 134
Coverture laws, 344–345
Cowpens, battle of (1781), 174
Cragin, Mary, 301 (i)
Crashes (financial). See Depressions (financial);
        Panics
Crawford, William H., 245–246, 246 (m), 247
Credit, 214–215, 315
    economic panics and, 257, 274
    sharecropping and, 401–402
Creek Indians, 17, 122–123, 237, 260, 309
    free blacks and, 190
    removal of, 262
Creek War (1813–1814), 237, 309
Creoles, 40, 114
"Crime against Kansas, The" (Sumner), 347
Crime and criminals, voting rights and, 243
Croatoan, discovery of word, 45
Crockett, David, 292
Cromwell, Oliver, 85
Crop lien system, 401–402
Crops
    in Carolinas, 68
    markets for, 63
    in middle colonies, 109–110, 111
    of Native Americans, 12, 13
    of Taino people, 30
    tobacco as, 50, 55–62
    of yeomen farmers, 324, 325
Crow Indians, 17
Cuba, 245, 311, 340
    in Seven Years' War, 134
    slave society in, 310
    Spain and, 33
Cuffe, John and Paul, 187
Culture(s)
    African American, 116, 321 (i)
    Anasazi, 14
    of Archaic Indians, 10 (m)
    Clovis, 7, 8
    divergence in North and South, 353
    of Great Basin, 11
    Hohokam, 14
    Hopewell, 15–16
    Indian, 16–20
    manifest destiny and, 288
    of Mexica people, 20–21
    Mississippian, 15 (m), 16
    Mogollon, 13–14
    of Paleo-Indians, 7
    of plain folk, 327
    public, after 1815, 252
    religious changes in, 264
    slave, 308
    southern, 374
    southwestern, 13–14, 13 (m), 15 (i)
    of Woodland Indians, 12, 15–16
Cumberland River region, in Civil War, 366
Currency, 257, 263. See also Money
    under Articles of Confederation, 192
    bank, 263
    national, 374
    pine tree shilling as, 93 (i)
Curriculum, in women's academies, 241
Curtis, Benjamin R., 348

Daguerre, Louis, 337
Daguerreotypes, 256 *(i)*, 337, 337 *(i)*
Dallas, George M., 294 *(i)*
Dalles, The (fishing site), 18
Dance, by plain folk, 327
Dartmouth College, 165 *(i)*
Daughters of Liberty, 142, 143–144, 210
Dave (slave potter), 306 *(i)*
Davis, Henry Winter, 387
Davis, Jefferson, 336, 352, 359, 360, 362, 371, 374
Davis, Paula Wright, 302
Dawes, William, 149–150
Dearborn, Fort, 237
Death of Jane McCrea (Vanderlyn), 170 *(i)*
Death rate. *See* Mortality rate
Debates, Lincoln-Douglas, 348–349
Debt, 257. *See also* National debt
   colonial, to Britain, 118
   Confederate, 392–393
   corporate, 257
   Revolutionary War, 169, 205–206
   of southern farmers, 402
   Spanish, 43
   state, 213
Decatur, Stephen, 234
"Declaration of Dependence, A" (loyalist document), 168
Declaration of Independence (1776), 160, 185, 187
"Declaration on the Causes and Necessity of Taking Up Arms, A," 158
Declaratory Act (1766), 142
Deep South, slavery in, 190
Deere, John, 281
Defense, intercolonial, 133–134
Deforestation, steamboat use and, 354
de Gouges, Olympe, 210, 211
Deists, in colonies, 119
Delany, Martin R., 302
Delaware (state and colony), 56 *(m)*, 108, 190, 359
Delaware (Lenni Lenape) Indians, 89 *(i)*, 91, 133, 136, 168, 172 *(m)*, 192, 215, 216, 217, 236
Delaware River region, 88 *(m)*, 163
Demobilization, after Civil War, 399
Democracy
   popular sovereignty and, 335
   vs. republicanism, 197
   in South, 327–328
   spread of, 258–260
Democratic Party, 274, 342 *(m)*. *See also* Elections
   collapse of Reconstruction and, 405–406
   emancipation and, 369, 370
   Jackson and, 259, 260–261
   "peace" Democrats and, 379
   popular sovereignty and, 341
   South and, 328, 400, 405–406
   Texas annexation and, 293
Democratic Republicans (Democrats), 258
Demonstration(s). *See* Protest(s); Revolts and rebellions
Denmark, 122
Dennis, John Q. A., 390
Departments of government. *See also* specific departments

   under Washington, 207–208
Depressions (financial). *See also* Panics
   of 1839, 253
   in 1870s, 404
Desertion, in Civil War, 372, 380
De Soto, Hernando, 35, 42 *(i)*
Detroit, Fort, 136, 137, 172 *(m)*
Dew, Thomas R., 308, 311, 319
Dias, Bartolomeu, 29
Dickinson, John, 142, 157, 158, 159, 160
Diet (food). *See also* Food(s)
   of slaves, 317
Dinwiddie, Robert, 132, 132 *(i)*
Diplomacy. *See also* Foreign policy
   in Civil War, 361, 366–367
   with France, 221, 223
   King Cotton, 367, 368
Discovery (ship), 51
Discrimination. *See also* Integration; Race and racism; Segregation
   in armed forces, 372–373
   against free blacks, 284, 303
   gender, 284, 302
   against immigrants, 284, 287
   during Reconstruction, 400
Diseases
   during California gold rush, 297
   in Columbian exchange, 32
   European in Americas, 41
   Indians and, 124, 289, 293
   in Jamestown, 53
   in Massachusetts, 80
   in Mexican-American War, 296
   during Revolution, 158
   slaves and, 115
Disfranchisement, 397. *See also* Voting and voting rights
   of African Americans, 398
   of women, 343
Disqualification Act (1787), 195
Dissent. *See also* Protest(s)
   in North (Civil War), 376–377
District of Columbia, 272, 337. *See also* Washington, D.C.
Diversity
   California gold rush and, 298–299
   in middle colonies, 88–89
   in Pennsylvania, 90–91
   in West, 298–299
Divorce, 240, 318
Dix, Dorothea, 375–376
Dollar (U.S.)
   Continental, 191
   depreciation of, 191 *(i)*
Domesticity, women and, 264–265
Dominican Republic, 404, 404 *(m)*
Dominion of New England, 96
Donelson, Fort, capture of (1862), 364 *(m)*, 366
"Doughfaces," northerners as, 339, 343
Douglas, Stephen A., 280, 359
   Compromise of 1850 and, 337–338
   debates with Lincoln, 348–349
   election of 1860 and, 351–352
   Freeport Doctrine of, 349
   Kansas-Nebraska Act of, 340
   on Lecompton constitution, 349
   popular sovereignty and, 341, 346

Douglass, Frederick, 302, 302 *(i)*, 333, 336, 339, 358, 369, 372, 395
Dove (ship), 62
Dove, Samuel, 389 *(i)*
Doyle, Mahala, 333
Draft (military), in Civil War, 370, 371, 372–373, 376–377
Drake, Francis, 288
Dred Scott decision (1857), 347–348, 349, 353
Drinker, Elizabeth, 210
Dueling, Burr-Hamilton, 229, 230–231, 231 *(i)*
Duke of York. *See* James II (Duke of York, England)
Duke of York (slave ship), 101
Dunmore (Lord), 150
Duquesne, Fort, 132, 134
Dürer, Albrecht, 43
Dutch, at New Amsterdam, 56 *(m)*, 88–89, 89 *(i)*
Dutch East India Company, 88
Dutch Reformed Church, 89
Duties. *See also* Taxation
   Britain and, 124
   on tobacco, 65
   Townshend, 142–144

Earl, Ralph E. W., 252 *(i)*
Earth
   circumnavigation of, 32
   Columbus on earth as sphere, 29
East (region)
   Civil War in, 363–365, 364 *(m)*
   suffrage in, 242–243
Eastern Hemisphere, sea routes to West and, 32
Eastern Woodland Indians, 12, 12 *(i)*, 15–17
East India Company (Britain), 146
East Indies
   Columbus and, 30
   Magellan and, 32
   Portugal and, 29
Eaton, William, 234
Economy. *See also* Depressions; Panics; Tariffs
   banking and, 257
   Bank War and, 264
   boom and bust cycles in, 257
   of Carolinas, 68
   in Civil War, 362–363, 371, 374–375
   colonial, 97, 103
   cotton exports and, 314
   free-labor, 279
   growth in, 280–281
   Hamilton and, 206, 209–215
   interdependence of, 308
   manifest destiny and, 288
   market revolution and, 252–257
   of New England, 85–86
   of New Spain, 40
   plantation, 311–315
   railroads and, 283–284
   in Reconstruction South, 400
   during Revolution, 169
   servant labor and, 65
   in South, 117
Edenton, North Carolina, women protesters in, 143 *(i)*
Education. *See also* Higher education; School(s)
   for African Americans, 266 *(i)*

freedmen and, 389, 401
free-labor ideal and, 285
plain folk and, 327
in South, 400
for women, 208, 240, 241–242, 241 (i), 318
of youth, 265–267
Edward VI (England), 77
Edwards, Jonathan, 120
Effigies, Taino, 30 (i)
Egypt, 367
Elastic clause, 197
"Elect," Puritans as, 82
Elections. See also Voting and voting rights
of 1796, 220–221
of 1800, 223, 228, 229
of 1804, 234–235
of 1808, 235
of 1812, 237
of 1816, 242
of 1820, 242
of 1824, 242, 245–246, 246 (m), 251, 272
of 1828, 251, 258–259, 259 (m), 272
of 1832, 251, 263, 272
of 1836, 272–273
of 1840, 274
of 1844, 293–294
of 1848, 336, 336 (m), 342 (m)
of 1852, 339–340, 341, 342 (m)
of 1854, 341
of 1855, 341
of 1856, 342 (m), 343–344, 343 (i)
of 1860, 342 (m), 349, 351–352, 352 (m)
of 1862, 370
of 1864, 377, 379, 392
of 1865, 394
of 1866, 396
of 1868, 385, 403, 403 (m), 405 (i)
of 1872, 385, 403–404
of 1874, 386, 404
of 1876, 403, 406–407, 407 (m)
elites in, 199
in Kansas (1854), 346
in Mississippi (1876), 406
of senators, 349
in South, 328
Electoral college, 242, 352, 403
in Constitution, 197
election of 1796 and, 220–221
election of 1824 and, 246
Electoral commission, for 1876 election, 406
Elites. See also Classes
in elections, 199
Jackson and, 258
of Mexica, 20–21
in New Spain, 40
southern, 328
of southern free blacks, 324
Elizabeth I (England), 77, 77 (i)
Emancipation, 386, 407
colonization in Africa and, 269
gradual, 187–189, 244
Lincoln and, 357
as military necessity, 370
preliminary proclamation of, 369–370
proponents and opponents of, 369
after Revolution, 323
in states, 188–189
status of slaves as contraband and, 369

Emancipation Proclamation (1863), 358, 370, 390
Embargo, by Jefferson, 234–235
Embargo Act (1807), 235
Emerson, Ralph Waldo, 300
Emigrant aid societies, Kansas settlement and, 346
Eminent domain, 257
Empires
British, 91–96, 97, 121 (m)
in eastern North America, 121 (m)
of Mexica, 20
Employment. See also Unemployment; Women; Workforce
black codes limitations on, 393
transportation and, 253
Empresario, 292
Encomenderos, 37–40
Encomienda system, 37–40
Energy, 281
England (Britain). See also British Empire; Colonies and colonization; Revolutionary War
abolitionism in, 268, 270–271, 270 (i)
American Revolutionary War and, 160–163, 164 (m), 169–177
Americas and, 44–45
boycott of trade with, 148
Civil War (U.S.) and, 367
colonial poverty compared with, 108
colonial trade and, 117
colonies of, 48–65, 66–71
control of Canada and, 134
cotton from South and, 361, 367
exploration by, 32, 44–45
French Revolution and, 219
impressment by, 235
Indians and, 53–54, 64
Jay Treaty with, 219
Native Americans and, 94
Oregon and, 288, 294
panic of 1837 and, 273
Protestantism in, 76–78, 77 (i)
Puritanism in England and, 76–78, 85
Puritanism in New England and, 78–81
Reformation in, 76–77
Roanoke settlement by, 44 (m), 45
rural resistance to, 147–148
Rush-Bagot treaty with, 238–239
in Seven Years' War, 130–132, 131 (m), 134–138
Texas and, 293
War of 1812 with, 228, 235, 237–238
women's rights in, 210
English Empire. See British Empire
English Reformation, 76–77
Enlightenment, 119
Entertainment. See also Leisure
in Chesapeake region, 62
Entrepreneurs, after 1815, 252
Enumerated goods, 92
Environment. See also Air pollution
of Great Basin region, 11
Native Americans and, 19
of Paleo-Indians, 7
steamboat use and, 254
Epidemics
from Columbian exchange, 32
Plains Indians and, 289

Equality. See also Gender and gender issues; Slaves and slavery
under Articles of Confederation, 187–190
gender, 344–345
slavery and, 187–190
Equiano, Olaudah, 114, 114 (i), 120
Erie, Lake, 134
battle in, 237
Erie Canal, 253 (m), 254–255
Ethnic groups
in colonies, 103, 104 (m)
in middle colonies, 108–109
Europe and Europeans. See also Colonies and colonization
ancient humans from, 5
Civil War (U.S.) and, 361, 366–367
colonies and (18th century), 104
exploration by, 27–42, 31 (m)
immigrants from, 69 (f)
migration to Americas from, 16
New World and, 21, 25–27, 42–45
North American influence of, 135 (m)
slave trade and, 115 (i)
trade routes of, 28 (m)
Evangelicalism, 252, 264, 267–268, 327
reform and, 269, 300
slaves and, 321
Everett, Sarah, 290
Evolution, Native American, 9
Executive. See President
Executive branch
under Articles of Confederation, 185
Jefferson and, 229, 232
Expansion and expansionism. See also Monroe Doctrine; Westward movement
in 1800s, 287
Indian lands and, 215
slavery and, 308
Texas and, 293–294
in West, 216 (m)
Exploration
by Columbus, 26, 29–31
European, 27–42, 31 (m)
by France, 43–44
by Norsemen, 27
by Portugal, 27, 28–29, 28 (m), 32
by Spain, 33–42
Exports
agricultural, 209
from Britain, 118–119
colonial growth and, 70–71, 92, 118
of cotton, 314, 368, 368 (f)
embargo on, 235
from English colonies, 117
from New England, 85–86
southern crops as, 117
of tobacco, 56
Extinction
of ancient large mammals, 7
of native horses, 11

Factionalism, 223
Factions. See also Political parties
Constitution and, 201
Factories
in Confederacy, 362
labor force in, 281, 319
workers and, 255–256

Fallen Timbers, battle of (1794), 216–217
Fall line, 56 (m)
Families
    African American, 116
    Civil War and, 358, 360, 381
    of free blacks, 323–324
    of freedmen, 389, 390, 401
    of loyalists, 168
    Mexican, 296 (i)
    in New England, 80–81, 86, 86 (i)
    of planters, 316, 317–319, 317 (i)
    separate spheres idea and, 264–265
    slave, 319, 320–321
    of southern poor whites, 326
    on trails, 289–290, 291 (i)
    women's rights in, 240
    of yeomen, 324–325
Famine, in Ireland, 287
Farewell Address, of Washington, 221 (i)
Farms and farming. See also Agriculture; Rural
        areas; Shays's Rebellion; Tenant farming
    Bacon's Rebellion and, 64–65
    in Chesapeake region, 59–62, 69–70
    free vs. unfree labor, 62
    mechanization of, 375
    in middle colonies, 109–110, 110 (i)
    Native American, 13 (i)
    in New England, 104
    on prairie, 281
    sharecropping and, 401–402
    slaves on, 319
    technology for, 281
    whiskey tax and, 214–215
    by women, 375
    by yeomen, 62–63, 324–325
Federal government. See Government (U.S.)
Federalist Papers, The, 201, 207
Federalists, 198–201, 200 (i), 235
    Alien and Sedition Acts and, 222–223
    Bill of Rights and, 208
    collapse of, 242
    election of 1796 and, 220–221
    election of 1800 and, 223, 228, 229
    Hartford Convention and, 238
    Jefferson and, 232
    Missouri crisis and, 245
    War of 1812 and, 237, 238
Federal slave code, for territories, 351
Feke, Robert, 111 (i)
Female academies. See Academies
Female Review, The, 156 (i)
Feme covert doctrine, 240, 243
Feminism
    Fifteenth Amendment and, 398
    in France, 210
Ferdinand (Spain), 25–26, 26 (i), 29,
        30–31, 38
Fifteenth Amendment, 398
"Fifty-four Forty or Fight," 294
54th Massachusetts Colored Regiment,
        372, 373
Figgins, J. D., 3–4
Fillmore, Millard, 337–338, 343, 343 (i)
Finances
    under Articles of Confederation, 183,
        191–192
    banking and, 257
    for Civil War, 362–363

credit and, 257–258
    Hamilton and, 205–206, 209–215
    during Revolution, 169
    tariffs and, 263
Finney, Charles Grandison, 267–268, 267 (i)
Fire, Indian uses of, 19–20
"Fire-eaters" (radical southerners), 336, 351
First Amendment, 208
First Bank of the United States, 213–214, 257
First Continental Congress (1774), 148–149,
        168, 182
First Great Awakening, 120
Fishing and fishing industry
    in New England, 85–86, 104–105
    in Pacific Northwest, 11–12, 18
Fitzhugh, George, 311, 318
Five Civilized Tribes, 365
Flag(s), 200 (i)
    at Fort Sumter, 356 (i)
Florida, 309
    Indians in, 66
    invasion by Andrew Jackson, 245
    Ponce de León in, 35
    secession of, 352
    Spain and, 42, 65–66
Folsom culture, 3–4, 4 (i), 11
Folsom points, 4
Food(s). See also Crops; Diet (food); Hunters
        and hunting
    in Columbian Exchange, 32
    in Confederacy, 362, 371
    of Eastern Woodland people, 12
    in Jamestown, 52–53
    for Pilgrims, 78
Foote, Henry S., 336
Force Bill (1833), 263
Foreign Miners' Tax Law (1850), 298
Foreign policy. See also Diplomacy
    of Grant, 404
    Monroe Doctrine and, 245
Fort(s). See also specific locations
    British and, 136–137, 219
    Indian attacks on, 135, 136
    in Ohio River region, 132
    along Oregon Trail, 289
    in Seven Years' War, 131 (m)
Forty-niners, 297, 299
Fossils, at Folsom site, 3–4
Founding Fathers, 206
Fourier, Charles, 300
Fourierist phalanxes, 300–301
Fourteenth Amendment, ratification by southern
        states, 395–396, 396–397, 400
4th U.S. Colored Infantry, Company E, 373 (i)
France. See also French Revolution
    alliance with, 160, 173, 175, 177, 221
    American West and, 232, 233–234
    Americas and, 43–44
    arms shipments to, 235
    Civil War (U.S.) and, 367
    cotton from South and, 361
    in eastern North America, 121 (m)
    English colonies and, 96
    Haiti and, 219–220
    Indians and, 94–95, 122–123
    Mexico and, 404
    Revolutionary War alliance with, 160, 173,
        175, 177

in Seven Years' War, 130–133, 131 (m), 134,
        135, 135 (m), 138
    warships of, 122
    withdrawal from North America, 135, 136
    women's rights in, 210
    XYZ Affair and, 221
Franchise, 302. See also Voting and voting rights
    for adult males, 242
Franciscans, in California, 293
Franklin, Benjamin, 112, 119, 120, 125, 135,
        195, 270
    Albany Plan of Union and, 133–134
    Constitution and, 180, 196
    Second Continental Congress and, 157
    slaves of, 109–110
Franklin, James, printing press of, 118
Fredericksburg, battle of (1862), 365
Free blacks, 323–324, 348. See also African
        Americans
    during Civil War, 377
    discrimination against, 284, 303
    economic rights of, 324
    elite, 324
    laws restricting, 323
    in Massachusetts, 189
    in Pennsylvania, 188
    violence against, 269
Freedmen
    black codes and, 393, 393 (i), 394
    education and, 389, 401
    freedom and, 388–392
    labor code and, 387–388
    land for, 388, 392, 401
    marriage and, 390
    during Reconstruction, 385–386
    in Republican Party, 399
    search for families by, 389, 389 (i)
    sharecropping by, 401–402
    taxes and, 405–406
    voting rights for, 395, 397
Freedmen's Bureau, 388, 396, 397
Freedmen's Bureau Acts (1865 and 1866), 395
Freedom(s)
    of free blacks, 324
    for freedmen, 388–392
    parable about, 100, 100 (i)
    for slaves, 102, 110, 150–151
    slave suit for, 188–189
"Freedom papers," 323, 323 (i)
Free labor, 284–287
    compulsory, 387–388
    as ideal, 284–285, 300, 302, 303
    in North, 303
    during Reconstruction, 387–388
    Republican Party on, 343
    vs. slavery, 311
    in West, 335
Free-labor economy, 279
Freeman, Elizabeth. See Bett, Mum
Freeport Doctrine, 349
Free soil doctrine, 335, 369
Free-Soil Party, 336, 337, 340
Free-soil settlers, in Kansas, 346 (i), 347
Free speech, 376
Free states, 329, 336, 337, 338 (m), 340 (m),
        346
"Freethinker," 344
Freewill Baptists, 240

Frémont, Jessie Benton, 343
Frémont, John C., 293, 343, 369
French and Indian War. *See* Seven Years'
  (French and Indian) War
French Revolution, 209, 218–219
Frobisher, Martin, 44
Frontier
  colonial, 104
  English forts and, 219
  Jackson, Andrew, and, 251–252
  in Revolutionary War, 171–172, 175
  settlers on, 287
Fuel, for steamboats, 254
Fugitive Slave Act (1850), 337, 338–339, 353
Fugitive slaves
  in Civil War, 357–358, 369, 374
  Compromise of 1850 and, 337, 338
  resistance by, 322
  underground railroad and, 303
Fuller, Margaret, 300
Fulton, Robert, 254
Fundamental Orders of Connecticut, 85
Fur trade, 85, 94, 95, 95 *(i)*, 96, 132, 288
  competition over, 122

Gabriel's Rebellion (1800), 229
Gadsden, James, 340
Gadsden Purchase (1853), 340, 340 *(m)*
Gage, Thomas, 113 *(m)*, 147, 149, 158
"Gag rule," in Congress, 272
Galloway, Joseph, 148
Gansevoort, Peter, 154 *(i)*
Garfield, James A., 396, 403
Garnet, Henry Highland, 302
Garrison, William Lloyd, 269, 270 *(i)*, 271,
  307, 336, 350, 407
Gary, Martin, 406
Gaspée (ship), 146
Gates, Horatio, 170 *(i)*, 171, 174
Gender and gender issues. *See also* Men;
  Women
  education and, 241–242
  equality and, 386
  in home, 264–265
  laws regulating relations, 240
  in Revolutionary War period, 156
  voting rights and, 186–187
  women's status and, 208–209
General Court (Massachusetts), 83, 84
Generall Historie of Virginia (Smith), 49
"General welfare" clause, 214
Genetics, Native American evolution and, 9
Geneva conventions, on prisoners of war, 167
Genoa, 27
Gentry
  land speculation by, 128
  slaveholding, 117
Geographic mobility, free labor and, 286–287
Geographic revolution, 32
George III (England), 135, 138, 142, 159
Georgia
  Cherokee removal and, 262
  Civil War in, 379
  population of, 112
  power of planters in, 328
  Revolutionary War and, 173–174, 173 *(m)*
  secession and, 352, 392
  slavery in, 190

Spanish exploration of, 35, 42 *(i)*
German Americans, 287
  Pennsylvania Dutch as, 108
German Reformed church, 109
Germany, immigrants from, 108–109, 287, 341
Gettysburg, battle of (1863), 377, 377 *(m)*,
  378 *(m)*
Ghent, Treaty of (1814), 238, 246
Giant bison, 3, 4
Gift exchange, with Indians, 136
Gilbert, Humphrey, 44
Girls. *See* Women
Glaciers, 6
Global issues
  European views of U.S. Civil War, 361
  international diplomacy during Civil War,
    361, 366–367
  in Seven Years' War, 130–138
  slave societies in New World, 310
  transatlantic abolitionism, 270
Glorieta Pass, battle at (1862), 366, 366 *(m)*
Glorious Revolution (England), 96
Godspeed (ship), 51
Gold
  as hard money, 191, 213
  in Mexico, 34, 36 *(i)*
  from Peru, 35
  as specie, 257
Gold Coast, 113 *(m)*, 115
Gold rush (California), 278 *(i)*, 297–299, 334
Goliad, massacre at (1836), 292
Gooding, James Henry, 372–373
Gorgas, Josiah, 362
Gould, William, 357–358, 370, 381
Government. *See also* Government (U.S.)
  of Massachusetts, 79
  of military districts in South, 396
  in New England, 82–84, 96, 104
  of New Spain, 36–40
  of Pennsylvania, 91
  Puritan, 78–79, 83–84
  state, 392–393, 396–397
  of Virginia colony, 54–55, 63–64
Government (U.S.)
  under Articles of Confederation, 183–185,
    190–195
  assumption of state debts by, 213
  branches of, 197
  Civil War and, 358, 374–375, 381
  Constitution and, 196–201
  Jackson and, 259–260
  Jefferson on limited, 232
  land policy of, 281
  Madison and, 182
  stability in, 206–209
  Washington and, 207–208
Governors, colonial, 124, 128
Gradual emancipation, 187–189, 244
Grain, taxation on, 214
Grandees, 64–65, 66–67. *See also* Elites
Grant, Ulysses S.
  in Civil War, 366, 377, 378–379,
    378 *(m)*, 380
  corruption and, 403, 403 *(i)*
  election of 1868 and, 385, 403, 403 *(m)*,
    405 *(i)*
  election of 1872 and, 403–404
  foreign policy of, 404

  presidency of, 403–404
  Reconstruction and, 404
Grasse (Comte de), 175
Graves, A. J. (Mrs.), 264
Gray, Thomas R., 308
Great Awakening, 120
  Second, 264, 267–268, 274
Great Basin region, peoples of, 11, 16
Great Britain. *See* England (Britain)
Great Compromise, 197
Great Lakes region, 96, 134, 254
  Indians of, 16–17, 135, 136, 227–228
Great Plains, 232
  buffalo (bison) in, 11
  Indians of, 16, 17
Great Salt Lake, 290
Greeley, Horace, 363, 404
Greenbacks, 374
Greenville, Treaty of (1795), 217–218,
  217 *(i)*, 219
Grenville, George, 138–140, 139 *(i)*
Grimké sisters
  Angelina, 269
  Sarah, 211, 269
Griswold, Roger, 222 *(i)*
Guadalupe Hidalgo, Treaty of (1848), 296
Guadeloupe, 134, 135 *(m)*, 138
Guerrilla war
  during Civil War, 359, 365–366
  in Kansas, 347
  in Revolutionary War, 173, 174
Gunboats, in Civil War, 366
Gun industry, interchangeable parts and, 282
Gutenberg, Johannes, 27

Habeas corpus, Lincoln and, 359
Haires, Francis, 58
Haiti, 219–220, 386
Hakluyt, Richard, 51
Halfway Covenant, 87
Hamilton, Alexander, 205–206
  Constitution and, 196, 199–200
  death of, 229, 230–231, 231 *(i)*
  economy and, 206, 209–215
  election of 1796 and, 221
  election of 1800 and, 229
  Federalist Papers and, 201
  Jefferson on policies of, 229–232
  as treasury secretary, 205, 207, 209
Hammond, James Henry, 320, 335
Hancock, John, 140, 150
Hannastown, Pennsylvania, 172 *(m)*
Hard money, 191, 213
Harmar, Josiah, 215
Harper, William, defense of slavery, 312–313
Harpers Ferry, Virginia, Brown's raid on (1859),
  332 *(i)*, 333–334, 349–350
Harrison, William Henry, 228, 236–237,
  273, 274
Hartford, 85
Hartford Convention (1814), 238–239
Hartford Seminary, 241
Hayes, Rutherford B., election of 1876 and,
  406–407
Headrights, 57, 67
Hemings, Sally, 232
Hendrick (Mohawk Indians), 133, 133 *(i)*, 134
Hendricks, Thomas A., 404

Henry, Fort, 172 *(m)*
    capture of (1862), 364 *(m)*, 366
Henry VII (England), 32
Henry VIII (England), 76–77
Henry the Navigator (Portugal), 28
Henry, Patrick, 128, 140, 146, 148, 196
Henry Frank (steamboat), 316 *(i)*
Herndon, William, 348
Herttell, Thomas, 344
Hessians, 163
Heyrick, Elizabeth, 271
Hierarchy
    of Catholic Church, 77
    Quakers and, 90
Higby, Richard, 59
Higginson, Thomas W., 373 *(i)*
Higher education, 266. *See also* Universities and
        colleges
    for women, 241–242
"Higher law" doctrine, of Seward, 337, 351
Highways. *See* Roads and highways
Hill, Aaron (Mohawk Indians), 192
Hillsborough (Lord), 143
Hispanic Americans, in California, 299
Hispaniola
    Haitian Revolution and, 219–220
    Spain and, 33
History and historiography, archaeology and,
        4–5
Hohokam culture, 14, 14 *(i)*
Holland, Puritans in, 78
Holmes, George F., 339
Holy experiment, of Penn, 90
Home front
    in Civil War, 368, 371–374, 374–377
    in Revolutionary War, 163–169
Home rule, for South, 403, 405
Homespun cloth, 144
Homestead Act (1862), 374
Homo erectus, 5
Homo sapiens, 5–6
Hone, Philip, 274
Honor
    Hamilton-Burr duel and, 230–231
    in South, 317
Hood, John B., 379
Hooker, Thomas, 85
Hopewell culture, 15–16
Hopi Indians, 14
Horses, 11, 283, 288
Horseshoe Bend, battle of (1814), 237
Hourglass, 27
Households, American furniture compared with
        European furniture, 81 *(i)*
House of Burgesses, 54–55, 63, 64, 140, 146
House of Representatives, 197, 229, 385
Housing
    in Cahokia, 16
    of free black elite, 324
    of poor planters, 63 *(i)*
    for slaves, 317
    on sugar plantation, 67 *(i)*
Houston, Sam, 292
Howe, William, 158, 163, 170, 173
Hudson, Carrie, 319
Hudson River region, 88, 88 *(m)*
Huitzilopochtli (god), 20
Hull, John, 93 *(i)*

Humans, writing and, 4–5
Human sacrifice, 19, 20, 21 *(i)*
Hunchback (ship), 358 *(i)*
Hunger, in Jamestown, 53
Hunley, H. L. (submarine), 367
Hunter-gatherers, Archaic, 8–12
Hunters and hunting
    ancient, 5, 6, 7
    of buffalo (bison), 11
    Indians and, 12, 19–20
    Paleo-Indians and, 6–7
Huron, Lake, 136
Huron Indians, 94
Hutchins, Thomas, 137
Hutchinson, Anne, 84–85
Hutchinson, Thomas, 130 *(i)*, 139, 141, 144
    Albany Plan of Union and, 133–134
    Boston Tea Party and, 146
    as loyalist, 165
    as Massachusetts governor, 129–130, 147
    Wheatley and, 150

Iberian Peninsula, 25–26. *See also* Portugal;
        Spain
Identity, of British North American colonists,
        124–125
Illinois, 236, 242, 243, 243 *(i)*, 244
    repeal of anti-black laws in, 281, 377
Illiteracy, 327
Illness. *See* Diseases
Immediate Not Gradual Abolition (Heyrick), 271
Immigrants and immigration. *See also*
        Migration; Slaves and slavery
    California gold rush and, 298–299
    to colonies, 102, 104 *(m)*, 108–109,
        111, 112
    free labor and, 287
    in gold and silver mining, 298
    indenture of, 58
    in middle colonies, 108–109, 111
    nativism and, 341
    in New England, 80, 85
    as percentage of state populations (1860),
        315 *(m)*
    South and, 315
    in textile industry, 255
    voting rights and, 398
Impartial Administration of Justice Act
        (1774), 147
Impeachment, of Johnson, Andrew, 397–398,
        397 *(i)*
Imports, 235
    English colonial, 93, 119, 144
    European cotton, 262, 368, 368 *(f)*
    in middle colonies, 112
    in New England, 104
    of slaves, 113 *(t)*, 310
Impost (import tax), 191
Impressment, 235, 238, 371
Inauguration, 353
    of Jackson, 259
    of Jefferson (1800), 223, 229
    of Washington, 207 *(i)*
Incan empire, 35
Incorporation, laws of, 257
Indentured servants, 57–59, 109. *See also*
        Slaves and slavery
Independence, in South America, 245

Independent treasury system, 274
India, 134, 367
    European exploration and, 29
Indian(s). *See also* Native Americans
    naming by Columbus, 30
Indiana, 236, 242, 243, 281
Indian country, 136–137, 171–172. *See also*
        Oklahoma; West
Indian policy. *See also* Native Americans
    concentration policy, 289
    of Jackson, 259, 260–262
    removal, 259, 260–262, 309
    reservations, 289
Indian Removal Act (1830), 261–262
Indian Territory, 261 *(m)*, 262, 365
Indigenous people. *See* Native Americans
Indigo, 112, 117
Individualism, 303, 317, 371
    parable about, 100, 100 *(i)*
Industrial capitalism, 381
Industrialization, Civil War and, 358, 362, 371
Industrial revolution, 281
Industry
    in North (Civil War), 375
    production, labor relations, and, 255–256
    profits from cotton and, 314
    railroads and, 282, 283
    in South, 314
Inflation
    in Civil War, 362–363, 371
    economic cycles and, 257
    in 1830s, 264
Inheritance
    in France, 210
    laws for, 240, 344–345
    partible, 104
Integration. *See also* Segregation
    of public schools, 303
Intellectual thought. *See also* Literature
    Enlightenment and, 119
    proslavery, 311
    transcendentalists and, 300
    utopians and, 300–301
    women and, 242
Interchangeable parts, 282
Intermarriage, 262. *See also* Marriage
Intolerable (Coercive) Acts (1774), 146–147
Inventions and inventors. *See also*
        specific inventions
    inflatable rubberized bags and, 280 *(i)*
Investments
    in English colonies, 51, 78–79
    by Southerners, 314
Iowa, 281, 377
Ireland, immigrants from, 108, 109, 287, 341,
        376–377
Iron and iron industry, 282–283
Ironclad warships, 358 *(i)*, 366
Iroquois Confederacy, 133, 165, 170, 192–193
Iroquois Indians, 17, 104, 111
    fur trade and, 94, 122
    during Revolution, 171, 172 *(m)*
    in Seven Years' War, 131 *(m)*, 134
"Irrepressible conflict" speech (Seward), 351
Irrigation, 13
Isabella (Spain), 24 *(i)*, 25–26, 26 *(i)*, 29,
        30–31
Isham, Edward, 325

Islam. *See* Muslims
Isthmus of Panama, 32

Jackson, Andrew ("Old Hickory"), 247,
    250 *(i)*, 251–252, 252 *(i)*, 317
  Bank of the United States and, 260
  Bank War and, 263–264
  California purchase and, 293
  civil service under, 259
  election of 1824 and, 246, 246 *(m)*
  election of 1828 and, 258–259
  election of 1832 and, 263
  Indians and, 245, 259, 260–262, 260 *(i)*
  marriage of, 259
  on moneyed interests, 257
  at New Orleans, 238
  nullification and, 263
  reform and, 274–275
  second American party system and, 258–259
  Van Buren and, 259
  in War of 1812, 237
Jackson, Rachel, 259
Jackson, Thomas J. ("Stonewall"), 365
Jamaica, Spain and, 33
James (James Amistead Lafayette, slave),
    175 *(i)*
James I (England), 51, 55, 77 *(i)*, 78, 89–90
James II (Duke of York, England), 89–90, 96
Jamestown, 49–50, 51–53, 52 *(i)*
  advertisement for settlers, 55 *(i)*
  Bacon's Rebellion and, 64
Jay, John, 195, 201, 207, 219. *See also*
    Jay Treaty
Jay Treaty, 219, 221
Jefferson, Isaac, 320 *(i)*
Jefferson, Mary, 320 *(i)*
Jefferson, Thomas, 146, 150, 158, 174–175,
    185, 232 *(i)*
  Articles of Confederation and, 184
  assumption and, 213
  Barbary Wars and, 226 *(i)*, 234
  Declaration of Independence and, 160
  election of 1796 and, 220–221
  election of 1800 and, 223, 228, 229
  election of 1804 and, 234–235
  Embargo Act (1807) and, 235
  Hamilton and, 206
  Hemings, Sally, and, 232 *(i)*
  limited government and, 232, 259
  Louisiana Purchase, Lewis and Clark
    expedition, and, 234
  Missouri crisis sand, 245
  Northwest Territory and, 193–194, 193 *(m)*
  presidential terms of, 228–235
  religion and, 119
  republicanism of, 229–232, 247
  as secretary of state, 207
  slavery and, 115, 117, 245, 316, 320 *(i)*
  on Whiskey Rebellion, 215
Jersey (British prisoner of war ship), 166, 167 *(i)*
Jesuits, in New France, 94–95
Jews and Judaism, in Spain, 26
Jim Crow, 400
John II (Castile), 25
John Brown Going to His Hanging (Pippin),
    350 *(i)*
Johnson, Andrew
  assumption of presidency, 381, 392

  black codes and, 393–394
  Fourteenth Amendment and, 396
  Freedmen's Bureau bill and, 395
  impeachment of, 397–398, 397 *(i)*
  reconstruction plan of, 392
Johnson, Jane, 320
Johnson, William, 134, 136, 137
Johnston, Albert Sidney, 366
Johnston, Joseph, 364
Joint-stock companies, 51, 79, 83
Jolliet, Louis, 95
Jones, Charles Colcock, 321
Journalism. *See* Newspapers
Judaism. *See* Jews and Judaism
Judicial review, 232
Judiciary. *See also* Supreme Court
  Federalists and, 223
Judiciary Act (1789), 232

Kansas, 340, 345–346
  "Bleeding Kansas," 346–347, 346 *(m)*, 353
  free vs. slave state settlers in, 346 *(i)*
  slavery in, 346–347
  statehood for, 349
Kansas-Nebraska Act (1854), 338, 339–340,
    340 *(m)*, 341, 343, 346, 348
Kaskaskia, battle at, 171
Kearny, Stephen Watts, 295
Kee-O-Kuk, the Watchful Fox, Chief of the Tribe
    (Catlin), 290 *(i)*
Kendall, Mary, 319
Kennesaw Mountain, battle of (1864),
    378 *(m)*, 379
Kentucky, 214, 359, 360, 365, 366
  Virginia and Kentucky Resolutions and, 223
King, Rufus, 242
King Cotton diplomacy, 367, 368
King George, Grandy, 101, 102
King Philip (Metacomet, Wampanoag
    Indians), 93
King Philip's War (1675–1676), 93–96
Kingsley, Bathsheba, 120
King's Mountain, battle of (1780), 174
King William's War (1689–1697), 95, 96
Kinship. *See* Families
Kiowa Indians, 288, 291
Kivas (ceremonial rooms), 14, 15 *(i)*
Klan. *See* Ku Klux Klan
Know-Nothing Party, 341, 343–344, 343 *(i)*
Knox, Henry, 207
Ku Klux Klan, 385, 399, 403
Ku Klux Klan Act (1871), 404

Labor. *See also* Free labor; Servants; Slaves and
    slavery; Strikes; Workforce
  black codes and, 393
  for building Catholic churches, 66
  in Chesapeake region, 57–59, 68–70
  Chinese, 298
  in colonies, 103
  in factories, 255
  indentured servants as, 57–59, 109
  of Irish immigrants, 287
  Native American, 50
  in New Spain, 37–40, 42
  in Pennsylvania, 109–110
  separate spheres concept and, 264
  of southern poor whites, 325

Labor code, during Reconstruction, 387
Ladies Association, 165
Lady's Magazine, woman's rights in, 211 *(i)*
Lafayette (Marquis de), 175 *(i)*
Lakes. *See* Great Lakes region
Land. *See also* Agriculture; Farms and farming;
    Public land
  in Chesapeake, 59–62
  in colonies, 103, 104
  of Creek Indians, 309
  federal policy for, 281
  for freedmen, 388, 389, 397
  Homestead Act and, 374
  Indian, 192–194, 215–218
  in middle colonies, 111
  Morrill Act and, 374
  in New England, 84
  return to ex-Confederates, 392
  speculation in, 104, 128, 132, 138, 194, 213
  taxes on, 328
  in West, 183–184, 184 *(m)*, 190–191,
    264, 288
Land bridge, between Siberia and Alaska, 6
Land-Grant College Act (Morrill Act, 1863),
    374
Land grants
  in middle colonies, 88
  to railroads, 283
Landowners, in Chesapeake, 62–63
Langhorne, James H., 370 *(i)*
Language(s)
  of ancient and modern Native Americans,
    5, 9
  of Mexico, 34
  in northern and southern colonies, 308
  of Powhatan, 54 *(i)*
  writing and, 4–5
L'Anse aux Meadows, Newfoundland, 27
Laramie, Fort, Indian conference at, 289
Las Casas, Bartolomé de, 38–40
Latin America. *See* America(s); Central America;
    South America
Latinos. *See* Hispanic Americans; specific groups
Law(s). *See also* Legislation; specific laws
  in British colonies, 124
  commercial, 257
  against southern free blacks, 323
  women and, 240
Lawrence, Kansas, 346 *(i)*
League of Five Nations, 17
Lecompton constitution (Kansas), 349
Le Dru, Pierre, 228 *(i)*
Lee, Richard Henry, 146
Lee, Robert E., 362
  in Civil War, 364–365, 378 *(m)*, 379, 380
  Harpers Ferry raid and, 333
Legal tender. *See* Currency
Legal Tender Act (1862), 374
Legislation. *See also* Law(s)
  in British colonies, 124
Legislatures, in Constitution, 197
Leisler, Jacob, 96
Leisure. *See also* Entertainment
  of plain folk, 327
  of plantation mistresses, 319
  in South, 117
Lenni Lenape (Delaware) Indians. *See*
    Delaware Indians

Leopard (ship), 235
Le Paon, Jean Baptiste, 175 *(i)*
Letters from a Farmer in Pennsylvania
    (Dickinson), 142, 157
Lewis, Meriwether, 232, 234
Lewis and Clark expedition, 233 *(m)*
Lexington, battle at, 149–150, 149 *(m)*
Lexington (steamboat), 254, 254 *(i)*
Liberal Party, 403–404
Liberator (newspaper), 269, 270 *(i)*, 307
Liberia, West Africa, 269, 303
Liberty(ies). *See also* Bill of Rights; Freedom(s)
    in bills of rights, 185
    meanings of, 142
    property and, 311
    Slave Power and, 343
Liberty Party, 293–294
Liberty Tree, as symbol, 148 *(i)*
Lien, crop, 401–402
Life expectancy
    of Eastern Woodland people, 12
    of slaves, 68
Lifestyle. *See* Society
Limited government, 232, 259
Lincoln, Abraham, 279–280, 280 *(i)*, 283–284,
    285, 294, 300, 339, 348, 352 *(i)*
    assassination of, 380–381, 392
    in Civil War, 361, 362, 363, 365, 367
    disunion and, 358–359
    election of 1860 and, 351–352
    election of 1864 and, 379
    emancipation and, 357, 369–370, 390
    first inaugural address (1861), 353, 358
    on Harpers Ferry raid, 334
    on Kansas-Nebraska Act, 348
    military imprisonment by, 376
    Reconstruction plan of, 386, 387
    on secession, 353
    slavery and, 368–369
Lincoln, Mary Todd, 279, 280
Lincoln, Nancy, 279
Lincoln, Thomas, 279–280
Lincoln-Douglas debates, 348–349
Lineages, African American, 116
Lipscomb family, 326
Liquor. *See* Alcohol and alcoholism
Literacy
    for blacks, 389
    newspaper expansion and, 258
    during Reconstruction, 400
    school enrollment and, 286, 286 *(f)*
    in South, 400
    tests of, 398
    for women, 241, 266
Literature. *See also* specific authors
    on slavery, 339
    Uncle Tom's Cabin, 338, 339
Little Turtle (Miami Indians), 215, 216,
    217 *(i)*, 218
Livingston, Robert R., 186 *(i)*, 233–234,
    233 *(m)*
Loans. *See* Bank(s) and banking; Economy
Lobo, 41 *(i)*
Locomotive, 282, 284 *(i)*
Lone Star Republic, 292, 293
Long Island, battle of (1776), 163
Loom, 256 *(i)*
Louis XIV (France), 94

Louisiana, 238, 311, 352, 387, 406
Louisiana Purchase, 228, 229, 233 *(m)*, 234,
    281, 340, 341
Louisiana Territory, slavery in, 334
Lovejoy, Elijah, 269
Lowell, Massachusetts, 255, 266–267
Lower South, 112, 309, 309 *(m)*, 310, 310 *(f)*.
    See also South
    secession and, 352–353, 352 *(m)*, 358–359,
    360 *(m)*
Loyalists (U.S.), in Revolutionary period, 130,
    163, 165–169, 168 *(m)*, 171, 177
Luther, Martin, 43
Lutheranism, 109
Lynchings
    in California goldfields, 298
    in San Francisco, 299
Lyon, Mary, 266
Lyon, Matthew, 222 *(i)*

Machine tool industry, 282
Mackintosh, Ebenezer, 140, 141
Madison, Dolley, 182 *(i)*, 235, 236 *(i)*, 238
Madison, James, 181–182, 182 *(i)*, 232
    Articles of Confederation and, 183–184
    Barbary Wars and, 234
    Bill of Rights and, 208
    Constitution and, 180, 196
    at Continental Congress, 182
    election of 1808 and, 235
    Federalist Papers and, 201
    finances and, 214
    Hamilton and, 206
    state debt and, 213
    War of 1812 and, 235, 237–238
Magellan, Ferdinand, 32
Mahican Indians, 104
Mail service
    political information and, 253–254
    by Pony Express, 374
Maine, 79, 244
Malcolm, John, 148 *(i)*
Male suffrage. *See also* Voting and voting
    rights
    white, 328
Malinali (**Marina,** Mexico), 34, 35 *(i)*
Mammals, 5. *See also* Animals
Mammoths, Clovis artifacts and, 5, 9
Manassas, battle of. *See* Bull Run (Manassas)
Mandan Indians, 17, 234
Manhattan, in Revolution, 163, 170
Manhattan Island, 88, 89 *(i)*
Manifest destiny, 297, 303
    California and, 293
    Pierce and, 340
    Polk and, 294
    westward movement and, 288
Manning, William, 191
Manufacturing
    American system of, 282
    expansion of, 255, 281–282
    Hamilton on, 214
    in South, 400
Manumission laws, 189
Maps, of New World, 32
Marbury, William, 232
Marbury v. Madison (1803), 232
"March to the Sea" (1864), 378 *(m)*, 379

Marines (U.S.). *See also* Military
    in Barbary Wars, 234
Market(s)
    for agricultural produce, 63
    colonial, 93
    domestic, 282
    for furs, 94
    transportation and, 253
    for western land, 264
Market economy, 252
Market revolution, 252–257
Marks, A. A., 394
Marquette, Jacques, 95
Marriage
    age at first marriage, 265, 265 *(t)*
    in Chesapeake, 58
    English-Indian, 53
    by free blacks, 323
    freedmen and, 390
    of immigrant female servants, 59
    laws governing, 239
    in New England, 86, 103
    Oneida community and, 301
    plural (polygamy), 290, 291
    of slaves, 321
    society and, 209
    southern women and, 318–319
    Spanish-Indian, 40
    woman's rights and, 240
Married women, rights of, 302, 318, 344–345
Marshall, James, 297
Marshall, John, 231
Martin, Anna, 168
Martinique, 134, 135 *(m)*, 138
Mary I (England), 77
Mary II (England), 96
Maryland, 214. *See also* Chesapeake region;
    Tobacco and tobacco industry
    Catholicism in, 62
    in Civil War, 365
    manumission in, 190
    population of, 56, 62, 112
    revolt in, 96
    secession and, 359
    slavery in, 151
Mason, George, 187
Mason, Priscilla, 210
Mason-Dixon line, 308, 329, 343
Mason family, 86 *(i)*
Massachusetts, 104, 129. *See also* New England
    charter of, 79, 83
    committees of correspondence in, 146
    debts after Revolution, 213
    in Dominion of New England, 96
    Iroquois Confederacy land and, 192
    Native Americans in, 93
    Plymouth colony in, 78–79
    protests in, 141–142, 143, 147–148
    public school integration in (1855), 303
    as royal colony, 96, 129
    Shays's Rebellion in, 194–195
    slavery in, 187, 188–189
Massachusetts Bay colony, 79–81, 79 *(i)*
Massachusetts Bay Company, 79, 83
Massachusetts Government Act (1774), 147
Massasoit (Wampanoag Indians), 78, 93
Mass markets, colonial, 118
Mather, Increase, 83

Mathews, John, 320
Maximilian (Mexico), 404
Maxwell, Henry, 373
Mayan people
    European diseases among, 41
    language of, 34
Mayflower (ship), 78
Mayflower Compact, 78
Maysville Road veto, 260
McClellan, George B., 363 (i), 364–365, 379
McCormick, Cyrus, 281, 375
McIntosh, Fort, Treaty of (1785), 194
McJunkin, George, 3, 4 (i)
Meade, George G., 377
Measles, 32
Mechanical reapers, 281
Mechanization, 282
Medicine, 296. *See also* Diseases
Mediterranean region
    Barbary States in, 226 (i), 234
    trade in, 27
Melrose, Andrew, 284 (i)
Melville, Herman, 154 (i)
Memoir on Slavery (Harper), 312–313
Memphis, 364 (m), 366, 396
Men. *See also* Gender
    height in 18th century, 162 (f)
    voting by, 186, 242
    women's rights and, 210–211
Menéndez de Avilés, Pedro, 42
Mennonites, 109
Mercantilism, in English colonies, 64
Mercenaries, Hessians as, 163
Merchants
    in Chesapeake, 63
    in New England, 105–107
    in South, 314–315, 401–402
Méricourt, Théroigne de, 210
Merrimack (frigate), 366
Mesa Verde, 14
Mestizos, 40, 41 (i)
Metallurgy, European vs. Native American, 24 (i)
Metcalf, Michael, 81 (i)
Methodists, 240, 321, 327, 392
Mexican Americans, during Mexican-American War, 296 (i)
Mexican-American War (1846–1848), 294–297, 295 (m), 361, 362
    casualties in, 295, 296
    land cessions after, 296, 297 (m), 335 (m)
    manifest destiny and, 294
    sectionalism and, 334
    Treaty of Guadalupe Hidalgo and, 296
Mexican borderlands, 291–293
Mexican cession (1848), 296, 297 (m), 335 (m)
    slavery in, 334–335, 353
Mexica people, 14 (i), 20–21, 34, 36 (i)
Mexico, 287, 340
    Cortés in, 26 (i), 33–34
    independence of, 245, 291
    Maximilian in, 404
    native peoples of, 20–21, 21 (i)
    silver from, 40
    Spanish conquest of, 33–34, 35
    Texas and, 292–293, 292 (m)
    after Treaty of Guadalupe Hidalgo, 297
Mexico City, assault on (1847), 296
Miami, Fort, 136, 217

Miami Indians, 215, 216, 236
Michigan, 236, 281
Michigan, Lake, 136
Michilimackinac, Fort, 136
Middle class, during Civil War, 375
Middle colonies, 108–112
    colonial unifying elements in, 117–124
    founding of, 88–91
    in Revolutionary War, 158–159
    in 17th century, 88 (m)
Middle East, Barbary Wars and, 234
Middle ground, free blacks and, 323
Middle Passage, 113, 114, 115
Midwest, 281
Migration. *See also* Slave trade; Westward movement
    African American, 101–102
    by Archaic Indians, 9
    by Europeans, 16, 69 (f)
    west of Mississippi River, 287
Military, 226 (i). *See also* Soldiers; specific battles and wars
    African Americans in, 369, 370–371
    British colonial, 138
    in Civil War, 362
    Continental army as, 157, 158, 161
    in Reconstruction, 396
    in Seven Years' War, 134, 135
Military districts, in South, 396, 396 (m)
Military Reconstruction Act (1867), 396, 397
Militia
    armed, 208
    in British colonies, 121
    in Massachusetts, 147–148, 150
    in Revolutionary War, 160–161
Militia Act (1862), 370
Milliken's Bend, battle of, 371
Mills, 255, 314
Mimbres culture, 14
Minavavana (Chippewa), 136
Mines and mining
    California gold rush and, 297–298, 298–299
    coal and, 281
    immigrants in, 298
Mingo Indians, 132–133, 192
Minié, Claude, 362 (i)
Minié balls, 362 (i)
Mining towns, 299
Minorities. *See* Ethnic groups; specific groups
Minuit, Peter, 88
Minutemen, 149–150
Miscegenation, 311, 317, 319
Missions and missionaries
    in California, 123–124, 123 (i), 124 (m), 293
    encomienda system and, 37–39, 40
    Indians and, 80, 260
    Jesuit, 94–95
    Quaker, 91
    Spanish, 37, 66
Mississippi, 242, 243, 352, 392, 393, 406
Mississippian culture, 2 (i), 15 (m), 16
Mississippi River region, 95, 134, 135 (m), 172, 254, 365, 366
Missouri, 243 (i), 346, 359–360, 365
Missouri Compromise (1820), 228, 243–245, 244 (m), 263, 334, 336, 340, 348

Missouri River region, exploration of, 234
Mixed-race people, 40, 41 (i), 220, 318 (i)
Mobilization
    in Civil War, 362–363
    in French and Indian War, 134
Mogollon culture, 13–14
Mohawk Indians, 17, 133, 134, 165, 170, 192
Mohawk Valley region, 170, 171, 172 (m)
Molasses Act (1733), 138
Monarchs and monarchies. *See also* specific rulers
    Spanish, 42–43
Money
    hard money, 257
    paper, 191, 257, 362
    during Revolution, 169
Money supply, 253
Monitor (ironclad), 366
Moniz, Felipa, 29
Monopolies, transportation company rights to, 254
Monroe, Elizabeth, 242, 245–246
Monroe, James, 229, 242, 245. *See also* Monroe Doctrine (1823)
Monroe Doctrine (1823), 245
Montecino, Antón, 38
Monterrey, battle at (1846), 295
Montezuma (Mexico), 34, 36 (i)
Montgomery, Alabama, Confederacy established in, 352
Montgomery, Richard, 162, 163
Montreal, 134, 162
Moral reform movement, 268, 274–275
Moravians, 109, 110 (i)
Morisco, 41 (i)
Mormons, 290–291
Mormon Trail, 289 (m)
Mormon War (1857), 291
Morrill, Justin, 374
Morrill (Land-Grant College) Act (1863), 374
Morris, Robert, 182, 191, 192
Morristown, New Jersey, Washington in, 163
Morse, Samuel F. B., 282, 283
Mortality rate
    in Chesapeake region, 62–63
    in Middle Passage, 114
    in New England, 103
    of slave children, 115–116
Mothers, 208–209. *See also* Wives; Women
Mott, Lucretia, 271
Mound builders, 15–16, 15 (m)
Mountain men, 288
Mount Holyoke Seminary, 266
Mulattos, 41 (i), 318 (i), 319
Murray, Judith Sargent, 208–209, 209 (i), 241
Music
    African, 70 (i)
    hymns as, 327
    of slaves, 102 (i)
    spirituals, 327
Musical instruments, of slaves, 321 (i)
Muskets, 157
Muskogean Indians, 17
Muslims, in Spain, 25, 26

Na Dené language, 9
Nahuatl language, 33, 34
Napoleon I Bonaparte (France), 209, 229
Narrative of the Life of Frederick Douglass, as Told by Himself (Douglass), 339
Narváez, Pánfilo de, 35
Nashville, battle of (1864), 378 *(m)*, 379
Nast, Thomas, on Grant and scandal, 403 *(i)*
Natchez Indians, 17
National Banking Act (1863), 374
National debt, 212–213, 264. *See also* Debt
Nationalism, 356 *(i)*
    in Confederacy, 373–374
National Negro Convention (Philadelphia), 269
National Republicans (Whigs), 258, 263
National Road, 254
National self-determination. *See* Self-determination
National Union Party, 396
Native Americans, 44 *(i)*, 290 *(i)*. *See also* Wars and warfare; specific groups
    as allies of whites, 133
    ancient, 2 *(i)*, 3–16
    Archaic hunter-gatherers and, 8–12
    British medal for, 138 *(i)*
    buffalo and, 288, 289
    in California, 11, 293, 299
    in Chesapeake region, 48 *(i)*, 53 *(i)*, 54
    Christianity and, 53, 65–66, 80, 94–95, 137
    "civilizing" of, 260
    in Civil War, 365
    colonial frontier and, 104
    diseases and, 41
    early groups of, 5–7, 8
    Eastern Woodland groups of, 12, 12 *(i)*, 15–17
    English settlements and, 49–50, 52, 53–54, 121, 136–137
    European weapons and, 24 *(i)*
    Fort Stanwix Treaty and, 192–193
    in 1490s, 16–20, 17 *(f)*
    about 1500, 18 *(m)*
    fur trade and, 94, 95 *(i)*, 122
    gold rush and, 299
    of Great Basin region, 11
    as hunter-gatherers, 8–12
    Jackson and, 245, 259, 260–262
    lands of, 192–193, 194, 215–218, 216 *(m)*, 309
    Lewis and Clark expedition and, 234
    as loyalists, 165–168
    in Massachusetts Bay colony, 80
    Mississippian mask and, 2 *(i)*
    Mogollon culture of, 13–14
    in Nebraska, 340, 340 *(m)*
    in New Amsterdam, 89 *(i)*
    in New England, 78
    in New France, 94–95
    in New Spain, 37–42
    North American cultures of, 10 *(m)*, 18 *(m)*
    in Ohio River region, 192–193, 194 227–228
    origins of, 5–6
    of Pacific Ocean region, 11–12
    Paleo-Indians as, 6
    in Pennsylvania, 91, 111
    Plains Indians, 288–289
    population in 1810, 236

Proclamation of 1763 and, 135–138
    religion and, 53, 66
    removal and, 261–262, 261 *(m)*
    resistance by, 64
    Revolutionary War and, 165–168, 165 *(i)*, 171–172, 172 *(m)*, 176–177
    in Seven Years' War, 130–138, 131 *(m)*
    Trail of Tears and, 261 *(m)*, 262
    treaties with, 260–261
    War of 1812 and, 237, 238
    in West, 215–218, 236–237, 236 *(i)*, 287, 288–289
Nativism, 341
Nat Turner's rebellion, 307–308, 308 *(i)*
Naturalization. *See* Citizens and citizenship
Nauvoo, Illinois, Mormons in, 290
Navajo Indians, 18
Navies. *See also* Navy (U.S.)
    British, 93, 122, 146
    in Revolutionary War, 175
    warships in European, 122, 122 *(f)*
Navigation Acts, 117, 118, 121
    of 1650, 63, 91
    of 1651, 63, 91
    of 1660, 64, 91
Navigational aids, 27
Navy (U.S.), 226 *(i)*
    African Americans in, 357–358, 358 *(i)*, 370
    Barbary Wars and, 234
    in Civil War, 357–358, 362, 364 *(m)*, 366, 367
Nebraska, as free state, 340
Necessary and proper clause, 197
"Necessary evil" argument, for slavery, 311
Necessity, Fort, 132, 133, 134
Negroes. *See* African Americans
"Negro first" strategy, 398
"Negro rule," 385, 400
Neolin (Delaware Indians), 136
Netherlands, warships of, 122
Neutrality Proclamation (1793), 219
Nevada, Comstock Lode in, 334
Neville, John, 214–215
New Amsterdam, 56 *(m)*, 80, 88, 89 *(i)*
New Bedford Mercury, 372
New England, 103–108
    as city upon a hill, 79, 80
    colonial unifying elements in, 117–124
    Congregationalism in, 119
    economy of, 85–86
    English governing of, 96, 104
    manufacturing in, 282
    Native Americans in, 93–96, 104
    partible inheritance in, 104
    population in cities, 314
    population of, 86 *(f)*, 103–104
    Puritans in, 75–76, 78–87
    Quakers in, 87
    resistance to British in, 147
    in Revolution, 169
    in 17th century, 80 *(m)*
    society in, 81–88, 103–108
    textile mills in, 255, 255 *(m)*
    town meetings in, 83–84
    in War of 1812, 237
New England Anti-Slavery Society, 269
New England Courant (newspaper), 118
Newfoundland, 27, 32

New France, 104
    fur trade in, 94, 95 *(i)*
    Jesuits in, 94–95
    in Seven Years' War, 131 *(m)*
New Hampshire, 79, 187
New Jersey, 88, 90, 108
    in Revolutionary War, 163, 164 *(m)*, 169
    slavery in, 188–189
    voting rights in, 186, 240
New Jersey Plan, 196
New Mexico, 65–66, 296, 340
    Indians in, 66
    Mexican-American War in, 295
    Mogollon culture in, 14
    Pueblo Revolt in, 66
    slavery in, 337
    Spanish colony in, 42, 65–66
    statehood for, 336
New Negroes (newly arrived slaves), 114
New Netherland (New York), 88, 89
New Orleans, 316 *(i)*
    battle of (1815), 238, 251
    Civil War in, 364 *(m)*, 366
    control of, 134, 135 *(m)*
    violence against blacks in, 396
Newport, Rhode Island, 175
New South, 386
New Spain
    English colonies compared with, 70–71
    mixed-race people in, 40, 41 *(i)*
    Russia and, 123
    in 16th century, 36–42
Newspapers
    of black abolitionists, 302
    Cherokee, 262
    colonial, 118
    expansion of, 258, 258 *(t)*
    Stamp Act protests in, 140 *(i)*
    telegraph and, 282
New World. *See also* America(s)
    Europeans and, 25–45
    Mexica in, 20–21
    migration from Europe and Africa to, 69, 69 *(f)*
    wealth from, 35, 43
New York (city)
    antidraft riots in, 376–377
    as capital city, 209
    evangelicalism in, 267 *(i)*
New York (colony), 79, 88, 89, 94, 108, 111
New York (state)
    debts after Revolution, 213
    emancipation law of 1799 in, 244
    Indians in, 135, 192–193
    Iroquois Confederacy land and, 192
    in Revolutionary War, 163, 164 *(m)*
    Treaty of Fort Stanwix and, 192–193
New York Female Moral Reform Society, 268
New York Tribune, 348, 404
Niagara, Fort, 134, 137, 171
Night riders, 406
Niña (ship), 29
Ninth Amendment, 208
Nobility, of Mexico, 20
Noble, T. S., 318 *(i)*
Nonconsumption, 143–144
Nonimportation
    agreements among merchants, 143, 145
    laws against British, 235

Non-Intercourse Act (1809), 237
Nonslaveholders, in South, 324, 327
Norsemen, 27
North (Civil War), 374–377
  draft in, 370
  emancipation and, 369
  inflation in, 362–363
  Lincoln's leadership of, 362
  mobilization of, 362
  resources of, 360–361, 361 (f), 375 (i)
North (U.S. region)
  abolitionism in, 269
  African Americans in, 310
  Civil War impact on, 381
  free blacks in, 303
  free labor in, 303
  Fugitive Slave Act (1850) and, 338–339
  mixed economy of, 314
  Reconstruction and, 404–405
  Revolutionary War in, 164 (m), 169–171
  South compared with, 308–309
  southern cotton and, 314
  southern Republican Party and, 399
  white supremacy in, 310–311
  Wilmot Proviso and, 335
North, Frederick (Lord), 145, 146, 147
North Africa, Barbary Wars in, 234
North America. See also Colonies and
    colonization; South America
  ancient peoples of, 5–7
  Atlantic trade in, 105 (m)
  empires in eastern, 121 (m)
  European influences in, 135 (m)
  Native American cultures of, 10 (m)
  population of English colonies in,
    102–103
  separation from Pangaea, 5
  Seven Years' War and, 130–138, 131 (m)
North Carolina, 44 (i), 56, 112, 174, 359. See
    also Carolina(s)
Northern colonies, 75–97
Northup, Solomon, 339
Northwest Ordinance (1787), 194, 243, 334
Northwest Passage, search for, 32, 44, 88
Northwest peoples, 11–12, 18
Northwest Territory, 182, 193–194, 193 (m)
Nova Scotia, African Americans in, 151
Noyes, John Humphrey, 301, 301 (i)
Nullification
  crises, 263, 336
  of tariff of 1828, 260, 262–263
Nursing, 375–376

Oath of allegiance
  in Lincoln's Reconstruction plan, 387
  in Wade-Davis bill, 387
Oberlin College, 266, 266 (i)
Occupation (military)
  British, of Boston, 144–145
  of South in Reconstruction, 396
Officeholders, in antebellum South, 328
Ohio Company, 132, 138
Ohio River region, 254
  cession to United States, 192–194
  Indians of, 135, 168, 192, 215
  massacre in, 132
  population of, 236
  Revolutionary War in, 171

in 1753, 132 (m)
  Seven Years' War in, 130–138
Ojibwa Indians, 136
Oklahoma, 262. See also Indian Territory
Old Calabar, Bight of Biafra, West Africa, slave
    trade in, 101–102
Old Northwest, Indians in, 236, 260
Old Ship Meeting House (Massachusetts),
    83 (i)
Old South Church (Boston), 146
Oligarchy, in South, 117
Oliver, Andrew, 141, 159
Olustee, battle of, 373
Omnibus Bill (1850), 337
Oñate, Juan de, 42
Oneida community, 301
Oneida Indians, 17, 134, 165
Onondaga Indians, 17, 165
Ontario, Lake, 134
"On the Equality of the Sexes" (Murray), 208
Opechancanough (Algonquian leader), 54, 64
Ordinance of 1784, 193
Ordinance of 1785, 194
Ordnance Bureau (Confederacy), 362
Oregon, 294
  settlement of, 288, 290
  Spanish exploration of, 36
Oregon Trail, 288, 289, 289 (m), 293
Oriskany, battle of (1777), 170, 171
O'Sullivan, John L. (editor), 288
Ottawa Indians, 94, 135, 136, 217
Ouiatenon, Fort, 136
Overseers, 316, 324

Pacific Coast Indians, 11–12, 18
Pacific Northwest Indians, 11–12, 16
Pacific Ocean region
  ancient Americans from, 8
  Balboa at, 32
  Lewis and Clark at, 234
  Native Americans in, 16
  settlement of, 123–124, 124 (i), 288
Pacific Railroad Act (1862), 374
Paine, Thomas, 159, 270
Paleo-Indians, 6–7, 8
Palmetto Guards, 346 (i)
Palo Alto, battle at (1846), 295
Panama, Isthmus of, 32
Pangaea, 5
Panics, 257. See also Depressions (financial)
  of 1819, 253, 257, 263
  of 1837, 253, 272, 273–274, 273 (i), 344
  of 1839, 253, 274, 344
  of 1857, 349
  of 1873, 404
Paper money. See Money
Pardons
  for Confederates, 387
  by Johnson, Andrew, 392, 394, 397
Paris, France, abolitionism in, 270
Paris, Treaty of
  of 1763, 134, 135 (m), 136, 232
  of 1783, 176, 192, 215
Parliament (England)
  Charles I and, 78, 85
  colonial control by, 140, 141–142
Partible inheritance, 104
Paternalism, of planters, 316–317

Patriotism, 226 (i)
  in Civil War, 374, 375
  in Revolutionary War, 163–169, 171
  by women, 143–144
Patriots, 141 (i), 143–144, 148
Patronage, colonial, 124
Patroonships, 88
Paupers, voting and, 243
Pawnee Indians, 17
Paxton Boys, 137
"Peace" Democrats, 379
Peace of Paris (1763), 136
Peale, Charles Willson, Madison portrait by,
    182 (i)
Pea Ridge, battle of (1862), 364 (m), 365
Peninsula campaign (1862), 363 (i), 364, 365,
    365 (m)
Peninsulares, 40
Penn, William, 88, 90, 90 (i), 91
Penn family (Pennsylvania), 111
Pennsylvania, 88, 108, 109–112, 214
  Bethlehem, 110 (i)
  emancipation in, 187–188
  Germans and Scots-Irish in, 108–109
  settlers in, 90–91, 108
  slavery in, 187–188
Pennsylvania Dutch, Germans as, 108
Penobscot Indians, 16
People, the, 185–187, 242
Percy, George, 52
Perry, Oliver Hazard, 237
Personal liberty laws, 338
Peru, 35, 245
Petersburg, Virginia, siege of (1864–1865),
    378 (m), 379, 380
Petersham, Massachusetts, 195
Petition, right to, 261–262
"Petition 'to the Union Convention of
    Tennessee Assembled in the Capital at
    Nashville,'" 391
Philadelphia, 91, 112
  as capital city, 209
  constitutional convention in (1787), 196
  First Continental Congress in (1774), 147,
    148, 182
Philadelphia (ship), 234
Philip II (Spain), 43, 77
Phillips, Wendell, 270 (i), 336, 387, 398
Photography. See also Daguerreotypes
  Brady and, 337, 351 (i)
  of westward movement, 291 (i)
Phyllis (New England slave), "dummy board"
    of, 103 (i)
Pickett, George E., 377
Pierce, Franklin, 339–340, 347
Pikes, of Brown, John, 332 (i)
Pilgrims, 78
Pinckney, Charles Cotesworth, 234, 235
Pinckney, Thomas, 220, 221
Pinta (ship), 29
Pioneers, on trails, 289–290, 291 (i)
Pippin, Horace, 350 (i)
Pirates, 229, 234
Pisa, 27
Pitt, Fort, 137, 171, 172 (m)
Pitt, William, 134, 135, 142
Pizarro, Francisco, 34–35

Plague. *See* Black Death
Plain folk
  politics and, 328
  in South, 324–327
Plains Indians, 288–289, 288 *(m)*, 340
Plantation belt yeomen, 324–325
Plantation economy, 311–315
Planters and plantations, 311, 316
  in Chesapeake region, 62–63
  during Civil War, 371, 373, 374
  cotton and, 310
  in 1860 and 1881, 402 *(m)*
  families of, 316, 317–319, 317 *(i)*
  grandees and, 64
  in Haiti, 220
  housing of, 63 *(i)*, 67 *(i)*
  Johnson, Andrew, and, 392
  labor code and, 387
  labor for, 57–59
  and paternalism, 316–317
  power of, 317, 327, 328
  during Reconstruction, 393, 401
  slavery and, 319–322
  southern economy and, 311–315
  sugar and, 66–67, 67 *(i)*
  tobacco and, 57 *(i)*
  white women on, 317–319
  yeomen and, 324–325
Plants, as Archaic American food source, 11, 12
Plattsburgh, battle at, 238
Plows, 281, 281 *(i)*
Plural marriage (polygamy), 290, 291. *See also*
    Polygamy
Plymouth colony, 78–79
Pocahontas, 49–50, 50 *(i)*
Political campaigns. *See* Elections
Political information, transportation of,
    253–254
Political parties, 220, 223. *See also*
    specific groups
  after 1828, 259
  in 1830s, 274–275
  formation of, 252
  realignment of, 341–344, 342 *(m)*
  second American party system and, 258
  sectionalism and, 341, 342 *(m)*
  in South, 328
Political reconstruction, 391
Politics. *See also* Conservatism and
    conservatives; Political parties
  borderlands and, 121–124
  democratization of, 327–328
  household objects expressing, 245 *(i)*
  in North (Civil War), 376–377
  planters in, 328
  race and, 243–245
  sectionalism in, 334, 342 *(m)*
  of slavery, 327–328
  slaves and, 68–69
  women and, 247, 343, 399
Polk, James K., 293, 294–295, 294 *(i)*, 296,
    336
Pollution. *See* Air pollution; Environment
Polygamy, 290, 291
Ponce de León, Juan, 35
Pontiac (Ottawa Indians), uprising by, 135,
    135 *(m)*, 136, 137 *(i)*
Pony Express, 374

Poor people. *See* Poverty
Poor Richard's Almanack (Franklin), 112, 112 *(i)*
Popé (Pueblo Indians), 66
Pope, American exploration and, 30
Pope, John, 365
Popular sovereignty, 335, 337, 340, 341, 346,
    349, 351
Population
  African in southern colonies, 68, 112
  black and white in South (1860), 310 *(f)*
  of Chesapeake region, 56, 64
  during Civil War, 360
  of colonies, 102–103
  in 1810, 236
  of English North American colonies, 86 *(f)*
  of Europe, 27
  expansion after Revolution, 212, 212 *(i)*, 215
  of free blacks in South, 310 *(f)*, 323
  immigrants in, 287
  indigenous New World, 16, 20
  male heights in 18th century, 162 *(f)*
  of Maryland, 62
  of middle colonies, 108
  natural increase of, 102–103, 112
  of New England, 86, 103–104
  of Pennsylvania, 91
  of Philadelphia, 91
  in rural areas, 280–281, 287
  slave, 310, 311
  of southern nonslaveholders, 324
  of Spaniards in Florida and New Mexico, 65
  of Spanish colonial settlers, 40
Port cities, in South, 314
Port Hudson, battle of (1863), 371
Portolá, Gaspar de, 123
Portugal
  Brazil and, 36, 37 *(m)*
  exploration by, 27, 28–29, 28 *(m)*
  Treaty of Tordesillas and, 30
"Positive good" argument, for slavery, 311
Potato blight, in Ireland, 287
Potawatomi Indians, 217, 236
Potosí, Bolivia, silver from, 40
Pottawatomie Creek, Brown, John, at, 333, 347
Pottery
  of African American slaves, 306 *(i)*
  of Eastern Woodland people, 12, 12 *(i)*
Poverty
  in Confederacy, 371–372, 373
  in New England, 107–108
  of whites in South, 325–327
Powder Alarm, 147
Power (energy). *See* Energy
Power (political)
  after Civil War, 381
  of planters, 327, 328
  Spanish, 65 *(i)*
Power loom, 256 *(i)*
Powhatan (Indian leader), 48 *(i)*, 49–50,
    52–53, 53 *(i)*, 54, 54 *(i)*, 71
Preachers
  in Great Awakening, 120
  women as, 240
Predestination, 82
Pregnancy, among immigrant servant
    women, 59
Prejudice. *See* Discrimination
Presbyterians, 266

President. *See also* Executive; Twelfth
    Amendment; specific individuals
  in Constitution, 197
  title of, 207
Presidential Reconstruction, 392–395
Presidios, in California, 123
Preston, John Smith, 352
Preston, Thomas, 144
Price of Blood, The (Noble), 318 *(i)*
Printing, 118, 258
Prisoners of war, in 18th century, 166–167,
    167 *(i)*
Privateers, Barbary, 234
Proclamation of 1763, 135–138
Proclamation of Amnesty and Reconstruction
    (1863), 387
Productivity, agricultural, 281
Property
  slaves as, 311
  for voting, 96, 186, 187, 242–243, 327, 398
  women and, 302, 318, 344–345
Property rights
  of free blacks, 334
  of married women, 318, 344–345
Prophetstown, Indiana, 228, 236, 237
Proprietors
  Baltimore, Lord, as, 96
  in Pennsylvania, 90, 91
Proslavery arguments, 308, 311, 312–313
Prospectors, 299
Prosperity
  in middle colonies, 111–112
  southern slavery and, 117
Protective tariffs, 246. *See also* Tariffs
Protest(s). *See also* Resistance
  against Stamp Act, 141–142
Protestant Association (Maryland), 96
Protestantism
  Calvinism and, 82
  vs. Catholicism, 62, 341
  in Chesapeake region, 62
  in colonies, 119–121
  in England, 76–78, 77 *(i)*
  evangelical, 264
  Irish immigrants and, 287
  in northern and southern colonies, 308
  women and, 240–241
Protestant Reformation, 43, 76
Prussia, 134
Public credit. *See* Credit
Public debt. *See* Debt; National debt
Public land, 375. *See also* Land
Public schools. *See also* School(s)
  in cities and towns, 285
  integration of (1855), 303
  in South, 315, 327, 400
  state-supported, 265–266
Pueblo, 13, 14, 35
Pueblo Bonito, 14, 15 *(i)*
Pueblo Indians, 66
Pueblo Revolt, 66
Puerto Rico, 33
Punishment
  of African Americans, 317
  of loyalists, 168
  of servant labor, 59
Puritanism
  Calvinism and, 82

Congregationalism and, 119
divisions in, 84–85
in England, 76–78
government by and for, 79, 83–84
Halfway Covenant of, 87
in Massachusetts, 79
in New England, 75–76, 78–87, 103
Puritan Revolution, 62, 82 (i), 85
Pynchon, William, 84

Quadrant, 27
Quakers, 87, 90–91, 112
abolitionism and, 270–271
Quantrill, William Clarke, 365
Quartering Act (1774), 147
Quasi-War (1798–1800), 221–222, 223
Quebec, 95, 134, 135 (m), 162–163
Quebec Act (1774), 146
Quincy, Josiah, 145

Race and racism. See also African Americans;
     Segregation
in armed forces, 370
against Californios, 299
in Chesapeake region, 58–59
against Chinese immigrants, 298–299,
     299–300
in Civil War, 357–358
in colonies, 103
Fifteenth Amendment and, 398
free blacks and, 303
Haitian Revolution and, 220
of Johnson, Andrew, 392
Missouri Compromise and, 243–245
mixed races and, 40, 41 (i)
Reconstruction and, 404
southern Democratic Party and, 405
in Union army, 370
voting rights and, 186–187
white superiority and, 311
Wilmot Proviso and, 335
Racial segregation. See Segregation
Radical Reconstruction, 396–397
Radical Republicans, 394, 396
Railroads, 253, 255
Chinese workers on, 298
in 1860, 283 (m)
expansion of, 282–284
financing of, 328
land grants to, 283
in South, 315, 362, 400
telegraph communication and, 282
transcontinental, 288, 340, 374
Raleigh, Walter, 44–45
Rancheros, 293
Ranchos, 293
Randall, A. B., 390
Randolph, Edmund, 207, 317
Rape, of Indian women, 124
Rapier, James T., 385–386, 386 (i), 405, 407
Rapier, John, 385
Ratification
     of Bill of Rights, 208
     of Constitution, 197–201, 199 (m), 200 (i)
Reapers, mechanical, 281, 375
Rebellions. See Protest(s); Revolts and rebellions
Recessions. See Depressions; Economy; Panics
Reconquest (Spain), 25–26

Reconstruction (1863–1877), 384–407
abandonment of, 404–405
carpetbaggers and, 384 (i), 399
collapse of, 402–407
congressional, 387, 395–398
Johnson impeachment and, 397–398
labor code and, 387–388
military rule during, 396
North and, 404–405
politics in, 399
presidential, 392–395
Radical, 396–397
Redeemers and, 405, 406
second, 407
of South (1869, 1873), 406 (m)
southern Republican Party and, 384 (i),
     399–400
wartime, 386–392
white supremacy and, 405–406
Reconstruction Acts (1867), 397, 398, 400
Recreation. See Leisure
Redcoats, in Revolutionary War, 163
Redeemers, in South, 405, 406
Redemptioners, in middle colonies, 109
Red Hawk (Shawnee Indians), 171
Reexport trade, 117
Reform and reform movements
abolitionism, 268–269, 302–303
in education and training, 265–267
moral reformers and, 268, 274–275
in Second Great Awakening, 264, 267–268
temperance and, 268, 300
women and, 301–302
Reformation. See Protestant Reformation
Regulation, of colonial trade, 91–93
Religion(s). See also Churches; specific groups
in Chesapeake region, 62
colonial, 117, 119–121
evangelical, 252, 264
of freedmen, 389–392
Indians and, 53, 66
in late 1700s and early 1800s, 240–241
in Maryland, 62
in Mexico, 20
in New England, 79, 82–83
in New York colony, 89, 90
in Pennsylvania, 91
of Puritans, 82–83, 84–85
of Quakers, 90
Second Great Awakening and, 264, 267–268
of slaves, 321–322
in Spanish borderland, 65–66
of Taino people, 30
women and, 239–240
Religious toleration
in New York, 90
in Pennsylvania, 90–91
Relocation. See Removal policy
Removal policy, for Indians, 259, 261–262, 309
Repartimiento reform, 40
Report on Manufactures (Hamilton), 214
Report on Public Credit (Hamilton), 212
Report on the Causes and Reasons for War, 237
Representation
colonial, 124
Constitution on, 196–197
in Virginia, 54–55
virtual, 139–140

Republicanism, 185
democracy vs., 197
Jefferson and, 223, 229–232, 247
Republican motherhood, 208, 211
Republican Party, 275. See also Elections
on Dred Scott decision, 348
ex-Confederates in Congress and, 394
growth of, 341–343
Liberal Party and, 403–404
presidential Reconstruction and, 394–395
Radical Reconstruction and, 396–397
radicals in, 394
sectionalism and, 344
in South, 399–400, 403, 404, 405–406, 407
women in, 343
Republicans (Jeffersonian), 223
Alien and Sedition Acts and, 222–223
election of 1796 and, 220–221
Republic of Haiti, 219
Republic of Texas, 294
Requerimiento, 38–39
Resaca de la Palma, battle at (1846), 295, 295 (m)
Reservations (Indian), 289
Resistance. See also Revolts and rebellions
to British rule, 124
by Indians, 262
by slaves, 116, 150–151, 322
to Stamp Act, 140–141
Resources, Indian labor as, 42
Revel, James, 59
Revenue Act, of 1764 (Sugar Act), 139
Revere, Paul, 149–150
Revivals and revivalism, 252
in colonies, 136
Great Awakening as, 120–121
Revolts and rebellions. See also Resistance
at Acoma pueblo, 42
Bacon's Rebellion, 64–65
Bear Flag Revolt, 293
Gabriel's Rebellion, 229
by Leisler, 96
at Lexington and Concord (1774–1775),
     149–150
by Opechancanough, 54
by Pontiac, 135, 135 (m), 136, 137 (i)
Pueblo Revolt, 66
Shays's Rebellion, 189, 194–195, 194 (m)
by slaves, 150–151, 322
in Spanish borderland, 65–66
Stono rebellion, 116
in Texas, 292
by Turner, Nat, 307–308, 308 (i)
Virginia laws covering, 61
Whiskey Rebellion, 214–215
Revolution(s)
in France, 209, 218–219
in Haiti, 219–220
Revolutionary War (1775–1783)
balance of power in, 176 (i)
British surrender at Yorktown, 175
campaigns of 1777–1779 in, 169–173
debts after, 191, 205–206
finances and corruption during, 169
first year of (1775–1776), 160–163
French alliance during, 160, 173, 175
home front in, 163–169
Indians in, 165–168, 165 (i), 171–172,
     172 (m)

Revolutionary War (1775–1783) (*continued*)
loyalists in, 163–169, 168 (*m*)
in North (1775–1778), 164 (*m*)
opening of, 149–151
reasons for British loss in, 177
in South, 173–175, 173 (*m*)
women in, 155–156
Rhode Island, 85, 124, 188, 255
Rice, 112, 117, 313
Richardson, Ebenezer, 144
Richmond, Virginia, 363, 365, 380, 380 (*i*)
Rifles, 157 (*i*)
Rights. *See also* Bill of Rights (U.S.); Bills of
rights; Women
of African Americans, 187–190, 347, 348,
393, 404
in Bill of Rights, 208
of colonists, 130, 140
of poor white farmers, 69–70
for wives, 344–345
Rights of Women, The (de Gouge), 210, 211
Rio Grande, 294, 296
Riots. *See also* Protest(s)
antidraft, 376–377
for bread, in Confederacy, 371
Rivers. *See also* specific river regions
steamboat travel and, 253, 253 (*m*), 254
Roads and highways, 104, 212, 212 (*m*), 253,
254, 259–260
Roanoke Island, 44 (*m*), 45, 51
Robards, Rachel Donelson. *See* Jackson,
Rachel
Robin John family, 101–102
Robinson, Solon, 316 (*i*)
Rochambeau (Comte de), 175
Rockingham (Marquess of), 142
Rolfe, John, 50, 56
Rolfe, Thomas, 50, 71
Roman Catholicism. *See* Catholicism
Rose, Ernestine Potowsky, 344–345, 345 (*i*)
Rose, William, 344
Rosecrans, William, 378
Royal colonies, 93, 124
Massachusetts as, 96, 129
Virginia as, 54–55, 63
"Royal fifth," Spanish, 36
Royal Navy. *See* Navies, British
Rum, 214
Runaway servants, 60
Runaway slaves. *See* Fugitive slaves
Rural areas. *See also* Farms and farming
population in, 280–281, 287
school enrollment in, 285
Rush-Bagot disarmament treaty (1817),
238–239
Russia, 123
purchase of Alaska from, 404

Sacajawea (Shoshoni Indians), 234
"Sack of Lawrence," 347
Sacrifice. *See* Human sacrifice
Sager family, 291 (*i*)
Sailors
impressment of, 235
lifestyle in 18th century, 106–107
St. Augustine, Florida, 42
St. Clair, Arthur, 215–216
Saint Domingue, 219

St. Joseph, Fort, 136
St. Lawrence River region, 43, 94
St. Louis, Missouri, 243 (*i*)
St. Mary's City, Maryland, 63
"Saints," Puritan elect as, 82, 87
Salem, Massachusetts
Williams, Roger, in, 75
witch trials in, 88
Salta abas, 41 (*i*)
Salvation
by faith alone, 85
in Great Awakening, 121
Puritans on, 79, 84
Samoset (Wampanoag Indians), 78
Sampson, Deborah (Robert Shurtliff),
155–156, 156 (*i*), 176
Sandusky, Fort, 136
San Francisco, 298–299
San Jacinto, battle at, 292
San Miguel de Gualdape, 35
San Salvador, Columbus in, 30
Santa Anna, Antonio López de, 292, 295, 296
Santa Clara, California, mission in, 123 (*i*)
Santa Fe, New Mexico, 42, 292, 295, 366
Santa Fe Trail, 289 (*m*), 292
Santa Maria (ship), 29
Santo Domingo, 219, 404
Saratoga, battle of (1777), 164 (*m*), 170–171,
170 (*m*)
Sauk and Fox Indians, 262
Savannah, Georgia, fall of (1864), 378 (*m*),
379, 380
Scalawags, 399
School(s), 265–266. *See also* Education; Public
schools
enrollment and literacy rates, 286, 286 (*f*)
in South, 327
for women, 241 (*i*)
Schurz, Carl, 386, 407
Schuyler, Betsey, 205
Schuylkill Canal, 254
Schwachheim, Carl, 3
Scotland, immigrants from, 108
Scots-Irish immigrants, 109
Scott, Dred, 347–348, 347 (*i*)
Scott, Winfield, 296, 339–340
Scriven, Abream, 321
Seasoning, slave acculturation as, 114–115
Secession, 263, 349
repudiation of, 392
of South, 352–353, 352 (*m*), 359–360,
360 (*m*)
southern calls for, 336
"Second American Revolution," Civil War as,
381
Second Bank of the United States, 257,
263–264
Second Continental Congress (1775), 149,
156–158, 183
Second Great Awakening, 264, 267–268, 274
Second Reconstruction, 407
Secotan Village, 51 (*i*)
Sectionalism
election of 1856 and, 344
election of 1860 and, 351–352
Mexican-American War and, 334
Missouri statehood and, 242
in politics, 334, 341, 342 (*m*)

Tallmadge amendments and, 244
transcontinental railroad and, 340
Security. *See* Defense
Sedgwick, Susan Ridley, portrait of Mum Bett,
189 (*i*)
Sedgwick, Theodore, 188–189
Sedition Act, of 1798, 222–223
Segregation
in California, 298
in South, 400
in Union army, 370
Self-determination, 366
Self-discipline, free-labor ideal and, 300
Self-government, in Massachusetts, 79
Seminole Indians, 190, 245, 260, 262
Senate (U.S.)
election to, 349
slavery violence in, 347
term in, 197
Seneca Falls, New York, 301, 344
Seneca Falls Declaration of Sentiments (1848),
301–302
Seneca Indians, 17, 165, 170, 192
Senegambia, 113 (*m*), 115
Separate spheres doctrine, 264–265
Separatists, 78
Serra, Junípero, 123
Servants. *See also* Indentured servants
body servants, in Civil War, 370 (*i*)
in Chesapeake region, 57–59, 62–63, 65
Virginia laws governing, 60–61
women as, 59
Settlement(s). *See also* Colonies and
colonization; Land
by Archaic Indians, 8–12
at Cahokia, 16
in California, 123–124
English colonies as, 48–65, 66–71, 78–81
along James River, 59 (*m*)
in middle colonies, 111–112, 111 (*m*)
in New England, 104
in Southwest, 13–114
in Spanish colonies, 33
by Woodland Indians, 12
Settler(s), free state vs. slave state, 346 (*i*)
Seven Cities of Cíbola, wealth of, 35
Seven Days Battle (1862), 363 (*i*), 365,
365 (*m*)
Seventeenth Amendment, 349
Seven Years' (French and Indian) War
(1754–1763), 123, 130–138
casualties in, 135
European areas of influence in, 131 (*m*)
in Indian Country, 136–137
Seward, William H., 337, 346, 351, 353,
362, 404
"Seward's Ice Box," 404
Sex and sexuality
in Oneida community, 301, 301 (*i*)
slave women and, 317, 319
Seymour, Horatio, 403, 405 (*i*)
Seymour, Jane (England), 77
Shadrach (runaway slave), 338
Sharecroppers and sharecropping, 401–402
Shawnee Indians, 133, 133 (*i*), 168, 171,
172 (*m*), 192, 215, 216, 217, 227–228,
236–237
Shays, Daniel, 195

Shays's Rebellion (1786–1787), 189, 194–195, 194 (m), 195 (i)
Sheffield, Robert, 167 (i)
Shenandoah River region
    Civil War in, 379
    settlement in, 111
Shepard, William, 195 (i)
Sheridan, Philip H., 379
Sherman, William Tecumseh, 378 (m), 379, 388
Shiloh, battle of (1862), 364 (m), 366, 372
Ships and shipping
    Barbary States and, 234
    caravels and, 29
    in Civil War, 366
    colonial trade and, 91–92
    of cotton, 316 (i)
    French privateers and, 221
    impressment and, 235
    in New England, 105–106
    pirates and, 229
    prisoners of war and, 166
    sailor's life in 18th century and, 106–107
    transportation changes and, 253, 254–255
    warships in European navies, 122
Shoe industry, 255–256
Shoshoni Indians, 288
Shurtliff, Robert. See Sampson, Deborah (Robert Shurtliff)
Siberia, humans in, 3, 5–6, 8
Sierra Leone, 151, 190
Silver
    as hard money, 191, 213
    in New Spain, 35, 40
    presentational, 195 (i)
    in Spain, 43
    as specie, 257
Sioux Indians, 288
Slater, Samuel, 255
Slaughterhouse cases (1873), 404
Slave catchers, 339
Slave codes (laws), 311
Slave drivers, 320
Slaveholders, 324, 327, 328, 374
    black, 324
Slave patrols, 324
Slave Power, 343, 347
Slaves and slavery. *See also* Abolition and abolitionism; African Americans; Fugitive slaves
    abolitionism and, 268–269, 270–271
    African, 29, 42, 67, 68, 69 (f), 113–114
    African American culture and, 116
    as artisans, 102 (i), 320, 320 (i)
    attacks on, 311
    in Chesapeake region, 57–58
    Civil War and, 368, 370 (i), 371, 372, 373, 374
    colonial growth and, 70–71
    colonization and, 269
    Constitution and, 271
    cotton and, 309–310
    defense of, 308, 311, 312–313
    in District of Columbia, 269, 272
    economy and, 314
    in 1820 and 1860, 309 (m)
    in 1830s, 263
    elimination in North and West, 284
    emancipation and, 357
    equality and, 187–190
    families and, 319, 320–321
    free labor vs., 311
    gender relations and, 240
    Haitian Revolution and, 219–220
    Harpers Ferry raid and, 333–334
    impressment of, 371
    Jefferson and, 245
    in Kansas, 346–347
    labor and, 66–70, 116, 319–320
    legal challenges to (1777–1804), 187 (m), 188–189
    Lincoln-Douglas debates on, 349
    Lincoln on, 348
    in Massachusetts, 187, 188–189
    in Mexican cession, 334–335, 353
    in middle colonies, 109–110
    Missouri Compromise and, 243–245
    mulatto children, 318 (i)
    in New England, 108
    in Northwest Territory, 194
    paternalism and, 316–317
    on plantations, 311–312, 319–322
    politics of, 272, 327–328
    pottery by, 306 (i)
    punishment of, 317
    rebellions by, 116, 150–151, 322
    religion of, 321–322
    representation of, 197
    Republican Party on, 343
    search for families of former, 389, 389 (i), 390
    secession of South and, 352
    slave ships and, 270, 271 (i)
    society of, 116
    in South, 112–117, 190, 306–322, 327–328, 353
    state outlawing of, 244
    suit for freedom and, 188–189
    Supreme Court on, 347–348
    task system for, 116
    in territories, 334, 353
    Texas and, 292, 293
    Turner's rebellion and, 307–308
    underground railroad and, 303
    in Union army, 372
    in upcountry, 325
    Van Buren and, 272
    in Virginia, 60–61
    voting rights and, 187–190
    Wilmot Proviso and, 335
    women and, 317, 319, 320
    yeomen and, 324
Slave states, 329, 338 (m), 340 (m), 346
Slave trade, 101–102, 112–116, 113 (m), 115 (i), 270, 318 (i)
    close of, 271, 316, 337
    Constitution and, 271
    domestic, 310
    Middle Passage and, 113, 114, 115
Smallpox, 32
    during Revolution, 158, 163
Smith, Gerrit, 302 (i)
Smith, John, 49–50, 52 (i), 53
    dictionary of Powhatan's language, 54 (i)
    on tobacco, 56
Smith, Joseph, 290
Smith, William Thompson Russell, 326 (i)
Smoking. See Tobacco and tobacco industry
Smuggling, colonial, 134, 139, 146
Sneden, Robert Knox, 363 (i)
Socialism and socialists, utopianism of, 274
Social mobility, free-labor ideal and, 286–287
Social welfare. See Welfare and welfare system
Société des Amis des Noirs (Society of the Friends of Blacks), 270
Society
    in Chesapeake, 62–65
    colonial, 97, 102–103
    after 1815, 252
    marriage and, 209
    in middle colonies, 108–112
    Native American (1490s), 16–20
    in New England, 81–88, 103–108
    in New Spain, 40
    in Pennsylvania, 109–112
    Puritan, 81–88
    servants in, 59
    slave, 308, 310, 328–329
    in southern colonies, 112–117
    women in, 239–242
    of Woodland Indians, 15–16
    yeoman, 324–325
Society for Effecting the Abolition of the Slave Trade, 270
Society for Promoting the Abolition of Slavery, 270
Society of Friends. See Quakers
Society of Republican Revolutionary Women (Paris), 210
Soldiers. *See also* Military
    black, 372–373
    British in North America, 134, 135
    in Civil War, 363 (i), 370 (i), 371–372
    colonial, 135
    equipment of, 169 (i)
    in Mexican-American War, 296
    in Revolution, 154 (i)
Sons of Liberty, 140, 141, 143–144, 146
South (U.S. region). *See also* Confederacy; New South; Reconstruction
    abolitionists and, 272
    African Americans and, 112–117, 323–324
    agricultural economy of, 314–315
    antislavery movement in, 328
    black and white populations in (1860), 310 (f)
    Brown's raid and, 334, 350–351
    cash crops of, 312–315, 314 (m)
    cities in, 314–315
    during Civil War, 371–374
    colonial, 112–117
    cotton and, 309–310, 324, 324 (m)
    economic development in, 315, 400
    economy in, 117
    emancipation in, 189–190
    Federalists and, 238
    Fourteenth Amendment and, 395
    home rule for, 403, 405
    honor in, 317
    impact of Civil War on, 381
    Indians in, 260
    military rule in, 396–397
    North compared with, 308–309
    plain folk in, 324–327

South (U.S. region) (continued)
    politics of slavery in, 327–328
    poor whites in, 325–327
    population of colonies in, 86 (f)
    railroads in, 315
    Reconstruction and, 386, 387–388,
        392–394, 396–397, 398–402, 406 (m)
    Redeemers in, 405, 406
    Republican Party in, 384 (i), 399–400
    resistance to Indian removal in, 262
    Revolutionary War and, 173–175, 173 (m)
    secession of, 352–353, 359–360, 360 (m)
    segregation in, 400
    sharecropping in, 401–402
    slavery in, 244, 306–322, 328–329,
        387–388
    tariffs and, 262–263
    taxation in, 405–406
    unifying elements in colonies and, 117–124
    Unionists in, 352
    upcountry in, 324, 325 (m)
    violence against blacks in, 396
    voting in, 117
    white supremacy in, 310–311
    Wilmot Proviso and, 335
South America. See also North America
    European colonies in, 37 (m)
    Monroe Doctrine and, 245
    Paleo-Indians in, 7
South Carolina, 112, 380. See also Carolina(s)
    nullification issue and, 262–263
    population of, 112
    Revolutionary War in, 173, 173 (m), 174
    secession and, 352, 392
    settlement of, 67
    Stono Rebellion in, 116
    Tariff of Abominations and, 263
    Yamasee War in, 123
Southeast, Indians of, 17
Southeast Asia, early Americans from, 8
Southern Literary Messenger, 339
"Southern Rights" flag, 346 (i)
Southwest
    native cultures of, 13–14, 13 (m), 17–18
    Spanish settlements in, 42
Sovereignty. See Popular sovereignty
Spain
    Adams-Onís Treaty with, 245
    American West and, 232–233
    Columbian Exchange and, 33 (i)
    Columbus and, 26–27, 26 (i), 29–31
    in eastern North America, 121 (m)
    English colonies and, 52
    exploration and conquest by, 33–42, 36 (i)
    Florida and, 42
    Golden Age of, 42–43
    Isabella and, 25
    Mexico and, 291
    missions of, 123–124, 123 (i), 124 (m)
    Mississippi River and, 172
    New Spain and, 36–42
    Seven Years' War and, 131 (m), 134, 135 (m)
    Treaty of Tordesillas and, 30
    wealth from Americas in, 43
    weapons used against Indians, 24 (i)
Spears, 4, 7, 7 (i), 8, 9 (i)
Specie payments, 257
Speculation

    economic cycles and, 257
    after 1815, 253
    in land, 104, 128, 132, 138, 194, 213, 281
    in railroads, 255
Spending. See Finances
Spoils system, 259, 403
Spotsylvania Court House, battle of (1864),
    378 (m), 379
Springfield, Illinois, 279, 348
Squanto (Wampanoag Indians), 78
Squatters, 281
Stagecoach travel, 212, 253, 254
Stamp Act (1765), 129, 139–142, 140 (i)
Stamp Act Congress (1765), 141–142
Standardization, of parts, 282
Standard of living. See Wealth
Stanton, Edwin M., 390, 398
Stanton, Elizabeth Cady, 301, 302, 344,
    395, 398
Stanwix, Fort
    battle at (1777), 154 (i), 170
    Treaty of (1784), 192–193, 215
State(s), 281
    Articles of Confederation and, 183–184
    bank charters from, 256
    bills of rights in, 208
    Constitution and, 196, 198, 199 (m),
        200–201
    constitutions of, 185, 187
    free, 336, 337, 338 (m), 340 (m)
    in Northwest Territory, 193–194
    during Reconstruction, 392–393, 396–397,
        399–400
    restoration to Union, 387, 395–396, 400
    slave, 329, 338 (m), 340 (m)
    sovereignty of, 185–190, 362
    voting rights in, 186–187, 242
    western boundaries of, 183
    western land claims of, 183–184, 184 (m)
State Department, 207, 232
Statehood
    for land in Northwest Territory, 194
    Missouri Compromise and, 243–245
State legislatures, 349
States' rights, 223, 371
    federal power vs., 263
    Indian removal and, 262
    Johnson, Andrew, on, 392
Steamboats, 253 (m), 254, 254 (i), 316 (i)
Steam power, 281
Stephens, Alexander, 352, 394
Stephens, Harry, family, 389 (i)
Stevens, Elizabeth Alexander, 186 (i)
Stevens, Thaddeus, 396, 397
Stewart, Maria, 269
Stirrups, Spanish, 65–66, 65 (i)
Stock(s), 214
Stone, Joseph, 156 (i)
Stone Age, 4
Stono rebellion, 116
Stowe, Harriet Beecher, 241
    Uncle Tom's Cabin by, 338, 339, 339 (i)
Strikes. See also Labor
    during Civil War, 375
    in textile mills, 255
Stringfellow, Thornton, 313
Stuart, Gilbert, 236 (i)
Stuart, James E. B. ("Jeb"), 365

Stuyvesant, Peter, 89, 90
Submarines, in Civil War, 366, 367
Subsidies, in transportation, 254, 283
Subsistence lifestyle, 12. See also
        Hunter-gatherers
Substitutes, in Civil War draft, 372, 376
Suffolk County, Massachusetts, 147
Suffrage. See also Voting and voting rights;
        Woman suffrage
    black, 386 (i), 387, 398
    in East, 242–243
    expansion of southern, 327
    for men, 186, 242
    for women, 186–187, 186 (i), 302, 343, 395,
        396 (i)
Sugar Act (Revenue Act, 1764), 129, 138
Sugar and sugar industry, 118, 312–313
    slavery and, 66–67, 113 (m), 117
    trade and, 104, 105
Sugar islands. See Guadeloupe; Martinique
Sullivan, John, 171, 172
Sumner, Charles, 293, 336, 347, 395, 396
Sumter, Fort, attack on, 356 (i), 359
Supreme Court (U.S.)
    Cherokee removal and, 262
    Reconstruction and, 404
    on slavery in territories, 347–348
Surplus (financial), 264
Susan Constant (ship), 51
Syphilis, in Columbian exchange, 32

Taino people, 30, 30 (i)
Tallmadge, James, Jr., 244
Tallmadge amendment, 244
Tanaghrisson (Mingo Indians), 132–133
Taney, Roger B., 347
Tarhe the Crane (Wyandot Indians), 217 (i)
Tariffs, 282
    of 1816, 262
    of 1824, 262
    of Abominations (1828), 260, 262–263
Tarring and feathering, of customs collector,
    148 (i)
Task system, for slaves, 116
Taxation. See also Duties
    under Articles of Confederation, 183, 191
    assumption of state debts and, 213
    in Chesapeake region, 65
    Civil War and, 362, 374
    in colonies, 129, 138–148
    impost as, 191
    Jefferson and, 232
    representation and, 139–140
    Shays's Rebellion and, 194–195
    on slaves, 328
    in South, 405–406
    of whiskey, 214–215
Taylor, Zachary, 294, 295, 296 (i),
    336, 338
Tea Act (1773), 129, 146
Teachers and teaching, 266, 285, 373
Technology. See also Tools; Weapons
    agricultural, 281
    for artificial limbs, 394
    exploration and, 27
    mechanization and, 282
    of Native Americans, 19 (i)
    printing and, 118, 118 (i), 258

of weaving, 19
women's lives and, 239 (i)
Tecumseh (Shawnee Indians), 227–228, 228 (i), 235, 236–237, 236 (i), 262
Tejanos, 292
Telegraph, 282, 283
Temperance, 268, 300
Tenant farming, 65, 117, 325
Tennent, William, 120
Tennessee, 251, 359, 366, 387, 395–396
Tenochtitlán, 20, 34, 35 (i), 36 (i)
Tenskwatawa (Prophet, Shawnee Indians), 227–228, 236, 236 (i)
Tenth Amendment, 208
Tenure of Office Act (1867), 398
Territories. *See also* Indian Territory; Northwest Territory
federal land policy and, 281
federal slave code and, 351
popular sovereignty in, 335
populations of, 236
slavery in, 334–335, 347–348
statehood for, 194
Terrorism
by Klan, 403, 404
southern Democratic party and, 406
Teton Sioux Indians, 17
Texas, 245, 309, 337
annexation of, 293–294
border with Mexico, 296
Lone Star Republic in, 292
rebellion in, 292
Republic of, 294
secession of, 352
settlement of, 292–293
Texcoco, Lake, 20
Textbooks, 285
Textiles and textile industry
cotton textile industry (ca. 1840), 255 (m)
cotton used in, 361
in Lowell, 255
in North (Civil War), 375
women workers in, 255, 256 (i)
Thames, battle of the (1813), 228, 237
Thanksgiving, Pilgrims and, 78
Thayendanegea (Joseph Brant). *See* Brant, Joseph
Third parties, 275
Thirteenth Amendment, 393
Thomas, Lorenzo, 390
Thompson, George, 270 (i)
Thoreau, Henry David, 300
Three-fifths clause, 197, 238
Ticonderoga, Fort, 134
Tilden, Samuel J., 406–407
Tippecanoe, battle of (1811), 236–237, 237 (m)
Title(s)
in French Revolution, 218 (i)
of president, 207
Tlaxcala and Tlaxcalan people, 34
Tobacco and tobacco industry, 30, 118
in Chesapeake region, 55–62, 57 (i), 64
in Columbian exchange, 32, 33 (i)
duties on, 65
in English colonies, 50
slavery and, 117, 311
in South, 117, 327
Tocqueville, Alexis de, 308

Todd, Albert, 319
Toleration. *See* Religious toleration
Toll roads, 212
Tools, of ancient Americans, 4, 5, 7
Toombs, Robert, 336, 350–351, 359
Tordesillas, Treaty of (1494), 30
Tories, loyalists as, 165
Toronto, Canada, 237
Toussaint L'Ouverture, 220
Town meetings, in New England, 83–84
Townshend, Charles, 142
Townshend duties, 129, 142–144, 145
Townships, in Northwest Territory, 194
Trade. *See also* Commerce; Ships and shipping; Slave trade; Transportation
in Atlantic region, 105 (m)
boycott of, 148
during Civil War, 367
colonial, 63–64, 91–93, 112, 121, 145–146, 148
Columbian Exchange and, 32, 33 (i)
exploration, colonization, and, 29
fur, 94
with Indians, 53
interregional, 16
manifest destiny and, 288
in Mediterranean region, 27
in New England, 85–86, 104–105
nonconsumption and, 143–144
nonimportation and, 143, 145
in Ohio River region, 130–132, 134
in Pacific Northwest, 18
warfare and, 123
westward expansion and, 300
Trade goods, 94, 123
Trade routes, European (15th century), 28 (m)
Trail(s)
California, 289 (m), 293
Mormon, 289 (m)
Oregon, 288, 289, 289 (m), 293
Santa Fe Trail, 289 (m), 292
to West, 288 (m), 289 (m), 291 (i)
Trail of Tears, 261 (m), 262
Traitors
Arnold, Benedict, as, 174
Burr as, 231
in Revolution, 168–169
Transatlantic region, 234–235
Transcendentalists, 300
Transcontinental railroad, 288, 340, 374
Trans-Mississippi West, 232–233
Transnational relations. *See* Global issues
Transportation
improvements in, 253–255
of products, 253, 253 (m)
routes of (1840), 253 (m)
segregation of, 400
in 1790s, 212, 212 (m)
Travel, 104, 212, 213 (m)
Travis, Joseph, 307
Travis, William B., 292
Treason. *See* Traitors
Treasury Department, 205, 207, 209, 232
Treaties. *See* specific treaties and wars
Trial by jury, 146
Trials, in colonies, 145, 147
Triple Entente, 234
Tripoli, 226 (i)

Troy Female Seminary, New York, 241
Trumbull, John, 232 (i)
Trumbull, Lyman, 395
Truth, Sojourner, 302
Tubman, Harriet, 303, 338
Turner, Nat, 307–308, 308 (i), 322
Turner, West, 320
Turnpikes, 253, 254
Tuscarora Indians, 165
Twelfth Amendment (1803), 220–221, 229, 246
Twelve Years a Slave (Northup), 339
Twentieth Amendment, 353
"Twenty-Negro law," 372–373
Tyler, John, 293, 294
Tyler, William, 63

Uncle Tom's Cabin (Stowe), 338, 339, 339 (i), 353
Underground railroad, 303, 338
Unemployment
in 1870s depression, 404
in North (Civil War), 375
in panic of 1819, 257
Uniforms, in Revolution, 154 (i)
Union (U.S.). *See also* North (Civil War)
under Articles of Confederation, 183
collapse of, 332–353
nullification and, 263
Unionists, in South, 352, 358–359, 359–360, 374, 391, 399
Union Ordnance, Yorktown, Virginia, 375 (i)
United States. *See* Constitution (U.S.); Government (U.S.); Supreme Court (U.S.)
U.S. Christian Commission, 376 (i)
U.S. Sanitary Commission, 375, 376 (i)
United States v. Cruikshank (1876), 404
Universities and colleges. *See also* Higher education
coeducational, 266, 266 (i)
Morrill Act and, 374
women in, 241
Unskilled workers, 282
Upcountry yeomen, 325
Upper South, 112, 309, 309 (m), 310 (f). *See also* South
emancipation in, 323
secession and, 352–353, 358, 359–360, 360 (m)
Uprisings. *See* Revolts and rebellions
Urban areas. *See* Cities and towns
Urbanization. *See also* Cities and towns
South and, 314–315
Utah, 291, 337
Utopians, 274, 300–301

Vagrancy, black codes and, 393
Vallejo, Mariano, 299
Valley Forge, Continental army at, 171
Van Buren, Martin, 259, 262, 272–274
election of 1836 and, 272–273
election of 1840 and, 274
election of 1848 and, 336
Vanderlyn, John, 170 (i), 230 (i)
Venice, 27
Vermont, 79, 242
Verrazano, Giovanni da, 43

Vesey, Denmark, 322, 324
Vespucci, Amerigo, 32
Veterans
    African American, 373
    of Mexican-American War, 335
Vetoes, 197
    colonial, 124
    by Jackson, 259–260, 263
    by Johnson, Andrew, 395, 397
Vice admiralty courts, 139
Vice presidency, 220–221
Vicksburg, Mississippi (1863), siege of, 377,
        377 (m), 378 (m)
View of St. Louis from an Illinois Town, A, 243 (i)
Vikings, 27
Vincennes, Fort, battle at, 171–172
Vindication of the Rights of Woman, A
        (Wollstonecraft), 210, 211 (i)
Violence. See Riots; Strikes; Wars and warfare
Virginia, 214. See also Chesapeake region;
        Jamestown; Tobacco and tobacco
        industry
    Algonquian Indians in, 48 (i), 49
    bill of rights in, 187
    Civil War in, 361, 363, 364, 365, 378 (m),
        379
    debts after Revolution, 213
    independence resolution in, 160
    Jamestown settlement and, 49–50, 51–54
    land cession by, 184, 184 (m)
    laws governing servants and slaves, 60–61
    as "Lincoln state" in reconstruction plan, 387
    manumission in, 190
    population of, 56, 112
    royal government of, 54–55, 63–64, 93
    secession of, 359
    settlement in, 111, 111 (m)
    Seven Years' War and, 131 (m), 132–133
    slavery in, 150
    Smith's map of, 52 (i)
    Turner rebellion in, 307–308, 308 (i)
Virginia (ironclad), 366
Virginia and Kentucky Resolutions (1798),
        223, 263
Virginia Company, 51, 53, 54
Virginia Convention, 181
Virginia Plan, 196
Virginia Resolves, 128, 140, 196
Virtual representation, 139–140, 141
Virtue, 207, 209
Visible saints, 82
Volunteers, in Mexican-American War, 294,
        296 (i)
Voting and voting rights. See also Elections;
        Woman suffrage
    for African Americans, 187–190
    in Bill of Rights, 208
    in Constitution, 197
    democratization of, 242–243
    disfranchisement of blacks and, 398
    in election of 1828, 258
    in election of 1840, 274
    Fifteenth Amendment and, 398
    Fourteenth Amendment and, 395
    for free blacks, 303
    in Massachusetts, 83
    property ownership for, 96, 186, 187,
        242–243

during Reconstruction, 386 (i), 396–397
    in South, 117, 327, 328
    in Virginia, 55, 63
    for women, 186–187, 186 (i), 240, 243,
        302, 386, 398
Voyages of exploration. See also Exploration
    of Columbus, 26, 29–31, 30 (m)
    European, 25–31, 31 (m)
    of Magellan, 32

Wade, Benjamin, 387
Wade-Davis bill (1864), 387
Wage labor, 285, 298. See also Labor
Wages
    for blacks vs. whites, in Union army,
        370, 373
    for factory workers, 255–256
    wife's right to, 345
    for women, 302, 375
Wagner, Fort, battle of (1863), 371
Wagon trains, 288, 289, 291 (i)
Waldseemüller, Martin, 32
Walker, David, 269, 307
Walker, Quok, 187
Wampanoag Indians, 78, 79, 96 (i)
    King Philip's War and, 93–96
War bonds, in Civil War, 362
War debts. See also Debt
    British, 138
    Confederate, 392–393
    after Revolution, 191
War Department, 207, 370, 372
War Hawks, War of 1812 and, 237, 239
War of 1812, 228, 235, 237–239, 238 (m), 247
Warren, Mercy Otis, 199
Wars and warfare. See also specific battles
        and wars
    English-Indian, 53–54, 64, 93–96
    guerrilla war, 359, 365–366
    among Native Americans, 18, 19
    prisoners of war and, 166–167
    Spanish, 43
Warships, in European navies (1660–1760),
        123, 123 (f)
Wartime Reconstruction, 386–392
Washington, D.C., 363
    abolition of slavery in, 369
    burning of, 238
    location of, 213
Washington, Fort, 215, 216
Washington, George, 180 (i)
    cabinet of, 207–208
    Constitution and, 196
    Farewell Address of, 221 (i)
    at First Continental Congress, 148
    Hamilton and, 205
    inauguration of, 207 (i)
    journal of, 132 (i)
    memorabilia about, 204 (i)
    Neutrality Proclamation and, 219
    in Ohio River region, 132–133, 132 (i)
    as president, 206, 207–208
    in Revolutionary War, 157, 158, 163,
        171, 175
    in Seven Years' War, 134
    slaves of, 116
Washington, Lawrence and Augustine, 132
Washington, Martha, 229

Water, travel by, 253, 253 (m), 254
Waterpower, 281
"Waving the bloody shirt," 403, 406
Wayne, Anthony ("Mad Anthony"), 216–217,
        217 (i)
Wealth
    from Americas, 35, 43
    from California gold rush, 299
    in 1860, 285
    of Mexica people, 20
    in New England, 107–109
    from New Spain, 43
    of Seven Cities of Cíbola, 35
    in South, 400
Weapons
    in Civil War, 362, 362 (i), 375 (i)
    European, 24 (i), 42 (i)
    Indian, 11, 18–19
    Revolutionary muskets and rifles, 157 (i)
Weathercocks, 108
Weaving, by ancient Americans, 19 (i)
Webster, Daniel, 263, 273, 337
Weld, Ezra Greenleaf, 302 (i)
Welfare and welfare system, in Confederacy,
        371
Werowance (subordinate chief), 49
Wesley, John and Charles, 102
West (region). See also Pacific Ocean region;
        Westward movement
    Civil War in, 364 (m), 365–366, 365 (m),
        367, 374
    diversity in, 298–299, 299–300
    free blacks in, 303
    free labor in, 335
    gold discoveries in, 353
    Indians and, 215–218, 287, 288–289
    Indian war in Revolution (1777–1782), 172
    land in, 183–184, 184 (m), 190–191
    manifest destiny and, 288
    Revolutionary War in, 171–173
    secession and, 359–360
    southern and northern views of, 334
    state boundaries in, 183
    territories in, 281
    trails to, 288–289, 288 (m), 289 (m)
West Africa, 269, 303
    African American culture and, 113,
        113 (m), 116
West Coast. See Pacific Ocean region
Western Hemisphere
    Europeans and, 21
    human migrations into, 5–6
    Monroe Doctrine and, 245
    sea routes to East and, 32
    Spain in, 33–45
West India Company (Dutch), 88, 89
West Indies, 219
    Carolina and, 67–68
    French, 219
    markets in, 92, 117
    in 17th century, 68 (m)
    slaves from, 66–67, 114
West Point, 174
West Virginia, 360
Westward movement, 280, 287–293
    cotton kingdom and, 309, 310
    after Creek War, 309
    families in, 289–290

under Jefferson, 232–234
Louisiana Purchase and, 234
after Revolution, 215–218, 216 (m)
trade and, 300
Westward the Star of the Empire Takes Its Way . . .
(Melrose), 284 (i)
Wheat, 109–110, 209, 281
Wheatley, Phillis, 150–151, 150 (i)
Wheelock, Eleazar, 165 (i)
Whig Party, 259, 342 (m)
collapse of, 341
election of 1836 and, 272–273
election of 1848 and, 336, 336 (m)
Lincoln in, 348
Mexican-American War and, 294
National Republicans as, 258
panic of 1837 and, 274
reformers in, 269, 275
in South, 328
Whippings, of blacks, 317, 320, 323
Whiskey, taxation on, 214
Whiskey Rebellion (1794), 214–215
White, Hugh Lawson, 273
White, John, 44 (i), 45, 51 (i)
White Eyes (Delaware Indians), 171
Whitefield, George, 120, 120 (i)
White House, 236
Whites, 288
in Chesapeake region, 69–70
emancipation and, 369, 388–389
freedoms for poor, 69–70
gender relations of, 240
in Haiti, 219
identity in British colonies, 117–118
master-slave relationship, 316–317
in Northwest Territory, 194
slavery and, 117
in South, 117, 329, 405–406
in southern Democratic Party, 405, 406
southern poor, 325–327
in southern Republican Party, 399
White supremacy, 405 (i)
free blacks and, 303
Ku Klux Klan and, 399
Lincoln and, 348
North and, 310–311
Reconstruction and, 405–406
in South, 310–311
"White terror," 399
Whitman, Marcus and Narcissa, 291 (i)
Whitney, Eli, 209, 314, 315
Whole Booke of Psalmes Faithfully Translated into
English Metre, 74 (i)
Wichita Indians, 288
Widows, inheritance laws and, 344–345
Wigglesworth, Michael, 87
Wilberforce, William, 270
Wilderness, battle of the (1864), 378 (m), 379
Wilkinson, Eliza, 165
Wilkinson, Jemima, 240
Willard, Emma, 241

William III (of Orange, English king), 96
Williams, Roger, 75–76, 84, 85
Williamsburg, Virginia, battle at, 174
Willing, (Mrs.) Charles, 111 (i)
Wilmot, David, 334, 335, 353
Wilmot Proviso (1846), 335, 337, 343
Winthrop, John, 75, 79–81, 84–85
Wisconsin, 281, 336
Wisconsin glaciation, 6
Witches and witchcraft, 87 (i), 88
Wives. *See also* Women
Republican, 208–209
rights for, 344–345
separate spheres and, 264–265
Wollstonecraft, Mary, 210, 211 (i)
Woman's rights movement, 300, 301–302,
343, 344–345
Woman suffrage, 186–187, 186 (i)
Fifteenth Amendment and, 398
Fourteenth Amendment and, 395
movement for, 395, 396 (i)
Women, 243. *See also* Gender and gender issues;
Slaves and slavery; Voting and voting
rights
in abolition movement, 269, 270, 271
academies for, 266
Adams, Abigail, and, 159–160, 159 (i)
age at first marriage, 265, 265 (t)
black, 401, 401 (i)
in Chesapeake region, 58
church governance and, 240–241
in Civil War, 358, 370, 371–372, 373, 374,
375–376, 376 (i), 381
in colonies, 53
as Daughters of Liberty, 142, 144
education for, 208, 241–242, 241 (i), 318
evangelicalism and, 266, 266 (i), 268
Fourteenth Amendment and, 395
French Revolution and, 218, 218 (i)
Indian, 12, 17, 53–54
Irish immigrant, 287
laws and, 239, 240
Madison's presidency and, 235–236
moral reform movement and, 268
as Native American farmers, 13 (i)
in New Spain, 40
in nursing, 375–376
petition for redress of grievances by,
261–262, 275
on plantations, 317–319
politics and, 247, 280, 343, 399
poor white, 326
property and, 318, 344–345
protests by colonial, 143–144, 143 (i)
as Quakers, 90
in Republican Party, 343
as republican wives and mothers, 208–209
Revolution and, 155–156, 165
rights for, 210–211, 301–302, 344–345, 386
separate spheres doctrine and, 264–265
as servants, 59

southern, 317–319
status of, 239–242
in teaching, 266, 285
in textile industry, 255, 256 (i)
in wage-earning labor, 255–256
wealth and, 285
in westward movement, 289–290
as wives of loyalists, 168
in workforce, 284
yeomen, 325
Women's rights, 210–211, 240, 269. *See also*
Feminism; Women
Woodland peoples, 12, 12 (i), 15–17. *See also*
Eastern Woodland Indians
Worcester v. Georgia (1832), 262
Workday, for slaves, 317, 319–320
Workers. *See also* Factories; Labor; Strikes;
Women; Workforce
in factories, 255–256
in North (Civil War), 375
standardized parts and, 282
in textile industry, 255
unskilled, 282
Workforce, women in, 375
Workplace
masculine, 265
young people in, 266–267
World Antislavery Convention (1840),
270 (i), 271
Worth, William, 296 (i)
Wright, Henry, 321 (i)
Writing
archaeology, history, and, 4–5
Indians and, 19

XYZ Affair, 221

Yamasee Indians, 122–123
Yamasee War (1715), 122–123
Yankee traders, 108
Yeoman farmers, 117, 324–325
in Chesapeake region, 62–63
during Civil War, 371, 372–373
plantation belt yeomen, 324–325
politics and, 328
in southern Republican Party, 399
taxation and, 405–406
upcountry yeomen, 325
York (slave), 234
York, Canada. *See* Toronto
York, Duke of. *See* James II (Duke of York,
England)
Yorktown, battle of (1781), 174–175, 175 (m)
Young, Brigham, 290, 291
Young, Lewis, 320
Young people, education and training of,
265–267

Zacatecas, Mexico, silver from, 40
Zuñi Indians, 14, 35